SCIENCE IN ELEMENTARY EDUCATION

JOHN WILEY & SONS, INC.

NEW YORK • LONDON • SYDNEY • TORONTO

PETER C. GEGA

SCHOOL OF EDUCATION
SAN DIEGO STATE COLLEGE

SECOND EDITION

SCIENCE IN ELEMENTARY EDUCATION

To Dale, Chris, and Suzanne

Preface

THIS IS A BOOK ON HOW TO TEACH SCIENCE IN ELEMENTARY schools. It should be especially useful in related college and in-service courses.

The second edition continues and enlarges upon the practical emphasis of the first edition. Significant findings from developmental psychology and government-funded science projects have been incorporated into this volume. For example, the six thinking skill categories developed in the first edition have been rearranged into five categories that more nearly reflect processes taught in the latest programs. Various open-ended activities have been added, as well as a thorough examination of the three major experimental programs currently taught or being introduced in leading schools throughout the United States and abroad. Many sections and activities have been improved, simplified or, in some cases, deleted, as a result of detailed feedback from previous text users.

The book now has three main parts. Part I introduces the basic things teachers need to know: how science is organized in elementary schools, strategies and tactics of science teaching, evaluation methods, how to get and use materials, and how to plan lessons. Part II applies these methods in many different ways, within the typical subject-matter fields of elementary science. Part III describes several experimentally developed science programs and their important effect on modern school practice.

The twelve units of Part II contain specific, model-lesson plans, arranged in teaching sequences that encourage children to learn through the development of their own thinking skills. These skills are clearly identified as they are used within each lesson (for details, see pages 70–71). An understandable subject-matter exposition before each sequence of lessons provides the background needed to teach the sequence confidently and successfully.

Four units each emphasize the primary, intermediate, and upper-grade levels—enough material to make up most of a year's work at each level. Overlapping has been purposely planned. Adjustments

vii

in vocabulary and teacher assistance, among other things, will enable all of these units to be taught at various levels.

For help received in the preparation of the second edition, I am greatly indebted to William H. Banks, Jr., Randolph Brown, Norman F. Dessel, Gerald F. Gates, Sharon C. Hartigan, Ruth Lofgren, John R. Mayor, Charles D. Oviatt, Dorothy L. Parry, Gretchen Peebles, Maxine H. Scott, Herbert D. Thier, Gerhard Wolter, David Salstrom, John M. Nickel, William Walsh, Bernard Auerbach, Ernest E. Snyder, Cyrus W. Barnes, and Dora Dean.

Peter C. Gega

Contents

PART II APPLICATIONS OF SCIENCE TEACHING
METHODS   139

Unit

1 *Molecules and Heat Energy*   *140*

SCIENCE IN ELEMENTARY EDUCATION

INTRODUCTION TO SCIENCE TEACHING METHODS

Part I

INTRODUCTION TO
SCIENCE TEACHING
METHODS

Science in Elementary Education

CHAPTER 1

CHAPTER ONE

Science in Elementary Education

WHEN YOU WERE A CHILD, YOU AND ALL THE OTHER BOYS AND girls wanted to know a great deal about the natural world around you. Children still do. Sooner or later, they will ask questions like:

"How do birds get in the egg?"
"Why doesn't a spider get stuck in its web?"
"How can you tell the difference between a boy and a girl tree?"

and

"Where does the dark come from?"
"What makes the wind blow?"
"Why is dirt different colors?"

and

"What makes water wet?"
"How does the picture get on television?"
"Where does smoke go?"

If you had asked these questions as a child, how thoughtfully would your teachers have handled them? Would you have been able to explore such a wide scope of knowledge? Or was learning more restricted? Were you guided to think through some problems for yourself? Or were answers always given? The ways in which your teachers worked with children depended greatly on their notions

Credit for chapter opening photograph. **Hella Hammid — Rapho Guillumette**

4

of good teaching in elementary science. The same truism applies today with you.

It would be convenient to state exactly what ideas are now most valued and practiced by teachers; but this is hard to do. For one thing, some ideas in the field have a disturbing way of not hanging on very long. Besides, no one knows accurately how much of what people say is actually put into practice. In spite of this, several broad contrasts in the teaching of elementary science have become apparent since 1930 or so. Although the older approaches are fading away their traces can still be found, perhaps in thousands of classrooms, and often in subtly changed forms. The following section should help you know what to look for when observing others teach. Not all practices are helpful; some can be inefficient and misleading.

HOW SCIENCE TEACHING IS CHANGING

Elementary science used to be considered a form of "nature study." There was much pressing of leaves and flowers, collecting of rocks, observation and sketching of trees, and observation of birds, for example. The object was to appreciate the beauty and wonder of the natural environment, as contrasted with the man-made environment. Often coupled was the thought that children's minds were not yet ready for "real" science study; this would be taken up later, and after the proper appreciation of nature was gained.

But over the years, most teachers have come to realize that children can learn in any area of science, from astronomy through zoology. Difficulty of learning appears less related to the topic than to the complexity of the ideas studied. When necessary, this complexity can be adjusted to the mental ability of the learner. Appreciation of the natural world can now be gained as well or better through activities which are more intellectually stimulating than nature study. Understanding can be produced without the mysticism or exaggerated reverence for nature which often was a side effect of such teaching.

Teachers used to be concerned almost exclusively with the teaching of science information. They were concerned with teaching the results or *products* of scientific investigation. Progress was noted mostly by how much knowledge the pupil had at the end of a specific period of time, usually a term or year.

We are still concerned with the acquisition of knowledge. But now there is also much interest in teaching science *processes* —that is, the ways scientists think and feel while discovering and ordering knowledge. Most modern educators realize that for intelligent living it is at least as important to learn science thinking skills and attitudes (processes) as principles and facts of science (products).

At one time, it was usual to assign narrow topics by grade levels. In one school, for example, the frog was a third-grade topic, while birds held sway with first-grade teachers. Mastery of facts—the moon is about 240,000 miles away, a spider has eight legs, and an insect has six—was the dominant theme. Often factual information within the topics studied was of a trivial nature, and unrelated to other portions of the curriculum. As a result, worrisome difficulties continually appeared. With fast-increasing science knowledge, what should be left out? What included? Are insects more important than frogs? Why is so much forgotten by the children a short time after they have learned about the topic? Why is there so little application of science knowledge in daily living?

To construct workable solutions to these and other problems, interested persons began to re-examine how children learn. Increasingly educators began reasoning: Since children can profit from experiences in most areas of science, why not broaden the scope of study? Since science information is increasing so fast, why not dwell on the big ideas, or major principles,[1] of science? Because one-time topic teaching is soon largely forgotten, why not use a developmental approach? Some ideas can be repeated several times through the grades, but with increased complexity and in different contexts. These thoughts became some of the guidelines in use today.

As implied, modern practices are not the result of educational thinking in just the last few years. A look at the 1932 and 1947 yearbooks of the National Society for the Study of Education [2] discloses the origins of much present thought and method. In addition, other educational organizations, such as the National Science Teachers Association, have continually emphasized curriculum development. So over the years there has been a continuous, though far too slow, transition toward more efficient practices.

Two elements were lacking for satisfactory progress: big money and contributions to children's science education by working scientists. The spectacular Russian space achievements in 1957 sharply boosted the rising motivation for these factors, and things still have not settled down. Since that time we have seen unparalleled activity in science course revision at all levels of precollege education. As the development of knowledge accelerates, there is mounting concern about the need to teach the truly fundamental ideas of science and ways to improve pupils' thinking abilities. How else can we achieve economy in learning? How else can we avoid teaching what is obsolete? These are

the nagging questions. Study groups have formed around the country to seek solutions, and it is the rare university or college whose personnel remain untouched by it all.

Although more and more attention to science education should do much to improve the way science is taught, there is always danger of confusion when many voices are heard. Whom do we heed? Since this is a continual problem in education, it will be helpful to understand some of the factors that enter into the selection of what to teach.

FACTORS INFLUENCING WHAT WE TEACH

Much of our guidance for what to teach comes from the broad field of science itself. Although there are different specialties within the field, scientists have shown time and again that their knowledge is "all of a piece." It has become increasingly necessary for different specialists to work together in solving problems, as evidenced by the growth of such fused sciences as astrophysics, biochemistry, geophysics, and others. As scientists have developed generalizations they have shown how these relate to one another, and how they cut across traditional subject-matter lines. Even entire subsciences emerge that defy older classification. The best example is oceanography. Therefore, it is possible to select broad generalizations for teaching— those that have many applications in the lives of children.

Even little Bobby's broad generalization, "Things expand when they are heated" helps him to relate and explain such apparently different happenings as sidewalks buckling and cracking in hot weather, telephone wires sagging on a summer day, rocks rimming a campfire cracking open, and his mother's loosening of a tightly screwed jar lid by running hot water over it. His later understanding of more

---

[1] "Science principles," "big ideas," "laws," and "generalizations" are terms usually used interchangeably in elementary science education. When several important ideas are combined into a broader statement, sometimes the term "conceptual schemes" is used.

[2] National Society for the Study of Education, A Program for Teaching Science, Thirty-First Yearbook, Part I, Chicago: University of Chicago Press, 1932; and Science Education in American Schools, Forty-Sixth Yearbook, Part I, Chicago: University of Chicago Press, 1947.

sophisticated statements of the same principle may involve molecular motion and coefficients of linear and cubical expansion. These refinements permit a more complete "explanation" of these events.

Does a science generalization truly "explain" natural events? Perhaps this is a good time to emphasize that, strictly speaking, few scientists pretend to fully *explain* or "understand" natural phenomena. These terms tend to lack significance for scientists. But they do try to *describe* natural events and, when they can, to *predict* or *control* these events. What we often call "explanations" (generalizations, laws, principles, and theories) are really descriptions — often brilliantly developed and useful — but only descriptions after all. How well a description permits us to "explain," predict, or control events becomes the chief measure of its worth.

Ideas change as more data and better thinking about data become available. Probably much of what we know today will be regarded as incomplete or faulty thinking some time from now, if the history of science is any indication. So scientists continually try to increase the sharpness of their observations and find ways to improve their thinking about these observations, rather than to discover immutable laws or truths. Such an approach breeds deeply the willingness to listen to others' ideas, readiness to try innovations, and many other characteristics we call "open-mindedness" or "scientific attitude." This does not come from some special quality of nobility and goodness in the scientist, of course, but from the ever-present and uncomfortable possibility that his thinking can be improved. (We shall consider attitudes again in a later chapter.)

Because broad generalizations, and also skills, are so useful, it is tempting to increase their scope so that they apply to more and more phenomena. But there is always the question of when to stop. Explanations become continually more abstract and remote from common experience as their "mileage" increases. As a teaching generalization or a technique more closely approaches the most advanced scientific model, it is less likely that children can learn it or will want to. To persist is simply to ask them to bite off more than they can chew.

In their efforts to teach broadly applicable ideas or skills to children, some curriculum developers have taken a learn-this-now, you-will-see-the-value-of-it-later approach. Even though a skill or a generalization may prove useful at some future time, this alone is not a sufficient reason to present it. It is important for children to maintain meaning throughout their studies and to see the purpose of what they are doing. Also, they need to reach short-range goals as they head toward those farther away. To do otherwise cuts down pupil interest, understanding, and personal meaning in what is taught. Because they are relatively inexperienced, and intellectually as well as physically immature, children usually learn best when working with the concrete and semiconcrete, the limited theories, and the here and now.[3] This is most obvious and necessary with younger pupils, as primary teachers are quick to tell us.

There is a related point. Science for children usually includes some study of technological and other life applications of scientific principles — the telephone, airplane, vacuum cleaner, simple engines, and so on. Should we abandon study of these inventions for study of basic scientific ideas alone? After all, we are told, some inventions and other present applications of science may be around for only a short while.

Frequently, the best way to approach study of an important generalization is through some of the technological products

[3] David P. Ausubel, "Some Psychological Considerations in the Objectives and Design of an Elementary-School Science Program," *Science Education*, April 1963, pp. 278–284.

that have resulted from it. Studying how something works becomes a convenient way for opening up study of far broader applications, which results in mastery of the generalization. A curriculum that provides at least some of these applications is in touch with children's interests. It tends to keep study alive. And when applications are at hand in the everyday environment, so much the better. Their concreteness and accessibility may make them easy to work with. But these applications should be tied to important generalizations; otherwise, most of their value is lost. Let us study the telephone, for example, but while we are at it let us make sure that the ideas which made it possible — electromagnetism and change of energy forms — emerge as the important learnings.

Contrary to popular view, many of the basic ideas of science *are* relatively lasting. Scientific thinking is always subject to change with new information. But the principles we use today involving the concepts of gravity, motion, interdependence, and the like, may last for generations in only slightly altered forms. The fastest changes we see are in *technology* (from black-and-white to color TV); in specific *"facts"* (from 186,149 miles per second for the speed of light to 186,282 miles per second); and in the thinking of scientists engaged in *frontier research* (from uncomplicated models of atoms to complicated statistical models).

Then there are children's needs to be considered. As they develop, what must they understand about their bodies and the physical forces that govern their safety and play? What can we do to help them interpret now the things they want to know and need to know about their environment? What will they need to know as adults?

Usual sources of the science principles we teach have been textbooks, yearbooks of learned organizations, publications of national commissions, and education research reports. We have also relied upon these sources to provide us with ideas about methods of thinking that children can use as they discover or otherwise learn these principles.

Presently, increasing numbers of subject-area specialists are finding time to show us the important ideas and inquiry methods in their fields. There is no question but that these scientists and college teachers have identified many worthwhile ideas and process methods for teaching. Who is more aware of what is obsolete or current, important or unimportant, in scientific thought than the persons continually engaged in such thought? It is hoped that their contributions to elementary science curriculum development can continue indefinitely.

However, children are not "scientists," in spite of a few superficial similarities in curiosity and explanation-seeking behavior. Teaching statements of basic science principles must be modified to fit in with what we know about children's capacities. Ideas must be simplified, known interests and needs of children considered, and their physical coordination and dexterity weighed. What they can apply now and in the future must be assessed, as well as the other goals of early general education. Judgments about all these factors and more must enter into elementary-school science. The best science programs require a broad spectrum of talent. Besides the important role of scientists, contributions are needed from classroom teachers, psychologists, science educators, technicians, and professional writers. We shall examine some noteworthy experimental programs in Part III.

THE GROWTH OF CHILDREN'S THINKING

What, precisely, can children learn? And how does their ability to reason grow? Jean Piaget, a Swiss developmental psychologist, is widely regarded as the researcher who has done most for our understanding of children's thinking. His books[4] and the work of other researchers suggest that the capacity for logical thinking develops sequentially through four indefinite and widely overlapping stages:

sensorimotor, from birth to about two years

preoperational, from two to about seven years;

concrete operations, from seven to about twelve years;

formal operations, from about twelve on.

In the first stage, the infant ceaselessly explores his environment. Through trial and error, he begins to coordinate his perceptions and physical responses. In the first half of the preoperational stage — from two to four years — he increasingly associates words with objects, and vague concepts begin to form. He also learns in a limited way that there are foreseeable consequences for certain actions.

From ages four to seven years in this second stage, which we can call an *intuitive substage,* the child begins a highly interesting phase of mental growth. He relies on quick sense impressions for his judgments. He finds it hard to break down complex sequences, or objects into separable parts, and to mentally keep the parts in order. The concrete operational child, on the other hand, can do much logical thinking. His major handicap is that the objects or ideas he considers must be concretely represented before him; or, at least, he must have had some physical encounter with them. From about twelve years, in the stage of formal operations, the child is able to think much more abstractly. There is far less need to refer to

concrete objects. With similar experience, he can handle the same operations of logic as adults.

As an elementary school teacher, your work is mostly with children who are in the intuitive and concrete operational phases of mental growth. It will be most worthwhile for you to study in some detail how children grow from intuitive to concrete operational thought. This can provide you with many ideas for teaching and some fascinating chances to reflect upon what children do or say. Even sixth graders regress frequently, and often primary level children will startle you with worthy examples of logical thinking. We shall take up, in order, the intuitive child's notions of relations, causality, and conservation.

Relational Thinking. The four-to-seven-year-old child finds it hard to interrelate time, distance, and speed. For example, if two toys are stopped parallel to each other on two adjacent pathways, he may assume that each has taken the same amount of time to get there. However, an adult will see that one pathway to the stopping point is obviously longer.

He usually orders objects well: light to heavy, small to large, thin to thick, and so on. But he matches only two objects at a time. In contrast, the concrete operational child can consider more objects simultaneously.

The intuitive child finds it hard to reverse his thinking. To observe this, you might let the child compare three sticks of different sizes, but not at the same time. First, give him stick A and let him see that it is shorter than stick B. Then remove A and show him stick C, which is longer than B. Ask if C is larger, smaller, or the same size as A. He probably will not be able to answer unless you show him all three sticks at once. Apparently, it is too hard to remember the first stick. His last perception seems to interfere with his earlier one.

Of special interest is the intuitive child's

[4] *The Language and Thought of the Child,* New York: Harcourt, Brace & World, 1926; *The Psychology of Intelligence,* London: Routledge and Kegan Paul, 1950; *The Construction of Reality in the Child,* New York: Basic Books, 1954. Also, with B. Inhelder, *The Child's Conception of Space,* London: Routledge and Kegan Paul, 1956; and *The Early Growth of Logic in the Child,* London: Routledge and Kegan Paul, 1964.

self-centered view of things. The moon and sun "follow him" as he walks. And, if you ask him to point to your right arm when he is face-to-face with you, he will point to your *left* arm. He finds it hard to put himself in another's position. This attitude is reflected in his language. He takes for granted that everyone understands (and is interested in) what he is saying. He assumes that words mean the same to others as they do to him. The idea of conventions or common agreements in language usage is a foreign one.

Causal Thinking. The logic of the intuitive child may be unpredictable. He may think nothing of contradicting himself to "explain" something. If you ask him why an object sinks in water, he may say it is too small to float. On another occasion, it is too large. If you remind him of this inconsistency, he may shrug indifferently and say, "Well, it is."

It is difficult for him to think of several properties of an object at one time. He selects a blue object, for instance, but finds it puzzling to pick out one that is also heavy, round, and rough. Or, he finds it hard to conceive that one can live simultaneously on a street *and* in a town *and* in a county *and* in a state.

The four-to-seven-year-old often gives magical explanations for events. Or he may suppose that lifeless objects have conscious awareness and other human qualities. Clouds move because they "want to." There is thunder because "the sky is angry." Or, he may say, "It rained because the farmers wanted it to."

Conservative Thinking. Perhaps the most widely known findings of Piaget and associates are the intuitive child's notions of *conservation*. Here, to "conserve" means the ability to realize that certain properties of an object remain unchanged or can be restored if the object is changed in some way. Take a paper bag, for instance. Even if you crush it, you realize

that it still weighs the same and can be opened again to its original capacity. The informed adult, of course, has few problems with the conservation concept. But the intuitive-stage child's reasoning can be astonishingly different. Let us examine next the ways in which he may fail to conserve volume, length, mass, and number—each important for science comprehension.

If you show the child two identical glasses filled with water, he will probably say each contains the same amount of water. But if you pour the contents of one glass into a taller, narrower glass, he is likely to say that the taller glass contains more water than the remaining, filled glass. The error is a result of an inability to keep in mind several ideas at one time. Here, a child at the concrete operations stage would realize that the narrowness of the glass compensates for its increased height. Mistakes within the other concepts that we shall consider in this section appear to be made for the same lack of compensatory thinking.

The intuitive thinker's notions of distance are equally interesting. He will agree that two yard-long strings are the same length when laid out together. But arrange one string into a Z shape, and he may say the unchanged string is longer. Again he centers on only one variable at a time. Or, put a small upright screen between two blocks that are several feet apart. He may tell you that now the distance between the blocks is shorter than before.

You might want to try another activity to see if he can conserve substance or mass. Show him two identical balls of clay. Ask if each ball has the same amount of clay. Probably he will say yes. Flatten out one ball into a large disk and ask the same question again. He is apt to say that now the flattened ball has more clay. In a like manner, a square foot of cloth does not contain as much cloth to him when it is folded as when it is spread out.

The intuitive-stage child also finds it difficult to conserve the notion of number or quantity. Put ten checkers in two rows and ask if the top and bottom groups contain the same number of checkers. Then bunch one row together and ask the same question. Surprisingly often, he says no. He may insist on counting them if told the number is unchanged. Similarly, a pie divided into parts is usually seen as more pie than before its cutting.

For some firsthand evidence of how children react to some conservation tests, use the material in Figure 1. Try working with children of different ages, from four to ten, for example. Then compare their statements.

Piaget's work on the growth of children's thinking has made a deep impression on modern science programs. More and more teachers agree on these points:

1. There is a positive need for children to explore the physical properties of a wide variety of objects. Not to do so in the

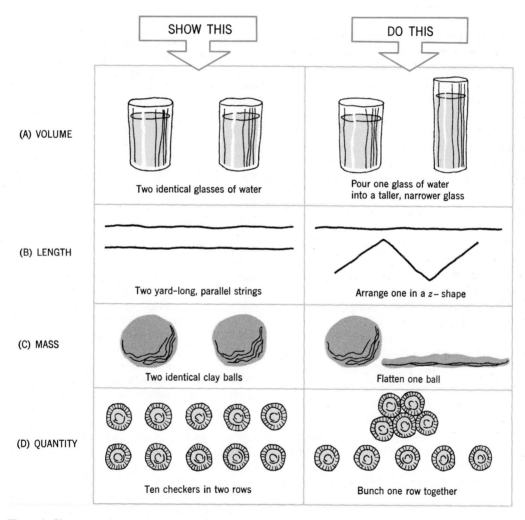

Figure 1 How to test for conservation concepts. Ask these questions twice, once when presenting the objects, and then after changing them: (A) Do the glasses have the same amount of water? (B) Is each string as long as the other? (C) Do the balls have the same amount of clay? (D) Do the top and bottom rows (or groups) have the same number of checkers? Also, each time the child responds to a question, ask why he said yes or no.

early years of schooling is wasteful and intellectually crippling in later stages of mental operations.

2. Besides handling objects and discovering their properties, children must actively transform them in different ways; that is, perform operations with them and think about how and why the objects have changed.

3. It is helpful in all stages for the child to share his experiences with others, to consider other viewpoints, and to evaluate critically these interactions.

Can the several stages of mental growth be greatly accelerated? The answers are unclear. Piaget and learning psychologists generally agree that an enriched environment seems to put the child on firm footing in each succeeding stage. In other words, he regresses less often; he operates much more successfully than peers from a stimulus-poor background. But American psychologists seem to be more optimistic about acceleration than Piaget. Jerome Bruner[5] believes it is possible through good teaching to "tempt" children into the next stage. Robert Gagné[6] would move children along by analyzing and breaking down the desired behavior into smaller, more easily acquired sub-behaviors. In a well-designed research, using a method like this, Richard Anderson[7] found that a group of above-average first graders performed mental functions usually associated by Piaget with the formal stage of mental operations. Despite these favorable signs, no one knows how broadly transfer of learning occurs when children's thinking appears to be accelerated. And thus far, there are few long-range programs designed to study the matter.

Specific applications of Piaget's work in the classroom are hard to pinpoint. His first concern has not been education as such, but the course of human development. Other psychologists, using his findings as a base, have forged additional ideas and methods useful in the classroom. Some of their work is applied in the experimental programs found in Part III.

Perhaps the most important reason to understand Piagetian theory is that it helps you to interpret children's thinking. Read this description of a class of seven-year-olds, written by an insightful observer.

As part of a unit about sand, second graders were asked to put an assortment of empty containers in order from largest to smallest. The containers varied in size and were of regular and irregular shapes. After much argument as to which container was bigger, most agreed that height (tallness) could be used to establish an order.

They then were asked whether or not there was a good way to order them when the containers were turned on their sides. The children thought that now they would have to change the order.

Then the class looked for ways to make an order for biggest that would work standing up or lying down. A few thought the biggest container would hold the most sand. How to find out which this was and which was next biggest and so on was a problem. (See Figure 2.)

Each youngster's approach was quite individual. One child started filling containers and overturning the contents on trays to compare the size of the piles. Another youngster measured how many handsful of sand were in a container. Another took a tiny cap and found out how many capsful it took to fill a small cup.

Then a girl thought of pouring the sand from one container to another. Her enthusiasm was contagious, but most of the others could not follow her idea because it was so different from their own thinking. A few children did follow her example. They would pour the sand confidently from one container to another, but with no regard for the overflow of sand. When asked which of two containers held more sand, sometimes one was singled out, sometimes another.

From an adult's standpoint it would seem that pouring sand from one container to another

[5] Jerome S. Bruner, *The Process of Education*, Cambridge, Mass.: Harvard University Press, 1960.

[6] Robert M. Gagné, *The Conditions of Learning*, New York: Holt, Rinehart and Winston, Inc., 1965.

[7] Richard C. Anderson, "Can First-Graders Learn an Advanced Problem-Solving Skill?" *Journal of Educational Psychology*, **56**, 283–294, 1965.

would be the easiest way to compare volumes. However, it appeared that unless children have had a great deal of experience — through water play, balancing volumes of materials, or other activities — this is an unknown strategy to them.

It took the children a long time to sort out what mattered, and in what way it mattered. In trying to solve the problem children said things like:

"I poured sand into the jar from the full vase and it didn't come up to the top. Does that mean the vase is bigger because it was full? Or, is the jar bigger, because I could put more sand in it?"

"If the sand flows over, that means there is lots of sand, so maybe the container is the big

one. If the sand doesn't fill the jar, the amount of sand looks smaller, so maybe that jar is smaller."

"If I pour sand from one container to another and some sand spills, I don't know whether or not I did it right or whether the spilled sand means these are different-sized containers."

"I poured all the sand from this tall one into the pail and didn't even cover the bottom."

When pouring from container to container it appeared to the children that the volume of sand changed as well as the size of the container. They observed the sand and the container as a single thing; when the sand looked too small, that meant the container was too small; when there was a lot of sand, that implied that the

Figure 2 The child's ideas about conservation of volume influence success in this activity. (Courtesy Education Development Center, Newton, Mass.)

container was big. The notion of *too much* was not available to them because everything was changing.

It took a great deal of practice, talking, and thinking before the children realized that in each case of pouring, the amount of sand remained the same. What looked like less sand meant really that there was more container space.[8]

THREE FORMS OF TEACHING

Science in elementary education is likely to appear in three forms. Mostly, it is taught as a *basic program,* with a definite allocation of time. Sometimes it is *correlated* with a broad content area; social studies or health lessons may present an opportunity to connect science ideas. It is also taught on an *incidental* basis, as pupil interest or the occasion arises.

Since all three approaches contain potential contributions to learning, let us examine them more closely. We shall consider each in terms of *scope*—the range or breadth of study, and *sequence*—the order in which learnings are taken up.

Science as a Basic Program. The scope of a modern science curriculum is likely to be almost as broad as science itself. Here is a composite list of concepts and topics commonly found in recent courses of study:

Physical Science
    Physical changes and properties of matter
    Atoms, molecules, and chemical changes
    Magnetism and electricity
    Laws of motion
    Mechanical energy
    Light and heat energy
    Sound energy

Life Science
    Life requirements of plants and animals
    Structures and functions

Diversity in plants and animals
Growth and development
Interrelationships of living things and the environment
Populations and life cycles

Earth Science
    Earth-moon-sun system
    The solar system and beyond
    Structure of the earth
    Changes and the earth's surface
    Earth history
    Oceanography
    Air and weather

Under the "expanding generalization" or "spiral" plan used with these topics, large generalizations are taught at least several times through the elementary grades. For example, "Heat is a form of energy that is transferred in several ways" may be studied in the primary grades as simple heat conduction from the source through solid materials, such as metal, plastic, wood, and so on. In the intermediate grades radiation and convection might be introduced, in addition to a more refined treatment of conduction. Upper-grade pupils may learn about heat transfer as molecular energy. Each of the experiences and smaller ideas studied contribute to understanding the overall idea of heat transfer. At the same time, progress is made toward understanding the very broad concept of "energy."

Many curriculum guides today contain generalizations and activities developed by blocks of grades—K–2, 3–4, 5–6—for instance. Others develop many of the larger ideas in every grade. Some guides list broad topics assigned to each grade level. Regardless of the organization of guides, at least two general practices seem clear. Most stress the study of larger ideas of science; and such study is usually developmental. In other words, some attempt is made for the child to study broad ideas more than once in the several grades. Because of this, you can see that it is highly important for representatives from all

---

[8] *ESS Newsletter,* March 1968, Issue No. 14, Elementary Science Study, Education Development Center, Inc., 55 Chapel Street, Newton, Mass. 02160. By permission.

school levels—elementary, junior high, and senior high—to plan together in curriculum construction.

It is general practice to organize convenient teaching segments of the entire curriculum into *units*. Although not everyone would agree with this definition, for our purposes *a unit is a sequence of related ideas and activities organized around a theme or topic*. Examples of units appear in Part II of this book. The trend at present is to teach fewer, but more intensive, units during the school year. Leading the trend are several elementary-school science textbook series.

In the Holt, Rinehart and Winston series,[9] for example, after introductory exploration activities in kindergarten and grade 1, four units are studied in depth within each grade:

Book 2
Animals
Water and Air
Seeing and Hearing
Hot and Cold

Book 3
Plants
Rocks and Soil
Simple Machines
Kinds of Matter

Book 4
Foods and Health
Heat and Energy
Changes in the Earth
Living Things and Their Surroundings

Book 5
Atmosphere and Weather
Solar System and the Stars
Electricity and Magnetism
Variety in Living Things

Book 6
Atoms and Molecules
Sound and Light

[9] Abraham S. Fischler, Sam S. Blanc, Mary N. Farley, Lawrence F. Lowery, and Vincent E. Smith, *Science—A Modern Approach,* New York: Holt, 1970.

Motion and Work
Interdependence of Living Things

An interesting side to such depth study is that concepts from several subject areas within science can be thoroughly related to one another. So in a study of the atmosphere, say, behavior of molecules, change of energy forms, properties of water, and the like are seen together in an understandable context.

The trend to fewer units is a reaction to needless repetition of topics and shallowness of study that marked elementary science programs some time ago. In many curricula today, similar topics are scheduled in two- or three-year cycles, rather than every year. Such planning still insures a developmental approach and a broad scope of study, but lessens such occasions where children say, "What, weather again?"

Some curricula have *topics* for unit titles ("Plants and Animals"), others generalization-based *themes* ("The Interdependence of Living Things and Their Environment"). Does the use of topics mean that the development of science principles from one level to another is being neglected? Actual differences between these practices may be trifling. It is just as easy to develop a spiral curriculum with topical titles as with themes, or their variations. To see how well the scope and sequence of major ideas have been woven throughout a curriculum, one must go beyond a superficial look at unit titles.

Sequence of learnings in a basic program is decided by the complexity of the ideas involved, ways they can be logically arranged in order, and how children tend to perceive the ideas. (We shall go into more detail in later chapters.) Often certain principles are "placed" at certain grade levels, after some trials to see if they can be efficiently taught. It is not unusual to see the same principle placed at varying levels in different curriculum guides and text series, and in somewhat different sequences. Ordinarily, these differences are unimportant.

The vital question is: Do children efficiently learn the principle? The fact is, we have a lot to discover about sequence in learning before we can be more exact in curriculum development.

It should be clear that we have used knowledge or "product" objectives as the foundation for both scope and sequence in the spiral approach just described. But how about thinking or "process" skills? How is the winning of these important objectives planned for in this organization? This is hard to answer specifically because again we find many different practices. Traditionally, process skills either have been ignored or not well-taught. While everyone seems to have had good intentions, the skills have been vaguely defined and hard to convert into practice. Probably most responsible for the neglect has been the scarcity until recent years of good curriculum models for guidance. Where taught, the commonest method of handling processes is to insure that at least several generalizations in a unit are developed in a problem-solving way.

Specific process skills used within this procedure might be like these:

Classifying	Observing	Making
Defining	Recording	Inferences
Problems	Discussing	Generalizing
Hypothesizing	Organizing	Applying
Researching	Verifying	Knowledge
Designing	Using	Predicting
Investigations	Models	

Correlated Teaching. It is only commonsensical to realize that learning in any subject area requires skills and knowledge from other parts of the curriculum. When a pupil looks up information in an encyclopedia, he is reading. He uses arithmetic when he determines differences in weight of a moist and dry food sample in a nutrition experiment. He employs language skills to make a well-organized report on theories of why dinosaurs became extinct. When several children draw a large panel picture to illustrate several conserva-

Figure 3 When studying about weather, it is natural to want to draw pictures about it. (Courtesy San Diego City Schools.)

tion practices, this is art. Such integration of "subjects" is not only desirable, but unavoidable when you use a variety of activities to bring about learning. (See Figure 3.)

There are times, however, when an entire subject, or an important part of a subject, is correlated with science. Social studies, and health and safety are usually the most likely areas of the curriculum to be treated in this fashion. The advantages of teaching health and safety with science are clear— there is less likely to be finger-wagging admonition and prescriptive rule-making. There is likelier to be clear understanding of cause-and-effect relationships, especially when real problems are studied: Why do most dentists recommend fluoridated water? Why should we play quietly after a large meal? Many educators favor integration of health and science. As far as they are concerned, good health teaching is good science teaching. Health study becomes an important emphasis within the overall science program.

Advantages also occur when carefully

16

selected social studies ideas are joined with science ideas. It is hardly likely that conservation practices and laws can be profitably studied without scientific information. And such questions as, How do we get our water? and, Why did they build Megalopolis City in that location? are also examples of times where social studies and science ideas intertwine. Such correlation makes it easier for cohesive, whole understandings to form in pupils' minds than when we teach these ideas in isolation.

Many relationships between science and social studies may be profitably planned. But some persons go beyond the point of effective learning. Consider the study of technological applications of science in a communications unit. The children may learn the names and biographies of several famous inventors, their inventions, and influences on cultural change. This is important and useful in social studies. Yet such an approach is likely to overlook the science principles themselves, unless specific provision is made for their study. It may become hard to build a structure of basic knowledge in science. The first choice for selecting subject matter in this case is social studies, and the tendency is to look for cohesiveness and completeness in it, rather than in science.

Even if enough time is allowed to explore science principles, both scope and sequence of science are likely to be impaired if first consideration for subject matter selection is given to social studies. Many important areas of science can be slighted, as they may not fit conveniently in the scope planned for in social studies. Also, attempts to develop an acceptable sequence in two areas at one time typically lead to the neglect of one subject or the other. It is just too hard to juggle both sequences at one time.

Sometimes correlation of subject matter is seized upon as an answer to the crowded time problem. The thinking goes, "Since there is not enough time for science, let's just correlate it with something else." A look at the number of principles taught usually discloses the now-you-see-it, now-you-don't quality of this approach. If there are ten science and ten social studies principles to explore, this makes a total of twenty principles. About the same length of time is needed to teach all of them whether taught together or separately. If anything, needed correlation should take somewhat longer if connections between the two areas are made clear.

Despite the long history of science teaching in some elementary schools, only in recent years have large numbers of schools elevated its status to a basic, rather than supplementary, study. It is only natural to see a real problem about time for teaching emerge as the importance of science education grows with our changing culture. But to meet the time problem we must establish a policy of priorities, rather than "lose" one subject in another.

Incidental Teaching. Children show much curiosity about the world around them. It is clear that some of the questions with which we began this chapter could have been asked because of interests or discoveries sparked outside of the classroom, while others may have been stimulated through in-school work. When questions are raised during study of a generalization and are pertinent, you may wish to handle them within the context of the study. But sometimes children's questions have little relation to what is currently being investigated. Or, they may come up at a time when no science unit is in progress. In these cases, questions may need to be handled on a separate, incidental basis. As important and interesting events occur in and out of the classroom, sincere questions cannot be ignored if the children's need to know is respected.

Incidental teaching is valuable in maintaining spontaneity, currentness, and some provision for individual curiosity and interest. Yet it cannot replace the need for an organized, basic program. Children's interests may flicker out quickly; perhaps only a few may be deeply interested in a topic at one time. Scope of study can be so narrow ("Let's study about rockets again!") that little is done in other vital areas of science. Sequence of learnings is likely to be haphazard, with little assurance that children are ready for more complex experiences in later years.

To summarize, all three provisions for teaching—basic program, correlated, and incidental—are useful. The basic program organization provides a teaching structure of big ideas within which children can develop important skills of inquiry. The correlated approach permits social and other relationships to be vitally joined with science phenomena. Provision for incidental teaching lends extra assurance that children's interests will be considered.

So far, we have been concerned with the overall setting and organization of science in the elementary school. Among other things, you have seen that modern programs are committed to the teaching of both process and product objectives. The next several chapters show how these two basic purposes may be accomplished. Chapter 2 considers the broad strategy that underlies modern science teaching. Chapter 3 presents specific tactics you can use.

Strategy in Science Teaching

CHAPTER TWO

Strategy in Science Teaching

OUR PRESENT CONCERN WITH THE TEACHING OF BOTH PRODUCT and process makes it important to organize activities that can best develop each objective. Accordingly, most of the experiences that children have in elementary science can be divided into two broad types: *background-centered* and *solution-centered*. Sometimes we are interested mostly in helping children become aware of certain factual information; the facts give a background of knowledge to draw upon when needed. Other times we are concerned more with their ability to think with facts; the thinking is pointed toward working out solutions to problem situations. But often we help establish purposes for either kind of activity by raising questions, or by capitalizing on questions children ask. Because of this, it will be helpful to know about the specific purposes behind each kind of activity.

BACKGROUND-CENTERED QUESTIONS

There are several reasons for using background-centered questions; the following four tend to complement and overlap one another:

1. To establish some background of knowledge before introducing a problem.

Example: "What sounds can be made with this instrument?" leads to the solution-centered problem, "What causes the differences between high and low sounds?"

Credit for chapter opening photograph. **S. L. Guiliani, San Diego City Schools**

22

Clearly the "what" of a subject usually precedes the "why." In other subject areas, children must be aware that food may spoil before the reasons are explored. They will be unable to guess (hypothesize) intelligently about the causes of night and day if unaware that the earth is in space and receives light from the sun. In short, a certain amount of informational background is necessary before children can work meaningfully with a problem.

2. To fill in gaps or omissions to form a more complete understanding after a problem has been studied.

Example: "We have discovered through experimenting that saliva changes starch to sugar as we chew. But how are other foods broken down and digested? Let's read and find out."

By establishing a context within which problem findings are related, the pupil is helped to see the big picture. Also, it would be impossible through problem solving alone to study more than just a fraction of the present curriculum. Many discoveries are beyond the abilities of children, and time for teaching is limited. While we should avoid superficially sailing over a sea of subject matter, a sizable part of human knowledge must be sampled by pupils if they are to become liberally educated.

3. To satisfy children's curiosity about things or ideas met before or during the unit which are not problems as such.

Examples: "What are shooting stars?"
"What do you have to know to be a jet pilot?"
"Who invented the Diesel engine?"

Often the reasons that cause children to ask such questions are like those in item 2. Sometimes personal interests are reflected in questions of this type.

4. To cope with special procedures that may have to be learned as the class studies science.

Examples: "How do we use and take care of a microscope?"
"How can this insect be mounted?"

"Can the yardstick help us measure how much taller this plant has grown?"

These needs are usually best handled as they come along rather than being pretaught. The pupil sees the need to develop skill with a procedure. Otherwise, he may just acquire easily forgettable knowledge about it. A desirable way to handle such needs is through demonstrations.

Questions within the above categories sometimes may be narrow and specific:

"How many legs does an insect have?"
"What are the main parts of a plant?"
"What are the highest clouds called?"

Or, they may be very broad and general:

"How does the weather bureau help us?"
"What objects are in space?"
"What are some of the ways in which animals take care of their young?"

Some background-centered questions lead to involved but prescribed answers:

"How is a photograph developed?"
"How is a microscope slide prepared?"
"How does blood circulate in the body?"

Notice that background-centered questions have several factors in common:

1. Their answers often are provided by some *authority,* whether it is the teacher, book, specialist, film, or other reference.

2. Answers are immediately or soon available.

3. Children's hypotheses as to possible answers are either not needed, or are hard to elicit because the children lack background.

We must realize that the foregoing comments refer to elementary-school children, as contrasted with scientists. Scientists are still trying to find out in detail, "How does blood circulate in the body?" as well as other questions that appear here.

Background-centered questions are helpful to establish purposes for many activities. But don't present them as "problems."

The elements that make up an interesting problem are not present. What these elements are, we shall consider next.

SOLUTION-CENTERED QUESTIONS

Many times we see statements of a "scientific method" supposedly useful in solving a problem. Usually, the method includes five steps: (1) defining the problem; (2) making a hypothesis or guess as to the solution; (3) testing the hypothesis; (4) assessing the findings; and (5) drawing a conclusion. Criticism of this method has become widespread. Scientists and educators rightly point out that problem solving cannot be so neatly described. But does this mean that it is useless to categorize problem-solving behavior? Not at all. As you will see in Chapter 4, a similar classification, using *categories*, rather than steps, is helpful in determining the kinds of process behaviors to teach.

Perhaps the commonest objection to the five-step "method" stems from the fact that many teachers present the steps as almost a guaranteed way to solve a problem. Of course, mindlessly following a ritual is likely to be unproductive in any endeavor. Consider for a moment the novice stock-market investor about to purchase some common stock. For financial success, all he needs to do is follow a two-step method: (1) buy at low prices, and (2) sell at high prices. But he soon discovers from his broker and other sources that there are numerous relative factors to consider, assumptions to be examined, and all-important judgments to be made *within* the two steps. Under proper conditions, these things can be learned to a considerable degree; but the investor hardly has a guarantee of success.

Productive thinking in science education also is based on the examination of relative factors, assumptions, judgments, and more. Actual problem solving seldom proceeds in an orderly, sequential way. There is much deviation and backtracking. However, the process does have elements within it that can be taught. As with the stock-market example, such teaching would involve helping the child learn how to ask questions, how to get the best information possible, and how to reason and make intelligent judgments with this information. But here, too, there is no guarantee of success.

Solution-centered questions are probably the best means we have to foster such a wide range of thinking procedures. Let us consider now some criteria we can use in developing these questions.

Almost everyone can agree that the school must be selective in the learning experiences provided for children. The purpose of the school is not to take up any or all things that may come up. It is instead to get children to reflect upon important ideas and thinking processes that will enable them to learn more efficiently than they would without schooling. When an important science generalization is selected and then set up in a problem-solving way, this purpose is likely to be realized.

Once a worthwhile generalization has been selected, it is helpful to think of cause-and-effect in attempting to develop a problem. A problem can generally be stated in terms of an effect or real-life application. Pupil hypotheses should be stated in terms of probable causes. Consider the following:

Generalization (Actual Cause). The greater the density of a liquid, the more buoyancy it provides.

Problem (Effect or Application). Why can a ship carry a heavier cargo on the ocean than on the Great Lakes?

Hypothesis (Pupil's Proposed Cause). Things float more easily in salt water than in fresh water.

Notice that a better hypothesis would resemble more the actual generalization, which offers the best cause. However, seldom does a child's hypothesis match a science principle in preciseness and completeness. We strive toward this, and progress does occur as the experiences and abilities of children increase through the years.

The answer to a worthwhile problem should not be obvious immediately. When possible, there should be some discrepancy or paradox present, apparently caused by a reason which demands some thought. This stimulates the children to develop more hypotheses which can be critically screened and tested.

Sometimes teachers state a problem in such a way that the venturing of a hypothesis is needless. There is a big difference between a real problem and a generalization merely cast in question form. A generalization turned into a question has a boring teacherish aura about it. Look at these contrasts:

Does air have weight?
What makes the liquid go up a straw when you drink pop?

Does warm air hold more moisture than cold air?
Why do our lips and skin seem so dry today?

Does sunlight cause a chemical change in colors?
Why do the sides of books have brighter colors than the ends, if they are stored on a shelf for a while?

The factor that makes a real problem intriguing is that at least several plausible explanations are possible. It is interesting to have potential disagreement; pupils tend to become committed to testing what seems to be the most plausible hypothesis. In the first example of each pair above, even the alternatives of "yes" and "no" are not truly present. The children know full well that if the answer were "no" the question would not have been raised in the first place.

Notice that the more desirable questions are formed from *applications* of the generalizations. Since an excellent measure of the understanding of a generalization is the ability to recognize its real-life applications, this is a fruitful way to begin teaching for such understanding. In addition, such an approach has the advantage of going from an observation to a proposed description or explanation (hypothesis). This enhances the possibilities for thoughtful inquiry. Such problems need not always be practical. But usually they tend to be more interesting and immediately understandable to children when rooted in their lives. Since forming effective problems from applications is important for developing worthwhile experiments, we shall consider it in more detail in the next chapter.

Less desirable questions from an inquiry standpoint are the kind that not only make a hypothesis unnecessary, but also make the selection of a test a foregone conclusion. Consider the following:

Will snow melt when heated?
Does running water move soil from one place to another?
Does paint prevent iron from rusting?

However, when you want to stress the teaching of experimental procedures or useful facts, questions like these may be in order. This assumes, though, that the tests would not be so obvious and restrictive. To improve these questions, you could rephrase them like this: What are some ways to melt snow? And, perhaps: How could you slow down the melting of snow? In what natural ways could this soil have been moved here? How could you keep iron from rusting?

Notice that these questions hint at multiple approaches. They open up exploration rather than restrict it. In the next chapter, we shall take up these "open-ended" questions more fully.

By and large, primary children do much better with questions that require them to think about ways to observe or manipulate concrete objects than those that call for abstract explanatory hypotheses. (The second group of questions above would be quite suitable for young pupils.) Solution-centered questions that call for "why" explanations sometimes can be ambiguous or too difficult for young children; also, pupils' explanations may not be testable. For example:

> "Why do fish go to the surface of the water?" can be interpreted as two quite different questions: "How are fish able to move to the surface?" and "For what reason do fish go to the surface?" Each has an appropriate but different response.
>
> Frequently, too, children answer "why" questions with interpretations which cannot be verified by observation or experimentation. It is impossible to obtain evidence in support or rejection of "God made the fish that way" or "The fish wanted to." [1]

To help ensure that children become involved in experimenting and make testable hypotheses, Strasser suggests that questions begin in these ways:

> What will happen if we . . . ?
> Will it work more or less quickly with . . . ?
> What might we do if we want this one to . . . ?
> Can anyone think of a way we might work to get the plant to . . . ? [2]

Sometimes well-intentioned persons say, "If a problem is presented by the children they are likelier to be motivated for study than if it comes from the teacher." What does this really mean? Perhaps the actual reasons for lack of motivation lie much more in the *form* in which the problem is cast, rather than in the source. It is true that personal interest in a particular problem arouses motivation, but only occasionally will a child state problems that immediately stir the attention and interest of the entire class. When this happens, usually it is because the problems reflect personal experiences and interests; in other words, this happens when there is self-relating in the children. If these elements are present in the teacher's problems, the chances are good for the same high level of enthusiasm and personal involvement.

Yet seldom will we achieve complete commitment and interest with everyone. Each of us has a hierarchy of personal needs that makes us more or less sensitive to the stimuli we encounter each day. Although we may hope to influence what a child considers is important, we can hardly expect to completely rearrange each child's hierarchy of needs.

What is the difference between a solvable problem and an unsolvable one? Certainly we must be sure that the problem is not beyond the intellectual capacity of the children. But when a problem situation is pitched at their level, what else must be present to assist its solution? At least part of the answer seems to be the presence of pupil background or *input* — any information, skills, and attitudes previously acquired by the child that can be used in coping with the problem. Although the term "readiness" is sometimes used in this way, it can be confused with physical maturation alone. The easy implication follows that we can do nothing except wait for the pupil to be ready for instruction. Yet a child is always "ready" to do *something*. Input makes us more aware of the need to examine what a child has experienced before our teaching begins and of ways to move him along. Remember, unless children already have or can develop with our help some process skills and information they can work with, the problem may be too difficult.

Sometimes analogies can provide input. (Refer to p. 239R,[3] activity 2, to see how work with hand lenses there enables pupils to explain how nearsightedness might be corrected in the next activity, on p. 240R). Other times, relatable information may be gotten through experiments or authoritative sources. But let us differentiate between consulting authority — a book, film,

---

[1] Science Curriculum Improvement Study, *Organisms*, Teacher's Guide, preliminary edition, Boston: D. C. Heath & Co., 1967, page 13. By permission.

[2] Ben B. Strasser, "Posing Productive Questions," *Science and Children*, April 1967, pp. 9–10.

[3] "R" means right column, "L" left column.

expert, etc. — for *data to use in developing a solution,* and consulting authority *for the solution itself.* What is needed to *solve* a real problem is not just related information, but data that the children can manipulate intellectually. (For an in-context example, see activity 6, page 351L.)

When we use background-centered questions along with problems needing solutions, we may face a real difficulty. The background source may reveal so much information in the form of connected facts and illustrative demonstrations that little material remains for the child's own reasoning. With care, a great deal of this difficulty can be avoided. Careful selection and the use of materials, interwoven with some teacher-given information, can provide much background or input for pupils without destroying the chances for thinking.

When the child lacks sufficient input, exposing him to a careful sequence of learning activities is probably the best means for developing it. By having enough input, we are saved later on from continually "feeding in" clues, so that all the child does is respond to our questions. Since the idea of input is important but elusive, this may be a good time to skim through several units in the second part of this book to note how it is developed in various activity sequences. (You might begin with some easy examples, as on page 145R, with contributing idea A, and follow the sequence through with ideas B and C. Also beginning on page 248L, activities 1 and 2.)

Let us extract now, in summary form, the important factors that make up a solution-centered problem. Keep in mind, however, that it is seldom possible to prepare or select problems that have *all* these characteristics:

1. Children have input, or can soon acquire enough to cope with the problem.
2. At least several hypotheses can be offered toward the problem's solution.
3. Appropriate activities are available.

4. Solutions develop through *reasoning* with test *data* or furnished *data.*

See if these criteria help you in distinguishing *probable* background-centered questions from solution-centered questions in the following list. (Answers appear in the next footnote.) Remember, there are no absolutely "right" answers.

1. How are magnets made?
2. What are things made of?
3. Under what conditions will a compass needle point other than north?
4. How far away is the sun?
5. Why do people wrap heater pipes with asbestos?
6. How does radar work?
7. Why does gas burn?
8. What makes a solar eclipse?
9. How does the engine in a car work?
10. How are fish classified?
11. What happens to the size, shape, and colors of a baby caterpillar as it gets older?
12. How can I make one light go on while the other goes off?
13. What makes the wind blow?
14. How do volcanoes get started?
15. Why is it daylight and then night?
16. What makes the fog come?
17. How do they know there is a neutron in an atom?
18. Why do they grease the wheels on a car?
19. Why is the earth hot in the middle?
20. Where does salt come from? [4]

QUESTION AND PROBLEM SOURCES

You have seen that questions and problems raised in class are usually pointed toward the learning of science principles and processes the teacher has in mind. You can find out what principles and processes to stress by referring to the course of study and textbook in use. But where will the problems or questions themselves come from?

[4] Items that tend to be solution-oriented: 3, 5, 8, 11, 12, 13, 15, 16, 18, 20.

Most district courses of study or teacher guides usually contain many excellent generalizations and activities. Unfortunately, only rarely do these aids indicate cause-effect type problems that pupils may explore in pursuing activities. Slightly more frequent are questions which you can use to establish purposes for the activities.

Although often overlooked, or used inappropriately, modern science textbooks for pupils commonly contain many possible problem and question situations that you can use if you know where to look. There are several places in the text to search for such situations. Pictures, particularly introductory pictures, may contain an illustration or application of a principle. The children can be asked to describe what they see. They may then close their books and develop likely reasons why the event has happened. The same picture may be portrayed by you on the bulletin board, or in a chalkboard sketch, or just verbally. In these cases, the book is not used at all by the children at the beginning.

Another place to look for problems and questions in the text is just before a demonstration or experiment. Usually there will be some need aroused at this place by the author for such activities. There is little reason why you cannot use these problems yourself, provided you have the children keep their books closed until after the thinking and activity take place.

Don't neglect the accompanying teacher's guide for the textbook. It may contain direct statements of useful questions or problems you can raise. These may also be found in the topical headings or sentences in the text. It would be helpful at this time to examine several children's textbooks and search for useful questions and problems in the places suggested here. You may be pleasantly surprised at the range and excellence of some that can be extracted from children's text series.

Some science text series for children have accompanying workbooks or activity booklets that contain problems, in addition to projects and tests. Many worthwhile ideas may be gleaned by looking over ways that the authors have used to approach a topic.

Sometimes pictures may be found in magazines and elsewhere which can be developed into problems; an eroded hillside, a rusted bridge, a caterpillar and butterfly — all may serve as vehicles for conjecture. Or, questions may be raised about things observed on study trips. In many cases, motion pictures can be used to raise questions if shown with the sound turned off. Without sound, it often becomes possible to raise questions as one would on a study trip or with a still picture.

Thus far, these techniques all permit a fairly firm measure of teacher control of problems and questions raised. Although children would no doubt make contributions as they moved along, it can be seen that the teacher would exercise primary responsibility.

There are times, however, when it is desirable to have more direct contributions from the children. An "arranged environment" can be used successfully to raise questions at the beginning of unit study to interest pupils, and at least partly reveal their background of knowledge. Such an environment might include a bulletin board of pictures, with the addition of many accompanying materials that children can explore on nearby experiment tables or at their seats. In the act of exploring the materials, questions almost inevitably are raised by the children. For example:

In a primary-grade unit on magnets, a teacher gathers a dozen magnets of several kinds and places them on several tables next to the bulletin board. In addition, there are assortments of nails and paperclips, straight pins (brass [5] and steel), three bowls of water, a bar magnet suspended from a string, and several thin sheets of plastic, wood, and metal. The unit is introduced through a discussion of pictures on the new

---

[5] Brass is not attracted by a magnet.

bulletin board. After desirable standards for conduct are reviewed, the children are invited to go to the materials and find out what they can about them. At the end of a prearranged time, the children return to their seats and are encouraged to tell first what they have found out and then to ask any questions they wish about their explorations. As expected, questions are posed by the class:

1. "How do they make a magnet?"
2. "Why can't the magnet pick up these pins [brass, but silver coated] when it picks up these [steel]?"
3. "Why does the [bar] magnet you spin stop in the one place all the time?"
4. "How can the magnet pull through water?"
5. "Why is this magnet weaker than this other one?" [They were otherwise identical.]
6. "Why does the magnet pull through the wood but not the tin [steel plate]?"

In the course of studying the unit, some of these questions are used by the teacher for establishing purposes for background activities (1, 4, 6); the others are used to motivate solution-centered activities.

Although desirable some of the time, raising questions and problems through an arranged environment is not always possible. When there are few materials, or few manipulative activities, it becomes difficult to set up a situation that incites much broad exploration. Then, too, it takes real skill to "build into" the materials latent problems which will be discovered by the children. For example, it was no accident that the teacher included identical-appearing steel and brass straight pins with the other materials. Although the pins looked the same, only some were attracted to the magnet. This was a real problem.

For these reasons, children's questions in the arranged-environment activity tend to be more the "what" kind than the "why" kind. In other words, we are far likelier to get from them incomplete, background-centered questions than solution-centered

questions.[6] An arranged environment is often desirable to develop motivation and to indicate areas of individual needs. It can serve as a preliminary set of investigations to acquaint children with the materials and subject matter they will study. This can set the stage for more analytical work or discovery of related examples. But we must realize the limitations of studying only questions or problems brought up by the children. Therefore, when the method is used, informed teachers contribute additional ideas, problems, and questions as needed.

Unexpected results in demonstrations and experiments can also be used to advantage in arousing problems and questions. Sometimes the most interesting problems are the result of some difficulty that comes up in such situations. When intentional on the part of the teacher, it is not hard to guide the children to think through a satisfactory solution. But when it is unplanned, many teachers may not be able to assist children to develop a systematic and efficient search for the reasons why the "failure" occurred. Since this is a common area of concern, we shall explore this matter further in a section of the next chapter entitled, "Analysis of Faulty Procedure."

Sometimes, children ask questions which arise from their experiences away from school. When they fall within the context of the generalizations you have planned, it is usually possible to incorporate them into regular study. But when they fall outside of this context, and are unfamiliar to you, they may be hard to handle. Of course, it is always easy to say, "That's a good question. Why don't you look it up in the encyclopedia?" or something similar. Though this approach is desirable with some children, and on some occasions, use it sparingly.

[6] As you can see on page 27R, questions containing the word "what" need not be background-centered; however, there is a tendency toward this type when the word is used.

29

There probably is no "best" way to handle all such questions. But if the question is important enough for class or individual study, it is usually not too difficult to postpone considering it until you have had time to consult some resource. Perhaps the best reason for this is not so much to find the proper answer, but to find out how the child can be assisted to think through the answer for himself. The reason for postponement need not be disguised. It is safe to say that no one in the world can immediately assist any pupil to think through an answer to any question in science. To indicate gracefully the need for such postponement you might simply say, "I think I can find a book by tomorrow that can help us with this question."

QUESTION AND PROBLEM STATEMENTS

How well questions and problems are stated is important in determining how well the rest of inquiry goes. This is why we see in most science books the reminder to make clearly defined problem statements before investigation begins. But children, like adults, tend to ask questions which make sense to them. In our haste to get children to define a problem "properly," we may introduce so many qualifiers and ramifications that the children become more puzzled than before.

One major reason why the teacher can break the problem down and define it well at the beginning is because he has previously acquired information about it, while the children have not. In order for children to break down a problem or introduce many qualifiers, they must study it first. In a true problem situation that involves many ramifications, stating precisely what we want to know is usually impossible until some work has been done toward the solution. This is one reason why there are objections to following "steps" in problem solving. Whereas stating the problem

would be the first step in theory, in practice we often return at later times to redefine it in the light of further knowledge. Notice how this occurs in a problem about the breathing of a turtle, in the next section on hypothesizing.

Most children can profit from some assistance in stating their questions. Typically this is a matter of helping them use clear language. Garbled and incomplete sentences are as undesirable in science as elsewhere. Or, if someone uses a term that is vague, it should be made clear, and so on. But we must be careful not to become analytical beyond the limited capabilities of children. Increased capacity to analyze is a by-product of further experience and maturation. To sense when to stop analysis somewhere short of tedium is an art only developed with practice.

On raising problems and questions with pupils, there is some disagreement among educators. Should we take problems *verbatim* as given by children (with minor corrections in language), or help the children restate them in a broader, more organized manner? For example, the upper-grade child's question, "Is aluminum as strong as steel?" might become, "What are the properties of aluminum and steel?" Many teachers tend to feel that such immediate improvements in children's questions are premature. They contend that the broader questions should be asked after activities have been studied relative to the initial question. Thus, in their minds, the initial question becomes a springboard into a larger pool of experiences. This seems more consistent with the ideas expressed in this chapter.

Operational Definitions. From time to time, you will discover the need for a different kind of "problem" definition, one that calls for a word or phrase to be used in an observable way. That is, you may need an *operational definition*. Let's begin with an example; then, how to detect the need for these definitions.

In one lesson, you invite the class to hold an evaporation contest: Which team can dry soaked paper towels fastest? The children plot feverishly with their teammates about how to outwit their rivals. But there is just one thing they will have to agree on before the fun begins. How will everyone know when a towel is "dry?" Momentarily stumped, they start coming up with answers:

> Squeeze the towel into a ball to see if water comes out.
> Rub it on the chalkboard; see if it makes a wet mark.
> Tear it and compare the tearing sound to that of an unsoaked towel.
> Hold it up to the light and compare its color to an unsoaked towel.
> See if it can be set on fire as fast as an unsoaked towel.
> Put an unsoaked towel on one end of an equal-arm balance and see if the other towel balances.

The class agrees that the last suggestion is easiest to observe and least arguable. It is stated as an operational definition: "A towel is dry if it counterbalances an unsoaked, identical towel." Work begins.

Our example shows two qualities of operational definitions: (1) They contain features that you actually observe or act upon; and (2) when more than one definition is suggested, you select the least arguable one for that situation.

When operational definitions are not used, it is easy to fall into the trap of circular reasoning: What is the condition of a *dry* towel? It contains no moisture. What is the condition of a towel that *contains no moisture?* It is dry.

Or, to borrow from children's humor, this example:

> He is the best scientist we've ever had.
> Who is?
> He is.
> Who is "he"?
> The best scientist we've ever had.

There are at least several predictable times in your teaching when the need for operational definitions will come up. Watch children's use of such relative terms as tall, short (How tall? Short?), light, heavy, fast, slow, good, bad (What is "bad" luck?) and so on. Or such times when comparisons are implied: "Brand X will make your sink whiter." (Than what?) Or times when ambiguities are present, such as on page 411L in extending activity 3. For some other in-context examples where the need for operational definitions come up in natural ways, see page 220L, extending activity 3; page 493L, activity 2; and page 521R, extending activity 1.

Above all, be sure definitions are linked closely to pupil experience. While we want to encourage precise thinking, the capacity to do so varies greatly among different age levels. By continually observing the two operational criteria, you are likely to be successful.

CAUSE-AND-EFFECT THINKING: HYPOTHESIZING

When an interesting problem is posed, immediately we begin casting about in our minds for possible explanations. In short, we hypothesize. The hypothesis is at once the germ of a generalization and a means by which we may avoid a chancy, trial-and-error attack on the problem's solution. But all hypotheses are not of equal value. How do we improve children's thinking? How do we help them hypothesize without doing it for them?

Sometimes pupils can be helped to improve their guesses by an indirect method, such as teaching them to identify and focus attention on key words in the problem.

Example: Why can't submarines go down to the *deeper parts* of the *ocean?*

In one class, by calling attention to the possible differences between shallow and deeper depths, a teacher elicited the hypothesis, "Water pressure gets greater the deeper you go."

31

Another indirect method to improve hypotheses is to teach children to question the inferences or assumptions that lead to the problem statement.

Example: How can a turtle breathe underwater?

The middle-grade girl who asked this question had observed a swimming turtle stay underwater "a while." She inferred from this that it could *breathe* underwater. Her observation was accurate, but her inference was not. This caused her to pose a faulty question which surely would have led to faulty hypotheses. When this was called to her attention, she changed her problem statement to, "Can turtles breathe underwater?" Perhaps an even better problem statement would have been, "How do turtles breathe?"

Elementary-school pupils, particularly on the primary level, often pose problems that are based on hearsay. Frequently, they assume that their source of information was correct. When we focus attention on this and other assumptions without necessarily labeling them as such, pupils can be helped to cast better hypotheses by asking better questions.

The psychological climate of the classroom apparently can make a significant difference in children's behavior in forming and testing hypotheses. Atkin[7] selected eleven classrooms where the climate was judged "permissive" in science instruction, and fourteen classrooms judged "less permissive." Criteria for "permissiveness" centered largely on how much pupils were allowed to participate in learning activities. All classrooms were distributed among the first, third, and sixth grades in one school system. Although findings were similar in several respects, pupils in permissive classrooms made significantly more "original" hypotheses, in contrast with the other group's more frequent reference to authority, specific observation, or experience. The permissive group also relied less upon authority and more on their own means in testing these hypotheses, to a significant degree. If these behaviors seem desirable, the implications are clear.

At various times, observations are offered by the children in place of hypotheses. What is needed is to get at the assumptions or inferences behind the observations. These, then, become the hypotheses. For instance:

An objective of a primary-level lesson[8] is to teach that sea water provides greater buoyancy than fresh water, because of its greater density. Two pictures are exhibited at the beginning of the lesson. Each shows a line drawing of a cargo ship that is apparently floating in water. The ships are identical in every respect save three: one ship is black, the other white; the black ship is low in the water, and the other is higher; cargo booms are down on the black ship, up on the white ship. The children are invited to note the similarities and differences in the pictures. It is established that the ships are identical in every way, except as noted, and that *they are carrying cargoes of equal weight*. Pupils are then invited to state the problem. After a brief discussion, this statement is considered satisfactory by the group: "Why is one ship floating higher than the other ship?" (Notice that "floating" is really an inference—at least one ship may be partially resting on the bottom.)

Now come the hypotheses, with the first several centered on the aspect of weight:

MIKE: "Well, one is black and one is white." (He means, "Black paint may be enough heavier than white paint to make it sink lower." By asking, "How would that make a difference?" the teacher helps Mike restate his observation as a hypothesis.)

LORIN: "The booms are down in one and up in the other." (This is the same kind of observa-

[7] J. Myron Atkin, "A Study of Formulating and Suggesting Tests for Hypotheses in Elementary School Science Learning Experiences," *Science Education*, December 1958, pp. 414–22.

[8] Adapted from a demonstration lesson taught by Mrs. Aileen J. Birch, Campus Laboratory School, San Diego State College.

tion as the preceding, and the teacher clears it up in the same way. "The booms are heavier when they are down," becomes a hypothesis.)

NANCY: "The black ship has a leak and the other one doesn't." (This becomes "The black ship may have a leak, and the extra water inside is heavy.")

Now, let us examine these hypotheses from another perspective. The first two are based on comparative differences, of course, but these are not likely to be *critical* differences. By examining the three in terms of *cause*-and-*effect,* the children most probably will pick the last as the best explanation.

It is highly important to let children screen out unlikely hypotheses before they plan ways of finding out. To accept and test every guess indiscriminately prevents the child from developing shrewdness in evaluating for the most probable reason. Children should develop a feeling for the "reasonableness" of a guess, whenever possible. Discussion as to what seems most promising for a solution enhances their critical thinking.

Interestingly, many of us do little "mental" experiments with the hypotheses at this time to discern the most reasonable one. This is why it is important to help children state their hypotheses in *testable terms.* However, this is not always possible immediately, particularly with younger children, or with older children who lack sufficient input.

Giving a few clues in question form to a child can cause him to re-evaluate his own hypothesis, and either amend or reject it in the new light of his thinking. For example, in the guess about the position of the booms ("The booms are heavier when they are down."), the teacher might say, "If you are weighing yourself and slowly put your arms up and then down, would it change your weight?" Where possible, for obvious reasons, we should give first opportunity for the evaluation of a hypothesis to the person who made it.

There is an issue as to *when* such evalua-

tion should take place. Basically, we have two choices: accept all hypotheses and let the class evaluate later; or let the group evaluate each hypothesis at the time it is presented. More hypotheses are believed to be advanced by the first means and fewer but possibly higher-quality guesses generated by the second approach. Older children tend to be more inhibited than younger ones. So it is good to delay evaluative screening until all contributions have been made. Otherwise, they may hesitate to contribute. Younger children are less likely to react in this way. Mild and positive criticism, and especially chances for self-criticism, may noticeably improve ideas without reducing participation.[9] Even so, each situation needs to be examined by itself.

Sometimes, hypotheses are few or irrelevant because the children fixate on the dominant feature of the scene or problem. In other words, they fail to consider all the elements that may be involved because of overattention to one or just several elements. Around and around the children go, in futile, circular thinking. Here, a suggestion may be needed to consider other aspects. Thus in the lesson above the teacher says, "In all our guesses, we have been thinking about differences between the ships. Is there anything else in the pictures besides the ships that might cause the difference?" Now more hypotheses are heard:

"The water is not so deep and the white boat is stuck on the bottom."
"Maybe one ship is on the ocean. Maybe ocean water is stronger [more buoyant] than lake water."

More clues through questions or information developed by the teacher could assist the pupils if the latter hypothesis did not materialize. Questions directed to past swimming experiences in fresh and salt

[9] Louis M. Smith and Bryce B. Hudgins, *Educational Psychology.* New York: Alfred A. Knopf, 1964, page 417.

water might help. Or, the teacher could say, "I've heard it's easier to swim in ocean water than in lake water, etc."

In this entire chapter, notice how important it is to give clues, especially somewhat indirect clues, to assist children in their thinking. This keeps them going, provided that sufficient input or background has already been developed. But is there any guide as to the number of clues we should extend to children? One teacher said, "I give my pupils the least number of clues I can for them to solve the problem within the time available." This may be the most satisfactory answer we have.

The Child Who "Knows" the Answer. You have picked out a fine experiment and a good problem. Much enthusiasm is expressed by the class when it is stated and discussed. Smilingly, you invite conjecture as to causes. Bill, your brightest pupil, sits with knitted brow. Suddenly it clears, and you have a sinking premonition of disaster. Bill quickly raises his hand and blurts out, "I know, it's because . . ." What do you do—within the law—when this happens?

One approach is just to treat the statement as you would any other hypothesis. Bill is reminded gently that he *thinks* he knows, which may be different from knowing. He is thanked for his contribution, additional hypotheses are invited, and evaluation takes place. If Bill's hand can be recognized after other children have had an opportunity to conjecture, this is better; there will be more hypotheses.

A variation of this technique is to ask Bill why he thinks he knows. In other words, he can be asked for evidence. Chances are he will quote some reference or a casual personal observation, rather than an experiment. If he has no direct experimental evidence, he will be more willing to offer his knowledge as a hypothesis. In the unlikely case he does have a valid test, his statement should be treated as another hypothesis—something that may

be worthwhile to try in turn. This may be particularly valuable if you have another kind of experiment in mind; two valid experiments will be more useful than one.

Another approach is to probe to Bill's level of ignorance. This can be done usually through the simple device of asking "why" just twice. Unfortunately, unless you know your subject matter, you inadvertently may be blocked by your own level of ignorance. Of course, this can happen to anyone, depending on the subject matter. Notice now how the two "whys" are employed here:

PROBLEM: "Why is one ship higher in the water?"
BILL'S HYPOTHESIS: "Because things float higher in salt water."
TEACHER: "Why is that?"
BILL: "I don't know."

What the situation now requires is first to confirm experimentally that things will float higher in salt water, and then to find out why. In other words, Bill's hypothesis could become a new problem, "Why do things float higher in salt water than in fresh water?"

There is another disadvantage to this approach, in addition to possible lack of teacher knowledge. Often it is unlikely that the second "why" can be tested through an experiment with children.[10] Probably, authority in some form would need to be consulted—a book, film, or whatever is available. In the hands of a knowledgeable teacher, however, and especially with gifted children, this approach may be excellent.

Actually, the individual differences of all the children need to be considered, if each is to learn as well as he can. Additional suggestions for coping with the individual

---

[10] In this case a partial test easily would be possible. Evaporating some sea water or salt water would reveal more mineral residue than in an equal volume of fresh water. A reference could then be consulted to verify and explain more fully the children's emerging concept of density.

differences of children are given in other sections as needed.

There are many in-context opportunities in Part II to help children suggest and screen their own hypotheses. See sections next to the marginal notes entitled "suggest hypotheses," beginning on page 146R and continuing in all units.

TWO SOURCES OF INFORMATION AND THINKING

Most everyone has had the experience of wanting to buy some household product without knowing much in advance about it. In the process of seeking the facts, good thinkers are likely to be more critical of this information than poor thinkers; therefore, they are likelier to emerge with a satisfactory product. Sometimes, we pick up criteria to use in the evaluation of such information without being too conscious of them, and at other times, we acquire criteria through having been "burned" by previous, unwise purchases.

Say someone wants to buy a new carpet. As usual, there are several conditions attached to its purchase: it has to be priced under so many dollars a square yard, not show excessive wear for at least five years around the heavily traveled areas, be stain-proof in case something gets spilled on it, and so forth. How does the prospective buyer know if the carpet will meet his conditions? First, he thinks of where he can find out: there are several carpet salesmen, a few friends, a consumer's magazine. Next, he mentally evaluates his sources: The salesmen recommend it highly. ("But they do have a vested interest.") *Consumer Reports* gives it a satisfactory rating. ("But will the carpet I buy be identical to the one tested?") A friend knows someone who seems satisfied with the same kind. ("But this is hearsay.") Another friend has found it to wear well. ("But he has only one child—not four.") We need to show children that getting information in science

education is something like this. We have to know what sources are available, but we also need to know how to evaluate these sources.

In seeking information, there are only two main sources available to us: *authority* —in the form of printed materials, audio-visual materials, knowledgeable persons; and *ourselves*—in the form of personal experiments and observations. Through many years, elaborate safeguards have been developed by thinking persons to reduce the likelihood of error and unreliability in both sources. Criteria we use for appraising the information from each are both *internal* (Does it make sense?) and *external* (How does this compare with what is known?) in nature.

Don't be discouraged if it seems hard to develop in elementary-school children much immediate ability to appraise the merits of authority used in schools. There are several reasons for this difficulty. Perhaps an obvious one is that elementary children just do not know enough yet. Also, they possess somewhat less logical ability than they will have later. Another is that materials used in the schools are likely to be reasonably accurate and reliable. After all, instructional materials must usually run the gamut of editorial supervision, numerous selection committees of educators, and other sources of appraisal; what survives is likely to be quite acceptable. If not, it is hardly likely that children will possess the intellectual skill and knowledge to detect error or otherwise evaluate critically. Certainly, they can be cautioned to watch for copyright dates, general conformity with what is known, to consult more than one source, to note the occasional conflict in fact, and the like. But the possibilities for critical appraisal of authority are relatively few, largely because of children's lack of background, limited logical capacity, and few appropriate materials. Therefore, we typically spend little time on critical analysis of materials. Instead, we help children learn the sources of authority that exist, ways to consult these sources efficiently, and how to comprehend what the sources say.

There are many more opportunities to teach critical thinking in the experiments and observations that children themselves make during the course of a unit. These activities are close to the raw, unadulterated facts—information minus the "thinking man's filter" already supplied when actual authority is consulted. Pupils must provide their own intellectual filter, with teacher guidance when needed, if the data are to be trustworthy. Gradually, they develop more understanding and skill in appraising their own methods of achieving information. In so doing, they also become abler to appraise critically, as well as appreciate, real sources of authority. Well before they complete high school, students with much experience of this kind do a skillful job of analyzing the assumptions, beliefs, and evidence behind the statements of authorities.

Anthropomorphism. Every child has read stories for entertainment in which animals talk, clouds cry, and steam locomotives suffer pitiably as they huff and puff up a steep mountainside. Giving such human characteristics to nonhuman things is called *anthropomorphism*. (See Figure 4.)

Most of the time children have no trouble in deciding whether events like these are true or fictional. But sometimes they do make anthropomorphic inferences without realizing it, especially when dealing with living things. Do plant roots really "seek" water? Do squirrels gather nuts with the specific purpose of surviving a long winter? Why is a lion "braver" than a mouse? Why is a fox "sly"? Why is a wolf "nastier" than a dog? Because a chipmunk is beneath a bush, are we justified in saying that it is "hiding"?

Make children aware of faulty inferences wherever they are made. It will help them to become better thinkers.

Superstitious Thinking. Most children have had some acquaintance with common superstitions, claims of magic, astrology, folk medicine, weather sayings, and the like. These conventions may offer excellent opportunities to teach the difference between genuine cause-and-effect, and mere correlation without causation. That is because two events—breaking a mirror and then badly stubbing a toe, for instance—occur closely together, there is no logical reason to assume that one event caused the other.

Children enjoy exploring actual reasons that might have prompted superstitions. They become quickly adept at providing thoughtful explanations after a little practice. Interestingly, one upper-grade class actually offered a *psychological* reason for the toe-stubbing accident: The person got "unstrung" because he thought breaking a mirror would bring bad luck. This caused poor muscular coordination, with the result of a stubbed toe!

We should encourage pupils to analyze conventional beliefs and offer explanations

Figure 4 It is easy to make anthropomorphic statements about some living things. (A. Devaney, Inc.)

as to how they got started and continue to be popular. A bright class can even be helped to differentiate between what is factual and what is merely plausible. One child offered these reasons for the popularity of the superstition that people who walk under ladders have worse "luck" than those who walk around them: Ladders are close to buildings. Things may fall off window ledges and strike people walking under a ladder, since they, too, would be close to the building. Also, workmen on ladders who drop objects would be likelier to drop things on persons walking beneath the ladder than around it. When the child was invited to show evidence that these things actually caused the superstition to develop or prevail, he began to see the difference between what is reasonable or plausible, and what has been factually determined.

Tactics in Science Teaching

CHAPTER THREE

Tactics in Science Teaching

NEARLY ALL CHILDREN ARE ABLE TO PERFORM EXPERIMENTS IN seeking solutions to problems. Although pupils cannot gather all the data they need this way, an experiment does give the capable teacher an excellent chance to stimulate their thinking. But how is the teaching capability acquired? We could study many examples, but experiments differ greatly from field to field; and elementary-school children range so greatly in mental ability. Examples at one level may not be applicable to another.

What may be needed is study of some mediating devices—suggestions specific enough for us to begin thinking of specific techniques that may be applied, yet broad enough to include many examples that may arise. In keeping with this thought, we begin this chapter with five ways of stimulating thinking in experimental activities:

1. Bridging and applying
2. Use of controls
3. Use of analogies
4. Use of substitutions
5. Analysis of faulty procedure

These methods are a combination of older and newer ideas useful at any educational level, from kindergarten through college. Though far from representing all the techniques that might be applied, these suggestions can help you get off to a good start.

Credit for chapter opening photograph. **Bruce Roberts—Rapho Guillumette**

BRIDGING AND APPLYING

We have seen that applications of science generalizations are good to use because they tend to improve the possibilities for thoughtful inquiry—children usually can relate their own experiences toward a solution. One method of stimulating thinking, *bridging* and *applying,* is a logical extension of this idea. Before children experiment, they must in some way be introduced to the problem, if they themselves have not raised it. Bridging is a process in which we introduce the problem by linking it to a life-like application, and then let children use their previous experience to think about it. Applying comes after the idea has been tested or otherwise verified. We go back to the lives of children and make other applications to extend their experiences.

Here is an example. The following generalization (or principle) has four common applications, shown at the bottom of page 42. (Examine these now.) Many more could be included.

Generalization: The evaporation rate of water increases as its surface area increases.

At first glance, these applications do not seem to be closely related. Yet all are applications of the same scientific principle. Most primary children are unaware of this principle, *even though they probably have experienced at least several of its applications.* By bridging and applying, it is easy to teach the principle in a meaningful problem-solving way. Let us convert application 4 into a bridge:

Boys and girls, does anyone here own a dog? What does it need, especially on a hot day? Let me tell you about a girl who found out something very interesting. Each day, she used to fill her dog's bowl with water. At night, it was usually about half empty. One day, though, the bowl got lost and she had to use another one. It held the same amount of water as the old one, but it was shaped in a different way. Now, each night, she noticed that the water in this bowl was almost gone. Why was there always less water in this bowl than the other one?

In this case, the teacher praises such sound hypotheses as the bowl was cracked, the dog drank more water, etc., and then helps the children to focus on the shape of the bowl as the significant factor. Pictures of the two shapes are drawn on the board for additional assistance. A hypothesis emerges: "Maybe water evaporates faster from a wide bowl." The experiment is conducted with two bowls of different diameters. Children draw a tentative conclusion. Further applications (1, 2, 3, and others) are learned through additional experimenting, observing, discussing, reading, or other means.

This is bridging and applying. By beginning and ending experiments (and other lessons) with understandable applications, purposes for doing things are clear to children. In addition, they learn science principles in a way that means something in their lives.

Now let us digress for a moment. Teachers are often puzzled as to how they can guide children from the hypothesis to a test or experiment. We shall first explain the area of decision open, and then show it in context with additional examples of bridging. Ways of handling this operation should then become clear.

Basically, your range of choices in helping the children make a test extends from no help at all to furnishing the test yourself in the form of a demonstration. In the absence of much input, few children can make experimental tests without some assistance. Note the range of choice in these examples:

"How can we test this idea?"
"What can we use on the table which can help us find out?"
"How can this assembled setup help us find out?"

In the first example, the children are left to their own devices. If they are capable, this is best; they will do all the thinking. The second example is a useful compromise. It permits pupils to develop their own ideas, yet it avoids the confusion that may accompany too much choice. With an able class, it is almost always desirable to have unneeded materials on the table with the essential materials. This forces pupils to select materials thoughtfully as well as to assemble them. Sometimes teachers place before a slower class only the materials needed for the test. The difficulty in using the materials then depends largely on deciding the best way to assemble them. The last example offers maximum help short of an actual demonstration by the teacher. It features an already assembled setup. The children's task is to figure out how it can be worked, and what data may be gleaned from its use.

In getting children to think of an appropriate experiment for an hypothesis, there is another idea that will be helpful to remember. Whenever you provide materials for an activity, at least some should *relate to the bridge*. In the evaporation experiment, for example, the teacher provided two bowls of different diameters because the bridge referred to bowls. Think of how confusing to the children it would have been if he had provided instead two wet bathing suits (application 1), or two aquaria (2), or a broom and a water puddle (3)! You realize that any of these materials could be used in an experiment to learn the same principle; but this is only because you understand the principle. Since the children do not, these materials—being unrelated to the bridge—would be confusing.

To return to more examples of bridging, observe how assistance with materials is provided in the following case. Assume appropriate responses after each question:

Have you ever noticed your shadow during the daytime? What causes the shadow? Does it always look the same? Why does the size of your shadow change? (Children offer hypotheses here.) How can we use this light to see if that can happen?

The bridge can be used to narrow the choices of hypotheses as well as materials:

Who would like to show us how to water this plant? Why did John water it that way? Well, do plants take in water through their roots or leaves? (A hypothesis is offered here.) How can this material help us find out?

The bridge may even furnish a hypothesis, in which case screening and testing it become important in stimulating the children's thinking:

How many of you live in homes where a dairyman leaves bottles of milk outside in the morning? When it gets cold enough for ice to form, do you notice anything strange that happens to the milk? What do you suppose makes the milk push out of the bottle like that? (Some opportunity for hypotheses is given here. If nobody has one, the teacher continues.) Some people think that the water mixed in with the milk gets bigger or expands when it freezes. Does this make sense? How could we use these materials to see if this is so?

It is also possible to pose several hypotheses in the bridge. The purpose would be to let the children select the most promising ones. Here, the teacher might say:

Some people think that the water in the milk expands when it freezes. Some think the milk

Application 1	Application 2	Application 3	Application 4
A spread-out wet bathing suit dries faster than when it is crumpled into a ball.	Water in a rectangular aquarium dries up faster than a round one with a small opening at the top.*	Water puddles on a sidewalk dry faster when spread out with a broom over a wide surface area.	Water in an animal's water bowl dries up faster when the bowl is shallow and wide than deep and narrow.*

* Assuming both containers have equal volumes of water.

bottle gets much smaller. Maybe air bubbles form on the bottom and push out the milk. What seems to be the best idea? (Choice here.) How can we use these materials to test this idea?

In all these examples, the teacher extends the children's understanding of the generalizations by applying them in different ways. The sun's apparent movement in changing shadows is used to tell the time of day. Water absorption through roots becomes more significant as children realize that irrigation can help transform rainless deserts into green fields. Expansion of frozen water takes on additional meaning as children understand that this is one reason the family car radiator is "winterized" against the cold. There are many additional applications.

Must we develop a special bridge and applications for *every* activity? The bridge is particularly important at the beginning of study of a generalization or a supporting idea. As a sequence of activities continues, each activity tends to lead to the next. Little or no formal bridging is necessary beyond relating one lesson to the next. Additional applications may be brought out or illustrated at the end of each sequence. The first unit of Part II contains specific examples of how this is done, beginning on page 145R.

The limitations of this method — like any other — depend on how it is used as much as on the method itself. Don't restrict applications to the common daily experiences of children out-of-school. Bridging and applying may become a straitjacket. Our object is to broaden the outlook of pupils and to give them more opportunities for learning than they would have without school. The thing to remember is that, before a problem is raised, pupils must be reasonably familiar with the objects or events involved. As pointed out in Chapter 2, an interesting demonstration, unexpected results in an experiment, or exploring arranged materials all may introduce thinking activities. In other words, when using bridges,

you can include understandable experiences *provided by the curriculum* as well as by daily living.

There are scores of bridges in Part II. Note especially page 173L, activity 2; page 174L, activity 2; page 194R, activity 1; and page 383L.

USE OF CONTROLS

In doing an experiment, children need to be reasonably sure that the results flow from what they have planned. They must plan their experiments so that there is some way of singling out the factor or factors responsible for the results. If two different-sized inclined planes (ramps) are used to see whether the longer requires less force to push up an object, both must be placed at the same height. Also, both should be of equal smoothness, and the same amount of weight should be pushed up along each. By keeping all conditions the same except length, this factor is easily identified as the one responsible for any decrease in force. Notice that friction, weight, and height are all variables which need to be controlled. These factors would have to be identical in each paired example.

But children are seldom able to recognize all of the variables which can affect results of an experiment. Therefore, we must help them to learn to be cautious about connecting a particular effect to a particular cause. They should learn to do the experiment several times, and perhaps later check with a book or other authority source to sharpen the accuracy of their conclusions.

If a problem based on an application is used by the teacher, the children's hypothesis will usually contain the factors that need to be tested and controlled.

TEACHER: Have you ever left your bike outside in the rain? What happens to the metal after a while? Where does it seem to rust first? Why is that? [1]

[1] Notice how much more natural it is to bring out a problem in this way than to say at the outset, "Will painted steel rust if it gets wet?" With this latter "problem" there is no real need for hypothesizing.

CHILDREN'S HYPOTHESIS: Paint prevents wet steel from rusting.

TEACHER: How can we test this guess?

The children now follow through by matching two pieces of steel, painting one and not the other, exposing each to the same moisture and temperature conditions, and allowing sufficient time. In addition, they could make a survey of some partly rusted toys, to see if there is a consistent relationship between no-paint and rust areas.

It is harder to use the idea of controls with primary children, unless they are given help. Younger children as a rule have not yet acquired sufficient reasoning ability and background to see for themselves the several variables that might change the outcome of an experiment. Those in the intuitive stage may become confused if they must control more than a single variable. But when given some assistance, they often rise to the occasion very well.

One way to help younger children (and older ones, too) see the need for controls is to give them a limited, contrasting choice of action, and then to help them consider the consequences. In a kindergarten class, the teacher wants to teach the generalization, "Air slows down the speed of objects according to their shape." This is an introduction to streamlining. The first of a series of experiments features a miniature parachute made of a handkerchief, some string, and an empty wooden spool to represent the parachutist. The example begins at the bridge:

TEACHER: What does a jet pilot wear when he goes flying?

CHILDREN: Miscellaneous answers and: A parachute.

TEACHER: Why does he wear a parachute?

CHILDREN: In case something goes wrong and he has to bail out.

TEACHER: How will the 'chute help?

CHILDREN: He'll fall slower that way. (This is the hypothesis.)

TEACHER: Will a pilot fall more slowly with a parachute than without one? (This is the first contrast the teacher draws to point up the need for a control.) How can we find out? Can these materials help?

CHILDREN: Let's drop the handkerchief there. It will fall pretty slow.

TEACHER: Where is the pilot on this little 'chute?

CHILDREN: He is the spool underneath.

TEACHER: We want to find out if he will fall slower with the parachute than without a parachute. What can we do? I notice there is another spool on the table. How can that help?

CHILDREN: We could drop that one, too. (Nothing more is suggested.)

TEACHER: Should we drop it first and then the 'chute with attached spool; or should we drop them both at the same time? (Another contrast is poised.)

The teacher then gets them to think of what will probably happen. By releasing them at the same time, the children can notice any differences that take place as they fall. The teacher can also inquire as to what difference it would make if the two were dropped at unequal heights, when released at the same time. The point to all this questioning, of course, is to make the children aware first that there are several variables present, and then to help them see the consequences of each. By beginning slowly in this or a similar way, children begin to grow sensitive to the need for controls. In some classes, perhaps only one of these controls could be brought meaningfully to the children's attention; in others, perhaps all three might be explored.

For some further examples of variables needing controls, see page 160R, page 223R, extending activity 2; page 385L, extending activity 2; page 449R, activity 1; and page 515R, activity 1.

USE OF ANALOGIES AND MODELS

How do you do an experiment with something that takes years to develop, like sedimentary rock? Or with a glacier, too large to bring to class? Many experiments and demonstrations in elementary-school science cannot deal directly with a real situation. Working with the real thing can involve danger, too much time, great difficulty, expense, and the like. However, there may be many opportunities to work with *analogies* of the real thing—in other words, materials and activities that reasonably resemble the actual situation you wish to take up. Analogous demonstrations or experiments are often helpful in getting children to understand causes as well as "what happens." At the same time, you can guide pupils to see that an uncritical acceptance of an analogy may result in error. They should try to determine similarities and differences between the analogy and real thing whenever possible.

"Why can't a submarine go down to the deeper parts of the ocean?" is an illustration of an upper-grade problem that requires an analogous experiment. Here is an abbreviated account of how it might be conducted.

CHILDREN'S HYPOTHESIS: The water pressure gets greater the deeper you go in the ocean.
TEACHER: How can we test this idea? Is there anything here that might help?
CHILDREN: Punch some holes in the side of that can. Make them the same size for the control.
TEACHER: What should happen if our guess is right?
CHILDREN: The water will spurt farthest out of the lowest hole, if the pressure is greater there.

(The experiment is conducted, and results occur as predicted. It is done again to "make sure." The tentative conclusion is made that water pressure increases with depth.)

TEACHER: How does this help us with the original problem?
CHILDREN: Probably the sub can't go down too far because it would get crushed by the pressure.
TEACHER: But we found out about the water pressure in a can, not the ocean. How is that like the ocean? How is it different from the ocean? Do we actually know that this happens in the ocean?

CHILDREN: Answers are varied as they attempt to note similarities and differences.

Most of the physical materials used in working with analogies are commonly called *models*. The globe is a familiar example. Other analogous models used frequently in elementary science demonstrations and experiments are the teakettle "cloud" for a real cloud; the globe and flashlight for causes of night and day; the string with attached weight to simulate an orbiting satellite; the Ping-Pong ball "chain reaction" with mousetraps for nuclear fission; the piece of paper bent to simulate an aircraft wing; and many, many more.

It is surprising how literal-minded children can be with models. ("You mean there *isn't* a real stripe painted around the earth? Then how can you tell when you've crossed the equator?") In the submarine example, the forces operating in the real situation are like those operating within the analogy. But at other times comparisons may be less complete. Therefore, when using analogies, give chances for pupils to reveal and examine their assumptions, and to critically compare likenesses and differences, within their capacities. Children will be far more likely to keep the model in proper perspective.

There is a second kind of model used in modern science education programs that we shall call a *mental model*. As you might infer, this is a theory constructed to explain what is happening when interactions between objects cannot be directly observed. It may or may not use physical materials. For example, a chemist may put together a ball-and-stick apparatus to explain the atomic structure of a protein molecule; but he might also choose to describe his model mathematically. For teaching, think of the first group of models as analogies useful to get points across in demonstrations and teacher-guided experiments. With mental models, however, you want to emphasize the *processes of*

45

developing theories to interpret observed data. The children are left more to their own devices. They are encouraged to come up with *different* models to explain or predict the *same* event. These are then tested or critically evaluated to select the most adequate model. Here is a working example.

Say you measure exactly five ounces of water in a marked vial of known accuracy and pour it into a graduated container. The water level, as expected, rises to the container's five-ounce mark. You next pour exactly five ounces of alcohol from the vial into the container, and quickly seal the top to prevent evaporation. The alcohol-water combination rises to *less than* ten ounces as shown on the container's marked side. How to account for this discrepancy? You theorize:

Maybe the container's markings are wrong. A check shows that they match those of other containers. But to make sure, you redo the procedure with water only. The water level now rises fully to the ten-ounce line, so you need a different theory.

Again you separately measure five ounces each of water and alcohol in the vial and pour each into the container. Again fewer than ten ounces are indicated. Further observation reveals that the alcohol is not thoroughly mixed with the water, but is concentrated to a degree on top. Maybe the water is being compressed, you reason. In other words, the alcohol may be heavy enough to "squash" it slightly. You begin to test your squashy-liquid model by comparing the weight of five ounces of alcohol with an equal volume of water. Unfortunately for your theory, the alcohol is *lighter* than the water.

Now you move farther beyond the directly observable in your reasoning. A more elaborate model emerges: if liquids are composed of tiny particles, then perhaps different liquids are made up of different-sized particles. You think of a further analogy. Bits of sand and play marbles are "particles" of different sizes. If the two substances are even slightly mixed, some sand particles will slip in between the marbles. The mixture will result in less volume than when the two substances are measured separately. This seems satisfactory because it makes sense and fits in with many further observations. However, sometime later you read in a science journal that all known liquids are slightly compressible! How to account for this new information? You will need to either revise or discard your mental model.

Notice that in building a mental model a continuous data-theory cycle occurs: you are confronted with data that need interpretation; you develop a theory to interpret the data; you use further data to verify, modify, or discard your theory, and so on. The process never ends, simply because most of nature is like a closed box. That is, we can seldom peer directly into natural phenomena and examine how they function. Instead, we glean what data we can from observation and make logical inferences from the data. But there is always the possibility that new, conflicting data may make the model inadequate.

Whether aware of it or not, we spend much of our lives inferring mental models to explain, predict, or control our perceptions of reality. Is there a difference between the ordinary garden variety of mental models and scientific models? Yes, but the difference is chiefly one of precision. How to teach for sharper mental models is a topic of considerable importance in modern programs.

For some in-context uses of models see page 185R, activity 3; page 347L, activity 3; page 390L, activity 4; page 405L, activity 4; and page 427R, activity 1.

USE OF SUBSTITUTIONS

Many times an experiment suggested by someone, or by some resource, includes materials that are unavailable or hard to get. When this is so, imaginative teachers and children are often able to substitute other materials that work almost as well or better than the original materials indicated. If a spring scale is suggested, perhaps a rubber band will do. A rubber comb (washed) may be an effective substitute for a rubber rod in a static electricity experience. A hot plate may be substituted for a Bunsen burner, and so on. Many examples of effective substitutions of materials are found in the units of Part II. The idea itself is a common one; for years, necessity has prompted teachers to devise substitutions of materials.

However, perhaps too much of the thinking about substitutions has been done by *teachers* rather than *pupils*. As most resourceful persons know, just any substitution may not do. There are criteria which must be met. These criteria boil down to the question: Will it work reasonably well? By letting children think through carefully the function of the material replaced and its probable effectiveness, they may become even more aware of what is taking place in the experiment than if substitution were not used. If very high temperatures are needed, for example, a hot plate won't do. Or if a permanent magnet is to be made, a steel object is preferable to one made of iron.

A visit to a large science fair for high-school students offers one of the best opportunities for observing the fantastic lengths to which effective substitutions may be carried. Of course, adequate essential equipment and materials should be a part of every school science program. But the potential resourcefulness and creativity that can be stimulated by inventing substitutions should be appreciated and exploited when possible.

So far, this discussion of substitution has been limited to materials that can be used in place of other materials. The experiment or demonstration remains essentially the same. Sometimes, however, it may be possible to substitute the experiment itself. In other words, an entirely different experiment may be used in place of that originally indicated by the book,

teacher, or someone else. Say we want to demonstrate that air takes up space. If a glass is inverted and carefully pushed down under the surface of a bowl of water, air in the glass will permit only a small amount of water to enter. If a small funnel is pressed into the vaseline-smeared opening of a small container, the air inside will prevent water poured down the funnel from entering. Both demonstrations show equally well that air takes up space. It is more effective to use both rather than one; there is reinforcement of learning and broadening of understanding as a result of seeing the generalization developed in more than one way.

Several things should be kept in mind if substitutions of experiments are used in teaching. These experiments can be analogous to the real thing; or they may directly involve the medium tested, as with air taking up space. Also, some topics—air and water, expansion-contraction of materials, and static electricity, for example—lend themselves more easily to substitutions than others. Lastly, as with analogies, the search for substitutions is a time when books and other resources can be employed in a specific, purposeful way.

For some Part II examples, see page 174R, activity 4; page 201L, extending activity 1; page 208L, extending activity 1; page 231R, extending activity 2; and page 325L, activity 6.

ANALYSIS OF FAULTY PROCEDURE

Frequently, in high-school and college laboratory sessions, students run into experimental results which are contrary to expectations. Though some of this must be expected as the result of testing out a faulty hypothesis, often it is the procedure itself that is at fault. In the past, it was customary for the instructor to diagnose the difficulty and then point out what was wrong. The student would then correct his faulty procedure and continue. Fewer instructors at present are providing such direct assistance—with good reason. A situation that involves faulty procedure provides one of the best means for stimulating thinking. By teaching the student himself to cope successfully with the situations, the instructor allows him to become more self-sufficient. Similar opportunities exist to stimulate the thinking of elementary-school children, but in less complex ways, of course.

Many of the mistakes children make in experiments involve their assumptions about *materials*. A balloon is old and slightly porous; a dry cell is worn out; insulation has not been removed completely from a wire and proper electrical contact is prevented; substitute materials may lack a factor needed to make the experiment work.

Sometimes assumptions about *controls* are to blame. In an upper-grade experiment on causes of bread mold, two children

bring in pieces of white bread. The "experimental" piece develops no mold but the control does! The children have assumed wrongly that the pieces are identical; in fact, one has been treated with a chemical to make it mold-resistant. In all likelihood the commonest cause of faulty procedure involving controls is simply the lack of enough of them.

Occasionally, *time* is a factor in faulty procedure—too much or too little. It may take several days, rather than a few hours, of sunshine before a piece of colored cloth fades. Some seeds take much longer to germinate than others. Two hours may be too long to wait before measuring the possible temperature difference of hot water in differently insulated jars.

Beyond elementary school, measurements and computational errors in arithmetic are often likely to be the causes of faulty experiments, because of the degree of precision needed. Since much less precision is expected of (or received from)

Figure 5 An experiment like this may bring out all five ways of stimulating thinking described in this chapter. (Courtesy San Diego City Schools.)

younger children, measurement and computation are less likely to cause difficulty in experimental findings. Even so, it will be worthwhile to be sensitive to such possibilities.

From the preceding examples we can see that an experiment can be conducted and results obtained without any sign that an error has taken place. Therefore, faulty procedure can lead to faulty conclusions. This happens in science laboratories as well as in elementary-school classrooms. So it is important to examine carefully where things may go wrong when thinking through an experiment. By critically examining procedures and assumptions, fewer errors are made.

Perhaps you have noticed that, in all activities described so far, the term "prove" is absent, and "test" or "find out" is used instead. Avoid use of the term prove for two reasons. It is seldom possible to experimentally prove anything in an elementary classroom. But more important, the idea itself is antiquated. The modern view is that well-designed experiments provide powerful data that lead to powerful theories. Poorly designed experiments yield less powerful data and theories. However *all* data and theories are subject to change with new information. Nothing is finally "proved." For the same reason, avoid saying to children that they are "right" or "wrong" when they propose explanations, theories, or hypotheses. Instead, simply ask, "What is your evidence?" The first practice fixes attention on the person; the second invites everyone to examine the data. This is where the attention belongs.

Sometimes children must be guided not to infer too much from the data at hand. When the familiar lighted candle under the inverted glass jar goes out, perhaps all we can say is that there no longer appears to be enough of something in the air needed by the candle flame. We cannot say from this experience that "Oxygen is required for burning" nor, "The air was all used up." Additional and different experiments may be needed before the inference can be made more specific. Yet, as indicated before, it may be difficult in some areas to find further experiments that can make the class more aware of the generalization in the teacher's mind. Rather than over-generalizing, what is needed at these times is reference to authority. This helps pupils to sharpen the generalization by supplementing the data received from the experiment.

For typical examples where faulty procedures occur, see page 146R, activity 2; page 190, extending activity 3; page 262L, extending activity 4; page 311L, activity 2; and page 443L, extending activity 2.

OPEN-ENDED ACTIVITIES

A striking difference between older and newer ways of science teaching is in the far greater number of *open-ended* activities available today to encourage creative thinking. To some people, an open-ended activity simply means putting some materials into children's hands and seeing what they can find out for themselves. But, with a few exceptions, unguided exploring results in only trivial gains toward either product or process objectives.[2]

For our purposes, open-ended activities may provide two functions: (1) chances to discover new *examples* of a phenomenon, process, or material; and (2) chances to discover the *conditions* (variables) that might change the phenomenon, process, or material in some way.

For children to discover many *examples,* ask questions such as these:

1. What materials rust?
2. On what materials will molds grow?
3. How powerful is the surface tension of different liquids?

[2] For a revealing research on the need for some structuring of learning activities, see David P. Butts, "The Degree to Which Children Conceptualize from Science Experience," *Journal of Research in Science Teaching,* Vol. 1, 1963, pp. 135–143.

4. How fast is liquid conducted up the stems of different flowers?
5. What will a magnet attract?
6. What liquids are basic? acidic? neutral?
7. Which of these objects can be charged with static electricity?
8. In what locations can we find sow bugs?
9. How many examples of single pulleys can we find around the school?
10. Which foods contain vitamin C?

For children to discover *conditions* that may bring changes, alter the preceding questions in the following ways:

1. What conditions affect whether a material will rust?
2. What conditions must be present for molds to grow?
3. How can the surface tension of liquids be increased (or decreased)?
4. What conditions affect how fast a liquid is conducted in flower stems?
5. How can the power of a magnet be increased (or decreased)?
6. Under what conditions do basic (or acidic or neutral) liquids form?
7. What conditions affect how long a charge is held by an object?
8. What conditions seem to be best for sow bugs to live?
9. How can single pulleys be rearranged to make work easier?
10. Under what conditions does a food lose its vitamin C content?

The possibilities for varying the conditions of an open-ended investigation are considerable. Pupils can vary temperature, shape, odor, size, texture, and many other physical properties. They may omit, rearrange, and increase or decrease other variables: time, moisture, friction, speed, sunlight, position, and so on. Moreover, these variables can be put together in different ways. For example, to study the problem, "What conditions must be present for molds to grow?" pupils may hypothesize singly about temperature, light, length of exposure to the air, location, and moisture. But they can combine these, too — "How much moisture with how much temperature?" for instance.

Exploration for examples — the first type — typically is easier than open-ended activities that require the manipulation of variables. Controls are usually easier, fewer possibilities exist for faulty procedures, and there is little need to consider several variables at one time. Therefore, it is especially suitable for young children, or older pupils of limited experience with inquiry.

The open-ended activity is good to use because it broadly extends children's knowledge. It enables many children to participate. It easily allows provisions for individual differences and may offer many chances for original thinking. It especially encourages the creative, playful child who explores for the sheer fun of it; who seeks variety and an outlet for his impulsivity. But there are a few cautions you should keep in mind. For one thing, there may be a study of detail or examples to an unnecessary degree. Notably where the example-centered open-ended procedure is used, the "what" aspect may overshadow the "why." Also, children's interest must be watched closely. If it begins to slacken noticeably, this may mean that it is time to end the exploration. Nevertheless, for reasons given, the open-ended activity is one of the most useful, inside or outside the classroom.

For some teaching examples, see page 199L, activity 4; page 216L, activity 2; page 236L, activity 3; page 279L, extending activity 1; page 316R, extending activity 2; and page 366R, extending activity 2.

DEMONSTRATIONS

We hear on every side that there is a distinct difference between an experiment and a demonstration. Indeed there is — if we stick closely to the classic definition of each. Strictly speaking, a demonstration is used to show something, to illustrate what is already stated as true or factual.

An experiment, as you have seen, is a quest into the unknown; it is finding one's own solution to a problem in a verifiable way. But in elementary science, there are many necessary and possible places to combine the two procedures. It sometimes becomes difficult to tell where one stops and the other begins. Perhaps this does not matter greatly in these cases, provided that children receive many excellent opportunities for doing independent thinking.

Sometimes demonstrations are needed to illustrate the use of materials or techniques, as when children are shown how to work with a microscope, make a measurement, construct a wind vane, properly store magnets, insert glass tubing into a stopper, and use vinegar to test for limestone. Although it is possible for these things to be "discovered" by the children, such discovery can be time-consuming and may imperil both children and materials needlessly. Demonstrations of this kind tend to be closest to the common definitions of the term.

At times, a demonstration may serve to introduce a problem in an interesting way:

1. A primary-grade teacher wants a class to learn some safety standards for bus travel. The children are asked to observe the demonstration, to tell what happened and why. A doll is placed in a standing position in a little wagon. The wagon is pushed and then suddenly stopped. The doll falls forward. Next, the doll is placed in a sitting position and again the wagon is pushed and quickly stopped. This time it stays about in the same position.

2. An intermediate-grade teacher slowly and deliberately wraps a wire around a nail and then touches the nail to some paper clips. Nothing happens. Next, the ends of the wires are connected to a dry cell, and the nail picks up several paper clips. One wire is disconnected and the paper clips fall. Now, a series of questions is posed by the teacher as to how and why this occurred.

3. An upper-grade teacher interested in teaching causes of winds has made a convection box. This consists of a topless cigar box placed on one side. Inside, at one end is a small candle, above which is a large hole. At the other end is another hole. The teacher lights the candle and then covers the open part of the box with a layer of Saran-Wrap. A piece of rope is set afire and then its flame is blown out; smoke rises from it. Suddenly, the teacher thrusts the smoking end of the rope near the hole farthest from the candle. The smoke goes down into the box and then out the hole above the candle. The candle is blown out and now the smoke from the rope no longer enters the box. The class is asked to tell what happened and why.

Notice that these demonstrations have some of the characteristics of an experiment. Each is controlled. Only the position of the doll is changed in the first example; only the dry cell added in the second. The candle flame is extinguished in the last illustration. In other words, children see the manipulation of only one variable. Their proposed explanations are really hypotheses which may be checked through other activities or use of authority. Notice also that these situations contain some possibilities for comparison of an analogy (bus versus wagon, for example), substitution, faulty procedure, as well as controls. While the teacher manipulates the materials in these cases, the children can participate, too.

When demonstrations are done in a "questing" manner, as contrasted with a "telling" manner, they may be as effective as experiments. Several illustrations in which the two approaches are contrasted may help us to understand the differences. Assume appropriate responses after any questions. Assume further that each activity would be followed by others to clinch the objective involved. Each of our paired examples begins with a "telling" approach.

1. In a primary-grade class, the objective is to teach what causes night and day. There is a globe and an unshielded lamp on a large table; the room is darkened.

"Boys and girls, we want to find out why we have night and day. We have found out that the earth is in space and that it gets its light from the sun. Notice where I have put the little sticker; this is where we live. We are in daylight now. The sun is shining on us. Watch what happens as I turn the globe. Is it day or night now?" (This continues until the teacher is assured that the children understand. In many cases, the children might be asked to turn the globe or help in some other way.)

In another primary-grade class—same objective, same materials:

"Boys and girls, it's daytime now and we have plenty of light to help us see. But what will happen later on after we have dinner and must go to bed? How will it be in the morning? Why do we have night and day?" (They are uncertain.) "Well, we have already found out that the sunshine gives us our light and that the earth is in space. How could we use this globe and light to find out about night and day?" (The teacher helps the children locate their area on the globe. A white piece of tape is stuck to this spot. The children try rotating the globe. The tape moves into and out of the light consecutively. That seems to "make sense." The children begin to conclude that this is the cause. Here, the teacher cautions them to see if there is another way the globe could become light and dark. Several think so, and try taking the "sun" —the teacher helps with the cord—around the "earth." Now, there is a dilemma and more data are needed. So the teacher asks them where they can find out. And so on.)

2. In an intermediate-grade class, the objective is to teach that coloration is important to the survival of some living things. Materials are a small bag of confetti, and a green lawn outside the classroom.

"Class, today we are going to find out how color helps protect animals. Fewer animals are destroyed by their enemies when they are colored like their surroundings, because they can't be seen as well. You can find this out yourself with this confetti. Let's sort out the colors first and count how many pieces you have in each pile. Notice that we have four colors: blue, green, red, and white. Let's have four children each take 100 pieces of one color—Mary, Donna, Harry, Frank— and scatter them evenly inside the area marked by the four stones on the lawn. We will have three minutes to gather the confetti. Which colors will be easiest to see? Of which colors will we gather the most pieces? Let's find out."

(The confetti is first distributed, then collected by the children. After returning to the classroom, children sort the colors and count them. There are 33 green, 48 blue, 65 red, and 70 white pieces of confetti. The teacher points out that this tends to verify his initial statement about color and its survival value.)

In another intermediate-grade class— same objective, same materials:

"Class, what are some of the conditions that help animals escape from their enemies? It does seem as though color might help. Let's say you are an insect that lives in or under a nice lawn, and you actually had a choice of green, blue, red, or white for your color. What would be the best color to have? Worst color? Why?" (Here, the teacher writes on the chalkboard choices of colors from best to worst: green, blue, white, red. Reasons for preference of rank are drawn out from the class.) "How could we use this confetti to find out if it is harder to locate colors which are like the background this insect lives in?" (The children themselves design the procedure. As they make mistakes or omissions in planning—not keeping track of the numbers of original colors, not planning for an even distribution of confetti, for example—the teacher asks pointed questions to help. After the search, pupils return to add and allot the data next to the four colors written on the board. The teacher asks the children what the data mean to them. Their conclusions are cautious, because the teacher brings out through questions the analogous nature of the activity. Animals may not perceive color as humans do. Besides, they reason, the sample is pretty small.)

The teacher also might have led the children to see the wisdom of having only confetti searchers who were ignorant of the hypothesis. This would eliminate the possibility of some persons trying to "prove" the point.[3] Another class could have been used, or several children excluded from the initial discussion. And the teacher does not always need to guide the children to see possible mistakes before they make them. When the data seem wrong or contradictory, this furnishes an excellent need to examine why.

3. In an upper-grade class, the objective is to teach that light is deflected downward when it enters water. Materials include an aquarium half filled with water, a white button (resting on the bottom of the tank), a pointer stick, and a book.

"Today we are going to learn that light does not always travel in a straight line. Bill, you aim at that button with the pointer, but make sure the tip doesn't enter the water. I will hold the grooved edge of this book under the pointer when you have made your aim. That way, you can't change your aim. Now slide the pointer into the water. Class, notice how he goes over the target. This is because when light enters the water it is bent downward. Now that we realize this, all we have to do to hit the target is to aim a little below where the button seems to be. Let's try it, Bill. Notice that now he just about hits it." (Several more trials are made until the

teacher believes the children understand.) "Why is this good to know if you are a spear fisherman?"

In another upper-grade class—same objective, same materials:

"Who likes to go fishing? What else do people fish with besides a rod and reel? Spear fishing is fun, but it helps if you know how light travels. Does anyone know where you have to aim at a fish to hit it when it is underwater and you are in a boat? Let's look at this setup. What could be the fish? The spear? What should we do? How shall we prevent the spear fisherman from changing his aim when the spear enters the water?" (Two children are chosen to come up in front and "spear the fish." Neither is allowed to watch and profit from the mistakes of the other. The class observes silently that each aim passes over the target. The teacher now asks for hypotheses to explain what might be happening to the light as it goes from the button to the eye of the observer and *vice versa*. Since the stick looks "bent" in the water the class hypothesizes that the light bends downward. The children are asked to reason in an "if-then" manner: If the light is bent downward, then what must the fisherman do? Proper advice is given the fisherman, and the target is struck. Now the class turns to its books to read the theory of why the light appeared to bend.)

The "telling" examples of these demonstrations may seem much more pallid than the "questing" ones, and demonstrations in general may seem inferior to experiments. Yet there are many times when you will want to use simple, straightforward demonstrations. When there seems to be little in the activity that may further process objectives; when the materials or concepts are complex; when you wish to begin a lesson with a discrepant event; when the materials are too fragile or hazardous for small children; when real-life examples are hard to find; when the activity is fitted into an involved, developmental sequence of activities—any of these may be

---

[3] For an interesting report on how children's preconceptions distorted their views of falling objects, see John D. Cunningham and Robert Karplus, "Free Fall Demonstration Experiment," *American Journal of Physics*, September 1962, page 656.

reason enough to try the direct approach. It is easy to develop an exaggerated reverence for "discovery," because it is often highly motivational and thoughtful. But the approach you use must remain a matter of judgment. Remember you do have two kinds of objectives — process and product. When there is little to be gained toward process objectives, and meaning can become clear through a straightforward demonstration, this is often the best thing to do. Of course, even at these times, some participation by the children is usually both possible and desirable.

TEXTBOOK EXPERIMENTS

An easy way to place a textbook author on the defensive is to say that his experiments are of a "cookbook" variety. That is, because problem, materials, directions, and conclusions are furnished, there is little opportunity for children to think. All that needs to be done by them is follow the recipe. Some criticism of this kind does seem to be in order, in spite of greatly improved modern texts and guides. At the same time, it is hard to avoid the conclusion that many critics simply don't know how hard it is to prepare textbooks or activities for wide use.

It is difficult for an author to include an involved experimental problem that arouses several or more "original" hypotheses. Unlike the teacher, he cannot change his material to correspond with whatever emerges in the classroom. Should he have suggested courses of action for any reasonable hypothesis that might come up? Plainly, this is too cumbersome. It becomes more manageable to turn a fact into a question (Do seeds need water?) or to give a forced-choice comparison (Does alcohol evaporate faster than water?). These or similar techniques are used frequently.

Then there are objections because pictures of experiments are included and conclusions are drawn for the children. At least several reasons prompt authors to include this matter. Some children are poor readers. It would be unwise to restrict science instruction to good readers. Also, in many cases the experiment just will not be done. Perhaps there is insufficient time, materials, lack of confidence by the teacher, and so on. The textbook author must prepare for "those who won't" as well as for "those who will."

Happily, more and more authors now use open-ended activities, which is one good way to deal with the problem. And conclusions for activities are now more often tucked safely into the accompanying teacher's manual, rather than right there on the page for all to see.

If used selectively and thoughtfully, a good textbook (even the "cookbook" type) can yield a surprising number of experiments and demonstrations for stimulating children's thinking. In examining a textbook experiment, especially note the way in which the author leads into the activity and his comments following it. Usually a purpose or question immediately precedes the experiment. Often it is based on an application of a principle ("Why does meat spoil?" "What makes airplanes fly?"). Or, the purpose may be in statement form ("Let's see how valleys are formed.") with extended applications written afterward.

If an application is available in the textbook experiment, or if you can think of one, this is a help in forming problems. With regard to materials, you have the options listed before: a range of choice from no materials at all to only those needed, depending on your judgment of what the children can do. Make provision — in moderation — for additional bridging and applying, or controls, or substitution, or analysis of faulty procedure and analogies. (Too much of this can be more confusing than helpful.) And perhaps most important, let the children draw their own conclusions.

The foregoing is much more thought-provoking when pupils' books are closed, rather than open. After the experiment is concluded, or at least planned, is the time to permit reading. The book, rather than the children, should serve as a source of verification. "It's fun to find out the book agrees with us," said one little girl, and she is right. It does not make sense to have pupils do the experiment to verify that the book is correct. The book is usually "right."

Now for a contrasting example of two ways of using a text "experiment." We begin with an unimaginative method.

"Today we will have a chance to do the experiment on page 161. Let's read the directions carefully so we will know exactly how to set it up." (The pupils follow in their books silently while someone reads orally.)

"Activity: Seedling Roots Grow Downward.

"Materials: ink blotter; wide-mouth glass jar; paper towel; water; bean seeds.

"What to Do: Place the blotter around the inside of the jar. Wad the towel and stuff it into the jar. This will hold the blotter against the glass. Arrange seeds in different positions between the blotter and glass. Add an inch of water to the jar to keep the blotter wet, and as needed later. Observe for two weeks.

"What Did You Find Out? Did all the roots grow downward? Roots grow this way no matter how they are turned. This is because they, like you, are attracted by gravity."

(The teacher selects from a thicket of waving hands two volunteers to set up the activity. Daily observations are made to see if the results conform to the book's statement.)

In another class—the same basic activity.

"No need for our books, class. We'll be working with experiments again. Has anyone ever seen some plant roots that were dug up? Which way did the roots seem to grow? What might happen if they didn't grow in that way? Well, here's a problem then. When you plant seeds, how do you know in which directions the roots will grow?" (The class responds.) "How can we test these ideas?" (The class suggests planting seeds in different positions in soil. Various substitutions are suggested for containers—Dixie cups, tinned cans, and so on. Since the teacher has a supply of bean seeds, everyone can do the activity. The planning includes procedures to water and then to dig up groups of seeds after staggered time intervals.) "It would be helpful to actually see the roots *as* they are growing. Can we think of some ways?" (She divides them into groups to "brainstorm" ideas. After a while, she places on a table the materials described in the book activity.) "Maybe these materials can give you some clues." (Several suggestions are made. The children evaluate critically: How will they tell if the water, rather than gravity, affects the roots? They set up controls. Will it work with other seeds? And so on. Later, the teacher asks the class to compare its findings with those of scientists, as found on page 161 of the class text. They are pleased with the favorable comparison, but find a variable they forgot to control. Next time, they vow, they will not be so careless.)

Sometimes the book presents a straightforward demonstration of a procedure or an idea. Instead of following the book you can introduce the topic and ask: How can it be demonstrated? In other words, after making the purpose clear, let the *children* figure out what to do with materials you provide or have them bring. Again, the book is opened and used for verification or comparison *after* the activity.

Here is another contrasting example. We begin again with the less desirable method.

"Open your books to page fifty-two for the directions on how to do this experiment."

"Activity: How can we separate materials by flotation and evaporation?

"Materials: hotplate, cooking pan, water, tablespoon, salt and pepper mixture.

"What to Do: To separate the salt from the pepper, pour the mixture into a half pan of water. Skim off the pepper with a spoon as

it floats to the surface. Heat the water until it completely evaporates. Examine the white material left on the bottom. Does it taste like salt?"

(The activity is performed and the class concludes, yes, it does taste like salt. They go on to the next page.)

In another class—the same basic activity.

"Does anyone have an idea of how we can separate the pepper and salt in this mixture?" (If suggestions are made, these are pursued. If not, the teacher continues.) "How could these materials be used to do this? When the mixture is separated, how will you know that you have the same amount of pepper and salt as when you began? (Various children try their ideas.) Now that we're finished, let's check our books to see a slightly different way of doing this. Which method do you like better? Why?"

With more complicated demonstrations, the materials can be set up beforehand. The children then "work" the assembled setup and try to explain how or why it works, with the text consulted later. A variety of subtle applications and changes is possible in these procedures, depending on the subject matter and the children.

Once in a while you may want to introduce a difficult or lengthy procedure, such as the three-stage technique for removing chlorophyll from a leaf and testing for stored starch. In these cases, perhaps it would be best to use the book as a guide for what to do. But even this can be done after the question is raised and some initial discussion has taken place.

"WRITING-UP" EXPERIMENTAL ACTIVITIES

One of the most frequent questions beginning teachers ask about experiments is, "Should they be written up?" As with a great many other questions in methodology, the best answer is, "It depends." There appears to be little, if any, need in the elementary school for a formal experiment sheet with spaces for the problem, hypothesis, test, data, and conclusion. It takes some spontaneity away from the situation and is likely to be an unwelcome chore. It can make a ritual out of a process that should be flexible and largely focused on what is going on, rather than on what has gone on.

Yet there are times when it is helpful for the teacher or several pupils to write things down. For example, when planning, it is desirable for everyone to be certain about the purpose of the experiment. This is needed especially when the experiment takes some time. Or, if several hypotheses are presented, these should be written down in order to keep track of them. If much data are to be gathered, particularly over a period of time, it is necessary to have a way of recording the facts. The children can then consider the cumulative total of facts before they draw conclusions. These illustrations are typical:

1. In a primary class, there is a seed-growing experiment in a corner of the room. A small sign above two coffee cans of dirt reads:

"Can our bean seeds start growing without water?
  We will water one pan of beans every day.
  We will not water the other one.
  We will see where the beans grow."

2. In a middle-grade class, there are five groups at work with litmus paper. (This chemically treated paper changes color when dipped in acidic or basic liquids.) The children want to find out which of five "unknown" substances are acidic, basic, or neutral. Each group has a chairman, who records findings on his group's data sheet. The form of recording has been previously agreed upon in the planning phase:

1. acid 2. base 3. neutral 4. base 5. acid.

At the end of the work session, the teacher has a brief discussion as to how the results of all the groups are to be recorded on the chalkboard. The following emerges:

Unknown Liquids

Group	1	2	3	4	5	
Jane	A	B	N	B	A	
Bill	A	B	N	B	A	A = Acid
Kathy	A	A	N	A	A	B = Base
Robin	A	B	N	A	A	N = Neutral
Joe	B	B	N	B	A	

Notice that the form used for chalkboard recordings is consistent with the chairmen's recordings. By keeping the two somewhat alike, it is easier for the children to interpret the accumulated data. By having a code (A = Acid, etc.) written to one side, the teacher cuts down on the time needed to record the findings. The data are now compared, discrepancies noted, and possible reasons discussed. Careful retesting is planned. At no time has the teacher written down the purpose or procedure. There is no need in this case. The thorough discussions, recordings, and individual participation have made each clear.

3. Although an upper-grade class has already completed a weather unit, there is a chart in a corner entitled, "What pattern, if any, is there to cloud movements in fall over River City?" There are three columns for September, October, and November which feature consecutively listed numbers for days. Next to about half of the numbers are written United States Weather Bureau cloud-code symbols for the dominant cloud cover, if any, each day. Even though it is only partly completed, a pattern of sequence is becoming evident. After it has been completed, this sample will be compared with data gathered by the local weather bureau for similar periods in previous years.

For more examples, see page 199L, activity 4; page 340L, activity 1; page 358R, extending activity 2; page 415R, activity 3; and page 508R.

OBSERVATION AND CLASSIFICATION

A child goes to a zoo and observes, among other things, a tiger, giraffe, hippopotamus, rhinoceros, baboon, sea otter, and rattlesnake. Ask him what he has seen and chances are the immediate reply is, "Lots of animals!" By placing the zoo's inhabitants into a single group, animals, the child has done what scientists do when they classify objects, processes, or phenomena. It is a natural tendency of the mind to group similarities or to form patterns among unordered data—in other words, to form concepts. The accuracy and completeness of our concepts help determine how well we think, whether they are about "democracy" or "density."

To classify things in science is to form concepts about them. Sometimes forgotten is the fact that a concept serves two functions. First of all, it identifies ideas or things belonging to a class or group, and thereby excludes dissimilar members. A concept also permits a chain of associations to be connected. When an informed person thinks of "wedge" many members of this class may spring to mind: ax head, tent stake, knife, teeth, even the bow of a boat. But he may also think of such associations as: narrowing the bow of a motorboat may increase speed with no increase in power; a sharp knife cuts more easily than a dull knife; it takes longer to get a sharp edge with a tempered steel blade than with ordinary steel, but it lasts longer; and a wedge is two inclined planes placed back to back, so it has the same increased-length, decreased-force relationship.

The goals of classification are the same as for other science inquiry practices: to *predict, explain,* or *control* natural events. Suppose a whale gets tangled in a strong fishnet twenty feet below the ocean's surface. Can you predict what will happen to the whale relatively soon? You might think: "Whale—that's a mammal. Mammals are lung breathers. It will probably drown."

Notice how the concept of mammal as a classification inclusive of the whale brings up the associated understanding. This enables you to make a reasonably certain prediction. Or, if a friend asks, "A whale *drown*? How?", you can explain by using the same process. The same understanding might also enable you to control the event, by swiftly cutting the net, for instance.

It is in the associations linked to concepts and generalizations that we get our best clues in choosing what to teach in observation and classification. Some time ago, a famous mountain climber was asked why he wanted to climb Mt. Everest. The reply was, "Because it's there." A more complete answer would have included the many associations that really motivated him.

Often the approach in science education has been to classify something just because "it's there." But this is not a satisfactory reason for most pupils. There is only one Mt. Everest. But there are over a million species of animals, and possibly half as many kinds of plants. In addition, there are the physical sciences to be heard from. Clearly, there must be some kind of selection to guide us.

One reason why some teachers get into trouble with observation and classification is that they begin with the idea of teaching specific identifications—so many rocks, so many birds, and so on. It is much better to start with an important generalization which leads to the need to look at some examples. ("Now that we know how sedimentary rocks are formed, can you pick some out of this mixed collection?")

There is practically no end to identification as such. The identification of an animal species every day of your adult life would cover little more than one percent of those in existence. Given five thousand years to finish the animals, it would then be possible to begin studying each species of plant— assuming that there are no mutant forms in the meantime to reclassify!

Often specialists themselves find it hard to identify specimens at a specific level. It is by no means uncommon for an entomologist to consult an insect key, or a geologist to make a laboratory test, before even a local rock specimen can be identified. Therefore, it makes good sense to keep classifications as broad as possible within the posed objective. (Note how this is done in Unit 11, beginning on page 466.)

Sometimes it is useful to teach specific identifications of certain insects, rocks, or other materials. In these cases, we might consider three things: *what* it is, *how* we know, and what *significance* or application it has. Say we want to teach examples of parasitism, an important concept in biology — this is a cowbird (what it is); this is how it differs from other birds (how we know); the female lays its eggs in the nests of other birds, which take care of the eggs and hatched young (significance).

To teach these elements, notice how the *reverse* of this order may present a more interesting approach: Sometimes we see a young cowbird being fed and taken care of by a completely different kind of bird. How does this happen? (Significance is brought out.) Let us learn some ways to identify cowbirds. (How we know.) Can we pick out the three cowbirds in this collection of pictures? (What it is.)

Of course, it is not always necessary to use this technique. When children have initiated the search for identification, for example, the "what" aspect usually precedes the others. However, we should use the same selective purposes when guiding children to observe and classify as when selecting experiments and demonstrations.

Children are interested in many things about them. The sheer availability of a variety of colorful birds, rocks, insects, seashells, or other things will prompt them to observe, collect, and want to name many of the specimens. Here, a small shelf of identification books is helpful.

Most classification "keys" are unworkable with younger children and many older children. Therefore, the best procedure in finding the name of a specimen, once its broad classification is determined, is to match the specimen with the picture in the book. This children can do with astonishing skill and speed, given some practice. A list of suggested identification books may be found on page 96R. Older children may find the identification keys in these books helpful in classifying some of the more difficult specimens. But with all children, the identification should be the introduction and not the end to inquiry.

All classification schemes ultimately can be divided into two kinds: (1) those based on possible *functions* or uses of an object, and (2) those based on an object's *properties*. In the beginning of Unit 11, "Animal Groups," children are asked to invent their own classifications based on uses — pets, farm animals, and so on. Later, they consider common properties of animals (skin covering, number of legs, etc.) in their groupings.

As you may realize, not all schemes within these two types are of equal value. The teacher down the hall, whose children spend most of the semester listening to records of birdcalls and identifying birds with flash cards, does use properties as a basis for classification. But her approach lacks mileage; pupils learn little else but identification. To explain, predict, and control, they need to study the interesting physiology of birds and their relationships with other organisms, both plant and animal.

Studying the relation between body structure and function is to relate cause to effect. The bill and feet of a bird may suggest the food it eats. Hollow bones and air sacs may permit easier flight. Properties of nonliving things can reveal similar causal relationships. Roundness of a stone found by a stream may indicate erosion through tumbling in a stream bed. Large crystals in a rock may result from slow, below-surface cooling.

One question perennially haunts those who would teach children to be better observers: Is observation a teachable "skill," or a by-product of subject-matter knowledge? In a less sophisticated period of educational history, many teachers believed that one's "powers" of observation could be strengthened by regular, studious attention to details, much as a muscle is strengthened by periodic exercise.

While more research needs to be done on transfer, it is becoming clear that children's knowledge of general techniques (rather than sheer practice) can be very helpful in improving observations. Here are three techniques you can teach:

1. *Use all five senses* — sight, sound, smell, touch, taste. Naturally, if any possibility exists that a substance is harmful, taste is not used.

2. *Keep observations separate from inferences.* "Some *liquid* has evaporated from the potato slice" is an observation. "Some *water* has evaporated . . ." is an inference. (How do we know it's water?)

3. *Make descriptions of observations as exact as possible.* Exactness can be improved by careful use of language and measurements. Nearly all properties can be operationally defined by children. How hard is "hard"? Does "roundish" refer to an ellipse, a circle, or what? What does "faster" mean? Can the difference in speed be expressed mathematically? Exactness can also be improved by noting *when* things happened during the observation. How did it look before, during, and after the event?

Children can learn well these general techniques within the limits of their maturity. And if we base our teaching on important concepts or generalizations, they can learn to detect noteworthy relationships. But we teach children who are inclined, like adults, to observe *only as carefully as their purposes motivate them to observe.* So when introducing an activity that requires observation and classification, try to begin with a bridge that either arouses or channels the children's interest. You have already seen how to bridge into lessons with a "significant" application. Let us expand this idea.

If we wish to study igneous rock, it is interesting to begin with volcanoes, then volcanic rock, and then other forms of igneous rock. Study of sedimentary rock in upper grades is begun interestingly through fossils and how they were formed. Or, in oil-producing localities, we might begin with oil and its origins. Metamorphic rock can be introduced through the odd appearance of sedimentary rock that is tilted or folded, where previous examples have been level. The identification of trees and shrubs might need to come about through the study of succession of plants in living communities. The usual succession is bare soil to grasses, grasses to shrubs, shrubs to softwood trees and then to hardwood trees. A survey can be made of the "stages" in local areas, with children's increased awareness of soil conditioning as an important factor in plant growth.

There are additional examples we can use: a small pond on the edge of town that will disappear before long because it is being filled by dying plants and growing plants invading the shoreline; the succession of clouds which indicates to some degree approaching weather conditions; the patterns of stars which give directional clues to navigators on earth and in space. All of these present reasons to observe, or to observe and classify, while each specific subject furnishes clues about what to look for.

ESTIMATION AND MEASUREMENT

For a long time in our schools, particularly beyond the elementary level, many persons have thought of two kinds of science education—one for "serious" students, and another for everyone else. Students with an interest or aptitude in science often take a different type of course than other students. There is good reason for varying the dif-

ficulty of some course work. But provisions of this sort have tended to make one science program highly mathematical and the other completely nonmathematical. Consequently, some teachers in the later grades have felt that with one student they can "pour it on" while with another they must teach a superficial, descriptive science devoid of quantitative thinking.

Such extremes can work out badly for both kinds of students. An unnecessary degree of precision and tiresome detail may be pressed onto the highly capable. The complete absence of measurement in studies of other students can result in far less learning of both process and product than is potentially there. In addition, many students who take further course work are surprised to find that science has taken on a very different character.

Mathematics, through measurement and simple computation, can be included from the earliest grades to help all children learn science. Primary teachers find and encourage a natural tendency in children to seek understanding of such concepts as temperature (Is it warm, cool, cold?), weight (Is it heavy, light?), size (Is it big, little, tiny?), and many more. Seen in this way, measurement can be merely a gradual introduction of refinements to processes long begun.

However, experienced teachers note that children generally are not interested in measurements as such, any more than they are interested in other scientific processes as such. They tend to be more interested in the physical activity and its outcome than in the intellectual processes used. They are likely to become disinterested if too much emphasis is placed on measurement. For this reason, deal with measurement (and other processes, too) as a natural course of action in finding answers or seeking solutions.

Occasionally, it may be convenient to teach a specific process in isolation. But usually it is better to relate new measurement techniques to ongoing needs. The teacher who announces, "Today we are going to improve our ability to measure very light weights," is seldom greeted with shouts of approval. Instead, as the class goes over the results of an evaporation experiment, he might say, "How do we know if the weight of the residues is the same in both pans? Can you invent a device that will show this? Do these materials give you any clues?" Children gradually can be helped to learn that the quality of the results they get in experiments usually depends on the accuracy of processes they use.

There are other factors in the use of measurement to keep in mind. For example, the mathematics curriculum must be considered. It is often easy to apply a process already learned in mathematics to science; but it may be harder to make a needed measurement not already introduced in the regular curriculum. Sometimes there will be no problem in introducing and teaching a new measurement or mathematical application in the science lesson. Other times, you may want pupils to skip an opportunity to measure something in science mainly because it is somewhat involved and can be studied later in the mathematics curriculum, perhaps in a more understandable way.

Learning in virtually any area of science is sharpened by the use of quantitative ideas. In electricity, the maximum load of a circuit is determined; cumulative voltages of dry cells are matched with the voltages of bulbs. In simple machines, an introduction to ratios is taught—distance to effort, speed to effort. Astronomy and navigation may demand some understanding of indirect measurement by triangulation. The mixing of soils may require some knowledge of fractions. The study of water and agriculture leads to the learning of such concepts as acre, acre-feet, and percentages of yield. Primary children measure lengths of shadows to help determine the time and relate the red line in a thermometer to feelings of warmth and coolness.

One way to improve the ability of children to estimate and measure accurately is to present specific *referents* (standards of measure) that can be borne in mind. If an acre-foot of water is the unit under discussion, it is helpful to measure off on the playground a square 208 feet on the sides to show an acre. A 1-foot ruler placed upright on the ground can help the class visualize the depth of water that would cover this area. If *g*-force is the unit, 2 *g*'s can be represented by a child holding "piggy back" another child of the same weight. The necessity of lying down during a rocket blast-off is readily seen when nine children are imagined to equal a force of 9 *g*'s.

Similar referents are needed for other concepts. Liquid volumes of ounces, pints, quarts, and gallons are easier to think about when there are appropriate containers in the room to which one can refer. With directions, north may be the front of the room. A mile may be a round trip to the local library from the school. Meanings associated with time and temperature can be developed by frequent references to the clock and thermometer.

Within several years, the United States may join most of the other countries of the world that have replaced the English measurement system with the metric system. Anticipating this, more and more school districts are teaching both systems. Scientists everywhere have long used the metric system because it is simpler for rapid calculating; all of its measures are defined in multiples of ten. Consider length, in which the basic unit (roughly forty inches) is called the *meter*.

a *kilo*meter = 1000 meters
a *hecto*meter = 100 meters
a *deca*meter = 10 meters
a *deci*meter = .1 meter
a *centi*meter = .01 meter
a *milli*meter = .001 meter

Incidentally, the italicized prefixes are consistent, whether one works with length, mass (grams), or volume (liters or cubic decimeters).

Children find the metric system faster to learn and easier to use than the English system. Some adults find this statement hard to accept, particularly if they have been victims of inept teaching. Why? Generations of high school students have been made to memorize the several metric units with very little exposure to concrete referents. With little or no practice in using and referring to real materials, whatever was learned was soon forgotten. Another widespread practice was to present the metric system as something that needed to be *converted* into the English system, or vice versa. This led to dreary and sometimes confusing sessions of learning formulas and mathematically finding equivalencies in both systems.

You can profit from these past mistakes by simply doing the opposite. If your district curriculum calls for work with both metric and English measures, give pupils much practice with concrete referents when working in both systems. Also, treat each system separately, instead of shifting back and forth. After much practice with concrete materials, pupils will naturally begin to conceptualize rough comparisons among units of both systems.

Very early, children should learn that there is a need for *standard units*. ("Mary Jo says the classroom is thirty-eight footsteps wide. Jason says thirty-*five*. Why the difference?") Variable inches are not permitted, a pint is a pint, and a quart is a quart. The markings on the Farenheit thermometer scale are always evenly spaced, as are those on the Celsius (centigrade) thermometer. If a balance is used to weigh things, and buttons are used for units, each button must weigh the same.

By the time they enter junior high school, many youngsters have had some experience with a variety of measuring instruments: the ruler, yardstick, clock, thermometer, barometer, balance or scales, graduated container, wind gauge, galvanometer, and protractor. Children themselves should have the opportunity to select with guidance the right instrument for the activity underway. Sometimes they can even invent, construct, and calibrate an instrument when one is lacking. This may be the best way to teach them how some instruments work. But this should not be interpreted as meaning that accurate, commercial instruments are unnecessary or undesirable.

The invention and construction of a measuring instrument can be as challenging and interesting to children as any other activity. Consider the upper-grade problem of how to determine wind speed when constructing a weather station. A light, wooden flap is hinged to the side of a

Figure 6   This child has made her own balance. (Courtesy Education Development Center, Newton, Mass.)

wind vane so that it swings freely. When the wind blows hard it pushes back the flap more than when there is a light breeze. But how can it be calibrated more accurately? Someone whose bicycle has a speedometer gets the idea to note the flap position while riding at various speeds. Another child points out that this had better be done on a windless day. Several others now suggest that it might lend additional accuracy to have the bicycle ridden in several directions and the flap positions averaged out. Even when this is done, some insist that the procedure be done several more times "just to make sure."

Take a primary class working with simple machines. The teacher mentions that only the child who is pulling a toy wagon up several different inclined planes can feel how much force is required. How can everyone tell how hard it is? To make visible to all the varying force required, the class suggests attaching a rubber band to the wagon handle. A ruler is placed next to the band to measure the amount it stretches.

When possible, bring out *variations* in *measurement*. It can be learned that even commercial products are somewhat inexact, as when several compasses give slightly different headings. When readings are hard to determine, as with a closely calibrated thermometer, it is instructive to have several children give their versions of the readings. This type of practice can illustrate the need for averaging and improving the instruments used.

The idea of *sampling* is also helpful here. A teacher working with a plant unit remarks to a class, "The seed box directions say that about 90 per cent of these seeds will grow under the proper conditions. How do we know that we won't pick out the 10 per cent that won't grow?" The time is ripe for discussion of assumptions and the need for random selection. These concepts are not too hard for children to understand when they are approached in this fashion.

Occasionally, there is need for *scaling* in elementary science activities. A group prepares a large panel picture or mural depicting some ancient animals. Since the children want everything to be as authentic as possible, some reading is done to find the probable dimensions of these animals. It is agreed that the scale should be one inch to one foot. This is so noted on the lower left corner of the picture.

Another class wants to make a model solar system. After reading the sizes of the planets and the relative distances between them, it is realized that only one scale — either distance or size — can be shown in the classroom model. Because of the huge distances involved, for the model to fit within the classroom some planets would have to be made too small for easy viewing. The class, therefore, decides that size will be scaled in the model. Proper distances according to the scale will be indicated neatly in black ink under the model.

Scaling may also be necessary in the construction of *graphs*. In some cases, graphs are the best way to present comparative data. In a long-range experiment on how soils affect bean growth in sandy soil, rich topsoil, and clay soil, fifteen coffee cans — five for each soil type — are used. Growth is measured every day with each plant, averaged, and recorded in bar graph form. The graph scale is 2 inches to each inch of actual growth, since the recording takes place on a large bulletin board. The reverse could be the case if the recording were done on a small sheet of paper.

Another class wants to find out the warmest time of day. Readings are made on the hour for five consecutive days and then averaged. Each child makes a small line graph that shows the gradual rise, leveling off, and decline in outside temperature according to the time of day. The graph's vertical axis lists degrees in intervals of five degrees to an inch. The horizontal axis presents time in hourly intervals spaced 1 inch apart.

Most beginning opportunities for scaling come in map study. And many younger children are introduced to graphs through recording in various workbooks their scores in spelling or other subjects. Therefore, it is unlikely, at least after the primary grades, that children will think of these operations as unusual. But these skills are somewhat abstract. So do not expect much success in the primary grades. Note other experiences of the children. In most cases it is unwise to plan much work of this kind until they have a mental age of eight to nine years.

For examples in Part II, notice the many places in the margins marked "reason quantitatively," especially page 160L; page 157L; page 216L; page 249R; page 418R; and page 502R.

Appraising Process and Product

CHAPTER 4

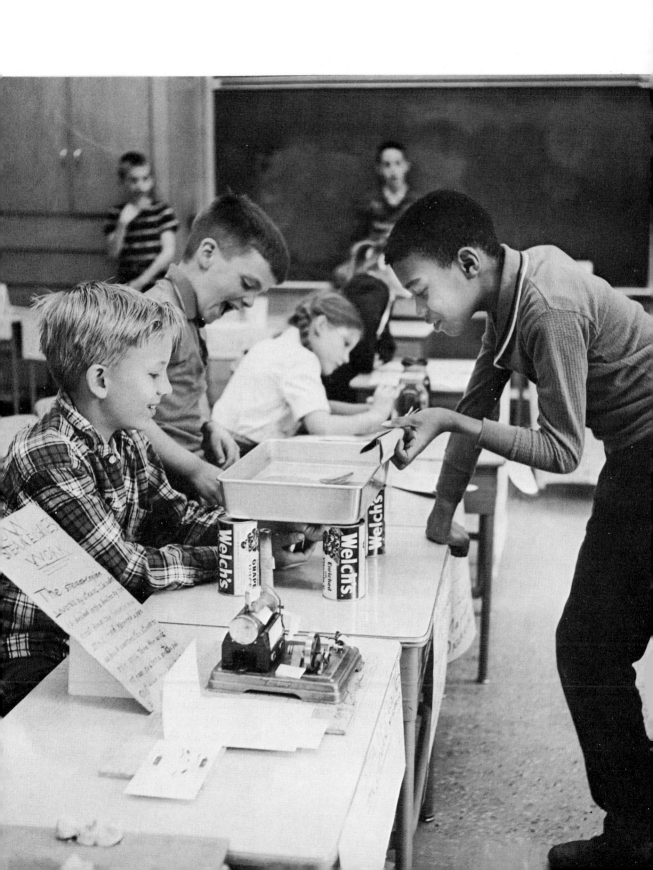

CHAPTER FOUR

Appraising Process and Product

HOW DO WE KEEP TRACK OF, LET ALONE TEACH TOWARD, THE great number of objectives suggested for the elementary school? When objectives in science education are added to those in all other subject areas, it is no wonder that much confusion exists about ways to appraise their achievement in children.

When we evaluate the work of children we need to make judgments about how well they have achieved our objectives. But before we can do this properly, our intentions must be clearly in mind. One way to ease the load of coping with so many objectives is to reduce their number. This can be done with knowledge objectives by working toward generalizations rather than isolated facts.

The learning of a generalization or concept cuts down the number of details that must be immediately remembered. Either includes or explains a great many things, and helps us to recall associated facts or ideas. That is, each becomes an intellectual peg on which to hang many facts or small ideas that might otherwise be forgotten after a short while.

The same idea can be applied to process or intellectual skill objectives in elementary science, as you shall see shortly. By using a relatively small number of broad classifications, each can help to recall a cluster of related subskills and techniques — provided these have been learned reasonably well. This is why a specific statement of objectives has been delayed until now.

Credit for chapter opening photograph. **Hays-Monkmeyer**

PRODUCT OBJECTIVES

Chapters in children's science textbooks typically are developed around a structure of large ideas or generalizations. This is also true of units found in school district guides, as well as the units in the second part of this book. In textbooks, supporting ideas, specific facts, and vocabulary are developed to aid the child's understanding of the major generalizations. Activities and pictures of one kind or another supplement the written material. In units, such supporting ideas, facts, and vocabulary are also developed. But you depend less on reading and more on the outcomes of several other kinds of activities to bring about understanding of generalizations.

When teaching, *it is wise to know the main generalizations which make up the whole structure of the text chapter or unit under study.* This permits you to see things in perspective, and to help children connect or relate ideas. It assists you to make judgments about planning and sequencing activities, and is useful in numerous other ways. You will find that about a half-dozen generalizations seem to be ideal for a teaching unit framework. Fewer may make the outline too broad to be useful, and many more tend to become fragmentary and hard to remember. For illustrations of knowledge objectives as shown in unit organization, examine now a portion of the primary-grade unit on magnets in Part II of this book (page 246).

The method used in teaching the generalization, "Magnets attract things made of iron and steel," is to begin with experiences that involve a fairly large number of facts. The children learn that a magnet attracts nails and metal coat hangers, for example, and that these are made of iron. They find that scissors and pins are attractable, and that these are made of steel. In addition, nonattractable objects are tested and discovered, both metal and nonmetal.

In the course of learning these facts, vocabulary is introduced as needed to label emerging concepts. Such words as "steel," "iron," "rubber," and others are used to begin mentally combining similar materials. Gradually, awareness grows of what is attractable and what is not. Children begin to generalize about their experiences until a reasonable approximation of the generalization develops in their minds.

For assessing how well children have learned this material, it is convenient to think of several levels of knowledge. At the simplest level the children can state such facts as the magnet attracted a nail, it did not attract a comb, and so on. Or they may identify steel or rubber objects and use the words "rubber," "steel," and other concepts in acceptable ways.

A higher level of understanding is revealed if the child can use his knowledge of a generalization to *explain, predict,* or *control* an event; hopefully, for a specific example that has not been taught or met before. This shows that the child can apply his knowledge as well as recall it. In a sense, to explain, predict, and control events is *the* behavioral objective of all product objectives. It does not change, while individual product generalizations do, depending on the subject matter.

An applicable level of understanding is most valuable. It can be extended to untaught examples. It tends to stick in our minds after some of the specific facts have been forgotten. While recognizing this, many teachers have come to the false conclusion that the facts can be bypassed and the generalization taught directly. This is unfortunate. A child's knowledge of a generalization is strongly related to the quality and diversity of the facts he studies. This is so whether these facts are learned before (inductively) or after (deductively) the generalization's introduction. It is largely because of this that we have continually stressed the idea of application.

In a more complex unit for older children, such as the one on electricity, the basic generalizations may be divided into sub-generalizations, or "contributing ideas," as we prefer to call them. It is typically convenient to assess understanding of a basic generalization through its contributing ideas, since they may more easily bring to mind examples of specific applications. This is illustrated later in the section on testing techniques.

PROCESS OBJECTIVES

Although it is important to possess knowledge one can apply, its attainment and use depend much upon the child's thinking abilities. But specifically what abilities must a child have to think clearly in science education? It is hard to find complete agreement among teachers and other concerned persons. Yet there are some indications that fewer than a half-dozen broadly inclusive skills can be used as guidelines in setting up objectives for teaching. Many curricula, and several of the nationally used science tests, now base their process objectives on problem-solving procedures. As suggested before, these procedures can be most helpful if used in the form of categories.

We shall state these outcomes as observable pupil behaviors and classify them according to five broad abilities. Page numbers after the following statements indicate places in the book where they were introduced.

The child states problems and makes operational definitions:

1. By questioning faulty assumptions that lead to a problem statement (p. 32L).
2. By detecting an unstated problem in a situation and stating it as a question (p. 32R).
3. By using clear English in stating the problem (p. 30R).
4. By identifying key words in a problem statement (p. 31R).
5. By returning when needed to a problem statement and restating it better (p. 30L).
6. By stating a problem that is testable (p. 26L).

7. By detecting the need for, and stating, operational definitions (p. 30R).

The child suggests and appraises hypotheses:

1. By identifying the several objects that may interact before he makes a hypothesis (p. 33R).
2. By stating a hypothesis in terms of a cause (p. 24R).
3. By stating the hypothesis in a way that can be tested (p. 33L).
4. By selecting the most promising hypothesis from among several alternate hypotheses (p. 33L).

The child develops and selects valid procedures:

1. By identifying the variables that need to be controlled in simple experiments (p. 43R).
2. By suggesting effective substitutions for materials (p. 46R).
3. By suggesting effective substitutions of experiments or demonstrations (p. 47L).
4. By pointing out faulty procedures, such as incorrect assumptions about materials, controls, and errors in measurement (p. 47R).
5. By stating, in his own words, the purpose for an experiment (p. 56R).

The child interprets data and makes inferences:

1. By recognizing when data need to be recorded and by correctly recording such data (p. 56L).
2. By correctly applying the data to the stated problem, and in the form of a tentative inference (p. 49L).
3. By distinguishing between an observation and an inference about the observation (p. 59R).
4. By limiting his inference to the objects tested until a broader inference is justified (p. 49L).
5. By constructing and changing his theories or models to account for data (p. 45R).

6. By noting, in observations, the relationship of structure to function or cause to effect (p. 59L).

7. By questioning the relevancy and accuracy of information (p. 35L).

8. By differentiating between cause-and-effect and correlation alone (p. 36R).

9. By detecting and avoiding anthropomorphic statements (p. 36L).

10. By consulting sources of information efficiently and accurately comprehending these sources (p. 35R).

11. By distinguishing among fact, hypothesis, and opinion (p. 35L).

12. By stating, after some study, similarities and differences between an analogy and what may be real (p. 44R).

The child *reasons* *quantitatively:*

1. By accurately pointing out or describing specific referents for units of measurement, such as inches, feet, yards, acres, meters, etc. (p. 61R).

2. By using correctly such common instruments as the foot rule, yardstick, clock, thermometer, barometer, balance, graduated container, galvanometer, and protractor (p. 62L).

3. By suggesting the need for averaging measurements when appropriate (p. 62L).

4. By performing correctly arithmetical computations when involved in science problems (p. 61L).

5. By constructing and reading correctly simple graphs and charts (p. 63R).

6. By constructing models and pictures according to proper scale (p. 63L).

7. By using correctly simple sampling techniques (p. 63L).

It is important to realize that there is no definite order to these five broad abilities. They are not "steps," but convenient *categories of mental operations.*

Note that each of the specific subabilities under each broad ability is a referent or standard by which to evaluate pupil behavior. Each broad ability is only as developed as the competency to apply the specific referents in real situations. In other words, the more subabilities one can apply successfully, the better is each general ability.

While only several are listed, many referents could be written under each broad heading. The open-ended nature of each ability is such that no one, not even an Einstein, ever acquires full awareness of all the applicable referents possible. Therefore, trying to teach just one way to "make inferences," for instance, might be worse than no method at all. Pupils need to make flexible adjustments to the different situations they meet, rather than rigid, set responses.[1]

The foregoing is a representative list of process outcomes that many children can exhibit reasonably well by the upper elementary grades. All are stated in a behavioral way. When objectives are expressed as observable behaviors rather than abstractions like, "To improve the mind," it becomes easier to judge how well they have been attained.

The idea behind behavioral statements is to increase the clarity of language. Most vague objectives are open to widely varying interpretations with different observers. Thus the more tangible and clear cut the definition of desired behavior, the easier it is to tell if the behavior is being expressed. Much the same reason has prompted the use of operational definitions in science, as you will recall from an earlier discussion.

Another important reason for clear referents is the need for pupils' intelligent self-appraisal. Teaching is worthless unless pupils themselves adopt useful behaviors. So we must make clear to children what the standards are, encourage them as they gradually develop these behaviors, and guide them when they need help.

Although these referents are put in behavioral terms, they do not tell how well

[1] For mainly this reason, the five broad process abilities are identified wherever they are used throughout the units of Part II. Seeing the many ways these abilities can be specifically taught may help you to use them flexibly.

or under what conditions the pupils must perform. For several reasons, *this must remain a matter of teacher judgment.* First of all, a standard of performance usually must be realistically attainable in the learner's mind before he will try to acquire it. So "Using clear English to state the problem" as a referent for a primary child might mean only that he is expected to state a complete sentence, or that his statement should make sense. An upper-grade teacher, on the other hand, also might be concerned with the expression of marginal grammar, redundant words, and shades of meaning. We clearly expect more from older children.

Moreover, as children advance in school, the material studied becomes more abstract. There are more things to relate. The material may be less connected to their present knowledge. Individual differences of children become more obvious. What is easy for one child in the class may not be for another. This is true of whole classes as well.

Lastly, our notions are changing about what children can do, or want to do, intellectually. Many goals thought unreasonably difficult for children even as recently as ten or fifteen years ago are now exceeded easily by many classes. We do not really know what children can do until they try.

For these reasons, we must use our judgment in appraising children's progress. To write down how well, and under what conditions, each child should perform is to become bogged down by unmanageable detail.

When confronted by the above list of over thirty specific objectives, one teacher remarked, "How on earth am I going to remember, *and* get my class to do, all of them?" It is natural to be concerned about this at first. But it is not as hard as it looks the first time around. For one thing, recognize that these are long-range outcomes. No one properly expects immediate, dramatic changes in behavior from lesson to lesson. Gains are slow and cumulative.

Also, remember that these abilities are planned for in other content areas as well. We need not pose an entirely different set of general abilities in social studies, for instance. Though some specific referents would change, as would the subject matter, "making valid inferences" is as necessary in social studies as in science.

For example, one guide for teacher education films in the social studies [2] includes these among several inquiry objectives listed:

To be able to recognize unstated assumptions and to distinguish facts from hypotheses.

To be able to determine whether evidence supports a hypothesis.

To be able to develop hypotheses.

To be able to assess the degree to which statements in an article are factually accurate, using internal evidence.

However, this similarity in objectives does not mean that abilities in either subject are necessarily transferable. Practice in both areas is needed.

The ways of teaching for process abilities recommended throughout this book may further lessen the need to remember a long list of skills. Proceeding in a problem-solving way, for example, tends to set up many opportunities for process thinking in children. By asking such questions as, "What's the problem?" and "What's our best guess?" and "What do these findings mean?" children demonstrate their skill — and lack of skill. We do not set out to teach children formal methods of solving problems from A to Z. Instead, we place them in situations where they actually work with subject matter and materials through questions, problems, and other purposes. It is in the natural course of try-

[2] Social Studies Curriculum Development Center of the Carnegie Institute of Technology, "An Introduction to the Study of History — A Viewer's Guide for Teacher-Training Films," New York: Holt, Rinehart & Winston, Inc., 1966, page 6.

ing to fulfill their purposes that needs arise.[3]

Therefore, your task is more to *recognize* when children need help than to recall everything in the way of process that is possible and then trying to cram it into lessons. At the same time, some intentional preplanning for process skills *is* important. We shall consider this in Chapter 6.

Scientific Attitudes. Besides the process and product objectives already mentioned, some persons would add a separate group of objectives for developing attitudes: the child is honest and objective, is ready to try innovations, is wary of hasty judgments, is curious about his environment, respects evidence, is willing to listen to the ideas of others, and so on. Often implied is that these attitudes are directly taught and evaluated.

This may be naive, for several reasons. Why does a scientist practice these desirable attitudes? He knows how easy it is to be "wrong" when he is not objective. He also knows how easily his work can be checked by his colleagues' methods of inquiry. Most attitudes are learned from two sources: (1) authority figures and other persons who furnish models for behavior; and (2) how we interpret the results that flow from the natural consequences of our activities. Although both are used, and perhaps needed, which is preferable? In an inquiry-centered program, attitude development happens in much the same way as with scientists: children compare the consequences of having and *not* having open-minded attitudes. Activities bring out these consequences at every turn. It is difficult, if not impossible, to separate attitudes from the thinking processes used. They are a long range by-product of inquiry itself.

Not everyone subscribes to this "by-product theory." Dissenters rightly point out that generations of students have left high school and college laboratories with few positive, and even some negative, attitudes. But they fail to recognize the difference between inquiry programs and those programs devoted to laboratory exercises from workbooks, uncritical reading, and continual direction from the top.

Another reason why many students have not become committed to scientific attitudes may be lack of application in both daily living and in other subjects. For an analogy, consider how handwriting is taught in elementary schools. To some teachers, handwriting is a subject taught for twenty minutes three times a week. To others, handwriting instruction may be needed anytime a child picks up a pencil.

Back again to our list of process skills. How much do you need it to help children become better thinkers? No educated person begins teaching with a blank mind. Most educated adults already have a reasonable stock of criteria for good thinking. Occasional references to a list, such as the foregoing, may serve to add a few helpful criteria to what you already possess. Over the years, the ability to detect and correct errors in thinking continues to improve. As your usable inventory of specific referents grows within each of the five broad abilities, so does your capacity to help children. But this kind of growth never ends. When a student teacher asked a professor how many referents for each ability one should have, the reply was, "How capable a teacher do you want to be?"

Some persons rely heavily upon formal, written statements of objectives. Although these may be of some help, you are likelier to get better results with process outcomes if your mind is organized than if the organization is only on paper. Teaching for process is often done best through the flexible, immediate tactics used in "teachable moments." These occasions arise continually if children are permitted to think for themselves. You need not be concerned if you know only a few usable

[3] A prominent and well designed exception to this practice is *Science—A Process Approach,* described in Part III.

73

referents at this time. If used continually, they probably will serve better than long lists of written outcomes. These are seldom translated into action.

Before we begin with specific examples of ways to appraise science achievement, a final point must be made: No child learns science in a vacuum. Progress in other academic areas, general interests and aspirations, home background, intelligence, social skills, and psychological makeup all have an effect on achievement in science. Any appraisal of growth in science must be seen in the light of all the information that is available. Therefore, view the upcoming ways of appraising achievement as a contribution toward the evaluation of children's growth in science rather than the entire operation.

TESTING FOR PRODUCT OBJECTIVES

As mentioned before, most of the product objectives appraised concern vocabulary, specific facts, and generalizations or, if the generalizations are unusually broad, contributing ideas. Let us look at several ways of testing for this material. To be specific we shall use a generalization from the electricity unit of Part II (p. 285L): "Short circuits and overloaded circuits may create dangerously hot wires; fuses or circuit breakers are used to eliminate this danger."

Testing Vocabulary (Terms and Concepts). A partial list of the vocabulary used in learning this generalization includes the following words and general definitions.

Fuse. A safety strip of metal that melts and breaks an electric circuit when the wires get too hot.
Circuit Breaker. A safety device used to open a circuit in place of a fuse.
Ampere. A measure of the amount of electric current flowing through a wire.

Volt. A measure of the force or pressure behind the flow of electricity.
Watt. A measure that tells how fast electricity is being used.

Notice that these definitions may be less precise than perhaps some persons would like. In other words, what "forgiving" considerations or conditions, if any, must be extended to children? These words are concepts, and grow in meaning with pupils as additional experiences are acquired, particularly in the mathematics of high-school physics. So the acceptable degree of precision must be largely a matter of judgment.

Here, now, are several methods of checking knowledge of these words, expressed in terms of definite pupil behaviors:

1. Given the term, the child selects a correct definition.

A *fuse* is a:
a. tool that joins two wires together without heating them.
(b.) safety strip of metal that melts when a circuit gets too hot.
c. measuring instrument that tells how much electricity is used.
d. plug that increases the flow of electricity when two wires cross.

In this multiple-choice item, an attempt has been made to keep the incorrect options plausible so that the answer cannot be detected through common sense alone. Note further that the options are about the same length.

2. The child identifies an accurate or inaccurate definition.

(T)F A *fuse* is a strip of metal that melts when a circuit gets too hot.

Although a true-false item like this seems easy to write, take care to avoid the exact words given in the book or other source. This tends to reward memorization rather than understanding. You will also want to avoid the use of such words as *all, always, never, no,* and *none.* Brighter pupils know that these "specific determiners," as they are called by test writers, usually indicate a false item. *May, generally,* and *should* typically indicate a true item, and should be avoided, too. A main defect in use of a true-false item is the likely chance that pupils will mark the correct answer without really knowing it. Although this makes little or no difference in a person's class rank — the chances either way tend to even out — you never can be confident about a child's actual knowledge.

3. Given the term, the child supplies an acceptable definition in his own words.

What is a *fuse?*
A fuse is a thing used for safety. It melts when a wire gets too hot and breaks the circuit.

While the short-answer method is excellent for revealing knowledge, a continual difficulty is the "originality" of the answers received. The answers are so varied their correctness is hard to judge. For this reason, restrict its use to situations that tend to have only one correct answer. This restriction may result in your emphasizing only simple, factual material. But several short-answer items demonstrated below show that it is also suited for reasoning items.

4. The child selects a proper synonym or analogy related to a given term.

A *fuse* is most like a bicycle:
a. horn b. speedometer (c.) brake d. tire

An item of this kind is somewhat harder than the others already shown because the pupil must abstract a common relationship between two apparently different things. These items often are more difficult to write.

5. The child states the main likeness and difference between two given, functionally related terms.

A. How is an electric *fuse* like an electric *switch?*

B. How are these two things different?
(A.) A fuse and a switch can both open a circuit.
(B.) A fuse opens the circuit only when it gets too hot. A switch is used to open and close a circuit anytime.

This is another item that calls for somewhat more reasoning than some of the others listed previously. Being a short-answer type, expect the same difficulty of variation in answers as has been pointed out before.

6. Given the definition, the child supplies the name of the term.

A safety strip of metal that melts when a circuit gets too hot is called a(n) __fuse.__

Observe the use of *n* with the article *a* to prevent it from becoming a context clue. The space allotted for the completion part may be another clue, and so should be of uniform length in other completion items. Although ordinarily it is less confusing to a child to respond to a question than to complete a statement, the meaning in this statement should be clear.

For an interesting variation of this method, use the form of a crossword puzzle. The number of spaces assigned each word provides an additional clue not present in the preceding example:

Down
1. A safety strip of metal that melts when a circuit gets too hot.
3. A measure of the amount of electric current flowing through a wire.

4. A measure of the force or pressure behind the flow of electricity.

Across

2. A safety device which shuts off a circuit that is too hot. (2 words)

5. A measure that tells how fast electricity is being used.

7. The child matches correctly given terms and definitions.

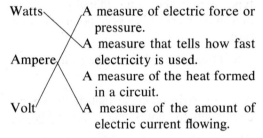

Watts — A measure of electric force or pressure.

A measure that tells how fast electricity is used.

Ampere — A measure of the heat formed in a circuit.

Volt — A measure of the amount of electric current flowing.

In using a matching item, develop some degree of likeness among terms in the first column as well as responses in the second column. Otherwise, it is easy for pupils to reduce the number of options through common sense alone. Note that such common-sense elimination can also be offset by employing a larger number of responses than needed.

Testing Factual Knowledge. Some of the specific facts presented before or during the development of the generalization on short circuits are these:

1. A penny has a high melting temperature.
2. A fuse has a low melting temperature.
3. Insulation is used to prevent electricity from leaving a wire.
4. A house appliance cord contains two wires.
5. Electric current for houses usually is supplied at a steady 110–120 volts.
6. Nearly all houses use parallel circuits in electric wiring.

Testing for facts is done much in the same way as vocabulary appraisal. Since this usually presents the least difficulty to teachers, only a few additional examples are presented. Numerals before the items refer to the facts listed above.

1. A penny has a (high, low) melting temperature.

1–2. Which has a higher melting point, a penny or a fuse?

A penny.

1–2. T(F) A penny has a lower melting point than a fuse.

3. Why is insulating material placed around an electric wire?

Insulation keeps the electricity from leaving the wire.

4. Inside an ordinary electric appliance cord, there is (are):
   a. 1 wire (b.) 2 wires c. 3 wires
   d. 4 wires

5. Electric current for most houses is supplied steadily at about:
   a. 40 volts b. 90 volts (c.) 120 volts
   d. 150 volts

6. Which one of these statements about house wiring is correct?
   (a.) Nearly all houses are wired in parallel.
   b. Nearly all houses are wired in series.
   c. About half are in series, the other half in parallel.

It may be worthwhile to note that in the last example, the words "nearly all" and "about" appear. Ordinarily, these could be considered specific determiners. However, when they are balanced among all the options or within an option, their clue value disappears.

Testing Applicable Generalizations. Some persons assume that understanding of a broad generalization may be tested adequately through the use of only one item. This is most unlikely. A broad generalization contains at least several parts that are usually hard to examine unless items are designed especially for this purpose. Moreover, the application of a generalization involves an adding and fitting together process in the mind. That is, when one uses a generalization, such use also involves previously acquired, lesser levels of knowledge—terms, facts, simpler concepts, and contributing ideas.

To check for thorough understanding of a broad generalization, it is a good idea to use items based on its several contributing ideas. This allows you to probe for soft spots in the child's total understanding of the generalization. In other words, it is less likely that an important aspect will be omitted.

Another advantage in testing for contributing ideas is that most direct, factual testing, and to some extent vocabulary testing, can be eliminated. As we have pointed out, these tend to be included in the several broader items. And because the contributing ideas are more specific than the generalization itself, applications are easier to think of when writing items. This last point becomes clear when the present generalization and its three contributing ideas are listed with possible applications:

Short circuits and overloaded circuits may create dangerously hot wires; fuses or circuit breakers are used to eliminate this danger.

1. A short circuit results when a resistor (light, appliance, etc.) is largely bypassed; the increased flow of electricity increases the heat of the wire. (Application: A lamp cord has been placed under a heavily traveled area of a rug. One night, the light goes out and part of the cord gets hot.)

2. Fuses are designed to open a circuit that is heating up before it becomes dangerous. (Application: A man replaces a fuse with a penny and the house catches fire.)

3. Arithmetic may be used to find out the number of resistors that can be replaced safely in a circuit. (Application: A woman wants to know how many of her electrical appliances can be plugged in safely at one time.)

Items directed toward these applications tend to be of the "how" and "why" type. This is in contrast with the "what," "who," "when," and "where" kind usually found in items that test for a lesser level of knowledge. Another way of looking at it is to think of how and why questions as being solution-centered, while the others tend to be background-centered. The latter type of question is seldom stressed when knowledge of the *applications* of generalizations is considered more valuable.

How will we know if a child can apply a generalization? *Our referent will require that he explain, predict, or control the applications tested.*

Test specialists tend to prefer the multiple-choice item for testing reasoning. Such items have many benefits. Choices of options can be made as subtle or easy as needed. The kinds of errors can be analyzed through the options. Further, such items are easily and reliably scored. Their form lends itself to several formats. Scores tend to correlate highly with free-response questions that are carefully scored, and more. Because of this, emphasis in the examples below is on the multiple-choice type, although several other types also are included.

As before, each item is preceded by a short, behavioral statement. Each will require the child to explain or predict or control an event. A further analysis of the child's expected intellectual behavior or the test strategy used occurs after each example.

1. Given an event the child selects the explanatory cause.

A lamp cord is placed under a heavily traveled rug. One night, the light goes out and part of the cord gets hot. The trouble is probably caused by a:

a. burned-out bulb   (c.) short circuit
b. disconnected plug   d. worn, separated cord

If proper reasoning takes place, it should be possible to select the proper answer in two ways: through a process of elimination— a, b, and d would all open the circuit—and by directly relating the "symptoms" to the cause.

2. Given several concepts, the child selects the one that does not belong and supplies the reason.

A. short circuit   C. hot circuit
B. overloaded circuit D. broken circuit

 D does not belong because all the circuits would be hot but the broken one.

Although we might assume proper knowledge of the reason through the child's correct choice, the requiring of a written reason for the choice helps to confirm such knowledge. Of course, as with any free-response answer, we are faced with the problem of interpreting the correctness of "original" answers.

3. Given an action, the child selects a related explanation.

It is unsatisfactory to replace a burned-out fuse with a penny because a penny:
(a.) has a high melting point
 b. conducts electricity poorly
 c. may cause a short circuit
 d. blocks the flow of electricity

This item goes beyond the simple recognition of a fact by requiring the child to grasp the significance of the fact as part of a larger picture. If there is objection that the other options are not factual but are merely plausible distractors, the above could be written in a recall or short-answer form:

Why is a penny considered an unsatisfactory substitute for a fuse? A penny has a high melting point and will not melt and open a hot circuit as will a fuse. The house can catch fire.

4. Given an event, the child selects a prediction and reason for the prediction.

A woman plugs in electric appliances that draw a total of 30 amperes. The house fuse is marked "25 amperes." Which one of these statements best describes the later condition of the fuse and the reason?

(a.) It has melted because it got too hot.
 b. It has melted because there was a short circuit.
 c. It is in good condition because a parallel circuit carries half the current.
 d. It is in good condition because a parallel circuit carries only half the heat.

Note that without the additions of reasons this would be better cast in some alternate response form, such as a true-false or yes-no item.

5. Given some data, the child first selects a correct condition and then a correct prediction.

Your mother wants to use at one time—without harming the 30-ampere house fuse—a coffee maker (360 watts), waffle iron (960 watts), toaster (600 watts), and iron (1200 watts). How many amperes will these appliances draw all together?

$$(A = \frac{W}{V})$$

a. 22   (b) 26   c. 30   d. 40

Which one of these statements would be correct?

 e. The fuse will probably burn out.
(f.) The fuse will probably not burn out.
 g. There is no way of telling what will probably happen.

Although the formula for calculating amperage is given, this problem requires knowledge of the amount of house voltage, how to apply the formula for the answer, and then the ability to think of the answer's significance. Were this item to be used, there would be little need for the preceding one. The problem's difficulty could be increased by omitting the formula. Note that an analysis by the teacher of the second answer would require knowledge of the child's first answer.

6. The child matches correctly given generalizations and applications.

Events

c A light goes out and part of the light cord gets hot.

d A door bell stops ringing

e A sound is heard in a telephone receiver.

b A five-cell flash-light is brighter than a two-cell flashlight

Reasons

a. An electric current can be produced by changing heat energy into electrical energy.

b. Circuits may be hooked up in series.

c. A short circuit takes place when a resistor is by-passed.

d. Current electricity flows only when there is a complete circuit.

e. A magnetic field is formed around a wire that carries electricity.

When applications for several generalizations or contributing ideas are to be tested, the matching item form may be convenient to use. Much material can be covered in a short time in this way. But remember that getting some appearance of likeness among the phrases in each column is a continual difficulty in writing a matching item.

TESTING FOR PROCESS OBJECTIVES

It is convenient to think of the five categories of abilities identified on pages 70–71 as broad generalizations, and the specific referents within each ability as contributing ideas. Seeing it this way, we can test for the broad ability from several angles, just as we did with contributing ideas. As before, the use of smaller, related ideas tends to make applications easier to think of than if the broad classification itself is used.

A main problem in evaluating process outcomes, as before, is to spell out clearly the behavior (referent) we wish to examine.

Once this is done, the task of writing an item is mainly to set up a situation in which the behavior may be expressed. The child then is expected to select or supply the appropriate behavior, which we compare to the referent. Let us say we wish to test for the ability to state problems. The specific referent is "questioning or avoiding faulty inferences and assumptions that lead to a problem statement." Here is an item that can help:

John read about Mexican bullfights. A bull charged toward the bullfighter when he flashed a red cape before its eyes. If John asked a question about this, which one of these would be best?

a. Why does a bull get so angry when it sees red?

b. How did they learn that a red cape was best to use?

(c.) What causes the bull to charge in the direction of the bullfighter?

d. Which causes the bull to get excited, the flashing cape or the color?

In the broad ability of suggesting and appraising hypotheses, an important referent is to select the most promising hypothesis from several alternative hypotheses:

Birds eat more food for their size than most other animals. To find out why, which of these possible reasons would be best for scientists to think about?

(a.) Maybe they use up their food faster.

b. Maybe they have better appetites.

c. Maybe it has become a habit to eat more.

d. Maybe they live longer.

The broad ability of developing procedures contains the referent of identifying variables that need to be controlled:

You want to find out if some mice will gain more weight on a milk diet than on a cola diet. What must you know before feeding the mice?

a. What brand of cola to use.

b. What the mice like to eat.

c. How old the mice are.

(d.) How heavy the mice are.

The broad ability of interpreting data and making inferences includes a referent to limit an inference to the thing tested; that is, until a broader inference is justified:

Sally has measured the heights of the girls and boys in the front row of her class. Each of these girls is taller than the boys measured. What is correct for her to say about these findings?

    a. "In my class, the girls are taller than the boys."

    b. "No boy in my class is taller than some of the girls."

    (c.) "Some girls in my class are taller than some of the boys."

    d. "Some girls in my class are taller than all of the boys."

The comprehensive ability of reasoning quantitatively includes the referent of constructing and reading correctly simple graphs and charts:

This is a graph Judy made of the changing water temperatures in two insulated cans:

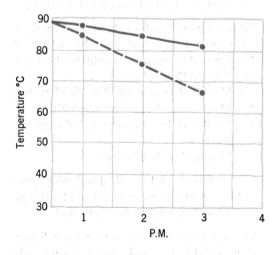

What probably will be the water temperature at 4 P.M. in the can that is cooling off faster?

a. 55°C   (b.) 60°C   c. 75°C   d. 80°C

Although it is possible to write acceptable items for some process skills, many others are very difficult to put into a reasonably short test-item form. It is mainly for this reason that test writers do not produce more of these items. Consider an important behavioral referent we should like children to adopt in stating problems: "The child returns when needed to a problem statement and restates it better." There is nothing very difficult in checking out this behavior. It is clearly spelled out and quite noticeable. But what if we wish to write a test item that measures the behavior? It can be done, but only with more effort and time than it is probably worth, *especially since we can observe the same behavior with little difficulty.* (Places marked in margins of Part II show when these observations can occur.) This is but one limitation to conventional tests. Shortly, we shall take up other limitations and what we can do about them in a practical manner.

STANDARDIZED TESTS

Several published tests are available which have been prepared for distribution and use on a nationwide basis. Since items are prepared by qualified test specialists, technically they are well developed and edited. Incorrect options are plausible, specific determiners are rare, and vocabulary is well selected. "Grade norms" are developed by administering the test to a widely scattered sampling of school districts over the entire country. In other words, typical scores received in grades of the representative sampling are charted so that customary performance on the test at each grade level or thereabouts can be known.

Overall scores made on the standardized tests are usually highly *reliable* — that is, scores received tend to be reasonably consistent from one administration of the test to another. But *curricular validity* — how relevant the test is to the goals of a specific school district—is often another matter. Before a standardized test is selected, it should be inspected to see if it agrees with local objectives. If items do not sample reasonably well the behaviors expected as a result of teaching, of what value are the findings?

Although validity remains a problem, it appears that newer standardized tests may be more widely usable than older versions. One reason for this is that emphasis on remembering specific facts is being shifted by teachers to understanding concepts and generalizations. Newer tests reflect the emphasis. In tests of this kind, therefore, it is less crucial to remember a specific, isolated fact to mark an item correctly. One group of facts may be as useful as another.

In addition, some tests include items designed to measure several process abilities. This innovation may be crude—a reliable measure of a broad ability cannot be determined from just one or two items. Besides, answers to such items may also depend on the recall of science generalizations. But there is hope for increased curricular validity in such tests as objectives in education change toward the broader, relatively permanent forms of learning.

Standardized tests in elementary-school science have a helpful but limited application in teaching. They can indicate where a child stands in general science knowledge compared to his peers. Still, this is meaningful only in terms of what is measured in the test, and how closely it samples the behaviors taught in the district. With this in mind, these tests may also show how closely a child's expectancy or aptitude score matches his science achievement.

Perhaps the best use for such tests is to partly show where the entire school district stands in relation to other districts, and how sizable segments of a large district compare with one another. When properly interpreted, this is useful knowledge. It can provide the spark for needed curricular or other changes.

But can standardized tests in science be used for evaluating a specific teacher's effectiveness? Or a child's success with several specific units? Or for diagnostic purposes? Most of the time we must say "no." The general nature of the science material sampled in the test prevents specific knowledge of where and how immediate teaching or curriculum is related to scores received. Such knowledge depends mostly on other means of assessment.

Typically, standardized tests in elementary-school science are included in overall achievement batteries, since most districts tend to test for several subjects at one time. However, separate science sections, from Grade 3 or 4 upward, usually are available upon request. Among the most widely used tests are these:

California Tests in Social and Related Sciences, California Test Bureau, Del Monte Research Park, Monterey, California.

Metropolitan Achievement Tests, Harcourt, Brace & World, Inc., 750 Third Ave., New York, New York.

Sequential Tests of Educational Progress, Cooperative Test Division, Educational Testing Service, 20 Nassau St., Princeton, New Jersey.

S R A Science Achievement Test, Science Research Associates, 57 W. Grand Ave., Chicago, Illinois.

Stanford Achievement Tests, Harcourt, Brace & World, Inc., 750 Third Ave., New York, New York.

Descriptions and critical reviews of these and other tests appear in the latest edition of *The Mental Measurement Yearbooks,* Oscar K. Buros, editor (Highland Park, N.J.: Gryphon Press).

LIMITATIONS OF WRITTEN TESTS

As you have seen, a main need in testing is to provide a situation that requires a behavioral decision by the child. But this is hard to do with all objectives, especially in the elementary school, through solely paper-and-pencil tests. A common process objective may be easy to observe but difficult to sample in written form. Also, *children's ability to learn science typically is farther advanced than either their writing or reading ability, particularly in the primary grades.*

Notice that thus far there has been no reference to essay questions. Besides the restricted sampling of learning that occurs with their use, and their unreliability when scored, writing itself may be difficult for pupils. Thus the essay test in science is an uncertain measure of what children can actually do, except perhaps with some children in the later elementary grades. This is why many teachers prefer to use a limited-answer item in its place, or essays whose answers are curtailed to a paragraph or two. Much the same problem is found with children's performance in reading. Items that are the most worthwhile, process and application-of-generalization types, are the lengthiest because a problem context first must be established before a behavior can be elicited. Although an item can be read by the teacher, it is better if the child is able to read the item for himself.

Few published paper-and-pencil tests exist for use below the fourth grade. Probably at least fourth-grade reading ability is necessary for achievement of average scores with published achievement tests in elementary science.[4] Readers at this level or lower achieve science scores far below the averages of their groups. Of course, this also may happen because too many persons still rely on the textbook to teach science. But certainly there is reason for caution in interpreting test results. Adequate tests in science are possible to construct below the fourth-grade

level. Simpler vocabulary can be used, numerous picture items can be developed, including tape recordings, slides, and the like. But these usually involve a great deal of time and skill, perhaps more than most primary teachers can afford or reasonably acquire.

Writing excellent application and process items at any level takes time and skill. Some help in providing tests is furnished in recent textbook series' teacher manuals and workbooks. Cooperative writing and exchanges by teachers of items is a worthwhile way to augment this help. More of this should be done among the faculties of schools and school systems that have similar objectives.

Certainly among the greatest limitations of typical tests is the unlikelihood that the results will materially affect the way in which the unit is taught. Tests are usually administered at the end of a unit. The immediate, corrective feedback often so necessary for highly effective teaching is thus absent. Since only limited time is available, it is hard to go back and effectively take care of omissions and mistakes. While results may be helpful in presenting a future unit or in correcting certain general procedures, this benefit is limited at best.

Because the task of teaching is inexact, it is helpful to view it as a whole series of consecutively developed hypotheses. That is, each action, statement, or expression we make is a kind of hypothesis which we cannot be certain will be "accepted" (learned) by the children. If much teaching takes place before feedback indicates that learning has taken place, we may be making a whole series of unwarranted assumptions. Tests are helpful to find out what children already know, or to confirm and check in a uniform manner what has been learned. *But much more important for good teaching is a host of informal, in-context practices which provide the teacher with data for fast self-correction.* An important necessity in these practices is that they in-

[4] Peter C. Gega and Bjorn Karlsen, "Situational vs. Non-Situational Casting of Items in the STEP—Elementary Science," *California Journal of Educational Research,* May 1962, pp. 99–104.

clude practical techniques for teachers of primary, as well as older, children.

The need for self-correction is no less important with children. One of the overall ideals in education is to progressively make each child as self-sufficient as possible. Yet before a child can work toward this goal, he must first know what the desired behaviors are. Evaluative methods which enlist his cooperation in everyday activities gradually give him personal reference systems. These can be used for self-appraisal of process and product outcomes in science. More on this shortly.

INFORMAL WAYS OF APPRAISAL

Observation. Daily observation of pupil behavior is the most frequently employed evaluation method of teachers. When done thoroughly, it probably furnishes the best classroom evidence of what pupils can do. It is also the most important procedure you have for the immediate, corrective feedback necessary for tactical changes in teaching procedure. Alert teachers have always been sensitive to the occasional blank stares, puzzled looks, frowns, faltering responses, or lack of upraised hands that signal the need to try another tack. But these are just a few of the general cues that changes may be necessary. What can you do to develop a more systematic basis for observation? (See Figure 7.)

Nothing is more crucial to successful assessment through observation than continual, active pupil involvement in learning experiences. In the absence of much pupil activity—intellectual and physical— there can be little evaluation. Corrective feedback comes from pupil responses. When responses are absent, so is feedback. To evaluate responses, you use your referents to make judgments, regularly and continually, as you teach.

For example, when a problem is to be stated by children, note their faulty inferences or assumptions, or how well they pose an unstated problem as a question, or the use of clear English, and so on. If the children do not show these behaviors at an acceptable level, the time to teach for improved behaviors is right at hand and ordinarily should not be postponed. The same is true when the time comes for the pupils to suggest hypotheses, develop valid procedures, interpret data and make inferences, and reason quantitatively. The important thing is *to provide the opportunity* for children to express the behavior, so that it can be assessed in the light of your referents. The purpose is not to "mark children down" for their mistakes, but to note what they need and do not need as you teach. (For specific chances to assess process skills note again the places marked in the margins of units in Part II.)

Similar in-context observations can take place when dealing with knowledge objectives. Some vocabulary referents might be: Do they use old and new terms correctly? Can they define the words? Can they give a synonym for the word? Factual referents can be: Do they answer satisfactorily when asked about important *what, who, when, where* facts? Do they use correct facts in discussions?

The generalization referent is clear-cut and always the same: Can they use the generalization to explain, predict, or control events? *This referent is the most useful to assess product objectives,* either orally or on written tests.

To get such evidence as you teach, use *questions* often in place of statements. When done properly, this stimulates the children to think through matters for themselves. At the same time it gives you a chance to evaluate their performance. Naturally, not all questions are of equal value. It takes a while to learn how to pose questions that are likeliest to bring out significant behaviors. You have seen material on questions in previous sections and chapters. But, hopefully, the activity sections of the units in Part II will be particularly helpful in furnishing examples.

Figure 7 **Activities like these present opportunities to evaluate through observation.** (S. L. Guiliani, San Diego City Schools.)

This would be a good time to skim through some units to note where and how such questions come up as the units are taught. Many questions can be found by the marginal notations and in the extending activity sections. In addition, a few quotes from the primary unit on machines (pp. 304–325) may help you know what to look for:

Ask them what the findings seem to mean. (p. 309L)

Ask why animals seem to choose a longer, zig-zagged route rather than a shorter, straight-up route. (p. 309L)

Ask them how a wedge is able to split objects apart when struck forcibly. (p. 309R)

If you want to balance three books with one book, where should they go? Four books with one book? (p. 314L)

When the board is centered on the fulcrum, which two people in our class can stand on the ends and be balanced? Which four people? (p. 314R)

Observation of the work that children do in everyday activities and discussion compares favorably with tests as a valid way to learn about what they can do. Yet this technique usually lacks the reliability and broad sampling—of children as well as subject material—possible in a well-prepared test. Fortunately, there are several things you can do to reduce these deficiencies. Let's take the idea of sampling first.

One method to learn what all the children, rather than just several, think about a problem statement, or hypothesis, or conclusion, and so on, is occasionally to ask everyone to write it down on a slip of paper and turn it in. Since the context has already been established by the activity itself, only a short, quickly written statement is needed. Statements are analyzed rapidly with the appropriate referent in mind; then appropriate actions are considered. A broad sampling of the material comes about by doing this with sufficiently different situations over a period of time.

Much the same thing is done with drawings. An experiment, demonstration, or picture is drawn to depict a test, illustration, or application, as the case may be. These need not even be turned in, but can be used as "flash cards," held under the chin so that you can observe the whole group at once. This also works well when there are measurement problems. When answers are written large and held up for teacher observation, you can note quickly if more help is needed. Of course, getting the right answer does not always mean it was arrived at properly.

But what if the children do not write or draw well enough, even though the problem has been made less complicated? In this case, seeking a representative sample may help. For instance, you can go around to a half-dozen or so children and ask them to whisper the needed control, conclusion, definition, application, or whatever. While not everyone may be heard from, some indication of class understanding can be received if children of varied competencies are checked.

Besides this procedure, some teachers ask their pupils to respond frequently to choices. Instead of asking for hands to show agreement with a hypothesis or an inference, thereby permitting anyone to go along mindlessly with the majority, children are asked to hold up one finger for agreement, two for disagreement. When done somewhat in the manner of flash cards, close to the body and under the chin, it is difficult to observe the choices of

neighbors. Reasons for agreement or disagreement are then explored.

This technique works very well with screening hypotheses. If several or more are to be evaluated for the best choice, assign numbers to each. A survey of choices can be made rapidly just by observing the number of fingers children show corresponding to the hypothesis numbers. Once the children are conditioned to responding in this manner, through your continual use of questions involving alternate choices, much feedback is possible. This is especially likely to happen if reasons for choices are also followed through on a selective basis. However, this does not mean that alternate-choice questions are always best to use. The technique is suggested as just another practical way to evaluate.

We saw early in this section that much pupil involvement is necessary for successful assessment. If children participate continually in learning activities over some length of time, an alert teacher receives many signs of their progress. Such indications present an easier and more reliable pattern to interpret when viewed cumulatively rather than separately. Also, we sometimes unknowingly neglect some children and overconcentrate on others in evaluating performance. For these reasons, it is worthwhile to make sure that all the children have had a reasonable opportunity to provide information about what they need to learn, and how well they are doing. Some teachers seem to remember unaided the needs of children and their progress. But many more find that taking occasional, brief notes is helpful in recalling information for this purpose.

Standard Setting for Product and Process. Experienced teachers realize the value of enlisting children's cooperation in setting standards for everyday activities. Besides the desirable side effects of higher interest and improved room control, this process gradually provides the child with the personal reference systems necessary for self-appraisal. It seems natural, also, to teach standards as an internal part of the activity itself. Typically children are interested in the activity and its outcomes rather than direct attempts to teach the "great truths" of science, whether they be process or product.

Some time should be set aside for group discussion of standards when working with activities. Brief discussion sessions just before and after the main activity of the lesson help to clarify purposes, develop or review needed standards, and evaluate performance. For example:

1. A primary class going on a study trip plans specifically what to look for and the kind of conduct appropriate for the site. A discussion after the trip helps the class to evaluate whether all went according to plan, and the reasons.

2. A middle-grade group working on several large panel pictures of ancient animals and plants decides that the animals must be drawn to scale and in relation to one another, that only animals of one epoch should be shown together, and that the plants must be as authentic as possible.

3. A competent, upper-grade group writing imaginative stories on space exploration decides that a realistic accounting of a trip would include the proper use of such previously studied terms as acceleration, re-entry, zero gravity, and micrometeorites.

Sometimes brief charts are helpful to keep standards of various activities in mind, although this can easily be overdone. In some cases, a chart may serve for several subject-matter areas:

A good reporter —
  uses his own words;
  uses the right vocabulary;
  can answer some questions;
  shows pictures or sketches when
    needed.

In other cases, a chart may be more specifically suited for science alone:

A good demonstrator —
  tells what the purpose is;
  uses controls if needed;
  handles materials properly;
  can answer some questions.

An excellent example of how standards are used to help children evaluate the designs of animal experiments is furnished by the Elementary Science Study.[5] While the criteria are given to the class in this case, in a later edition they are worked out cooperatively by teacher and pupils:

How to Experiment with Animals

Before proceeding with more investigations of mealworm behavior, thought might be given to some of the errors commonly made when experimenting with animals. To help accomplish this, a list of six criteria for good experimentation is given to the students.

1. In order to know if the animal is doing something different, one must first know its usual behavior.
2. An animal must be given a choice if it is to show a preference for one thing over something else.
3. What is done to an animal must be described in detail.
4. The description of what the animal does in the experiment must be complete.
5. The same experiment should be done more than once.
6. The conditions should be controlled so that the animal responds only to what is being tested.

Descriptions of ten hypothetical experiments are distributed and students decide which of the six criteria are violated in each example. There is no single right answer. In many cases, two, three, or even more responses may be considered correct. The purpose of having the children write an answer is to force them to consider the experiments carefully. Discussion of the "answers" in class should elicit a lively debate.

[5] Elementary Science Study, *Behavior of Mealworms*. Education Development Center, Newton, Mass. (n.d.), pp. 7–9. By permission.

1. I wanted to see if mealworms liked high places. I put my mealworms on a book and raised it five feet above the floor. This was done about 25 times with several different worms. Every time except once the mealworm crawled around the book until he fell off onto the floor. It took from 8 seconds to 6 minutes and 15 seconds for this to happen. The one mealworm which didn't fall off just sat on the book and didn't move. I don't think mealworms like heights.

2. I tested my dog to see his reaction to music. So every night after his dinner, for two weeks, I put him in the playroom and turned on some music. On almost every night he was asleep within 10 minutes. It seems that music makes my dog go to sleep. . . .

8. Does temperature affect the number of times a cricket cricks? To answer this question I performed the following experiment. I used 17 adult male crickets in separate outdoor screened cages. Between 2:00 and 3:00 in the afternoon of March 12th, I counted the number of times each cricket made a noise in a minute. The average was 38 times. The temperature was 67 degrees F. On the same night from 8:00 to 9:00, when the temperature was only 42 degrees F., the average of cricks was 21. I have concluded from this experiment that temperature does affect the cricking of crickets.

In sum, we can say that our main job in helping children set standards is to know some usable referents for process and product, recognize when they need to be applied, and be able to translate each referent into terms that children can grasp. Eventually, the children will acquire their own standards, patterned largely after those learned from a succession of teachers and other competent sources. Hopefully, our pupils will then no longer need us.

Evaluation—Maintaining a Balance. The conventional wisdom, as sometimes heard in the school lounge, is that teachers simply don't have the evaluative instruments they need to do an effective job in science instruction. However, the question arises: If we had more data, what would we do with it? *A good rule is, work only for data you can do something about instructionally.* Data collecting takes time—time you could be spending to plan and instruct. The preceding techniques will furnish more feedback than you can use, if applied well. To be sure, some subtle and long range learnings resist measurement with present techniques. But there is probably more need for present modes of teaching to catch up with what we know about evaluation, than the other way around.

Providing and Using Materials

CHAPTER 5

CHAPTER FIVE

Providing and Using Materials

ARE EDUCATORS TODAY REALLY TAKING ELEMENTARY SCHOOL science seriously? A good sign is the increasing attention paid in school districts to providing adequate instructional materials. It is true that in far too many cases teachers are still given little more than a set of science texts with which to conduct a program. But in some situations science materials go unclaimed because teachers don't know how to get them, or gather dust because teachers are uncertain of their uses. This chapter should help you learn many sources of materials commonly available, along with some considerations in using materials.

GETTING EQUIPMENT AND SUPPLIES

Most of the materials used in elementary science are simple and easy-to-get: the kind found around the home, in local stores, or other convenient places. Frequently the children themselves can bring in a share of the items needed for experiments, demonstrations, and other activities. This is a good practice, for several reasons. When common things are used, pupils can do many school-inspired activities at home as well as in class. Participation in getting materials usually includes some participation in planning for their use. This can increase pupil understanding and responsi-

Credit for chapter opening photograph. **Ben Gumm, San Diego City Schools**

bility. Materials are usually brought in by children as a result of previously stated purposes. Unfortunately, prestated purposes may not always be present when supplies and equipment are purchased by the school district. Purchases may be made solely on the basis of recommended lists appearing in various publications, with little tie-in to the local science program itself.

It is desirable for children to participate in gathering materials from time to time. But it is plainly unreliable and inadequate to base a complete program on the materials they contribute, however cooperative they may be. Commercial sources must be consulted — science supply houses, hardware stores, drug stores, and department stores, for example. All science supply houses provide catalogues that describe available materials and how to order them. A usual practice among several school districts is to circulate periodically to teachers and administrators an equipment and supply list that is at least partly based upon the items found in supply-house catalogues. The district representative then orders for everyone at one time; all benefit from the usual price discount that accompanies large orders.

Some general supply companies have developed special elementary-school catalogues. These reduce the difficulty of selecting materials suitable for children from the innumerable items intended for research or education at more advanced levels. In spite of this, commercial materials available for younger pupils can be disappointingly inappropriate. It is no longer difficult to find large thermometers with thick, red-colored columns, and large numerals for use in the primary grades. But easily handled and durable electric switches, lamp sockets, large pulleys, and the like still are rare. Instead, many supply houses offer only items that are too tiny or fragile for small, uncoordinated hands and fingers. Since much attention is being given to this problem, desirable changes for the better are sure to increase.

Information about materials for elementary-school science may be requested from:

Cambosco Scientific Company, Inc., 37 Antwerp Street, Brighton Station, Boston, Massachusetts;

Central Scientific Company, 1700 Irving Park Road, Chicago, Illinois (also at 6446 Telegraph Road, Los Angeles, California);

General Biological Supply House, 8200 South Hoyne Avenue, Chicago, Illinois;

Hubbard Scientific Company, Department C9, P.O. Box 105, Northbrook, Illinois;

The Learning Center, Elementary Department, Princeton, New Jersey;

Nasco Science Materials, Fort Atkinson, Wisconsin;

Ward's Natural Science Establishment, Inc., P.O. Box 1712, Rochester, New York (also at Box 1749, Monterey, California);

The Welch Scientific Company, 1515 Sedgwick Street, Chicago, Illinois.[1]

It is important to consider quality when ordering instructional supplies and equipment. Passage of the National Defense Education Act of 1958, Title III, made available large sums of money to local school districts for programs in science, mathematics, and foreign languages. This resulted in the sudden formation or expansion of hundreds of supply companies, some selling products of marginal quality. It became increasingly important for educators to learn desirable specifications and performance standards for materials and equipment. To meet this need the Council of Chief State School Officers developed purchase guides for programs in the three fields. The following excerpt from page 172 of the science and mathematics guide [2] illustrates the kind of assistance it provides:

---

[1]Sources of supply for the newer experimental programs are listed in Part III.

[2]Council of Chief State School Officers, *Purchase Guide for Programs in Science and Mathematics,* 1965. Boston: Ginn and Company. By permission. (Neither the Council nor any State Department of Education officially endorses any specific product described in the guide.)

2450
MAGNIFIER, READING GLASS

- **Biology** · Basic, one for each student
- **Earth Science** · Basic, one for each student
- **Elementary Science** · Basic, one classroom set for each school
- **Physics** · Basic, 4 for each classroom

For magnification in elementary biological and other laboratory work, including reading topographic maps.

• *Specifications:* The reading glass shall consist of a lens, approximately 2 in. to 4 in. in diameter, mounted in a durable rim and ferrule, and set in a durable plastic handle.

It shall be available with focal lengths ranging from 4 in. to 10 in. and corresponding magnifications ranging from 2× to 1×. Purchaser shall specify focal length and magnifications desired.

Besides descriptions of "hardware," the guide contains lists of annotated professional books and trade books, descriptions of new curriculum studies, and ways to use materials. Every school should have one of these useful guides, and, of course, every purchasing agent.

Another concern of importance is the quantity of materials that should be used. In a program where children are to be active participants, ten magnets, for example, are more appropriate for a class than one. The expense may prevent each teacher from receiving this number of magnets. However, a policy of cooperation and different time scheduling for teaching the same units in the school may make sufficient supplies available. This assumes that an adequate total number of items has been ordered in the first place.

Despite elaborate order lists provided by numerous schools, it is difficult to anticipate everything that will be needed in teaching. Sometimes articles are needed between order periods. In these cases a petty cash fund, administered through the principal's office, is most useful. Besides being convenient, such a fund lends encouragement to the teacher willing to depart from routine.

Many elementary schools possess self-contained *science kits.* Consisting of a durable box or chest with a teacher's manual and a wide array of materials stored inside, the science kit provides for many activities without most of the storage and distribution problems that accompany the ordering of individual supplies.

But the gain in convenience is offset by several important disadvantages. The kit is likely to be much more expensive than items gathered separately. Also, there is the natural tendency to want to use fully what has been purchased. The materials tend to dictate the program, rather than the other way around. Finally, the program is likely to consist more of cookbook demonstrations than inquiry activities. Yet it would be unjustified to disapprove of kits in all school situations. Their availability has without doubt assisted greatly in the improvement or development of science programs where little or nothing existed before their use.

In the past few years, publishers have developed kits containing equipment and supplies to accompany their science text series. These kits hold several advantages over the usual variety. They contain mul-

Figure 8 Sometimes parent-teacher organizations volunteer to assemble improvised science kits. (Courtesy San Diego City Schools.)

tiple items for activities, and so allow most class members to participate individually or in small groups. In contrast, traditional kits are limited more to individual demonstrations, since only single items are typical. Another advantage of the text kit is that it is, in a sense, correlated with a curriculum. You can more easily extend and enrich the concepts taken up because the materials and text go hand in hand. However, the text kit also may be more expensive than warranted by the materials it contains, especially if many common items such as straws, paper clips, and so on, are included. For this reason, personnel of some schools assemble their own kits to complement an adopted text series.

Look for exciting science kits of all kinds to be developed commercially in the near future. The new education development companies have employed some of the most creative minds available in the fields of learning and industrial designing. They are cooperatively developing materials for children in science and mathematics, and in other disciplines, too.

It is becoming more common for elementary schools to have a special *science-supply room* for supplementing and replenishing materials used in the classroom. Replacements may be stored for such consumable supplies as dry cells, miniature light bulbs, balloons, simple chemicals, candles, and so forth. Other items may include those that are used by various classes only some of the time, or that are too expensive to buy in quantity. Typical examples are cages of various types and sizes for animals, microscopes, commercial weather instruments and models, hot plates, and telephone sets.

A well-organized supply room reduces classroom storage problems. It saves you from continually rushing out to purchase consumable items, and makes a wider range of instructional devices available to everyone in the school.[3]

[3] For a comprehensive discussion of science kits, supplies, equipment, and science-supply rooms, see

READING MATERIALS

A great deal of reading matter exists for use in the classroom. Most common is the textbook, usually distributed on the basis of one per child. The modern textbook in elementary science is a great improvement over earlier editions. The range of subject matter is broader and more interesting; numerous "doing" activities are included, along with attractive pictures and an appealing format. In spite of improvements, criticism of textbooks continues.

The chief objections, as implied before, are that the text may try to substitute words and pictures for firsthand experiences so needed by children for real understanding. Some children may not be able to read the words. In addition, the text activities may merely illustrate the explanations and conclusions that make up the reading matter. There may be few possibilities for process-rich situations in which answers are unknown. As one teacher said, "Why even try the 'experiments'? The text spills the beans."

At least some of this criticism is due to *misuse* of texts or is the result of unrealistic expectations. Even a good text is only one of several tools in a science program, rather than a complete program in itself. (An analogy is the carpenter who threw away his hammer because it did a poor job of sawing wood.) You have already seen here and there some sound teaching techniques with textbooks. Let's now list in review, and in one place, some of the ways you can profitably use a basic text and its accompanying teacher's manual.

1. *As a source of experiments, activities, bridges, problems, and basic generalizations.* When used for these purposes, the

"Science Equipment and Materials for Elementary Schools," by Albert Piltz, Office of Education Bulletin No. 28, 1961, 30¢; and "Science Equipment and Materials: Science Kits," by Albert Piltz and William J. Gruver, Office of Education Bulletin No. 30, 1963, 15¢. Order from Supt. of Documents, U.S. Government Printing Office, Washington, D.C. 20402.

children's books *are closed at first;* the textbook author's ideas are used by the teacher.

2. *As a check-up source for experiments, analogies, and theories.* In these cases, the book serves as a check for the children to compare the completeness and accuracy of *their* ideas and activities with those in the book. The book is opened for verification or comparison only *after* the initial thinking and doing have taken place. Slow readers are helped individually or in small groups.

3. *As a data and background source.* Now the book is consulted for details as needed to answer previously established questions or purposes. Note that these purposes may have developed through item one above. In a primary text consisting mostly of pictures, the pictures may be examined in detail.

4. *As a source of additional examples to reinforce a previous activity.* Study of open-ended experiments, generalizations, or concepts can be enhanced by learning of additional examples. Frequently, such examples are either mentioned or illustrated in the text. The same is true of possible substitutions for previous experiments or demonstrations.

5. *As a summary of important ideas in the unit.* The clear, careful organization of subject matter typical in modern texts is ideal to summarize firsthand experiences within important segments of a unit, or even the entire unit itself. The additional filling in of detail, and seeing previously studied material in a new context through summary reading, provides reinforcement and more completeness in learning.

You may be aware that we have omitted using the text to overview or explore a unit. This practice is unsatisfactory in most cases. Children are likely to get the idea that they already know well the material of the unit. While they may be urged to read quickly for a general overview, many will read for details. If you pose the author's problems, the class will tend superficially

to "know" the answers. Therefore, the author's ideas will not be as convenient to use, should you be fresh out of your own approaches.

Naturally, even the best of textbooks cannot always do an ideal job in each of the five uses mentioned. They would soon grow too heavy to carry and too expensive to buy. But there are other printed materials that can help. Children's *trade books* are excellent for additional detail. Usually developed around one topic, such as simple machines, weather, soil, or electricity, they can provide the richness in depth difficult to put into a textbook unit. Less useful are those trade books of a survey type which deal with many topics. These tend to have the same deficiency in depth as many textbooks.

Some school districts prepare collections of books, or at least bibliographies, to accompany units. Local libraries may permit up to thirty or more trade books to be checked out to teachers for a limited period. Children can go to the local library, too, and find books which are helpful with the unit. An advantage in self-selection is that children usually choose books that they can read.

Trade books are probably the best means we have of providing for individual differences in reading. If a variety is available, it almost insures that excellent readers will have challenging materials. Slower readers, also, will usually have at their disposal books that are both interesting and within their more limited capabilities.

Many trade books and other books are printed every year. It is a continual problem just to keep up with what is published, much less to pick out quality material. Fortunately, we have several places to which we can turn for help. Among the more useful sources is an organization called "Books on Exhibit, Incorporated." This concern publishes yearly annotated listings of new elementary and secondary science trade books of most leading publishers. No book is listed unless it has at least three recommendations from among twelve top reviewing sources in the United States. A free exhibition of these books may be provided to school districts upon request. For a free catalogue and more information, write to:

Books on Exhibit, Incorporated
North Bedford Road
Mount Kisco, New York 10549

In 1963, the American Association for the Advancement of Science published a comprehensive (1219 titles), annotated list of trade books called, "The AAAS Science Book List for Children." This careful selection serves well as a basic acquisition guide for a district science library. In addition, the association publishes a quarterly review of newly printed books in science and mathematics at the elementary through junior-college levels. Unlike many review guides, this one has "bite." The four ratings given range from "highly recommended" to "not recommended." Here is a sample excerpt from a low-rated book: ". . . this books deals with the topic in a highly superficial manner, and the text is filled with scientific inaccuracies, poor grammar, and vague explanations." Specific references of both publications are:

Science Book List for Children, Second Edition, 1963 ($1.25 paper, $2.50 cloth), Hilary J. Deason, editor.

SCIENCE BOOKS: A *Quarterly Review,* Hilary J. Deason, editor. Subscription: $4.50 per year; $3.00 for additional copies to the same address.

For both references, write to: American Association for the Advancement of Science, 1515 Massachusetts Avenue, Washington, D.C. 20005.

One of the latest magazines to review children's science books is *Appraisal,* which appears three times a year. The publication is written by the Children's Science Book Review Committee, a non-profit group sponsored by the Harvard Graduate School of Education and the New England Round Table of Children's Librarians. Interestingly, each book is reviewed by *two* persons — a librarian and a subject specialist — thus combining a literary and technical evaluation.

For a subscription, write to *Appraisal,* Children's Science Book Review Committee, Harvard Graduate School of Education, 207 Byerly Hall, Cambridge, Massachusetts 02138.

Encyclopedias are also useful in providing additional information to children. But most of them are difficult for younger children to read without some help. Above all, discourage the usual practice of simply copying information out of the encyclopedia. When this happens comprehension may reach the vanishing point. Help the children interpret information when necessary. It may even be advisable occasionally for you to read short segments aloud, so individual pupils can jot down in their own words facts they wish to report or know.

To make many reference books available, and provide for differences in reading ability, many schools buy a half-dozen or more series of textbooks instead of one. In these cases a third-grade teacher with thirty-six children, let us say, may have six copies from each of six different series of books. Often some of the books are one grade below regular level, some at grade level, and at least several above grade level.

There appears to be no good reason for this practice. Some series may contain nothing at all on the unit being studied. And developmental sequences of concepts in each series rarely are fully exploited. Perhaps the major objection is that textbooks are not intended for reference use in the first place. They lack the detail of a good trade book and the comprehensive, logical organization of an encyclopedia.

On the other hand, a worthwhile textbook series with teachers' manuals can offer a useful base for a science program. It can provide security for the teacher unfamiliar in science. It can enable the pupil to refresh and reinforce his knowledge of generalizations at several grade levels and in several different contexts. Yet even an excellent text series needs to be supplemented with other reading materials and used with local emphases in mind. Merely buying several sets of texts does little to help in these respects.

From time to time we need to use *identification books* in the classroom. These are references whose major value is to group or order natural objects in a logical way, so that they can be classified or named. As brought out in Chapter 3, it is important to have books that are well illustrated. Most pupils rely more on matching pictures than on use of keys for identification. An excellent and inexpensive shelf of books with colored illustrations is the *Golden Nature Guides* series. It is available in inexpensive paperback or cloth editions from Simon and Schuster, Inc., Rockefeller Center, New York, New York. Titles include *Birds, Flowers, Trees, Insects, Stars, Reptiles and Amphibians, Rocks and Minerals, Fishes,* and *Seashores.*

Besides reference, trade, and text reading materials, many teachers discover that magazines, newspapers, charts, workbooks, catalogues, almanacs, bulletins, and the like are worthwhile for seeking information. Not surprisingly, they find that using a variety of reading matter often has double benefits. Not only do children become better at locating science information, but they may also increase their ability to locate information in other curriculum areas.

A less familiar reading resource is the *programed text* or *self-instructional program.* These materials differ from the conventional textbook. The pupil is required to respond continually to questions concerning the material learned as he proceeds through the program. After each response is made, it is compared with the correct answer. Subject matter encountered later presumes mastery of previous material.

Therefore, the child cannot continue properly unless he understands what he has read. Such mastery is not too difficult. Programs are typically presented in small steps learnable by most children for whom they are intended. When the program is used in a machine, there may be an automatic recording of errors. Errors may also be noted by requesting pupils to write their responses before comparing them with the correct answers.

A great many programs in elementary school science are becoming available.[4] While not all are verbal in nature, most can be used in somewhat the same manner as other supplementary reading matter. The primary advantages of programs are in the greater comprehension that may come about, and the self-pacing in speed of learning. There is little question that this form of instruction represents a promising step forward in providing for individual differences of learners.

Vocabulary and Meaning. Take care not to rush into reading activities. Our ability to understand words relates directly to our experiences. When a child explores problems and his environment before he reads, he begins to acquire percepts, ideas, and a vocabulary. All are needed to understand the printed material. In other words, we should provide experiences first, then the words to label them.

The difficulty of words is often deceptive. Consider this question, for instance: Which is harder for a child to read, "tyrannosaurus rex" or "energy?" If you chose the first item, by "read" perhaps you mean being able to decode and pronounce words. A choice of the second word may mean that to read is to comprehend. You can easily supply the first term to a child, and he may never forget it. What child wouldn't like to go around the neighborhood babbling

[4] For further information, write to The Center for Educational Technology, Teachers College, Columbia University, New York, N.Y. 10027.

"tyrannosaurus rex?" It is much more impressive than "king of the dinosaurs" or "terrible lizard." On the other hand, "energy" is an elusive, difficult concept that builds slowly in the child's mind only after many firsthand experiences.

It is easy to equate glibness with understanding. The child who rattles off words may be only hazily aware of what he is reading or talking about. Ironically, the child who "reads" less well can have a mind that is well-stocked with intuitive concepts. He may simply lack verbal labels to pin to what he already understands. In one way, then, teaching children to read science material is much like teaching science itself. To read in the full sense of the term, of course, a child needs to decode *and* comprehend. Still, it is important to understand the distinction.

Perhaps now you are wondering, when does one introduce actual science vocabulary, rather than simpler, childlike words? It depends on whether you are dealing with *objects* or *concepts*. Why have a child learn two or more names for an object, if one will do? Call a Florentine flask by its proper name right away. However, take longer to supply names for concepts. Wait until the children have sufficient experiences to possess some meaning for the label supplied. Mere association and repetition may be sufficient to clinch the names of objects, but not concepts.

The Elementary Science Study (see Part III) recognizes the distinction. Sometimes pupils are encouraged to invent their own labels for emerging concepts. In one unit,[5] for example, molecular adhesion is "stickiness" and molecular cohesion may be called "grabbiness." Whether this is always a good idea is arguable. Will communication be interfered with? Will associations be less clear? As with so many other methods in teaching, when and how to apply them remains a matter of teacher judgment.

NONREADING MATERIALS

We come now to the many nonreading materials broadly available in the classroom, often called *audio-visual aids*. These include still pictures, films and filmstrips, constructions, microscopes and microprojectors, television, and records or tapes. (Strictly speaking, even these materials may involve some reading—captions in films, descriptions of pictures, and the like.) As with books, a valid purpose should always precede their selection and use.

It is wise to vary the ways in which these materials are applied. For instance, using a film solely to begin science units or lesson series can eventually dampen pupil interest and enthusiasm. This unnecessarily restricts an instructional aid that is helpful in at least several other ways. Since there are excellent books[6] available devoted entirely to instructional materials, there is no need here to make a comprehensive analysis of these aids. However, a brief section about their specific applications in elementary science can sharpen your awareness of their possible contributions to teaching.

Pictorial Materials. Let us begin with *pictures, filmstrips,* and *films.* Each of these familiar materials may be used in at least three general ways:

1. To introduce or overview lessons and raise problems.
2. To help answer questions or explain difficult ideas.

---

[5] Elementary Science Study, *Kitchen Physics,* Boston, Mass.: Houghton Mifflin Company, 1965, page 29. (Now published by the Webster Division, McGraw-Hill Book Company, Manchester, Missouri.)

[6] For example, see: Walter A. Wittich and Charles F. Schuller, *Audio-Visual Materials: Their Nature and Use,* Fourth Edition, New York: Harper and Row, 1967; R. Murray Thomas and Sherwin G. Swarthout, *Integrated Teaching Materials,* Second Edition, New York: Longmans, Green and Co., Inc., 1963; James W. Brown, Richard B. Lewis, and Fred F. Harcleroad, *A V Instruction: Media and Methods,* Third Edition, New York: McGraw-Hill, 1968.

3. To summarize or extend with more examples what has been studied.

Pictures or illustrations probably are the most common aids used in elementary science, perhaps because their sources are so accessible. Among the many magazines where suitable illustrations may be found are *Life, National Geographic, Holiday, Look,* and *Arizona Highways.* Books also may contain numerous, helpful photographs or drawings. Sometimes you can get valuable pictures from old or discarded books. District and local libraries frequently furnish collections of pictures to interested teachers. A large supply is also obtainable from free and inexpensive commercial sources. These are listed later.

For most purposes the best kinds of illustrations are large and easily seen, with a single, central emphasis, and minimum of detail. This is especially important in the primary grades. An occasional difficulty with such pictures may be the absence of clues to indicate relative size, as with some animal pictures, for example. The *opaque projector* may be used to project and enlarge an image of a small picture, as well as any other illustrations that you may wish to trace with pen or crayon.

Pictures furnish an excellent means of introducing lessons and raising problems. There are also times when you may want to develop your own sketches. It is somewhat awkward and difficult to describe a situation for children, so they can sense and define a problem by themselves, without using language that gives it away. But when confronted with an illustration that contains a visual paradox or application, the job of describing what they see and stating the apparent problem is the children's own. (Notice how the sketch on page 147L can help to introduce a problem.)

All of us have had the experience of hearing someone describe a scene, person, or object, and of then being surprised to see a picture of what was described. This is why pictures furnish an excellent way of clari-

fying ideas and procedures. Because one scene may contain a great deal of information, it can be used to advantage where there is need for review or summary of ideas.

The Part II unit on machines (page 304) contains numerous places where pictures may provide additional applications and illustrations of science principles. Check especially the extending activities. When children find pictures of applications, this extends and broadens meaning. Other ideas for using pictures may be found in the section on bulletin boards, page 110R.

After only a short time of collecting pictures or illustrations, the need for a handy way to file them becomes obvious. You can solve this problem by first mounting the pictures on tagboard or stiff-paper backing of uniform size, then filing the pictures upright in an orange crate or a cardboard box of the right dimensions. Almost any careful system of cataloguing should assist in retrieving desired illustrations. A system that seems to work well is to file illustrations first by units and then according to specific generalizations within units. Be sure to use cross-filing notations on any pictures that can be used with more than one topic.

Carefully chosen *filmstrips* have most of the advantages of pictures and can be used in as many different ways. A helpful feature of the filmstrip is its sequential ordering of frames. At the same time this is a potential inconvenience. When a process involving details needs to be shown—as with the steps to develop photographs, set up an aquarium, propagate plants, and so on—a good filmstrip develops the several aspects involved in a logical, carefully ordered way. Static details are brought out clearly. The captions supplied with each frame help clarify the pictures. But in many cases there is little need to present all the frames of a filmstrip. The class may already be familiar with part of the process or some of the events. Part of the filmstrip may not apply to the specific idea being investigated.

A partial solution to the problem is to select and show just the specific sequence of frames needed. Since the frames are numbered, a rapid skimming through unneeded frames should lead to the section wanted. Yet sometimes this is not too useful, because the sequence itself may not be in the order desired. There may also be some pupil dissatisfaction with being "short changed" — children like to view all the frames. These are the reasons why some teachers prefer individual slides in place of filmstrips.

When *motion pictures* are well-constructed and properly used, they make available in the classroom vicarious experiences that are otherwise difficult, hazardous, or impossible to realize. Through the technique of animation, molecular theory is seen and understood better in dynamic

form. Microphotography enables children to see cell division, rare and active microscopic life, and body defenses reacting to invading germs. Time-lapse sequences enable the movements of developing plants to be recorded. Slow motion permits the leisurely analysis of swift and complex movements. Photography also makes possible the repeatable, safe viewing of solar eclipses, volcanoes, and other natural events. These are just a few examples of techniques and applications available in educational films.

While they possess a variety of useful and entertaining characteristics, many films contain shortcomings of some concern. Perhaps the most noticeable defect of many motion pictures prepared specifically

Figure 9 An individual filmstrip viewer may help provide for individual differences of children. (Courtesy Ben Gumm, San Diego City Schools.)

for elementary science is that they illustrate experiences children could engage in directly, rather than view on a screen. Besides, many films encompass far too broad a scope for the short time of presentation. This forces us to use films of this kind almost exclusively for introductions or superficial reviews.

Part of the difficulty lies in the economics involved. No commercial producer wants to prepare films for which there is only a very small and unprofitable market. But perhaps a more important reason is simply lack of insight into what this medium can contribute.

In recent years such educational organizations as the American Institute of Biolog-

ical Sciences and the Education Development Center have developed or encouraged the making of "single-concept" films — motion pictures that concentrate on a specific process, topic, or idea. Often these are in the form of *film loops* — short, silent motion pictures sealed into plastic cartridges. The film cartridge is easily and quickly inserted into a simple projector without threading. The film runs continuously without end, since both ends are joined. The specific idea shown in the film can be viewed over and over as needed. (See Figure 10.)

As more interest is expressed in films such as these, and market activity is stepped up, it seems likely that the tendency for

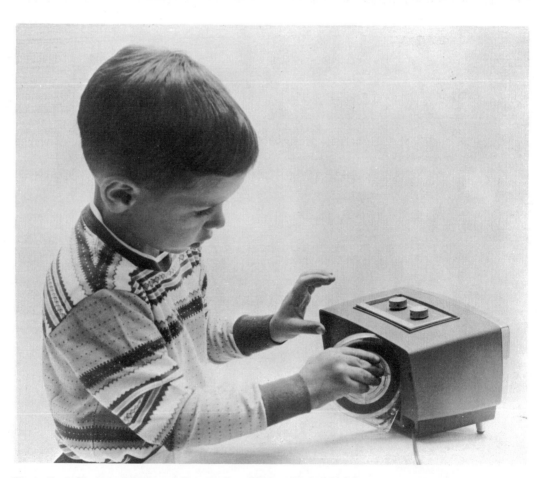

Figure 10   A film loop projector and film cartridge. (Courtesy Technicolor Corp., Costa Mesa, Calif.)

comprehensive or broad-scope films will be lessened.

Another difficulty with some elementary science films is the vocabulary of the accompanying vocal commentary. Some of this may come from choosing a film that is too advanced for the class involved. But even films that contain easy-to-learn concepts become hard to understand when adult terms are used. There is no reason why we must "utilize" instead of use water hoses, see a "holocaust" instead of a large fire, and view "extensive" rather than much damage. It is desirable to improve children's vocabularies. But the use of a large number of unfamiliar words in a short time can make an otherwise understandable film somewhat vague. It becomes hard to introduce important words to the children before showing the film. Instead of concentrating on just a few vital terms, we must decide and note what will cloud meaning in the entire commentary. Frequently, the list grows too long for effective presentation.

A subtler defect in too many motion pictures for elementary science is the authority-centered context in which the action takes place. Children are typically seen to seek adults to define their problems, provide materials, explain things, or otherwise provide counsel. Less frequently are children seen to think things through for themselves or to plan for ways of tracking down information. While the latter can be overdone, it is strange that educators have stressed for so long the need for children's growing independence in learning without this emphasis being reflected in our educational films.

Fortunately, newer films are including more inquiry. Probably most responsible for the change have been the several science-curriculum projects sponsored by the National Science Foundation.

Let us look now at some points in ordering and using films for teaching. "I ordered a film but it came too late." "The A-V department returned my order with a note saying the film was not available." These comments are heard all too frequently. What can we do when this happens?

In a large conference for instructional-materials specialists a few years ago, there was an informal discussion of such comments. The twelve discussants involved represented different-sized districts in several parts of the United States. Each of these persons had obtained much experience with the problems of supplying materials. Each had made a careful study of the criticisms of teachers in his district. The consensus of these specialists, and our own observations, lead to these points:

1. Much of the time films or other aids that are late in arrival are not ordered with an eye on recommended time deadlines. Occasionally it is possible to fill the request in spite of this. At other times it is impossible.

2. Audio-visual aids are often not obtainable because nearly everyone teaches the same thing at the same time. Perhaps an obvious remedy is to stagger unit times throughout the semester. This may have to be arranged in the school or on the district level.

3. Many teachers organize their lessons around narrow topics and facts rather than generalizations. If a generalization involves animal homes or ways of caring for young, for instance, it may be possible to order alternate films or other aids. In these cases, it may make little difference if your first choice fails to arrive. On the other hand, if a specific subject is considered, such as frogs, beavers, or white mice, then only a film directed toward the exact animal will do.

Keeping these ideas in mind can help reduce the problems of ordering films or other instructional materials. Naturally, when too few materials or inefficient distribution systems exist, such inadequacies must be corrected at the source.

When possible, carefully preview a film before showing it. A previewing reveals how you can best use the film. If the scope is broad and somewhat superficial, perhaps the best use is as an introduction or review. If some detail or depth is presented, the film may serve for background or solution-centered information. It is worthwhile to reshow detailed treatments to the class, just as it is desirable to reread a text that develops much detail. A previewing also tends to disclose if the level of presentation is suitable for the class. Sometimes a film is unrealistically recommended for six or more grade levels in the accompanying producer's guide or descriptive brochure.

During the previewing it is worthwhile to make a brief outline of the film, and note significant or important scenes and details. If there are other useful ideas or processes given besides those that originally prompted placing the order, it may be desirable to bring these out with the pupils before the film is shown. Difficult vocabulary, obscure sequences, and unusual photographic techniques may need to be explained to the class. An accompanying producer's guide can be helpful in providing information about all the points mentioned here.

Just before the film is viewed by the children, be sure to clearly state the purpose for its presentation. You may also wish to give a brief outline of its content. In addition, it is important to write some of the more difficult terms on the chalkboard and to use them in several understandable contexts.

Sometimes it is desirable to leave off the sound while viewing a film. This might be done in a review lesson, with children supplying the commentary. Or the children might be asked during viewing what they see to discover their present level of knowledge. When the commentary contains many difficult terms, you may wish to turn off the sound and substitute your own commentary.

A final comment on films. It is easy to cut down the effectiveness of a good film through overanalysis of a few ideas or exposure of too many ideas at one time. If a great deal of material is presented perhaps it would be wise to show only part of the film, or to reshow the film on a later occasion. Exposing too much material at one time may result in less learning than if only a few important points are taken up. This comment especially covers younger children.

Microscopes and Microprojectors. When we need to work with real objects or specimens that are too small to observe in detail, the microscope is an asset. It used to be difficult to find a microscope in elementary schools. The situation now is often very different. Although some elementary schools still lack this aid, others may have several microscopes for each classroom above the primary-grade level. In addition, some children have microscopes at home which occasionally are brought to school.

Children typically desire to see the highest possible magnification of a specimen.

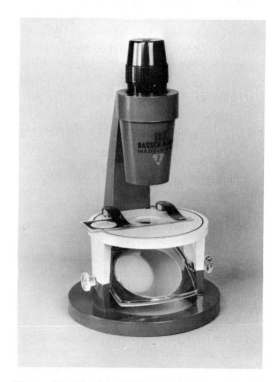

Figure 11 (Courtesy Bausch & Lomb, Rochester, N.Y.)

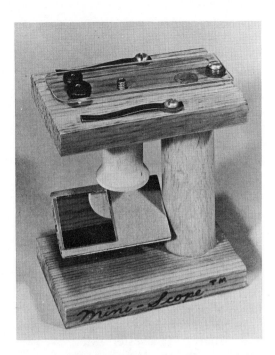

Figure 12 (Courtesy Kimtec, Inc., Houston, Texas)

The result is usually unsatisfactory. It may be difficult to focus the instrument properly. The field of observation may be too narrow to locate the desired area on the specimen; any minor movement or shifting of the slide is greatly exaggerated when viewed through an eyepiece. Moreover, it is possible that children will not understand what they are observing. For these reasons, well-built microscopes of lower power — and somewhat lower cost — are satisfactory for elementary schools. (See Figure 11 for an inexpensive Bausch and Lomb model. See Figure 12 for a Kimtec "Mini-Scope" pupils can assemble from kit form.)

A useful instrument for children is the "wide-field" type. In this case a magnified view of a whole insect or other small object is possible. Necessity for focusing and slide-making is held to a minimum. In a primary grade, it may be best to avoid entirely the use of microscopes. A dozen or more good quality hand lenses can be purchased at the same price. The portability of hand lenses, their greater total use, and

relative unimportance of high magnification at this level, commonly indicate this choice. (See Figure 13.)

Since we can seldom be sure of what children are viewing, and since it is likely that only one or a few microscopes can be available for use at one time, many teachers prefer the *microprojector*. (See Figure 14.) With this instrument it is possible to project an enlarged image of the specimen onto a screen, much like other visual projectors. It is convenient when instructing a whole class because everyone can view together what is taking place. When both kinds of instruments are available, you may find microscopes convenient for individual viewing or projects. (See Figure 15.)

"We know that microscopes and microprojectors are useful in secondary-school activities, but are they really important in elementary-school science?" This question is asked frequently in both preservice and in-service science education classes. Perhaps the best way of finding out is to investigate some sample uses of these aids in

Figure 13 There are times when nothing is more useful than a hand lens. (Hays-Monkmeyer.)

103

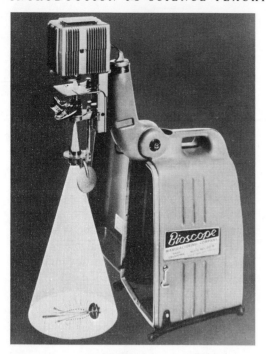

Figure 14 A microprojector. (Courtesy Bioscope Manufacturing Co., Tulsa, Okla.)

modern textbooks. A superficial examination of almost any text series might reveal such opportunities as these for viewing on a microscopic level:

Compound eyes of the housefly, various insect eyes. Fiber structure of wool, cotton, and other materials. Penetration of inks and dyes into several materials. Newly laid insect, frog, and snail eggs. Anatomy of the mosquito and bee. Pores and creases in human skin. Composition of human hair, several kinds of body cells, blood cells. Crystals of salt, sugar, other common substances. Algae, fresh-water protozoa. Effects of disinfectants on protozoa. Composition of mold growth, bacterial colonies. Parts of a flower, leaf, seed. Onion, root, stem, leaf cells. Root hairs, capillary action with colored water. Circulation of blood in the tail of a goldfish. Heartbeat of a water flea. Mouthparts of harmful insects. Fiber structures of various kinds of paper.

Additional activities described in detail, with numerous suggestions for making or

purchasing slides, may be found in the following publications:

The Microprojector and World of Microbes, Norfolk County Public Schools, Norfolk, Virginia.

Working with Animals, by J. Myron Atkin and R. Will Burnett. New York: Holt, Rinehart and Winston, Inc., 1959.

Working with Plants, by J. Myron Atkin and R. Will Burnett. New York: Holt, Rinehart and Winston, Inc., 1959.

Microscope Instruction Manual, Testa Manufacturing Co., 10126 East Rush Street, El Monte, California.

Elementary Explanation of Microscopic Slides and Classroom Experiments, Ken-A-Vision Manufacturing Co., Inc., Raytown, Missouri.

Small Things, by The Elementary Science Study. Manchester, Mo.: Webster Division, McGraw-Hill Co., 1967.

Teacher's Manual for the Bioscope, Model 60, Bioscope Manufacturing Co., Box 1492, Tulsa, Oklahoma.

Figure 15 Microscopes are best used for individual projects. (Shackman-Monkmeyer.)

Some suppliers of elementary-school microscopes are:

Bausch and Lomb, 83109 Bausch Street, Rochester, N.Y.;

Kimtec, Inc., 3625 Westheimer, Houston, Texas;

Testa Manufacturing Company, 10126 East Rush Street, El Monte, California.

Television. One reason why the scientific literacy of children is increasing is found in the numerous television programs devoted to science topics. Almost any weekly schedule of programs for the general public contains several or more titles of interest. Encourage your pupils to view or listen to a regularly scheduled series and then discuss or demonstrate ideas learned with other class members. Notify them in advance when a particularly pertinent telecast will take place. Encourage pupils to be on the lookout themselves for notices of future programs of unusual value.

Special educational programs for school systems or regions are increasing. Often these programs are important parts of large-scale experiments to study the usefulness of television instruction. Some large school systems—New York City is a typical example—have found that television is a useful medium for inservice instruction of teachers in elementary science, as well as in other aspects of the curriculum. Some school districts have regularly scheduled televised programs for science instruction of children. The classroom teacher acts as a resource person, discussion leader, or in some other related capacity, after the telecast has been completed.

Many programs are outstanding. Eminent scientists may appear and speak or demonstrate. Excellent demonstrations are conducted. Clearly illustrated instructional aids are shown, usually in a well-organized context and interesting format. However, it is probably too soon to judge how effectively television can be used for inquiry activities in elementary science instruction.

Certain problems have already been identified which should be considered when plans are made for such instruction. A common problem is the overly ambitious attempt to cover too many grade levels at one time. Some children inevitably are bored. Others may struggle with ideas for which they are not ready. Another drawback is the customary discontinuity of the presentations. Numerous, unrelated topics are less useful to an individual teacher than a more sustained approach. Perhaps the most important objections are the lack of feedback from pupils to the television teacher, and the all-too-frequent passive role of children in the lesson. Of course, letters can be written to the studio teacher. This is some help. And activities can be planned *after* a televised lesson. But frequently these methods are less desirable than working directly with the class. Specialists in television instruction are well aware of the difficulties which attend this form of teaching. Expect this important medium to be more effective as measures are taken to cope with such problems.

Recordings. Although usually given more limited use than some of the materials mentioned above, recordings, especially tape recordings, can be employed in at least several functional ways. Excellent radio programs broadcast after school hours can be recorded and played back at more convenient times. Interviews with science authorities, or sounds heard during a field trip, can also be recorded.

If a "listening post" or multiple plug-in device is attached to the recorder, and several sets of earphones are available, it is possible to provide assistance to either fast or slow learners without disturbing the rest of the class. (See Figure 16.) It is much easier to prepare a simplified version of a difficult passage from a book through reading it aloud in a simplified way and taping it, than it is to rewrite it. It is likewise possible to tape more difficult material for children whose reading vocabularies have not

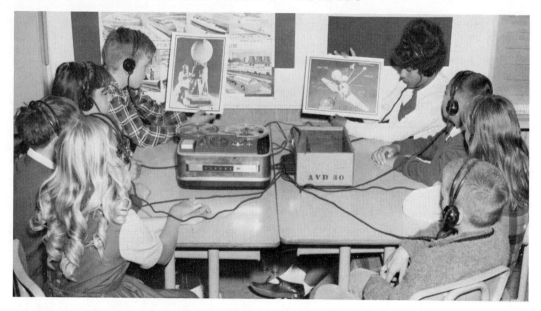

Figure 16 A listening post provides for individual differences while freeing the teacher for other possibilities. (Courtesy Ben Gumm, San Diego City Schools.)

yet caught up with their ability to think. Doing these things frees you for other possibilities. Also, evaluation sessions with children are helped by analysis of their taped oral discussions or reports that may accompany science activities.

Constructions. A great deal of time is given in some classrooms for constructing ap-

paratus and physical models. When attention is focused on the intellectual part of the activities—in learning the ideas and processes involved—such experiences are usually worthwhile. But unless the construction involves some useful science knowledge, the time taken may merely result in less opportunity for thoughtful learning.

Figure 17 This wind-tunnel model really works. (Courtesy Ben Gumm, San Diego City Schools.)

How much time should be spent in model making and other constructions? There are few definite answers, but the following observations may give you some guidance in thinking of desirable practices. The best kinds of constructions are *functional;* that is, they work by teaching an idea, a process, or helping to gather data. Such working constructions as telegraphs, weather instruments, electric circuit boards, and so forth, usually involve thoughtful planning on the part of the class. Less useful are constructions that might be called *props* — materials that are more decorative and atmosphere-lending than functional: a "spaceship" made out of cardboard, a paper "glacier," a chicken wire and papier-mâché "dinosaur," etc. This is not to say that such materials are useless. They often have a worthwhile purpose in dramatic play, or art-centered activities, for example. But time for science should not be largely used up in this way.

Perhaps in the past we have tended to overstress the possibilities for home and improvised materials. When constructions are too intricate for pupils or too time-consuming to assemble, try to get commercial items. There are many true-to-life scale models and other constructions available through local hobby shops and supply houses. These may bring about more actual understanding and interest than inadequate constructions developed during the neglect of more important learning activities.

Free and Inexpensive Materials. You can borrow or permanently acquire a host of instructional aids from commercial and institutional sources through request only, or at nominal cost. Films, filmstrips, charts, pictures, booklets, samples of raw or processed materials, models, posters, recordings — all these and more are available. But before requesting these, check the policy of your school district about such materials. Many commercial, institutional, and other donors in the past have used free and inexpensive materials as an advertising or propaganda medium. Educators have been forced to develop restrictions regarding their use. However, lately the supply of obviously objectional materials has decreased significantly.

Distributors of free and inexpensive materials usually have a large inventory of items available, so be very specific when requesting things. If a stock number appears in the catalogue consulted, be sure to include it in your request along with an exact description of what you want. As there are usually many requests for material, allow at least four to six weeks for its receipt. Processing takes time, and requests of this type typically are given low priority. Most free and inexpensive materials are two-dimensional. So when received, you can store them like pictorial materials.

The supply of donated and low-cost materials is notoriously unreliable. It is wise to use current and reliable listings in making requests. The following compilations of sources are revised each year. Efforts are made to edit out those sources that either have misrepresented their materials or have otherwise proved unsatisfactory:

Educators Guide to Free Science Materials
Educators Guide to Curriculum Materials
Educators Guide to Tapes, Scripts and Transcriptions
Educators Guide to Films
Educators Guide to Filmstrips

All of the *Educators Guides* are available at reasonable cost from Educators Progress Service, Randolph, Wisconsin 53956.

CLASSROOM FACILITIES

No one in an elementary school needs a shiny laboratory to have interesting and worthwhile activities take place. But good science teaching is greatly aided by a few conveniences or special arrangements easily provided in most self-contained classrooms. At least one electric outlet is desirable, so that a hot plate or other electrical device can be plugged in. However, it may be possible to substitute a propane tank burner, an alcohol lamp, or "solid alcohol" (Sterno) as a source of heat. A sink with running water is also handy in many experiments and demonstrations. Yet it is possible to get by with a bucket and pan. If you have constructions in mind, several hand tools and materials are indispensable — hammer, saw, pliers, screwdriver, lumber scraps, nails, and so on. A few of these items may be borrowed occasionally for brief periods from children's homes.

Seating Arrangements. "My children complain that they can't see when we do demonstrations in front of the room." "What do you do when attention seems to drift away after the first few minutes in a demonstration?" Teacher remarks like these may call for a more satisfactory furniture or seating arrangement.

A sturdy table and movable chairs are helpful when planning for demonstrations or experiments for an entire class, notably with smaller children. If there is a reading "circle," the same chairs can be arranged into a U-shaped pattern or semicircle around the table (Figure 18). Girls sit on the chairs. Boys sit on the floor, Indian-fashion, one in front of each chair. Everyone is close to the table. No one's view is obstructed. There is ready access to the table as individual children are called upon to participate. With some reminding, participating pupils will remember to stand *in back of* the table, so that everyone can see what is happening. An arrangement of this kind is especially needed with younger children. It is easy for them to lose interest or become distracted when seated some distance away from the activity source. A nearby chart holder or chalkboard in back of the table can serve for any needed recording.

The semicircular pattern is also convenient when there are enough materials for everyone to experiment or demonstrate at the same time. You can set standards with pupils for small-group activities, and assign areas of the room for working. After the several groups or committees have

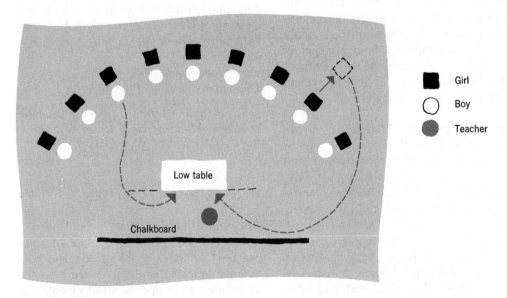

Girl
Boy
Teacher

Low table

Chalkboard

Figure 18 This arrangement makes it easy to either view or participate in demonstrations.

completed their work, having them reassemble into the initial seating pattern makes for easier reporting or discussion.

With older children there is less need for this type of seating arrangement. Short attention spans and distractions are less of a problem. An initial, functional grouping of desks and chairs may serve for most occasions. But keep the materials table reasonably close to all the children when experiments and demonstrations are done before the entire class. There is usually no trouble with class control when everyone can see what is happening. In cases where class desks are permanently fixed to the floor, use a higher-than-usual table for adequate viewing. It may be necessary to let some children change seats or move to a more satisfactory location.

Experimenting with Few Materials. The new science coordinator, who strongly praises inquiry at the district's first in-service session, is apt to hear this impatient cry for help: "It's alright for you to talk about inquiry because you can put thirty-five materials in the hands of thirty-five children. But what about those of us who can't? What I want to know is, how do you get everyone involved when you only have a few things to work with?"

It would be ideal if *every* child could *always* manipulate materials individually or with a partner. But for the present, this is something only a few experimental science projects have been able to achieve— at substantial cost. In the meantime, what's a teacher to do?

First, let us separate experimenting, perhaps artificially, into two parts—thinking and manipulating. We would like all the children to do both, if possible, but of the two, probably you will agree that the thinking part is more important. One solution then, while not wholly satisfactory, is possible along this line.

Assume that you want the class to do some problem solving with concealed electric circuits as described in this book.

(See page 277 if interested in details.) Materials are suggested for every pupil. But the only materials available are a flashlight battery and bulb, several wires, five brass paper fasteners, and a shoebox.

You connect the wires inside the box to paper fasteners that have been pushed through the box top. The brass heads will act as terminals. The box is taped shut. As different terminals are touched by the circuit tester—rigged from the battery and bulb—sometimes the bulb lights, sometimes it does not light. The circuits remain hidden inside the box. Can the class hypothesize about how the hidden wires are connected? Can everyone be involved in thinking, although materials are few? Try the following organization:

1. Divide the class into small groups or teams to develop their hypotheses and plans.

2. Leave the materials on a table in full view, perhaps in the center of the room, with persons in the several groups equally able to see or occasionally walk over to inspect the materials as needed.

3. Within each group, encourage the children to hypothesize, discuss, evaluate critically, suggest testing procedures, draw diagrams, and otherwise attempt to convince their fellow group members about their reasoning.

4. When the groups are ready to report to the entire class, have each chairman present his team's diagrams, hypotheses, and predictions (sometimes there is a minority report) about what will happen when they are tested.

5. Let the other class members closely question assumptions and faulty thinking as they occur. *Then have them select the group with apparently the best ideas to test them first.* Other groups may follow later.

A similar organization is possible with almost any activity. A main difference from the situation with adequate materials is in the manipulating part of the activity. Almost everything else occurs as it would when adequate materials are present.

Arranging the class in this way can be mentally stimulating, even exciting. However, its effectiveness is influenced by the following considerations. Try to distribute the talented and slower learners evenly among the groups. Keep groups small, no more than four or five members each, so that everyone participates. Circulate among the groups as they plan. Give hints to those who seem bogged down. This will keep them going and interested. Also, while the organization can be successful with children of all ages, useful returns gradually dwindle with declining age levels. Nothing is as good as firsthand experience.

Another way to cope with the materials problem is to use activities that involve easy-to-get, everyday objects. This is one of the reasons such activities are emphasized in this text. But any final solution requires adequate funding in the first place. This seems to be happening in more and more school districts.

A Science Area. The self-contained classroom in elementary schools often contains several *center-of-interest areas.* These are places in the room where several pupils at one time may go to work independently on art, language, science, or other activities. A desirable science center may contain a work bench, a display table for specimens, several collections, a microscope or several hand lenses, an aquarium, one or more small animal cages, and a collection of science books. An attractive bulletin board nearby may be set up to provide additional interest, or for use in a unit under study. In the science center a child can observe more closely the results of an experiment performed before the whole class. He can repeat a demonstration if materials are provided. He can work on unfinished projects, or look up information on a special science interest. Here, he may also wish to display his favorite collection of rocks, or proudly ex-

hibit his latest lizard. (See Figure 19.)

A worthwhile science center takes some care. Materials should be changed reasonably often. When it lapses into an isolated table for display of a few uninteresting and dust-covered objects, opportunities for worthwhile learnings may disappear entirely.

Making Bulletin Boards. The writer who looks in frustration at a blank sheet of paper has his counterpart — the teacher who stares hopelessly at empty bulletin board space. Does making up these aids need to be so difficult? So time-consuming? Here are some short cuts to consider.

A good way to begin is to start with an *idea,* not bulletin-board materials. That is, have a clear purpose in mind. "I want to do something about an aquarium" is a vague notion that probably will get nowhere. A better statement is, "I want to show what objects are needed for a small aquarium, and how to set them up in several easy-to-follow steps."

Of course, bulletin boards can be used for many purposes. But, for science, usually you will need to think of only three. Recall the description of pictorial materials on page 97R and their main functions: to *introduce,* to *explain,* to *summarize* ideas. You can use bulletin boards in these three ways. Consider them now one at a time.

An *introductory bulletin board* is a bridge put into pictorial form, and is conceived like any other bridge. You begin with a generalization the children will work toward ("Matter expands when heated and contracts when cooled."), and think of an application ("Telephone wires sag slightly in summer and are taut in winter.") Instead of making this into a verbal bridge, sketch the application in the form of a picture, such as Figure 1-6, on page 147L. You can add the problem in the form of a caption or elicit it verbally from the children in a discussion, as done on that page.

The foregoing introduces a problem related to only *one* generalization. It is also possible to introduce problems from several or all of the generalizations in the unit to be studied. Figure 20A shows problems from each of the four generalizations of Unit 9, "The Earth in Space," p. 395L.

Explanatory bulletin boards make plain in a pictorial way a concept or principle that is hard to visualize from a verbal description alone. The idea that the moon can rotate and revolve simultaneously becomes easier when portrayed with arrows in a picture. Or an analogy compared with the real thing, such as a teakettle "cloud" and an actual cloud, is also clarified in pictorial form. Figure 20B is an example. While intro-

ductory boards are almost always teacher-made, the explanatory kind is excellent for children's projects. Committees even in the primary grades can sometimes "research" and plan for simple explanatory presentations of extending ideas or enrichment projects.

A *summary bulletin board* may be used to show applications of one or all of the generalizations studied. Usually it can be planned and constructed by the children, and is an excellent vehicle to evaluate how well the class has learned. In the work shown in Figure 20C, each of five committees has printed on tagboard strips the

Figure 19 This science area encourages pupils to perform many individual, open-ended explorations. (Courtesy Ben Gumm, San Diego City Schools.)

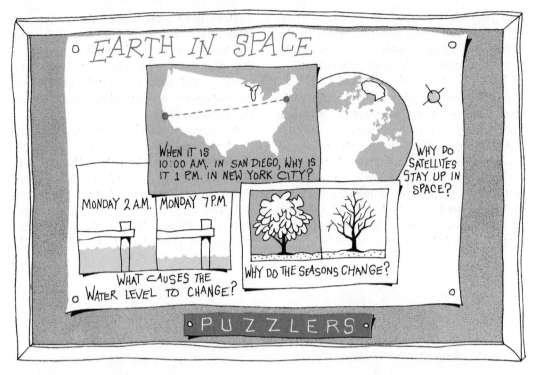

Figure 20A   An introductory bulletin board.

Figure 20B   An explanatory bulletin board.

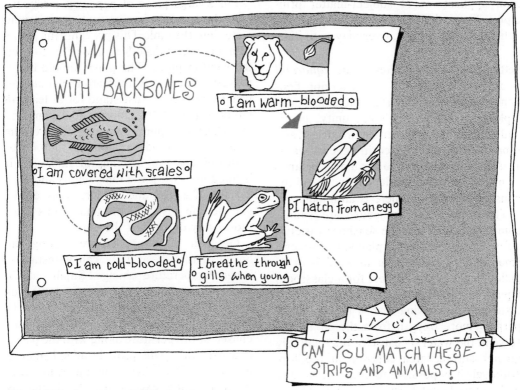

Figure 20C A summary bulletin board.

characteristics of one animal group. In discussing what to print, each committee has given the teacher much feedback. It is now the job of the entire class to pick the strips from the box and allocate them to the proper spots. Some animal groups have similar as well as different characteristics. So this is an interesting and challenging test of how well the children have learned some animal classifications. The bulletin board would be useful to help summarize Unit 2, "Animal Groups," page 464.

Most summary bulletin boards are open-ended, in the sense that children can search for any applications that relate to the principle studied. The children can bring in pictures from magazines or attempt to draw applications. Some good sources of pictures you will want to check for all bulletin boards are free and inexpensive materials, the district instructional materials center,

and the specific periodicals mentioned earlier in the chapter.

It is easy to draw enlarged pictures by using the opaque projector—a help to anyone, and an indispensable tool for the untalented. With it, you can enliven your bulletin boards with familiar comic strip or story characters for child appeal: Dr. Dolittle, Peanuts, Snoopy, and Dr. Suess' menagerie. (Don't worry about anthropomorphism; the caricatures are obvious.) It is also interesting to use mystery, surprise, oddities, contrast, personal application, and drama in captions or in the pictorial arrangement. Of course, you will want to avoid combining the children's work with commercial matter, or your work with theirs.

Can these three bulletin boards be used to illustrate process abilities? It can be done, but such skills are harder to pictorialize because they are more abstract than applications of subject-matter principles. These abilities are better displayed in action, during regular, everyday activities.

Setting Up an Aquarium.[7] An *aquarium* is an excellent source for observing first-hand examples of important biological principles. In this watery community, plants and animals adapt to their environment, and reproduction takes place in several ways. It is likewise possible to see a near balance of nature through interdependence, and the consequences when there is an imbalance.

The basic materials needed are a tank, some clean sand (not the seashore variety), a few aquatic snails and plants, and several small fish. A rectangular tank of 5- or 6-gallon capacity serves best for a classroom aquarium. The rectangular shape has less distortion in viewing than a bowl. It also permits more oxygen from the air to dissolve in the water, because of the relatively greater surface area exposed at the top. Although it is possible to construct a tank with properly-cut glass, tape, and cement, the very high probability of leakage makes this venture impractical for most beginners.

The tank must be clean. Dirt, grease, or caked lime can be removed by scrubbing thoroughly with salt and water. The salt is abrasive enough to have a scouring effect. Should detergent or soaps be needed, repeated rinsing of the tank is essential. Any residue may be harmful to future inhabitants. About two inches of clean sand may then be placed and spread evenly on the bottom of the tank.

A pet store can supply several varieties of inexpensive plants, any of which will serve well. *Sagittaria* and *vallisneria* will produce more oxygen than others, and are rooted plants. Anchor the plants firmly in the sand. If needed, several clean stones can supply support. Placing the plants toward the back of the tank will permit easier viewing of the fish.

Put a large piece of paper or cardboard over the plants before pouring or siphoning water into the tank. This prevents the plants from becoming dislodged and helps to keep the sand in place. The paper should be removed immediately thereafter. Should tap water be used, it must stand for at least 48 hours to permit the chlorine to escape and the water to acquire room temperature. The water level should be about an inch lower than the tank top. Moving the tank after it is filled may warp the tank seams and start a leak. (If a leak does occur, apply epoxy glue to the inside joints and seams after thoroughly drying out the tank.)

Goldfish and guppies are among the best fish to use, as they can withstand a broad temperature change. Small catfish, sunfish, minnows, zebras, and bullheads are also easy to keep and interesting to observe. If several water snails are purchased at the pet store along with the plants and fish, they will provide added interest and value. Snails keep the aquarium clean by scavenging excess fish food and by eating the green slime (algae) that may form on the glass. Only a few are needed, as they multiply rapidly and can become a problem. Children delight in examining snails' eggs, laid on the glass sides, and in seeing the snails scrape off and eat the algae. A few hand lenses placed around the aquarium make the viewing easier.

A properly set-up aquarium needs little attention. Plants give off some of the oxygen needed by the animals, and absorb some of the excrement. The animals also provide carbon dioxide needed by the plants to photosynthesize. What if the aquarium is not properly set up? Here we can look for clues that may indicate improper light, temperature, oxygen, feeding, or cleanliness.

If algae grow rapidly on the sides, there is too much light. A northeast corner location or other place of good but indirect light should work best. Adding more snails and wrapping black paper around the tank for a while can retard growth of algae. However, it may also be necessary to clean the tank.

[7] For a free set of detailed leaflets on keeping animals and plants in the classroom, see page 468L.

While algae will not hurt the fish, visibility is hampered.

If the temperature is too low reproduction will slow down noticeably, or stop. Some fish may die. The best temperature range for fish recommended here is 50-70°F. An exception is the guppy, which requires 70–85°F water if you want it to reproduce. When most kinds of tropical fish are used, a heater is a necessity. This can be in the form of a light bulb placed in the cover of the tank, although an immersible heater works better.

Insufficient oxygen is indicated when fish stay very close to the surface of the water. This is where the greatest amount of oxygen dissolved directly from the air is located. Occasionally, some fish might be seen to break the surface and gulp air directly. Insufficient surface area or overcrowding can cause this condition. About an inch of goldfish (not including the tail) per gallon is proper. If guppies are used, about six per gallon are satisfactory. Having too many snails will also contribute to an oxygen-poor condition. Planting more *sagittaria* and *vallisneria* will give some extra production of oxygen. But a motor-driven aerator, purchasable at pet stores, is a surer way to take care of the problem.

Cloudy water occurs from overfeeding the fish or not removing dead plants and animals. Bacterial action on uneaten food and other organic matter poisons the water and contributes to the growth of other microorganisms. The most practical solution is to discard everything, carefully clean the tank, and begin again.

Only a small sprinkling of packaged fish food once a day—enough to be completely eaten in two or three minutes—is required for feeding. Tiny bits of chopped beef and earthworm can also be used. No provision need be taken for weekends, but some means for feeding during vacations is necessary.

In spite of reasonable care, it may be necessary to clean the tank more frequently than is convenient unless the aquarium has an automatic water filter. This may consist of a combination charcoal and spun-glass filter through which water is pumped by a small electric motor. Purchasable for about five dollars and up at pet stores, an automatic filter can reduce cleaning periods to once a year. A filterless aquarium needs to to be cleaned once a month or oftener. Although the filter needs to be washed occasionally, this is a simple and quickly performed task. A filter also takes the place of an aerator, should one be needed.

A glass top or piece of Saran-Wrap may be used to cover the aquarium. For better air circulation, leave some space open, or punch a few holes in the Saran-Wrap cover. A top helps to maintain clean water, cuts down on loss of water through evaporation, or loss of an overly athletic fish. It also serves to illustrate condensation and precipitation, since water droplets form on the bottom surface and fall back into the tank.

Setting Up a Terrarium. A *terrarium* is a container in which a miniature land environment may be set up to feature several small plants and animals. Almost any large glass receptacle will do for the basic structure—a large pickle jar turned on its side, a leaky aquarium tank, or other sizable glass container. After the tank or jar has been cleaned, about an inch of small pebbles and bits of charcoal may be placed on the bottom. The pebbles provide drainage, and the charcoal can prevent the soil from turning sour. Equal parts of peat moss, soil, and sand mixed together with a little additional charcoal should be spread evenly over the base to a height of roughly 3 inches. Dwarf ivy, ferns, liverworts, and lichens are ideal plants. Partridge berry and mosses provide satisfactory ground cover, if desired.

A small, shallow dish pressed partly into the soil can serve as a source of water for the animals. Although the ground should be sprinkled until moist, it must not be left wet as molds and other fungi may develop. In about a week, the plants should take hold and the animals can be introduced. A land snail, earthworms, small land turtle, salamander, or small frog are quite suitable for this miniature woodland environment. A little lettuce will feed the snail and turtles; earthworms receive nutrition from the soil. Satisfactory food for frogs and salamanders include small live insects, such as flies, sow bugs, ants, and the like.

Keep the terrarium covered, and out of the sunlight to avoid buildup of heat. A glass sheet placed over the top of the terrarium, loosely fitted to permit air circulation, will help keep the humidity high and reduce the need to water the soil. Here, too, water will evaporate from the soil, condense on the underside of the glass cover, and fall as "rain," in a miniature water cycle.

Commercial Aquaria and Terraria. If you have never started and maintained an aquarium or terrarium, understandably you may be reluctant to begin. However, almost any biological supply house (see the list on p. 91R) has dependable sets of animals and plants, with detailed directions. At the time of this writing, they cost six to seven dollars. Safe delivery is guaranteed and can be made at any time of the year.

SCHOOL AND COMMUNITY RESOURCES

It is possible for us to get so engrossed in acquiring books, films, and other materials for classroom use that we forget there is an out-of-class environment for science exploration. The school building itself is a good place to start. Why are there cracks in the masonry and plaster? How do the fire extinguishers work? Why are the stairs worn in the middle and not at the sides? What's causing some of the paint outside to peel? How is the school heated? How many simple machines does the custodian use?

Things are happening on the school-grounds, too: Why are they planting ground cover on the hill? Why is the hot asphalt the playground "steaming" after the cloudburst? How does the seesaw work? What are the names of the birds around the schoolyard, and where do they nest? Why are the shrubs planted on the north side growing more slowly than those on the south side? Why is snow still on the roof of the main building when it has melted on the other roofs? Why are shadows longer in the afternoon?

The surrounding community may contain many places to visit for direct observations: a zoo, wooded area, garden, nursery and greenhouse, pond or brook, pet store, bird refuge, observatory, natural history museum, road cut, stone quarry, "vacant" lot, construction site, waterworks, sewage-treatment plant, dairy, airport, and weather bureau. All these and more are rewarding places for elementary-school pupils to visit. Specific suggestions for study trips to some of these locations are made in several units of Part II.

Before a study trip is taken, some preparation is needed to help make it worthwhile. A school district catalogue may be available of suggested places to visit in the community. This can assist in giving most of the necessary details for educational trips. In general, however, you will want to keep the following points in mind:

1. Be clear about the purpose for leaving the classroom. A common reason is to stimulate interest and problems at the beginning of a unit. Sometimes a study trip is helpful to give additional topical information or to see applications of generalizations.

2. Check with the principal for school policies. Chances are several procedures will need to be followed—notification and permission of parents, a phone call to the site-of-visit, transportation request made, and so forth.

3. Visit the site yourself. It is much easier to make plans when you actually know what conditions are like.

4. Plan with the children what to look for. A list of questions or purposes may be needed, and some background, to enable them to observe intelligently.

5. Develop with the class some behavior and safety standards to be remembered. A "buddy" system can be used—each child helps to keep track of another. Less reliable children can be placed at the head of the line. Several parents or monitors at the end of the line can prevent straggling.

6. At the site, make sure everyone can see and hear adequately, and can ask questions if desired. If the class is large it may be necessary to divide it into smaller groups.

7. After returning to the classroom, help pupils evaluate the trip. Did they achieve their purposes? Were safety and behavior standards observed?

When it is impossible to arrange visits away from the school, resource persons from the community may be able to visit the classroom. Numerous districts compile lists of informed persons who are willing to donate some of their time and talent for the education of children. As with study trips, maximum benefits from a classroom visit are likelier to happen if there has been some preplanning.

The class should decide what questions it wants to ask the visitor. Give the person's name and some background—occupation, qualifications, experience, and other information useful to the children. In some classes it may be worthwhile to have a brief rehearsal of how the class will participate before the guest arrives, just to make sure that things will go according to plan.

Inform your guest beforehand of the grade level, interests, and general characteristics of the children. Provide him with a list of questions the class wants to ask. These preparations can insure a more effective experience. If the speaker will respond informally to questions rather than give a formal speech, the chances are better for a more understandable and pertinent lesson. Should your guest have a tendency to drift from the subject or use difficult vocabulary, you may want to ask tactful, clarifying questions as needed. Above all, make sure the length of time for the presentation is well understood in advance. Most primary children grow restless after a half-hour. The maximum length of time for older pupils is usually about an hour.

Marshaling Community Resources. Many communities, especially the larger ones, have an enormous wealth of scientific and

Figure 21 A study trip to the seashore provides many interesting specimens for examination. (Nestor-Monkmeyer.)

other resources potentially available for instruction. But identification and organization of such resources are needed before they can be used. Typically, some of this is done in school district study trip guides and the like, but seldom is full value obtained from what is there.

A shining example of what can be done to marshal local resources for school use is found in the Community Educational Re-

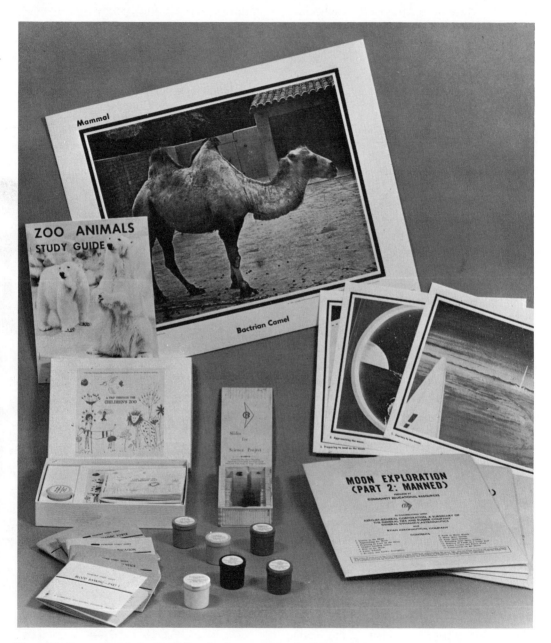

Figure 22 Some materials developed from local resources by the Community Educational Resources Section, Department of Education, San Diego County, California. (Courtesy Dept. of Education, San Diego County, Calif.)

sources Section of the San Diego County (California) Department of Education. In 1960, several task groups were formed of volunteers from local industrial, technological, scientific, educational, and military organizations. These persons thoroughly surveyed the Greater San Diego area for possible educational resources in their respective fields. The search turned up a gold mine of potential materials — films, charts, maps, models, photographs, sites for study trips, and more.

Since the project's beginning, hundreds of instructional materials have been rapidly and expertly processed from primary resources in such areas as oceanography, space exploration, nuclear energy, botany, marine geology, zoology, and mathematics. These materials often contain the latest contributions of persons on the cutting edge of scientific research and technological innovation. This has drastically reduced in many instances the lengthy time lag which normally occurs between actual discovery and classroom study of the discovered. (See Figure 22.)

Perhaps in the future we shall see regional or even nation-wide networks composed of similar educational resource groups, each sharing the unique features of its community resources with communities elsewhere.

Planning for Teaching

LIBRARY

CHAPTER SIX

Planning for Teaching

IN EVERY SCHOOL THERE ARE SOME TEACHERS WHO ARE MORE effective than others in teaching science. If you try to find a specific reason for their effectiveness it is often hard to pin down. There are so many differences in their teaching behavior. But at least one of their general characteristics stands out clearly: they are likely to be well organized. You will want to know some of the ways that successful teachers use to plan learning experiences for children.

THE THREE BASES OF PLANNING

Three questions reveal the gist of planning: *What* do we teach? *How* do we teach it? *How well* are we teaching it? This is what we have been discussing in the first five chapters. So far, though, the approach has been analytical, fine for studying one by one the elements that go into good science teaching. But unless you already have a structure to assimilate these ideas, they are hard to use in a systematic way. In this chapter, then, we shall tie together many of the preceding ideas *in a form convenient for teaching*.

The "What" of Planning. The *what* consists of process and product objectives. You remember that the many ways of investigating can be sorted conveniently into five broad processes. The child:

Credit for chapter opening photograph. **S. L. Guiliani, San Diego City Schools**

(1) *states problems* and makes operational definitions;

(2) *suggests* and appraises *hypotheses;*

(3) interprets data and *makes inferences;*

(4) *develops* and selects *procedures;*

(5) *reasons quantitatively.*

Each of these classifications can help to recall some subskills which can be used as specific referents to guide teaching. (For a review of some thirty subskills, see page 70.)

Do these specific referents need to be written down each time you make plans? Only if you are vague as to what they are. At first, it is probably a good idea when planning to jot down several which seem hard to remember. Later there will be no need. They become a permanent part of your teaching behavior when used often enough. As for the broad categories, these are potentially part of most lessons you teach, not just in science, but in social studies and some other areas as well. Having different process objectives for every subject area is confusing to both teaching and learning.

Product objectives should also be small in number. Six subject-matter generalizations or so are adequate for most units. Most textbook chapters feature no more, and many have fewer. These specific generalizations may change from one topic to the next. But *the behavioral referent we use to evaluate a child's knowledge of generalizations stays the same, just as referents for process behaviors stay the same.*

For example, we have said there is reasonable assurance a child knows a generalization when he can explain, predict, or control events; in short, apply his knowledge. This kind of mastery, then, is the classroom goal. *This behavioral referent can be used with any properly stated generalization,* and in almost any subject.

In Chapter 4 you also saw referents for concepts and facts. But, as explained there, in many cases you may not want to use these directly, since the generalization referents usually include the correct use of concepts and facts. As with process behaviors, there is no need to always put in writing the broad or specific knowledge behaviors you wish to bring about unless you are vague about what they are. With continual application, they become a permanent part of your teaching behavior.

These ideas emphasize the pervasive nature of both process and product objectives, when they are well-constructed. So, *the only "objectives" that typically need to be written down in planning are the specific generalizations that point toward the subject matter of the lessons to be taught.*

Do you need to think of specific behavioral objectives in process and product for each child? Some educators would firmly say "yes!" What are the implications of such a view? An important process referent when a child develops procedures for an experiment is his ability to identify needed controls. But how many controls? How subtle should they be? How difficult is the experiment? What are the limitations imposed by the materials?

An important product referent with generalizations, as you have seen, is the child's power to explain specific examples of applications. But how many applications? How subtle should they be?

It is physically impossible in classroom teaching to develop specific behavioral goals for each child. There are too many individual differences, too many children, too many subjects. "Granted," some teachers say, "but shouldn't we at least state the minimal behaviors we expect to develop?" Ironically, this can become a way of ignoring individual differences. *The best teaching rapidly and continually widens individual differences.* In fact, it is one of the best indications you have to tell how successful you are in meeting the needs of pupils. Goals in teaching should be clearly stated. The best way to make them clear is to state them as observable behaviors. However, statements of these behaviors must be *open-ended,* because you can never be sure how far children can go. You can and should develop *general* expectancies for individual children and help them grow toward increased performance through the referents. To go much beyond this is not only impractical but also undesirable.

Another way of saying this is: The specificity with which we state behavioral objectives can reach a point of diminishing returns. Some specificity is needed for clearness. Yet to go too far gets us tangled in a web of unmanageable details, and *may set unnecessary limits on children's performance.* We need referents to make *judgments* about our teaching and the children's learning. This we cannot avoid any more than the courts can rigidly state once and for all what is "due process," or "a clear and present danger."

Perhaps needless to say, these statements are directed toward conventional teaching with a group of thirty or more pupils. This contrasts with programed instruction or related forms, directed toward individual learners in tightly controlled learning sequences.

The "How" of Planning. Basically, your task in planning *how* to teach science is to expose children to activities where they can gradually learn generalizations in an understandable, process-rich context. This develops *both kinds* of objectives. When generalizations are not so broad as to be vague, and not so narrow as to lack significant applications, a great many teaching-learning activities become available. (How to quickly locate these activities we shall consider shortly.)

Emphasis on *activities* as the data source, rather than the teacher, has advantages. Data are likelier to be meaningful. The children have chances to develop their own abilities to locate and interpret data. There is no need to attempt the impossible task of

becoming an "expert" in every area of the curriculum. This is not to slight the importance of being a well-informed person, but rather to stress the wisdom of using the many resources at hand.

The more activities you can find to choose from the better, but they should be relevant to the generalizations. A common fault of learning activities found in many curriculum guides is that they are only loosely related to the generalizations involved. Note the variety of learning experiences you can use:

experiments	discussions
demonstrations	lectures
reading	interviews
audio-visual materials	reports
study trips	observations
constructions	written work
collections	art work
exhibits	

Having a variety of experiences gives the children opportunities to explore from different angles facts and ideas leading to generalizations. In addition, it gives you the chance to suggest assignments of varying difficulty to take care of individual differences.

A valid purpose should precede each activity, otherwise the likelihood of aimless busywork increases. Sometimes purposes are background-centered. Our role here is to make available books or other materials that can directly give the class awareness of facts and ideas. We may also want to explain directly some ideas or teach some skills. Sometimes purposes are solution-centered. In these cases, we are more inclined to guide children's discovery of ideas, which involves a greater degree of process methods than before. In other words, activities may be arranged to provide input and opportunity to work in a problem-solving way.

The "how" of teaching process and product requires more on our part than just collecting a group of activities that correspond to generalizations and then turning the children loose. We need to select and arrange available activities in a teaching order that yields the most learning for the time and energy expended. Ordinarily, learning increases when the sequence goes from the simple to the complex, the familiar to the unfamiliar, the present to the past, the more interesting to the less interesting, and the specific to the general. Occasionally, these and other criteria mentioned conflict. The unfamiliar may be more interesting than the familiar, the general more teachable than the specific. These are the times to exercise judgment about what should come first.

The "How Well" in Planning. Evaluation is probably the most neglected of the three bases of planning. But it need not be. Once you have some behavioral referents in mind, pupil involvement in activities and discussions provides much feedback for corrective action. The work the children do, the things they say, how they respond to your questions — all take on significance. Much of the time referents are mental criteria by which you observe and judge progress. But you have also seen how they can be built into tests. The "how well" aspect is largely an internal part of planning what to teach and how to teach it. If you have done a thorough job with the first two aspects, the last becomes much easier. Evaluation, then, is a process that begins with the first lesson, rather than a single paper-and-pencil test given when your teaching ends.

RESOURCE AND TEACHING UNITS

One of the best means of turning the three bases of planning into a teachable and interesting framework is the *unit of work*. We have already said that a unit "is a sequence of related ideas and activities organized around a theme or topic." Units found in curriculum guides supplied by school districts are likely to be *resource units*. That

is, each of these contains many more suggestions for study than is possible with any one class. The idea is to select from the resource unit only those objectives and activities that seem best to fit the needs of a specific class within the time available for study. When organized into a teachable sequence of learning experiences, the resource unit becomes a *teaching unit*. A well-done resource unit has sections that contain suggestions for nearly everything needed in teaching, from start to finish:

Objectives
Initiation suggestions
Learning activities
Local references and resources
Evaluation suggestions
Culminating activities

Let us briefly examine each of these.

1. *Objectives.* Long lists of such mind-numbing statements as "To learn the nature of the skies" thankfully are disappearing. There is a trend toward a small number of objectives, clearly written in terms of intended behaviors (but open-ended) toward which to teach. These reflect both process and product goals. Generalizations are listed for product goals which reflect the more important ideas of the subject, instead of facts or minor ideas.

2. *Initiation Suggestions.* Ways for initiating study of the unit may involve one activity or a combination of activities. For example, the room environment may be arranged to include a stimulating bulletin board with accompanying materials on a nearby table; pictures, various trade books, and other printed materials may be spread out on the library table; a film may be shown with the sound turned off, while the teacher asks the children questions about what they see, and so forth.

These activities differ from the usual in that they encompass a broader scope of study and raise more questions than they answer. So, besides getting the unit started, the initiation serves several other functions.

It arouses interest. It gives the teacher some opportunity to learn what the group already knows, and what it wants to know. It provides the class with at least a partial overview of what it will be studying.

Sensible though it may seem, whether a specific initiation phase is *always* the best way to do these things is an arguable point with experienced teachers. Therefore, we shall consider initiations again later in this chapter.

3. *Learning Activities*. The best units contain a large number of varied activities. As mentioned before, this helps teachers to cope with individual differences among pupils. Local environment and facilities are emphasized when applicable. The surrounding terrain, nearby museum of natural history, and district-sponsored study trips give an immediacy and vitality to learnings that are hard to achieve in other ways. Activities in such units are usually placed under or next to pertinent generalizations. Often there are accompanying questions or problems that can provide purposes for the activities. Unfortunately, when such questions do appear, they are seldom more than restatements of generalizations or facts, and are mostly background-centered.

4. *Local References and Resources*. Local materials and resources not already included under specific activities are placed in a special section for convenient reference. All the instructional materials available in the district which pertain to the unit may be found listed here: trade books, grouped according to difficulty levels; teacher references; audio-visual aids: free and inexpensive materials; special equipment, and so on. Although the same information might be scattered among a half-dozen or so catalogues, curriculum specialists find that placing it in the unit itself insures greater use of available resources.

5. *Evaluation Suggestions*. Sometimes tests are provided, and suggestions for teacher observation of significant behaviors. As with activities, the teacher is selective. Items are chosen which closely correspond to what is done in the teaching unit itself. Other aids might include pupil work standards which can be developed with the class, self-rating checklists for pupils, and other evaluation ideas.

6. *Culminating Activities*. To reinforce learning, it is good to summarize and review important parts of the unit. Culminating experiences are designed to bring this about at the unit's close. Typical activities suggested may be a "quiz" on the ideas studied, a small science fair that features constructions made during the unit, pupil reports, or a large mural which reflects important ideas studied, planned and painted by the entire class.

The modern trend is to play down or eliminate specific closing activities. Many teachers like to summarize learnings regularly throughout the unit, and prefer a smooth transition from one unit to another. Perhaps partly accountable for the trend are educators' adverse reactions to the extravagant preparation and near-theatrical atmosphere which accompany some culminations.

As you might expect, the quality of district-supplied units varies enormously. It is clear that an excellent resource unit takes care of a great many instructional problems. But what do you do when the unit-at-hand consists of little more than a declaration of good intentions? Or when there are no units at all? In these cases, the best course of action may be to develop a unit based on the organization of the pupils' textbook.

TEXTBOOK-BASED UNITS

A chapter in a well-written textbook is more than just a logical exposition of subject matter, supported by a few supplementary activities. It is a psychological presentation of ideas and activities that, used properly, can help to bring about effective teaching. Two of its most serious defects are likely to be lack of depth—although this is fast improving—and absence of local resources. When you know how to overcome these handicaps, what often emerges is a unit not just comparable to one that is wholly developed in the local district, but one that can be greatly superior. We cannot present here a detailed accounting of why textbook-based units are often desirable to construct. But as some justification for this recommendation might be expected, here are a few reasons.

Only a very few school districts can provide the money, personnel time, and expert study needed to develop a curriculum "from scratch" in any one field. When they can, we see worthwhile results. Districts that attempt ambitious programs of curriculum construction in science without fulfilling the necessary conditions develop curricula that are disappointingly ineffectual. In addition, such disappointment may provoke contempt and skepticism toward the usefulness of cooperative practices. That this is wholly unreasonable and unwarranted scarcely needs to be stated.

Fortunately, other educators take a more sensible approach to the problem. They realize that a soundly conceived textbook series in science contains the nucleus of an entire curriculum. They know that much attention has been given to principles of child development; that activities are carefully tested; that the teaching order in each chapter helps to indicate a learnable sequence, and so on. But they also know that teaching the text itself usually results in page-to-page following, with more opportunities for background learning than for thoughtful inquiry; that additional activities are needed, especially those which take advantage of local resources.

These reasons, and more than we can mention here, explain why many school districts base their science units upon the adopted text or texts. Chapter organizations are expanded or deepened, and "localized" with an abundance of resources. Suggestions for additional approaches and improvements are contributed. In effect, much of the same desirable cooperation and trying-out of ideas takes place as before, except that a better product emerges, and in far less time, than when attempts are made to start from no structure at all.

The three main things you need to know in developing a textbook-based unit are how to determine the *generalizations* which may be taught, how to compile *activities* which may be used to teach the generalizations, and how to prepare *bridges* for activity sequences.

Determining Generalizations. The chapters of nearly all textbook series are organized around large generalizations, from about three to ten. Rarely are there fewer or more than this, and the average seems to be about six. The teacher manuals of some series contain outlines with the large generalizations clearly labeled. When this is the case, all that is needed next, if the scope seems satisfactory, is to begin locating activities. In other series, generalizations are lumped together with facts, concepts, contributing ideas, and so forth, into "learnings," "understandings," or other broadly inclusive categories. Your job here is simply to figure out what the basic generalizations are. Try the following procedure:

1. Read the entire chapter quickly. This enables you to sense what it includes. Topical headings may reveal at least some of the large ideas involved. The pictures may illustrate them.

2. Check the accompanying teacher's manual. It probably contains at least a general outline of the chapter, or a list of

"learnings." Either can help point up generalizations and aid in checking others.

3. If the chapter is long and thorough, the broad generalizations you compose may each contain several ideas that should be emphasized individually. These can become "contributing ideas" and should be placed under each appropriate generalization. Your outline may then consist of, say, five or six generalizations, with several contributing ideas under most of them. Don't be concerned if there are no contributing ideas under some generalizations, if you have checked the outline carefully for completeness. This probably only reflects the present structure of the chapter. Later, when gathering activities, or teaching the unit, you may decide to add some contributing ideas of your own.

4. To check the accuracy and completeness of the outline, go through the text chapter again. Notice how the outline corresponds to the topical headings and sentences and also the amount of material allotted to each topic. When there is a long list of learnings in the teacher's manual, another check can show how well the generalizations encompass them. If all of the learnings can be placed under appropriate generalizations, the outline is probably satisfactory.

It is easy to get the impression from looking at these suggestions that a long time is needed to determine the large ideas. This is unlikely. Pick out a chapter in a child's text and carefully read it, along with the accompanying section in the teacher's manual. After doing so, with average ability in outlining, you can probably synthesize the main generalizations in ten to twenty minutes.

Whether you use the text chapter as a base for a unit or as the entire program, *it is extremely important to think through its basic organization*. When making a unit, you need to know the generalizations to compile activities, but the importance of

analysis goes beyond this. It contributes to your confidence by providing a sense of direction. It leads to the feeling that, if needed, you can make a few changes, and add some children's ideas. It helps you to decide what is important and what is not. In contrast, when merely following the book, you go wherever it leads.

Determining Activities. One advantage in using the book as a base is the assurance that at least some activities are "automatically" available and tied to each generalization. The text contains reading matter, pictures to examine, and other things to do. It is your job, then, to expand its present inventory of activities. The more the activities, the easier it is to select exactly what is most fitting at the time of planning specific lessons.

Many school districts provide for this purpose books and catalogues that contain collections of activities. The following titles collectively contain several thousand experiments, demonstrations, and other things to do:

David E. Hennessy, *Elementary Teacher's Classroom Science Demonstrations and Activities,* Englewood Cliffs, N.J.: Prentice-Hall, Inc., 1964.

Elizabeth B. Hone, Alexander Joseph, and Edward Victor, *A Sourcebook for Elementary Science,* New York: Harcourt, Brace and World, Inc., 1962.

National Science Teachers Association, *Space; Matter and Energy; Earth Sciences; Motion; Living Things; Waves* (Each is a separate publication.), Darien, Conn.: Teachers Publishing Corporation, 1968.

UNESCO, *700 Science Experiments for Everyone,* Second Edition (Originally published as *UNESCO Source Book for Science Teaching*.), Garden City, New York: Doubleday and Company, Inc., 1964.

Having a sourcebook that contains many activities is beneficial. You can usually find additional activities without wasting time, if the generalizations selected in the first place are truly fundamental. When working with some units, this text can serve in a similar way.

Besides a good sourcebook, consult your local audio-visual and other catalogues. Write down under each generalization what experiences will assist you to teach it. Also record recommended study trips.

Don't neglect other local facilities, such as the school building and grounds, and local resource persons. It may be worthwhile to check a free and inexpensive materials catalogue for other possibilities. Trade books may be available on the subject, either at the school district library or the local public library. After the primary grades, encyclopedias are worthwhile for additional information and reports. Further, children can check newspapers and magazines for stories and pictures.

Determining Bridges. As discussed in Chapter 3, a bridge can be developed from any understandable application of the generalization you want to teach. However, recall that the bridge must relate to the first activity you plan to use. Otherwise, it may be confusing.

What if you can't think of a bridge? Either the text or curriculum guide may contain an introduction that can be adapted. In most texts, a purpose or question usually precedes an activity. Sometimes, excellent application questions are asked at the end of each topical section. These may be easily used as bridges. The accompanying teacher's manual, too, may be a source of problem introductions. A good way to learn how to extract possible bridges from these sources is simply to leaf through them with this specific purpose in mind. With some practice (and a well-written text) potential bridges will leap to your attention.

Another source of ideas for bridges is this book. It has scores in Part II. To locate them, refer first to the topic, then to the generalizations that most closely resemble those in mind for your teaching unit.

Whether your unit is based on a resource guide or text, a convenient way to keep track of the generalizations, activities, and bridges is to use 5- by 8-inch cards. Write one generalization at the top of each card, next a bridge under the generalization, then the several activities below the bridge (Figure 23). Be sure to relate the bridge to the first activity. Sometimes, a generalization is broad enough to be subdivided into several contributing ideas. If so, it may be easier to keep track of your specific purposes and activities by using one card for each contributing idea, rather than for each generalization.

The use of cards has advantages. They can be shuffled in any desired sequence. It is easy to add and take away generalizations and activities. Special sections can be fitted in and items filed: outstanding bulletin board ideas, news clippings, evaluation suggestions, or whatever else is desired to help make the unit easier to teach. You may also want to put marginal notes next to the activities about which process skills to stress.

A fine unit does not spring full-blown from the first organization. The more it is taught, the more you will want to modify it. Activities may be strengthened, the teach-

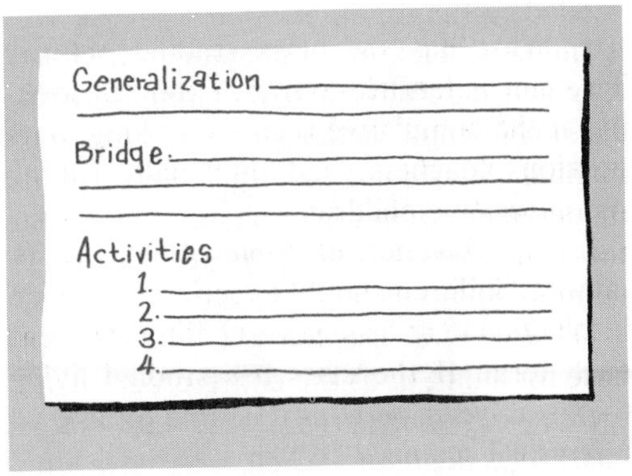

Figure 23 Essential parts of a card system for a teaching unit.

ing order changed, scope added to, and so on. With much experience, you can often detect from inspection alone where your first organization will falter with your classes. In the meantime, you learn largely from teaching it and noting what happens.

PLANNING BEFORE UNIT TEACHING

Just before teaching a unit, you need to make decisions about some practical problems. These decisions involve the choice of unit, your subject-matter background, the making of a general plan for teaching, and how to begin.

Choosing a Unit. Some school districts leave the choice of units entirely to the teacher. Others prescribe that thus and so shall be taught. Many districts have both required and optional units. This arrangement seems to work well. The required units are planned so that there is some continuity in ideas among the several grade levels, and a reasonably wide scope is represented. At the same time, some leeway is allowed for the desires of children and teachers. When there is a choice, these are some considerations that should enter into your decision:

1. What has the class studied before? This can be learned to some extent by looking at the cumulative records, talking to its previous teachers, and informally asking representative children.
2. Is a balance of topics being maintained? Children should experience science instruction in at least several different areas each term. If the class has studied living things all year, perhaps it is time to take up a physical science.
3. What are the children interested in? If motivation is present and strong in most

of the children, it would be unwise to ignore it. On the other hand, there are few topics in elementary science that fail to arouse interest if they are well planned.
4. What is the possibility of correlation with other curriculum areas? Should the material correlate well with whatever else is being studied, this offers a chance to reinforce and extend learnings by showing them in another context.
5. How much time is available? The best answer is stated in *hours*, unless the definitions of other terms used—"weeks," "days," "lessons"—are clear.
6. Is the unit seasonal? In most places, a class garden is a better activity in spring than fall. Observation of certain animals may be inconvenient or impossible in winter, and so on.
7. How many others will teach the unit at this time? If many teachers in the district plan to teach the unit at the same time probably district materials will be few and unpredictable in arrival.

Developing a Subject-Matter Background. Once the decision is made as to what unit will be taught, it is wise to assess your own subject-matter background. Of course, if you have no background at all in the unit topic, this might be a factor to consider when choosing the unit. Most of the time, gaps in background can be overcome without too much effort. The activities planned will provide most of the needed subject matter, and you can learn along with the class. However, it is important to do some background reading if you feel insecure about the *basic generalizations* to be studied.

When using a text-based unit, read the children's text chapter and correlated section in the teacher's guide. Most guides now contain subject matter for quick reference along with suggestions for teaching. A child's trade book on the topic, or a teacher's reference book available from the school or district, may also be worthwhile to ex-

Table 1 A Block Plan for a Primary Unit on Simple Machines, Scheduled Forty-Five Minutes Daily for Fifteen Days

	April 6–10	April 13–17	April 20–24
MONDAY	**1.** *Inclined plane; force changes with its tilt.* Introduce with pictures. Do experiments 1, 2, 3.	**3.** *Lever; force changes with force-arm length.* Do experiments 1, 2.	**4.** *Windlass; force changes with size of wheel.* Do experiments 1, 2. Remind class for extending activity.
TUESDAY	Do experiments 3, 4, 5. Remind class for extending activity.	Do experiments 3, 4, 5.	Do experiment 4. Do extending activity.
WEDNESDAY	Do experiments 6, 7. Do extending activity 1. Make bulletin board.	Do extending activity 2.	**5.** *Pulley; force changes with number of supporting lines.* Do experiments 1, 2, 3.
THURSDAY	**2.** *Screw; force changes with pitch.* Do experiments 1, 2. Remind class for extending activity.	Do extending activity 2. Remind class for extending activity 1.	Do experiments 4, 5, 6.
FRIDAY	Do experiment 3, and extending activity. Order film 370.15 for April 24.	Do extending acitivity.	Show film 370.15 "How Simple Machines Help Us" (20 min.) Discuss and evaluate whole unit.

amine. The purpose for reading should be to get acquainted with some facts and ideas *related to the generalizations in the unit,* rather than to acquire an encyclopedic background on the topic from which to draw. You need to understand the generalizations to teach them satisfactorily. But there is no need to know "everything." That is what reference books are for. Besides reading, you will find it helpful to try your hand with unfamiliar demonstrations or experiments that seem appropriate for class study.

Making a Block Plan. With some background, you are ready to go on. Select the generalizations and activities from the resource unit (or text unit, or text) which seem most appropriate for the class. Lay out a tentative block plan for study. It is better to plan *large blocks of time for daily study* than to schedule science for twenty minutes or so a day, two or three days a week. It takes too much time to set up and distribute materials — and otherwise have a program where children actively do things — for short periods to work well. Forty minutes or more may be satisfactory with most primary children, and about an hour is desirable with older pupils.

The day-to-day contact with ideas and activities of the unit is important for continuity and reinforcement in learning. It also contributes to a continuing sense of participation and interest. Daily teaching of science may mean that part of the year science will not be formally scheduled in the school day. This is far better than having brief, discontinuous sessions during the whole year where little can be done except textbook reading.

An exception to these suggestions is when the class grows plants or otherwise waits for slow changes to take place. Here, you may find it convenient to let the readiness of the objects influence when lessons are taught. Even careful advance preparations cannot guarantee that living things will always act in predictable ways.

Observe the block plan in Table 1, drawn up by a student teacher for Unit 6 of this book, page 304. (Although the units in this book are not truly of the resource type, the form of laying out a block plan is much the same.) The school district involved commends that social studies or science units be taught during the first hour of the day, after opening exercises and current-event reports. This leaves from forty minutes to almost an hour for unit teaching, depending on how much time is taken up at the start of day and the amount of time judged desirable by the teacher. Three "weeks" have been alloted for a science unit in this case; that is, fifteen sessions of about forty-five minutes each are available.

Note that only the broad aspects of planning are considered: shortened statements of the generalizations to keep purposes in view; probable days when experiments will be taken up; reminders to inform the class about materials needed on different days; a notation to order a film, and so forth.

The student teacher may find that her judgment is not completely accurate. For example, it may take more than two sessions to clinch understandings with the pulley, and fewer sessions with the inclined plane. For the last day, she has scheduled a film that reviews all simple machines, rather than the trip suggested in the unit. If it is a good film, it may reveal more than the study trip site available to the class. At the same time it can help culminate the unit.

The planning shown in Table 1 does not mean rigid restrictions have been placed on the time, activities, or sequence in question. Flexibility is encouraged in virtually all school districts. Although a certain amount of time has been set aside, it can be expanded or cut down, depending on what happens in the classroom. So the block plan is what you *start* with. It may be changed, and frequently is, when you see how your lessons go from day to day.

Should everyone put into block plans what appears in this one? Planning is a highly individual matter. When thirty experienced teachers in a college summer-session course were asked to make a block plan for another unit, wide differences appeared in the notations they felt were necessary for their own guidance. Nearly all these teachers strongly endorsed the making of a block plan, but few agreed as to exactly what it should contain.

The Opening Activity. Usually the last aspect of preplanning is to decide what opening lesson or lessons to use. Should you begin right off with a "regular" lesson? Or should there be a specifically planned initiation phase in which you attempt to (1) find out what the children know and want to know, (2) heighten interest, and (3) give the children an overview of what they will be studying?

There seems little point in having a formal initiation if the children are enthusiastic at the outset about the unit topic, and you have a reasonable idea of what they know. You will find out much more about their knowledge when they engage in specific activities. If you encourage them to ask questions during the entire unit, they will be far likelier to ask significant "why" questions instead of "what" questions. What about the overview? This is useful, but a complete overview at the very beginning of study is questionable. It may be much more understandable, especially with primary children, to give several smaller previews of future study at different points throughout the unit.

Teachers often ask, "Should pupils take part in long-range planning?" What we have been discussing requires much more knowledge than pupils have of the teaching-learning process, subject matter, and activities of the unit. It is desirable to involve pupils in planning, but this should be in specific, short-range situations, within an overall framework developed by the teacher. Some of these situations are pointed out in the next section.

LESSON PLANNING

Students of public speaking quickly catch on to the Big Secret of Success: "Tell 'em what you're going to say, say it, and then tell 'em what you've said." Or, translated: "Briefly establish the purpose of your talk, give the talk, and then briefly summarize it."

We do much the same thing in lesson planning:

1. A background or solution-centered purpose is established.
2. The children engage in background or solution-centered activities.
3. They summarize and then apply what they have learned to extend and clinch the ideas.

Here is your possible role in each of these three phases.

Purpose Setting. When you teach a lesson, you start out with a certain amount of "good will" from the children. Whether it grows or dissipates depends on the interest worked into the lesson. When you start a lesson with a bridge it provokes interest, and naturally leads to the need to find out and apply what has been learned. If the bridge contains a background-centered question, you help the children determine what to look for if they consult authority. If the question is solution-centered, you help the children plan ways in which they will test their hypotheses about the question—the materials needed, what they will do, the controls they will need, and so on. In the course of finding answers to the questions raised, the children begin to learn the generalization you have in mind. At the same time, they learn process methods which are developed in an understandable, purposeful context.

The beginning of the lesson, then, is when you motivate, pose questions, and plan how to find out. You need to know the generalization prompting the lesson, the activities and materials to be used, and the bridge.

Activity Phase. The next part of the lesson is where the children pursue the purpose raised. They perform experiments, see demonstrations, view films, read books, and engage in any of the other possibilities for activity. When there are enough materials to go around, the children work in small groups, or individually. You circulate around the room to iron out problems, assist slow readers, and so on. If you work directly with the children, as with a demonstration, you now ask questions and give clues to help children think about what is happening.

This is also the time when individuals work on reports or constructions. Or, if they have prepared them already, they give their reports or show to the class what they have made. The best reports and projects

Figure 24 The best reports and projects relate to generalizations studied by the entire class. (Courtesy Ben Gumm, San Diego City Schools.)

are those that relate to generalizations (not necessarily facts) studied by the entire class. It is hard for all pupils to benefit from these activities unless they have some background for understanding. (See Figure 24.)

Summary and Applying Phase. The last part of the lesson is when, through discussion, you help the children grasp the meaning of what they have done. Through your questions, based on process and product referents, you find out more about what they have learned. You guide them to evaluate their successes and failures, and to make generalizations.

Sometimes it seems hard for a class to generalize. More activities may be needed. But even when enough time is taken for finding out, generalizing may be difficult for many primary children. They may be at the intuitive, preverbal level—a condition in which they seem to understand, but cannot put it into words. In this case, you might let them "improve" a generalization you write. Or let them complete a partial

statement of a generalization that you have begun for them. But never press the matter if the going seems very hard. Otherwise, the tidy statement that emerges may be more yours than theirs, with little meaning for the children.

Some teachers record the important ideas discussed on a "We Found Out" chart. When placed next to a chart of related questions, it provides a record of progress, and a means for reviewing learning.

The end of the lesson is also the time when you do some planning with the children for the next lesson. Are materials needed? Perhaps the children can bring some from home. But you remember that children, especially the younger ones, are unreliable. So you ask several pupils rather than one to bring in an item. Have some children asked questions during the lesson? Perhaps these can be studied within the generalizations you have planned. If not, you must decide whether they should be studied individually, or by the entire class. Was process thinking satisfactory? Perhaps some particular skill needs stressing in future lessons. How much of this planning is done with the children depends, of course, on their maturity and ability.

When the children seem to understand the essentials of a generalization, use the last part of a lesson for applying and extending what they have learned. Bring up numerous examples of applications. Encourage the class to find other examples out of school. Assign activities of varying difficulty to provide for individual differences.

Although we have analyzed the lesson as to phases, in practice the transition from one phase to another is almost unnoticeable. And not always will all of these phases be completed in one class session. For example, there may be occasional need to spend several sessions on the activity part alone.

Summary of Planning (the GAB-BAG Approach). Because many details are presented in this chapter, it is easy to lose sight of the overall strategy of planning for thoughtful teaching and learning. The following device should help make this strategy clear.

Boiled down, you need to plan for three essentials in your teaching: *generalizations, activities,* and *bridges.* The *generalizations* comprise the basic structure of the unit and provide for the overall continuity of learning. These are furnished by the district curriculum guide. When there is no guide, you can extract them from a basic district-adopted text. *Activities* provide the means for learning the product and process objectives. Some sources for activities are the curriculum guide, basic text, district audio-visual guide, and various supplementary books. A *bridge* is needed for each activity sequence to insure that process learnings will receive attention. The sources of bridges are the guide, texts, or yourself.

In *planning* a unit, then, you select
G eneralizations, then find
A ctivities, then develop
B ridges, for the first activity of each sequence.

However, in teaching the unit, this sequential order won't do. In a teaching pattern for inductive thinking, it is usually important to begin with problems or similar purposes, and end with inferences that can be more broadly applied. This means that the order in which you plan is *reversed* when you teach.

In *teaching* a unit, then, you begin with a
B ridge, which leads the children to
A ctivities, which cause them to form a
G eneralization.

If your teaching unit is on 5- by 8-inch cards, once the unit is thoroughly familiar, you may be able to teach directly from a combination of the cards and your block plan. That is, the need for making detailed lesson plans may vanish except for occasional notes (such as for materials) jotted down in the appropriate spaces of the block plan.

By planning and teaching in a GAB-BAG way, process opportunities develop naturally, one after the other. To help you see how these opportunities arise, notations have been placed in the margins of each unit in Part II.

There is an efficient way to learn these processes that can be challenging and interesting. Mask the marginal notations with a 3/4-inch wide strip of stiff paper. As you read each unit, try to think of the process category the child uses in a particular part of a lesson—"suggests hypotheses," "reasons quantitatively," and so on. Then slide down the strip a little to see if you agree with the adjacent notation. Three facts should become quickly obvious. First, there is no set sequential order to the process categories. The start of a lesson may just as well call for pupils to reason quantitatively as state problems, for instance. Second, only about half of the places are noted where process skills are used. This was done partly to avoid clutter, but mainly to provide chances for your original thinking. Third, there are many specific subskills one uses to help children master the broad processes. To learn these, be sure to consult often the list in Chapter 4, page 70.

Continue to allocate the specific subskills to the broad categories throughout Part II. After studying all twelve units, you probably will know the subskills well enough to teach them "on your feet." That is, after all, a mark of the master teacher.

Some of the same shortcomings exist in setting down steps in planning as were found in our two-step method for beating the stock market (page 24L). Good planning or teaching is not a routinized, rule-of-thumb activity. It calls for imagination, personal innovation, and adaptability. It requires knowledge of when to "break the rules," and to adjust to the press of things that come up unexpectedly. In previous chapters pains were taken to present many of the considerations involved in making decisions. And some examples have been referred to in Part II. But so far, there has been little opportunity to study lessons that put together these ideas. Part II will provide such lessons.

HOW PART II OF THIS BOOK CAN HELP YOU

The units found on the following pages are designed to reflect the typical kinds of subject matter, activities, and materials found in the better elementary school science programs. They depart from the usual resource units in that they illustrate specific lessons arranged in teaching sequences. The lessons are instructional models which together contain applications of all the ideas of process and product development brought out in the previous chapters.

Few instructional models can be described which will work perfectly for everyone and in every situation. As you work with children or try out these instructional sequences in your methods class, you will begin to see where changes are desirable. But first you need something concrete to work with. In the course of thoughtfully going through the units, the ways of teaching that have been emphasized should become more familiar. The second part of this book, then, is an attempt to teach deeply what is introduced in the first part.

There are twelve units in Part II, selected from the three representative, broad-field areas used in elementary teaching: physical science, earth science, and life science. There are four units each with emphasis on primary, intermediate, and upper-level pupils, approximate ages five to thirteen. *The levels are only generally suggestive, as considerable overlapping has been carefully planned for.* The purpose of this book is not to provide a curriculum, but a wide range of activities you can explore in order to learn more about science and children. At the same time, it is important to learn the different teaching strategies needed with children of different ages and to have a solid core of activities you can rely on. But don't hesitate to try most of the activities over a broad age range, particularly the open-ended ones.

Each unit is constructed around a framework of important generalizations. Before every generalization is a subject-matter section to give you ample background. Following each generalization are the important aspects needed for teaching: materials, an interesting bridge, basic activities, vocabulary, and extending activities.

The sequence in each model unit generally goes from simpler ideas and activities to those more involved. When working with children you will want to start where they are. If they have little or no background for the material, begin with the first activity. With children who have some background, begin teaching at the place in the sequence for which they seem prepared. When insufficient time is a problem, *consider cutting down the number of generalizations* you teach in a unit. This should bring better results than lightly touching on all the suggested activities.

APPLICATIONS OF SCIENCE TEACHING METHODS

Part II

Molecules and Heat Energy

(Intermediate Emphasis)

UNIT ONE

Molecules and Heat Energy

(Intermediate Emphasis)

MODERN SCIENCE EDUCATION EMPHASIZES FUNDAMENTAL UNDER-
standings. Perhaps nowhere is this attention to fundamentals better seen than in units on energy. In the present one on heat, intended for children of the middle grades, some effort is made to
acquaint them with molecular theory. Children also will explore
through concrete experiences such concepts as heat and temperature, conservation of heat energy, expansion-contraction, heat
transfer, and changes of state. As is typical at this level, we shall be
concerned mostly with physical, rather than chemical, changes.

GENERALIZATIONS

I. Most materials expand when heated and contract when cooled.

II. Adding or taking away heat can cause materials to change
state; different materials change state at different temperatures.

III. There is a difference between temperature and heat; heat
energy is conserved when objects interact.

IV. Heat energy may come from several sources; it travels by
conduction, convection, and radiation.

Credit for chapter opening photograph. **Fundamental Photographs**

Expansion and Contraction.

QUESTION: How tall is the Empire State Building?

ANSWER: I don't know; it keeps changing.

Although answers like this seldom win prizes on television quiz shows, it is a valid one. The height of a tall structure may vary a half-foot or more, depending on temperature differences in effect when the measurements are taken. Similarly, a steel bridge may change more than a foot in length, and a ship captain may stride a slightly longer deck in southern, in contrast with northern, waters.

The molecular theory of matter offers an interesting explanation for these and many other events. To understand molecules, let us look for a moment at a drop of water. If we could subdivide it with an imaginary eyedropper for years on end, eventually we would get to a point where one more subdivision would produce two atoms of hydrogen and one of oxygen. Both are gases, and of course look nothing like water. From this we can say that a molecule is the smallest particle of a substance which can exist by itself and have the properties of that substance when interacting with other molecules.

Strictly speaking, only some gases are exclusively made up of molecules. Some liquids and many solids are composed of electrically charged atoms or groups of atoms called *ions*. A typical example is table salt, which is revealed through X-ray pictures to contain a boxlike, crystalline structure of sodium and chloride ions. However, since virtually all ionic particles possess physical characteristics very similar to molecules, it will be convenient to treat them as such at the elementary science level.

Is there any direct proof that molecules exist? Recently, yes. Pictures of some larger molecules have been taken through powerful electron microscopes. But for the most part scientists have had to rely on indirect evidence. It is a remarkable tribute to the intellectual ability of earlier scientists that they were able to forge so powerful a theory from their secondhand observations.

Many early experiments were so simple they may be duplicated today by children. An ounce of alcohol added to an ounce of water results in slightly less than two ounces of liquid. When gold and lead bars are clamped together for a long period there is a slight intermingling of these elements. Solid sugar crystals disappear when stirred into a hot liquid. Fine powder sprinkled into a water drop may be observed through a microscope of good quality to jiggle and move erratically.

From these and scores of other experiments and observations, the following ideas have been advanced:

Matter is composed of tiny particles that have an attractive force (cohesion) between them.

There is space between molecules. In a solid material, molecules are very close together, and are relatively "fixed" in place because their cohesion is greater than that of gases or liquids. Molecules of most liquids are slightly farther apart; their weaker cohesion permits them to slide about and take the shape of a container. Gas molecules are widest apart and have almost no cohesive attraction. Therefore, they can conform to a container's shape, or escape from an uncovered container.

Molecules are always in motion, but come almost to a standstill at absolute zero (−460°F or −273°C). Those of solids vibrate in place, while liquid and gas molecules move faster and more freely. With increased heat energy motion increases and the molecules move farther apart. The reverse happens when heat energy is decreased. This is why most matter expands when heated and contracts when cooled.

Although this theory states that liquids contract when cooled, we note an interesting exception when water temperature drops toward freezing. Water does contract in volume with decreased temperature, until about 39°F. Then its molecules begin to assemble into a crystalline form which takes on a solid appearance as ice at 32°F. The latticelike arrangement of these crystals takes up more space, about four percent more, than an equal amount of free-moving water molecules. This is why water pipes and engine blocks of water-cooled automobiles may burst in winter, and why frozen milk may push up and out of the bottle. Milk is largely water.

It also explains why a lake freezes from the top down, rather than the reverse. At 39°F water is densest and sinks to the lake bottom. Colder water, being less dense, floats to the surface. It freezes into surface ice, and traps the heat energy possessed by the slightly warmer water below. Unless the air temperature is extremely cold, this trapped energy is sufficient to keep the pond from freezing completely.

The importance of this phenomenon to living things can hardly be overestimated. Though it is clear that aquatic life is saved, consider what would happen to the world's climate if bodies of water froze from the bottom up. Since the heat now trapped by ice would escape, ice formation would increase. Gradually, the earth's climate would become increasingly cold, and eventually fatal to most life forms.

Different materials vary in their rates of expansion and contraction, because their cohesive forces vary. It is easier to tear a paper sheet apart than a thin steel

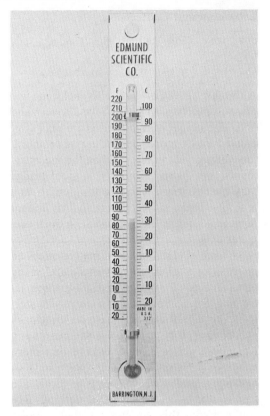

Figure 1-2 An appropriate thermometer for this unit. (Size 5¼ by ⅝ inches.)

sheet because steel molecules attract one another with much greater force. A cohesive disparity is likewise true of alcohol and water. Notice the difference in surface tension of water and alcohol in Figure 1-1. The cohesive force of water molecules is greater than that of alcohol. This helps explain why equal amounts of heat energy cause alcohol to expand more than water. It is easier to overcome the weaker cohesive force. It also indicates why alcohol evaporates faster than water.

Expansion-contraction, and as we shall see later, changes of state from solids to liquids and gases, are the results of a relentless tug-of-war between heat energy and cohesive force. Which "side" wins depends upon which force is the more powerful.

Before you begin the activity section, a

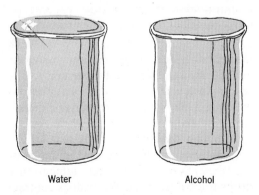

Water   Alcohol

Figure 1-1 Surface tension in alcohol and water.

note about materials may be useful. As with all of the following units, this one can be taught with supplies found about the school or home. However, there are several items which should be bought or borrowed to gain the greatest benefit from several forthcoming activities.

Several small, inexpensive thermometers, like the one in Figure 1-2, will be helpful. These should be marked for both the Celsius (centigrade) and Fahrenheit scales, with a full range from freezing (0°C, 32°F) to boiling (100°C, 212°F) points. We shall use both scales, although normally you and the children will find it easier to use the Celsius scale for graphing and other calculations. Expect cheap thermometers to vary several degrees from each other.

Especially useful will be some glass tubing, several one-hole rubber stoppers, flasks, and a large test tube. All the glassware heated in this unit should be of the Pyrex type. Ordinary glass expands more, and more unevenly with heat, and may

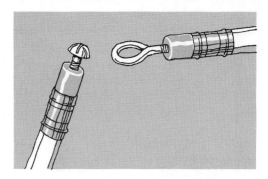

Figure 1-4   Screw and screw eye.

crack. For the hottest heating source, a propane gas burner is best. However, an alcohol lamp or even a candle will serve in many experiments (Figure 1-3). It will also be useful to have an electric hot plate.

Some experiences will require use of fire. Supervise these occasions closely. Probably it will be advisable to handle any burning materials yourself. Never allow a child with long hair or with a loose, trailing piece of apparel to work by an open flame. Always extinguish an alcohol lamp (by putting the metal cap over the wick) before carrying it to a new location. Always use a metal tray or other fireproof material to contain a burning substance. Develop standards about not touching a hot plate or other materials at random. No activity in this unit is even remotely dangerous, provided common-sense precautions are taken.

Generalization I: Most materials expand when heated and contract when cooled

Contributing Idea A. Solids expand when heated and contract when cooled.

The first activity is a demonstration in which a screw and screw eye are heated and cooled. This provides input for an experiment in the second activity.

1. *Materials:* ball-and-ring apparatus, or substitute a large screw eye and screw in two pencils, as in Figure 1-4 (the screw head must just barely fit through the screw

Figure 1-3   Two sources of heat. A propane gas burner and alcohol burner.

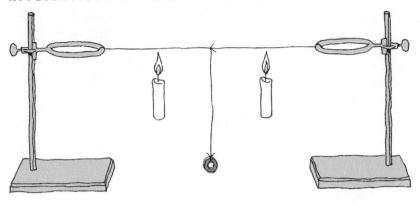

Figure 1-5

eye—turn the screw eye and screw into the erasers); candle and match; glass of water.

Ask the children to observe closely what you will be doing. Pass the screw through the screw eye. Now heat the screw in the candle flame for about ten seconds, and try to pass the screw through again. It should be impossible. Plunge the screw into the water and try again to pass it through the screw eye. This time it should go through. Invite the children to direct you to place in the flame or water either screw or screw eye, or both, as they wish so that they can gather as much information as possible from the demonstration.

make inferences Let the children summarize their observations, then attempt to explain in a general way what happened. Probably they will say that the heat caused the metal in either case to "get bigger" and the tap water caused the metal to "shrink" or get smaller. But did either screw or screw eye "shrink" or get smaller than original size? How can this be tested? Would either metal have "shrunk" back to the original size without plunging it into water? How can this be tested? (Be sure they keep the sequence straight, as they suggest various trials.)

make inferences Help the class infer that the metal in the screw and screw eye apparently become larger from the heat, and that the tap water merely hastened the return to the original size. With this input, they should be

ready to think about the problem posed in the next activity.

2. *Materials:* 3-foot copper bellwire, with insulation removed; two candles or propane burner; matches; string and small object to use as a weight; two ring stands (set up as in Figure 1-5—two front legs of a chair may substitute for the stands); bulletin board or chalkboard sketch of Figure 1-6.

Call attention to your sketch of Figure 1-6 and tell the class, "These sketches show how some telephone wires looked at two different times of the year. Do you notice anything odd? What seems to be the problem?" Guide the children toward a simple, clearly worded statement, such as, "Why are the wires sagging in June and not in December?" state problem

Encourage hypotheses. Acknowledge such reasonable guesses as, "The wires stretched after a while because they are heavy, etc." Give clues as needed: "When it is December again, the wires will look as they do in the top picture. What time of year is it in the second picture? How does the weather differ in most parts of the United States at these two periods of the year?" Help them to include heat as a possible cause. suggest hypothe

Lead an evaluative discussion of each hypothesis. Invite the children to test their most reasonable guesses. A hypothesis that

[1] For complete statements of marginal notations and specific subabilities, see pages 70–71.

146

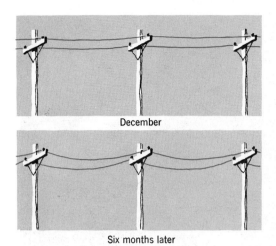

December

Six months later

Figure 1-6

heat will lengthen wire can be tested with the above materials. Let pupils suggest how to set up the experiment. Bring out the analogous nature of the materials, if needed: bellwire for telephone wire; stands or legs of a chair for telephone poles, between which the wire may be stretched and fastened; for the sun's heat, two candle flames passed up and down the wire will do. But if the wire only sags slightly, how will they tell? A small weight or object may be suspended from the center of the wire by a string or paperclip, so that it just misses the floor when slightly swinging. If the wire sags when heated, the weight should touch.

make
inferences

Permit several trials. Guide them first to describe, then infer what happened. If needed, suggest the usual vocabulary: the wire *expands* when heated and *contracts*

develop
procedures

when the candle flames are taken away. Capitalize on possible faulty procedures. For example, only one candle may not produce enough heat for expansion to be noticeable.

3. *Materials:* sketch of Figure 1-7.

To explain what happens on a molecular level, you might use this approach: "Scientists think they know why a solid material like our wire expands and contracts. Any material is made up of very tiny bits called *molecules*. Molecules of different

materials are of different sizes. But all are so small that only a few of the very largest have been seen by scientists with special microscopes. The molecules which make up our wire are too small to be seen. But we can pretend that they look like this." (Show your sketch of Figure 1-7.)

Develop the following ideas slowly and carefully:

a. In a hard, solid material like wire, molecules are very close together. But there is a small space between each molecule and the next one.

b. Each molecule stays in place because it is attracted to others next to it.

c. Molecules in a solid material are always vibrating or jiggling in place because they contain heat energy. When extra heat is applied to a solid the vibrating motion becomes faster, and wider in range. Therefore, spaces between the molecules get larger. This is why a solid expands.

d. When a solid loses some heat energy, the opposite happens. Vibrations are slower and smaller in range. The solid contracts.

4. *Materials:* glass Mason jar and metal screw lid; transparent bowl of very hot water; bimetallic strip, as in Figure 1-8 (Get from a scientific supply house or borrow from a junior high-school science teacher.); two ice cubes; candle; matches; tall glass of tap water.

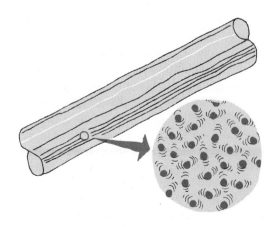

Figure 1-7

147

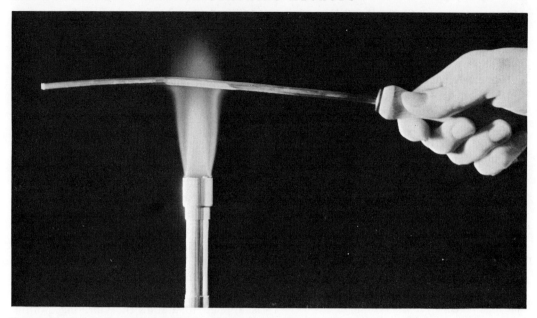

Figure 1-8 A bimetallic strip. Metal in the bottom layer is expanding slower than the top layer. (Fundamental Photographs.)

To help children learn that different solids expand and contract at different rates, try the following activities.

Tighten the screw top on a Mason jar until it cannot be unscrewed by a child. Show the capped jar to the pupils. Tell them the cap is stuck and ask for advice on how *select procedures* to unscrew it. After several children have tried and failed, ask how their knowledge of molecules might help. Indicate the bowl of hot water, if a clue is needed.

If the jar top is inverted and placed into the water for a moment, it should be possible to easily unscrew the lid. Guide an explanation of what happened on a molecular level. But point to a flaw. Glass is made of *state problems* molecules, too. What's the problem? (Doesn't the glass expand along with the metal?)

suggest hypotheses Lead to a tentative hypothesis: Maybe the metal expands more than the glass. Will one material expand more than another? Exhibit your bimetallic strip. Explain that it is made of two different metals fastened together. If one part expands more than the other, what should happen? (The strip should bend.)

Let someone hold the strip sideways and slightly above a candle flame. The strip will bend. Cool it back to the straightened position with tap water. Now invite conjecture *suggest hypothese* as to whether ice will produce an opposite effect. Will one metal contract more than the other? Hold the strip sideways between two ice cubes for a brief period. It will bend the opposite way. Help the class understand *make inferences* that different materials will expand at different rates.

Explain that bimetallic strips are useful. For example, in some houses, they may turn heaters off and on automatically when connected to an electric circuit.

Contributing Idea B. Liquids expand when heated and contract when cooled.

In the next investigation pupils observe how a heated and cooled liquid rises and falls in a glass tube inserted into a flask.

1. *Materials:* Pyrex baby bottle or flask or large test tube filled with water; one-hole

rubber stopper to fit the bottle opening; 12-inch glass tube (Insert about one-third of the tube into stopper. Always use a twisting motion when inserting glass tubing into a stopper. A paper towel wrapped around the tube will protect hands should the glass break. Wetting either the stopper or glass reduces friction.); red ink or food coloring; glass bowl, partly filled with a mixture of ice cubes and water; small rubber band; hot plate or substitute. (Set up as in Figure 1-9. A cafeteria tray or shallow pan will contain any spilled water in this or subsequent experiments with water.)

Bridge into the experiment with these comments:

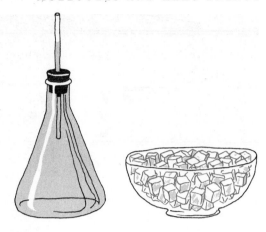

Figure 1-9

One summer day, the driver of a tank truck was asked to deliver a tankful of water to a distant road-building project high up in the mountains. At noon, he had the tank filled to the top; it held exactly 1000 gallons. (A gallon referent would be useful here.) He then started up the mountain and arrived at the project location in the evening. When he unloaded the water, he *suggest* was puzzled to find that only 990 gallons came *hypotheses* out of the tank. How many gallons less is that? What do you suppose happened?

Acknowledge but counter the idea of evaporation. Say that the tank was so designed that only a gallon or two might have been lost this way. If needed, provide clues as to possible temperature differences of the starting and ending places of travel. Remind the children of their previous experiment, and that water—a liquid—is made of molecules, too.

When contraction through cooling is suggested, ask for a test with the provided ma-*develop* terials. The flask can be filled with water *procedures* at room temperature. A few drops of red ink or food coloring will improve visibility. Cap with a one-hole stopper through which a tube is inserted and press down firmly. This will seal the liquid in the flask and cause it to rise slightly in the tube. When the flask is placed in a bowl of ice and water, the colored water will contract and go down the tube. Draw out the need

for a *control*. A rubber band placed around the tube will indicate the previous level. If available, an identical flask setup can be put alongside the first, but not placed in the water. Its water level should remain constant.

suggest hypotheses

Invite your pupils to predict what would have happened if the driver had started with a tankful of water at a cold location and had driven to a very warm one. (The tank would have overflowed.) This may be *develop procedures* tested with the same setup; but now the flask should contain chilled water, and be placed on a hot plate. As the water warms, some will flow up and out of the tube.

2. *Materials:* sketch of Figure 1-10. (It will be helpful for comparisons to place this sketch next to that of Figure 1-7.)

To acquaint the class with what happened on a molecular level, exhibit the sketch of Figure 1-7. Explain that it shows a small puddle of water, and the imagined behavior of its molecules. Develop the following ideas slowly and carefully.

a. In most liquids, molecules are farther apart than in a solid of the same substance.

b. Although the molecules are attracted to one another, this attraction is weaker than in a solid. Therefore, the molecules can slide and move around from one place to another. This is why a liquid takes the shape of its container.

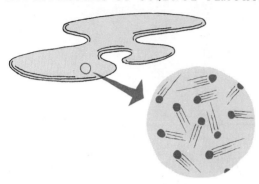

Figure 1-10

c. When liquid molecules gain heat energy they move around faster, bump one another oftener, and spread wider apart. This is why a liquid expands.

d. When they lose heat energy, the molecules move around more slowly and come closer together. This is why a liquid contracts.

3. *Materials:* hot plate; two small, identical Pyrex flasks or large test tubes with one-hole stoppers and glass tubes, one filled with red-colored alcohol, the other with red-colored water; two rubber bands (to mark the water level in each tube); two rectangular baking dishes or pans, one filled with very hot water, and another containing ice and water; thermometer (optional). See Figure 1-11 for the setup.

A previous activity demonstrated that different solids expand and contract unequally. The next experiment will teach that this is also true of liquids.

suggest hypotheses   Invite pupils to give a molecular explanation of how thermometers work. If an ordinary wood-backed thermometer is available, warm the bulb slightly over a hot plate. Let them see that the liquid column does expand, and then contract when taken away. Should the children be unable to read a thermometer accurately, draw a simplified scale on the chalkboard and help them to learn. Discuss various uses of thermometers, such as taking one's temperature, recording meat temperatures in cooking, in making candy, and so on.

Now confront your group with an apparent paradox. You have two homemade thermometers. The liquid in each is of the same temperature, and the tubes and flasks are identical. But they are acting strangely. *state problem* If the class observes closely, perhaps it can tell what is odd about the behavior of these liquids.

Place both flasks in the baking dish that contains the very hot water. (*Never put a container of flammable fluid such as alcohol directly over an open flame or glowing hot plate.*) Within a short period the liquid in each tube will rise. The rate of rise in one (alcohol) will exceed the other (water). Remove the flasks before they become too warm and overflow.

After several moments for discussion—this will also give time for each liquid to cool—put both flasks in the baking dish of ice water. The alcohol rate of contraction will exceed that of the water. How can this *suggest hypotheses* be explained? (The previous input with solids should help their thinking.)

Gradually help the class to focus on the liquid itself. Probably most of the children assumed—"took for granted," is an understandable way to express it with children—that the liquids were identical because they appeared that way to the eye. Identify the fast-acting liquid as alcohol,

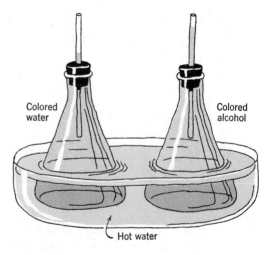

Colored water   Colored alcohol

Hot water

Figure 1-11

if pupils' noses have not already told them.

Remind them that different solids may expand and contract unequally; the same is true of liquids. If alcohol and mercury thermometers are available, compare them. Be sure to bring out that a thermometer's size of bore would also play a role in the expansion-contraction rate. Or, if glass tubes of different sizes are available, let the children discover this.

For an open-ended activity, let the children predict, and then try comparing, the expansion rates of different liquids and glass tubes of different diameters.

Contributing Idea C. Gases expand when heated and contract when cooled.

1. *Materials:* toy balloon; warm, sunny window area or hot plate.

Have your class try to help a mythical little child who is in trouble with his mother. John got a new balloon one morning. His mother warned him not to break it. When he was called to lunch, he carefully placed it on a window ledge. After lunch, he found that his balloon had burst. His mother was angry and reminded him of her warning not to blow up the balloon too hard. When John said he hadn't blown it up very much his mother replied, "How can a soft balloon break by itself?"

Encourage conjecture as to what probably happened. If necessary, provide clues. If the window ledge was sunny, maybe warmth played a role. What will happen to a soft balloon when heated? What test can the children set up?

If there is no sunshiny ledge on which to leave it for twenty minutes or so, a balloon can be warmed at a distance of about six inches over a hot plate. If slowly rotated while warmed, the balloon and its air will heat up quicker and more uniformly. Let pupils feel and compare the increased firmness of the balloon after it has been heated. Allow it to cool and contract for the opposite effect.

Assist the children in a brief summary. They know that air is made up of different

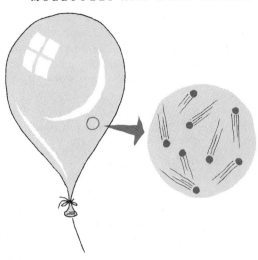

Figure 1-12

gases. It seems that gases expand and also contract. (Before going on to the next activity, however, perhaps someone can provide a pleasant ending to John's sad story.)

2. *Materials:* large sketch of Figure 1-12. (It will be helpful for comparisons to place it next to your sketches of Figures 1-10 and 1-7.)

Reveal the sketch of Figure 1-12. Indicate that it is a balloon and that they have an imaginary microscope so powerful it can detect the gas molecules which make up the air inside. With their previous knowledge about molecules, can the children explain why the balloon expands and contracts? Be sure to bring these ideas out carefully in the discussion:

a. In a gaseous material like air, molecules are even farther apart than in a liquid.

b. Although the molecules still have some attraction for one another, it is very slight. Therefore, they move about freely, and take the shape of their container.

c. When gas molecules gain heat energy they move around faster, bump one another oftener, and so spread wider apart. When heat energy is lost, the opposite happens.

d. A balloon may get firm in two ways. We can blow more and more air molecules into it until the molecules become "crowded." Or through heat, we can make

select procedures

make inferences

the fewer molecules inside a soft balloon move around faster. This causes them to bump oftener against the inside skin of the balloon and with one another.

3. *Materials:* balloon; small Pyrex flask or bottle (with a neck small enough for the balloon's open end to be stretched over it); hot plate; a container of cool water (optional).

select procedures

Assess understanding to see if the class can set up and explain a substitute experiment for activity 1. Exhibit the above materials unassembled. Challenge pupils to devise an experiment which shows that air expands and contracts.

make inferences

Stretch the balloon's opening over the bottle's open end, and set the bottle briefly on a hot plate. In several moments, expanded air will enter the balloon and inflate it. When the bottle is cooled (by placing it in or under some water, or simply waiting) the balloon will deflate.

Encourage a molecular explanation of what happened.

EXTENDING ACTIVITIES

make inferences

1. Press for a molecular explanation of this event: A partly filled milk bottle is taken out of a refrigerator and placed on a table. About ten minutes later, the top suddenly pops off. How can this happen "all by itself"?

2. Encourage children to locate many different kinds of thermometers or pictures of them. All will operate on the expansion-contraction principle, whether air, liquid, or a solid is used. Have children explain how they operate.

make inferences

reason quantitatively

3. Let several able children calibrate a homemade water or alcohol thermometer by comparing it with a commercial instrument. A white card taped in back of the tube will serve for recording marks. After several weeks, a wide temperature range will be established. A drop of oil placed on top of the liquid column will reduce evaporation.

4. Motivate a home and neighborhood search or magazine picture search for expansion-contraction effects and devices. Fathers can show the radiator overflow tube on the family automobile. Sidewalks have cracks, bridges expansion joints and rollers at one end. Railroad tracks have small openings between individual rail lengths. Concrete roads include tar separators between sections, which are squeezed up or pulled apart. Rivets in steel girders and beams are hammered in while hot; when cooled, they contract and form a tightly binding connection. Tank trucks and railroad tank cars often have several dome-like expansion chambers visible on top. Let pupils report, show, and discuss what they have found.

Changing States of Matter. Sometimes we get so accustomed to our environment it is hard to think of the things about us in new ways. Most everyone knows that air is a mixture of gases. Yet a favorite stunt of science demonstrators at high-school assemblies is to grandly pour liquid air from one container to another. Many persons know that carbon dioxide is a gas. Yet it is possible to trip over some, or drop it on your toe when it is in the form of dry ice. Steel is certainly a most durable solid. But high-temperature tests for possible spaceship uses turn it into vapor.

The state of matter at any given moment depends on the temperature. Temperature is a measure of the average speed of molecular movements. When increased heat energy is applied to a solid, its molecules vibrate faster. If the motion is powerful enough to overcome the molecules' cohesive forces, the molecules move farther away, and the solid becomes a liquid. If further energy is applied, the molecules move even faster and farther apart to become a gas. With loss of heat energy the opposite occurs. The decreased speed of molecules enables cohesive force to be reasserted, thus forming a liquid, then a solid, should sufficient heat be lost.

Does a solid become a liquid before it becomes a gas? Or a gas a liquid before it becomes a solid? Usually, yes. But a moth ball changes to a gas directly; so does dry ice. Frost is an example of vapor freezing directly into a solid state. This phenomenon is called *sublimation.*

Different substances change state at different temperatures. Adding salt to fresh water lowers its freezing point. Sea water, for example, freezes at 28.5°F, instead of 32°F. Unless the temperature is very low, sprinkling rock salt on an icy sidewalk melts the ice. We add an antifreeze liquid (ethylene glycol) to our automobile radiators to prevent freezing. A heavy salt solution would be even more effective, except for its unfortunate tendency to corrode metal.

Pressure also has an interesting effect upon changes of state. As a liquid warms, some of its molecules move so fast they bounce off into the air. We recognize this as evaporation. The same thing occurs with boiling, except the process is faster. To leave the surface of a liquid, however, molecules must overcome not only the cohesive pull of nearby molecules, but also the pressure of air molecules immediately above. At sea level, a square-inch column of air extending to outer space weighs 14.7 pounds. At the top of a tall mountain there is much less air—and thus weight—pressing down. With less pressure it is easier for liquid molecules to escape into vapor form. So, at 90,000 feet, water boils at room temperature. Astronauts or pilots of high-altitude airplanes wear pressure suits, or are enclosed in a pressurized cabin to avoid the possibility of their blood boiling.

Since we normally associate boiling with a temperature of about 212°F, it is important to realize another practical effect of decreased pressure. Boiling point temperature decreases about 1°F for each 550-foot increase in altitude. At a high location it is difficult to cook foods satisfactorily in an open container, because of the low temper-

ature at which boiling occurs. A pressure cooker is almost a necessity.

The effect of a different kind of pressure is readily observable with ice. Why is it possible to skate on ice, when we cannot on other smooth surfaces? The answer is that we do not skate directly on the ice. Our body weight exerts enough pressure through the ice skate blades to liquefy the ice. This furnishes a water-lubricated surface on which we slide. As the temperature drops, however, it takes increasing pressure to melt the ice. It may be difficult to skate at all.

A change of state always results in the absorption or release of heat energy. It requires energy for the fixed jiggling molecules of a solid to acquire a more freely moving liquid state. Interestingly, until an ice cube melts completely in a container of water, there is no appreciable rise in water temperature. The heat energy absorbed first changes the state of the frozen water, then raises the water temperature once the cube has melted. The next time you have an iced drink, try stirring the liquid until the last bit of ice has melted. You should sense no variation in temperature until after the frozen cubes have changed state.

Additional energy is required for liquid molecules to move fast enough and far enough apart to become a gas. Heat is absorbed from whatever accessible substance is warmer than the changing material. Therefore, if you hold an ice cube in your hand, it removes heat from your body. More heat is required as the liquid evaporates. This is why evaporation has a cooling effect. As the speed of evaporation increases, so does cooling. Ethyl chloride, for example, evaporates so quickly it is used by physicians to numb flesh for painless surgery.

Conversely, heat energy is released when a gas condenses to a liquid or a liquid freezes to a solid state, since molecular motion continually decreases. It used to be common in rural homes to place tubs of water near cellar vegetable bins. As the water freezes, enough heat is given off to prevent the vegetables (which have a slightly lower freezing point) from freezing.

The knowledge that heat is absorbed in evaporation and released through condensation is applied in modern electric refrigerators. A liquid refrigerant is released at low pressure into the freezing unit. As it flashes into a vaporous state, it cools rapidly and absorbs heat. As the now slightly warmed vapor leaves the unit, a motor-driven pump continually compresses the vapor until it has changed to a hot liquid under high pressure. The liquid next circulates in a condenser and releases its heat to the air. The cycle then begins again.

Generalization II: Adding or taking away heat can cause materials to change state; different materials change state at different temperatures

Contributing Idea A. Solids melt and become liquids when heated; liquids freeze and become solids when cooled.

In the next activity, pupils melt different solids to see how their melting times vary.

1. *Materials:* hot plate; 10-inch frying pan; several similar-sized solid materials for melting, such as candle wax, margarine patty, solder, lead (an old fishline sinker will do); four small (6½ oz.) empty tuna cans; pair of pliers or tongs.

Ask the class what happens to a tray of ice cubes after it is removed from a refrigerator and left standing in a warm room. Elicit that it melts, changing from a solid *state* (condition) to a liquid state. Bring out that the water would refreeze, or go from a liquid to solid state, if placed back in the freezer compartment of a refrigerator.

Hold up a candle. Mention that it is a solid, although it has never been in a refrigerator. Ask, "Why doesn't it melt? (Not warm enough.) Will all solids melt at different temperatures?" (Answers will vary.)

Indicate the several solids—for example, wax, margarine, solder, and lead—that might be tested. Have pupils try to predict

the correct order of melting. Put each item in a separate tuna can. It should be possible, if small cans are used, to put all in the pan at one time. Place the frying pan on the hot plate. suggest hypotheses

While waiting for the materials to heat sufficiently for melting, invite everyone to detect solid materials in the classroom that might once have been in a liquid state. Encourage discussion and speculation about these suggestions, but avoid any definite conclusions at this time. make inferences

In a short while, all the heated materials should be in liquid form. Remove the cans carefully from the pan with tongs or pliers and set them on a metal tray for cooling. Soon, the materials will resolidify.

2. The next problem and experiment will help pupils understand that different liquids may solidify at different temperatures. Because refrigeration is needed, it is convenient for children to do this experiment at home. Begin with a bridge that contains an unstated problem, such as this:

One cold winter day an airplane pilot was flying over a small ocean harbor. He saw several small boats speeding around in the harbor. Just half a mile away he saw a very large lake on which some children were ice skating. This puzzled him. What do you suppose there was in this scene that didn't seem right?

Draw out a concise statement of the problem. Why was the lake frozen and not the harbor? Guide the discussion eventually to the composition of the two liquids; one is salt water, the other fresh. Hypotheses that will probably emerge are salt water will not freeze, and salt water will freeze at a lower temperature than fresh water. state problems suggest hypotheses

Have pupils plan specifically how they might perform an experiment at home. Paper cups are adequate containers. Different concentrations of salt, measured in teaspoonfuls, may be dissolved in the water and then compared with equal volumes of fresh water. A check of the freezer every hour—mothers may become impatient with more frequent inspections, and the freezer develop procedure inefficient—will help determine which solutions freeze first, if at all.

On the following day let children report their findings. Although precise data cannot be expected, of course, it will be obvious that adding salt does lower the freezing point of fresh water. Bring out through reading or another authoritative source that even the ocean freezes in cold climates. Perhaps some pupils can find pictures showing the earth's polar regions.

develop procedures

Speculate about the addition of other substances to water to lower its freezing point. Mention that alcohol is sometimes added to automobile radiators in winter. If the children seem interested (and their mothers still patient), an open-ended experiment can be tried to determine the effect of adding alcohol or other liquids to water in various proportions.

3. Bring out an explanation of melting and freezing on a molecular level:

a. When molecules of a solid are heated, they vibrate faster and faster. If enough heat energy is present, the molecules break away from their places and slip around every which way. We say the material has *melted*.

b. When molecules of a liquid lose heat energy, they slow down and then settle into specific positions. They continue to vibrate as long as some heat is present, but they do not move around. In some cases we say the material has *frozen*.

Be sure pupils understand that any hard substance formerly in a liquid state is "frozen." Since this word is usually associated with cold temperatures, however, make clear it is more typical to use such other expressions as "become hard," "cooled to a solid state," etc.

Contributing Idea B. Liquids evaporate and become gases when heated; gases condense and become liquids when cooled.

1. *Materials:* hot plate; two identical pans each containing the same amount of water; pan lid.

Draw out of the class that spilled water,

rain puddles, and so on, dry after a while. Most children will know that this water disappears into the air, or *evaporates*. Let them see the word "vapor" in the larger word. Clarify it as a gaseous state of matter. The water has changed from a liquid to a gas.

Exhibit one pan of water. Elicit that after a while the water will evaporate. Inquire as to how this evaporation might be speeded up. The hot plate probably will be suggested. Establish the necessity for controls: one pan can be left off and another placed on this heating unit. After some boiling, it will be obvious that the evaporation rate in the control pan is far slower.

develop procedures

Now hold the pan lid about a foot above the water. Some of the escaping water vapor will condense back to a liquid on the lid and fall back into the pan.

Guide a molecular explanation of these events:

a. Heat energy causes the moving molecules in the water to move faster. Some molecules move fast enough to escape from the others, and go off into the air. Adding extra heat to one pan of water speeds up the movement of molecules. That is why the water evaporates faster.

b. The lid is cooler than the escaping molecules. This slows down the molecules and makes them more attracted to one another. Some molecules slow down enough to come together again and change back into a liquid state.

Explain that when spread out gas molecules come together again, they *condense*. This means that they now take up less space. This process, which is the opposite of evaporation, is called *condensation*.

2. *Materials:* hot plate; pan of boiling water; ice cubes; two metal pie plates or ice trays; paper towels.

Tell the class, "We found out that adding heat energy to water molecules made them evaporate faster than usual. Can we do the opposite thing? Can we make evaporated water molecules condense faster than usual?"

Discuss this briefly. Now show the children the boiling water, two pie plates (both should be at room temperature), and ice cubes. Have them do some reasoning. A surface cooler than the vapor slows down molecules. Will a still cooler surface slow them down even more? Challenge them to predict which tray—one cooled by ice cubes or another at room temperature—will cause more condensation. Some children may predict no difference.

Develop needed controls. Each pan will held in turn about the same distance and time over the water. The falling drops will be counted, if possible. Try the untreated tray first. While this is being done, place some ice cubes on the second tray. If you do this too soon, some moisture may condense out of the surrounding air, and spoil the experiment. Placing the cubes in the tray just before the trial should produce satisfactory results. Much more condensation from the evaporated water will appear on the cooler plate. Discuss.

Wipe off whatever moisture is underneath the two plates. Hold each up high. Have children observe them closely. They will notice condensation occurring on the colder metal. Bring out that this moisture is coming from the air itself. A surface that is sufficiently cool causes *dew* to form when the air contains sufficient moisture. Let them recall common experiences with dew formation.

make inferences

EXTENDING ACTIVITIES

1. Encourage pupils to develop a list of specific objects around the home and school which have been in liquid form but are now "frozen." Help them classify the specific objects into broader categories, such as candy, plastics, glass, dairy products, wax, and metal.

2. Most children know from personal experience that evaporation is a cooling process. For example, let them recall how cool wet skin and a wet bathing suit feel after emerging from water.

Now ask, "Why are hospital patients who have very high temperatures sometimes given an alcohol rubdown? Why don't they just use water?" When someone suggests greater cooling, challenge the group to develop a comparative test of alcohol and water as cooling agents.

suggest hypotheses

develop procedure

An easy method is to wrap the bulbs of two identical thermometers with small pieces of cotton, one saturated with alcohol, the other with water. Fan rapidly with cardboard. After a moment or so, the alcohol-treated thermometer will show a significantly lower temperature.

Spill identical, small amounts of alcohol and water on a surface. Have everyone note how much more rapidly the alcohol dries. Bring out that the faster a substance evaporates the faster heat energy is removed from the surface on which it rests.

make inferences

3. Get a porous ceramic pot or canvas water bag and fill with water. Fill another similar-sized, but nonporous container (a rubber hot water bottle, for example) with an equal volume of water. Have pupils take the temperatures of both containers periodically throughout a school day. The porous container will be consistently cooler through evaporation. A good bridge for this activity is to inquire why porous materials are often used to store water in hot climates. Isn't some water wasted that way? Then conduct it as an experiment.

suggest hypotheses

4. Try this activity to teach your pupils that, as a floating ice cube melts in ice water, it absorbs heat energy with little or no temperature change in stirred water. You will need a hot plate, a steel pie pan, two small Pyrex beakers or deep dishes containing ice cubes and ice water, a small thermometer, and graph paper for the class. (If there are enough cups, ice cubes, and thermometers for each pair of pupils, omit the hot plate. Pupils can do the whole experiment themselves.)

For the bridge, ask the class to discuss

what happens to the temperature of an iced drink after the ice has melted. Now show them one beaker of ice water and ice, remove the ice and place the beaker on the hot plate. Tell them that the hot plate will permit a speeded-up version of what happens. Distribute the graph paper and ask the children to record the temperature data on a line graph as the cold water warms up. Have a child or different children take the water temperature every thirty seconds and call out the reading. For a proper reading, he should stir the water a bit each time and keep the thermometer from resting on the beaker bottom. (If needed, show the class how to construct a line graph as in Figure 1-13 before beginning.) After the first several readings, ask the children to predict each forthcoming reading.

suggest hypotheses   Now invite the class to speculate on what a graph would look like if several ice cubes in ice water were left inside the beaker as heat is applied. Have them recall what a cold drink feels like as the ice cubes melt away. Does the drink get warmer as the ice cubes get smaller? Let everyone draw a light line on his graph to record his prediction. Place the second beaker containing an equal volume of ice water and two ice cubes, on the hot plate. Again have the temperatures recorded every thirty seconds. After several readings, ask the pupils if they wish to change

reason quantitatively   their predictions. Many will. Continue until the ice cubes have melted and the second line graph climbs upward to parallel the first one.

Help the children interpret their findings: the heat energy is apparently absorbed by

make inferences   the melting ice cubes until they have completely changed state.

(A note on preserving ice cubes for lessons. Ice cubes may be successfully stored for up to several hours in a styrofoam picnic basket. Wrapping a full ice tray in many layers of newspaper is also practical. The school cafeteria refrigerator may be used in some cases. For extra insurance, have

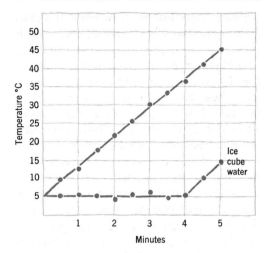

Figure 1-13

ice-cube lessons at the start of the school day and in cool weather. When experiments require identical ice cubes, commercial ice makers are likely to provide the best.)

Temperature and Heat Energy. We have stated that the temperature of a material depends on the speed of its molecules. Molecules of a cold substance move less rapidly than those of a hotter substance. The beginning activity of this section offers pupils a test of this statement through observation of colored water drops as they diffuse through water of unequal temperatures.

Although the concept of temperature is understood by many intermediate children, quantity of heat is a subtler idea. Consider a white-hot horseshoe just removed from a blacksmith's forge, and a large bathtub of warm water. Which contains the most heat? Very probably the water. The amount of heat a material contains depends on how many molecules it has, as well as how fast they are moving. This is why the owner of a large house pays much more for his winter fuel (heat energy) bill than someone who owns a small house, although the same air temperature may be maintained. It also explains why it takes about twice as long

157

to bring a quart of water to a boil as a pint. There are twice as many molecules to move.

Different materials have different capacities for heat energy. For example, it takes more heat for iron to reach a given temperature than equal weights of glass or lead. More energy is required to heat water to a given temperature than any other common material, liquid or solid, and water retains this heat longer. The most important effect of water's high heat capacity is found in weather and climate. Since the earth's oceans and lakes gain and lose heat more slowly than the land, they moderate changes in air temperature throughout the world. The most noticeable effects are found in coastal regions. Summers are cooler and winters warmer here than they are inland.

Two measures are commonly used to determine heat capacity: the calorie and British Thermal Unit (BTU). A calorie is the quantity of heat needed to raise the temperature of a gram (about $1/28$ ounces) of water 1° Celsius. The caloric value of a food is found simply by burning a dry sample of known weight in a special chamber of a carefully insulated container of pure water. The temperature rise is multiplied by the weight of water in the container. For example, assume 50 grams of water rises 20°C. $50 \times 20 = 1000$ calories. To make calculations less cumbersome, a "large" calorie is used in finding heat value of foods. Equivalent to 1000 small calories, the large calorie is what you see published in diet lists and nutrition recommendations.

The British Thermal Unit is used widely by engineers. Defined as the quantity of heat needed to raise 1 pound of water 1° Fahrenheit, it is also found by multiplying the mass of water by the temperature increase. Thus, to raise the temperature of 5 pounds of water 30°F requires 150 BTU.

Of course, this information is intended more for your use than for the pupils' at this level. However, it is not too early for many children to grasp the general idea of heat quantity. It is for this reason we have included several appropriate activities in the following material.

Another concept that middle-grade children can begin to acquire intuitively is that heat energy is *conserved* when liquids are mixed; that is, not lost but transferred in proportion to the original amount. A quart of warm water has twice the heat energy as a pint at the same temperature. Also, if two equal volumes of water at different temperatures are mixed, the resulting temperature is halfway between that of the two samples.

Experiences like these lead to several activities in which the concept of *equilibrium* is introduced. When water is brought to a boil, its temperature stays at 212°F or 100°C (sea level) until all the water has evaporated. Since it loses heat energy as fast as it gains the energy, we see a state of dynamic equilibrium—a stable condition that remains until the water disappears.

The second activity takes up a related phenomenon. You know that, when a jar of hot water is left standing long enough, it loses heat energy to the surrounding air and surface on which it rests. Eventually the water temperature becomes stable when it reaches *thermal equilibrium* with these interacting objects. The air, of course, is the chief interacting object that influences the water's final temperature. You can introduce pupils to this idea by asking them to extrapolate (predict by extending the data) from a few temperatures they record on a line graph. Don't be surprised if some children extrapolate down to a zero reading! This will help them to understand the danger of careless extrapolating along with the concept of thermal equilibrium.

Generalization III: There is a difference between temperature and heat; heat energy is conserved when objects interact

Contributing Idea A. Temperature is the measure of how fast molecules are moving.

In the next investigation, pupils observe the varying times needed for drops of colored liquid to diffuse in glasses of water of different temperatures.

1. *Materials:* two medicine droppers; two large, identical drinking glasses; blue food coloring; water. (Fill one glass with clear hot water, and the other with water at room temperature. Let each stand for at least three minutes to settle the water. Do not move after settling.)

Review that heat energy speeds up the motion of molecules. The higher the temperature, the faster molecules move. Indicate the two glasses of water. Inform the children that one — do not specify which — contains hot, and the other cooler, water. Draw out that a drop of coloring will spread (diffuse) throughout water when placed in it.

Develop the problem: If the hot water molecules are moving around faster than the cold water molecules, how will this affect a drop of coloring placed in each? Let pupils discuss and defend their predictions through reasoning about molecules. (The more rapidly moving molecules should scatter the food coloring molecules faster.)

suggest hypotheses

Hold each medicine dropper over a filled glass and release one food coloring drop from each at the same time. Request everyone to observe carefully. A white piece of background paper will assist observation. After several minutes, it will be interesting to check quickly the accuracy of the pupils' inferences. Label one glass "1" with a small card, and the other "2." Ask everyone to hold up guardedly one or two fingers to indicate which container holds hot water.

make inferences

Have several children report what they saw. Guide a related discussion. This will help their reasoning, and also give additional time for more complete diffusion to take place. A pupil might now check the two water temperatures with his finger for verification. Should one or two thermometers be available, they will be preferable to use.

If your group is able, it may be more challenging to use three water temperatures, rather than two — cool, warm, and hot. Avoid extreme temperatures, however.

Water vapor condenses on a cold glass. Very hot water may "steam" somewhat and also provide a clue.

2. Try faulty procedure on retrials. For example, stir the cooler water on some pretext ("This water is cloudy; let's clear it up a bit first.") before dropping in the ink. This will bring an indignant chorus of protest from an alert, thinking class. If the faulty procedure goes undetected, help them analyze the conflicting data.

develop procedures

Contributing Idea B. The amount of heat a material contains depends on how many molecules it has, as well as how fast they are moving.

What causes some ice cubes to melt faster than others? You can use this lesson to introduce the concept of heat energy as a variable quantity in melting ice cubes; and to bring up at least four other variables that the children can identify and try to control in further experiments: temperature, type of container, effect of stirring the water, and size of ice cubes.

1. *Materials:* for a class of thirty-two, you will need eight clean tinned cans, about 12-ounce capacity; eight styrofoam hot drink cups, about 12-ounce size, also; about four dozen ice cubes (half should be large, half smaller); 1-gallon each of hot and warm water; paper towels; clock or watch with second indicator; masking tape; crayon.

With a crayon, write one numeral on each container, from one to sixteen; use odd numerals for the cups, even numerals for the cans. (Put torn strips of masking tape on the cans to write numerals legibly.) On a low table, line up the containers in two columns, cups on one side, cans on the other.

Pour *different amounts* of hot water into four cans; do the same with four cups. Repeat this procedure with warm water in the remaining cans and cups.

Invite the children to have an ice cube "race." Each team of four pupils will have its chairman and a helper file by the front table, pick up one cup and can of water, and a paper towel. Mention that two ice cubes per team will be distributed shortly. Each team is to note when the ice cube in each cup completely melts. A raised hand and the container numeral spoken aloud will alert you to noting the times for chalkboard recording. Have the numerals and headings written on the chalkboard to show how the times will be recorded (see following). If no one asks, mention that stirring is allowed, but in only *one* container of each pair.

Now rapidly distribute the ice cubes, one large and one small to each group of four children. Put the cubes on the paper towels. The teams will put them into the containers upon your signal.

The melting times should be recorded in seconds on the chalkboard next to the appropriate numerals. Probably you will need to keep track of the times, as many children at this level will be unable to do so accurately. Ask someone to record the times for the odd column and another child to do the even column as you call them out. This will make it easier for you to note the times without looking away from your watch. Have a practice recording session for a few minutes before the race starts to make sure things will go smoothly.

The completed data may look like this:

Melting Times

Seconds	Cup Number	Can Number	Seconds
51	1	2	60
73	3	4	73
32	5	6	79
29	7	8	41
47	9	10	38
39	11	12	75
63	13	14	81
37	15	16	35

Help the children interpret their data by asking some questions:

What do you notice about the data? *(reason quantitati...)*
Which container is the overall winner? Loser? Are there ties?
Which came in second? Third?
Which came in fourteenth? Fifteenth?
Which "side" won the most times?
Why are the results so different? Why didn't the cubes all melt about the same time?

Invite the children to examine the three winning and losing containers to help them *(suggest hypothese...)* form hypotheses. Also, have the team members describe their previous observations. Assist in recording some observed differences:

1. Some containers have more water.
2. Some have hotter water.
3. Some are tinned cans, some are plastic cups.
4. Some were stirred.
5. Some ice cubes were bigger.

Would these differences make the melting times change? How can we find out? Ask the teams to discuss how they will test these differences. Help them to set up *(develop procedure...)* five controlled experiments by pairing containers that reflect a single difference:

1. Vary the *amount of water* in the pair; keep temperature, type of container, and ice cubes the same. Do not stir.
2. Vary the *water temperatures* in the pair; keep all else the same.
3. Vary the *material of the container;* keep all else the same.
4. Vary the *stirring.* Stir one but not the other; keep all else the same.
5. Vary the *size of the two ice cubes;* keep all else the same.

As experimental findings are reported, assist pupils to keep their observations separate from their inferences. Don't be *(make inferences)* too concerned about unpolished inferences at this stage.

Observations (What We Saw)	Inferences (Why We Think It Happened)
1. Ice melts faster with more water.	There probably is more heat energy with more water.

2. Ice melts faster in hotter water.

There probably is more heat energy with hotter water.

3. Ice melts faster in a plastic cup than in a can of the same shape.

A plastic cup holds the heat better than a can.

4. Ice melts faster when stirred.

Stirring makes the hot water get to the ice cube faster.

5. Ice melts faster when it is smaller.

It takes more heat to melt a big cube.

2. *Materials:* two small identical Pyrex beakers or bowls; hot plate and steel pie pan; two identical ice cubes; two thermometers; water; empty 6-fluid ounce can; hot pad or tongs; graph paper (optional).

In this activity pupils follow up the idea that a greater mass of water has more energy than a smaller mass at the same temperature. The energy must come from somewhere. Now they will see that with more water, more heat energy is needed to increase temperature.

Have the children recall that the ice cube melted faster in the cup with more water. Suggest that this information can help them with another problem: How long will two measures of water take to boil as compared with one? (In discussing reasons for their predictions, you will get valuable feedback about their knowledge.)

Let them discuss and set up what to do. They might empty a full can of water into one Pyrex beaker, two cans of water into the second beaker. Water temperature and heat source should be the same. Small-size beakers will allow both to be placed on the hot plate at one time to keep the heat source constant. (Be sure to place a steel pie plate under objects, especially those of glass, when using a hot plate.)

Inform them that everything looks set, but one thing is troubling you. How will they know exactly when the water is boiling? Encourage conjecture briefly but don't spend much time on developing an operational definition yet. This will alert them to the need for keener observations. Pupils might graph the temperatures, from readings taken every thirty seconds, while they are waiting for the water to boil.

reason quantitatively

After both samples are boiling, turn off the hot plate and discuss the results: it took longer for the larger amount of water to boil; there were more molecules to speed up.

make inferences

Bring the water to boil again and then take the beakers off the hot plate. Emphasize that the temperature in both beakers is the same. In which one will an ice cube melt faster? Discuss reasons; then drop one cube into each beaker, simultaneously. The cube in the larger mass of water should melt first. Help the class conclude that the larger mass contained more heat energy.

Now might be a good time to try for an operational definition of boiling. By observations and use of thermometers, children may say that water boils when bubbles appear over the entire surface of the water and the measured temperature will go no higher using the hot plate.

state problems

3. *Materials:* alcohol lamp or propane burner; one small nail and one large bolt, two small, identical tinned cans (6-ounce frozen orange juice cans are ideal), containing equal volumes of water at about room temperature; two small thermometers; pliers.

Hold the bolt and nail together with the pliers and heat them in a flame for about two minutes. Call attention to the two heated nails. State that they are now both at about the same temperature. But one object is larger than the other; it is made up of more molecules. Now ask, "Which object contains more heat energy?"

develop procedures

Refer to your materials. How can they be used to find out which object contains more heat energy? Guide pupils toward a test that calls for putting an object in each can to heat the water. If there is more heat energy in the nail, it should raise the water temperature higher than the bolt does.

But first the water temperatures will need checking to see if they are the same. Note if the children suggest this.[2] After the nail and bolt are immersed, the thermometers can be used for stirring the water in each glass to an even temperature. When the temperature rise in each can stabilizes, degree readings should be recorded. Of course, it is wise to get as many procedural ideas as possible from the class itself.

Data might be recorded like this:

reason
quantitatively

	Before	After	Difference
Large bolt can	70°	76°	6°
Small nail can	70°	72°	2°

make
inferences

Assist class reasoning toward a conclusion of more heat energy in the larger nail. Point out that the amount of heat energy in a fuel or food is determined similarly by scientists. A fuel or food is burned to see how hot it can make a certain volume of water. The measure used is a *calorie.* Another is the *British Thermal Unit,* or *BTU.* Tell pupils they will find out more about these measures of heat energy in later grades.

Contributing Idea C. Heat energy is conserved when different water samples are mixed.

In the next sequence, pupils mix different volumes of water of varying temperatures and attempt to predict temperatures of the mixtures.

1. *Materials:* one gallon each of hot and cool water (cold tap water will do); for each child or small group, three empty tinned cans, two 6-ounce and one 16-ounce size (any two small-size identical cans, and one larger one will do); thermometer; paper towels.

Review that a larger amount of a material object has more heat energy than a

smaller amount at the same temperature. But how about temperature? Bring up a specific example. Adding more hot water to a container of hot water increases the heat energy, but does it increase the temperature? Develop speculation, then have the children try it.

A typical procedure may be to pour hot water in each of two small cans and measure the water temperature in each can. Then pour both small containers of water into the larger one and measure the temperature. It should be the same as before.

2. Invite the children to speculate next what the temperature will be if two equal volumes of water of *different* temperatures are mixed. (In this case, pour hot water into one small can, cold into the other.) Careful measurements will reveal that the temperature of the mixed water is halfway between the high and low temperature found before the water is mixed.

3. Now ask the pupils to predict what the temperature will be if *unequal* volumes of water at different temperatures are mixed. Note the quality of the predictions. An intelligent estimate will place the final temperature above the midpoint of the two initial temperatures if a large volume of hot water is mixed with a smaller volume of colder water. For example, if the initial temperatures were 60°C and 20°C, the final temperature would be *above* 40°C. Likewise, a small volume of hot water mixed with a larger volume of colder water cannot raise the final temperature to the midpoint. It will be somewhat lower than this. Encourage open-ended investigations with different volumes of water at different temperatures.

make
inferences

develop
procedure

(Although it is possible for some children to calculate the exact temperatures resulting from the mixtures, it will be better to reserve the procedure for later grades. The intuitive knowledge gained now will be helpful then.)

Contributing Idea D. Equilibrium is demonstrated when water boils, and when the

[2] For an interesting variation of this experiment, use containers of water of *different* temperatures to begin with. If the children fail to check both temperatures before they measure the final difference, the results will be puzzling if the small heated nail has been placed in the hotter water.

temperature of an object becomes the same as surrounding objects.

1. *Materials:* clock or watch with second hand; alcohol lamp; candle; propane gas burner; three small Pyrex beakers, or three empty six-ounce tinned cans; three ring stands and wire gauze, or substitute stand apparatus; tongs; water; three small thermometers, three rubber bands and three pencils (to hold the thermometers when taking temperatures of boiling water); graph paper (optional). Set up materials as in Figure 1-14. Be sure to use only about four or five ounces of water in each beaker, else the candle may fail to appreciably heat the water.

Show the class the three sources of heat: candle, alcohol burner, and propane burner. Ask them to predict in which order, if **develop** any, these heat sources will cause water to **procedures** boil. Go over some control procedures before you begin. Someone should make sure the water volumes and temperatures are equal. The two burners and candle should be lit before placing them under the beakers, and all three slowly slid under the beakers at the same time. Some alert child may observe that objects periodically will have to be placed under the candle dish

as the candle burns down. Otherwise the candle flame distance from the beaker bottom will continually increase. (A stack of 5- by 8-inch cards should serve.)

If possible, have the children record the temperatures on graph paper each thirty seconds. Three pupils can be stationed at the thermometers to call off the readings as you signal each 30-second interval. All three records can be plotted on one graph or three separate graphs. If separate graphs are used for each heat source tested, you might assign each one-third of the class to plot records for one of the three heat sources. As before, a little practice will help things go smoothly.

After about five or six minutes, the water **reason** over the propane burner may be evaporating **quantitatively** too fast to continue. Withdraw the three heat sources and help the pupils evaluate their data. Graphs may look like Figure 1-15.

Guide discussion around some inferences **make** to be drawn from the data. The propane **inferences** burner provided the most heat energy, the candle least. Help children think about why the curves finally stabilized. Heat energy was being lost as fast as it was gained. Ask the class for evidence that the beaker water

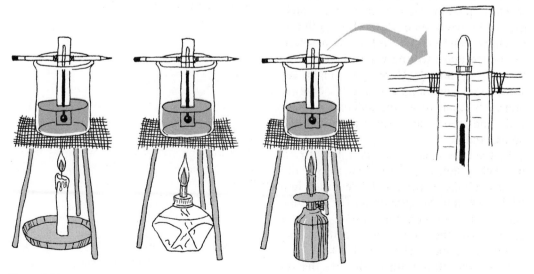

Figure 1-14

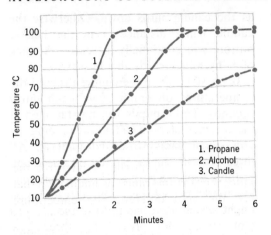

Figure 1-15

1. Propane
2. Alcohol
3. Candle

heated by the propane gained and lost heat faster than water in the other two beakers. (It had the fastest evaporation rate.)

2. *Materials:* for each child or group of children, one small thermometer; 6-ounce tinned can half-full of hot water. (Start this activity about fifteen minutes before lunch time.)

Tell the class that they have had some experience using graphs to predict future conditions. Now, they can have a contest to see who can come closest to predicting the correct temperature of hot water left alone over the lunch period. Each person will have ten minutes to take as many read- reason
quantitatively ings as he would like. But before going to lunch he must predict on his graph where the temperature will be when the class returns from lunch. (Here, you might set some exact time. Allow a total of about an hour. By that time, thermal equilibrium with the room air temperature should be assured.)

Instruct the class, as needed, how to set up their graphs. (Figure 1-16 shows the eight readings that one child recorded in a trial class, and his prediction for the time set by the teacher. Of course, he later found that the actual temperature had stabilized at about 21°C, or 70°F).

make
inferences When the class returns, discuss the results. Bring out that the water is now at the

same temperature as the air. The two temperatures are now in *equilibrium* with each other, that is, in "balance." You might mention the term again in several contexts, but for now it probably will be best to leave the concept as an intuitive notion.

Invite the children to predict from their reason
quantitatively data the probable temperatures at various times while the class was out to lunch. They will soon see that reasonable predictions are possible for short time periods if they work backward from the time they returned from lunch, or forward from the time they left for lunch. But they will also see that, as they go much beyond their observed data, predictions become more and more uncertain.

EXTENDING ACTIVITIES

1. Use the following discussion as an appraisal activity to gauge how well the class grasps the difference between the concepts of temperature and heat.

A man wants to buy a swimming pool, but can't decide whether to get a large or small one. He does not want to spend much money to heat it. Will there be a difference in heating costs for these two pools? Ask for an explanation on a molecular level. Look for the following ideas:

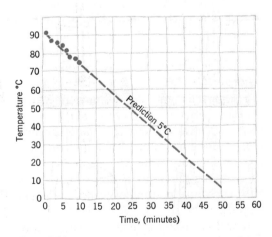

Figure 1-16

a. A large pool has more water molecules than a small pool.

b. Heat energy is used to speed up molecules to the desired temperature.

c. The more molecules there are, the more heat energy it takes to reach the desired temperature. The heating bill will be higher for the large pool.

2. Pupils will enjoy and profit from the following experience. It should help them understand the unreliability of determining temperature by touch. Fill three pans with water—one very cold, one hot, and one at room temperature. Label the pans "cold," "hot," and "room temperature" for easy reference. Keep the room temperature pan out of sight while choosing a volunteer. Have a blindfolded volunteer place one hand in hot, and his other hand in cold, water for at least two minutes. Let him withdraw the "cold" hand and put it into the room temperature water. He will say it is "warm." Pretend to remove this third pan, and replace it with another. Now have the volunteer withdraw the "hot" hand and put it into the same room temperature pan. He will say it is "cold."

3. Challenge the class with this question: "What is the *smallest* temperature difference you can feel by dipping your fingers into two cups of water of different temperatures?" Hypotheses will probably range from more than twenty degrees Fahrenheit to one. (The average child can detect about a three-degree difference.)

Each pupil pair will need two paper cups, one half-filled with hot water, one half-filled with cooler water; and a small thermometer.

develop procedures

See if they can decide how they will proceed. A good way is to pour some of the water from one cup into the other until the water temperatures of both cups feel almost similar. From that point on, it is wise to take the temperatures of both cups after each tiny pouring of water and finger dipping.

It will be useful to make a histogram of the fifteen or so reported findings:

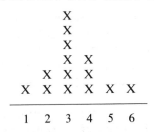

Least degree (F) difference felt

Allow time for pupils to interpret the data: What is the range of findings? What was the least difference in temperature someone said he could feel? What was the most common finding? Next most common?

reason quantitatively

Why didn't everyone report the same finding? Pupils may make several hypotheses: some people are more sensitive; some thermometers were read wrong; some people poured too much water without taking the temperatures first; some people soaked only one finger—it's better to alternate; and so on. All these guesses can be tested. Bring up related questions: Are girls more sensitive to temperature than boys? Blonds more than brunettes? Children more than adults? and so on.

suggest hypotheses

4. Invite pupils to give a molecular explanation for this situation. Two persons in a restaurant order tea—one iced, the other hot. Both use one lump of sugar for sweetening. Which one will stir his tea longer, and why?

make inferences

5. Challenge the class to develop bulletin-board ideas to illustrate the difference between temperature and the amount of heat energy present in a substance.

Conduction, Convection, and Radiation. Until the nineteenth century it was generally thought that heat was a fluidlike substance ("Caloric") which could be poured from one material to another. Scientists now realize that heat is a form of energy—energy being defined as the capacity to do work.

Many experiments have shown that energy can be transformed from one form to another. Our practical experience also indicates that this is so. Electrical energy changes to heat in toasters and hot plates; chemical energy yields heat through fires and explosives; mechanical energy (motion) provides the force necessary to overcome friction, and in the process heat is released.

Heat, in turn, changes to other forms of energy. Hot fuel turns a generator to produce electricity; gasoline is burned in automobile engines to produce mechanical energy, and so on. The initial activities of the present section are intended to help children achieve some understanding of this important idea.

If you put a pan of hot water in a cool room, after a while the water cools to room temperature. But place a pan of cool water in a hot oven and the water warms to oven temperature. In moving toward thermal equilibrium, as we saw before, heat energy always travels from a place of higher temperature to one of lower temperature. In moving from one location to another, heat energy may travel in one or more of three ways—by *conduction, convection,* and *radiation.* Let us consider these ways one at a time.

If you grasp the metal handle of a hot frying pan you quickly let go. How is it possible for the heat energy to go from the hot stove grid to the handle? Molecular conduction is responsible. As heat energy enters the pan bottom, its molecules begin to vibrate faster. This motion is passed along, molecule by molecule, up the pan's sides to its handle. Eventually all the particles are vibrating faster, and you feel the heat.

Of all solids, metals are the best conductors. Their molecules are very close together and transmit the heat energy quickly. But each type of metal varies somewhat in conductivity. Copper is the best common conductor, followed by aluminum, steel, and iron. Other solids are comparatively poor conductors, including ceramic materials. This is one reason we use a ceramic cup to hold hot coffee. As any army veteran knows, drinking hot coffee from a metal cup can be a painful experience.

Since molecules of liquids are farther apart than solids, it is reasonable to expect that they conduct heat less efficiently than solids. Ordinary experiences with bathwater help confirm this thought. When hot water is added to cooler water, it takes a long time for the heat to reach all portions of the tub. For this reason, most persons stir the water a bit to hasten the process.

Gases are the poorest conductors of all. Their molecules are spread so far apart they do not collide often and regularly enough to pass on increased energy to any appreciable extent. This is why it is possible for frozen-food sections in supermarkets to have open counters. Very little heat energy is conducted downward from the warmer air above the counter.

Although liquids and gases conduct poorly, it is easy to heat a pan of water quickly to boiling temperature, or quickly roast a frankfurter in the hot air over a fire. This means that there must be another, more efficient method of heat transfer in liquids and gases than conduction. To identify it, let us examine first what happens when air is warmed.

Watch the smoke from burning material. Why does it rise? Is it unaffected by gravity? A clue to its behavior is found when smoke is pumped into a vacuum chamber. The smoke particles fall like lead weights. Therefore, smoke does not just "rise"; something must push it up.

When the glowing part of burning material warms the adjacent air, the increased energy agitates air molecules to increased speeds and they spread farther apart. Since now fewer molecules take up a given volume of space, they are lighter than an equal volume of the surrounding air. The lighter air is pushed up with the smoke particles as it is replaced by heavier, colder air. As the mass of lighter air rises, it carries increased energy with it. This is why air near the ceiling is warmer than air near the floor.

When there is an opening for warm air to escape and cool air to flow into a room, a *convection current* is set up. This is a principal method by which our homes are heated. It is also the primary cause of winds in the atmosphere.

Similar convection currents are set up in heated liquids. Warmed, expanded water in a pan rises as it is continually replaced by cooler, heavier water until the same temperature is reached in the entire container. Because of the way convective currents move, a heating unit is usually located at the bottom of a hot-water tank and a cooling unit at the top of a refrigerator.

Convection also helps to set up ocean currents. Warm water at the equator is continually being replaced by cold water flowing from the polar regions. Air convection currents form winds which contribute to the distribution of these giant water currents. A third important factor is the earth's rotation. Because water has a high heat capacity, ocean currents are responsible for altering the climates of many countries.

A common example of the third method of heat transfer, radiation, is found in the fireplace of a house. This is especially noticeable when the air temperature is low. As you warm yourself in front of the fire, only the portion of your body that faces the fire feels warm. Conduction is poor, since air is the conducting medium. Convection is negligible, since most of the hot air escapes up the chimney. Heat reaches you by radiation.

All vibrating molecules release a certain amount of energy through invisible heat rays, called *infrared waves*. These waves largely pass through transparent materials like air and glass, but are absorbed by opaque objects, which become warmer as a result. We are conscious of radiant energy only when the emitting source is warmer than body temperature. The sun is by far our most important source of radiant energy. In its rays are found visible light, invisible infrared waves, and other forms of radiant energy. We shall go into more detail in the unit on light energy (page 212).

Knowledge of how heat travels permits us to control it. We use *insulation* to pre-

vent or retard heat energy transfer. For example, to retard conduction, we use poor conductors. Since air is a poor conductor, materials with air spaces, such as wood and wool, make excellent insulators.

In homes, convection and conduction are reduced by using hollow walls designed to trap the air. Since some convection takes place anyway, some homeowners fill the walls with a light, fluffy material, such as rock wool.

An excellent way to insulate for radiation is to reflect it away, since it behaves like light as it travels. This is why insulating materials in the home may use a shiny foil exterior, particularly in the attic. It explains, too, why silver-colored paint is used on large gasoline storage tanks.

One of the concluding activities of this section presents an opportunity for children to discover, in an open-ended way, the efficiency of many insulating materials.

Generalization IV: Heat energy may come from several sources; it travels by conduction, convection, and radiation

Contributing Idea A. Several sources of energy can be changed to heat energy.

Materials: magnifying glass; sandpaper and block of wood; hammer, large nail, and block of wood.

Bring out that, although the class has learned much about the effects of heat energy, not much has been said so far about its origins. In how many different ways can molecules be made to move faster? Invite a discussion of how the materials might be employed to produce heat energy. Permit groups of pupils to explore their ideas. Help organize on the chalkboard activities which convert some other energy forms to heat energy. For example:

suggest hypotheses

Electrical energy—a plugged-in toaster; heat from a light bulb.
Chemical energy—a burning match; burning candle.
Mechanical energy (energy of motion)—

friction produced when rubbing hands together, and rubbing sandpaper on wood; a hammered nailhead gets warm.

Light energy—a magnifying glass focuses the sun's rays.

Add several forms which the children cannot easily investigate:

Sound energy—absorbed sounds speed up molecules in the sound absorbers.
Nuclear energy—heat is released in atomic reactions.

Emphasize that, regardless of its origin, heat travels in only several ways. Now the children will have an opportunity to explore these ways.

Contributing Idea B. Sometimes heat travels by conduction.

1. *Materials:* candle and match; 10-inch piece of heavy, solid copper wire with insulation removed or a piece of straightened-out iron coat hanger wire; four paraffin balls. (About pea size. Make from warm paraffin wax. Arrange materials as in Figure 1-17.)

Have everyone recall experiences of taking hold of a hot metal pan handle, or spoon immersed in a hot liquid. Draw a large spoon on the chalkboard. Bring out that its molecules are vibrating but relatively fixed —that is, moving only within a small space —since it is a solid. When the spoon's oval end is immersed in hot liquid, its molecules must vibrate more rapidly. But what about

the handle? How does it become hot? Elicit that only three ways seem possible:

   a. the whole handle becomes hot at once;

   b. the handle tip gets hot and heat energy moves toward the immersed part;

   c. the heat gradually travels from the immersed end through the spoon's entire length.

Guide a discussion as to which of these ideas seems most reasonable. Encourage molecular explanations.

Invite a test of the children's ideas with the materials. (An old spoon may be used instead of the wire.) Several wax balls may be fixed to the wire, starting about two inches from the end of the wire, at ½-inch intervals. The weaker your heat source, the closer the wax must be affixed to the wire's end. When the wire end is held in a flame, the order in which the melted wax balls drop off should indicate which idea is best.

The order of dropping will be from flame to the wire's opposite end. Encourage a molecular interpretation. As molecules in the heated end begin jiggling faster, they agitate others. Finally, increased motion is passed along the wire's entire length. Write *conduction* on the chalkboard. Emphasize that heat energy travels by conduction when one molecule passes on its increased energy when striking another molecule.

If additional clarification seems necessary, set up on end a row of closely spaced dominoes. When one domino is pushed, all the others will fall in turn.

suggest hypothes

develop procedure

make inferences

Figure 1-17

2. *Materials:* candle and match; small steel kitchen pan with copper-coated bottom; six small balls of wax; 10-inch piece of heavy, solid copper wire with insulation removed; 10-inch piece of heavy iron wire from a wire clothes hanger.

Exhibit the kitchen pan. Draw out that heat from the stove is conducted through the pan metal to heat food. Inquire as to why the bottom part is coated with copper. Guide toward an hypothesis of better conductivity with copper than steel. Mention that you have iron wire, which is similar to steel, and copper wire on hand. (If steel wire is available, of course it would be better.) Encourage a test with these materials.

Three wax balls can be attached near the end of each wire, about ½ inch apart. As ends of the two wires are held at the same time in a candle flame, conductive efficiency will be revealed as the wax pellets drop off.

Bring out that copper appears to be a better conductor than iron. Also, the order of conductive efficiency among common metals is copper, aluminum, brass, and iron. (If identical rods of these materials are available, it would be worthwhile for pupils to discover this through a similar experiment.)

3. *Materials:* metal pie plate or substitute; brick; piece of wood; piece of cloth; folded newspaper page.

The following experience will help children place some common solids in descending order of efficiency in conducting heat energy. It will also lead to an understanding of why one material may feel colder than another, although both are at an equal temperature.

Say, "Let's learn more about how well solids conduct heat energy. How many of you like to walk barefooted outdoors?" Develop that some surfaces seem colder to the touch than others. Elicit the most obvious reason: some are in shade and some are in the sun. But now the children are going to discover something very odd.

Point out your materials. Will they all

suggest hypotheses

develop procedures

make inferences

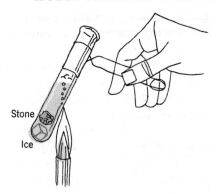

Figure 1-18

feel equally warm or cool to the touch? You will need two barefooted volunteers.

Have each person stand on two different materials at one time for comparisons. Let each, without the other's knowledge, indicate his ranking of the materials, from cooler to warmer. The pupil's opinions will tend to agree. Metal will feel the coolest, then probably the brick, wood, cloth or newspaper, in that order.

But how can this be? All have been in the room for some time and have about the same temperature. (The bulb of a thermometer can be held against each object to see if a temperature change will occur.) If adequate references are available, they might be consulted. Lead toward an explanation that features conduction of heat. Some materials conduct heat well and some poorly. Good conductors conduct heat energy away rapidly from our warm skin at the point of contact. This makes them seem cool. Poor conductors pass along heat slowly. This makes them feel warmer, since less heat is lost from our skin.

suggest hypotheses

4. *Materials:* large, Pyrex test tube; ice cube; small stone or piece of steel wool; propane burner and match; pliers or test-tube holder; water (Figure 1-18).

State that thus far the class has considered solids as conductors. Now there will be opportunities to investigate liquids, then gases. Review briefly what conduction means. Is conduction likely to be as good

169

in most liquids as in solids? Entertain discussion. (Since the molecules are farther apart, it would seem less likely.)

Place an ice cube fragment in the test tube. The ice cube may be broken up by placing it in a handkerchief and tapping it with a hammer or substitute. Use a stone or a bit of steel wool to keep the ice at the bottom of the test tube. Fill two-thirds full with *ice* water. (Warmer water may melt the ice prematurely.) Place the tube diagonally in the flame while holding the open end with pliers. Have everyone observe closely that water boils on top while the ice fragment remains largely unaffected. Elicit that water is a poor conductor of heat. Avoid touching the heated part of the tube.

make inferences

Empty the test tube. Place inside another ice fragment of similar size, and ice water, but no stone. Hold the tube vertically with the holder or pliers and place it directly over a candle flame. In a short while, the floating ice will melt. Can any pupils explain this odd event? (Probably not. The water has been heated by convection, not conduction.) Mention that shortly they will learn about another way in which heat

make inferences

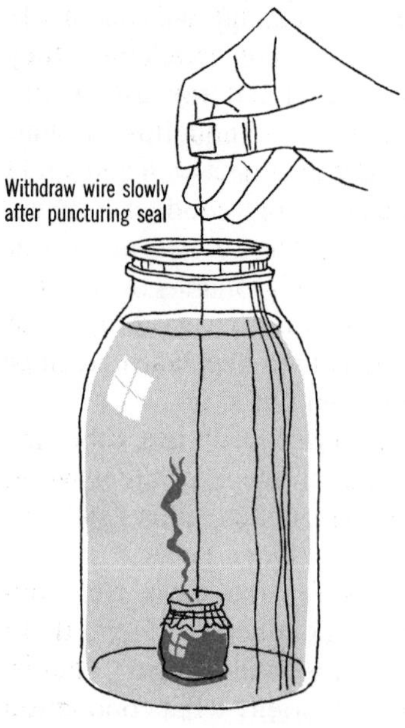

Withdraw wire slowly after puncturing seal

Figure 1-19

170

travels. They will then understand more clearly what happened.

5. *Materials:* candle; matches; pliers.

Remind everyone that air molecules are even farther apart than water molecules. Is air likely to be a good conductor? (No.) Ask for keen observation of the next demonstration.

Use pliers to hold an unlit match. Position the match head at one side of a candle flame, about one-half inch or less away. Have someone count slowly to 10. No ignition should occur. If it does, increase the distance slightly. Bring out that air seems to be a poor conductor.

Now place the match head *above* the flame at a similar distance. Again have someone count slowly. In several seconds, it should burst into flame. How can this be explained? After some discussion, mention that this and the preceding demonstration will be cleared up now as the children learn about the second way in which heat energy travels.

suggest hypotheses

Contributing Idea C. Sometimes heat travels by convection.

1. *Materials:* small bottle containing hot colored water (seal top with foil and a rubber band.); open Mason jar two-thirds full of cold water; stiff 10-inch wire (Figure 1-19.)

Review briefly that a liquid expands when heated. Show the bottle of hot water. Bring out that it weighs slightly less than an equal volume of cold water because of expansion. Place the bottle inside the container. Ask pupils what they thing will happen to the colored water when you puncture the cap. (It will rise.) Now puncture the cap and withdraw the wire from the water. Do this gently to avoid disturbing the water excessively. Entertain an explanation of what happened. (The hot expanded water was lighter than the surrounding water. It was pushed up while being replaced by the colder, heavier water.)

make inferences

Ask the children to think of a related

select procedures experiment that might check their explanation. (Fill the small bottle with *cold* colored water. Will it go up?)

2. *Materials:* two identical clear glass pop bottles, one filled with hot, red-colored water, the other with uncolored, cool tap water (Figure 1-20); 3- by 5-inch card; 8- by 11-inch piece of white paper; pan.

Put the card over the hot-water bottle opening. Invert the bottle, and place it gently on top of the second bottle. Explain that the top bottle contains hot, and the bottom bottle cold, water. Invite predictions and reasons as to what will happen suggest hypotheses when you remove the card. (There should be almost no mixture, as the cold water is heavier.) Hold white paper in back of the bottles for easy viewing.

Now grasp the two bottle necks in one hand, wrist turned in and thumb facing downward. Quickly reverse the bottle positions. The heavier cold water will quickly displace the hot water. The hotter water will rise into the other container as the colder water empties. Use a white background again for good viewing.

Discuss to insure understanding. Identify this means of heat transfer as *convection*. The lighter mass of fast-moving molecules conveys or carries heat energy along with it as it moves from one place to another. Draw out how, in a previous demonstration, the floating ice cube melted rapidly when the test tube was heated at the bottom.

make inferences Some children may recall personal experiences with unevenly heated swimming pools and lakes. Sometimes a distinct current of warmer or colder water is noticeable. Help them to understand also that one cause of ocean currents is convection set up in unevenly heated water.

3. *Materials:* 6-inch piece of clothesline; matches; yardstick or 3-foot dowel; cellophane tape; string; two identical paper bags; lamp or substitute. (Set up materials as in Figure 1-21. A hole drilled in the top third of the yardstick will permit more stability. Use a tiny lump of clay to achieve

Figure 1-20

a perfect balance. If no overhead hook is available, suspend the balance from a stick placed across the tops of two separated chairs. Leave the bulb unlit for the present.)

Light a rope end and blow out the flame. A clearly visible stream of smoke should result. Ask why it rises, rather than falls. Aren't smoke molecules affected by gravity? Lead toward a reasonable explanation. Maybe the air is also heated by convection. How can we see if warm air rises? develop procedures Invite a test with the assembled materials.

The warmed air rising from the bulb will cause the bag above to rise. Help pupils to reason that wind is probably moving air make inferences caused by cooler air replacing warmed, expanded air. To check this idea further, they will want to do the next activity.

4. *Materials:* schoolroom with a top and bottom window opening; two thin, tissue paper streamers, about 10 inches long; cellophane tape; thermometer; stick or window pole. (This demonstration works well when the outside temperature is much lower than that of the schoolroom.)

Guide this activity one step at a time to develop maximum understanding:

a. Is the warmed air in the room rising? (If so, air at the ceiling should be warmer than air at floor level. Encourage thermometer readings. Air temperature near the ceiling may be measured by strapping a thermometer to a long stick or window pole.)

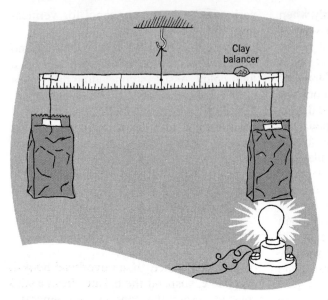

Clay
balancer

Figure 1-21

b. Is there a place for warm air to move out of the classroom? (An open top window is needed. Since air is invisible, taping a streamer at the opening should reveal air movements as they occur.)

c. Is there a place for cooler, heavier air to enter the room? (An open bottom window is needed. Another streamer taped at the bottom should also reveal air movements.)

Emphasize through reading and discussion that all winds basically are caused by convection resulting from the unequal heating and cooling of the earth's surface. Help pupils realize that many heating systems use convective currents in heating homes, schools, and factories. Have someone point out hot-air registers in the room or other places where warmed air sets up air currents in the room.

make inferences Pupils should now understand why the match held above the flame in a previous demonstration ignited quickly. Most of the heat energy traveled upward through convection.

Contributing Idea D. Sometimes heat travels by radiation.

1. *Materials:* electric iron; magnifying glass.

Plug in the electric iron and let it get moderately hot. Hold the iron parallel to the floor. Have a pupil place his hand 6 inches or so under the iron. He will sense the heat immediately. Ask why he feels the heat. Is it traveling from the iron by conduction? (No. Air is a very poor conductor. Also, he feels the heat immediately. Conduction takes more time.) Is it traveling by convection? (No. Any warmed air currents would rise.) *make inferences*

Through purposeful reading or your exposition, inform the class that the heat energy travels through *radiation*. Bring out that heat rays are like light rays from the sun, except that we can only feel them and not see them. Elicit that the iron itself would glow and be visible in the dark if made hot enough.

Emphasize that when heat travels by radiation, there need not be any molecules to pass along (transfer) the energy as in conduction and convection. Let someone focus the sun's rays with a magnifying glass on a piece of paper. Help pupils to understand that the sun's energy is radiating through largely empty space to the earth. Only when the radiant energy causes the paper's molecules to move fast enough to burn is the heat noticed.

Develop that nearly all objects give off some radiant energy, but this is not noticeable to us until they are fairly warm. Have children recall the warmth that exudes from a fireplace for some time after the fire is out, or the warmth radiated from sidewalks and stone buildings shortly after sunset.

2. *Materials:* two thermometers; two identical tinned cans, about 12-ounce capacity (one painted black inside and out); cardboard lids; hot water.

Inform the class that we use radiators to give off as much heat energy as possible. Examples are radiant heating in homes, steam or hot-water room radiators, and automobile radiators. Describe, or have pupils read about these cases.

Now introduce a related problem. Most room radiators are painted silver, or some other light color. Most automobile radiators are painted black. Yet in both cases we want these objects to lose (radiate) as much heat energy as possible. Whey aren't both painted the same color? Develop speculation, and a possible test with the available materials.

suggest hypotheses

To determine which radiates heat faster, pour hot water into each can and cover with a cardboard lid. For continual temperature readings, a hole may be cut in each lid just large enough to accommodate a thermometer. Have children record temperatures within both cans, and times taken, on a chalkboard graph. Readings might be taken ten minutes apart over an hour for good results. Assign times to six pupils to avoid interference with other classwork. If no thermometers are available, temperature differences will be noticeable by touch after a short while.

develop procedures

At the hour's end, help pupils conclude that the darker color apparently helps to increase the radiation, since the drop in water temperature is greatest in the dark-colored container. Encourage duplicate ex-

make inferences

periments at home or school for verification.

Request a pupil survey of parents and friends who have painted home radiators a light color. Assist in concluding that this is done for appearance, rather than efficiency.

Contributing Idea E. Knowing how heat travels allows us to control it through insulation.

1. *Materials:* large sketch of Figure 1-22; Thermos bottle. (Borrow one from a child who brings his lunch to school.)

Hold up a Thermos bottle, and establish its dual purpose of keeping liquids cold or hot for an extended time period. Point out that to do this, the bottle designer must have developed ways of controlling conduction, convection, and radiation. Invite the class to speculate how this was done by looking at a cross section of a vacuum bottle (your sketch of Figure 1-22). Use a series of questions to assist reasoning:

Why is a glass container used instead of metal? (Glass is a poor conductor. Heat from a warm liquid will not pass easily to the outside; the reverse is also true if the liquid is to stay cool.)

make inferences

Why is air removed from the hollow glass

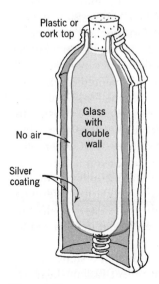

Plastic or cork top

No air

Glass with double wall

Silver coating

Figure 1-22

walls of the container? (No air conduction can take place. No convection can take place.) Develop that the removal of air leaves a *vacuum*—a space in which no molecules are present. Mention, however, that it is presently impossible to remove all the air. Therefore, it is not a perfect vacuum.

Why are the two inside surfaces of the glass walls given a silver coating? (Probably most of the children will only be able to speculate that it might have something to do with radiation. This will help lead into the next experiment.)

2. *Materials:* two identical tinned cans of about 12-ounce capacity, one with a shiny metal exterior, the other painted black; tap water; silver foil lids, one painted black; sunshine; two thermometers and two ice cubes (optional).

Should a picture be available of large, silver-painted gasoline storage tanks, show it. If not, it is likely that enough children have seen these tanks to have a discussion. Bring out that gasoline is highly flammable, and it is wise to keep the storage tanks as cool as possible. But why are they painted bright silver? Why not black? Both paints would protect the steel tanks from rusting.

suggest hypotheses

Guide toward a reasonable hypothesis. The sun's radiant energy may be largely reflected from a silvered surface, which would keep the gasoline cooler than if black paint were used. Help pupils develop an appropriate controlled experiment.

develop procedures

Two tinned cans, one painted black, may be filled with water, capped with foil, and left in the sun. About an hour's exposure to strong sunlight should be more than adequate to notice the difference of water temperature in the two cans, even if thermometers are not used. (Many pupils can detect with their fingers a temperature difference of only 3°C.) If you want faster results, an identical ice cube can be put in each can to observe melting times.

make inferences

Help pupils conclude that a shiny, silver surface is useful to reflect radiant heat. In the case of a vacuum bottle, two such surfaces help to keep heat from entering or leaving the container.

Call attention to the shiny, foil bags used to transport ice cream home from a market, or the foil wrapper on a popsicle. These, too, are used to block radiant energy.

3. *Materials:* a piece of wool and piece of cotton cloth; scissors; glass of water.

Have the class discuss the need for clothing to conserve body heat, particularly in winter. Bring out that woolens are worn oftener in winter than in summer. Develop speculation as to why woolens are warmer. Let some children closely inspect the weaves of cotton and wool cloth. Comment about the wool's looseness of weave. They have found out that air is a poor conductor of heat. Does wool contain more trapped air than cotton?

suggest hypotheses

Encourage a test. Equal-sized pieces of cotton and wool can be pushed under water, one at a time. The cloth releasing the most bubbles probably holds the most air. Develop the need for retrials and careful observation.

develop procedure

Comment that the children have been discovering about *insulation,* the ways of slowing down or preventing the movement of heat energy from one place to another. Draw out how animals use insulation for warmth. A polar bear has heavy, fluffy fur that traps air. This is such a good insulator that zoo bears in summer sometimes are supplied with large cakes of ice and chilled water to maintain good health. Birds fluff their feathers often in chilly weather. This traps more air, which provides more insulation. Through reading or reporting, let pupils find out that many Eskimos wear animal fur inside out. The skin deflects wind, while the trapped still air inside the fur offers excellent insulation.

4. *Materials:* for each team of pupils, two small (6-ounce), identical tinned cans; two 16-ounce identical cans (these will be large enough to hold the smaller ones); cotton; two cardboard lids for the larger cans; two thermometers; graph paper (optional).

Bring out that one reason a house is constructed with double walls is to take advantage of the still air trapped between. Develop that, in spite of this, many homeowners have this space filled with fluffy, cottonlike material. How helpful is this practice in conserving heat?

select
rocedures

Assist pupils in setting up some materials to find out. Place the two smaller cans in the larger ones. Pack loose, fluffy cotton around one smaller can. Fill both with hot water. If thermometers are available, have someone record the initial temperatures. Cap both large containers with cardboard lids. Have periodic readings taken. Use of a simple graph, such as in Figure 1-23, will be profitable.

select
procedures

This can be made an open-ended activity by children experimenting with many insulating materials at home or school and exhibiting their graphs with oral or written reports.

5. For an interesting variation of the insulation activity, announce the opening of the "The Great Ice Cube Preservation Contest." Instead of matching two containers of hot water, as in activity 4, children can try to prolong the melting time of an ice cube. A cube will be placed in the small can, and this put into the large can. Both cans will have a cardboard lid. The test will be to see which secret insulation formula works best—sawdust, cotton, wool, foil, rice crispies, shredded paper—anything pupils want to try, singly or combined. Pupils will want to set up such rules

develop
procedures

as:

   a. Everyone must use identical containers and lids.

   b. Containers must stay in the room in the same location.

   c. Ice cubes must be of equal size to start with.

   d. Any insulation can be used, but must be enclosed by the larger can.

(Notice that, in setting up "rules," pupils are controlling variables.)

Start the contest at the beginning of the day. Permit children to peek into their con-

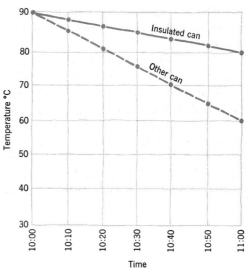

Figure 1-23

tainers from time to time. Most will not overdo this if they realize that each time they open their containers they reduce their chances to win.

Contrast the materials in the five best- and least-performing containers. What properties made them perform so? Could the variation in the number of "peeks" have made the difference? How could this be tested?

suggest
hypotheses

EXTENDING ACTIVITIES

1. Invite an explanation of why a freezing unit is usually located in the top section of a refrigerator and a heating unit beneath a hot-water tank or hot-water heating system.

make
inferences

2. Lower a small piece of metal window screen (or wire gauze) over the tip of a candle flame. No flame will appear above it, although most of the gas continues upward. Encourage able pupils to find out why. (The metal screen conducts heat energy away so fast the gas is no longer hot enough to burn.)

make
inferences

3. Show a film or filmstrip on heat transfer by conduction, convection, and radiation.

4. Have a committee report on how homes are heated by the three ways of heat transfer.

5. Encourage the children to conduct a hunt for insulators in the kitchen and elsewhere in their houses and list them. Some items that may be recorded are: hot pads, cloth pot holders, wooden and plastic handles on cooking utensils, oven and refrigerator insulation, insulation in ceilings, walls, and floors, weather stripping around doors and windows, double-pane glass windows and sliding doors, storm windows, and asbestos coverings on hot-water or steam pipes.

6. Conduct a study trip to a nearby home construction site to observe heating and insulation provisions. Also visit and inspect the school heating plant. Ask the custodian to explain how it operates.

7. Contact a local building insulation contractor or dealer for possible display of some materials available for home insulation.

Sound Energy

(Intermediate Emphasis)

UNIT 2

UNIT TWO

Sound Energy

(Intermediate Emphasis)

PLAY A RADIO LOUDLY, AND THE WINDOWS RATTLE. WATCH A parade at a distance and the marchers seem to be out-of-time with the music. Sing in the shower and suddenly your voice takes on new dimensions.

There are few topics that present so many available materials and interesting "whys" to explore as sound energy. In this unit, children learn what sounds are and how they are made. They measure distances at which echoes appear, experiment with changes in pitch, and find the natural vibrating rates of different objects. This is a "doing" unit virtually all the way through.

A few investigations include simple models of molecules to assist children in thinking about why different sound waves occur. Use or omit this material according to the children's age, experience, and ability. It is not essential to the unit's overall purposes. Late fourth graders (especially the talented) and older children usually profit from some discussion of theory. Beginning third graders, on the other hand, are less likely to gain from such study. There is a significant difference in the intellectual makeup of a child who has recently left the second grade and one is only a few months away from the fifth grade.

Credit for chapter opening photograph. **Shackman-Monkmeyer**

GENERALIZATIONS

I. Sounds are produced by vibrations that travel in waves.

II. Sound waves travel in gases, liquids, and solids – at different speeds.

III. Sound waves can be reflected and absorbed; echoes are reflections at a distance.

IV. Pitch changes as the rate of vibrations changes.

V. Sound waves can produce forced and sympathetic vibrations.

VI. Some sound waves can be heard by man, some cannot be heard.

Vibrations as Sounds. Every so often in science fiction a sinister scientist invents a machine capable of collecting and playing back all the sounds that have ever been made. At first he uses the machine to help historians determine what King John *really* said at Runnymede; but shortly he is offering the enemy military secrets discussed at the Pentagon.

Of course, all indications are that such a machine could never be invented. Sounds are simply waves of compressed molecules pulsating outward in all directions from a vibrating source. Consider the air about you. It is composed of tiny, individual molecules of different gases mixed with relative uniformity throughout the lower atmosphere. These molecules are rapidly and randomly moving about. A fast vibrating source – hummingbird's wings, bell, guitar string, a "twanged" ruler held on the edge of a desk – compresses billions of these molecules with each back-and-forth movement, because the molecules are in the way. Since air molecules are apparently quite elastic, they quickly assume their original shape after moving out of the vibrating object's path. But before this happens, they transfer energy to other molecules over a distance.

Let us emphasize that it is the *wave of energy* that may travel a great distance, rather than the molecules. Each molecule may move less than a billionth of an inch;

but this is enough to bump the next randomly moving molecule and so pass on the outward movement. Figure 2-1 shows a wave motion resulting from a compression and rarefaction effect on the molecules started by the vibrating source.

A sound fades away when energy behind the original vibrations is used up in the transmitting process. As one molecule bumps another it uses a tiny amount of energy. As more molecules are bumped, there is less energy available. The sound stops when energy of the randomly moving molecules exceeds the wave's energy. The molecules simply resume their normal helter-skelter movements.

How is loudness explained? First of all, let us call it *intensity*. "Loudness" is what we actually hear. If our ears are functioning poorly, a very intense sound may be barely discernible. So loudness is a matter of individual perception. On the other hand, intensity can be consistently and accurately

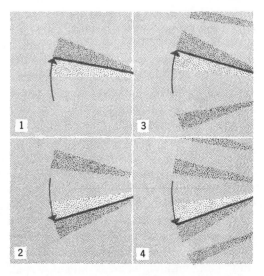

Figure 2-1 A vibrating ruler producing sound waves. In (1) the ruler is pushing the air molecules together (compression). Notice the thinned out space below it (rarefaction). Picture (2) shows the opposite happening, with the first part of the sound wave now moving away. Pictures (3) and (4) show another sound wave being produced. The wave moves outward as the molecules push others in the way, which in turn squeeze other molecules.

recorded by a sensitive sound detector in terms of the *decibel,* a unit of measurement in sound. The distinction between loudness and intensity may be too subtle to be worth teaching at the intermediate-grade level.

Shouting requires more energy than whispering. Expenditure of more energy forces any vibrating medium to vibrate to-and-fro more widely than usual, but in the same amount of time. This compresses molecules more forcefully, and the greater energy is able to move more molecules.

Of course, distance is also a factor in sound intensity. The farther away we are from the source, the weaker the sound. Molecules are pushed less because there is progressively less energy available. Interestingly, the same mathematical relationship is found in sound loss as exists with such other forms of energy as light, gravity, magnetism, and electricity. Intensity diminishes as the square of the distance between any sound source and perceiver. At 20 feet a sound has only one-fourth the intensity it exhibits at 10 feet from the source. With a distance of 30 feet intensity drops to one-ninth of the original sound. At 40 feet only one-sixteenth of the original intensity remains.

Sometimes the analogy of a water wave is used to teach how sound travels. A pebble is dropped into water and a circular series of ripples spreads out on the water's surface. This may be useful to show to your class. However, this example contains two main defects. Water waves are up-and-down motions which travel at right angles to the line of the waves. These are called *transverse* waves. Sound waves come from back-and-forth motions that result in *longitudinal* waves. Also, water waves move only horizontally, whereas sound waves travel outward in all planes. Many science teachers ask students to imagine sound waves as they would a series of rapidly blown soap bubbles, each enveloped within another that is slightly larger, all quickly expanding outward in all directions.

The wave idea is useful to distinguish be-tween *sounds* and *noises*. A sound consists of regularly pulsating vibrations – the time interval between each compression and rarefaction is the same. Noise is heard when irregular vibrations are transmitted.

Generalization I: Sounds are produced by vibrations that travel in waves

Contributing Idea A. Sounds are produced by vibrations.

Tell your pupils that they are going to see and participate in a number of demonstrations with sound makers. (Five are suggested.) You have decided to be completely silent except to give occasional directions. Each demonstration will feature something that makes a sound. Everyone should independently try to develop a satisfactory answer to this question: How are the sound makers alike?

1. *Materials:* desk or table; a thin 1-foot ruler or flat stick or hacksaw blade.

Hold down firmly about one-third of a ruler with the heel of one hand on a table edge; the remaining two-thirds should stick out over the edge. Press down the projecting end with the other hand and quickly let go. Repeat several times. The humming sound made will be loud and prolonged if about an inch of ruler is left between your hand and table edge.

2. *Materials:* tuning fork; one grain of puffed rice suspended from a foot-long thread. (Thread it with a needle and knot the end, or glue it.) Any small, light object can be substituted – puffed wheat, bit of cork, bit of a soda straw, balled tissue paper, pith ball, and so on.

Sharply strike the tuning fork against a *rubber* heel. (Striking a tuning fork against a hard object may damage it or alter its designed vibrating rate.) Draw the suspended object closer to the vibrating fork until it touches and bounces away. Repeat several times.

3. *Materials:* tuning fork or triangle (the kindergarten usually has one); small, shal-

low dish or small, transparent bowl; a few ounces of water.

Sharply strike a fork or triangle to make it vibrate. Hold it loosely against an empty dish. A loud ringing noise will be heard. Now pour some water into the dish. Strike the fork again, and thrust the vibrating ends into the water. It will splatter.

4. *Materials:* toy drum (One can be made from a large coffee can or cylindrical oatmeal container by covering the open end with a plastic top or a piece of balloon or inner tube. Fasten down with rubber bands, string, or tape.); a tablespoon of sand (or some bits of anything light—cork, salt, sugar, puffed rice, and so on).

Sprinkle sand or substitute material over the drum head. Strike the drum. Particles will bounce up and down as the head vibrates, thus making vibrations easier to see.

5. *Materials:* rubber bands. (One for each child is ideal. Children will bring them from home if reminded a day in advance.)

Ask the children to clench one end of a band in their teeth, and to stretch the other end slightly with their thumb. (A brief word here about standards will prevent some from stretching the rubber bands to the breaking point.) Have them pluck the strands with their fingers. Ask them to stop the sound before it stops by itself. Most will find out they can do this by pressing a finger against the vibrating bands. Does sound start again when they take their fingers off the band? (No.)

_{make inferences} Elicit from your class the thing common to all the demonstrations: a to-and-fro movement called *vibrations*. Without vibrations there is no sound. It might be worthwhile to have children briefly demonstrate the sound makers again to clinch this idea. Or it may be useful to divide the class into small groups. Each group can manipulate one set of materials for a short time and then move on to another set.

6. *Materials:* a rubber band for each pupil; chalkboard or chart sketch of human vocal cords (see Figure 2-2).

The children should be ready now for

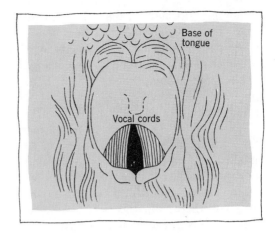

Figure 2-2 **Voice box (larynx) seen from above.**

learning how they make sounds with their vibrating vocal cords. Inform them that shortly they will be asked to explain how they make sounds with their voices. Have each child stretch his rubber band slightly, with the two strands close together. Tell them to hold the band very close to their lips, and gently blow out air. Vibrations will be heard. Many children will feel a ticklish sensation as the moving strands touch their lips.

Now tell them to take a breath and hum softly with mouths closed, while touching their "Adam's apples" gently with their fingers. Direct them to pinch their noses gently with thumb and forefinger of the free hand, and to notice what happens. (Sound stops.) The sound can be interrupted and started again by alternately closing and opening the fingers.

Now ask the children to open their mouths, expel all the air they can, and then try to make a sound. (They will be unable to do so, unless they breathe in.)

Get them to reason how they make _{make inferences} sounds with their voices: Air is forced from the lungs, up the throat, and through something in the Adam's apple that seems to vibrate. When the air is stopped or there is no air, vibrations are not possible. Show them a sketch of the *vocal cords*. Develop that their vocal cords are two elastic-like

183

membranes located inside the Adam's apple. These membranes vibrate when air rushes past. It would be advisable to avoid an explanation at this time of how changes of pitch are accomplished. This will become more understandable after later experiences.

The class will be interested in learning that such animals as cats and cows, for instance, are easily able to make sounds with their vocal cords as they *breathe in*. Let the class practice for a moment saying, "Are you there?" in this way. It can be done, but it is awkward and unsatisfactory.

Contributing Idea B. Sound travels in waves that spread out in all directions and planes.

1. *Materials:* a bell, or any other sound maker; several chairs.

Point out to your pupils that they have discovered there is no sound without a vibrating object. But how does sound travel outward from a vibrating object? Does it travel only in one direction? Does it go high and low? Develop conjecture. The children may hypothesize that sound travels in all directions from the source. Whatever their guess, get them to set up a way of testing it by positioning themselves in various places in the room and using their sound detectors (ears). Some may use chairs to stand on; some may crouch low. Others may form circles of increasing size and distance from the sound source. When they reach the tentative conclusion that sound travels outward in all directions from the source, it will be interesting and challenging to them if you give another explanation.

You might say, "What *real* proof do we have that sound travels through air in all directions? In every case we were connected in some way to the floor. Maybe the sound is just traveling through the floor and up our bodies. How could we find out if sound can travel through the air?" For proof, someone may offer that airplane noises can be heard; that skyrocket explosions can be heard on the Fourth of July, or that thunder can be heard. All

suggest hypotheses

develop procedures

these indicate that sound can travel through air. But invite pupils to develop their own test. If clues are needed, tell them that two jumpers might be able to find out. (Both children can jump up high simultaneously while one calls to the other.)

develop procedures

2. *Materials:* ten marbles; two yardsticks; ruler or stick.

Tell pupils they are going to see several demonstrations which will help them understand how sound travels. Explain that everything is made up of *molecules*. A molecule is a very tiny bit of anything—gas, liquid, or solid. Most are too small to be seen even under powerful microscopes. Atoms are even tinier, and join together to form molecules. Develop that gas molecules which make up the air move about every which way, bumping against one another. A sound starts when a vibrating object pushes against some molecules, which push other molecules, which in turn push others. Tell the class it will be able to understand this better by seeing the following demonstration.

Arrange two groups of five marbles each about one-half inch apart in a groove formed by two yardsticks. (See Figure 2-3.) Ask the class to pretend that the marbles are molecules. Wave a ruler to and fro from the wrist a few times to remind the pupils it is now pushing air molecules. Place the ruler between the two groups of marbles. With a slow vibratory motion knock one end marble into the rest on one side, then repeat on the other side. Establish that each "molecule" travels only a short distance, while

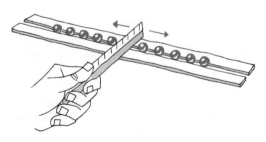

Figure 2-3

184

the wave motion itself continues. Repeat several times.

3. *Materials:* "Slinky" toy spring (available at toy stores or borrow from a child); table.

A "Slinky" toy (Figure 2-4) will better show wave motion. Lay it on a table, and have someone hold one end. Stretch it as far as it will go without widely separating the individual coils. Pinch together several coils at one end and release them quickly. A wave motion will travel from one end to the other. Elicit that one coil pushes the next, and so on. When the energy wave reaches our ears, we hear sound.

4. *Materials:* small rubber ball; set of dominoes.

Arrange a set of dominoes as shown in Figure 2-5. Drop a ball into the center. A wave motion will travel outward.

make inferences Children should criticize the models used in the three preceding demonstrations. Their chief criticism should be that the models showed only horizontal movement, while sound appeared to travel outward from the source in all directions (planes). Mention again that air molecules are in constant random movement.

Contributing Idea C. Loudness of a sound depends upon its energy and distance traveled.

1. *Materials:* drum or substitute; tablespoon of sand or substitute; pencil.

Ask, "Who knows how to make a soft sound with this drum?" Before the drum is struck with a pencil sprinkle sand on top so that vibrations can be seen. The sand will move up and down slightly. Now inquire how a loud sound can be made. Everyone should note greater sand movement as the drumhead is struck with greater force. Being out that more *energy* is used to strike the drum the second time. Explain that energy is the ability to move things. Movement in this case is a vibrating drumhead and the arm used for striking the drum. Develop that the children would get more tired from pounding a drum loudly for an hour than

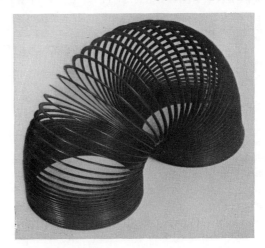

Figure 2-4 A slinky toy. (James-Industries, Inc.)

from striking it gently for an hour, because they would use more energy when pounding.

2. *Materials:* thin 1-foot ruler; table or desk. Permit a few children to made loud and soft noises by vibrating a ruler on a table edge with varying degrees of force. Call attention to the greater force (and so greater energy) needed to make the sounds louder.

3. *Materials:* ten to fifteen marbles, one-half inch apart; two yardsticks; cellophane tape. Arrange as in Figure 2-6.

Mention that you will demonstrate two "sounds" with an air molecule model. The pupils are to distinguish between a

Figure 2-5

185

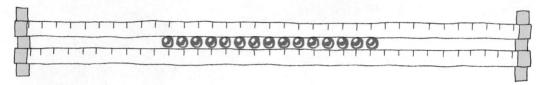

Figure 2.6

soft and loud sound. Gently push the end marble into the next so wave motion stops after a distance of several marbles. (A little practice will make this easy.) Also, if a stretched cloth or desk blotter is placed under the yardsticks, marbles will be prevented from rolling too freely. Rearrange the marbles. This time give a slightly harder push, so that wave motion continues past the previous point. Bring out that the second "sound" wave travels farther because it has more energy and can push more molecules.

Emphasize that the class has been working with a model (analogy), and that one way to test how well a model explains things is to see how it matches actual experience. *Does* a soft sound travel as far as a loud sound? *Is* it easier to hear a sound when close to or far away from it? Answers should be related to the model. Help the children reason that loudness of sounds depends on both the energy of a sound wave and the distance it has traveled. Even a loud sound ceases when it has used up its energy to move molecules.

make inferences

EXTENDING ACTIVITIES

1. Divide class members into several discussion groups to evaluate the following statement: An inventor claims that he has developed a sound-gathering machine. He says it can collect all the sounds from the air that have ever been made—the voices of George Washington, and so on. Is this possible if our understanding of sound waves is correct? Why or why not?

2. Encourage children to bring in as many sound makers as possible. Each contributor can explain how sound is produced

in his material. A display table and bulletin board may be arranged.

3. Pupils can read and consult authorities to learn how animals of many kinds make sounds—insects, fishes, mammals, reptiles, amphibians, birds, etc.

4. Ask an able child to make a report on the loudest sound ever reported—a volcanic explosion on what was once the island of Krakatoa, in Indonesia. The sound wave was so powerful it traveled thousands of miles.

The Variable Speeds of Sound. Watch a parade from afar and band members appear to be out-of-step with the music they are playing. Observe a carpenter hammering a nail on a distant roof top, and you hear the sound as he lifts the hammer instead of when he strikes the nail. Note the increasing speed of aircraft, and be assured that protests to the Federal Aviation Agency over sonic booms continue to mount!

The speeds at which sound waves travel lie behind each of these events. Light travels so fast—about 186,000 miles per second—it seems instantaneous to our eyes. But sound is another matter. At sea level and 42°F, sound waves move about 1100 feet per second in the air—only as fast as a low-powered rifle bullet. (This number is rounded off to 1000 in the unit to make computation easier.) Sound also travels in liquids and solids. It moves about five times faster in water than in air; in steel, sound may travel fifteen times faster than in air.

Three conditions determine the speed of sound: temperature, density, and the elasticity or "springiness" of the molecules conducting the sound.

Density by itself does not increase the speed of sound. In fact, the speed of sound may decrease with density. But often associated with density is greatly increased elasticity of molecules. When highly elastic, close-together molecules of a solid transmit sound, it travels much more rapidly than in either air or water. In the following section, construction of a simple molecular model (see Figure 2-7) is suggested to demonstrate speeds of sound in three mediums. A principal defect of this model is that comparative elasticity of molecules is not shown.

A temperature increase results in increasing the speed of sound about 1 foot per second for every 1 degree Fahrenheit. Have you ever wondered why sounds carry such large distances on certain days? On a cold winter day with snow on the ground, for example, air next to the ground is often colder than higher air. Instead of a sound wave spreading out uniformly and rapidly dying out, the temperature difference causes parts of the wave to travel at different speeds. The upper part begins to travel faster than the lower part and bends back down toward the ground some distance away.

Given the same medium and temperature, all sounds travel at the same speed. If this were not so, it would be difficult, if not impossible, to conduct concerts in large auditoriums. The reedy sound of an oboe and brassy timbre of a trombone always reach your ears at the same time, if they are begun at the same time.

If they live in a community where sonic booms occur with some frequency, it is likely that children will ask what happens when an airplane "breaks the sound barrier." We know that a sound-producing object sends out sound waves in all directions. When the object is set in motion it continues to send out waves in all directions. But let us continue to increase this object's velocity. As it goes faster it is more difficult for waves to travel outward in front of it. When an airplane reaches a certain speed

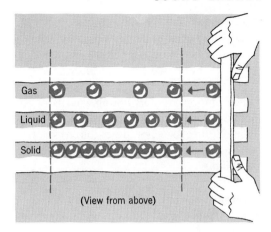

Figure 2-7

(about 750 miles per hour; but it varies greatly with altitude and temperature) air compressions of these sound waves pile up into a dense wall of compressed air. This can subject the airplane to severe stresses.

A powerful engine and proper design enable an airplane to slip through the dense air barrier. Sound is largely left behind to anyone riding in the airplane. But what happens to the wall of compressed air? The tremendous energy is passed on—molecule to molecule—until it hits the earth as a booming shock wave. The shock wave continues on the ground several or more miles wide and traces the airplane's flight path. It stops only when the pilot slows down his aircraft below the speed of sound. Sonic booms that cause the least damage start at very high altitudes. By the time energy in the original wall of compressed air is transmitted to the ground, much of it has been dissipated.

Similar shock waves are formed by an explosion, except that they move out equidistantly in all directions. Very rapid expansion of gases in an exploding bomb compresses the surrounding air. As the shock wave of compressed air moves outward, it flattens virtually anything in its path until such pressure finally dissipates over a distance.

Since energy in a sound wave is always

187

transmitted onward molecule to molecule, it is impossible to have sound waves in a vacuum. The moon appears to be virtually airless. These two findings often lead persons to observe, "There can be no sounds on the moon." Contributing idea B of this section closes with a problem based on this idea. Your class should be able to see how a solid might be used as the transmitting medium.

Generalization II: Sound waves travel in gases, liquids, and solids – at different speeds

Contributing Idea A. Sound waves travel much more slowly than light.

1. *Materials:* small piece of scrap wood; hammer; playground.

Point out to your pupils that if they watch a parading band from some distance, the band members will appear to be out-of-step with their music. Entertain hypotheses *suggest hypotheses* that would account for this. When travel time for sound is suggested, invite them to test this guess with a block of wood and hammer. They will need to do this outdoors, of course. A distance of 100 yards or more will provide a dramatic and obvious difference between when they see the block struck and when they hear the resulting sound. It is interesting to shorten this distance gradually to note decreases in the time lag.

Back in the room, help the children to recall other experiences they may have had of this kind: hearing the crack of a baseball bat after a ball has been struck; hearing thunder after a flash of lightning. Explain that light travels so fast it reaches us almost instantly; light can travel a distance equal to seven and one-half times around the world in just one second! In comparison, sound travels through the air about 1000 feet a second. (This figure is rounded from 1100 to make calculations easier in the next activity.)

2. Introduce the idea that by knowing how fast sound travels we can tell how far away some sounds are, if we can see the

sound maker in action. You might say, "Since there are about 5000 feet in a mile, how many seconds will sound take to go a mile? Remember sound travels about 1000 feet a second." The simplicity of your approach, of course, will need to vary with the mathematical ability of your class. An easy method might feature a column of 1000's to add, with a corresponding column of seconds. After each five 1000's, mark off one mile. By using the chalkboard and round numbers or combinations of fives, it should be possible to do such problems as these: *reason quantitativ[e]*

a. You see lightning; 10 seconds later you hear thunder. How far away was the lightning?

b. You see a tug boat blow its steam whistle far up river; 15 seconds later you hear it. How far away is it?

With practice, some children will develop the ability to estimate a second's duration. Repeating the words, "a thousand in one" in time to a clock's second sweep will aid in developing this ability.

Contributing Idea B. Sound waves travel faster in liquids than in gases, and fastest in most solids.

1. *Materials:* aquarium tank, about half-filled with water; small metal tongs (or two hard objects that can be knocked together to make a sound).

Tell the class you have learned that some swimming pool owners are interested in radio speakers that will play music underwater. Can sounds be sent through water? Would they be louder or softer than if made through the air? Encourage pupils to think of a test for the two problems by using an *develop procedures* aquarium tank and small tongs clicked together (or substitutions). Although no one can – or should – put his head underwater, an ear can be pressed against the outside of the tank under the waterline while tongs or two stones are clicked together underwater. To test for the second question, the tongs can be clicked slightly above the waterline with a child's ear also above the waterline, and again pressed against the tank. For controls, ear and tongs are the same distance away in both cases. The tongs are clicked with equal force. Many children will be surprised to find that sound does travel underwater, and that it is louder.

2. *Materials:* yardstick (or window pole or broomstick); wristwatch.

suggest
hypotheses

Use a controlled experiment to bring out that a sound can be heard better through wood than air. Mention that sometimes an automobile mechanic will put an end of a broomstick to his ear and touch various parts of a running motor with the other end. Press for reasons. If someone suggests that the mechanic can hear motor noises that way, inquire why he does not just lean close to the motor and listen without a stick. Someone may immediately guess that sounds are heard better through the handle than through the air. How can this guess be tested?

develop
procedures

If needed, suggest a wristwatch and yardstick for materials. A child can press a wristwatch tightly against one end of a yardstick placed on the table. (Pressing the watch assures maximum transfer of vibrations to the stick.) A second child should put his ear to the yardstick's other end. Can he hear the same ticking noise through only the air? The same distance will need to be measured. For example, the listener's ear might be three feet *above* the watch on the second trial.

What can be done to give more people a chance to listen at the same time? Perhaps the watch can be held or taped (put paper over the watch face) at the center of a long window pole, either metal or wood. Try two or four persons at a time. Some sound loss will occur as more ears are held against the pole, since this dampens vibrations.

In discussion, bring out the old practice of Indians putting their ears to the ground to listen for hoofbeats. Also, how a railroad maintenance worker may place his ear on a rail to listen for an approaching train. Tell your pupils to place an ear against one end of their desks, and to scratch the top softly with a fingernail at the other end. Then have them raise their heads slightly while continuing the scratching motion.

3. *Materials:* old spoons or forks; wire hangers; scissors; string. (These materials for everyone, if possible.)

This activity shows how the beautiful tones produced by common objects can be detected through an attached solid conductor, such as string.

Have everyone tie a string about 2 feet long to his spoon or other object to be tested. Holding the string, each person should gently swing the spoon against his desk. The usual, small clanking sound will be heard. Now have each child put the string next to an eardrum and again swing the spoon against his desk. Sounds will dramatically appear louder and like cathedral bells or chimes.

Encourage pupils to experiment to see what they can discover. They might use two strings, one for each ear with the spoon tied in the middle. They might substitute other objects, strike metal against metal, and bang two spoons or hangers together. Some may shorten or lengthen the string. Some may stop the vibrating string with their fingers and then release it. A few may try a chain of hangers or other objects on one or two strings.

develop
procedures

Let everyone report his findings and demonstrate, if needed. Bring out that a sound appears to travel better through a solid (string) than through gases (air).

make
inferences

4. *Materials:* four yardsticks; a ruler; twenty-two marbles. Arrange materials as in Figure 2-7.

Call attention to results from the children's several preceding experiences: Sound appears to travel "better" (with less energy loss) in water than air, and in a solid substance better than water. Entertain theories that will explain why. Few will be forthcoming. Suggest that a model can help them to understand what happens to a sound wave in a gas, liquid, and solid substance.

Explain that liquid and solid materials are also made up of jiggling molecules, but that they are closer together than in a gas. Help pupils to identify which rows of marbles represent a gas, liquid, and solid. Tell them you are going to start a "sound wave." But first invite them to predict which wave will *make inferences* travel most quickly. Push the three "molecules" resting against the ruler into the three groups. (Be sure to stop the ruler's forward motion *before* the marbles collide.) The wave will be fastest in the solid, slower in the liquid, and slowest in the gas model. In addition, the last "molecule" in each model will be knocked away to varying distances, with the solid molecule going farthest and the gas molecule going least far. *make inferences* Help the children observe that not only does the solid molecule wave travel fastest, but it also seems to have the most energy at the end; this, because of the distances each end molecule travels. Guide them to understand that the sound wave with the most energy will be loudest, as they have noted before.

5. Continue by emphasizing that they have observed a model, and it would be wise to check its accuracy. Have someone look up speeds of sound in air, water, and steel, for example. Or, provide these speeds:

Air—about 1000 feet in one second (more than three football fields).

Water—about 5000 feet in one second (a little less than a mile).

Steel—about 15,000 feet in one second (a little less than 3 miles).

Once again local referents for these distances would be helpful.

Establish that for every foot sound travels in air it would travel about 5 feet in water and about 15 feet in steel. This may *reason quantitatively* be drawn to scale on a chalkboard or bulletin board and labeled.

Contributing Idea C. Sound cannot travel in a vacuum.

Reveal through reading, a report, or telling that scientists believe there is no air or water on the moon. Suggest that this may raise a problem if astronauts on the moon want to chat with their companions, especially if they have no radio. Ask the children to define the problem in terms of sound. Help them to state it *state problems* clearly and concisely. "In what ways, if any, will sound travel on the moon?" might be one such statement. Through reasoning, they should tentatively conclude that sound might be transmitted through *make inferences* the ground, or by talking with space helmets touching. Bring up possibilities of communication other than sound: wig-wag, flashlight signals, etc. Introduce the word *vacuum* — a space where there are no molecules of any kind. Let pupils read to confirm that sound cannot travel unless there is a substance to transmit the wave.

EXTENDING ACTIVITIES

1. Let someone consult an encyclopedia for information on how a hydrophone is used to detect many different sounds in water. Although children at this level will be unable to understand exactly how this water microphone works, it is interesting for them to note the various kinds of sounds that have been detected with it.

2. Try to get a film which demonstrates that sound cannot travel in a vacuum. A usual setup features a glass jar containing a suspended electric bell. As the bell is rung, air is quickly pumped out of the jar. By the time a near vacuum exists, sound can no longer be heard. Then, as air is introduced again, the sound gets louder and louder.

3. Encourage the children to make string "telephones." Each pair of pupils will need two large, durable paper cups (or round cereal boxes, or clean metal cans free of jagged edges and open at one end); also, about 15 feet of strong string.

Punch a hole with a nail in the closed end of the cups. Thread the string through both cups and knot each end to prevent it from pulling out. When in use the string is stretched tightly while one child talks into one container and another holds the second container to his ear.

Sound waves coming from the mouth set the diaphragm (end of container) in motion. This, in turn, transmits vibrations to the string. These vibrations travel the string's length and set the other diaphragm in motion. Air is set in motion by the second diaphragm and sound enters the ear. The children themselves should be able to both provide and partly test this explanation.

This apparatus works *unlike* a real telephone. In a real telephone sound energy is changed to electrical energy and back to sound energy again. (An explanation of how the telephone operates may be found on pages 291–293.)

Children will gain much information and enjoyment if this activity is treated in an open-ended way. Asking questions like, "What can you do to make it work better?" and, "How far away can you talk before it stops working well?" yields many facts. Some of the variables to explore are (1) loudness of the voice; (2) container size; (3) elasticity of the diaphragms and type of container; (4) type of string—a "hard" string or a waxed string works better than a soft one; and (5) tautness of the string. No matter how hard the children try, eventually the sound waves will die out when a certain string length is reached. There will not be enough energy to push molecules in the string or move the diaphragm in and out.

develop procedures

make inferences

Pupils may also want to make a "party line" by crossing the strings of two or more pairs of telephones and tieing them tightly at the crosspoint with a small piece of cord. If the strings are held taut, there should be little or no noticeable sound loss.

develop procedures

Note throughout these investigations if pupils can detect such faulty procedures as a slack line interfering with free vibration of the line, or dampening diaphragm vibrations by holding the cup at its closed end.

Sound Absorption and Reflection. One reason why singing in the shower or bathroom is so popular comes from the nature of sound reflections. As a sound hits the smooth walls, it bounces back and forth, increasing in loudness and prolonging the notes a little. This is pleasing to the ear. The smoother the reflecting surface, the better sound reflects. On a very smooth wall, sound reflections bounce off like light reflections from a mirror. The angle of reflection equals the angle of incidence.

Have you ever noticed how different sounds seem in a room before and after furnishings are installed? Rugs, drapes, and cloth-covered furniture absorb more sound waves than we may realize. However, even a furnished room may have a "hollow" sound if the walls and ceilings are hard and smooth. The use of porous acoustical tile on ceilings aids in cutting down sound reflections. So does the use of rough, porous plaster blown on with a compressed-air applicator. Besides absorbing some sound waves, a rough surface interferes with the wave reflection, like the way in which light is diffused when it hits an irregular surface.

Sometimes children ask, "What happens to the molecules when they enter a porous material?" It appears that sound energy is changed to heat energy. The regular pulsating movements of a wave are broken up into the normal, irregular motions of individual molecules. As this happens, any energy passed into the porous substance is transmitted to other air molecules, thus very slightly raising the temperature. (Temperature is determined by the average speed of molecular movements. The faster they jiggle about, the higher the temperature.)

Because sound can be reflected, we can direct or channel it in certain directions by using different devices. Open-air theaters often have a large shell-like structure surrounding the stage. This enables sounds to be directed toward an audience with re-

191

duced energy loss. The same principle is used with cheerleaders' megaphones.

An even more efficient way to conserve sound energy is to enclose it in a tube. Since the sound is kept from spreading out by continual reflections within the encircling wall, such concentrated sound loses energy slowly and may travel a long way. Physicians' stethoscopes and speaking tubes in older apartment houses and ships are familiar applications.

A reverse application of this reflection principle is found in the old-fashioned ear trumpet, and in the ears of such animals as rabbits and donkeys. In these cases sounds are "gathered," or reflected inward. Besides large ears, many animals have the additional advantage of being able to cock them separately in different directions.

Since sound takes time to travel and can be reflected, it stands to reason that at a certain distance you should be able to hear a distinctly separate reflection of an original sound—an echo. Most persons need an interval of at least one-tenth of a second to distinguish between two sounds. If the interval is shorter than this, you hear one sound, much in the same manner your brain interprets separate frames of a motion picture as continuous motion.

Assuming that a sound wave travels at a speed of 1100 feet per second, in one-tenth of a second it travels 110 feet. To hear an echo—a distinguishable, separate sound —we must stand far enough away from a reflecting surface for the sound wave to travel a total distance of 110 feet. Since the sound travels *to* the reflecting surface and *back* to our ears, a distance of 55 feet from the surface is adequate to hear an echo. Remember, this distance varies a bit with temperature variations.

Sometimes the combination of a loud sound and many distant reflecting surfaces produces multiple echoes, or *reverberations*. A common example is thunder, which may reverberate back and forth from cloud to earth and among air layers of varying densities.

Figure 2-8 A bat's ears are well suited for echo-ranging. (Courtesy American Museum of Natural History.)

A few ship captains still use echoes from fog horns to gauge the distance from icebergs or a mountainous coastline. However, the use of radio waves (radar) for this purpose is much commoner, since it is more convenient, accurate, and reliable. A variation in temperature at different air levels could result in misleading calculations with sound echoes.

An interesting application of echo detection is found in a U.S. Navy device called *Sonar*. (The term is coined from the words, "SOund NAvigation and Ranging.") This apparatus sends a sound wave through the water and detects reflections from any direction. The time between an initial sound and its received echo enables a Sonar operator to know the distance of a reflector, whether it is a submarine or an underwater obstruction. Similar devices are used on fishing vessels to detect schools of fish.

A strange use of sound reflections is found in the bat. By listening to reflections of its cries, a bat flying in total darkness avoids collisions and may even catch insects in mid-air. An interesting aspect of this odd form of echo-ranging is that these sounds are so high they are inaudible to humans. How was their "secret" detected? The answer lies in the ability of scientists to cast shrewd hypotheses and make careful tests. In the last activity of this section, children are challenged to do similar thinking.

There is a related point which you may find intriguing. In addition to ultrahigh sounds inaudible to humans, bats not in flight make squeaky sounds which are clearly audible. Scientists have discovered that ultrahigh sounds are reflected more strongly from small surfaces (such as an insect in flight) than sounds of lower frequency. Since bats can make lower or higher sounds, why do they make the higher sounds in flight? Are they "choosing" to do so because better echo-ranging occurs?

Generalization III: Sound waves can be reflected and absorbed; echoes are reflections heard at a distance

Contributing Idea A. Sound waves can be reflected and absorbed.

1. *Materials:* metal wastebasket (empty).

In this investigation, the children observe how well an empty container reflects sounds.

You might begin by inquiring, "Have you ever noticed how your voice sounds in an empty house or room, before the furniture and curtains are put in? Or when singing in the shower?" Most children will be aware that their voices seem louder than usual in these places. Someone may venture that sound is reflected off the walls. Withhold verification until after the next experiment.

suggest hypotheses

Give someone a wastebasket. Have him hold it up sideways, with the open end close to his face. His back should be toward the class. Instruct him to count slowly and loudly into the open end. Next, have him

try it without the wastebasket. (He should be at least 10 feet from a wall, to avoid a strong reflection from it.) A difference in loudness will be even more noticeable if one note is sung for 10 or more seconds without interruption, while the container is alternately raised to his face and then lowered. Elicit that sound waves were apparently reflected off the container's sides and bottom and sent out the open end, past the child, and toward the class. Draw out similarities between this demonstration and sound reflections in an empty room.

make inferences

2. *Materials:* metal wastebasket; several old rags; small bell. (A ringing sound can also be made by hitting a spoon against an empty glass.)

In this activity, a comparison is made of sounds reflected when a container is empty and lined with cloth.

Let a few children recall how sounds change after carpeting, drapes, and furniture are put into an empty room. When decreased loudness is brought up, invite some pupils to devise an experiment with the materials to verify their common experiences. A bell can be rung with equal force near the bottom of the container, once when empty and then lined with rags. A noticeable difference in loudness of the two sounds will be heard. Clarify that sound is largely *absorbed* by soft or porous materials.

develop procedures

make inferences

3. *Materials:* large megaphone (make from tagboard, fasten with tape or staples).

Reveal how a megaphone directs sound by reflecting it in a specific direction.

Call attention to the common practice of cupping hands to the mouth when shouting at a distance. Have the children recall experiences of observing megaphones in use. Lead to a possible explanation of these practices: sound waves cannot spread out as easily; sounds are reflected from the cupped hands or megaphones, and are thus sent toward a specific direction.

suggest hypotheses

Tell your pupils they can test how well their explanation fits the known facts. This should be performed outdoors, preferably on a windless day. If there is some wind, have the demonstrator face it and the class. Position him about 20 feet from the other children, who should be bunched closely together. The demonstrating child sings and holds a single note with uniform loudness for about 10 seconds. During this time he slowly turns in place at least one full circle. Let him repeat this procedure with the megaphone. There will be a noticeable difference in variation of loudness, with the megaphone's variation dramatically obvious. Repeat both procedures with different children. Back in the classroom, help them to discuss the demonstration and how it tends to verify their previous explanation. Encourage them to think of other ways in which sound can be directed through reflection. (For example, see extending activity 4.)

4. *Materials:* megaphone; wristwatch.

A megaphone can be used to gather sounds besides reflect them. This can be found out in an experiment.

suggest hypotheses

Remind pupils that occasionally they see a person cup his hand to an ear while listening. Develop conjecture as to why. When increased loudness is suggested, let them cup one or both hands to their ears while someone sings or talks in front of the room. Establish that once again sounds seem to be reflected, but this time into the ear. Contrast with directed sound sent outward, as in the last activity. Point to a megaphone and watch. Ask how a controlled experiment could be set up to learn if sounds are "gathered" with a megaphone and are therefore easier to hear. Their directions might be similar to the following:

develop procedures

Place the megaphone over the ticking watch. Put an ear to the smaller opening. Gradually raise the megaphone. The ticking sound can barely be heard. Remove the megaphone. The ticking should be inaudible.

Object (if no one else does) that the group has no visible proof that sound is or is not being heard. Since there is not enough time to have everyone try it, what could be done to show everyone that sound is heard with

develop procedures

the megaphone? If no one can suggest a way, provide the clue that a listener may have to keep his eyes closed or be blindfolded during this experiment.

Let the class try the experiment again. But once distance is established for barely hearing a ticking sound with the megaphone, the watch can be stealthily removed or replaced, as the listener uses his megaphone. He can be asked at random if he hears the watch. This gives proof of whether it is heard or not, provided he cannot see. It now would be interesting to have the blindfolded listener move beyond the point of audibility and guess as to when the watch is in place. Any discrepancy between these guesses and the experiment should become quickly apparent.

make inferences

Enhance class understanding of the sound-gathering efficiency of large reflectors by discussing such examples as donkey and rabbit ears, and the old-fashioned ear trumpet.

Contributing Idea B. Echoes may occur when sounds are reflected over a distance.

1. *Materials:* hammer; block of wood; 10-foot string; chalk; suitable outdoor location.

In this investigation, children can discover how far one must be from a sound reflector to hear an echo.

Have everyone recall the nature of sounds in an empty corridor, bathroom, or other place where sounds reflect well. Bring out that in addition to loudness the sound seems to be slightly prolonged. Establish that as an empty room or other reflecting place gets larger, the sound is increasingly prolonged. Help the children reason why this is so: sound takes time to travel. When it reflects back we hear it in addition to the original sound. Thus, it lasts a little longer, and is louder.

Let the class guess what would occur if distance were gradually increased between a sound reflector and listener. *Echoes* will probably be mentioned. If not, ask pupils if an *echo* seems likely. Explore their understanding of this concept for a moment. Recall with them the physical conditions present in their previous experiences with echoes. Establish that three factors appear necessary: a reasonably large sound reflector, such as a wall; a sound maker; and some distance between the reflector and listener. Inform them that the school building wall (or some other appropriate reflector) might serve to reflect sound. Invite them to discover the distance, if any, that an echo should appear.

Together, design procedures. A string of known length (10 feet is a handy size for both addition and rapid measurement) can be used to mark the distance from a reflecting wall. At each 10-foot interval the wood block can be struck with a hammer to give a sharp sound, while everyone listens

reason quantitatively for a possible echo. The first discernible echo should appear at some point between 50 and 60 feet. If sounds are made at increasingly far distances, the echoes will

make inferences appear at later time intervals. Have pupils reason why this offers proof that sound does take time to travel. Dramatically compare the pupils' measurement of when the echo first appears with the 55-foot distance calculated by scientists. Everyone will be delighted with the close "agreement." You might mention, however, that the speed of sound varies with air temperature.

2. It may be useful and interesting at this time to inform the children of how echoes enable bats to fly safely in total darkness. This information can lead to a "thought" experiment. You might say, "Scientists now know that a bat can fly safely and catch insects in the air even if it is blindfolded and there is complete darkness. It does this with echoes. The bat makes very high sounds that bounce back from anything in the way, even from tiny flying insects. When it hears the echoes it can tell in what direction an insect or object is, and how far away. It wasn't easy for scientists to find this out, though, because the sounds bats make are so squeaky-high that human ears can't hear them."

"Let's say that we are scientists who want to find out how bats can fly in the dark without bumping into things. We think that maybe a bat makes high sounds, and then listens for echoes. But we aren't sure. Say we have several bats. We also have a large room with posts sticking up into the air and wires strung from floor to ceiling. How could we test to see if echoes are used by the bats to fly safely?"

develop procedures

Suggestions may vary. One method would be to blindfold the bats or otherwise eliminate vision. The sound factor could be taken care of in either of two ways or both: plugging both ears, and taping the mouth shut. If the class is alert, inquire as to which of these two latter measures would be better, if only one could be employed. (Plugging the ears. It might be possible for the bat to "hum" through its nose, someone may surmise!)

If designing the test seems too difficult for the children without clues, you could merely ask, "What could we do with its ears? Mouth?" and so on.

After the children have designed and reasoned through their experiment, inform them of what scientists actually did. Let them compare their procedures with the scientists' and try to make inferences. Reveal the following:

make inferences

(1) Bats were blindfolded and flew just as well as before. What did this show? (Sight was unnecessary.)

(2) The noses and mouths of some bats were covered and they flew into objects. What did this show? (The bats probably needed to make sounds.)

(3) The ears of bats were plugged, and they again flew into objects in their way. What did this show? (The bats probably needed to hear the sound reflections.)

EXTENDING ACTIVITIES

1. Have the class evaluate this statement: "A man shouted loudly at a far-away mountain. Several days later he heard the

echo." Is this possible? Why or why not? (It is impossible. No one possesses enough power to shout the thousands of miles the sound would need to travel for such a long-delayed echo.)

2. Ask a capable pupil or group to report on *Sonar* and its uses.

3. Visit places in the school building that feature sound insulation. Point out such provisions as porous plaster, soft wall-board, heavy drapes and curtains in the auditorium, and acoustical tile.

4. Encourage several pupils to bring garden hoses to use for speaking tubes. Point out the similarity between these "tubes" and those still used in some apartment buildings and ships. Because the sound waves cannot spread out, sound energy may travel as far as several thousand feet in properly designed tubes.

5. Let the children check their heart-beats with a homemade "stethoscope" — a funnel fitted into the end of a short hose or rubber tube. The funnel is placed over the heart while a listener holds the tube's free end to his ear. Have pupils listen to heart-beats before and after moderate exercise, such as running in place. They will be surprised at the more powerful sound vibrations produced by a rapidly beating heart.

Changing the Pitch of Sounds. Many pilots of certain crop-dusting airplanes actually rely on sound to gauge the safeness of their air speed. It is difficult while skimming low to watch both an air-speed indicator in the cockpit and ground obstructions. Flying speed is estimated by listening to the pitch of sound produced by the vibration of the airplane's struts and wires as the relative wind rushes past. Some seasoned pilots can judge their margin of safety to within 5 miles per hour by this method.

Sometimes children fasten small cards against the spokes of their bicycle wheels to simulate a motor sound while riding. As the spokes go around and hit the card, it vibrates and makes a sound. The pitch rises with increased speed of vibrations, and lowers with decreased speed of vibrations.

In a stringed instrument pitch is determined by the length, tightness, and thickness of the strings. Shortening a string causes the frequency of vibrations to increase, raising pitch. Lengthening it has an opposite effect. Tightening a string also increases pitch, whereas lessening tension decreases it. A thick string vibrates more slowly than a thin one, and thus produces a lower sound.

You know that different instruments — a violin and a cello, for instance — may play a note at the same pitch and yet sound different. This is because of the *quality* of tone produced by these instruments. Most vibrations include more than just simple back-and-forth movements along a string's entire length. Although there is a fundamental vibration which governs the basic pitch, other parts of the string vibrate at faster frequencies. The combinations of vibrations are different with each string and with various stringed instruments. Together they produce tones of distinctly recognizable qualities.

In wind instruments, sound is produced by a vibrating column of air. The vibrations may be started by a player's lips, as with trumpets and tubas, or by blowing past a reed, as with the saxophone and clarinet.

Pitch is regulated by changing the length of the air column vibrating within the instrument. In a wind instrument such as the saxophone, air-column length is changed by opening and closing valves with the fingers. In a trombone, air-column length is regulated by pulling or pushing a long, closed, double tube, called the slide.

The characteristic of quality is also present in wind instruments. In this case it is caused by the combinations of additional air vibrations set up within each instrument. Quality of voices is produced in much the same way. This is regulated by the size and shape of air cavities in the mouth and nose. An interesting way for children to learn about pitch and tonal quality is to make their own string and wind instru-

Figure 2-9

ments. Rubber bands of different sizes make pleasant sounds when placed around shoe boxes or their lids. Strong nylon fishline, fastened on pieces of wood with nails and screw eyes, is even better. (See Figure 2-13 A-C.) When the line is fastened to a screw eye, its tension may be adjusted by turning the eye in the appropriate direction. Tuned properly, nylon fishline sounds like the string on a regular instrument. Simple tunes can be composed and played on the stringed instruments children fashion.

Soda straws and bottles make acceptable wind instruments. For best results with straws, get the large diameter, plain paper kind. "Sunshine" brand straws have been very effective in trial use.

Interestingly, opposite results in pitch occur with partly filled soda-pop bottles, depending on whether they are used as wind or percussion instruments. That is, if you blow over the tops of soda bottles containing varying volumes of water as in Figure 2-9, the scale will go from low to high, left to right. If you *strike* the bottles sharply with a pencil, the scale will go from high to low, left to right. With blowing, the bottle's *air* mainly vibrates; when striking the bottle, the *water* and glass mainly vibrate.

Generalization IV: Pitch changes as the rate of vibrations changes.

Contributing Idea A. Length, tension, and thickness affect the pitch of a vibrating string.

1. *Materials:* various shoe boxes and lids, or empty quart milk cartons (with one side cut open); rubber bands of varying size and thickness; scissors.

Invite the class to explore different kinds of sounds they can make with the materials. Can they make high and low sounds? Can they make louder and softer sounds? Can they make a scale? Play a simple tune? Some children will stretch their bands the long way over the boxes or lids, some around the shorter way. Several may not use the boxes to hold the bands until they wish to make louder sounds. A few may try to set up a musical scale, with heavy and lighter rubber bands, as in Figure 2-10. Tension across the top is adjusted by pulling the bands up or down on the sides. A few pupils will quickly find that the sounds are greatly magnified when an ear is held against the box or lid. *(develop procedures)*

After enough time to thoroughly explore the possibilities, have different persons report and demonstrate what they found. Toward the discussion's end, concentrate on *pitch*. How was it changed? Pupils probably will say that tightness, thickness, and length were factors. *(make inferences)*

(Should you wish to do three controlled experiments with these variables, do activities 2 and 3. If you want to have the class explore more sophisticated string instruments, try activity 4.)

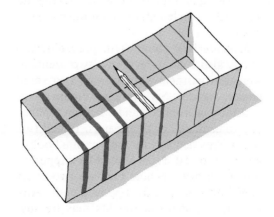

Figure 2-10

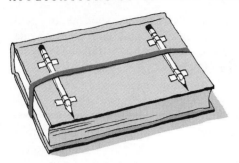

Figure 2-11

2. *Materials:* two rubber bands, thin and thick; two pencils; cellophane tape; book. Set up as in Figure 2-11.

How does length affect the pitch of a vibrating rubber band? Let the class express what must be done for a test. Pupils will probably suggest what they seem to have discovered: By stretching a band to varying degrees, pitch changes. Develop that this procedure *also* increases tightness.

develop procedures

Ask how length *alone* can be tested. If ideas are not forthcoming, show the setup as found in Figure 2-11. Challenge the children to use it for length. By placing a finger at various points between the two pencils while plucking, pitch is raised and lowered. Tightness remains the same. This happens with bands of any size.

Question how tightness can be tested using the same setup. Bring out that this time length must remain constant. (Someone can tighten the band while keeping the same vibrating length between the two pencils.)

3. *Materials:* same as in preceding activity; also four paper clips; two identical weights (two heavy scissors or two small books will do). Set up as in Figure 2-12. Cut the two rubber bands. Fasten a paper clip to each end of both bands. Imbed two paper clips deeply into the top of a book— about 40 or 50 pages should be clipped to provide a firm anchor. Fashion two other clips into hooks at the opposite ends. Any two heavy, identical weights may be suspended, including books. For the time

being, leave off the weights. When using this setup, hold the book at its open side to prevent it from opening. Put the book on a table edge so that the weights hang freely.

Point out that the children have tested satisfactorily for tightness and length, but a test for thickness remains. To do so, they must think of a way to set up properly a thick rubber band and a thin one. Both must be pulled with equal force. Length of the vibrating strings must also be equal. Encourage conjecture and criticism of the various methods suggested. If ideas bog down, reveal the Figure 2-12 apparatus. Draw out from the children what is needed. Two identical weights which pull with equal force should be attached. Equal vibrating lengths can be taken care of by placing a finger on each band at the bottom pencil while strumming. If variables are controlled, the thick band will make a noticeably lower sound.

develop procedures

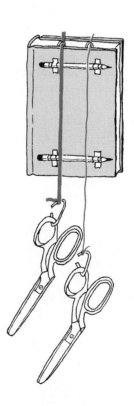

Figure 2-12

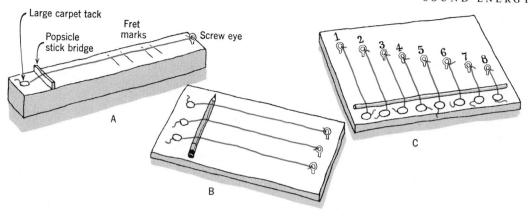

Large carpet tack

Fret marks

Popsicle stick bridge

Screw eye

A

B

1 2 3 4 5 6 7 8

C

Figure 2-13 A — B — C

4. *Materials:* various pieces of scrap wood, about ½ of an inch thick; box of 100 medium-size screw eyes (eye about ⁵⁄₁₆ of an inch inside diameter, screw— ⅝ of an inch long); box of large carpet tacks; several large nails, hammers, scissors; 100 feet of strong nylon fishline (40-pound test).

Invite the children to make some permanent stringed instruments with the materials. They might try various constructions of their own design, including *develop procedures* instruments like those in Figure 2-13 A–C. Strings can be attached with large carpet tacks at one end, and screw eyes on the other end to adjust tension. A bridge will be needed under the strings to hold them up off the board. Pencils, dowels, and popsicle sticks will serve as bridges. If screw eyes are used at both ends, no bridge is needed, since they are high enough to hold the strings off the boards. Nail holes can be tapped into the wood to start the screw eyes. If the screw eyes are hard to twist with fingers alone, a large nail can be inserted crosswise into the eye to help the twisting. Be sure that the carpet tacks are fastened securely to the wood to prevent them from pulling out when the strings are tightened.

Encourage children to play simple songs on their instruments, such as "Merrily We Roll Along," "Three Blind Mice," and "Twinkle, Twinkle, Little Star." Some children might compose their own melodies. *develop procedures* They can key the notes to numbered strings, as in C. Or crude fret (fingerboard) marks can be penciled on the instrument, as in A, to reliably reproduce certain notes of a melody. Penciled fret marks can also be made on paper tacked to the board under the strings, and changed for each new song. Let pupils exchange their musical compositions (and instruments) and try to play them.

Contributing Idea B. Length of the vibrating air column affects pitch in wind instruments.

1. *Materials:* for each small group, eight soda pop bottles (plain glass works better than rippled glass), a "six-pack" of empty soda bottles and two identical extra bottles; half-gallon plastic container of water; funnel; paper towels or newspaper; for you, two identical soda bottles, one about half-full, the other one-third full of water.

How is pitch adjusted in a wind instrument? With your two demonstration bottles, let a volunteer show how to make a sound by blowing over the top of one bottle, then the other. (Be sure to stress to the class that there is no need to touch the bottle with one's lips.) Why the difference in

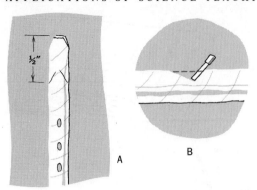

Figure 2-14 How to make a soda straw clarinet. (A), flatten the straw end and snip off two corners. (B), make a shallow V-cut with a safety razor. Holes should be about one inch apart, all in the top two-thirds of the straw.

pitch? Challenge children to make an eight-note scale with their bottles, varying the volume of water as in Figure 2-9.

After they have stablished a full scale by blowing, suggest *striking* the bottles sharply with a pencil. See if they can detect that **make inferences** the scale is reversed. Pupils will enjoy using the bottles both ways to play simple songs. Encourage them to compose scores to exchange with other groups. Can they guess the titles of familiar melodies?

2. *Materials:* for each child, several large paper soda straws, one small diameter straw (to fit easily into the larger straw); scissors; some cellophane tape.

Show how to make a soda-straw clarinet. Flatten about one-half inch of the end on a large straw and snip off the corners, as in Figure 2-14. (Don't make the finger holes now.) Put about one and one-half inches of the straw into your mouth. Keep lips closed but somewhat loose. Blow hard and then gradually slacken force. You will soon discover the right force to produce a sound. If there is some difficulty, it may help to bite down gently on the straw just below the flattened part. This will open up the "reed" slightly and let it vibrate more easily. Try blowing again in the same way.

Let the children experiment with chang-ing the pitch of their straws. This can be **select procedure** done in at least four ways:

a. Snip off parts of the straw from the bottom while blowing. The problem, of course, is that there is no instrument left after playing one scale!

b. Insert a smaller straw into the larger one, and slide it up and down like the slide of a trombone. A little cellophane tape around the inner straw end will insure a snug fit without interfering with the sliding action.

c. Cut several small, oval finger holes, about one inch apart in the top half of the straw. You might do this for the children, since it requires a safety razor. Simply make a shallow V-cut with the razor for each hole, as in Figure 2-14.

d. Extend the overall length of the straw clarinet by joining another straw of the same size to its end. To do this, pinch slightly the end of the second straw and insert about an eighth of an inch into the end of the straw clarinet. It probably will fall out unless a bit of cellophane tape is wrapped around the place where the straws are joined. The tone will be lowered dramatically. Try adding another straw in the same way. The right combination of joined straws and a good "reed" will produce a beautiful tone, somewhat like a low note of an oboe.

Contributing Idea C. Pitch changes with the rate of vibrations.

Materials: bicycle (upside down, resting on the handlebars and seat); small card.

In the preceding activities, *why* did the pitch change? See if pupils can give an explanation that includes the rate of vibrations. If not, suggest that they observe this demonstration to assist their thinking. They are to listen carefully for how sounds of a vibrating card change in the demonstration.

Hold a card against the rear wheel spokes of a bicycle, near the rim, while someone slowly turns the sprocket by cranking around a pedal arm. The cranking speed should be gradually increased, then decreased. As the wheel spins faster, the pitch of the vibrating card rises. As it slows, the pitch lowers.

Discuss what happened. Introduce *pitch* as the word for highness and lowness of sounds. Draw out that pitch seems to go up as the card vibrations go faster; that pitch **make** **inferences** goes down as vibrations go slower. Relate this idea to their other experiences.

EXTENDING ACTIVITIES

1. Invite the group to make chimes from five or six tinned cans of varying sizes. Punch holes in the bottoms, thread through and knot strings. Individually suspend each inverted can from a yardstick placed between the backs of two chairs. When struck with a spoon or stick, sounds of different pitch are emitted—the larger the can, the lower the pitch. Flower pots may be used in similar fashion.

2. Show how to make a pin "harp" from eight straight pins or finishing nails. With a hammer, tap the pins into the side of an open cheesebox or 8-inch block of soft wood. Gradually increase pin height from low at one end to high at the opposite end. By tapping gently here and there, it is possible to approximate a musical scale. To play the harp, pluck it sharply under the pinheads with another pin or small nail.

3. Let the children examine several wind and string instruments brought to school by pupils. Have the players of wind instruments demonstrate how they control pitch through closing or opening air valves and adjusting lip vibrations. Let the string players show how they tune and play their instruments.

4. Let everyone count to 10 by alternately saying a number aloud, then whispering the next. If fingers are held to throats, vocal cord vibrations will be noticed only when numbers are spoken aloud. Explain that we speak by using the air

cavities in our mouths and noses in addition to our vocal cords.

Have pupils whisper o-o-o-h, ah-h-h-h. Each will notice a slight change in pitch and quality caused by the changing air cavity in his mouth, although his vocal cords are unused.

Have each child pinch his nose a few times while speaking some words aloud. A distinct difference in voice quality will be noticed.

Forced and Sympathetic Vibrations. If you place a vibrating tuning fork handle against a table top, the sound suddenly gets louder. The vibrating fork forces the table top to vibrate with equal speed. This sets in motion many more air molecules than would the fork alone. Try putting a vibrating tuning fork against other objects. Almost any hard object can be forced to vibrate at the fork's natural frequency.

Similar results can be obtained if you hold a pocket comb against an object and vibrate the comb by running a finger over the teeth ends. Note the decrease in loudness when you vibrate the comb away from the object.

A peculiar example of forced vibrations can occur when a group of soldiers marches over a bridge. If there are enough persons marching in step, the entire structure can be forced to vibrate in time to the step. The bridge may weaken or collapse. For this reason, a standing military order is, "Break step when crossing a bridge."

Thomas Edison used his knowledge of forced vibrations when inventing the phonograph. He attached a sharp needle to a thin diaphragm which vibrated when sound waves struck it. The needle was placed against a cylinder wrapped with soft tin foil. As he spoke, he slowly cranked the cylinder around and around. The vibrating needle cut a series of impressions into the metal. To play back his sounds, he placed the needle in the impression first scratched and cranked the cylinder. As it followed the impressions, the needle was forced to vibrate, thus causing the diaphragm to vibrate. Edison could hear his recorded voice!

A similar basic principle of recording and playing back sound vibrations is followed today. But now electricity is used to assist in the initial cutting of a wax record and for playing back recorded vibrations. Sounds sung or spoken into a microphone are changed to spurts of electricity. The variable electric current causes an attached needle to vibrate as it cuts a wavy groove in a wax disk. Duplicate records are pressed from forms of the initial master disk. When playing a record, the moving wavy groove forces the needle to vibrate. This motion is changed into variable electrical impulses which vibrate the phonograph speaker, and recorded sound is heard.

Have you ever heard windows vibrate in their frames as a low-flying airplane passes overhead? Or noticed dishes faintly rattle occasionally as a loud radio is played? To see why this happens, consider two identical tuning forks. If one vibrates and is held near the other, it also begins to vibrate. But with two tuning forks of different pitches, only the struck one vibrates.

When forks are of identical pitch, sound waves arrive at the proper time to set the still fork in motion. Each additional air compression pushes a prong as it starts to bend in from a previous one. Each rarefaction arrives as the prong starts to bend back out. The steady, timed, push-pause-push-pause sets the fork vibrating, in almost the same way as you would push someone on a swing.

When forks are of different pitch, the timing is wrong for this to happen. For example, a prong may bend inward properly with a compression, but as it starts to bend back another air compression may strike it prematurely, and slow or stop it. The same thing would occur with a moving swing that is pushed while only part-way back on a downswing.

Every solid object has a natural frequency of vibration. If sound waves of that frequency push against an object, it may start vibrating sympathetically (or resonating). Remember that objects vibrate sympathetically only when they possess the same natural pitch as the initial sound maker. On the other hand, objects *forced* to vibrate always do so at the frequency of the vibrating object placed against them, regardless of their own natural frequency.

You may have learned that a very loud note sung or played into a thin glass can shatter it through violent sympathetic vibrations, provided such vibrations represent the natural pitch of the glass. However, it is not true that "seashore sounds" may be detected in shell souvenirs, unless someone is listening at the beach. What is heard are only sympathetic reflections of nearby sounds. The section closes with an experiment designed to test this misconception.

Generalization V: Sound waves can produce forced and sympathetic vibrations

Contributing Idea A. A vibrating object can force another object to vibrate.

1. *Materials:* open shoe box and rubber band; tuning fork; for each child, a small pocket comb.

Have pupils recall strumming rubber bands both on and off shoe boxes in a previous investigation. How did the loudness compare? If there is some uncertainty, let a child first strum a stretched rubber band held by someone else and, then, when the band is slipped around an open shoe box. Why is it louder now? Ask the children to try giving an explanation after the following activities.

Sharply strike a tuning fork against a rubber heel to get it vibrating. As the sound begins to die away, place the fork base against a desk top or table. The sound will suddenly get louder. Try the same procedure with as many objects as possible: door (a thin plywood door makes an excellent sounding board); window; up-turned drinking glass; various boxes; and so on.

Let pupils try a similar procedure with small pocket combs. They can make the comb vibrate by running a finger across the ends of the teeth. They should press one end of the comb firmly against the object in which vibrations will be forced and then vibrate the comb. For a comparison, they should also vibrate the comb *without* touching the object.

Help the children reason about what happened with the tuning fork and combs. When the vibrating tuning fork or comb was held against an object, it was forced to begin vibrating, too. Because the object was larger than the tuning fork or comb in each case, it set many more air molecules in motion than before. This made the sound louder.

develop
procedures
Ask groups to locate the *object* in the room on which the loudest noise is made with the comb. How do we know for sure? What variables will we need to control? (Comb, stroke, background noise, etc.) How will we agree on "loudest"?

2. *Materials:* record player; old 78 r.p.m. record; needle; three tagboard cards of different sizes, such as 2 by 2 inches, 3 by 3 inches, and 4 by 4 inches; small megaphone; magnifying lens.

Show how the sound of a vibrating needle can be magnified by forcing an increased surface area to vibrate.

Invite some children to examine a phonograph record with a magnifying lens. The grooves will appear wavy. Explain that record grooves are made by a sharp needle which has been forced to vibrate by electricity.

Now stick a needle into a corner of the smallest card and turn on the record player. Place the needle into a groove. A faint sound will be heard. Ask someone to explain what is happening. If no one can, provide this explanation: wavy grooves in the record are forcing the needle to vibrate. The needle is forcing the card to vibrate, and the vibrating card pushes air molecules into sound waves.

Hold up all three cards and ask which one would cause the most air molecules to begin moving in sound waves. Then ask which would cause the loudest sound. Try the remaining cards. The loudest sound, of course, will come from the largest card. Bring out that the children have heard *forced vibrations*—one object forcing another to vibrate at the same speed. suggest
hypotheses

Now stick the needle into the small, folded end of a megaphone. Point the open end toward your class and lower the needle into a groove. An even louder sound will be heard than with the cards. Link this to the children's previous experiences with megaphones.

You might close by saying, "Scientists have found they can make the best records if electricity is used to make vibration grooves in the records. Electricity is also used now to make sounds louder when we play records. But the ideas we have learned about forced vibrations are still needed."

Contributing Idea B. Sympathetic vibrations may occur when a vibrating object is in tune with another object.

1. *Materials:* piano. (An autoharp is a less satisfactory substitute.)

This activity reveals how piano strings may resonate to voices.

Try this bridge. "Have you ever noticed that dishes on shelves rattle slightly when the volume of a radio is turned up too loud? Have you ever heard windows vibrate when a large, noisy airplane flies low over your house? What causes this?" Anticipate some explanations based on forced vibrations. In this event, bring out that these vibrating sources of sound are *not* touching the dishes or window panes. You might then say, "Let's learn another way in which sound vibrations take place."

Take the class to a piano. If the instrument is in another classroom, do the following demonstration during a brief recess. Only several moments are needed.

Lift up the piano top—whether concert or upright. Have someone depress the "loud" pedal. This lifts felt dampers off the strings and permits them to vibrate longer. Sing a short, loud note into the strings. Several strings will begin vibrating. Let several children try singing short notes of different pitches. They should detect shortly that only those strings vibrate that are in tune (pitch) with their voices.

make inferences

2. *Materials:* three tuning forks (two identical, and one of different pitch).

Back in your room, encourage pupils to discuss what they found: only those strings that seem to be "in tune" with their voices made vibrations. Now strike the tuning forks one at a time and ask which two appear to be in tune. They will immediately pick the two identical forks.

Hold one of these in each hand. Strike a fork to get it vibrating and hold it an inch or less away from the other. After a few seconds, stop the vibrating fork and listen to the other. It should now emit a faint sound, indicating that it is vibrating. Let several children hear and verify what is taking place.

Now try this procedure with one of the tuning forks and a *dissimilar* one. This time there will be no sound from the second fork.

Invite pupils to express what they have found out. Then provide the following summary: "We learned before that we could *force* almost anything to vibrate by holding a vibrating object against it. We have now found that we can get some things to vibrate without touching them. But before this can happen, both objects must have the same natural pitch, or vibrating speed. Otherwise, the sound waves cannot push at the right time to get the second object moving." Mention and write on the chalkboard the term *sympathetic vibrations*. Tell the class this term is used to describe the vibrations just experienced.

3. *Materials:* three small soda bottles (two identical, and one of different size).

This and the next activity show how resonance can occur with air vibrations in identical bottles.

Remind everyone that air vibrates inside wind instruments. Have someone blow over the mouth of one of the identical soda bottles. It should emit a tone. Point out that this tone is the bottle's natural pitch. Try commenting as follows: "We have found that a string vibrates when in tune with a sound, and a tuning fork vibrates when in tune with another one. Will the same thing happen with a wind instrument, such as a bottle? In which of these two other bottles should air vibrations start when the first bottle is blown?"

Have one child sound short, forceful notes with one bottle while a second child stands close by and holds another bottle about a half-inch from his own ear. When identical bottles are used a clear sound should be heard in the second bottle as well as the first. If a dozen or more identical soda bottles (small ones work best) can be obtained, more children will be able to listen at one time. Emphasize that vibrations in the "listening" bottles are sympathetic vibrations. Sound waves in these bottles move up and down at the same speed as in the first bottle and so make the same sound.

Let someone blow a note with the dissimilar bottle. Its pitch will be different from that of the other bottles. Invite someone to try sounding a note of the same pitch with two different bottles. He will be unable to do so. Point out that the natural pitch of an object cannot be changed unless the object is changed. Review how pitch was changed in previous activities by adding water.

4. *Materials:* several or more identical, empty milk bottles.

Hold up a milk bottle. Challenge pupils to find its natural pitch by singing into it. This can be done by holding the open end of one bottle about one-half inch from an ear while singing directly into the other bottle. Let them discover the natural pitch by singing a musical scale. When the right note is sung a loud sound will be heard from the "listening" bottle.

After the *key note* or natural pitch is found, let several or more children (depending on how many milk bottles are available) stand close to the singer. Have them listen as he sings the key note and then a note of another pitch. The key note will dramatically appear in each listening bottle as it is sung into the first bottle. For variation, take away the first bottle. Have the key note sung. Each listening bottle will continue to emit its key note.

5. *Materials:* a large sea shell; several small glass jars or drinking glasses.

Here is an experiment children can do to test a common misconception about sea shells.

Tell your group some persons believe that "sounds of the sea"—such as waves splashing—may be heard in a sea shell. *suggest hypotheses* Raise conjecture about the possibility of this belief being true. Develop how the class might explain sounds heard from a sea shell through sympathetic vibrations. Draw out that possibly some sounds nearby or in the room might cause air in the shell to vibrate sympathetically.

Invite children to test if someone can detect special "sounds of the sea" in a sea shell, as contrasted with sounds from other *develop* hollow containers. Someone can be blind-*procedures* folded. Several glass containers and a shell might be held near his ear by someone else. The listener can then attempt to tell when he hears "sounds of the sea."

EXTENDING ACTIVITY

Encourage pupils to find the key notes of containers of many kinds. With cardboard boxes, the key notes cause the most vibrations. They may detect this by lightly touching the containers while humming a half-tone scale.

Hearing and Locating Sounds. The ear must be ranked among the body's most remarkable organs. In our hearing, sound waves are channeled into the ear canal by the outer ear, which acts as a megaphone in reverse. As sound waves collide with the eardrum, this thin membrane of stretched skin begins vibrating at the same frequency as the waves. Just inside the eardrum are three tiny, connected bones: the hammer, anvil, and stirrup. (See Figure 2-15). A vibrating eardrum starts the attached hammer shaking and this movement is transmitted through the connected bones to the cochlea, or inner ear. This snail-shaped apparatus is filled with a watery fluid and lined with sensitive nerve endings that trail off to the auditory nerve and brain. The transmitted vibrations pass through the fluid and excite the nerve endings. These excitations are converted into electrical impulses which reach the brain. The Eustachian tube is a narrow opening that leads from the back of the mouth to the middle ear. It equalizes air pressure on the eardrum.

Children should learn some reasonable rules for ear care and safety. A sharp object jabbed into the ear may cause a punctured eardrum. This greatly impairs or prevents eardrum vibrations, and results in hearing loss in the affected ear. They should beware of a sharp blow against the outer ear. This compresses air within the ear canal, and may cause a ruptured eardrum. Blowing the nose forces air up through the

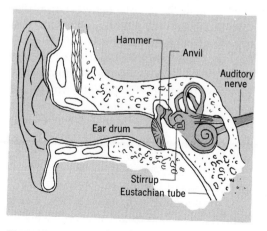

Figure 2-15

205

Eustachian tube. If a person is suffering from a cold, excessively hard blowing may force germs up the tube and infect the middle ear.

Elementary-school pupils find it interesting to learn how animals without visible outer ears detect sounds. Frogs, toads, and turtles have clearly noticeable eardrums of tough skin located slightly below and back of the eyes. Crickets and katydids hear through a tiny eardrum located on each foreleg, just below the "knee" joint. Look for an oval spot of slightly different color. Grasshoppers also have visible eardrums. These are located on each side of the abdomen's first section. Lift up the insect's wings and look for a disklike membrane just above where the rear legs are attached. Fishes hear with auditory capsules located deep within the head. In addition, many fishes have a lateral line of sensory scales which extend from head to tail. These are particularly sensitive to sounds of low pitch. Earthworms and snakes feel ground vibrations through the underneath portions of their bodies.

Although our ears are sensitive to a wide range of pitches, there are limits to what we can hear. Virtually no one can detect a sound that vibrates less than about 16 times per second, or more than 20,000 times per second. As we grow older, this range is gradually narrowed.

Hearing ranges in animals often exceed those of man. A bat may detect sounds that vary between 10 vibrations to 100,000 vibrations per second. A dog's hearing begins at only several vibrations and goes to 40,000 vibrations per second. This is why it is possible to use a "silent" whistle for calling a dog. The sound is simply too high for humans to hear. A cat can detect sounds up to 50,000 cycles. Sounds inaudible to man are called *infrasonic* when they vibrate too slowly, and *ultrasonic* when vibrations are too fast.

A forthcoming activity requires a dog trained to respond to an ultrasonic whistle. If no one has a trained dog, it is easy as a rule to train one in a short while. Children are delighted to participate in this process. At meal times, the dog is called by voice, and the whistle blown immediately afterward. Several times a day, between meals, the child may repeat this procedure and reward the dog with a pat, or give it a tasty tidbit. After several days, only the whistle is sounded on every other occasion. After four days or so, the dog should react to the whistle alone.

Ultrasonic sound is presently employed in many ways. Surgical instruments immersed in a container of liquid are thoroughly cleansed and sterilized when ultrasound is passed through. Milk and paint are homogenized, and clothes in experimental washers made flawlessly clean. Delicate surgery in some instances may be performed with ultrasound focused on diseased tissue without cutting into skin or bone. In industry, metal castings are examined for invisible flaws through ultrasonic echoes recorded on a machine. These are but a few examples. Ultrasonic sounds seem certain to play a vital part in everyone's future.

Generalization VI: Some sound waves can be heard by man, but many cannot be heard

Contributing Idea A. We hear only those sounds that cause our eardrums to vibrate.

1. *Materials:* Borrow from the school nurse a large chart which shows a cross section of the ear. (Or project Figure 2-15 with an opaque projector.)

With chart or projected drawing, explain how the ears work. Air molecules of a sound wave enter the ear and push against the eardrum, which vibrates. These vibrations are passed on to three small, connected bones—the hammer, anvil, and stirrup. The stirrup causes tiny nerve endings in the inner ear (cochlea) to vibrate. These little nerves start tiny electric currents which flow up to the brain through a large, connected nerve. The brain tells us about the sound.

2. *Materials:* thin, wooden ruler or stick; "silent" dog whistle (This may be purchased at pet shops, or obtained from dog owners in the class.); a dog (If this demonstration and the following experiment are done immediately in the morning, perhaps a parent can bring the family pet to school and take it home.)

Use this activity to reveal the superior hearing range of a dog.

Wave the ruler slowly up and down from the wrist. Ask the children what sound they hear. Express mock surprise when they say they are unable to hear the vibrations. Ask them to explain why. Help them understand that the air molecules were not pushed rapidly enough to vibrate their eardrums.

Hold down a ruler on the edge of a desk with most of its length sticking out over the edge. Press down the projecting part with your free hand and quickly let go. A low sound will be emitted. Shorten the length of the projecting ruler and again start it vibrating. Continue shortening the length and vibrating the projecting part.

Draw out facts from the children's observations: with very slow vibrations they heard nothing at all. Gradually, as the speed of vibrations increased, so did the pitch. Briefly review their previous experiences with pitch to confirm this. Now tell them that some sounds are pitched so high our eardrums cannot vibrate fast enough to send the sound into the middle ear.

Produce a dog whistle and blow it. No one will hear a sound. If a dog is available, ask the children to observe the dog's ears each time the whistle is blown. They will **make inferences** stiffen slightly in reaction to the "silent" sound. If a dog is not available, perhaps a child can try this demonstration at home and report what happened to the class.

3. *Materials:* trained dog; silent dog whistle; playground or other appropriate location.

An interesting experiment can be designed by the class if someone has a dog that has been trained to respond to a silent whistle. Have pupils set up an experiment to test if a dog responds to a silent whistle **develop procedures** blown by its owner. Bring out that a dog usually has a keen sense of smell and fairly good eyesight. A good design might involve a location where the wind is blowing at the dog's back. This will prevent it from using scents to find its owner. Perhaps the owner might be stationed just around a corner of a nearby building, so that he is out-of-sight. When he blows the whistle, his dog can be released. It should run immediately to the whistle source. This experiment can be tried again with the whistle blown by someone else after it is sterilized with some alcohol and rinsed with water.

Invite the dog's owner to tell his classmates how he trained it to respond to a silent whistle.

Contributing Idea B. Two ears are better than one ear for locating sources of sound.

Materials: eight pencils.

"If you lost your hearing in one ear, would it really make any difference?" Guide the children to speculate if a hearing loss in one ear would make a difference first in loudness, then in being able to detect the location of sounds.

It will be easy for the class to think of a test for loudness. For example, someone might read aloud in front of the class while **develop procedures** the children cover and uncover one ear. They will notice some loss. Point out that often persons learn to use the "good" ear more effectively than before the hearing loss, although it cannot fully make up for the loss.

Now ask your pupils to design a test for **develop procedures** the second problem: Can sounds be located as well with one ear as with two? Divide the class into small groups to design a testing procedure. A child might be placed in the center of the room, with other children in each corner. The center child should keep his eyes closed while he listens for sound locations with both ears. The corner children, in any order, may individually tap two pencils together. The listener should try to indicate the direction from which the sound came immediately after hearing it.

This procedure can be tried again, but now with the listener's hand held tightly over an ear. He should have great difficulty locating sound sources.

See if the children can explain why it is more difficult to detect sound sources the second time. You may need to tell them that the explanation involves two facts learned before: sound takes time to travel; and loudness of a sound decreases with distance.

Develop that with normal hearing one ear hears sound slightly before the other, if the head is at an angle. Also, one ear possibly hears a slightly louder sound than the other. The brain is then able to tell from which direction the sound comes. With one ear, there is no comparison of either speed or loudness. Thus locations are harder to judge.

in various directions while a sound is made (two pencils clicking together, shuffling feet, bell ringing, etc.). Ask the listener to describe where the sound is coming from. The children will discover that it is possible to completely reverse the listener's orientation. For example, in Figure 2-16, the child will identify a sound coming from his *right* side as coming from his *left* side.

2. Ask the school nurse to give an illustrated talk on ear care.

3. Have an able pupil report an interview with a local dentist or physician on how ultrasonic devices clean surgical instruments.

4. Let the children bring in a grasshopper, cricket, katydid, frog, toad, and turtle. Have them search for the external eardrums on these animals. Several hand lenses will be useful for this purpose. (See the preceding background information for details.)

EXTENDING ACTIVITIES

1. Here is an interesting variation you can use to follow up the last activity. Get two 24-inch narrow, flexible tubes and attach a funnel to one end of each. Let a volunteer "listener" close his eyes and hold the tubes' opposite ends tightly to his ears. Have another person point the funnels

Figure 2-16

Light Energy

(Upper Emphasis)

UNIT 3

UNIT THREE

Light Energy

(Upper Emphasis)

WHY DOES SOMETHING LOOK LARGER UNDER A MAGNIFYING GLASS? What makes a rainbow? Why do some people wear eyeglasses? Children want to know many things about the behavior of light. The broad range of ideas and activities developed in this unit will help pupils become aware of the very significant part light energy plays in their lives.

Several activities in this unit are best done in a darkened room. If the regular classroom cannot be darkened, perhaps an auditorium or substitute facility can be made available on these occasions.

GENERALIZATIONS

I. Light usually travels in straight lines; its reflections are affected by the texture of the reflecting surface and slant at which light strikes the surface.

II. Absorbed light energy changes into heat energy and chemical energy.

III. Slanted light rays are refracted when they pass from one medium to another of different density.

IV. White light is composed of different colors; the color of objects depends on which colors are transmitted, absorbed, and reflected.

Credit for chapter opening photograph. **Fred Lyon-Rapho Guillumette**

V. The eye is a complicated organ that operates with the brain.

The Pathways of Light. Imagine reaching for something that is visible in front of you and not finding it there. Or shining a flashlight in the darkness and having it illuminate only something in *back* of you. This, of course, is not likely to happen, since light travels in straight lines. It's true that a beam of light can "bend" under certain conditions, such as when going from air into water, glass, or the reverse. (We shall go into this more deeply in the next section.) And scientists now know that light passing through space is attracted and curved by the gravitational fields of massive objects in space. But with these exceptions light does appear to travel in straight lines. This property makes many interesting things take place.

For example, look at the pinhole "camera" in Figure 3-1. Light from the candle flame shines through a narrow pinhole in the cereal box end. At the other end, an *inverted* image appears on wax paper taped over the opening. Why? The numerals suggest an answer. If light travels in straight lines, the light going from spot 1 on the left can only go to spot 1 on the right, and so on.

There are several ways in which we can alter the pathways of light; some are sur-prising. For instance, why does a lady powder her nose? Psychological reasons aside, she does it to scatter light reflections. You know that a ball thrown straight down on smooth, level pavement bounces back up. Try it on rough gravel, however, and its return path is unpredictable. A smooth, shiny surface reflects light rays with very little scattering. However, a rough or uneven surface may scatter the rays so thoroughly that reflections may be scarcely visible. What makes makeup powder so effective? Put some under a microscope. Greatly magnified, it resembles gravel!

Of course, even better reflections are possible with mirrors than noses. Sprinkle some powder or chalk dust over half of a mirror; leave the remainder clear. Shine a flashlight on both sections of the mirror. Does the powder help to reduce glare? Scattered light rays are called *diffused* reflections. Light rays which are not scattered are *regular* reflections.

When you deal with flat or *plane* reflectors, a special kind of regular reflection becomes possible. If you stand by a mirror and can see the face of another person, that person can also see you. No matter from what position or angle you try it, the same results occur, provided both of you are close enough to the mirror to see a reflection. The angle at which light strikes a

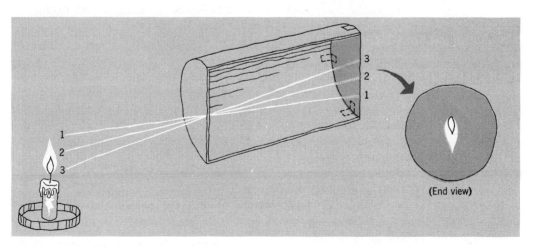

(End view)

Figure 3-1

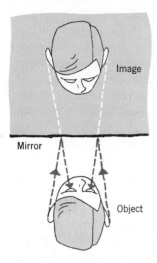

Figure 3-2 Why a mirror image is reversed.

plane reflector (called the angle of incidence) always equals the angle at which it is reflected. In activities designed to help them understand this idea, children can make several measurements to discover this equality of angles.

No attempt is made in this unit to develop an understanding of curved mirrors. The optical explanations of convex and concave mirrors are beyond most elementary school pupils. However, they can note that convex mirrors—those with a bulging center—reduce a wide field to a small area. This is why they are used for rear view mirrors on some automobiles, for example. Concave mirrors—those with a scooped-out center—magnify images. Thus they are useful for such purposes as cosmetic work or shaving.

If we could not look at our photographs, or double reflections in two mirrors, we would never know how we appear to others. A mirror always produces a reversed image of the observer.

To learn why this is so, study Figure 3-2. In a sense, a mirror image is an optical illusion. Light rays reflect off the mirror into the boy's eyes. He stares outward along the lines of the incoming rays. To him, his image appears to be just as far in back of the glass as he is in front of it. An interest-

ing demonstration in this section will help pupils verify this fact about mirrors for themselves.

It is customary to think of clear glass as completely transparent to light. Yet a small amount does reflect off the surface. Ordinarily, we do not see the reflected light, because it is only a fraction of the rest that passes through. But at night, when there is darkness in back of the glass, even dim light striking the surface results in noticeable reflections.

Symmetry. Work with mirrors will enable you to introduce the concept of symmetry to pupils—the idea of balanced proportions in objects and geometric forms. The concept is of value in many fields, including biology, mathematics, and the arts. A butterfly, for example, has symmetry. If you draw an imaginary line down the middle of its body, the left half is a near-duplicate of its right half. A starfish has another kind of symmetry. If you turn its body around on an imaginary axis, a rotational balance is evident.

An investigation in this section takes up the presence or absence of mirror symmetry in letters of the alphabet. Children will be surprised at the ways a mirror can reveal balanced proportions. They can learn to predict which letter shapes will reveal the property of symmetry. Notice in Figure 3-3 that each of these letters is symmetrical. The left and right sides of A are opposite but alike. The remaining letters are different

Figure 3-3 Symmetry in letters of the alphabet. Dotted lines show how to hold a mirror to reconstruct the original letters.

in that the symmetry is vertical; that is, found in the tops and bottoms, but not laterally. A few letters — X, O, I, H — have both lateral and vertical balance. Some, such as L, F, and J, have none at all.

Mirrors have always held a fascination for man. In prescientific times, many superstitions were developed to explain what seemed to be a magical image. Even today, many persons cling to the belief that breaking a mirror brings "bad luck." We close this section with an experiment which children can use to test this notion.

Generalization I: Light usually travels in straight lines; its reflections are affected by the texture of the reflecting surface and slant at which it strikes the surface

Contributing Idea A. Light usually travels in straight lines.

Materials: chalkboard sketch of pinhole camera, as in Figure 3-1 (leave off for now the numerals, broken lines, and inverted image); candle on dish; match; pinhole "camera." (To make this, cut about a square inch out of the bottom of a cylindrical cereal container. Tape a small piece of aluminum foil over this opening. With a large pin or narrow nail, make a sharp hole in the foil. A hole in foil gives a sharper image than one in the box end itself. Remove the top from the box and tape waxed paper or thin tissue paper over this opening.)

Lead into an examination of the pinhole camera by first asking about the pathways of light. For example, you might ask someone to draw with chalk and yardstick a picture of a beam of light shining from a spotlight to some object. Why is the beam straight? If the beam were made increasingly narrow, would it still be straight? Most of the class will agree.

Show the pinhole camera sketch. If light does travel in straight lines, then what should a candle image look like if it goes through the tiny pinhole? Let pupils discuss this problem in small groups.

Darken the room and place the pinhole camera about 12 inches in front of a candle flame. The waxed paper end should face the class so that the image is observable. Make sure the hole is in line with the flame. A book can prop up the container. Move the camera back and forth a bit until a sharp, inverted image appears on the paper.

Were the groups' predictions successful? Challenge the groups to explain why the candle image is inverted. If clues are needed, first put numerals in the sketch, as in Figure 3-1, then a single light ray. Pupils should be able to fill in correctly the rest of the sketch. Bring out the reason an inverted image appears: if light travels in straight lines, each part of the light going through the narrow pinhole would reach a diagonally opposite location.

make
inferences

Contributing Idea B. When light travels to a smooth, flat reflector at a slant, it is reflected at the same slant in a new direction.

1. *Materials:* powerful, narrow-beam flashlight; mirror about 4 by 6 inches; masking tape; yardstick; 12-inch ruler.

Set up this activity as in Figure 3-4. Select seven pupils of about the same height. Tape a mirror to a wall at the face height of these pupils. Put a ruler or stick marker on the floor about 10 feet away from the mirror, pointing toward the mirror's center. It will be used as a place from which side distances will be measured. Have six pupils stand close together on one side of the ruler and one pupil with a flashlight on the other side. At your signal the child with the flashlight should hold it to

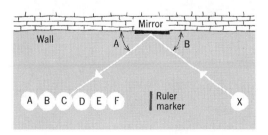

Figure 3-4

215

his eye, sight along the cylinder toward the mirror, and switch on the light.

Invite someone to pose the problem: Which child's face, if any, will the beam shine on? Encourage conjecture, then darken the room and proceed with the trial. What will happen if the flashlight holder moves one pace to the right? Left? Can the yardstick help to make the predictions more accurate? If they use the yardstick to measure, children will find that the side distance is the same from the flashlight to the marker, and from the marker to a standing child receiving the reflected light. They may also find that each time the flashlight child looks at the mirror he can see his reflected "target." (In Figure 3-4, this is child C.) What's more, the target child can see in the mirror the flashlight child, assuming the room is not totally dark. If none of the six children's faces is visible in the mirror to the child holding the flashlight, the reflected beam will probably pass *between* two faces, or outside of the end children, as the case may be. In discussion, a few pupils may observe that angles *A* and *B* (Figure 3-4) are always equal.

reason quantitatively

2. *Materials:* four or five small mirrors; powerful flashlight or filmstrip projector.

Suggest a multiple-mirror light relay, in which a light beam is reflected from two or more mirrors to hit a pre-selected target. You might start with a two-mirror example, then a three-mirror one, as in Figure 3-5, and go on to more mirrors. (After about five mirrors, the reflected light is dim. This

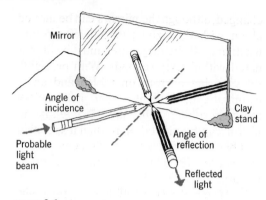

Figure 3-6

may help teach that the light spreads out more with distance and that mirrors *absorb* light besides reflecting it.)

For a target area, tape a piece of paper to a wall. After a period of fumbling the relay children will learn how they must hold their mirrors in relation to their partners' mirrors. Like most open-ended activities, this one offers a host of conditions and examples that may be varied: different light sources, sizes and numbers of mirrors used, various locations of target areas, and degree of precision required.

Some classes will be able to plan precision relays by using mirrors on desk tops, and by making careful estimations of light-beam angles. Here, a simple tool will be needed. In Figure 3-6, two pencils assist in predicting the light beam's probable reflected path. A child with another mirror can align his "incoming light-beam" pencil in the same direction as the reflected light-beam pencil used in the first mirror. He then adjusts his second pencil to make a straight line, as shown.

reason quantitati

After they are reasonably familiar with using mirrors to reflect light, the children will enjoy setting up relay teams. They can compete in illuminating different (but equivalent) target areas chosen by lot. A few rules should be set up. For example, with hand-held mirrors these may be specified by the class: (1) positions of mirror holders are set before the flashlight is turned on; (2) after the flashlight is on, no position can be

develop procedure

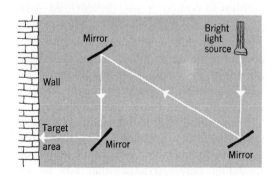

Figure 3-5 A three-mirror light relay.

216

changed, although the mirrors can be moved about with the hands; (3) all mirrors are used; and (4) the target area must be illuminated within sixty seconds. With precision relays using mirrors on tables and angle estimating instruments (such as pencils), the main rule probably should state that no mirror can be moved more than a specified number of inches after it has been placed in position. The team that comes closest to its target wins.

3. *Materials:* stack of books; two mirrors; empty wastebasket; ball; table. Set up these or substitute materials as in Figure 3-7, except for the mirrors.

See if the class can apply its knowledge about reflected light using a vertical dimension, as in a periscope. You might remark, "We know light travels in straight lines and is reflected from a mirror at the same slant it strikes the mirror. Let's say someone's eyes are near level with this table top and he has two mirrors. How could he see over the pile of books to tell what is on the upturned wastebasket?"

suggest
ypotheses

If clues are necessary, gradually lead the class to understand that one mirror will be held above the books, while the lower one is left on the table. Encourage pupils to draw various angles of the mirrors on the chalkboard. When several drawings appear valid to the pupils, let them try the activity.

Are they aware of the mirrors' similarity

Figure 3-7

of slant? This is just another example of the reflection principle they have learned.

make
inferences

Some children will realize they have made a *periscope,* even though there is no tube into which the mirrors are fitted. Bring out that periscopes are useful to see over crowds at a parade, or to see around corners at play. (Should some pupils wish to make their own periscopes, see extending activity 1 of this section.)

Contributing Idea C. A flat mirror produces a reversed image which appears to be the same size and distance away from the mirror as the reflected object.

1. *Materials:* large mirror (at least 8 by 6 inches); chalkboard sketch or projection of Figure 3-2 (withhold showing until needed).

To show how mirror reversals occur, position a child before a mirror in front of the room. His back should be to the class and his reflected face visible to all. Try tilting the mirror slightly and holding it just above his eye level to make good visibility possible for the class.

With mock seriousness, extract a solemn pledge from the volunteer that he will obey your instructions to the letter. Ask him to close his *left* eye. His mirror image will close its *right* eye. Instruct him to close his left eye. The image's opposite eye will close. Why is this happening?

Reveal the sketch of Figure 3-2. Can someone explain why reversals occur? (Light rays bounce off the mirror and are reflected into the boy's eyes. His eyes stare outward along the lines of the incoming light rays. To him, it appears as though his image is beyond the mirror's surface.)

Bring out that the image distance and size appear to be identical to the original. But are they? There is a demonstration which will help them to decide if mirror images accurately reflect these two factors.

2. *Materials:* two identical small candles; small piece of transparent glass (a microscope slide may do); two small lumps of modeling clay. Arrange materials as in Figure 3-8, and darken the room a little.

Figure 3-8

Position a child in back of the lit candle. Have him direct another child to move the unlit candle until its image appears to be burning at the wick. Let the class note the identical distance of the two candles from the improvised mirror. Only one candle image seems to appear in the glass mirror. An image always appears to be the same distance and size as the reflected object.

Draw out pupil experiences where window glass or water reflected images. Develop that this occurs when it is dark behind or below the normally transparent surface. While much light passes through, some is reflected back to the observer. You might place a strip of black and white paper under a piece of flat glass to illustrate the point. Only the black background makes the glass a visible image reflector.

3. *Materials:* for each child, a sheet of lined paper; pencil; small mirror. (Refer to Figures 3-3 and 3-9 for specific reference to letters and words mentioned in the following procedures.)

Acquaint the children with problems involving mirror symmetry. Draw the right half of a capital A on the chalkboard, but don't identify the letter. Ask the children to do the same on their papers. What is it? Can a mirror held the right way complete the figure? Follow the same procedure with B, C, D, and E. Acquaint them with the terms *lateral symmetry* (for side to side balance) and *vertical symmetry* (for top and bottom balance). Ask the children to classify all the capital letters of the alphabet according to those with (1) lateral symmetry, (2) vertical symmetry, (3) both kinds of symmetry, (4) no symmetry. You might circulate around the room to help some children as needed. After a while, have a discussion to compare results and test disagreements with mirrors.

Follow a similar procedure with words, such as those in Figure 3-9. Can the chil-

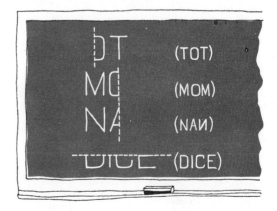

Figure 3-9 Symmetry in words. (Notice the exception in the third word down.)

make inferences

dren think of other examples? Only a few are possible with perfect lateral symmetry, since the first and last letters must be the same. However, many are possible with vertical symmetry. Each word can be tested with a mirror.

After a practice session, draw up teams to compose words. Each team must list its words on the chalkboard *before* using a mirror. Any word will be tested if challenged by other teams. The team with the largest number of symmetrical words (including unchallenged words) wins. If thoughtless or capricious challenges become a problem, suggest a one-word penalty for every unsuccessful challenge. This probably will bring about frequent, intense discussions within a group before a challenge is decided upon.

suggest hypotheses

Contributing Idea D. Rough, dull surfaces provide diffused reflections; smooth, shiny surfaces provide regular reflections.

Materials: filmstrip projector or flashlight; mirror; aluminum foil (both the shiny and dull sides will be used); one sheet each of black and white paper; book; sticky tape.

Have the children recall experiences when lighting conditions appeared too bright, glary, and hard on the eyes. Possibly they will mention reading a book with glossy paper under a bright light, or walking on a white, sandy beach, or in the snow on a sunny day. Briefly discuss conditions present in these experiences. Bring out that light *reflections* are responsible for the glare.

Write on the chalkboard the following words and numerals: (1) white paper, (2) mirror, (3) shiny, crinkled foil, (4) dull, crinkled foil, (5) shiny, smooth foil, (6) black paper. Tape under each word an equal-sized sample of the appropriate material. Comment that each of these materials will reflect some light, but some more than others. Invite the children to renumber the materials listed in order of their probable ability to reflect light. Accuracy of this

suggest hypotheses

order can be tested with the materials provided.

With the room darkened, each material can be placed against a book and held vertically toward the class, while light is beamed on it from the projector. Reflections will be more obvious if the book is turned from side to side as light shines on the material.

If you have several flashlights and enough materials, it will be worthwhile to use small groups in this activity. Each group can record its own data, then compare results with other groups for verification. Differences can be worked out through retesting.

Careful test results will show this order of decreasing brightness in reflections: (1) mirror, (2) shiny, smooth foil, (3) shiny, crinkled foil, (4) dull, crinkled foil, (5) white paper, (6) black paper.

Help the children think through why there was a difference in glare. The smooth, shiny objects gave *regular reflections*. Most of the light was reflected right back to their eyes. Rough, dull objects gave *diffused* or *scattered reflections*. Although some light was reflected back to their eyes, most of it bounced off the rough surfaces in many different directions.

Remind them of their common experiences in bouncing a ball. When a ball is dropped straight down, on a smooth, level sidewalk, it bounces back straight up. But if tried on very rough ground, it bounces in any direction. Develop that light acts in a similar way.

EXTENDING ACTIVITIES

1. Constructing a periscope is instructive and interesting. Needed are a long narrow container, two mirrors, a razor, and cellophane tape. Since the mirrors are taped inside the container, select a container with a flap, as found on a waxed-paper or kitchen-foil carton. Construct as in Figure 3-10. Finish by wrapping several rubber bands around the box to prevent it from opening.

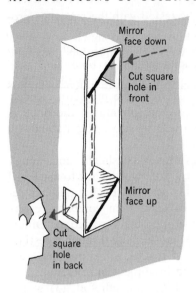

Figure 3-10 A periscope.

reason quantitatively
2. Challenge able pupils who can work with protractors to make up reflection experiments with a flashlight and mirrors positioned at various angles. They will soon discover complementary angles and some other geometric understandings. Ideas can first be worked out on paper and then tested.

3. Many preadolescents believe the superstition, "Breaking a mirror brings bad luck." An experiment may help dispel this belief. Several or more children can bring small, inexpensive mirrors from home. The experiment can be designed in two ways. The "luck" experienced by several mirror breakers can be compared with that of a matched group for, say, three weeks. Or the mirror breakers' luck alone can be noted *develop procedures* for a given period before and after they break their mirrors. In either case, get pupils to set up the procedure, method for recording data, and ground rules. What, for *state problems* example, will be "bad luck?" An operational definition is needed. This experiment can be thought provoking and instructive in scientific procedures if some effort is put into it.

From Light to Heat and Chemical Energy. An air traveler who goes from a cold to a tropical climate in a matter of hours can scarcely fail to notice many differences in his new surroundings. Among the most impressive are house colors—largely light pastels and dazzling white. Similar differences can be noted in clothing colors. Although most adults know the basic reason —dark-colored materials absorb more sunlight than light-colored materials—the practical consequences of this fact are most impressive in a tropical climate.

Figure 3-11 reveals why persons in tropical countries find a greater need for lighter colors than those who live farther away from the equator. Light is most intense when it is received from directly overhead. If the same amount of light is spread out over a larger area, any part of that area receives less light.

The transformation of light energy to heat energy is most noticeable when there is an effective way of preventing the heat from escaping. A common example is the temperature rise within a tightly closed automobile parked in sunlight. The rapidly vibrating short waves of sunlight can pass through the windows. When they strike the upholstery they are absorbed, then reradiated as longer, slower-vibrating heat waves. The longer waves are largely unable to penetrate glass, however, so most of the heat stays inside, building up in intensity as sunlight continues to stream in. Since the same thing occurs in greenhouses, this

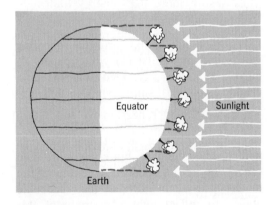

Figure 3-11

phenomenon is aptly called the *greenhouse effect*.

Our atmosphere also is warmed largely by reradiated heat waves. The atmosphere is like a giant glass cover that traps the longer, reradiated heat waves. However, this analogy is not perfect. Fortunately for us, the atmosphere is far less efficient than glass. A substantial amount of reradiated heat escapes into space. Were this not so, the earth's air temperature would become intolerable to life.

Because of the greenhouse effect, air temperatures get warmest in the afternoon, rather than at mid-day. Although the sun is most nearly overhead at noon, the buildup of heat continues for several hours afterward.

This section ends with a brief study of *photochemical* reactions—the transformation of light energy to chemical energy when light is absorbed. Materials that react photochemically do not just change in physical appearance. A permanent change occurs in molecular structure. Although this can be annoying when a favorite sweater fades, the phenomenon makes possible many important events, from photography to photosynthesis.

Generalization II: Absorbed light energy changes into heat energy and chemical energy

Contributing Idea A. Dark-colored materials absorb more light energy than light-colored materials.

1. *Materials:* two different-sized sheets of construction paper, one white and one black; scissors; two thermometers; sunshine.

You might say, "When we did our experiments with light reflection we found light reflected least of all from black paper. Actually, with the right kind of black paper, there is practically no reflection at all. If so, where does the light energy go? What happens to it?"

suggest hypotheses

Provide clues as needed: "What colors

seem more popular in summer than winter? Why is white worn so much in tropical countries? Why are light colors preferred for houses in the tropics?"

A reasonable guess is that light energy is changed to heat energy in materials of dark color. Pursue a hypothesis about the white paper. The children should reason that not as much heat energy would be produced because white paper largely reflects light. Press for a test of this thinking. If necessary, inquire as to how the materials might be used.

develop procedures

An easy test is to place the black and white sheets over two thermometers in a sunny area. Leaving the upper-third of each thermometer sticking out at the top will provide advance notice of a temperature rise sufficient to break the thermometers. Someone should check temperatures every several minutes. Be prepared to bring out such needed controls as equal size of paper, recording identical thermometer temperatures before the test, and equal exposure time. When test results are in, guide toward a tentative conclusion: black paper seems to *absorb* light energy more efficiently than white paper. Therefore, it becomes warmer.

make inferences

2. If thermometers are unavailable, a similar test can be made with two small cans of water. Encircle one in black paper, the other in white. Place in strong sunlight for at least an hour. Pretest and post-test temperatures can be taken by dipping a finger into the water. This is less accurate, of course, but the difference should be noticeable. Children can also do this experiment at home and report their findings.

Contributing Idea B. Vertical light rays striking a surface produce more heat energy than slanted rays.

1. *Materials:* two sheets black construction paper; two thermometers; stapler; sunshine.

Have pupils recall how warm it feels when sunlight shines on them. Develop that sometimes the sun's rays feel warmer than at other times. Establish the time of day when this occurs. The sun usually feels warmer in the early afternoon, as contrasted with morning or late afternoon sunlight. Ask for a reason. If clues are needed, let the class recall when shadows are longest. When light slant is suggested, invite the children to set up an experiment. If needed, suggest use of the stated materials.

develop procedures

A pocket can be made for each thermometer by folding over the black paper once and stapling it at the bottom and side. Again it will be useful to leave the tops of each thermometer sticking out to receive advance warning of possible breakage. Both thermometers should be placed with tops pointing away from the sun. One thermometer should be level and the other propped up to receive vertical light. (Figure 3-12.) Again pretest temperatures must be identical.

Guide pupils in finding the correct angle for propping. A pencil can be placed upright on the covered thermometer. When there is no shadow, the light will be perfectly vertical. Prop up the thermometer with books or other handy material.

make inferences

One pupil should check temperatures every several minutes. When the temperature difference is obvious, discuss findings and conclusions.

2. *Materials:* filmstrip projector or flashlight (narrow-beam type); 6-foot string; chalk; chalkboard; piece of cellophane tape.

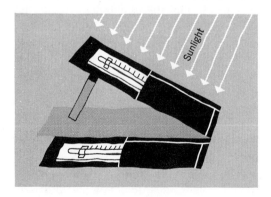

Figure 3-12

Inquire as to *why* vertical light results in more heat absorption than slanted light. If no satisfactory answer is given, ask your group to explain the following demonstration.

Fasten one end of the string to the projector; stick the other end to a spot on the chalkboard. Darken the room. Shine the light on the chalkboard. Let someone carefully draw a line around the light received. Now move the projector several steps to one side, and shine the light at a slant of 45 degrees or more on the same spot. (The string will insure a similar distance.) A line should be drawn around the second area of illumination.

make inferences

Draw out the idea behind this demonstration. An equal amount of light is distributed over a larger area the second time. This is like spreading out jam or butter over more bread; it has to be thinner. Each part of the larger area received less light. Therefore, there is less heat in each part.

Elicit why the string was used. Show that light can also be spread out by increasing distance between the chalkboard and flashlight. Shine the light from a point close to the chalkboard and have someone trace a line around it. Gradually move the light source back farther and farther. As the illuminated area increases, the intensity of light will decrease.

Contributing Idea C. Light energy passes through glass, while heat energy is largely blocked by glass.

Materials: Mason jar with lid (a milk bottle may be substituted. Use Saran-Wrap and a rubber band for the lid); piece of dark-colored cloth; two thermometers; scissors; sunshine.

Do an experiment on the greenhouse effect. Try this sequence of questions to develop need for the experiment:

"Have you ever opened the door of a car that has been tightly shut and standing in the sun for a long time? What did it feel like inside?" (The air and upholstery were hot.)

suggest
hypotheses

"Where did the heat come from?" (The sunlight entered the closed windows and was changed into heat when absorbed by the upholstery.)

"Why didn't the heat go out through the closed windows?"

develop
procedures

"How can we do an experiment to find out if heat energy is blocked by glass?"

If necessary, exhibit the materials. A well-designed experiment might have the Mason jar or bottle in a horizontal position. A swatch of dark cloth placed inside will simulate upholstery. One thermometer can be placed inside, on the cloth. The other thermometer can be laid on an identical piece of cloth placed outside and next to the closed jar. When placed in sunshine for several minutes, the inside thermometer should show a noticeable rise over the outside one. (To avoid breaking the inside thermometer on a hot day, have it watched continuously.)

Contributing Idea D. Light energy may bring about chemical changes.

Materials: construction paper sheets of six different colors, and several white sheets; scissors; bulletin board space or window space for mounting the paper.

For an interesting bridge to this experiment on how light fades colored materials, look for some common examples: faded dark paper on a bulletin board with darker outlines of letters; cloth garments with noticeable differences between inside or lined portions and outside parts; shelved books with faded cloth covers, especially on the part exposed to light; and so on. Examples are found in abundance with a little searching.

suggest
hypotheses

Show pupils your examples. Ask them to name conditions which may have caused these materials to fade. Focus on the light factor. Get them to hypothesize about the relation of color type to rapidity of fading. Show the construction paper. Will some colors fade more rapidly than other colors? Children can record the probable order of fading, and then test it.

develop
procedures

There should be little difficulty in setting up the design. Small, white squares can be pinned or taped to each colored sheet. The sheets can be placed on a bulletin board facing the windows. A week's exposure to light should produce some changes. But portions under the white squares will remain unfaded. For quicker results, tape the colored papers to windows, instead of a bulletin board.

make
inferences

Guard against sweeping conclusions from this experiment. Although darker colors often tend to fade more rapidly than bright colors, the color "fastness" and composition of materials vary so widely no reliable single generalization can be drawn.

EXTENDING ACTIVITIES

1. Visit a nearby greenhouse. Let children learn how light, shade, and temperature are controlled throughout the year.

2. Encourage children to look for examples of fading through light. Discuss each example to determine if other factors may have been responsible. Let them look for controls. For example, blue jeans will fade with repeated washings. Looking at the cloth inside a back pocket will help reveal how washing alone faded the cloth. A sample is valid only when it contains faded and unfaded portions, and when both portions have received the same treatment, except for light.

make
inferences

Light Refraction. We have stated that the speed of light changes as it travels in media of different densities. If a light beam enters or leaves a different medium at a slant the change in speed may cause the beam to *refract,* or change direction of travel.

This phenomenon is readily observable. A pencil half-placed in water looks bent. Distant images shimmer through unevenly heated air as we drive along a hot road. The scenery looks distorted through a cheap glass window, since its thickness is uneven. Interestingly, the function of an automobile windshield wiper is to restore the rainy, outside surface of a windshield to a plane surface. As rain is wiped away, the light rays enter the plate glass at a uniform angle, rather than unevenly.

Man has learned to control light refraction with lenses. Magnifying glasses and optical instruments of many descriptions extend the power of sight far beyond that available to the unaided eye. In this section there are opportunities for children to work with both convex and concave lenses, the two principal types.

Commercial lenses can teach much; but children may learn even more by fashioning their own lenses from a variety of transparent objects, containers, and fluids. A clear glass play marble magnifies objects; so does a water drop or drops of other fluids. A small drinking glass with vertical sides (not tapered) magnifies things well when it is filled with water or other fluids. Narrow olive jars make especially powerful magnifiers. However, the best possibilities for controlled study of "home-made" lenses will occur if small plastic pill vials are available.

Small plastic vials can be purchased through most drug stores for about five to ten cents each. The plastic cap is easily removable and leakproof. Convenient sizes to get are the 1-inch and 1½-inch diameter vials; height about 2 to 2½ inches. The capacity of these vials is large enough for excellent study of light refraction, yet small enough so that only a small quantity of any one fluid will be needed.

Since one of the most interesting aspects of refraction study is finding out how various liquids "bend" light rays, you will want to use at least several different kinds of liquids: light corn syrup, rubbing alcohol, transparent dish detergent, cooking oil, and water. Details are provided in the following activities.

Generalization III: Slanted light rays are refracted when they pass from one medium to another of different density; lenses are made to control refraction

Contributing Idea A. Slanted light rays bend when passing from one medium to another of different density.

1. *Materials: straight* yardstick or pointer; flat-sided aquarium tank, two-thirds filled with water; white button or chalk (placed inside the tank); book. See Figure 3-13B for a sketch of this activity.

It will be interesting to start this sequence with a bridge that leads into a problem and a need to understand why the problem has occurred. You might say, "Who likes to go fishing? What else do people fish with besides a rod and reel? (Bring out that some people spear fish while standing in a boat or on a dock.) Spearfishing is fun, but you are likelier to get good results if you know how light travels. Who thinks he can spear the 'fish' (chalk or button) in this tank?"

Accept several volunteers, but let each observe only his own trial. Let one child sight along the yardstick. (He should use the wide portion, rather than edge, for his sighting. If the yardstick is slid into the water on its edge, the extra width of wood may permit him to hit his target even though his aim is off.) When his angle of aim is set, ask how a control can be developed to insure that the angle does not shift when the stick enters the water. A book may be used for this purpose. Hold it firmly while the yardstick is slid down a groove formed by the outside covers.

Have the class observe silently while each volunteer consistently goes over the target. Ask for hypotheses to account for the misses. Let the pupils discuss each hypothesis. Three probable guesses are:

a. The volunteers could not aim. (This is unlikely, because several were used and all missed.)

b. The stick is bent. (This can be checked. If necessary, the stick can be turned over and tried again.)

c. Something happens to the light when

suggest hypotheses

Figure 3-13 A–B

it enters or leaves the water. (Let them discuss this briefly; then move to an explanation of the principles involved.)

Bring out that anything in motion will slow down or stop when something is in the way. It is easy to run across an empty room at top speed. But scatter some people around it and the runner must slow down. If the room is completely filled, it is impossible to run across it. The population of the room has become *denser* each time. A greater amount of matter is taking up the same space.

Continue by stating that a similar thing happens with light as it travels through air, water, and glass. Water is denser than air—it has more molecules in the same space—and glass has more density than water. When light enters a denser medium, it slows down. The reverse is also true. How this happens can be understood through using an analogy, in the next activity.

2. *Materials:* chalkboard sketches of Figure 3-13 A–B.

Exhibit sketch A. Explain that two wheels attached to an axle are rolling freely in the direction indicated. Bring out what happens when the leading wheel strikes a sandy road. The device moves on, but at a slightly different angle. Now show the reverse. If the wheel-axle device travels diagonally upward, one wheel will hit the paved portion sooner. The direction will again change, but in an opposite way. Inform the class that a similar change in directions takes place when a beam of light enters and leaves materials of unequal density.

Place sketch B next to A. Let them study this drawing for a moment. Can they provide an explanation of why the "spearfishermen" consistently overshot their mark? It may be worthwhile to use small discussion groups to form explanations.

suggest hypotheses

Develop that, as *light* leaves the water, *it changes directions slightly.* We sight along a path where the button seems to be, because it seems to be in a straight line. But when our *stick* enters the water, *it continues at the same slant as it began.* Therefore, it overshoots the target.

Have the children apply their thinking. How should the aim be changed? Be sure they reason this through, as now it is easy to suggest only altering the aim. By aiming below the perceived target, accuracy should improve. Let class members try it.

make inferences

3. *Materials:* shallow paper cups, or shallow teacups; straws, or pencils; paper towels. (Two paper cups, one three-fourths filled with water, and one straw are needed for each experiment. It is desirable to have children to this activity in pairs.)

It will be most interesting to the class if

everyone can try the above "spearfishing" activity in miniature. At the same time, this will provide an opportunity to discover that light "bends" only when it enters or leaves water at a slant.

If children are to work in pairs or groups, remember to review briefly standards and procedures. Paper towels should be available to soak up any spilled water.

Have children draw a pinhead-sized circle on the inside bottom of each empty paper cup. It should be reasonably centered. (If ceramic teacups are used, substitute a small iron washer or coin.) These cups should be placed on desks and viewed from an angle, so that the penciled circle just barely disappears from view. Direct partners to pour water slowly from the unmarked cup into the marked cup. Viewers should keep their heads perfectly still. As water is poured in, the circle will appear, slightly farther away and higher than before. Let partners trade roles and try this demonstration several times.

Bring out that light must have bent slightly as water filled the cup; the penciled circles obviously could not move.

The children can sight their target through straws and try to hit it from all angles. Again a book can be used to maintain an unchangeable angle once a sighting has been made. Pupils will discover that when they are directly over the target, there is no difficulty in hitting it. The circle is where it appears to be. They should realize no bending occurs unless the light enters or leaves at a slant, even though its speed changes.

make inferences

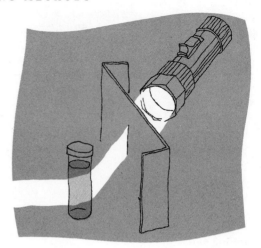

Figure 3-15

4. *Materials:* for each small group, a flashlight; a small plastic vial filled with water (or a filled, small, plain drinking glass with straight sides); scissors; 5- by 8-inch card; chalkboard sketch of Figure 3-14. (Leave off the dashed lines. These are to be drawn by pupils.)

You can use this activity to see how well the children can predict the path of light rays by applying the wheels-axle analogy to a real problem.

make inferences

Show the chalkboard sketch. Mention that this is a top view of a water-filled vial (or substitute). Lines *A, B,* and *C* represent three narrow beams of light entering the vial. What will be the paths of *A, B,* and *C* after they enter and leave it? Invite predictions. If needed, suggest they apply the wheels-axle analogy again, as in activity 2. Encourage the drawing of numerous circles and predicted beam pathways.

For the tests, materials can be arranged as in Figure 3-15. Pupils can use scissors to cut a very narrow slit, about 2 inches high, in each card to let the light through. The card ends can be folded in opposite directions to keep them upright. Pupils may move either the flashlight or the vial as they try to achieve, one at a time, beam patterns *A, B,* and *C.* The degree of room darkness will partly determine how clearly each beam

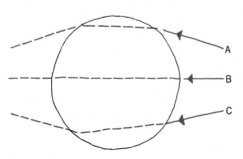

Figure 3-14

is visible in the water itself. However, it should be very easy to see the entering and leaving beam paths. These should resemble · the paths in Figure 3-14.

Contributing Idea B. A convex lens converges light rays; lenses with shorter focal lengths magnify more than those with longer focal lengths.

1. *Materials:* hand magnifying lenses of varied thicknesses; ruler; sheet of lined paper; sunshine or flashlight; sketch of Figure 3-16 A-B-C. (For now, omit the dashed lines in B and C.)

Many children are surprised to learn their magnifying "glasses" work because of refraction. The next several activities will help them understand this application.

Have everyone recall how they use a hand lens to focus the sun's rays. If necessary, someone can demonstrate this. Show your sketch, and indicate drawing B as a *convex* lens refracting light rays. Explain that the sun's parallel rays enter the glass and are refracted or bent when entering and leaving. Once again it will be helpful to draw or use an axle with two wheels to show how the refraction takes place. (Some teachers use a large cardboard cross section of a lens, with a toy wheel-axle combination, so pupils may see this more clearly.)

Once the children understand how the refraction takes place, move to drawing A. Most of the light rays enter the eye from two opposite slants. As the eye follows these slanted rays to the lens they seem to continue outward, and so form an enlarged image of the object.

Compare drawings B and C. Bring out that the two lenses are different in thickness, although their diameter is the same. Each will bring the sun's rays to a point or *focus* at a different distance. Distance from point of focus to the lens is the *focal length.*

Develop conjecture as to whether lenses with shorter focal lengths give more powerful magnification than those of longer focal

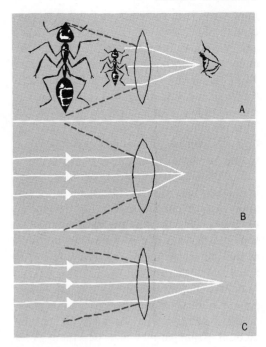

Figure 3-16 A–B–C

lengths. Encourage the children to use drawings A-B-C as they reason this through. Extend the angled lines in B and C from the focal points outward, as in A. They should reason that B would be more powerful than C. Challenge them to test this notion.

The first step is to determine focal lengths for each hand lens available. This can be done quickly with rulers and lenses in the sun. (Caution pupils not to focus on any flammable substance while measuring.) If there is no sunshine, substitute a narrow-beam flashlight. Darken the room and place the flashlight in a parallel position at least 15 feet away from the lens. Hold the lens in the light beam and focus it on a wall. A lens is focused when the light rays are converged to the smallest point. Most focal lengths will be about 4 to 8 inches. Of course, written notations will be helpful to keep track of lenses and their focal lengths.

Magnification can be tested by placing a lens parallel to and over lined paper, as in Figure 3-17. Put an X on the paper. Center it in the lens. Move the lens up and down

make inferences

reason quantitatively

227

until the X is most clearly defined. This distance will be somewhere between the paper and the lens' focal length. Count all the lines visible through the lens. Then count all lines *outside* the lens that fall between the first and last lines visible through the lens. Divide the larger figure by the smaller. This provides the lens' power of magnification. In Figure 3-17, lens power is 2. Images would be twice life size.

reason quantitatively

2. Pupils can try a variety of open-ended investigations with everyday materials to apply and further clarify their understanding of lenses. Or you may decide that the following activities are useful to *begin* study of this subsection. Both ways seem to work satisfactorily.

a. *Materials:* medicine droppers, waxed paper; books; one pint each of various liquids, such as water, cooking oil, rubbing alcohol, transparent dish detergent, and light corn syrup; paper towels; plastic cups to hold the liquids.

Let the children experiment with water-drop lenses. One drop from a medicine dropper on waxed paper makes a good lens. Pupils can slide the waxed paper around on a book page. How much larger does a single letter appear? Will two or more drops together magnify more? (No.)

Some pupils may discover that adding more drops tends to flatten out the water "bump," or profile. If no one does, sug-

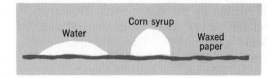

Figure 3-18 A one-drop profile of two liquids.

gest that they hold up the waxed paper to eye level and compare the bumps. Have them add a corn syrup drop next to the water drop. Since its molecules cohere more strongly to one another, it will have a higher profile than water, as in Figure 3-18. How well does the syrup drop magnify compared to a water drop? (A good way to tell is to select a common alphabetical letter and to find two places on a book page where this letter will be magnified under each drop.)

develop procedures

If several liquids are available, let the children observe these in drop form and then try to rank them in order of magnifying power. You might ask the pupils to predict what they may find before they make the observations. See if they use relative "bumpiness" as a criterion; it will be helpful. There probably will be some disagreement as to the exact magnifying power of these drops, as the test is a very crude one.

make inferences

b. *Materials:* various clear drinking glasses and jars with straight sides, containing water; pencils.

Have pupils explore the refraction characteristics of many glass containers by placing pencils, fingers, and other objects both inside and in back of them. They will note the greater magnification when two containers of water are placed together, one behind the other.

They also may discover that the image of a pencil moved back and forth behind a jar may suddenly reverse directions. This happens when the pencil is moved from side to side just beyond the focal length of the jar lens. Children will find it interesting to compare this reversal of motion in two containers, one narrow, and the second of larger diameter, as in Figure 3-19. The

Figure 3-17

make inferences image's reversal of direction will occur at different distances in the two containers, that is, only when the pencil is beyond the focal point of each lens. By extending the converging broken lines in Figure 3-19 beyond the focal points, you can see that the light rays reverse positions at these points. That is why the image is reversed.

c. *Materials:* for each group, several or more capped, plastic vials 1 inch in diameter, about 3 inches long; several medicine droppers (optional); one pint each of various liquids as in activity a; plastic cups; candle.

This activity can reveal the different magnifying powers of various liquids. At the same time, it can bring up interesting comparisons of the relative densities of liquids.

Remind pupils they found that single drops of various liquids magnified differently. Suggest that they pour individual liquids in separate plastic containers and observe how they magnify. But before they do this, can they predict which ones will magnify more? To surprise them, and to develop the need for careful hypothesizing, ask them to predict whether alcohol or

Figure 3-20 The focal lengths of many liquid-filled vials may be found at one time by the light of a single candle.

water will be the more powerful magnifier. If they worked with alcohol in activity a, the children probably will firmly state that water will magnify better. (A single-drop profile of alcohol is quite flat on waxed paper.) They can fill one vial with alcohol, another with water, and see for themselves. Probably the alcohol will magnify objects *more*. How can that be? Perhaps some measurements may help to explain the difference in power.

Show them how to measure the focal length of a liquid-filled container. Light a candle (it should be about the same height as the vials) and place it about six inches away from the two *capped* vials (alcohol is flammable) filled with alcohol and water. If the room is darkened a little, the candle light will plainly shine through the vials and come to a focus a short distance away. (You can use a flashlight instead of a candle for a light source for single containers. A candle will be more convenient for several or more, since its flame shines in all directions. See Figure 3-20.) The alcohol container will have the shorter focal length. Children may recall that powerful hand lenses they worked

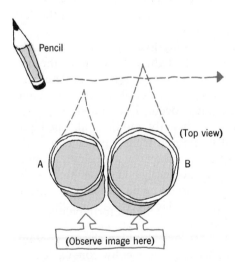

Pencil

(Top view)

A   B

(Observe image here)

Figure 3-19 Reversing the direction of a moving image. If the pencil is moved to the right, its image will move to the *left* in A, to the *right* in B. The broken lines show how a broad light beam would be brought to focus at different lengths by the two containers of water.

229

with in previous activities also had shorter focal lengths than weaker lenses.

make inferences Encourage pupils to make predictions about the magnifying power of several liquids. They might use the focal length test to order the liquid fillers from weakest to most powerful, before they view objects through the vial lenses. *Direct them to cap all the vials before lighting the candle.* Also, any candle used by children should be firmly anchored to a fireproof dish. If there is any doubt about safety, you can have all the measurements done under your immediate supervision or use flashlights only.

Some groups may have difficulty in comparing the focal lengths. If you can provide either graph paper or drawing compasses, these will help. Pupils can draw a series of circles a slight distance apart, beginning from the vials outward, to make a circular grid. See if the children realize the need for consistency in interpreting where the focal point is in each case, since it may not be sharply evident. It does not matter if groups disagree, as long as the measurement within each group is consistent. In effect, each group will need to define operationally the focal point for itself.

state problems

Get the several groups to compare their

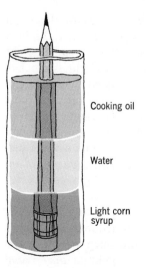

Figure 3-21 Light refraction in different fluids.

Cooking oil

Water

Light corn syrup

predictions. Any disagreements? After comparisons are made, either the same or different objects may be viewed through the lenses by the groups, as long as each group consistently uses an identical object with each lens. For example, five identical pencils may be used to get a simultaneous comparison of five vials.

d. *Materials:* liquids and vials used in the previous activity; medicine droppers (optional).

Point out the difficulty of trying to compare magnifications of liquids in five vials at one time. It would be nice to have all five liquids in *one* container. That way, only one pencil or other object would reveal the different magnifying powers of the liquids. As the children begin protesting ("they'll get mixed together, etc."), get them to define the problem; for example: Can different liquids be poured into one container and stay separated? state problems

They might try two liquids first, such as light corn syrup and water, and gradually try more. Figure 3-21 shows results with three liquids. Suggest the need for a test and recording plan to eliminate aimless develop procedures trial and error with all groups. It might be interesting to compare the relative success make inferences of two groups that record and share the data with two that do not.

An interesting five-layered effect can be achieved with light corn syrup at the bottom of the vial, then liquid dish detergent, water, oil, and alcohol at the top. Some mixing may occur if a liquid is poured abruptly or heavily into the vial. The liquid should be poured from a paper cup as the vial is held at a slant. Or a medicine dropper can be used to gently add fluids. Most of the time there should be no difficulty as long as the added liquid is less dense than the liquid layer below.

Jars, vials, and drinking glasses containing liquids are not wholly convex lenses. They are more properly called *cylindrical* lenses. No doubt you have observed that in every case the images they produce are distorted. Images are magnified only in width and not height because these lenses are convex only in one direction. A regular convex lens forms a perfect candle flame image on a sheet of paper held several inches away. But if you form the image with a cylindrical lens, it will be tall and narrow. Try it and see.

Contributing Idea C. A concave lens causes light rays to diverge; therefore, images appear smaller.

Materials: sketches of Figure 3-22 A–B; concave lenses. In your sketch of A, leave out the diverging lines. It will be challenging for your pupils to draw these in later.

Exhibit sketch A, but withhold B at this time. Tell the class this is a cross section of a *concave* lens. An easy way to remember the shape is with the words "caved in." A concave lens has a caved-in center. Invite someone to predict where the parallel lines will go after they enter the lens. Again a wheel-axle device may be used. After diverging lines have been drawn, emphasize the opposite curvature of this lens in contrast with that of a convex lens. Since they are curved in an opposite manner, the refraction is also opposite. Convex lenses *converge* light rays, or bring them together. Concave lenses cause light rays to *diverge,* or spread out.

make inferences

Now show sketch B. Help pupils think through what happens when an object is viewed through a concave lens. Most of the rays slant outward, as in X and Y. As the eye follows many of these slanted rays back to the lens, they seem to continue inward at a slant, and form a smaller image of the object.

Let pupils look at objects through concave lenses. If none is available, perhaps substitutes can be provided. Thick drinking glasses and glass egg cups often have concave-shaped bases. Check by seeing if images are smaller when viewed through them. Nearsighted children who wear eyeglasses are another available source of supply. It will be worthwhile to record, but temporarily postpone, questions about why

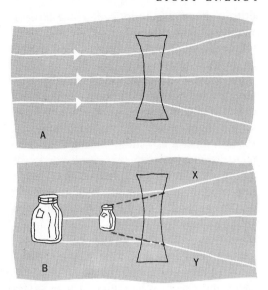

Figure 3-22 A–B

some eyeglass lenses are concave. This will be taken up shortly in an overall and applied context when the eye is studied.

EXTENDING ACTIVITIES

1. Almost everyone has seen wavy, shimmering images produced when viewing objects through heated air. A similar effect can be achieved by a hot plate. Place a picture in back of a hot plate before and after it is turned on. The children should understand that the effect is produced through air convection. Warm air rises and is continually being replaced by cooler air of different density. Light rays passing through the area of unequal density are refracted unevenly.

2. Several additional kinds of liquid lenses can be made. Here are two.

a. Make a "wire loop" liquid lens. Form a loop of thin, soft wire around a large nail. It is important to get the loop perfectly round, as otherwise a distorted image results. For best results, use only enough wire to close the loop without having any wire left over. Pliers will help. Scoop up a drop of liquid in the loop. Surface tension will hold it in place. Try different liquids. Glycerine (available at drug stores) makes an especially powerful magnifier.

b. A more elaborate setup may be constructed for viewing thin cross sections of objects. In this case it is important to have strong light going *through* the objects. Place a clear glass slide bearing the specimen on end between two small stacks of books. Position a small mirror at an angle underneath the specimen. Prop it with an eraser or stack of cards so light is reflected strongly upward through the specimen. View with any of the lenses previously suggested. (For an illustration, see p. 500L.)

Light and Color. When ancient man saw a rainbow, he was probably inclined to give a magical or supernatural explanation to account for it. Later, people thought that the colors came from the rain droplets through which the sunlight passes. It was not until Isaac Newton (1642–1727) performed experiments with prisms that it was realized these colors were the components of visible sunlight itself.

There are seven universally recognized colors in the visible spectrum of sunlight: red, orange, yellow, green, blue, indigo, and violet. (Many teachers remember these colors and their spectral order through the name Roy G. Biv.) Since indigo is virtually indistinguishable from its adjacent colors, it is common to exclude indigo at the elementary level of study.

A prism separates light because each color has a different wavelength and rate of vibration. Red light has the longest wavelength, with about 30,000 waves to one inch. Violet light has the shortest wavelength, with about 60,000 waves to one inch. As a light beam passes through a prism the longer waves are refracted least, the shorter waves most (Figure 3-23).

Differences in colors are often compared with pitch differences in sound. A low sound is a result of relatively slow vibrations. Its visual counterpart is the color red. A high sound results from fast vibrations. Its counterpart is violet.

There are two basic ways in which we can mix colors, one with colored beams of light and the other with paints or dyes. When light beams of only three primary colors—red, blue, and green—are added together in the right proportions on a white screen, different color combinations occur. These are shown in the overlapping sections of Figure 3-24. When red, blue, and green are used as colored light beams they are called the additive colors.

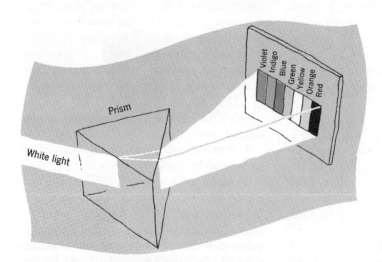

Figure 3-23 **A prism separates white light into a spectrum of seven colors.**

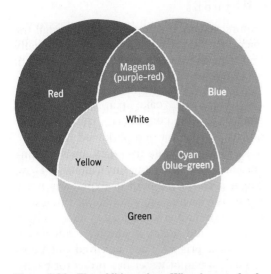

Figure 3-24 The additive colors. When beams of red, blue, and green light are added together in the right proportions the overlapping colors result. Color television is produced by an additive process.

Scientists have found that three certain colored pigments can absorb these additive colors. That is, if you shine a red or blue or green light on these pigments there is practically no color reflection at all. The pigments look black. Blue light is absorbed by a yellow pigment, and red light by a blue-green pigment called cyan. Green light is absorbed by a purple-red pigment called magenta. If a *white* light beam shines on these colored pigments, each will absorb or "subtract" the specific color mentioned above and reflect to our eyes what is not absorbed. We can mix these pigments to get various colors, but the results we get from mixing all three are the *opposite* from mixing the three light beams. This is shown in Figure 3-25.

The foregoing ideas boil down to this: When viewing an object the color we see depends on (1) the color of light shining on the object; and (2) the color reflected by the object to our eyes. The children can do some experiments with colored construction paper and colored light beams to help them understand these ideas and their practical effects. With ordinary materials it is very difficult to predict the exact hues that

will emerge from the many possible combinations. But at the elementary level, simply discovering the interesting effects of combining colored lights and pigments is highly rewarding.

Even the best artificial light does not contain the exact colors of sunlight. For this reason, we can never be sure a garment purchased at night will look the same in daylight. For example, most white light bulbs are somewhat deficient in blue. Therefore, a blue garment will look a bit darker under this light than in daylight. Fortunately, many clothing retailers recognize this problem and install lights whose color qualities differ only slightly from sunlight.

Don't be surprised if you find several boys in your class to be at least partly color blind. One male in twelve has this deficiency, contrasted with only one in two hundred females. Most commonly, reds and greens are seen in shades of gray; other colors are perceived normally. Rarely, are all colors seen only in black and white, and shades of gray.

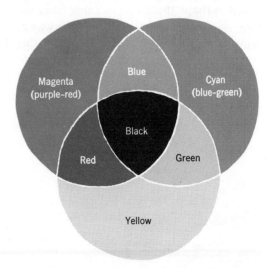

Figure 3-25 The subtractive colors. Paints and dyes absorb or "subtract" some colors from white light and reflect what is left. When the three primary pigments are mixed in the right proportions we see the overlapping colors.

Generalization IV: White light is composed of different colors; the color of objects depends on which colors are transmitted, absorbed, and reflected

Contributing Idea A. A prism separates white light by refracting the colors which make up the light.

1. *Materials:* glass prism; sunlight (or filmstrip projector and darkened room).

You might begin by asking if anyone has seen a rainbow. What makes a rainbow? Where do the colors come from? Develop that it is reasonable to think they may come from the sunlight itself. Mention the children can find out for themselves with several activities. In the first one they will use a glass *prism.* Show them a prism.

Hold the prism in sunlight and rotate it slowly until a spectrum appears on a wall or ceiling. (If there is no sunlight, put the prism on end in front of a filmstrip projector beam, as in Figure 3-26.) Have pupils identify the colors: red, orange, yellow, green, blue, and violet. There appear to be six main colors (excluding indigo) in sunlight. If a projector light is used, its spectrum will be similar.

But perhaps these colors came from the glass. Encourage pupils to think of a way in which they could be reasonably sure this was not the case. When needed, provide hints. If light can be taken apart, then we should be able to put it back together. How could *two* prisms help?

Establish now, or later through authority,

that although difficult to do in a classroom, light refracted into separate colors can be reconstituted. Two prisms are used, the second in reverse position of the first. The end product is again white light.

2. *Materials:* cake pan of water (or shallow glass container); small mirror; filmstrip projector and darkened room.

Remind everyone that they are still concerned about understanding rainbows. How can a glass prism help in explaining what happens? Encourage discussion. Elicit that two factors are always present in rainbows: sunshine and water in the air. Can water act like a prism? They can find out now.

Place a pan of water in a projector beam, as in Figure 3-27. Hold a mirror vertically against the pan's inside rim, then gradually tip it back. Light must strike part of the mirror below the water's surface. Depending on the angle of light, a beautifully clear spectrum will appear on a nearby wall or ceiling.

Stir the water slightly and have the class note that white light appears. When the water becomes still, the spectrum again appears. Bring out that colors were recombined when the water was stirred.

3. *Materials:* attached garden hose, with fine spray nozzle; slanted morning or afternoon sun. (If the sun or school custodian are uncooperative, children can do this activity at home sometime after its introduction.)

Briefly review what they have learned: White light is composed of rainbow colors.

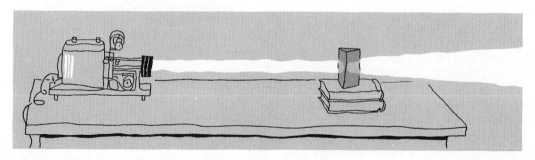

Figure 3-26

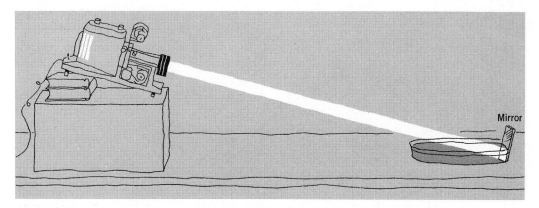

Mirror

Figure 3-27

White light can be separated by a prism. Water can act like a prism. But water in the air is made up of fine droplets. Rainbows appear when the sun is at an angle. Can tiny droplets act like prisms in slanted sunshine?

Encourage pupils to think of what to do. Give clues as needed. When are the sun's rays slanting? (Morning and late afternoon.) What can break up water into tiny droplets? (Garden hose and fine spray nozzle.) Where is the sun when they see a rainbow? (In back or at an angle.) If essential factors are observed—slanted sun in back of the observer, and fine spray—a rainbow will be observed.

Contributing Idea B. An object's color depends on the color of light striking it and the color it reflects.

1. *Materials:* glass prism; filmstrip projector and white screen; three small sheets of cellophane, red, blue, and green; three sheets of construction paper, red, blue, and green; darkened room.

This activity will reveal that a colored cellophane filter tends to block all the colors in a white light beam except the color it lets through the filter.

Shine the projector on a white screen. Draw out that the children are viewing all the rainbow colors combined to form white light. Now place a double thickness of red cellophane over the lens. Invite anyone to explain why there is now a red light shining. "Is the red cellophane turning the rainbow colors to red? Or is the cellophane letting just the red through? Let's see if we can figure out what is happening."

Take off the red cellophane and place the prism in the white light beam. Place it on end on a pile of books, as in Figure 3-26. Reposition the projector if needed so that a spectrum appears on the white screen. Ask pupils to note carefully the exact position of red in the spectrum. Place red cellophane over the projector lens. All but the red part of the spectrum will disappear. The position of red in the spectrum will be identical before and after the red cellophane is used.

Invite pupils to use what they observed in explaining how the red cellophane functioned. Guide them to reason that the cellophane probably prevented all but the red waves from getting through. Additional trials with green and blue cellophane blocking spectrum colors may be tried, but will probably be less successful. It is difficult to obtain perfect filtering action with ordinary cellophane.

2. Demonstrate now the effect of shining a colored light on a colored object. Ask, "When the sun shines, do you feel warmer in a dark blue sweater or a white sweater?" (Blue.) Develop that only one color, blue, is being reflected and all other spectrum colors absorbed and changed into heat energy.

make inferences

235

"If blue is the only color that can be reflected, what color must shine on the sweater to see it?" (Blue.) Hold up a blue sweater or, preferably, blue construction paper in front of the projector. (If there is inadequate darkness tape the paper to the bottom of a large, empty carton or wastebasket. Lay it on its side and shine the projector light into it.) Put folded blue cellophane over the lens. The construction paper will continue to be visible and blue in color.

suggest hypotheses Raise conjecture about the paper's color if red and green lights are used. Try each in turn. Bring out that these colors were absorbed. Since there was no blue light in either color, the paper looked black. Objects appear black when there is no (or very little) reflection of light waves.

3. *Materials:* filmstrip projector; variety of colored cellophane sheets; variety of colored construction paper; darkened room; empty carton or wastebasket (if needed).

Try an open-ended activity in which colored lights and papers are combined.

Mention that even a careful person can make mistakes when buying colored clothing in stores with inadequate artificial lighting. Challenge the class to detect the true colors of the construction paper samples as they are exposed to various colored lights. Be sure to mention that neither cellophane paper nor construction paper will be perfect in filtering and absorbing colors. Therefore, resulting colors should be unpredictable.

Have someone change construction paper samples as you change cellophane filters. Use one colored filter for a whole series of construction papers, then another, and so on. It will be especially interesting if a guess-verification procedure is adopted. For example, have pupils keep their eyes closed while the paper sample is changed. Show the example in colored light. Let each pupil write his guess. Then remove the filter and let the children see the paper in white light. After sufficient practice, they should have little difficulty in understanding

that color is a function of the light striking an object as well as the color it reflects. make inferences

4. *Materials:* opaque projector (microscopes are less adequate, hand lenses least adequate); one black-and-white newspaper photograph; several colored pictures from comic strips and magazines featuring these colors: orange, green, and purple; yellow, red, and blue crayons; and white paper for the children.

This investigation will bring out how different colors in published drawings or photographs are achieved by combining only several colored pigments.

With the class observing, take a black-and-white newspaper photograph and project its image onto a white screen with an opaque projector. Elicit that the photo is composed of unevenly spaced black dots. Explain that colored drawings or photographs in printed publications also consist of dots—*but of only three colors,* such as red, yellow, and blue. Does this seem odd? (Why are other colors than these visible in publications?) state problems

Probably the children will hypothesize that combinations of colored dots are used. Invite them to predict these before viewing some colored illustrations. If children are unfamiliar with the hues that result from combining colored pigments, you might have them experiment with red, yellow, and blue crayons. They can rub one crayon on white paper, and then a different crayon on top of the mark to see what color results. To keep track of results, the following table will be helpful.

	R	Y	B
R	red	orange	purple
Y	orange	yellow	green
B	purple	green	blue

Will colored illustrations reveal dots with these combinations? Project portions of colored illustrations with the foregoing colors. How do their results with crayons compare with the colored dots? (If only hand lenses are available, two can be placed together for greater magnification. Perhaps cylindrical lenses made in a previous activity can be used if there are not enough hand lenses for small groups. Several colored illustrations should be available for each group.)

Many printed illustrations employ three slightly different colored pigments. However, children should understand that virtually any color can be produced by varying the number of dots with just several colors.

EXTENDING ACTIVITY

Students will enjoy using paper chromatography to discover the several colors that may be used in a single dye or ink. In this process, the separate compounds making up the colored fluid are adsorbed at different rates by the paper. This has the effect of "spreading out" the ingredients, which makes them visible.

Figure 3-28 shows a convenient way individuals or small groups can set up their investigations with shoe boxes. Strips

Figure 3-28 Paper chromatography can reveal the several colors that may make up a dye or ink.

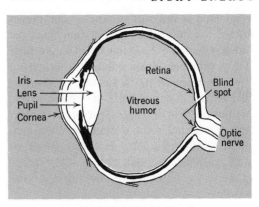

Figure 3-29 A simplified eye.

from white paper hand towels work well. In addition to analyzing commercial inks or dyes, pupils might want to try their own colored mixtures. Good results may take less than an hour. In some cases, several or more hours will be needed.

Perception and the Eye. In the closing generalization of this unit, children learn how their eyes function, and apply some ideas met before. Although the eye has many parts, we shall concentrate on three directly involved in sight: the *iris, lens,* and *retina.* (See Figure 3-29.)

The iris contains pigment which absorbs some colors and reflects others. Since the kind and amount of this coloring matter varies in individuals, some eyes appear brown, some blue, and so on. Two sets of tiny muscles control the size of a small hole (pupil) in the iris. This regulates the amount of light entering the eye.

The eyes of cats have a capacity for pupil dilation far in excess of humans. This is one reason why they see better than humans in near darkness. A dramatic example of this capacity appears when the headlights of an automobile suddenly shine into the eyes of a cat on a dark night. The two shiny round spots we see are the headlight reflections from *inside* the cat's eyes.

Our eyes make a second important adjustment when light varies in brightness. The retina contains two kinds of light-

237

sensitive cells, named *rods* and *cones.* Cones are less sensitive than rods and are clustered near the back of the eyeball. They function most efficiently in strong light, and enable us to see color. Rods are distributed in other parts of the retina and are sensitive to dim light. Chemical changes sensitize either rods or cones under appropriate conditions. For example, when we walk into a dark theater on a sunny day, it takes several moments before the rods work well. To achieve optimum sensitivity, up to a half-hour may be required.

It is thought that cones are most sensitive to three basic colors—red, green, and blue. According to this idea, we see many colors because the basic colors are seen in various combinations. An experiment is provided to test this theory.

An eye lens is convex in shape and works like any other convex lens—with one important difference. A muscle permits it to change shape. If a large, close object appears before you, the lens thickens. This refracts light rays entering the eye sharply enough for a focus to occur on the retina. However, light rays from a small or far-away object enter the lens in a near parallel fashion. Only a small refraction is needed to bring the rays to a focus on the retina. Look at a distant object, than suddenly look at something a foot away. Do you feel the tug of your lens muscles pulling the lens? Do you find the near object is fuzzy for the brief instant it takes for the muscles to adjust lens thickness? In a camera, of course, focusing is achieved by moving the lens back and forth.

Two principal defects in vision are introduced in this section. In *nearsightedness,* the lens may be thicker or the eyeball longer than normal. This causes an image to focus in front of the retina rather than on it. In *farsightedness,* the lens may be thinner or the eyeball shorter than normal. In this case, an image can be focused only some distance in back of the retina. Activities are provided to help children apply this knowledge of lenses in correcting these defects. This may be an ideal time to help pupils develop a mature attitude about the wearing of eyeglasses.

An excellent example of how the brain and eyes work together takes place when we judge distance. Each eye sees an object from a different angle. The closer the object, the more each image appears to be different. We actually see a tiny bit "around" the object. At the same time, we feel our eyes turn inward. With greater distances, the angle gets smaller. The brain interprets this accordingly.

Beyond about 50 yards, we rely mainly on size to judge distance. A small telegraph pole looks far away mostly because we know that telephone poles are large. We also use such other clues as increased haze and the surrounding perspective.

Several activities are provided to acquaint children with the subjective nature of vision. A study of common optical illusions can cause them to become more aware of how these interesting phenomena occur.

The apparent motion of a motion-picture projection results from *persistence of vision.* It takes about one-sixteenth of a second for an image to fade from our vision after it is withdrawn. By flashing twenty-four images a second on a screen, a projector creates the illusion of motion.

It took some experience before the present speed of projecting individual motion-picture frames was adopted. Early motion pictures were photographed and projected at much slower speeds. The short, unlighted pause between frames was noticeable. This is how the term "flickers" got started.

Develop with pupils the necessity for protecting and conserving their eyes. Particular care should be taken with sticks, stones, and other potentially dangerous objects. Children should consult a responsible adult when a foreign object is imbedded in an eye. Good lighting is important in reading and studying. Television watching should take place a reasonable distance from the screen. At night, an extra light will soften the harsh contrast between the screen and surrounding darkness. Be alert for signs of eyestrain or poor vision. The school nurse can decide if medical attention is necessary.

Your class will find it interesting to learn that the eyes of certain animals are peculiarly adapted for how or where they live. A snake's eyes are protected by a horny, transparent cover. The hippopotamus and alligator have eyes on top of their heads. The excellent side vision of rabbits makes it difficult to approach them undetected. So-called "flatfish," such as the flounder and halibut, lie on one side. Both eyes are arranged on one side of the head. Since these fish are typically bottom-dwellers, this eye arrangement permits greater vision.

Generalization V: The eye is a complicated organ that operates with the brain

Contributing Idea A. The eye has three main parts—iris, lens, and retina—each of which works in a special way.

This activity will enable pupils to learn about several main parts and properties of the eye.

1. *Materials:* large sketch or projection of Figure 3-29; pencils; paper.

Have your pupils recall what it is like to go into a darkened movie theater from the bright outdoors and the reverse. Briefly pursue an explanation of what happens when their eyes "get used to" the light or darkness. Mention that a demonstration will help them to understand one important adjustment of the eye.

Let pupils work in pairs, facing each other. Each should cover one of his own eyes with a hand, and wait fifteen or more seconds. Then have each remove his hand quickly and note if his partner's eye changes in any way as it undergoes sudden exposure to light. After several trials most pupils will realize that the black spot (pupil) changes in size.

Exhibit your sketch. Identify the *pupil* and *iris*. Help the children understand that the pupil of the eye is an opening in the iris. Develop that the pupil looks larger and smaller because the iris automatically adjusts in size as the brightness of the light varies. When it is dark, a larger opening helps us to see. If it is very bright a smaller opening prevents us from being temporarily blinded. Explain that chemical changes inside the eye are also involved in its adjustment to light and darkness. Emphasize that eye pupils change size very quickly, but that the chemical changes take much longer.

Acquaint the class with other eye parts:

Cornea—a transparent covering in front of the eye. It gives protection to more delicate parts beneath it, and partly focuses entering light rays. Let the children examine others' eyes from the side. The cornea is easily seen.

Lens—a transparent convex-shaped part through which light passes into the eye. Mention that they will investigate this part more closely later.

Vitreous humor—a jellylike material that helps the eyeball keep its shape.

Retina—nerve fibers sensitive to light. When light strikes any portion of it, a signal is sent to the brain through the *optic nerve,* which is connected in back of the eyeball.

Children will be interested in learning that there is a blind spot in the retina where the optic nerve is connected. Have them pencil on paper a dot at left and a cross at right, about three inches apart. With the left eye closed, they should stare at the dot with their right eye. The paper should now be slowly drawn closer to the eye. At some point, the cross will disappear.

2. *Materials:* for each group, two hand magnifying lenses and a piece of white tagboard; sketch of Figure 3-30 A-B-C.

This and the next activity develop why eyeglasses may correct some defects in vision.

Remind the children that in the previous sketch, a convex lens was shown in back of the iris. Have them recall a common con-

239

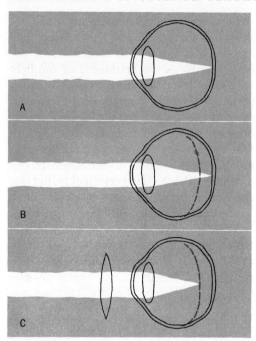

Figure 3-30 A–B–C

vex lens they used before — a hand magnifying lens. Does it work like the eye lens?

To find out, have persons with a hand lens stand 10 feet or more from an open window and focus the window image on a piece of tagboard or wall. The proper distance for focusing probably will be under 12 inches. Draw out the analogy: a hand lens for the eye lens; a piece of tagboard for the retina.

make inferences

Most children are surprised to find the image is upside down. Is this also true in our eyes? Let them find out that it is. The brain learns by experience how things are really arranged, and we adjust our thinking accordingly.

Ask why some people wear eyeglasses. Develop that images often appear fuzzy or blurry to them; eyeglasses help make these images sharp and clear. Exhibit your sketch of Figure 3-30 A-B-C. Explain that drawing A shows a normal eyeball with an image properly coming to a sharp focus on the retina. However, drawing B shows what happens when an eyeball is shorter than

normal. Help pupils explain what is happening. (The image must be blurry, because it has not yet been brought to a focus.) Assist them in explaining C. (A convex lens slightly converges the light rays before they enter the eye. This helps the eye lens to converge the light rays a little sooner, and thus achieve a proper focus.)

make inferences

Tell the children their explanations may appear reasonable, but should be tested for accuracy. They can use two hand lenses and a piece of tagboard.

Guide the experimenting children to parallel the drawings closely. A clear focus of the window on the tagboard represents a normal eyeball. When the card is brought closer to the hand lens the image is fuzzy, or out of focus. When a second lens is held in front of the first, a sharp image appears on the shortened "retina." If there is a far-sighted child with glasses in the room, one lens of his glasses will dramatically substitute for a hand lens.

3. *Materials:* one hand lens; a concave lens (a nearsighted person's eyeglasses can be used); sketch of Figure 3-31 A-B-C.

Exhibit your sketch as an example of how eyeglasses correct for the opposite problem — an eyeball that is longer than normal. The children should have little difficulty in explaining these three drawings. Again ask for a test of their explanations.

make inferences

A proper focus on the card represents a normal eyeball. Moving the card a few inches farther away will lengthen the "eyeball" and cause a fuzzy image to appear. When a concave lens is held in front of the convex "eye" lens, a sharp image appears on the card "retina."

These demonstrations may be verified through reference to authority. Also, it will be worthwhile to develop briefly that our eye lenses continually change shape to accommodate for viewing objects at varying distances. When eye lenses cannot accommodate satisfactorily, proper glasses will help to achieve a proper focus. Thus, lenses correct both eyeball and eye-lens defects. (Many children find it difficult to un-

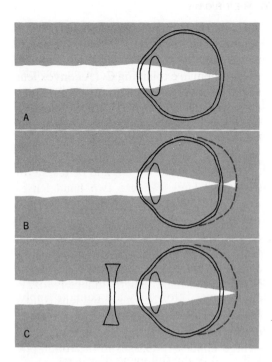

Figure 3-31 A – B – C

derstand lens accommodation at this level. Therefore, it may be better to treat this aspect as a readiness experience rather than a definite teaching objective.)

4. *Materials:* several small, colored objects; sketch of Figure 3-29.

Do an experiment to test which part of the eye is more sensitive in perceiving color.

Show the eye sketch of Figure 3-29 again. Point out that the retina contains millions of nerve fibers which react to different amounts of brightness and color. However, emphasize that color sensitive cells have been found to be largely clustered in back, near the optic nerve.

Aid them in thinking through the implications of this idea. If we are to see color, some colored light must reach the back of the eyeball. But what if we view a colored object from the "side" of an eye? When we are first able to detect it is there, can we also tell its color?

To test this, a child can stare fixedly at a designated spot while a colored object is slowly moved forward at the side of his head. When he barely detects the object, he should immediately say so. The object then is held motionless, while he tries to detect its color, eyes still staring fixedly on some forward spot.

Let all the other pupils try it in pairs. But first, draw out needed controls. The viewer must not know before hand what colors are used, and must stare fixedly forward. They will find color is detectable only after the object is moved some distance forward of where it is first noticed.

develop procedures

make inferences

5. *Materials:* large, white paper screen; three 8-inch diameter circle cutouts of colored construction paper—green, blue, and red; sketch of the additive color diagram of Figure 3-24.

In this investigation pupils can test a theory about how the eye detects color.

Mention that many scientists believe the color portion of the retina is mainly sensitive to three basic colors: red, green, and blue. We are able to see many different colors because the three "retinal" colors are seen in different amounts.

Ask the children to look at the white paper screen. Establish that it looks white because nerves are stimulated in the retina which are sensitive to red, green, and blue. Have children note that in the sketch the three-color combination results in white.

Speculate what "white" light would look like if we were able to see only two of these colors. Elicit these combinations and record them on the chalkboard:

make inferences

a. If we could not see blue, white light might look yellow.

b. If we could not see red, white light might look blue-green.

c. If we could not see green, white light might look purple-red.

Inform the class that there is a way of temporarily tiring the nerves which are sensitive to colors. This can be done for each color, so that only two groups of color nerves operate together, instead of three, when white is observed.

Pin a blue circle in the center of the white screen. Have everyone stare fixedly at it for about thirty seconds. Now quickly remove the colored circle, while everyone continues to stare at the same spot. A yellowish circle will appear on the white paper. Try the other two colors, but allow several moments between trials for discussion and eye rest. Have pupils reason through what happened in each case.

Contributing Idea B. Two eyes are better than one for judging distance.

Materials: pencils.

Discuss some of the many reasons we must be careful with our eyes. Bring out problems that might emerge if only one eye were operable, rather than two. Bridge into the story of a baseball player who temporarily wore a bandage over one injured eye. He began having trouble catching high pop flies. The ball kept dropping in front of him.

Do two eyes make a difference in how we judge distance? Have each pupil hold a pencil vertically at three-fourths of an arm's length away from his face. With one eye closed, let each try to touch the pencil with another pencil held in the opposite hand. This pencil should be held sideways, parallel to the body, and brought down slowly over the vertical pencil. The children will be astonished at how difficult it is, especially if the vertical pencil distance is changed slightly after each trial. Bring out the need for trying it with two eyes, also.

Before inviting the class to explain why two eyes make judging distances easier, provide some input:

Tell children to look down a pencil, eraser end placed against the nose, with fingers holding the sharpened tip. How many pencils do they see? (Two.)

Ask everyone to look at a room corner. With one eye closed have them line up a thumb with the corner, then alternate the other eye. Elicit that the thumb seems to move.

With both eyes open, have each child look over a thumb at a corner. Each will see two thumbs.

Guide them to express why judging dis-

tance is better with two eyes. Each eye views an object from a slightly different perspective; often this helps us to see slightly "around" an object. Bring out that this advantage decreases with distance. Decreased size of objects and other cues are likelier to be important in judging distances.

Contributing Idea C. We cannot always believe what we see.

1. *Materials:* paper; pencils; sketch of Figure 3-32 A-B-C.

This and the next activity take up some common optical illusions.

Remind the children that their past experience has been helpful in judging size and distance. Now they are going to apply their experience in judging size and distance in another way.

Exhibit your sketch of Figure 3-32 A-B-C. Ask the following questions:

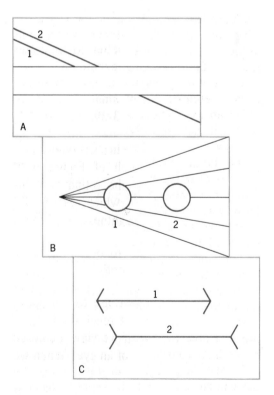

Figure 3-32 A–B–C

For A, "Which top slanted line belongs with the lower slanted line, one or two?"

For B, "Which circle seems larger, one or two?"

For C, "Which inside line seems larger, one or two?"

After children commit themselves, let them connect the lines in A with a yardstick, and measure sizes in B and C. Most will be surprised to discover slanted line 1 connects to the lower slanted line in A, and circle sizes in B are the same, as are line lengths in C.

Help pupils understand what happened. They are accustomed to using many cues in interpreting things. Ordinarily, this is helpful. In some cases, however, the cues can mislead us.

make
inferences

Discuss how moods may also influence perceptions. Bring out examples: When are some people likely to interpret a white sheet as a "ghost"? When does a cold glass of lemonade appear the most refreshing? Help the class realize that the eye is only a gateway to the mind; it is the mind that sees.

2. *Materials:* reel of motion-picture film; film projector; small paper pads; pencils; crayon; watch with second hand.

Introduce motion-picture projection as another case in which we see something that is different from reality. Have some children unwind several feet of film and examine the individual frames of a sequence in which action is occurring, such as a moving vehicle. They will note that in each frame the vehicle appears in a slightly different position.

If small paper pads are available, guide children to draw a head-on view of a bird with wings, on the bottom and center of the first page. A small circle for the body and two curved lines for wings will do. On succeeding pages, in the same spot, have them draw the wings in ever higher positions. Subsequent drawings should show the wings in gradually lower positions. A total of twenty pages is more than adequate. When the pad pages are flipped over rapidly, a sequence of flapping wings appears.

Why the illusion of motion? Develop these facts:

a. We observe a series of rapidly flashed still pictures in a "motion" picture.

b. Our eyes cannot see more than about sixteen separate images in one second. When more than that number appear, the pictures appear to run together.

Get pupils to reason: We cannot see more than sixteen separate images in one second. If true, would motion pictures be flashed on a screen faster or slower than sixteen frames per second? (Faster, the children should reason. It is actually about twenty-four frames per second.) make
inferences

Now present this problem: How can we discover the number of frames flashed through a movie projector each second? (Lightly mark with crayon the film frame closest to the projection slot. Run the projector for exactly 10 seconds. Mark with crayon the frame just beyond the slot. Count the number of frames between the crayon marks and divide by 10.) develop
procedures

Ask the class to calculate how many separate frames are flashed in an hour-long movie. (24 frames × 60 seconds × 60 minutes = 86,400 frames.) reason
quantitatively

EXTENDING ACTIVITIES

1. Let children investigate insect eyes with hand lenses. Some are compound eyes, as in the housefly. Each of the hundreds of facets seems to record a separate image.

2. Encourage several children to check encyclopedias and trade books for information on animal eyes. Have them report on the special ways in which such animals as snakes, cats, rabbits, and bottom-dwelling fish benefit from their visual organs.

3. Invite a school nurse to give an illustrated talk on eye safety and care.

Magnets and Their Properties

(Primary Emphasis)

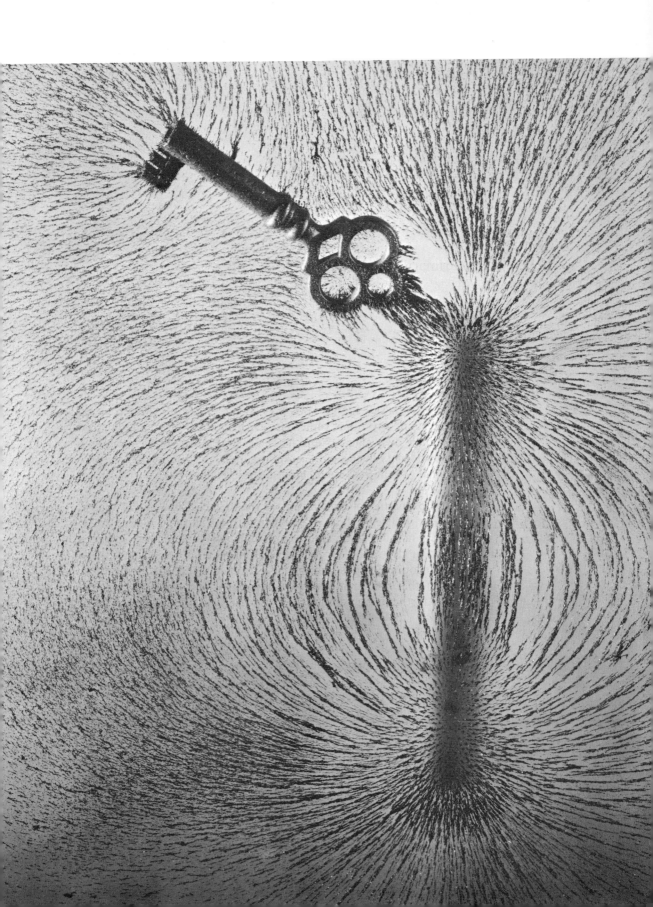

UNIT FOUR

Magnets and Their Properties

(Primary Emphasis)

AT THE PRIMARY LEVEL MAGNETS ARE PROBABLY STUDIED MORE
widely than any other topic. Growing numbers of young children
have their own magnets and magnetic toys. Many learn something
about magnets even before enrolling in school. For these reasons,
we shall go into the subject more deeply than has been customary at
this level.

The properties of magnetism are the theme. Among other things,
children will learn how magnetism attracts through different materials;[1] how it can be studied although invisible; and how it is preserved or destroyed. If only several magnets are available for this
unit, encourage pupils to bring theirs from home. Also, the third section of this unit includes some directions for "making" magnets.
Many forthcoming activities are suitable for either groups or individuals.

GENERALIZATIONS

I. Magnets commonly attract objects made of iron and steel.

II. A magnet attracts objects without touching them because
there is a field of force around it; the field is most powerful at the
ends, or poles.

III. Magnetism can pass through many materials.

[1] Wristwatches should be removed before working with magnets.

Credit for chapter opening photograph. **Bernice Abbott-Photo Researchers, Inc.**

246

IV. Iron or steel are the commonest materials magnetized by a magnet; steel holds its magnetism longer than iron.

V. The field of force around a wire carrying electricity can be used to magnetize iron or steel objects.

VI. Compasses are magnets that show directions because of the earth's magnetism; unlike poles of magnets attract, like poles repel each other.

VII. Dropping, heating, or storing a magnet improperly will weaken its force.

Magnets and What They Attract. There is no scarcity of magnets about us for examples in teaching. In kitchens, cloth pot holders containing magnets are placed conveniently on the sides of stoves. Automatic can openers contain magnets to hold opened can lids. Cabinet doors remain closed because of magnets. Some women wear magnetic earrings. Beauty operators use magnets to pick up dropped hairpins. Physicians sometimes employ them to extract pieces of metal from wounds. Toy stores contain a variety of toys that in some way use magnetism.

In nearly all these cases, the metals attracted to a magnet are iron and steel. Less well-known magnetic metals are cobalt and nickel. Among the commoner metals not attracted by magnets are brass (an alloy of copper and zinc), aluminum, tin, silver, stainless steel (an alloy of several metals), copper, bronze (an alloy of copper and tin), and gold.

It will be helpful to know several facts about situations that may cause some confusion in this unit unless they are understood. For example, a question may arise about the attractable property of so-called "tin" cans. These are made of thin sheet steel and coated lightly with tin. Although tin is not attractable, steel is. Confusion may also result if some straight pins are attracted by a magnet and other identical-appearing pins are not. Scraping off some silver coating on the nonattractable pins will usually reveal that they are made of

brass. Also, whereas pure nickel is ordinarily magnetic, the United States five-cent piece is largely composed of copper and so should not be used as an example.

Natural magnets are sometimes called "lodestones," or "leading stones," perhaps because ancient mariners used them as crude compasses. Lodestones are composed of magnetite, an iron ore found in different locations on the earth's crust. Since only some of these deposits are magnetized, theories have been developed to explain this phenomenon. One such theory holds that lightning may have been responsible. It is thought that electricity discharged into the ore may have arranged many atoms within the ore in a manner similar to that found in magnets. Traces of magnetite are common in soils. A magnet dragged along the ground or in a playground sandbox may attract many particles. These particles can be an effective substitute in experiments where iron "filings" are used.

Man-made or artificial magnets are often composed of steel and magnetized by electricity. Named for their shape, there are *bar, V, U, horseshoe,* and *cylindrical* magnets, to give the more familiar varieties. (Figure 4-1.) Each of these magnets attracts substances most strongly at the ends, or poles. The U, V, and horseshoe magnets are more powerful than the others, when all factors are equal; they are bent so two poles attract instead of one.

Powerful *alnico* magnets are now available to teachers at scientific supply houses and in commercial kits. These are made from aluminum, cobalt, nickel, and iron. Alnico magnets are used for such home and commercial purposes mentioned at the beginning of this section, as well as for a variety of others.

So far, we have described permanent magnets. Though useful, they do not compare with the enormous importance of temporary magnets, or more accurately, *electromagnets.* These will be discussed more fully later.

The strategy of the first sequence is to

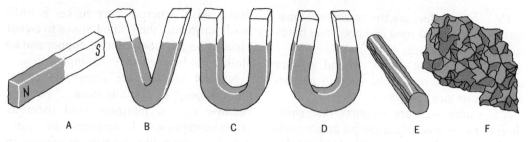

Figure 4-1 Magnets. (a) bar, (b) V, (c) U, (d) horseshoe, (e) cylindrical and (f) lodestone.

build an understanding in the children of the materials that magnets will attract. This understanding can then be used to figure out why, given a number of apparently identical objects, only some are attractable. An extending activity will require thinking about how to control variables, and how to interpret data.

Generalization I: Magnets commonly attract objects made of iron and steel

1. *Materials:* several magnets (have one attached to a 2-foot string); iron roller-skate key; shoe box of numerous attractable and nonattractable objects, metals and nonmetals, including the following chart materials or substitutes. (Be sure to have examples of the six metals listed. Children can bring these objects from home, although the exact purpose should not be revealed; all can be returned.) If the children can read, have this material written on the chalkboard and concealed by a pull-down map:

Name:	Made of:	We Think:	We Found Out:
nails	iron	–	–
wire	copper	–	–
pins	steel	–	–
hair curler	aluminum	–	–
penny	bronze	–	–
scissors	steel	–	–
screws	brass	–	–

You might begin with this bridge: "Let's say one day you are walking over some

very large rocks. You have a roller-skate key in your hand. While jumping from one rock to another the key slips out of your hand and falls in between two very big rocks. The space is too small to get your arm into, even though you can see the key is just an arm's length below. How can you get the key back?"

Be prepared for a variety of approaches, some ingenious. (One trial class child said, "I'd use a stick with chewing gum on the end.") Finally, if no one suggests it, ask how a magnet and string can be used. Does it make any difference what the key is made of? What metals *will* a magnet pull?

Reveal the chalkboard material. Hold up one listed item at a time. Will a magnet pull this kind of metal? Ask pupils to make a guess about each of six to eight different objects of varying metals. Before and after each one is tried, write "yes" or "no" in the appropriate columns. (You need not be concerned about children learning the names of most of the metals. The important thing is for them to realize gradually that only a few metals are attractable.)

How about other objects and materials? What will a magnet attract? Distribute all of the materials to small groups and invite the children to follow a similar guess-test procedure. They can separate the materials into two piles, one "yes" pile for attractable objects, one "no" pile for unattractable objects. After a short work period, the several smaller piles can be added together to make two large "yes" and "no" piles on a table in front of the class.

develop procedure

248

Have a class discussion. What do the "yes" materials look like? What do the "no" materials look like? Let someone make a subset of "no" metals. What do "no" metals look like? Help pupils infer *make inferences* that it is more likely that materials in the "yes" pile were made of iron or steel than the other materials. Now hold up a skate key. What metals does it most look like? (Iron or steel.) Will a magnet attract it? Let someone try it.

2. *Materials:* nail file, or small coarse rock; magnifying glass; magnet; several identical-appearing straight pins of brass and steel on a table. (Test with a magnet to determine which are steel.)

Ask someone to put the straight pins in a box. Have him use a magnet to make the task "easier." When failure is experienced with some (brass) pins, let the children first *state problems* define the problem, then raise hypotheses as to why failure occurred.

suggest hypotheses Their previous input with nonattractable objects including metals should prompt some children to guess that some of the pins are made of one or more nonattractable metals. If not, review their initial experi- *develop procedures* ence. If this guess is made, ask for a test.

Pupils may decide that attracted and un- attracted pins may be rubbed against a nail file or rough stone. As the thin coating is worn away, steel pins will appear dull gray, and brass pins yellowish. Let the test continue until a pattern develops. All at- tracted pins will be one color, all unattracted pins another. This will help verify the hy- pothesis. Have them compare the ma- terials with the half-dozen metals identified in activity 1. Can they identify the two *make inferences* different pin metals?

Bring out that some pins were made of steel, and some of *brass* — a metal that is not attracted by magnetism.

EXTENDING ACTIVITIES

1. Have a magnet power test. You will need six or more magnets, a box of *small* paper clips, a box of carpet tacks or brads (small nails), masking tape and crayon for marking the magnets. (You might mark the magnets with a masking tape strip of a different color to help the class learn colors, or letters of the alphabet to aid this learn- ing.)

Line up all the magnets on a table. Which magnet is most powerful? Ask for reasons why some are picked. (Most chil- dren will cite larger size.) Suggest that they test the magnets and order them from strongest to weakest. But there will need to be some "rules" (controls) to make sure *develop procedures* everything is fair. Work these out with the children, but keep the list small:

Only one end (pole) is used.

The same size paper clips are used.

Clips are completely picked up, end to end in a chain (not bunched).

Record the data on the chalkboard:

Magnet	Clips	Rank
A	3	
B	2	
C	4	
D	5	
E	2	
F	3	

Probably there will be a few ties, since the paper clips are a crude measure. How to break the ties? See if the children suggest a more sensitive test, such as using carpet tacks or brads. After ties are broken, *reason quantitatively* get pupils to rank the magnets in order of power (first, second, etc.) by interpreting the numerical data. This can be done on individual worksheets while you circulate around the room checking the work and helping where needed.

Why weren't the magnets equally power- ful? Develop that not all magnets are made of the same materials or made in the same way. Another reason is that some are not properly cared for.

2. Acquaint the class with some stand- ards for the care and keeping of magnets. It is suggested that no attempts be made at this time to reason through these stand- ards, as this requires input that will be ac-

the unit. However, tell the chil-
~~t~~ these standards will help keep
~~mag~~nets in good condition. See Figure
~~3~~ for some model charts. Chart A
~~so~~ft iron "keepers" in two instances.
~~If regu~~lar keepers are not available, nails or
other soft iron objects will do. Two strips
cut from a tinned can work well with bar
magnets. (Caution: File down jagged or
sharp edges to make them safe for handling.)

3. If possible, provide several different
kinds of magnets for exploration. Teach
their proper names. Some magnets might
be brought by class members.

Magnetic Field of Force. As children explore with magnets, they will observe that
a magnet will attract from a distance. For
example, a small nail or paper clip will
"jump" to the magnet. They will also see
that the attractive force is strongest at the
poles. This offers an opportunity to illustrate the field of force surrounding a magnet.

Although it is impossible to see the field
directly, its presence may be inferred.
Sprinkle iron filings on a sheet of stiff
white paper placed over a magnet. Observe
that their distribution is orderly, with the
greatest concentration of filings at the poles.

(Figure 4-3.) Theoretically, a magnetic
field extends outward to an infinite distance. But for practical purposes the field
ends where its presence is no longer detectable.

**Generalization II: A magnet attracts ob-
jects without touching them because there
is a field of force around it; the field is most
powerful at the ends, or poles**

Materials: for each small group, container of iron filings (a salt shaker is useful);
a sheet of stiff, white paper; carpet tacks or
small paper clips; two powerful magnets.

Place the foregoing materials on a table.
You might want to begin with a demonstra-
tion-discussion. Hold up a magnet and ask,
"How close must this magnet be to attract
iron or steel objects?" Allow several children to try different distances with a magnet
and carpet tacks or small paper clips. Have
them find which part of the magnet appears
most powerful. If several magnets of differing strengths are available, let the children
demonstrate that some will attract over a
greater distance than others. "How is it
possible for these magnets to pick up things
without touching them?" Most children
will realize that "something" is causing

Figure 4-2 A–B

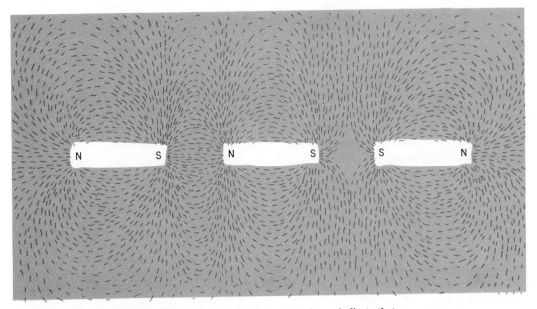

Figure 4-3 Besides revealing fields of force, iron filings in this picture indicate that like poles of magnets repel and unlike poles attract each other.

interaction between the two objects, but will not be able to identify what the "something" is. After the class reacts, you might remark, "Here is a way we can find out."

Lay the magnet on a table and place a sheet of stiff white paper over it. Explain that the container holds small bits of iron, called "filings." Sprinkle some filings on the paper above the magnet. Tap the paper gently to assist in the distribution of filings. Have the children observe that the filings are arranged in an orderly pattern some distance around the magnet. Tell them that this area is the magnet's *field of force*. The idea of field (area) and force (push or pull) might be explained simply here, if needed.

Note that concentrations of "lines" of force shown by the filings seem greatest at the poles. Bring out that this is probably the reason the ends of the magnet seemed more powerful than its other parts. Observe that this force is invisible, but that we can see what it does through this demonstration. Help the class to realize that an iron or steel object can be attracted without being touched as long as it is within the magnet's field of force. Point out that the magnet's

make
inferences

strength and weight of the attracted object determine whether this attraction becomes noticeable.

Encourage groups to explore various patterns they can make by arranging one or two magnets in different positions and sprinkling iron filings on white paper placed over the magnets. Who can tell how the magnets are arranged underneath just by looking at the iron filing patterns?

make
inferences

EXTENDING ACTIVITY

Prepare several simple-to-harder "magnet inference sheets" from permanent records of lines of force made with one or several magnets. The object is for the child to observe the magnetic field record, then try to duplicate it. He should be given the permanent record sheet, the original magnet or magnets used, a stiff sheet of white paper, and a shakerful of iron filings. A sketch of the original magnet positions on the back of the magnet inference sheet may help to verify these positions for some pupils, but is not needed if the patterns are reasonably

make
inferences

251

clear. Some ambiguity is desirable to require careful observing and interpreting of possible matching patterns. It is also good for pupils to learn self-reliance in getting answers.

Permanent records can be made in several ways, including blueprint paper or plastic spray. Arrange one or two magnets in various positions on a cardboard tray. Put blueprint paper on top and sprinkle with iron filings. Place this carefully in a windless, sunny area, without disturbing the pattern or magnets. Expose for 5 to 10 minutes, then remove the filings. A blue-and-white record of the lines of force will remain. (Look on the blueprint paper package for possible extra steps to insure a permanent record, such as running cold water over it.)

For a more realistic-appearing record, use plastic spray to fix the filings on a stiff sheet of white paper. Hold the aerosol can at sufficient distance so filings are not blown away. For best results, be sure to use fine, powder-like filings and to sprinkle lightly. *Let the spray dry before removing the sheet* from the magnets.

Magnetic Transparency. An intriguing phenomenon of a magnetic field is that it can pass through many substances without apparent loss of effect. It seems as though

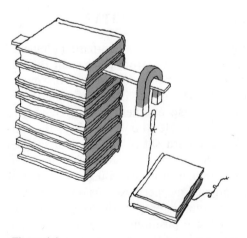

Figure 4-4

these materials are "transparent" to the passage of the lines of force. This makes it possible for magnetic earrings to be worn, and for wristwatches to be affected unless precautions are taken. Plumbers may use magnets in locating pipes (iron or steel) behind walls or under floors. In fact, the field of force will penetrate any nonmagnetic materials the class may test.

Materials of iron and steel are considered "opaque" to this force. When touched by a magnet, the force passes inside them and back into the magnet.

Generalization III: Magnetism can pass through many materials

Materials: for you, a brimful glass of water with a paper clip inside; a magnet; for each small group, flat, thin pieces of glass, steel (can tops), plastic, aluminum or aluminum foil, wood, and so on; magnet; thread; small paper clip; ruler; books. (Place the objects on a table and set up the magnet as in Figure 4-4. However, leave the attached paper clip lying on the table until after your bridge.)

Hold up the brimful glass of water with a small paper clip inside. Who can get this paper clip out of the glass with a magnet without putting the magnet into the water? Probably someone will show that a strong *develop procedures* magnet can be touched to the glass adjacent to the paper clip to attract the clip. If the magnet is moved carefully up the side of a glass, the paper clip will follow. Bring out the apparent reason. Probably the *make inferences* magnetism went through the water and glass.

Now, suspend the paper clip, as in the model of Figure 4-4. Pull the thread end gently to lower the clip to just above the point of falling. Elicit that the magnetic *develop procedures* field is attracting it through air. "How can we use this setup and materials on the table to see if magnetism will go through objects?"

Have some children try slipping various flat objects in the space between the magnet and paper clip. Relate their findings to the initial problem.

When a tinned can top and other attractable objects are placed in the space, they will note that the paper clip falls. Guide them to understand that magnetism will penetrate nonmagnetic materials, but does not seem to pass through magnetic materials.

make inferences

EXTENDING ACTIVITIES

1. Try this little problem to help pupils apply their knowledge, and for appraisal. Hold up a tinned can full of water with a paper clip inside. Have a magnet in full view. Ask for ways in which the paper clip might be gotten out of the can. (Naturally, the iron will block the magnetism if a magnet is used.) If someone does suggest using a magnet (as with the glass of water previously), find how many agree and disagree, hold an evaluative discussion, and then test the idea.

suggest hypotheses

2. Prepare some "hidden object" boxes. These can give children a chance to make inferences from indirect evidence, and to improve in communication skills. The activity can take three or more forms, each progressively harder.

In the first form the child receives a shoe box and a magnet. On the box is a card that identifies several hidden objects which have been taped by you anywhere inside except on the bottom. (Figure 4-5.) The box is not to be opened, picked up, or shaken, although it can be turned around for convenience. The child tries to find the exact locations of the objects by sliding his magnet around the box's outside surface. He also tries to identify the proper objects in these locations and to infer whether they are in a parallel or perpendicular position relative to the box base. (The last task can be skipped to make it easier.)

make inferences

For a second version of the game, the searcher tells someone else what he thinks the objects might be, exactly where to find

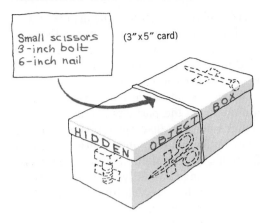

Figure 4-5

them, and their positions relative to the box base. The "catch" is that he must verbally give the directions once, and without gestures.

In the third version the searcher is the data source for someone else. Tape only one object, or two at the most, inside the box. If two objects are used, one need only be identified as the "big object," and the other the "small object." After the searcher has used his magnet to explore all over the box surface for possible box contents, a partner (who has not observed the exploration) tries to extract the data from him by asking questions that can only be answered by a "yes" or "no" response. The measure of success is to ask the fewest questions possible to locate and describe the object. (This can be discussed in an evaluative session.) Here is an example of how the third version might go, using one taped object:

"Is the object in the half of the box nearest me?"

"Yes."

"Is it on one of the long sides?"

"No."

"Is it on the top?"

"No."

"Is it parallel to the box bottom?"

"Yes."

The questioner now states his inference about the contents and location. So that

make inferences

253

make
inferences

there is no doubt about it, he also points to the box end facing him as the object's location, and moves his forefinger from side to side to show its parallel position. The box is opened for verification.

When the inference and actual location are different, the partners discuss possible reasons for the discrepancy. Perhaps the searcher has made some faulty inferences from his search data. Perhaps the questioner has made a faulty inference from the information he received from the searcher.

When two objects are used (each should be taped in a different location), the game is played in the same way. The effect is simply to introduce another set of variables that must be discovered by the searcher and questioner.

All taped objects in these games must be both attractable and sizable for successful inferences. Probably none should be smaller than a 3-inch iron nail. If more than one object is used, each should vary at least 50 per cent in size from other objects.

Making Magnets. A magnet can be made from a piece of iron or steel by stroking it in one direction with one pole of a permanent magnet. Its power increases with the number of strokes applied. If a piece of over six or eight inches is used, stroke with one pole from the object's center outward for at least twenty strokes. Repeat the procedure on the remaining half, but this time with the magnet's opposite pole. This should produce good results. Be sure to lift the magnet clear at the end of each stroke before bringing it back to start another. Merely rubbing it back and forth will produce unsatisfactory results.

Although it takes longer to induce magnetism in steel than in iron, steel retains its magnetism longer. Common materials made of steel include scissors, some knitting needles, sewing needles, screwdrivers, hacksaw blades, and knife blades. Perhaps the commonest useful examples of soft iron are nails and wire coat hangers.

A more efficient way to induce magnetism is by using electricity. This is developed in another basic generalization of the unit.

Generalization IV: Iron or steel are the commonest materials magnetized by a magnet; steel holds its magnetism longer than iron

This activity leads to four controlled experiments with magnets. The beginning phase provides some of the input necessary to perform these experiments intelligently.

Materials: several large (4-inch) nails; box of carpet tacks; magnets; steel straight pins; paper clips; large steel sewing needles; needles; screwdriver; or similar objects.

Place your materials on a table. Invite a child to pick up a carpet tack and try to attract another tack with it. Then have him use a magnet to attract a tack. Guide him to build a "chain" of tacks, using each magnetized tack to attract another. Permit him to continue until the chain is broken. Probably by this part of the unit the children will have made many "chains" in magnet play.

If a powerful magnet is available, hold a pole of the magnet just above the head of a tack without touching it. It should be possible to make a small chain of tacks dangle from the first tack. (If the tacks you use are too small to be held conveniently in your fingers, just use a small nail in place of the first tack.) Magnetism is induced in the tacks by the magnet's field of force. Ask a few questions. "What could we call each tack that attracted another tack? Was each tack a magnet to begin with? What caused each tack to become a magnet?" Bring out that magnets can be made out of steel and iron objects.

Now demonstrate how to induce magnetism in several objects. Use a large nail, a large steel sewing needle, or similar materials. Show first that these are not magnetized by touching them to a tack. With either pole of a magnet, stroke the object its entire length *in one direction only*. Call this to the children's attention. Lift the magnet at the end of each stroke for about twenty to thirty strokes. Demonstrate that the object is now a magnet.

For follow-up activities, say, "Here are some questions that need experiments to find the answers. Let's see if you can think of ways we can find these answers." (Each experiment will need controls the children can construct, if they are guided to see the necessity for them. After each question, briefly discuss how the experiment should be done. Substitute appropriate materials where necessary.)

develop procedures

a. "Will this nail's magnetism get more powerful the more it is stroked?" (First, test the nail for magnetism by seeing if it attracts paper clips. It should not. Test again after each ten strokes with a magnet.)

b. "Which can be magnetized more easily—a soft iron nail or a sewing needle made of hard steel?" (Each object is first tested for magnetism, stroked once before each test, tested again with tacks, and so on.)

c. "Which will keep its strength longer—the magnetized, soft iron nail, or the magnetized needle made of hard steel?" (Same procedure as above is followed, except that objects are initially stroked more times and tested after a 10-minute or longer interval. The difference will be greater if the objects are used normally rather than left undisturbed during the waiting period.)

d. "Will a magnet you make be more powerful if stroked in one direction or back and forth in two directions?" (Use two identical nails. Test to see if magnetized. Stroke each thirty times—one in a single direction and one fifteen times each way. Test with tacks.)

If you have a capable primary class, assign the problems to various small groups so procedures can be thought through. Allow enough time for thinking to take place, and for the experiments to be tried several times.

Discussion afterward can begin by asking first for the problem, then for specific procedures followed in individual groups. With your aid, procedures can be constructively analyzed by the children. After discussion of specific findings, summarize by asking, "How can a magnet be made?" and "How can a long-lasting magnet be made?"

EXTENDING ACTIVITIES

1. What objects can be magnetized? Have children try to magnetize any object they wish. (First, each should be tested for magnetism.) If the same "yes" and "no" materials are used as in the first activity of Generalization I, pupils will discover that all the objects that were attractable in that activity also can be magnetized. Those that were nonattractable cannot be magnetized.

make inferences

2. Here is a difficult but interesting problem for children: Give two large sewing needles to each child or group. One needle is magnetized, but one is not. Which one is the magnet? The only permissible way to find out is to touch the needles, rather than to use a compass, suspend a needle from a thread, etc. The key to finding out is to know that a magnet is weakest in its center part. The children should have found this out in the previous activities in order to do well in this one. For example, if you try to place small nails or tacks along the entire length of a bar magnet, they will fall from, or adhere very weakly to, the center portion. Studying iron filings in a field of force also confirms this area of weakness. (Later, when your pupils find out more about positive and negative poles, you might ask them why the center part of a magnet is weaker. When one third-grade teacher did, the reply was, "Since it is right in between the poles, the magnet is undecided.")

Notice in Figure 4-6 A–B how the magnetized needle is discovered. In A there is no noticeable attraction when the nonmagnet is held against the middle part of

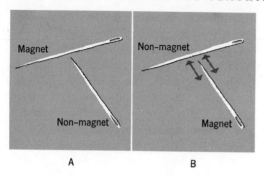

Figure 4-6 A–B

make
inferences the magnet. When the needle positions are reversed (B), the nonmagnet leaps to the pole of the magnet.

The Electromagnet. Connect a wire to a flashlight battery or dry cell, and the wire will attract iron filings. It is an *electromagnet*. If the wire is fashioned into a coil, this concentrates the effect, making it a more powerful magnet. Other ways of boosting magnetic force are to use an iron or steel core in the coil, and to increase the flow of electricity going through the wire.

Variations and applications of electromagnets are virtually endless—motors, doorbells, generators, telephones, and so on. (We shall examine a few of these in the next unit.) One of the easier and more in-teresting applications for children is the electromagnetic crane. (See Figure 4-7.)

Basically the same things are present in the crane as are needed in a related, up-coming lesson: a source of electricity, wire to carry the current, and a soft iron core around which the wire is wrapped. (See Figure 4-8.)

Children need to be made aware that a soft iron core is used in electromagnets rather than hard steel, since steel tends to become permanently magnetized. If they have studied the previous generalization, most should have no trouble understanding this fact. They will also realize the advantage of having a magnet that can be shut off or turned on whenever needed.

A question may be raised if certain lightweight materials such as tacks or pins continue to be attracted to the electromagnet after electricity is shut off. This is due to "residual" magnetism, or the small amount that remains for a while in the soft iron nail or core. These materials will usually fall off when shaken slightly. Stove bolts typically have less residual magnetism than nails of comparable size.

Generalization V: The field of force around a wire carrying electricity can be used to magnetize iron and steel objects

Figure 4-7 An electromagnetic crane at work. (1) shows the metal cover, (2) where the wire is coiled around an iron core and how the wire leads to the cab, (3) where the storage batteries or generator are housed.

256

1. *Materials:* for each pair of pupils or group, a 6-foot length of plastic insulated Number 20 copper wire (remove an inch of insulation from each end so proper contact can be made when it is connected to a battery); a large iron bolt or nail; a steel rod (a screwdriver will do); several tacks or steel straight pins; a "D" flashlight battery; a projection of an electromagnetic crane, as in Figure 4-7.

state problems

Show your class the crane sketch and ask, "What is happening in this picture?" If necessary, draw attention to the manner of lifting. Scrap metal objects appear to be sticking to the device suspended from the crane. Bring out that probably some kind of large magnet is attached to the crane and its apparent purpose is to move scrap iron and steel from one place to another.

suggest hypotheses

"If this is a big magnet, how can the crane operator remove materials from his magnet?" Observation of the electric wire may help the children in guessing. Guide toward a hypothesis that permits the crane operator to turn the magnetism on and off. Ask *how* this is possible. If no one knows, tell the class the crane has a magnet attached to it that operates through electricity. It is called an *electromagnet.*

Using the sketch, point out three features: (1) a metal core; (2) wire wrapped around the core inside the cover; and, tracing the wire from the core to the crane's cab, point out (3) a place where batteries or generators are kept to provide electricity. Indicate the materials and ask, "How could these objects be used to make an electromagnet?"

develop procedures

Pupils may need assistance in touching the wire ends properly to the terminals of the battery (Figure 4-8). Although the wire ends can be taped to the terminals, a direct connection of this kind will completely drain the battery's power if left for a length of time. Both wire ends can be touched to the terminals when power is desired, and pulled away when power is to be shut off. Or a single wire end can be taped and the other end touched and pulled away to control the electricity.

Give the children time to play with the electromagnets. They will try touching and removing the wires alternately from the terminals. They will note that nails or other attracted objects fall off after the wire is disconnected. (Remember, if lightweight objects are used, residual magnetism in the electromagnet may continue to attract them for a time even after the wire is disconnected.) If needed, suggest that they experiment with the number of turns of wire. They will observe that increasing the number of turns increases power.

2. Review that in a previous lesson they had magnetized hard steel and soft iron objects. Steel retained its magnetism longer. Ask which metal should be used in the core of an electromagnet to work properly. Encourage reasons for answers. Guide toward the hypothesis that a steel core will become a permanent magnet but that a soft iron core will lose its magnetism quickly. Invite a group to set up an experiment to find out.

A large nail and small screwdriver can be used for the cores. Guide the children to realize needed controls: same wire and number of turns on each core; cores should be about the same size; the same battery should be used, and same objects attracted.

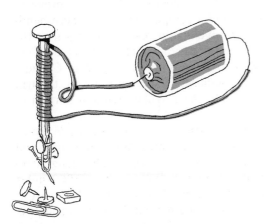

Figure 4-8 A wire carrying electricity makes an effective electromagnet when wrapped 20 or more times around a large nail.

Both iron and steel cores must be tested for magnetism before the experiment.

make
inferences   Children should find that a steel core will become a permanent magnet, and is therefore unsatisfactory for this purpose.

Magnetic Poles. Suspend a bar magnet from a string in North America and a curious thing happens; it points toward the north magnetic pole. Do the same in South America and it points toward the south magnetic pole. (This assumes no interference from nearby metal deposits or objects.) A magnetized needle placed horizontally on a floating wood chip or slice of cork also points toward a magnetic pole.

To see why this is so, consider the poles of a magnet. When another magnet or magnetized object is held near a suspended or floating magnet, the like poles (north-north or south-south) repel each other. The opposite poles (south-north or north-south) attract each other.

The earth itself acts like a giant magnet. No one knows why, but there are some theories. One explanation holds that several parts of the earth's interior rotate at different speeds. The resulting friction strips electric particles from atoms. This causes an electric current to be generated which creates a magnetic field. Since the earth's core is supposedly made of nickel-iron, the effect is that of a huge electromagnet buried within the earth.

Recall the activities before that dealt with magnetic fields of force. When iron filings were sprinkled on paper placed over a bar magnet, they revealed lines of force looping from one pole to another, and concentrating at both poles. On a gigantic scale, somewhat the same type of magnetic field is evidenced with the earth's magnetism.

Lines of force from the earth's magnetism run roughly north and south far into space and then loop down to concentrate at the north and south magnetic poles. Therefore, a freely swinging magnet—bar, horseshoe, or any other type with dominant poles—tends to assume a direction parallel to these lines of force. Since lines of force terminate at the magnetic poles, properly following a compass in the northern hemisphere eventually results in arrival at the north magnetic pole. This is located above the upper Hudson Bay region of Canada. If a southernly direction is taken, the trip terminates near Wilkes Land, a portion of Antarctica.

The north and south *magnetic* poles should not be confused with the north and south *geographic* poles. The geographic and magnetic poles are about 1000 miles apart in the north and 1500 miles apart in the south. In other words, when a compass points north, it does *not* point true north, or toward the north star. Charts must be made for navigators which show the angular

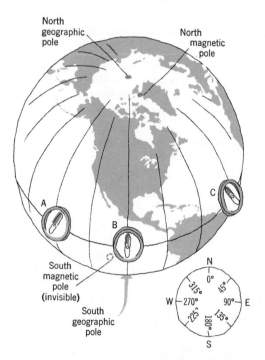

Figure 4-9 Note in A, B, and C an angle between the meridian on which the compass is located and the direction toward which the needle points. These are variations that must be added or subtracted from a compass heading to determine true north. For example, true heading for A, B, and C should be 0°, or north. Actual readings are 35°, 5°, and 315°. A chart would indicate the need to subtract 35° from A, 5° from B, and to add 45° to C.

variation between true north and the direction toward which a compass points. These charts must be periodically changed, as the magnetic poles are slowly but continually shifting. (See Figure 4-9.)

Many persons are surprised to discover that a bar magnet or compass points with its "N" or *north* pole toward the earth's *north* magnetic pole. Yet it is known that *like* poles *repel* and unlike poles attract. How is this apparent paradox explained? The answer lies in antiquity. Compasses were used long before reasons for their operation were understood. So it became customary to speak of the end of a magnet that points northward as the north pole. It is more accurately called the *north-seeking* pole, and its counterpart the *south-seeking* pole.

Of course, these explanations of magnetic variation and misnaming of the magnet's poles are intended more for your background than for presentation to most pupils at the primary level. Compasses and earth magnetism are not easy for primary pupils to understand. Unless you have a very able group, you may want to consider skipping this generalization or using it only with older pupils.

Generalization VI: Compasses are magnets that show directions because of the earth's magnetism; unlike poles attract, and like poles repel each other

This sequence is designed to gradually introduce the functions of magnetic compasses and what makes them work.

1. *Materials:* two bar magnets (or two magnetized steel knitting needles, or rods, or hacksaw blades); 18-inch thread; four cards marked *north, south, east* and *west* respectively; cork; needle; brimful glass of water; masking tape; compass; 6-inch piece of copper wire.

Place directional cards prominently on the walls. If the walls are not aligned with reference to a cardinal direction, cards can

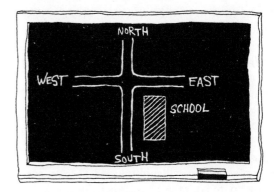

Figure 4-10

be affixed to chairs or taped down on the floor.

You might ask, "What do you notice today in our room that you have not seen before? What do these words tell us? Who lives north of our school? South? East? West?"

Draw a chalkboard sketch of the school and two main streets that run north-south and east-west. If this is impossible, use a sketch of Figure 4-10.

Picking out various locations on this "map," ask the children directions they would take to come to school, go home, and so on. Continue until it is obvious that most everyone knows the four cardinal directions.

2. Suspend by a thin thread a bar magnet or substitute. (A 6-inch copper wire bent into a J-shaped "cradle" will save fumbling around in attaching the string and balancing the magnet. First, make an oval of the wire; twist the ends together. Turn the oval sideways and bend it into a J shape. Attach a thread to the top of the cradle. For a stand, use an overturned wooden chair, or pile of books with a ruler tucked part way into the top book. Cover the magnet's poles with masking or adhesive tape, so that pupils will need to identify poles for control purposes. To save time, it will be helpful to set up these materials before working with the class.)

Ask a child to spin the magnet around *lightly*. (Otherwise the spinning takes too long to stop.) After the magnet stops, ask the class toward what main direction the magnet is pointing. Repeat this procedure. When the children again say the magnet points north, ask how they can be sure, since both taped ends are alike. They should then see the need to mark one end for control purposes.

develop procedures

Use the same procedure with another suspended magnet (at least 10 feet away). Are similar results obtained? (Make certain no iron or steel objects are close enough to affect the magnets.) Elicit that these magnets seem to point reliably in one direction. Develop that if one direction is known, then other directions are also known.

3. Continue this sequence with a floating needle demonstration. (Figure 4-11.) Have ready a needle, a magnet to magnetize the needle, a brimful glass of water, and a thin cross section of a cork top. (Make a shallow groove across the top to cradle the needle, otherwise it may roll off.)

Hold up the needle, and ask someone to magnetize it. To avoid confusion, the needle should be stroked from its blunt end to its point with the magnet's "S" pole. This will insure that the sharp end points north. Develop speculation as to what direction it will point if placed horizontally on a cork and floated in water.

Again an approximate north-south align-

Figure 4-11

260

ment should be indicated. Elicit that a magnetized needle, too, can point out directions.

(Sometimes this demonstration is interfered with by the cork's tendency to drift against a container's sides. This is caused by the attraction of the water molecules to the sides, which creates a slight rise around the rim of the water line. Since a floating object floats to the highest possible point, it naturally drifts toward a container's sides. By using a *brimful* glass of water it stays centered, since this tends to be the highest area.)

4. Keep the bar magnets in activity 2 and needle in activity 3 set up and pointing northward. Produce a compass, or several, for close inspection by everyone. Establish that it is pointing in the same direction as the other materials. Elicit that it, too, is probably a magnet.

Set up some hypothetical situations in which the children can use a compass. For example, they are at sea; no landmarks exist. They know, however, land is northward. In what direction shall they sail? Continue with south, east, and west. Use at least several compasses, if possible, for maximum pupil participation and understanding. For further clarification, draw a simple chalkboard sketch of a compass, with only four principal directions and a needle. Bring out the advantages of being able to use a compass when lost in a wooded area, sailing at sea, or flying at night.

5. *Materials:* two bar magnets, one suspended from a string; magnets and compasses for the children.

If the class is above average, it will be worthwhile in this and the next activity to go into *why* magnets point north. With one magnet suspended and the other in his hand, have a child demonstrate what happens when the like poles are brought together. Have him try opposite poles. Use often and together the words "pull" and "attract," "push" and "repel" until the children are reasonably aware of their meaning. Have pupils try a similar procedure with compasses and magnets. A similar effect will be observed with the compass needles. After sufficient trial, bring out as clearly as possible the fundamental law of magnets: unlike poles attract and like poles repel each other.

6. Ask someone to explain why magnets point north-south, rather than in other directions. A satisfactory explanation will probably not be given. Now draw a chalkboard sketch of Figure 4-12.

Explain that deep inside the earth are huge amounts of magnetized metals. Although these metals do *not* look like the big bar magnet drawn in the picture, they do attract and repel magnets in much the same way. Have the children recall how they previously discovered that magnetism could penetrate many substances. Bring out that the earth's magnetic field of force exists everywhere on earth. Its effect can be seen with magnets or compasses, whether underwater, in the air, or on land.

EXTENDING ACTIVITIES

1. Try several additional activities to clinch the important idea of like and unlike poles. You will need two strong bar magnets, one with the poles clearly marked and the second with concealed pole markings; several small nails.

Suspend three or four small nails in a "chain" from a pole of the marked magnet. Elicit from the class that each nail is now a tiny magnet, each with a pole. Speculate *suggest hypotheses* where the N and S poles are on the first nail, second nail, and so on. Have various children draw on the chalkboard their versions and describe their supporting reasons.

Now have someone bring a pole of the *unmarked* magnet near the end of the last nail in the chain, as in Figure 4-13. Let him reverse the poles. The nail will be either *make inferences* repelled or attracted in turn. Can we predict what pole is next to the nail? Discuss reasons for the predictions, then reveal the

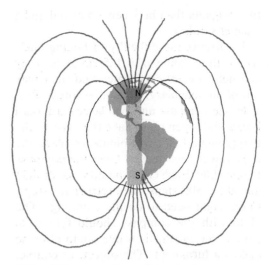

Figure 4-12

poles' identity. Like poles repel, unlike poles attract.

2. Suspend several "mystery objects" around the room. Are they magnets or not? Children can use a magnet to find out. (The objects may be prepared by wrapping a bar magnet in construction paper and suspending it from a string; a wrapped nail of similar length can serve as a nonmagnetic object. When a magnet is brought close to the concealed magnet one pole will be repelled. Children may also notice a more powerful *make inferences* attraction between the unlike poles of the

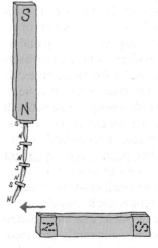

Figure 4-13

261

two magnets than between a nail end and a magnet's pole.)

3. Discuss the difficulty of finding one's way without landmarks. Inform pupils they can help several classmates find their way out of an imaginary, unfamiliar forest. Provide one compass and two large cardboard boxes with open tops. Take the class to the playground. Let two volunteers place the boxes over their heads. Give the compass to one child. Each child should walk straight ahead for 300 steps, then retrace his steps. (You might need to do the counting.) The child with the compass should follow its needle due north, then due south after he makes a turnabout. The object, of course, is to see which child will come closest to the starting point.

develop procedures Take caution to insure that ground markings, noises, and so on do not give directional clues to the participants. A discussion in the room before the demonstration, about procedures and needed controls, will be worthwhile.

develop procedures 4. For an agreed time period, have all those with compasses try to discover a location where their compass needle will *not* point north. Caution them about nearby interference from iron or steel objects, or let them discover such faulty procedure for themselves.

Magnetic Theory and Magnet Care. Important as magnetism is, science has yet to provide a satisfactory explanation of its cause. One theory, capable of being understood by young children, is based on observations they can make for themselves. It has been known for many years that heating or repeatedly dropping a magnet will cause it to lose its magnetic properties. And, although a magnet may be broken into smaller and smaller pieces, each fragment continues to have a north and south pole.

It is believed that small clusters of atoms within these materials each contain north and south poles. Such clusters, called *domains,* are normally randomly arranged. When an object is stroked in one direction

with a magnet, or otherwise magnetized, the domains tend to line up in a single direction. Heating a magnet forces the domains into more violent motion, and so they are likelier to become disarranged. Repeatedly dropping a magnet jars the domains out of line, with the same result. Since steel is harder than soft iron—the molecules exert a more powerful attractive force on one another—it is more difficult to rearrange the domains' makeup. But once this is done, magnetism is retained longer for the same reason. (See Figure 4-14.)

The closing experiments of this unit are based on standards for magnet care. They can be performed at an earlier time, but placing them at the end permits more pupil planning and thinking than would be possible without these experiences. It is recommended that only the effects of heating and dropping magnets be tested. Experiments on improper storage and use of a keeper are too subtle and time consuming for most primary classes.

Generalization VII: Dropping, heating, or storing a magnet improperly causes it to lose its magnetism

1. *Materials:* propane burner or alcohol burner; two large, identical nails; magnet; pliers; carpet tacks; can of water.

Try this bridge: "You have learned that to take good care of magnets they must be stored properly, and never dropped or heated. What do you think would happen to a magnet that is dropped a few times?" (Pause for comments, then hold up the nails.) "Rather than perhaps ruin our regular magnets, what could we do with these materials?"

develop procedures To avoid confusion, treat the magnetizing of the nails and "dropping" test as two distinct activities. Make sure both are stroked the same number of times, and tested with tacks. The same number of tacks should be attracted in both cases. If not, apply additional strokes as needed.

With the "dropping" test, drop only one

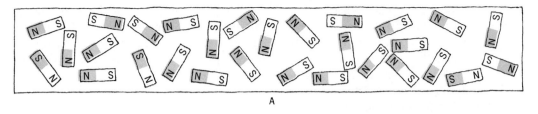

Figure 4-14 A-B An unmagnetized (A) and magnetized (B) steel bar.

magnetized nail, about thirty times. This should produce a noticeable difference in its attractive force. Help pupils to record their pretest and post-test results in this or a similar way:

	Dropped Magnet	Other Magnet
Before:	5 tacks	5 tacks
After:	2 tacks	5 tacks

(Since iron nails do not retain their initial magnetized strength very long, it is possible that the control magnet will also be weaker on the post-test. The change should be slight, however.)

make inferences Help them reason that dropping one magnet probably causes the difference in tacks attracted. To gain additional assurance of this conclusion, guide them in testing the second (control) magnet in the same way.

2. Remagnetize the nails. Develop a similar procedure with heat as the critical factor. Pliers or tongs should be used to grasp the magnetized nail while it is held vertically in the flame of a propane burner. A minute is usually long enough for significant results. (Cool it instantly by dropping make inferences it into a can of cold water.) As before, use tacks for pretest and post-test comparisons. Follow through by testing the control magnet to affirm conclusions.

3. *Materials:* magnetized, old hacksaw blade, four 18-inch pieces of strong thread; four wire cradles; bar magnet; carpet tacks; pliers; paper towel; opaque projection or sketch of Figure 4-14.

Present the projection or sketch of Figure 4-14. Explain it shows an unmagnetized and magnetized steel bar. Develop the following ideas:

a. Magnets seem to have inside them tiny bits called *domains*. Domains in the sketch do not look like real domains. They are drawn that way to help pupils learn what happens when something is magnetized.

b. When domains are lined up, they act like tiny magnets which are pointed in one direction. Stroking a needle or nail with a magnet is one way to arrange them in a line.

c. When heated or jarred, the domains get out of line and repel each other. Storing like poles together pushes the domains out of alignment, too. This causes a magnet to lose some of its force.

Call attention to the way the poles are aligned in Figure 4-14B. Elicit that the left end is the N pole and right end the S pole. What would happen to the poles if the bar is broken into two pieces? (Remain the same.) Broken into four pieces? (Remain the same.) Produce the magnetized hacksaw blade. Show that it is magnetized by picking up some tacks with both poles. If desired, suspend the blade from a string and show with a bar magnet that one end is repelled and the other attracted. Will it still act like a magnet with opposite poles if it is broken into two pieces? Four pieces? Invite predictions on the basis of how they interpret Figure 4-14B.

make inferences

After marking the poles, break the blade in half with pliers, with the blade wrapped inside a paper towel. This will prevent any pieces from flying should the blade be brittle. Let pupils use the same, previous test on each half to show no change in the magnetic poles. Also, carpet tacks will continue to be attracted. Break the parts into smaller parts and test. Pupils should infer that when a magnet is broken into smaller and smaller pieces, each retains its magnetic properties, and continues to have two poles.

make inferences

EXTENDING ACTIVITIES

1. Invite the class to draw their versions of a *partially* magnetized steel bar. In this case, some "domains" should appear aligned and some unaligned.

2. Have a display of many magnetic toys gathered by the children. Each should be explained before exhibited. Where possible, bring out ideas learned during the entire unit as such explanations are made.

The Energy of Electricity

(Upper Emphasis)

UNIT FIVE

The Energy of Electricity

(Upper Emphasis)

ONE WAY TO APPRECIATE THE ADVANTAGES OF A READY SOURCE OF electricity is to count the number of electrical devices in a modern home and then try to devise nonelectrical substitutes for them. Yet appliances alone do not represent the full importance of electricity in our lives. The atom itself is composed of electrical particles and forces. Thus it seems that anything that exists cannot escape the influence of electricity. In the study of this unit, children should begin to appreciate some of the instruments that make electrical energy available, and, more importantly, the principles that make them work.

GENERALIZATIONS

I. Current electricity flows when there is a complete circuit; circuits may be opened and closed through the use of switches.

II. Circuits may be designed in series and parallel.

III. The kind, size, and length of materials used affect the flow of electricity.

IV. Short circuits and overloaded circuits may create dangerously hot wires; fuses or circuit breakers are used to eliminate this danger.

V. Electromagnets can be made because a magnetic field is generated around a wire carrying electricity; electromagnets may be used in many ways.

Credit for chapter opening photograph. **A. Devaney, Inc.**

VI. Matter contains electrons which may be accumulated through friction into electric charges; unlike charges attract, and like charges repel one another.

Circuits and Switches. Each time we push a button or flip a switch that "turns on" electricity, there is a flow of electrical energy in wires continuously connected from the generating plant to our appliance and back again to the plant. On a smaller scale, much the same thing happens when a battery is connected to a miniature lamp. If there is a continuous connection between the source of electricity and the appliance or device using it, lights go on, bells ring, or motors spin. This continuous connection is called a *closed circuit*. Anytime there is a break or gap in the circuit, the electric flow stops. This condition is called an *open circuit*.

Regardless of their shape, size, or method of operation, electric switches serve only to open or close a circuit. They offer a safe and convenient method of supplying the flow of electricity when we want it by merely providing a linkage through which the energy can flow to the connecting wires. In studying the first generalization, pupils can discover how to make circuits and switches.

Much of the work in this unit calls for the use of dry cells, copper wire, and flashlight bulbs. Number 6 dry cells or "D" flashlight cells should be used because they are safe, fairly long lasting, and relatively inexpensive. When fresh, they deliver one and one-half volts of electricity, as contrasted with 110 to 120 volts or so supplied in the home. In other words, it would take as many as 80 of these cells connected together to have a force usually supplied by the current found in the home. *Caution the children that house current is dangerous for electrical investigations and should never be used by them for this purpose.* For an experiment needing a relatively large supply of current, twelve D or Number 6 cells connected together are a very safe

maximum. However, in this unit and most other units at the elementary level, three or four connected cells are all that will ever be needed. D-size flashlight "batteries" can be substituted for Number 6 dry cells, though being smaller they become weaker and wear out faster than the larger dry cells. Incidentally, although individual flashlight cells are often called "batteries," it is correct to use the term "battery" only when a combination of two or more cells is used.

Since the unit calls for experiments with miniature bulbs (flashlight-type bulbs), it will be helpful to understand how to use them properly. Miniature bulbs are designed to be used with a loosely specified number of one and one-half volt dry cells. Thus there are 1-cell, 2-cell, 3-cell, etc. bulbs. One-cell bulbs are sometimes marked ".1.2v," 2-cell bulbs "2.5v," and so on. If three dry cells are connected to a 1-cell bulb, it is likely that the thin tungsten filament in the lamp will burn out quickly. So it is best to use the proper bulb for the number of cells employed. Too many cells will cause the bulb to burn out quickly; too few will cause it to glow feebly, if at all. A good compromise for this unit is the Number 13 (3.7 volt) bulb.

Many unit activities call for the use of commercial-type miniature bulbs and sockets. While several substitutes are possible, these are usually cumbersome and less useful. For maximum ease in using miniature sockets, large ($3/4$ by $3/8$ of an inch) Fahnestock clips should be fastened to each side of the socket with the screws found there. See Figure 5-1 for an example. Notice that the large Number 6 cell is also supplied with clips, rather than the usual binding posts with screw caps. The suggestion to use Fahnestock clips may seem to be a minor one, but they can make a big difference in your time and overall accomplishment.

The wire you use should also be selected with an eye to convenience. Number 20 wire is excellent for almost every activity. You will need a spool of about one hundred feet. Get plastic-covered solid copper wire,

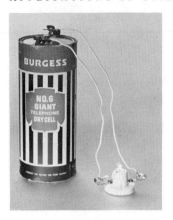

Figure 5-1 A number 6 dry cell and two D cells connected in complete circuits.

rather than cotton-covered wire consisting of many small twisted strands. These become unraveled at the ends, and cotton insulation is harder to strip off than a plastic covering. Insulation can be quickly removed with a *wirestripper* (Figure 5-2); this device also cuts wires efficiently. However, with the wire suggested here, scissors may serve both purposes almost as well.

There are several easy ways to connect cells and bulbs, depending on the kinds of materials you have. Figure 5-1 shows how a D cell can be substituted for a Number 6 cell. (Since the smaller cell is much cheaper and easy to get, more pupils will be able to participate directly.) A small, wide rubber band will hold the stripped wire ends snugly against the D-cell terminals. The center terminal (positive), recognizable by the bump, corresponds to the center terminal on the large cell. The opposite terminal (negative) is equivalent to the rim-mounted terminal on the large cell. The third arrangement needs only a single wire touching the terminals and bulb base to complete the circuit. One end is wrapped around the bulb base to serve as a bulb holder.

The investigations in this unit have been carefully worked out to help insure teaching success. However, occasionally an investigation may not go as planned. If this happens, use the occasion as an opportunity for learning. Most difficulties with materials in this unit can probably be handled by posing one or more of the following questions. Through knowing about them in advance, you should experience little difficulty in tracing the source of the "trouble."

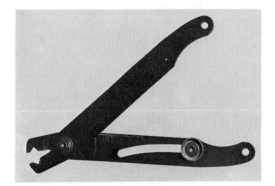

Figure 5-2 A wirestripper.

Bulb — Is it screwed in tightly? Burned out? Is there correct voltage?

Wire — Is it in good condition? Is the insulation stripped from the ends where contact is made? Is a complete circuit made? Short circuit?

Dry Cell — Is it in good condition? Is it powerful enough for the circuit?

Connections — Are they secure? Is enough contact being made for the current to flow easily?

Other Materials — Are the devices used in good operating condition?

Generalization I: Current electricity flows when there is a complete circuit; circuits may be opened and closed through the use of switches

Contributing Idea A. Current electricity flows only when there is a complete circuit; there are several ways to make a bulb light.

1. *Materials:* for each pair of children or small group, D cell; two bulbs; two 8-inch wires. (Either bare or insulated wires may be used in all the activities except where otherwise indicated. If insulated wire is used, be sure about 1½ inches on each end are stripped for effective contact with cells or bulbs.)

develop procedures

Invite the children to make *one* bulb light up by using the cells and wires they have been given. Suggest that they find as many ways as possible to do so, and sketch on the board any method that is successful. Some will use one wire, some two, in a variety of ways. In all cases, however, a connection must be made with both terminals (or ends) of the cell, and the side and bottom of the bulb's base. (Figure 5-3.) Notice that in the center connection of Figure 5-3, one wire could be eliminated without affecting the light. Observe in the right side example that the top wire does not need to touch the cell's top terminal. This is because the entire top is metal.

Figure 5-4 A–B

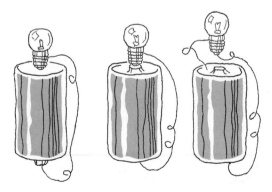

Figure 5-3 Three ways to light a bulb. Since the terminals on most D cells are joined to a metal plate at each end, touching the plates anywhere may complete a circuit.

When the cell top is not metal, the wire must touch the terminal for the bulb to light.

2. Now challenge them to make *two* bulbs light up at the same time with one battery. Again methods may be sketched on the chalkboard. Some typical results to anticipate are shown in Figure 5-4 A–B.

develop procedures

Most of the children will notice that bulbs connected as in A are much dimmer than they are in B. Reserve for later extended discussion as to why this occurred. (These are examples of series (A) and parallel (B) connections, which we shall take up in the next generalization.)

3. *Materials:* for each small group, three 8-inch wires; miniature bulb and socket; D cell and rubber band; two brass paper fasteners; 5- by 8-inch piece of cardboard; paper clip.

This activity will reveal how to connect a complete circuit with a bulb and socket, and how to make a paper clip switch for the circuit. (Figure 5-5.)

Ask the class to connect two wires to the battery and socket so that the bulb lights. Most pupils will realize quickly how to slip the wires under the rubber band to connect the D cell. Ask for several ways in which the light might be turned off. (Unscrewing the bulb, disconnecting or cutting the wire.) Bring out the several ways lights are turned off and on in the home. Stress the incon-

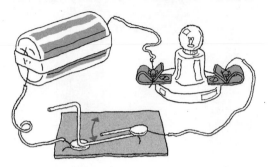

Figure 5-5

venience and hazard of closing or opening a home circuit unless some kind of switch is used.

develop procedures   Invite the children to make a paper clip switch for their circuits, so that they may be closed and opened conveniently. Let them try to work this out independently for the most part. Many finished switches may look like the one in Figure 5-5.

4. *Materials:* as in activity 3; one extra brass paper fastener; 4-inch wire.

Here, small groups can pair off and pool some of their materials to arrange *two* switches to control a single light. A good real-life example for discussion is a hall light controlled by an upstairs and downstairs switch. Notice in Figure 5-6 that the "hall" light may be switched on "upstairs," then turned off "downstairs," or the reverse. A few hints may be needed to get the children on the right track, but don't be

surprised if several see almost instantly how the connections might be made to accomplish the purpose. A good way to spark such insight is to get various children to draw their suggested models on the chalkboard for discussion. After tryouts, let pupils relate their constructions to such switches in their homes.   *develop procedures* *make inferences*

Review the work accomplished so far. Develop that in each case a continuous connection was necessary between two parts of the bulb and the cell's two terminals for the bulb to light. If needed, introduce the term *circuit,* and that switches are used to *open* and *close* circuits.

EXTENDING ACTIVITIES

1. For extra appraisal of how well pupils grasp the circuit concept, draw on the chalkboard or a ditto worksheet the sketch of a two-cell flashlight shown in Figure 5-7. See if they can trace the circuit by drawing in a dotted line with colored chalk or crayon.   *make inferences*

2. Ask the class to make a list of all the places in the home where switches are used and tell how they are turned on and off.

3. Encourage the children to bring in switches of all kinds to examine how they work. (Electric appliance repair stores are often willing to donate worn materials.)

4. Have the group examine different

Figure 5-6

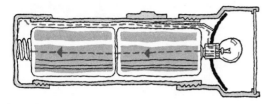

Figure 5-7

kinds of flashlights and make diagrams of how they work.

Series and Parallel Circuits. There are only two basic ways to connect electrical devices in a circuit: through series or parallel wiring. (Figure 5-8 A–B.) In series wiring, all of the usable electricity flows through each bulb or appliance. A chief disadvantage of this circuit is obvious to anyone who has had a bulb burn out in a series-type string of Christmas tree lights. When one bulb burns out the circuit is broken and all the lights go out. All the bulbs must then be tested to discover which one needs to be replaced. When flashlight cells are the source of power, adding extra bulbs to the series circuit steadily decreases bulb brightness.

To avoid the difficulties of series circuits, most wiring for home and commercial use is parallel wiring. In this kind, electricity flows through a main wire and through branching wires connected to it as well, as shown in Figure 5-8 A–B. (In this Figure, the Fahnestock clips represent the branching wires.) If a light or other fixture should burn out, no other light or fixture is affected. They receive electricity whether or not the others are in use. In their parallel circuits, children will notice no change in bulb brightness as bulbs are added.

Cells also can be arranged in series and parallel, as shown in Figure 5-9 A–B. In the series examples the top drawing shows the easier way to connect D cells. A wide rubber band can serve to affix wires, but the cells will buckle where they join unless they are enclosed. A sheet of rolled, stiff paper or a cardboard cylinder from a roll of bathroom tissue can be used for this purpose. If children work in pairs, these holders will not be required, as four hands should be able to hold everything together. To keep the cells from rolling, they can be placed between two books. Note that in all the series examples, negative terminals (−) are

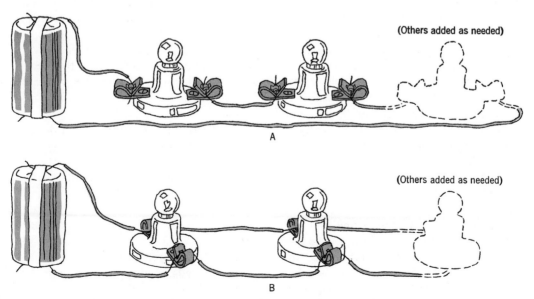

Figure 5-8 A–B   Two contrasting circuits. (A) lights are in series, (B) in parallel.

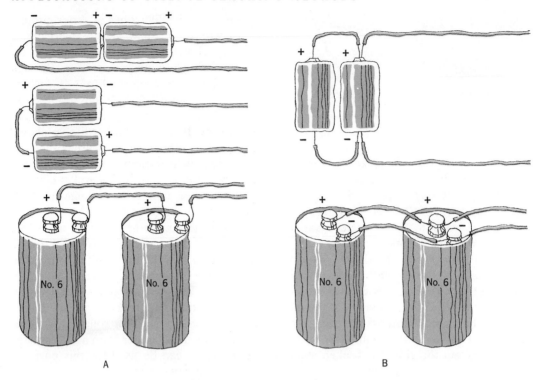

Figure 5-9 A–B Batteries arranged in series (A) and parallel (B).

joined to positive (+) terminals. In the parallel examples, positives are joined to positives and negatives to negatives.

Hooking up cells in series increases the *voltage,* or pressure, behind the flow of electricity. In contrast, arranging several or more cells in parallel makes available a longer lasting supply of current without increasing the voltage. For example, a bulb connected to two cells in series will burn about twice as brightly as if the cells are connected in parallel. However, the bulb will burn about two times longer with the parallel arrangement.

An analogy, as shown in Figure 5-10 A–B, can help to clarify why these differences take place. Cells in series are like connected tanks of water, with one mounted higher than the other. The force of the flow is directly related to how many tanks are used. In contrast, cells in parallel are like water tanks mounted on the same level. The water flows at about the same rate as

it would with one tank. Therefore, the water supply lasts longer than in the other setup, up to twice as long.

In studying circuits, children can have many interesting opportunities to make predictions about which bulbs will light, and to make inferences about hidden wires. Such activities are included in this section after introductory experiences with the two kinds of circuits.

Generalization II: Circuits may be designed in series and parallel

Contributing Idea A. Batteries may be connected in series or parallel.

Materials: for each small group, two D cells; miniature bulb and socket; four 8-inch wires.

Ask the children to make the bulb light with *two* cells as the power source. Hint that there is more than one way. Have successful and unsuccessful arrangements sketched on the chalkboard. The successful setups will resemble those in Figure 5-9 A–B. Label the connections *series* and *parallel* as needed.

Most of the pupils will notice that the parallel connection is not as bright as the series connection. Get them to describe how much brighter the light shines when the cells are in series. Descriptions probably will be vague. How can we *measure* brightness? (Through how many pieces of paper will the bulb be visible in each setup?) Children can use small, torn pieces of notebook paper in "sandwiches" of varying layers to place on the lit bulb. Have them all use the same kind of paper and record the number of paper layers needed to obscure the light in each case. Compile the data on the chalkboard:

Group	Series Battery	Parallel Battery
Bill	14	8
Dana	18	7
Alice	15	8
John	13	7
Ann	10	6
Peter	16	9
Darlene	12	5
Totals:	98	50
Average:	14	$7\frac{1}{7}$

reason
atively Can they describe the difference in brightness more accurately now? (The bulb

was about twice as bright when the cells were in series.) Have them examine the data closely. Why are there so many differences among the groups? Bring out the variables that might have affected the measurements. suggest
hypotheses

Contributing Idea B. Bulbs may be set up in series or parallel circuits.

Materials: for each small group, two D cells; six 4-inch and two 8-inch wires; three miniature bulbs and sockets; extra Fahnestock clip.

To begin with, suggest that the children try to set up a circuit with three bulbs and *one* D cell. Probably most will arrange the bulbs in series and the bulbs will barely glow. If no one has discovered how to arrange the bulbs in parallel, hint that there is another way. When it is discovered, contrast the two circuits and discuss why the brightness varied. How can the series bulbs be made brighter? (Use two cells in series.) make
inferences

See if children can make predictions about which lights will go out when a series and parallel circuit are disconnected in several places. Sketch Figure 5-11 on the chalkboard. What will happen if the wire is disconnected at 1 or 2 or 3? Pupils can test their predictions with their materials. All the bulbs will go out in each case. What will happen to the other lights if any bulb is removed? (The remaining bulbs will go out.)

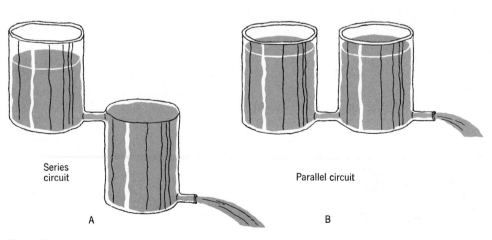

Series circuit

A

Parallel circuit

B

Figure 5-10 A–B (A) is twice as forceful as (B), but (B) will flow twice as long.

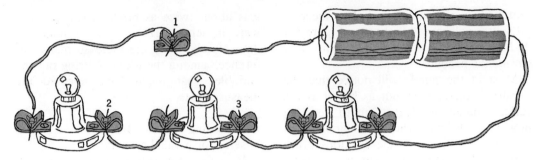

Figure 5-11

make
inferences

Sketch Figure 5-12 on the chalkboard for more predictions. Mention for clarity that a Fahnestock clip connects two wires at place 1. What will happen to the lit bulbs if the wires are separated at place 1? (All will go out.) Separated at place 2? (All will go out.) Separated at place 3? (Only the bulb opposite place 2 will stay lit.) Separated at place 4? (The two inside bulbs will stay lit.) Let them test their predictions with the materials.

Sketch a variation of the last circuit as in Figure 5-13, for a more challenging test of pupil's predictive ability. In this circuit one bulb is wired in series and two in parallel.

make
inferences

Ask questions like these:

What will be the brightness of bulbs 1, 2, and 3? (Bulb 1 will be bright, 2 and 3 dim.)

If bulb 1 is removed, will any other lights go out? (Both 2 and 3 will go out.)

If bulb 2 is removed, will any other lights go out? (No.) If not, what will be the rela-tive brightness of 1 and 3? (About the same.)

If bulb 3 is removed, will any lights go out? (No.) If not, what will be the relative brightness of 1 and 2? (About the same.)

After predictions are made and recorded, children can test them with their materials.

Contributing Idea C. Circuits may be inferred from tests if the wires are hidden from view.

1. *Materials:* three regular-size (9 by 11¾ inches) manila folders or substitutes; D cell with rubber band holder; seven 8-inch wires; bulb and socket, with Fahnestock clips; paper clip.

Your class will be interested in learning that it is possible to detect how a circuit may be connected even though the wires are out of sight. In the process, they will discover that several inferred patterns may explain a circuit equally well. To introduce

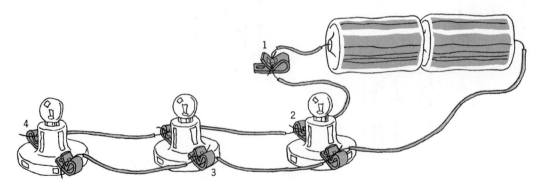

Figure 5-12

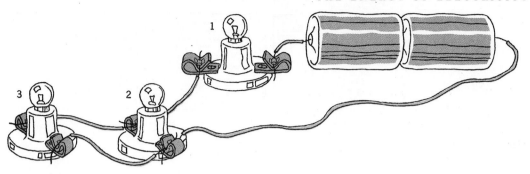

Figure 5-13

some simple hidden circuits, you will need to prepare circuit "boards" from the materials, as in Figure 5-14 A–C. Punch three holes in one cover of the first folder (A), and number them as shown. Insert three paper fasteners into the holes. Open the folder and attach inside the ends of one wire to fasteners 2 and 3. Spread out the fastener ends as needed to keep the paper fasteners secure and to hold the wire. A paper clip will keep the folder closed and the wire location hidden. Boards B and C can be prepared in the same way except that the wiring patterns are different as shown, and C has an additional paper fastener terminal.

The "circuit tester" is simply a disconnected circuit of two wires, D cell, and bulb with socket. To make the bulb light in

pattern A, just touch one end of the wire to terminal 3 on the folder, and the outside Fahnestock clip to terminal 2. If your bulb socket does not have clips attach a wire at the appropriate place on the socket; touch the bared end of the wire to terminal 2 to light the bulb.

Pin circuit board A to a suitable place in front of the class. Mention that it has a concealed circuit. Show how to check the possible circuit by using the tester. Elicit from pupils the combinations tested and the results. (Reversals of combinations should be omitted to keep the data more manageable.)

Terminals Tested	Light?
1–2	No
1–3	No
2–3	Yes

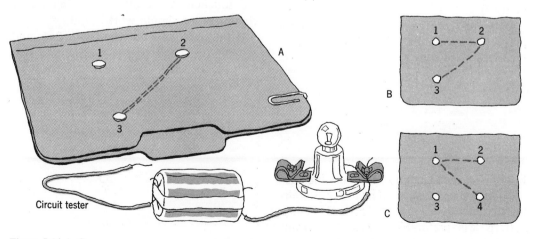

Figure 5-14 A–C

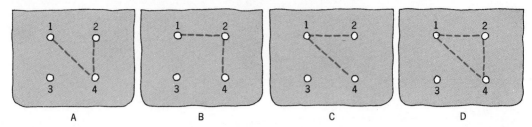

Figure 5-15 A–D

make inferences Can the circuit be inferred from these data? Most pupils will realize that a wire is attached to terminals 2–3. Open the folder cover and verify that this is so.

Now try board B.

1–2	Yes
1–3	Yes
2–3	Yes

make inferences Suggest pupils draw the possible wiring pattern or patterns on a sheet of paper. While they are doing this, circulate around the room and check the results. Some patterns will resemble Figure 5-14 B, *but some may have an additional wire drawn between 1 and 3.*

Does this additional wire do anything that cannot be performed or explained with just two wires? (No.) Bring out that when several possible ideas or models explain something equally well, it is usually more efficient to choose the simplest one. (In science, this is called the "law of parsimony.")

With this input, the children should be prepared for circuit C. With four terminals, there are more data to consider:

1–2	Yes
1–3	No
1–4	Yes
2–3	No
2–4	Yes
3–4	No

make inferences Pupils can again sketch all the possible patterns on a sheet of paper. The four possibilities are shown in Figure 5-15 A–D. Is any pattern less preferable? (Yes, D.) Draw out that A, B, and C account equally well for the data. Reveal the actual wiring pattern, but emphasize that it should not be considered more "correct" than the two others.

2. *Materials:* chalkboard sketch of Figure 5-16.

Given some data, the children should now be able to predict which combinations would light up a bulb tester. Elicit the fifteen possible combinations (excluding duplicates) in the six-terminal chalkboard model:

1–2	2–3	3–4	4–5	5–6
1–3	2–4	3–5	4–6	
1–4	2–5	3–6		
1–5	2–6			
1–6				

Pose some problems; allow plenty of time for pupils to think through and record responses:

make inference If the tester bulb lights when 1–4 and 3–4 are touched, what other combination or combinations should work? (1–3.)

If the light goes on when 1–2, 2–6, and

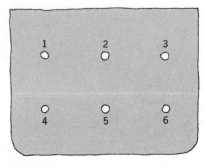

Figure 5-16

278

Figure 5-17

3–6 are touched, what else should work? (1–3, 1–6, 2–3, 3–6.)

If 1–2, 2–5, 5–6 work, what else should work? (1–3, 1–5, 1–6, 2–3, 2–6, 3–6.)

Should enough materials be available, let small groups construct boards to test their predictions. Or, the possible circuit patterns may be drawn on paper or chalkboard for checking.

EXTENDING ACTIVITIES

1. Invite the children to pair off and make their own circuit boards, either on paper or with real materials. If materials are used, each pair will need a bulb-and-socket tester, D cell, six paper fasteners, six wires, and a manila folder or substitute (chipboard folded in two, 5- by 8-inch cards, cardboard, etc.). Each child should try to challenge his partner's ability to make inferences by creating an original pattern. Can the partner discover it or the equivalent through testing and reasoning?

2. Have a contest to see which team can figure out how to light the most miniature bulbs at one time. Mention a few restrictions: it must be done without socket holders, using only one D cell and two bare wires. (Up to about six bulbs can be lit at one time by the method in Figure 5-17. One wire serves as a bulb holder. Make six single loops along the wire by bending the wire once around a pencil for each loop; then screw in the bulbs. The second wire touches the negative cell terminal and a bulb base.) If the supply of bulbs is limited, proposed models can be drawn on the chalkboard. An evaluative discussion can serve to select likely prospects for testing. (For this to work the cell's ends must be of metal.)

3. Let the children construct an electrical questioning board, as in Figure 5-18. Use chipboard, masonite, or plywood for the base, bell wire for the circuits. Paper fasteners are useful for terminals, but stove bolts and nuts are more durable. To permit

make inferences

develop procedures

suggest hypotheses

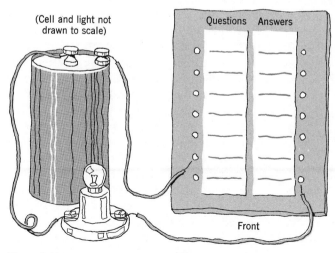
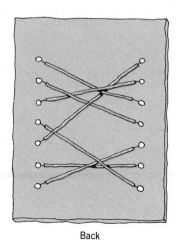

(Cell and light not drawn to scale)

Questions   Answers

Front

Back

Figure 5-18

easy interchange of the wire pieces, Fahnestock clips are more satisfactory to use than nuts. Otherwise, nuts must be loosened and tightened each time if the wiring setup is changed to avoid the possibility of children memorizing the correct positions of the connectors, in place of knowing the correct answers. Fahnestock clips may be purchased at radio-TV repair stores.

An easy way to prepare questions and answers is merely to type them on two long sheets of paper. Have spaces between questions and answers corresponding to the spaces between the connectors on the board. Sheets may be fastened with a tack at each end. Be sure that the answers are "scrambled" out of order with regard to the questions.

When children prepare questions and answers, it is convenient to have them written on 3- by 5-inch cards. These can be tacked next to the terminals or placed in shallow pockets made from paper folded at intervals to correspond with the terminals.

Conductors and Their Properties. The term "conductor" is usually given to any substance that permits an easy flow of electricity. Metals are by far the best conductors of electricity and so are commonly used for wires. Although several of the precious metals are better conductors, copper is most often used as it is comparable in efficiency and yet cheap enough to produce in quantity.

We often hear the term "nonconductor" applied to such materials as rubber, glass, plastic, cloth, and other nonmetallic substances. This is a misnomer, as virtually anything will conduct electricity if given sufficient voltage. These materials may be more properly considered as poor conductors, or *insulators*. This is why electricians may wear rubber gloves, and electric wires are covered with cloth, plastic, or rubber. It also explains why appliance plugs are covered with rubber or plastic and glass separators used on power line poles to keep apart high voltage lines.

Some poor conductors become good conductors when wet. Pure or distilled water is a poor conductor, but with the addition of dissolved minerals it becomes a fairly good one. Wet human skin is a far better conductor than dry skin. For this reason it is safer to turn appliances on and off with dry hands.

Although metals conduct electricity much better than nonmetals, there is still some resistance in metal wire to the flow of electrons. Of course, the longer the wire the greater will be the resistance. You may have experienced the gradual dimming of lights in a theater or adjusted the brightness of dashboard lights in an automobile. The change in both cases was probably achieved by a *rheostat*. A rheostat is a device that increases or decreases the length of wire through which electric current flows, thereby increasing or decreasing the wire's resistance. A simple model is shown in Figure 5-19.

Some metals have so much resistance to the flow of electricity that they glow brightly when there is enough electrical pressure or voltage to force relatively large quantities of electricity to flow in them. Unfortunately, most metals melt or evaporate within a short period of time when hot enough to give off light. This caused an agonizingly long search by Thomas Edison for materials to be used as bulb filaments before he was able to achieve reasonable success. Some of the materials he tried indicate the exhaustive character of the search: bamboo slivers, sewing thread,

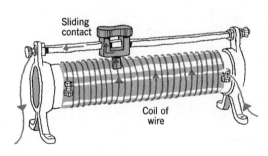

Sliding contact

Coil of wire

Figure 5-19 A simple rheostat.

even human hair, were carbonized and tested!

Tungsten, sometimes called wolfram, is the metal used in *incandescent* bulbs today. (Any bulb that gives light from a very hot filament is called an incandescent bulb.) With a melting point of almost 6200 degrees Fahrenheit, tungsten is well able to withstand the temperature caused by the movement of electricity through its highly resistant composition. An inactive gas, such as argon, is pumped into the bulbs to help prevent burning away of the filament. However, some of the tungsten evaporates eventually and the filament is separated, breaking the circuit. The ever-darkening appearance of the portion of the bulb next to the filament indicates the deposition of the evaporating tungsten.

Electric heaters also have wires of highly resistant metal. Most heaters today use nichrome wire, a combination of nickel and chromium.

So far, length and composition of wire have been mentioned as important factors in resistance to the flow of electricity. Another factor is the diameter of the wire. Perhaps the use of an analogy here will be helpful in explaining why size of wire affects resistance. Imagine part of a large crowd in a sports stadium converging into a narrow passageway. As some of the people begin to enter the passageway the forward speed of the crowd slackens. At the end of the passageway the forward pace again picks up.

A thick wire presents a broad pathway for the flow of electricity. A narrow wire constricts the flow. In the "effort" to crowd through the narrow pathway much friction is created and the wire grows hot. If thin enough, and when made of material such as tungsten, it can also produce much light as it glows.

Most devices that produce heat, such as heaters, toasters, and electric irons, have relatively thin, long, highly resistant wires. The wires cannot be as narrow in diameter as a light filament—one reason is that they

are exposed to the open air and would rapidly evaporate away—but they are relatively thin compared to other wires designed to carry a similar voltage.

It would be helpful when teaching this section of the unit to acquire some real examples of toasters and heaters for observation. Discarded electric irons, toasters, and heaters can often be obtained free of charge from electrical repair shops. These can be taken apart and closely examined—something that perhaps better not be tried with someone's new appliance!

Generalization III: The kind, size, and length of materials used affect the flow of electricity

Contributing Idea A. Conductors are materials through which electricity passes freely; materials that tend to block the flow of electricity are called insulators or nonconductors.

Materials: poor or fair conductors, such as plastic, wool, cotton, glass, pencil lead, chalk, paper, rubber, etc.; good conductors—objects made of various metals; miniature bulbs and sockets; wire.

In this activity, pupils can distinguish between conductors and insulators. Set up a simple circuit with two wires, bulb and socket, and D cell. Disconnect one from a Fahnestock clip. Now this becomes a circuit tester like the one used in the preceding activities (Figure 5-14 A–C). Remind the children that the circuit tester bulb lights when a wire bridges the gap between the two ends of the tester. Are there any materials on the table that could also make the tester bulb light? If needed, touch the tester ends to some metal object to demonstrate that a circuit results and the bulb lights.

Point to a table on which many materials are displayed and raise conjecture as to which will or will not let the bulb light when the tester is used. Materials can be tentatively divided into two piles before testing. With some objects (pencil lead, for ex-

suggest hypotheses

ample) pupils may discover that adding more cells in series to their tester will enable the bulb to glow at least feebly.

Mention that materials that permit the easy passage of electricity are called *conductors;* those that block or retard the passage of electrical current are called *nonconductors* or *insulators.* Discuss the kinds of materials they have observed covering plugs, commercial switches, or other devices that must be touched by the hand or foot to be operated. These are insulators, for safety reasons. Bring out that, by adding more cell power, some so-called "nonconductors" conducted enough electricity to make the tester bulb light. Help them understand that almost any material will conduct electricity if the electrical source is very powerful.

state problems

To avoid confusion in their own discussions, perhaps the children can develop their own operational definition of a "good conductor." One class decided that an object was a good conductor if, when touched by a tester using one new D cell, the bulb glow was visible through eight or more thicknesses of arithmetic paper held against a 2.5 volt bulb.

Contributing Idea B. Thinner wire has more resistance than thicker wire.

Materials: several worn-out house bulbs; house bulb with transparent glass (if possible); paper bag; hammer; short strand of iron picture wire; Number 6 cell; two pliers.

Let the class examine a transparent light bulb to observe the filament. If no transparent bulb is available, get a worn-out bulb and place it in a bag. Holding it downward and against a wall or other solid structure, tap it lightly with a hammer until it breaks.

suggest hypotheses

The filament may now be observed. Ask the class why it is so thin. When someone hypothesizes that a thin wire will "light up" faster than a thicker wire, point to the strand of picture wire and dry cell. Ask how an appropriate experiment can be performed with these materials.

develop procedures

A thin strand may be unraveled from the

picture wire for the smaller diameter wire. The remainder of the strand can serve for the larger diameter. Place the thin strand across the posts of the dry cell to observe how long it takes for the strand to glow. Record the amount of time needed to glow for the thin wire first; abandon attempts to make the thicker wire glow after it becomes obvious that it is taking longer. *Caution:* Use two pliers or clothespins to hold the wires, as the wires will heat up fast. Hold the wires on the posts as short a time as possible, since this quickly dissipates the cell's energy.

make inference

Let some pupils read to confirm their tentative conclusion that thinner wires offer more *resistance* than thicker wires.

Contributing Idea C. Longer wires offer more resistance to electricity than shorter wires made of the same material.

Materials: 3-foot Number 32 bare nichrome wire (sold in radio stores); piece of sticky tape; D cell; miniature bulb in socket; two wires.

Use the analogy of a garden hose to help the children think through the next experiment. Inquire whether a very long hose would have as much pressure at the nozzle as a short one. Point out that the friction taking place inside the hose as the water slides along gradually reduces the force of the water. Now, raise conjecture about whether longer wires have more resistance to electricity.

Connect the materials as shown in Figure 5-20; slide an end of the connecting wire up and down the nichrome wire. Encourage the pupils to observe keenly the brightness of the light. Explain that this is a *rheostat*—a device that decreases or increases current by decreasing or increasing the resistance to the flow of electricity. Mention that the thin wire used is nichrome wire, made of nickel and chromium rather than copper.

make inference

Have the children read to confirm their conclusion that the length of the wire affects the resistance.

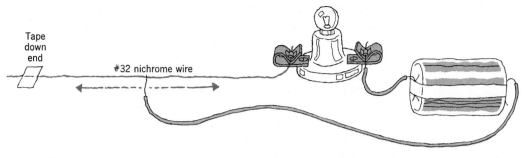

Tape
down
end

#32 nichrome wire

Figure 5-20

Contributing Idea D. Some metals have more resistance to electricity than others.

Materials: two bare 3-foot wires, one nichrome and one copper; D cell; sticky tape; miniature bulb and socket; two wires.

Set up this demonstration just like the previous one, except now substitute for the nichrome wire a piece of copper wire of equal length. Have the children observe the brightness of the bulb as the connecting wire is slid up and down the substitute wire. The bulb should burn brightly with the copper wire with no detectable change in brightness.

Ask the children what can be concluded from their observation. They may forget that the *diameter* of the wire might also be a factor. If so, you might ask them to recall what they previously learned about wire and resistance. How could the control be set up? Ideally, now is the time to have pieces of iron picture wire and copper wire of equal diameter and length for testing. If not, the class might read to confirm that the composition of the metal does affect its resistance to electricity.

make
inferences

select
procedures

Contributing Idea E. Devices that produce heat, such as heaters, toasters, and electric irons commonly have relatively thin, long, and highly resistant metal wires or ribbons.

Materials: new or old toasters; electric heater; hot plate; worn-out electric iron that may be taken apart.

Review with the class that size, length, and kind of wire affect resistance. Have the children recall that greater resistance resulted in greater heat. Bring up the idea that man attempts to apply the scientific principles he may learn about. Ask the children for some names of devices that provide heat. Invite them to predict what the heating elements would look like.

Let them observe the above devices for confirmation or rejection of their predictions.

It will be helpful to use several questions to stimulate their thinking during the observations of these devices. For example:

Why aren't the wires as thin as those in the bulb? (They would otherwise burn out soon in the open air.)

make
inferences

Why are the wires a different color from ordinary wire? (They may be made of a different material, such as nichrome.)

Why are the wires partly coiled or zig-zagged? (This enables more wire, and thus heat, to be provided in the available space.)

EXTENDING ACTIVITIES

1. Invite someone to report on Thomas Edison's invention of the first practical incandescent lamp. Emphasis might be on the long and frustrating search for materials that would not quickly burn away, with illustrations of these materials where possible.

2. Have an interested child read and report why bulbs appear to explode when dropped. (They are filled with nitrogen

gas to retard the burning of the filament. If the filament were not enclosed and surrounded by this gas, it would quickly burn out — oxygen supports burning.)

Circuit Hazards and Fuses. We have seen that when bulbs or appliances are wired into a circuit they show resistance to the flow of electrical energy. At the place where the energy enters these resistors, however, a transformation of energy takes place — some of the electrical energy becomes converted into heat (if it enters a heater) or light (bulb) or sound (radio) or motion (motor). In other words, a significant amount of electrical energy is "used up," or changed. Suppose, however, there is no resistor connected in the circuit. Since the copper wire has relatively low resistance, a great surge of electricity flows through the wire. The wire now heats up rapidly, even though it normally offers little resistance to a current.

In house and commercial circuits intense heating of the wires may come from a "short" circuit. This may happen when two bare wires touch each other, thus preventing the main supply of current from flowing through the resistor. Since the resistor is largely bypassed, a huge amount of electricity flows. A common cause of short circuits occurs when an appliance cord is placed under a heavily traveled rug. If the insulation between the two internal wires wears away they may touch and a "short" develop. Notice in Figure 5-23 that a circuit is not necessarily shortened in length for a "short" circuit to occur. The essential thing is that the resistor — in this case, the bulb — is bypassed. Since children are sometimes confused by the term "short circuit," an activity in this section is designed to clarify it.

Overloading a circuit is perhaps an even more frequent cause of wires overheating. Many older houses, for example, were wired when only a few of today's common appliances were in widespread use. Small-diameter, lightly insulated wires were formerly adequate. However, as more and more of today's appliances continue to be plugged in, intense heating occurs that is a potential source of fire.

Fuses and circuit breakers protect us from the fire hazard. A screw-in type fuse contains a narrow metal strip that melts at a fairly low temperature. When a fuse is placed in a circuit, the electricity must travel through the strip. Should the wire heat up dangerously, the strip melts and the circuit opens, thereby shutting off the current.

Occasionally, someone will replace a burned-out fuse with a penny to avoid the "inconvenience" of another fuse burning out. Unfortunately, if the initial source of the difficulty is not corrected the wires may grow so hot the house may catch fire. An acceptable fuse has two requirements: it must be a good conductor, and have a low melting point. A penny meets only the first requirement!

A bimetallic strip circuit breaker may be used instead of a fuse. This consists of two thin, metal ribbons fused together. The ribbons are made of two different metals. When placed in a circuit and heated, the bimetallic strip bends away from one of the contact points, opening the circuit. The bending, as mentioned in Unit 1, is due to different expansion rates of the metals.

Another modern type of circuit breaker works from the fact that any wire containing current electricity generates some magnetism. Increasing the supply of current has the effect of increasing the magnetism. When a movable steel rod is enclosed in a coil of wire placed in a circuit, it may be pulled upward as the current (and so magnetism) increases. If the rod is connected to a contact point, its upward movement will result in the circuit being opened. A spring catch that can be reset by hand is used to prevent the rod from dropping down again. An electromagnetic device that operates this way is called a solenoid. (Another section will present more on electromagnetism.)

Children can be taught to calculate the number of resistors that can be safely placed in a circuit. In order to do this they will need a bit of general knowledge about the meaning of the terms *ampere, volt,* and *watt.* An *ampere* is the rate of flow of electricity. Technically, it is defined as the flow of 6.3 billion billion electrons per second past a given point. This figure can be presented to the class (a six, followed by eighteen zeroes), but, of course, will be meaningless. The idea to stress is that ampere means the rate of flow. If a fuse is rated at 30 amperes, then only those appliances can be operated whose total rate of current used is under 30 amperes.

We have indicated before that the term *volt* is a unit of pressure. A dry cell has an electrical pressure of one and one-half volts, house current 110 to 120 volts. Sometimes a special line which carries 220 volts is attached to a house circuit for such heavy users of current as electric clothes dryers and ovens.

The term *watt* is used to measure power, or the rate at which electricity is used to do work. It is found by multiplying amperes by volts. A watt-hour is the amount of energy needed to keep a one-watt device functioning for one hour. Since a houseful of appliances may use hundreds or thousands of watts per hour, wattage usually is expressed in kilowatt-hour units (1000 watts for one hour).

Activities are included in this section to help children understand how electric power company bills are calculated for consumers.

Generalization IV: Short circuits and overloaded circuits may create dangerously hot wires; fuses or circuit breakers are used to eliminate this danger

Contributing Idea A. A short circuit results when a resistor is largely bypassed; the increased flow of electricity increases the heat of the wire.

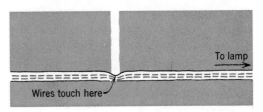

Figure 5-21

Materials: miniature bulb and socket; insulated wire; D cell; wire stripper.

Have on the chalkboard the sketch shown in Figure 5-21.

Use this bridge: "We are often warned not to place electric wires under a rug, particularly where they are liable to be stepped on or pushed down. Why is this so?" Discuss this for a moment. Now turn to the sketch and inform the class that it shows a table leg pressing on a wire whose insulation at one point has gradually worn away. Explain that the lines to represent the wires are drawn as broken lines; this shows that the wires are invisible because of the insulation. Point out that electricity is streaming into the top wire. Encourage the pupils to hypothesize as to the probable path of the electricity at the point where contact is made. Also, seek a prediction as to whether the lamp will light at this time. suggest hypotheses

Indicate the materials and ask how they can be set up to test the hypotheses. The insulation must be scraped away on the two wires where contact will be made. The assembly may look like Figure 5-22. *Caution:* Do not permit anyone to hold the bare wires at the contact point, as the wires will quickly grow hot. It will also be best to do this demonstration fairly quickly, to avoid greatly draining the cell's energy. develop procedures

After it is observed that the light goes out, have several children feel the insulated part of the wire in front and in back of the bare contact point. Have someone notice that the short-circuited part is hot while the wires beyond the contact point are cool. Draw out from pupils that this helps confirm the hypothesis of electricity not flow- make inferences

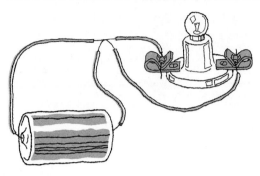

Figure 5-22

ing beyond the contact point. It should be pointed out, however, that there is a very small current still flowing through the other part.

Bring out that this experience is an example of a *short circuit.* Try to elicit a reasonable explanation as to what happened. The children should understand that when a resistor such as a lamp is bypassed, a huge amount of current will surge through a wire when contact is made; there is very little resistance to check its flow. Again call attention to the great heat produced as a result of this short circuit.

Contributing Idea B. Fuses are designed to open a circuit that is heating up before it becomes dangerous.

In the following sequence pupils observe how several kinds of short circuits may melt their improvised fuses, and find out why lack of a fuse might be dangerous.

1. *Materials:* 2 D cells connected in series; miniature bulb and socket; four pieces of wire; scissors; fuse device. (To prepare the fuse you will need two all-metal thumb tacks, a piece of heavy cardboard for the base, and several strips of metal foil about one and one-half inches long and three-sixteenths of an inch wide. One strip is used at a time. Gum wrapper foil, with paper removed, is satisfactory; also the wrappers for Hershey's chocolate kisses. Make a V-shaped nick in the foil. This will make it likelier that the foil will burn out instantly.) Set up the materials as in Figure

5-23, but for the present keep out of view the extra wire used in method 2.

Get your pupils to speculate about the fire hazard when a short circuit takes place. Bring out that, because of the hazard, measures are taken to avoid it. Ask the children if any heat would occur if the circuit were opened. Ask for a logical way a circuit might be broken with heat. Help them reason that a device introduced into the circuit which would conduct electricity well and yet have a low melting point would be applicable. *make inferences*

Show the improvised fuse and other materials. How can these objects be used to see that will happen if the circuit is "shorted"? Several children might set up and "short" the circuit, as in method 1. Bring out that the circuit size was decreased when the bulb was largely bypassed. *develop procedures*

Now hold a piece of wire by the bulb socket terminals as in method 2. Point out that if the wire ends are touched to the terminals *you will be increasing the size* of the circuit. Will a "short" circuit result here, also? Why or why not?

After the demonstration, suggest that pupils develop an operational definition for a "short" circuit. The essential ingredient in the definition should be the bypassing of the resistor rather than change in circuit length. *state problems*

2. *Materials:* same as above; substitute a penny for the foil.

Review reasons the fuse worked: (1) it conducted electricity satisfactorily while the circuit was normal; and (2) having a lower melting point than the copper wire, it melted when the increased current created increased heat. Now repeat the previous demonstration, but this time use a penny instead of a foil strip between the two tack heads. The tacks, of course, will need to touch the penny. The penny and wires should begin heating up.

Bring out that while the penny is a good conductor, it has a high melting point. Ask the class if it would be sensible to substi-

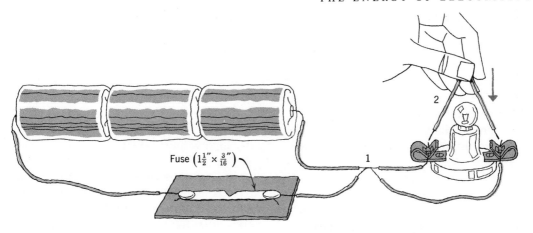

Figure 5-23 Two ways to make a "short" circuit and burn out a foil fuse. In 1, the circuit length is decreased, in 2, it is increased.

tute a penny in place of a fuse when it burns out. Bring out the foolishness of ignoring a warning sign or symptom by "correcting" the symptom and not the cause.

Help pupils understand that overloading a parallel circuit may also overheat the wires. Remind them that a house usually has parallel wiring. The power station supplies a steady voltage regardless of the number of resistors used in the circuit. If too many resistors are used, excessive current will pass through the wires and make them very hot unless a fuse or other device opens the circuit.

3. *Materials:* various commercial fuses including automobile electric fuses.

If several commercial fuses are available, it would be especially helpful to show them at this time. Electrical shops may be good sources for worn-out fuses.

Contributing Idea C. Arithmetic may be used to find out the number of resistors that can be safely placed in a circuit.

1. Develop the idea that we do not need to leave to chance whether a fuse or circuit breaker will open a circuit. If a 30-ampere fuse is available, mention that the label reads "30 A." Otherwise, mention that there are 30 A fuses. Such fuses melt when 30 amperes flow through the circuit. Explain that the safety margin can be calcu-lated through the use of arithmetic. To understand how to do this, first the term *ampere* must be learned.

Begin with the analogy of two water hoses. Both are the same length. But one is a narrow garden hose and the other a wide fireman's hose. Both are hooked to the same fire hydrant. Ask which has the larger amount of water flowing out of the nozzle and why. (The larger hose, because it can carry more water.) Apply the idea to elec-tricity now, and acquaint pupils with the word ampere, used to mean the rate of flow. Tell them that one ampere is a flowing of more than six billion billion tiny particles of electricity a second. Have them recall their previous experiment with thick and thin wires. Will a thick copper wire have more flow (amperes) of electricity than a thin copper wire of the same length? (Yes.) Mention some typical house appliances, and the amount of electricity each might need to operate. For example:

	Amperes
Coffee maker	5
Toaster	5
Waffle iron	8
Sun lamp	5
	23

Point out that by adding the amperages of these appliances one knows whether they are totally within the capacity of a 30-ampere fuse.

Have the pupils add an 11-ampere iron and five 1-ampere bulbs to the list. Inquire if the new total will exceed the rated capacity of a 30-ampere fuse.

2. Continue with the analogy of the water hose. Many children have noticed the water pressure varying to some noticeable degree while playing with or using a hose. This happens when someone else in the house or a neighbor is also using outlets. Point out that sometimes the water will shoot out powerfully for a great distance from the nozzle, but sometimes only a short distance. Mention that the push or force behind the water is greater in one case than the other. Would more water flow into a bucket within 10 seconds with a forceful stream or with a weaker one? (Forceful stream.)

Help the children to summarize the two ways they could increase the amount of water flowing at any time: by using a bigger hose, to provide a wider pathway; and by increasing the push or pressure behind the water. Continue by making the application to electricity. Point out that the unit of pressure is the *volt*. Have someone read the voltage rating of a D cell and a No. 6 dry cell (one and one-half volts). Inform them that the pressure of house current is about 120 volts. If class members can work with decimal divisors, request them to calculate how many new dry cells it would take to equal this voltage by dividing 120 by 1.5. (80 cells.)

Remind the children that in the lessons on series and parallel wiring they have already learned how to increase the voltage of dry cells by attaching them in a series. Have them recall that the light got brighter as the second cell was added in series, but that the brightness did not change as the cell was added in parallel. Repeat this demonstration, if needed.

3. *Materials:* five D cells; miniature bulb and socket; wire.

If a bulb can be sacrificed in the interest of science education, let the children connect the bulb to a dry cell, and then gradually add more cells in series until it burns out. Allow a half-minute or so of bulb burning time for each additional cell. Five cells will probably have more than enough voltage to burn out the bulb, unless it has a fairly high voltage rating.

4. Mention that household appliances may not have the amperage rating stamped on them, but have instead the number of *watts* used. Explain that the wattage is merely the flow of electricity times the pressure, that is, amperes times volts. Thus, 5 amperes × 10 volts = 50 watts. In other words, a watt tells how fast electricity is being used. Show the class that it is possible to figure out amperes if the voltage and wattage of the appliance is known. Write on the board the formula:

$$\text{Amperes} = \frac{\text{Watts}}{\text{Volts}}$$

Pose some problems such as the following:

reason
quantitative

An electric drill uses 240 watts on regular 120-volt house current. How many amperes does it use?

$$\frac{240\ W}{120\ V} = 2\ A$$

An electric iron uses 1200 watts on regular house current. How many amperes does it use?

$$\frac{1200\ W}{120\ V} = 10\ A$$

5. Ask the class to calculate the following problem to determine if all the appliances could be used without overloading a house circuit. (Assume a 120-volt supply.) The circuit breaker is rated at 30 amperes.

reason
quantitative

	Watts
Coffee maker	360
Waffle iron	960
Toaster	600
Iron	1200

The class should total the wattages (3120W) and divide by 120 V. The answer is 26 amperes. It would not actuate the circuit breaker.

EXTENDING ACTIVITIES

reason quantitatively 1. Invite the pupils to find out the rated capacity of the fuse or circuit breaker used in their home or apartment. Have them find the wattages or amperes used by the lights and appliances and total them. The total may then be compared with the circuit capacity. If a few children are unable to find the wattage rating of some appliances, perhaps the following list of typical appliances may be convenient to use:

	Watts
Electric blanket	600
Electric frypan	1100
Dishwasher	1200
Oven	3000
Washing machine	1600
Electric dryer	5000
Vacuum cleaner	700
Waffle iron	1100
Iron	800

2. Pupils who excel in arithmetic may wish to determine the quantity of volts, watts, or amperes used when only two of these factors are known. Present the formula $A = W/V$. Next to it place $4 = 8/2$. Tell them that these numerals can help them to think through the relationships of the symbols in the formula. Now ask them if they can discover a formula that will reason quantitatively determine volts, if only watts and amperes are known. In a like manner the other quantities may be thought through.

3. Invite a local fireman to class for a talk on safety with electricity. This courtesy is extended by many fire departments as a public service.

4. The class may be interested in determining how electric power bills are calculated by the local power company.

The essentials of the arithmetic involved reason quantitatively are to multiply watts times hours, which yields watt-hours. Dividing this figure by 1000 gives the kilowatt-hours. This figure is then multiplied by the kilowatt-hour charge.

Example:

1700 watts for 200 hours = 340,000 watt-hours

$$\frac{340,000}{1,000} \text{ watt-hours} = 340 \text{ kilowatt-hours}$$

$$\begin{array}{r} 340 \text{ kilowatt-hours} \\ \times \ \ 0.05 \text{ per kilowatt-hour charge} \\ \hline \$17.00 \text{ bill} \end{array}$$

Electromagnets. In 1820 a professor of physics at Copenhagen made a discovery that opened up for development one of the most useful devices ever conceived: the electromagnet. *Hans Christian Oersted* had believed for years that there was a relationship between magnetism and electricity. In spite of much research, however, Oersted had not succeeded in discovering a useful connection between these phenomena. One day, while lecturing to a class, he noticed that a wire carrying electric current was deflecting a nearby compass needle. Oersted realized immediately that the wire was generating a magnetic field. His subsequent experiments, writings, and lectures helped spread to the world the new concept of electromagnetism.

The telephone, electric motor, and many other indispensable tools of modern living had their origin in Oersted's work and related discoveries. This section of the unit goes into some detail on how several of these devices work. It would be most helpful to the children if the tremendous impact of these inventions on their lives can be discussed as they are studied.

Generalization V: Electromagnets can be made because a magnetic field is generated around a wire carrying electricity; electromagnets can be used in many ways

Contributing Idea A. A magnetic field is generated around a wire carrying electricity; the strength of the field can be increased in several ways.

Materials: for each child or group a D cell; large iron stove bolt or nail; 8-foot insulated wire (Number 22 enameled magnet wire is best); small box of carpet tacks or brads (small nails).

In this activity, pupils can experiment with electromagnets. It is like a previous investigation in the magnetism unit, except that a more precise measurement technique is used.

Does anyone know how to make a magnet from the materials and how to test it? Chances are that a good portion of the class will. (Remove an inch of insulation from each end of the wire. Leave about a foot of one wire end free, and wrap the rest as needed around the bolt. Touch the wire ends to the D cell and touch the bolt to the brads at the same time. Pick up the brads, *end to end,* then drop them on the table by disconnecting the D cell.)

Discuss possible ways to make an electromagnet stronger. Ask questions such as: How many more brads do you think a twenty-turn electromagnet will pick up compared to a ten-turn one? Thirty turns compared to twenty turns? (Pupils should understand that, since a wire carrying an electric current generates magnetism, wrapping the wire closely around an object concentrates the magnetism into a smaller area and so increases its practical effect.)

Suggest that each team keep a record of the number of turns used, ten turns each time, and the results in brads picked up. (It is important that small objects be picked up *end to end* to counter the effect of "leftover" or residual magnetism, and to have a uniform procedure for assessing power. But let pupils discover these things.)

A graph can easily be made by each group, with number of turns on the horizontal axis, number of brads on the vertical axis. Since a fairly straight-line relationship will be noted after three or four recordings on the graphs, you might ask individual groups if they can predict the results of the next ten-turn trial. (Although a scientifically controlled procedure will show a doubling of power with doubling the turns, children will rarely achieve this finding.)

Look for variations among the teams' results. Help the class analyze why these variations happened. Even though the same number of turns was used by each group, there must have been other variables that were not controlled. Help them isolate and check possible variables:

Were the bolts the same? Used in the same way?

Was the wire the same? Wrapped around the same?

Were the D cells equally strong? Was more than one used?

Were the brads all the same? Picked in the same way?

Was the counting correct? Recording correct?

Is there a way that every group will get *exactly* the same results? This is a challenge that some classes relish. (Probably it will be impossible, especially if the material to be picked up is made smaller and smaller. It might be interesting for your class to learn that greater relative variations may occur as the measurement unit becomes smaller. That is, a variation of *one* nail may be equivalent to *three* brads or *five* small wire staples.)

Contributing Idea B. Electromagnets may be used in the construction of an interrupted circuit for a bell or buzzer system.

1. *Materials:* for each small group two nails, about 2½ inches and 2¾ inches in length; 10-foot enameled (Number 22) magnet wire; 7- by 3- by ¾-inch block of wood; large thumb tack, hammer; pliers; 1- by 8-inch bare metal strip. (Cut the strip from a discarded large can with tin shears. Use gloves to avoid cutting fingers on sharp edges. File jagged or sharp parts so that

reason quantitativ

develop procedures

develop procedures

reason quantitative

290

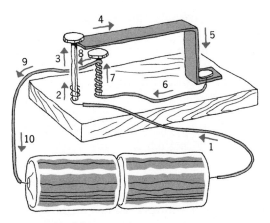

Figure 5-24   A buzzer system.

the strip may be safely handled. Scrape or sand away paint or other covering, especially at the ends on both sides. Several fathers of pupils may be willing to prepare a number of strips, given these instructions.)

Have the children build a buzzer to learn how an electromagnet may be used in a circuit. Let them use a projection of Figure 5-24 to build the system and describe how it works. About one hundred turns of wire are needed around the smaller nail to make an electromagnet powerful enough to pull down the strip end. Make sure they understand that this circuit is alternately opened and closed as the contact point opens and closes at the nail head. The end of the metal strip must touch the bottom of the larger nail head. If it does not, tap the nail down with the hammer until it touches.

2. Remove the cover of a door bell. Compare the buzzer and bell. (See Figure 5-25.) Develop that the circuitry is practically identical. The main differences are in materials used and sounds made.

make
inferences

Contributing Idea C. Telephone receivers contain electromagnets that help change spurts of electrical energy to sound energy; the transmitter uses sound energy to turn on electrical energy.

1. *Materials:* carbon rod from an old dry cell; hammer; two 25-cent pieces; small,

clear-glass egg cup; wire; cellophane tape; three D cells; miniature lamp and socket; large sketch or projection of a telephone transmitter and receiver (Figure 5-27); if possible, a real telephone. (Local telephone companies are usually cooperative in lending many useful materials to schools.)

This sequence should give children some understanding of how a telephone works. Begin by asking the pupils if they have ever made a long distance call on a telephone. Bring out distances involved. Cite the case of a person who phones someone 2250 miles away. The two people seem to hear each other instantly. Yet it is known that sound travels about 750 miles per hour, about the speed of some jet aircraft. What is the problem? (How is it possible to hear a person almost instantly when a telephone is used?)

state
problems

It is doubtful that your pupils' explanations will be entirely correct. However, ask which explanation seems most reasonable,

suggest
hypotheses

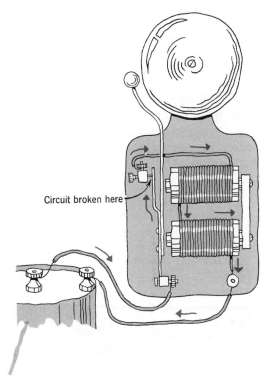

Circuit broken here

Figure 5-25

then continue. Tell them they now have almost enough background to understand how a telephone works, and will be able to figure out shortly for themselves what happens when a telephone is used.

It will be helpful to begin the sequence with a demonstration. Show that the amount of electrical current sent through a wire can be varied by increasing or decreasing the distance between conductors. Recall the children's previous experience with the nichrome wire rheostat, where length was an important factor in varying the resistance. In the following demonstration with carbon granules, the varying distance of the granules to one another will alter the amount of electrical current that flows in the circuit. This will cause light to burn with varying brightness.

Place the carbon rod on some paper and break it into small pieces with a hammer. Take two large coins, and attach the bared ends of two wires with cellophane tape to the coins. Complete the rest of the circuit as in Figure 5-26, placing the carbon granules between the coins to make a "sandwich." A small, clear-glass egg cup or plastic container will keep the granules from scattering and yet permit observation. Tell someone to press down on the coin gently, then harder. Ask the children to tell _make_ _inferences_ what they see and to explain why it happens. (More electricity is conducted when particles are squeezed together; this makes the light brighter. The opposite happens when the particles are not squeezed together.)

2. Have the children recall the ways in which an electromagnet can be made stronger. Emphasize that increasing the current by hooking up more dry cells in series makes an electromagnet more powerful. Ask if an electromagnet would gain or lose power through the same reason that the light's brightness varies. If there is any difficulty at this point, substitute an electromagnet for the light. Note its varying power of attraction with paper clips as the coins are pressed and released.

3. Place on the chalkboard or project the sketch of a telephone transmitter and receiver in Figure 5-27. Point to the two diaphragms and inform the class that they are made of very thin metal that can *vibrate,* or move back and forth rapidly. Note that the carbon granules or particles in the transmitter are like those used in the coin "sandwich" demonstration. Now ask the class to study the sketch and give an explanation of how the telephone works. _make_ _inferences_

With a little assistance, it should now be clear to the children why it is possible to hear someone speaking over the telephone almost instantly. Sound vibrations from the voice variably squeeze the carbon granules. This causes the granules to conduct variable electrical impulses, rather than a steady current. The electrical impulses rather than the voice itself are transmitted in the wire. Therefore, they travel thou-

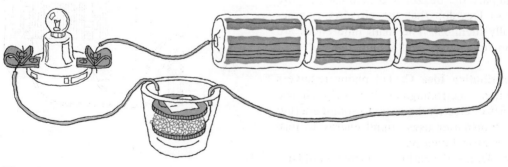

Figure 5-26

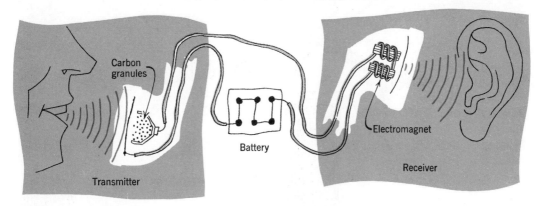

Figure 5-27 A telephone circuit.

sands of miles almost instantly instead of at the much slower speed of sound. The varying currents or impulses cause the electromagnet in the receiver to set its diaphragm vibrating. This creates the sounds. To summarize, you might emphasize the idea that one kind of energy may be changed to another. In this case, sound energy is used to provide the electrical energy, which is then used to provide sound energy. For reinforcement of learning, this would be an ideal time for pupils to read a textbook explanation.

If an actual telephone is available for inspection, unscrew the transmitter and receiver. Let pupils compare the parts with those in the sketch.

Contributing Idea D. Electric motors spin because they contain electromagnets which alternately push and pull as their poles change.

1. *Materials:* two bar magnets; string; electromagnet; Number 6 cell or D cell.

Tell the children that one of the most important applications of the electromagnet is in electric motors. Draw out names of common appliances that use electric motors, such as sewing machines, washers, fans, etc. Mention that the class will begin to understand how electric motors function after the following demonstration.

Suspend a bar magnet from a string.

Bring the opposite pole of the second bar magnet close to the suspended magnet. Demonstrate that unlike poles attract each other, and like poles repel each other. Now start the suspended magnet rotating in one direction by alternately attracting and repelling each pole. Twist the bar magnet so the poles are attracted at first, then repelled. If timed properly, the suspended magnet will rotate somewhat uniformly.

Now demonstrate a similar technique with an electromagnet. First, find the pole on the electromagnet that is the opposite of the bar magnet's nearer pole. It will attract. Next, reverse terminal connections and the poles will also be reversed. The nearer pole will now be repelled. (See Figure 5-28.) It should be possible to rotate the suspended magnet smoothly by touching the binding posts—first one way, then the opposite way. (A child can do this at a given signal.) Explain that in electric motors there is a device which reverses the current automatically, and thus reverses the poles. The alternating attraction and repulsion of the poles keeps the motor turning.

2. *Materials:* commercially made St. Louis motor; bell wire; dry cell.

A St. Louis motor is excellent for illustrative purposes. (See Figure 5-29.) Point out the main moving part, the *armature,* which is a rotating electromagnet. Show the

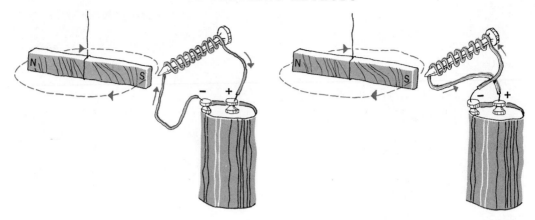

Figure 5-28

commutator. This device automatically reverses the armature's current—and thus its poles—just as the poles line up with the poles of the *field magnets.* These two permanent magnets are fastened on opposite sides of the armature. Also point out the *brushes,* which enable electricity to flow through the commutator to the electromagnet and back again.

EXTENDING ACTIVITIES

1. Have short reports on contributions of the following men to the technology of communication:

Samuel F. B. Morse (invented the first practical telegraph and code for each letter of the alphabet).

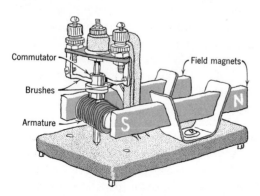

Figure 5-29 A St. Louis motor.

Commutator

Field magnets

Brushes

Armature

Cyrus W. Field (major contributor to research information used in laying telegraph cables across the Atlantic Ocean, through which messages called cablegrams are sent).

Guglielmo Marconi (invented the wireless telegraph, making possible transmission of electrical waves through air for communication purposes).

Alexander Graham Bell (invented the first practical telephone).

Hans Christian Oersted (conducted early experiments in electromagnetism).

2. A few advanced pupils may wish to build their own electric motor and demonstrate it. Directions for construction of simple motors may be found in many children's books on electricity.

Static Electricity. Not all electricity is useful. Almost everyone has experienced some form of *static electricity:* the crackling sound of hair when it is combed after having been washed and dried; the slight shock felt when a metal door knob is touched after scuffing across a rug; the flash of lightning that briefly illuminates a darkened sky. In each case an electric charge appears to build up on an object and then stay there (hence the name static) until a conductor provides a route through which the charge can escape. Although forms of static electricity vary considerably, their causes are fundamentally the same. To understand these causes, it will be helpful for us to peer briefly into the composition of molecules and atoms.

We know that most matter is made up of *molecules.* A molecule is the smallest bit of any substance which retains the chemical properties of that substance. If we subdivide the molecule further, it no longer resembles the original substance; we have arrived at the atomic level.

Only two of the particles of which an atom is composed need concern us here: *electrons* and *protons.* Each of these particles has a tiny electric charge that is the opposite of the other. The electron's charge is called a *negative charge* and the proton's charge a *positive charge.*

In their "normal" state, atoms possess as many electrons as protons. Since these particles attract each other with equal force they balance or neutralize each other. The atom is said to be *neutral,* or uncharged. However, electrons are easily dislodged or torn away from atoms by rubbing and by other means. Free electrons, as these dislodged particles are called, may be attracted to another atom. If an atom loses one or more electrons it will have an excess of protons, and hence a positive electric charge. If it gains one or more electrons the atom will have an excess of electrons and a negative electric charge.

When neutral, unlike materials are rubbed together one tends to lose electrons to the other. For example, when a hard rubber rod is rubbed with a wool cloth, the cloth loses some of its electrons to the rod. This gives the cloth a positive charge and the rod a negative charge. When a glass rod is rubbed with silk, however, scientists have found that some electrons leave the glass and go onto the silk cloth. This gives the silk a negative charge and the glass a positive charge. Although almost any unlike materials rubbed together will produce some static electricity, usually these materials—hard rubber and wool, silk and glass—give the best results.

A modern conception of the atom is needed to understand reasonably well the nature of static electricity. But early scientific discoveries helped at least to make it a less mysterious phenomenon than it must have been to primitive man. Benjamin Franklin's contribution to the understanding of static electricity is an interesting example.

To find out if lightning was associated with electricity, Franklin flew a kite during a thunderstorm. Attached to the kite was a metal rod, and at the end of the string a key was fastened. Franklin hypothesized that a spark would jump to the key as electricity traveled down the string. To avoid being shocked, he held the key by means of a silk ribbon. (Silk is a fairly good insulator.) Franklin took the additional precaution of standing under a shelter so the ribbon would remain dry. He realized that moisture increases conduction of electricity. His success with this and other experiments helped prove that lightning was a form of static electricity.

(Discourage anyone from trying Franklin's experiment. We know now that a severe electric charge would have electrocuted him in spite of the silk cloth insulator.)

What causes lightning? Basically, it is produced by friction. A cloud contains varying amounts of dust particles, rain drops, air (gas) molecules, and sometimes ice crystals. When violent air currents occur in clouds, these substances rub together in various combinations. If a huge electric charge is built up, it may be attracted by an oppositely charged cloud, or the ground. When this happens, we see lightning.

Since metals are excellent conductors, usually anyone is safe from lightning in a steel-framed building, or in a building equipped with a lightning rod. If the object is struck, the charge is harmlessly conducted by the metal down into the ground. Electricity always takes the path of least resistance. Lightning rod systems have the extra advantage of permitting excess charges on the ground to leak off the rod into the air, thus lessening the chance of a lightning stroke. Teach children to stay away from tall trees and other tall objects during a storm, especially if these are isolated and wet. The least resistance effect occurs here, too.

Static electricity can be dangerous or annoying in other ways. When spots or stains are rubbed off clothing through use of a flammable fluid, sparks may ignite the explosive vapor. Air inside flour and grain mills is often laden with fine particles of dust. Almost any material is highly combustible if reduced to small enough particles. Again there is danger of a spark causing an explosion.

Gasoline trucks have a strap or chain dangling from the chassis to the ground. This drains off static electricity built up from the gasoline jostling around in the tank. Toll booths on bridges and highways usually have thin metal rods imbedded in the ground immediately before each station. These rods drain off whatever static charges a vehicle has accumulated, thus preventing either driver or attendant from receiving a shock when the toll is paid. In the forthcoming activities, charged objects may be "grounded" (neutralized) by touching them. In the case of a balloon, you may have to touch several parts before it becomes neutralized all over.

Experiments with static electricity may be disappointing unless performed on dry days. Cold days are often ideal, because the air holds less moisture than on warmer days. When there is much moisture in the air, whatever static charges are built up may leak off rapidly into the air and ground.

Generalization VI: Matter contains electrons which may be accumulated through friction into electric charges; unlike charges attract, like charges repel each other

Contributing Idea A. Matter is made up of atoms which contain tiny particles of electricity called electrons and protons.

1. *Materials:* rubber comb; small bits of tissue paper; wool cloth; new balloon.

Invite a child to rub a comb briskly over some cloth and then place the comb near bits of tissue paper. The two will be attracted. Have another pupil rub a balloon with cloth and then place the balloon against the wall. It usually will stay there. Ask the class what is causing these phenomena to occur. They are almost sure to say "electricity."

Mention that this kind of electricity is called *static* or *frictional* electricity. Briefly, go into the meaning of the two words. Continue by inquiring whether someone has washed his hair a day or so previously. Have him recount what he noticed if he had brushed or briskly combed his hair after it dried. Invite the children to tell of other instances when they have noticed static electricity. They may mention experiences of sparks after rubbing their pets' fur, or sliding across a plastic automobile seat and then touching a metal door handle. Someone may have scuffed across a deeply piled rug and then touched a metal door knob.

After experiences have been told, develop that in each case rubbing one thing against another brought on a charge of static electricity. Now, ask the children where the electricity came from. Some may volunteer an explanation. Perhaps no one can. This will arouse the need for finding out how electric charges are built up on objects.

2. Permit the class to read or view visual materials to find out about the electrical particles of which atoms are partly made. Or your simplified exposition will help. Some ideas to stress are:

a. Everything in the world is made up of atoms. Atoms are very, very tiny. No one has ever seen one. But scientists have formed some ideas about them through their experiments and mathematical calculations.

b. Atoms have two different kinds of tiny electrical particles, of equal but opposite forces. One kind is the electron, whose electric charge is called a *negative* or minus (−) charge. The other is the proton, whose electric charge is called a *positive,* or plus (+) charge.

c. Electrons may whirl in many different orbits around the center of an atom. Protons usually stay located in the center of the atom.

d. Different atoms may have different amounts of electrons and protons, but usually they have an electron for every proton. When there is a balance of this sort, the atom is said to be *neutral,* or *uncharged.*

e. Protons usually stay where they are. However, some electrons are rather easily removed from atoms by an outside force, such as rubbing. When that happens, there is no longer a balance of electrical charges.

f. When electrons are rubbed off a neutral object, there are more positive protons left than electrons. The object has a positive charge.

g. A neutral object that gains negative electrons now has more electrons than protons. It has a negative charge.

h. Therefore, objects that have more electrons than usual have a negative electric charge. Those that have fewer electrons than usual have a positive charge. Atoms that have the same amount of electrons and protons have no charge, or are neutral.

make inferences Review to insure understanding. Place on the board the material in Figure 5-30:

Atom A has four electrons but only three protons. What charge, if any, does it have? (Negative.)

What charge, if any, does atom B have? (Positive.)

What charge, if any, does atom C have? (It is neutral, or uncharged.)

Contributing Idea B. Materials which have unlike charges attract each other.

1. *Materials:* glass rod (or piece of glass tubing or test tube or plastic object); piece of silk; hard rubber rod (or comb); piece of wool cloth; new inflated balloon; 18-inch string.

Suspend a balloon by a string from an upturned chair or other support so that it hangs freely. Have someone rub the balloon with a cloth. Explain that wool loses electrons easily and that electrons are going onto the balloon. Ask the class what charge the balloon may now have. (Negative.)

Ask a child to rub a glass rod vigorously with some silk. Explain that silk can remove electrons from a glass rod. Ask what charge the rod now has. (Positive.) Inquire as to what the children think will happen when a positively charged object (glass rod) is brought near a negatively charged object (balloon). After trying it, elicit that the objects tested had unlike charges, and therefore attracted each other. make inferences

2. *Materials:* glass rod or substitute; string and clothespin rod holder; silk cloth; rubber rod or substitute; woolen cloth.

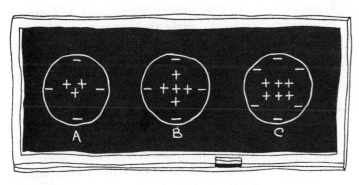

Figure 5-30

Suspend the glass rod from a string. (A wooden spring-type clothespin attached to the string and clamped to the rod makes this easy to do.) Charge it positively with the silk cloth. Let someone charge a rubber rod negatively by rubbing it hard on some wool. Be sure everyone knows the rubber is negatively charged and the glass is positively charged. Have someone explain what is happening to the electrons. Again request the children to predict what will happen when the unlike charges are brought close together. After they find the same result, draw from them the idea that unlike charges attract each other.

make inferences

Contributing Idea C. Materials which have like charges repel each other.

1. *Materials:* string; inflated balloon; wool cloth; rubber rod or comb.

Allow a class member to suspend the balloon again and recharge it with the wool cloth. The rod should also be recharged with the wool cloth. Make sure that everyone understands both items are negatively charged. Invite predictions as to what will happen if two negative charges are brought near each other. After trying it, draw from the group that the two negatively charged objects pushed or repelled each other.

make inferences

2. *Materials:* two glass rods or substitutes; silk cloth; string and clothespin rod holder.

Let a glass rod be suspended again. Have both rods rubbed with the silk cloth. If only one-half of each rod is rubbed, make sure that only those parts are brought near one another, as the charge will be built up only on the portion of the rod that is rubbed. Again call for predictions of what will happen when two positively charged objects are brought close together. After trying it, draw from the children that the two positively charged objects repelled each other.

make inferences

Recall with them the previous experiment. Through questions, bring out that in both experiments the objects had the same charges; in one case, negative charges, in the other, positive charges. Press for a tentative conclusion which states that like charges, whether negative or positive, repel each other.

make inferences

At this time, or perhaps after the children try several of the extending activities, discuss the difficulty of using static electricity in productive ways. Stress the need for a sustained and reliable source of electrical power.

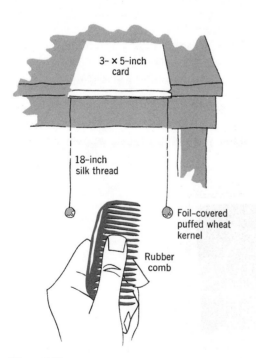

3- × 5-inch card

18-inch silk thread

Foil-covered puffed wheat kernel

Rubber comb

Figure 5-31

EXTENDING ACTIVITIES

1. This activity (Figure 5-31) will require pupils to apply their knowledge of static electricity in a problem-solving way. In other words, the previous investigations may be thought of as input for this activity. For this reason, you can also use it for appraisal purposes.

Each child or group will need a 3- by 5-inch file card; one piece each of silk and wool cloth; glass rod or substitute; hard rubber rod or substitute; 2-inch square piece of thin kitchen foil or substitute (chewing gum wrapper foil with paper removed, clean wrapper from Hershey chocolate candy kisses, etc.); 18-inch silk thread; scissors, puffed wheat kernels.

Inform the class that they can make an *electroscope* to figure out some of the strange ways of static electricity. Show them how to assemble the materials as in Figure 5-31. With scissors, make two small nicks in the card about one-half inch from the end. This will keep the thread from sliding off. To suspend each wheat kernel, just put one end of the thread next to the kernel and wrap it in foil together with the kernel. The card will stay secure if about three-fourths of an inch protrudes over a table edge.

Let the children explore for several minutes actions of the suspended pellets as uncharged and charged rubber or glass rods are brought close or allowed to touch them. If needed, help them discover that the pellets may be charged together by touching them with one charged rod; or may be charged separately with opposite charges by holding the strings farther apart and touching each pellet with a differently charged rod. Also, that the pellets may be neutralized by holding them for an instant.

make
inferences Have them explain why a pellet may be attracted to a rod, touch it, then flit away. (At first, the pellet is either neutral or has an opposite charge from that of the rod. As soon as it touches the rod, it instantly acquires a like charge and is repelled.) Review that rubbing silk on a glass rod produces a positive charge on the rod, and rubbing wool on a rubber rod produces a negative charge. Also, that like charges repel and unlike attract.

Now bring up the problem; perhaps in the form of a chalkboard sketch of Figure 5-32 A–E (left side only). Mention that the five sketches show the behavior of the pellets when a rod is put between them. They are to figure out what charge the rod has (if any), and the charge (if any) on the pellets. To make descriptions simple, a code will be used: N for neutral or no charge, +

for positive, and − for negative charges. (Worksheets here would be ideal for recording findings and evaluative feedback.) Suggest that pupils hypothesize first, then suggest hypotheses test the hypotheses with their electroscopes.

Treat all findings as tentative until the make inferences class seems ready for an evaluative discussion. Then have individual children test before the entire class their ideas about pellet behavior in the five situations. Thirteen combinations of charges and neutral states are possible. Try to bring out the valuable idea that the same phenomenon may have more than one valid explanation.

2. Get a committee to find out what causes lightning and what safety precautions may be taken to protect people and property.

3. Invite someone to report on how Benjamin Franklin experimented with a kite to find out about lightning. Have the class

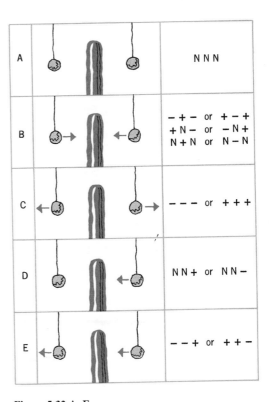

Figure 5-32 A–E

discuss the danger of this experiment and the danger of flying kites near power poles.

4. Draw up two teams. Each team can find out how the following things or places may be affected by static electricity; also, what precautions are necessary to prevent static charges from piling up. Develop with the class criteria for choosing valid and reliable information sources. Illustrative questions to pose before the pupils begin their search will also be helpful. *develop procedures*

Dry cleaners	Spray paint shop
Flour mill	Gasoline truck
Automobiles	Highway and bridge toll stations

Machines and Force

(Primary Emphasis)

UNIT SIX

Machines and Force

(Primary Emphasis)

IMAGINE A PARADE OF THE WORLD'S MACHINES—AIRPLANES AND tweezers, bulldozers and baby carriages, computers and egg beaters —an almost endless line of inventions, without which we would fare far less well. But perhaps the most remarkable thing about these applications of man's ingenuity lies in their construction. All machines, no matter how complex, are made from variations of just six simple machines. These are the inclined plane (ramp), wedge, screw, lever, wheel and axle (windlass), and pulley.

Many scientists classify simple machines into only two types— inclined plane and lever. To them, a screw and wedge are only variations of the inclined plane, and a windlass and pulley variations of the lever. Our agreement with this idea is reflected in the sequence and emphases within the unit. However, each of the six machines will receive some examination.

When simple machines are taught, we are often tempted to plan for an analysis of more complex types. This is not advisable with primary children, except perhaps for some familiar tools and less complicated machines. Variations and combinations of simple machines are limitless and hard to perceive, unless pupils have much experience and thorough understanding.

Although anyone who has just sat and thought hard for a while may disagree with this definition, to a scientist "work" can only be an applied force that moves a resistance or load over a distance. Force applied is measured in pounds, and distance measured in feet, to yield foot-pounds of work.

Credit for chapter opening photograph. **Shackman-Monkmeyer**

For any machine to do work, force must be exerted to overcome gravity, inertia, or molecular attraction. (*Friction* can be considered a form of molecular attraction; another is *cohesion,* the binding force that holds materials together.) Machines may be used to (1) reduce the force needed to do work, (2) speed up work, or (3) change the direction of a force.

Most of the following lessons concentrate on making work easier or, more accurately, how to reduce applied force. Children will learn that it is possible to gain an advantage of force in each case, but this is done at the sacrifice of moving a resistance over a greater distance than before. They will also see that friction is a counteractive force which reduces efficiency of machines. *The trading of distance for force and the inhibiting effect of friction should be brought out wherever applicable.* If these ideas are coupled with the following generalizations, pupils should learn many significant relationships. These should prepare them for more precise ideas in later experiences.

GENERALIZATIONS

I. Force needed to use an inclined plane changes as its tilt is changed; a wedge is like an inclined plane.

II. Force needed to use a screw changes as its pitch is changed.

III. Force needed to use a lever changes as length of the effort arm is changed; equal lever arms or loads, or combinations, permit objects to balance.

IV. Force needed to use a wheel and axle (windlass) changes with wheel size; the speed and direction of rotation of linked wheels can be changed.

V. Force needed to use a pulley changes as the number of ropes supporting the load is changed.

Inclined Planes. Although they may not have thought about it, even small children have had such experiences with inclined planes as climbing stairs, walking up a hill, coasting down a slanted driveway on roller skates, and the like. They know from these experiences that it is harder to climb a steep hill than a gradual hill. Boys and girls may even unknowingly use the idea that distance may be increased to decrease force, as when a bicycle rider rides diagonally up a hill, back and forth. This background of common experiences permits us to focus on relationships fairly quickly in the present generalization. It should also permit relatively easy applications of learnings to the wedge and screw, since these machines are variations of the inclined plane.

Perhaps it is wrong for us to say that an inclined plane or other simple machines make work "easier," if by that we mean that some part of the total effort is saved. In terms of work, or force moving a resistance over a distance, it is impossible to get out of a machine any more than is put into a machine. Another way of saying this is: *effort times distance equals resistance times distance*, or $ED = RD$.

Let us apply this idea to the inclined plane in Figure 6-1.

We wish to push a 50-pound barrel to a height of 5 feet and the inclined plane is 10 feet long. A measure of the force required to roll the barrel up would theoretically average out at 25 pounds. Using this figure and the distances involved, it can be shown that the total effort is the same:

By using the inclined plane—Effort (25 pounds) times Distance (10 feet) = 250 foot-pounds of work.

By lifting straight up—Resistance (50 pounds) times Distance (5 feet) = 250 foot-pounds of work.

The foregoing assumes that we are physically capable of performing the work in both cases. However, it is physically easier for us to apply less force for a longer distance and time. Muscles become tired quickly when subjected to heavy work. This is mentioned because many persons think that

305

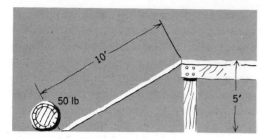

Figure 6-1

since the total foot-pounds of work are equal in both cases of a comparative situation, a simple machine never makes more actual work possible.

So far, we have left out friction. In reality, there would be some friction between the barrel and board. Since this would increase the actual resistance, effort would also need to be increased. In a lesson that follows, roller-skate wheels are used to reduce friction with a pushed box.

The reduction of force provided by a simple machine is called its *mechanical advantage*. This is found by *dividing force of the resistance by the force of the effort*. In the foregoing example the mechanical advantage is

$$\frac{R(50 \text{ pounds})}{E(25 \text{ pounds})} \text{ or } 2$$

In other words, it is twice as easy to lift the barrel with the inclined plane as without it. Or we can say it takes half as much effort. Since distance for both resistance and effort varies inversely in each case, inverting the two distances and dividing can also reveal the mechanical advantage. Thus

$$\frac{10 \text{ feet}}{5 \text{ feet}} = 2$$

However, this disregards friction.

By including frictional resistance with the resistance of the load moved, and by measuring actual effort needed to overcome this combined resistance, the real mechanical advantage is found. Since this would differ greatly with many objects moved—for example, a box with wheels, and an equally heavy box without wheels—it is the preferable way to measure mechanical advantage.

Friction makes it impossible for any machine to produce exactly as much work as the effort put into it. Since work "spread out" over additional time is easier, and because today so many machines use other than muscle power, this fact is not quickly obvious.

Of course, no one properly expects typical primary children to be taught the mathematical formulas in this exposition. But pupils can make many crude measurements and perceive, in a limited way, some of the relationships involved. For instance, a string can be employed to compare the length of an inclined plane with the height to which it rises. A rubber band attached to an object may have a ruler held beside it to measure different degrees of applied force in terms of "stretch." Or a spring scale will be even more effective than a rubber band. However, forces translated into ounces or fractions of a pound tend to have very limited meaning for young children. This is especially the case when differences of only a few ounces are involved.

We suggest that only whole numbers be used in gathering data, unless pupils are quite advanced. If measurements are awkward and difficult with a ruler because of the relatively wide spaces between numerals, cut out a cardboard "ruler" with numerals at half-inch intervals or less.

Wedges. A wedge can be thought of as two inclined planes placed back to back. Although the classic use of this machine has waned along with professional railsplitters and woodchoppers, the wedge principle is employed in numerous other ways. For example, "streamlining" is a way of better enabling objects to pierce air and water. Thus more speed can be achieved with the same amount of applied force. Paper cutters, knives, pencil sharpeners, nails, needles—all these are everyday wedges used for cutting or piercing functions.

Generalization I: Force needed to use an inclined plane changes as its tilt is changed; a wedge is like an inclined plane

1. *Materials:* cardboard box weighted with books; smooth, sturdy board about 4 feet long; 4-foot string; low table. Also, several pictures of inclined planes from magazines, perhaps including a stairway, a gangway for ships, an airplane ramp, and a trucker's loading ramp. In the absence of pictures, copy the sketches in Figure 6-2 on a chalkboard or chart. (Use an opaque projector for easy tracing.)

This investigation will contrast the force needed to pick up an object with that needed to push it up an inclined plane.

Ask such questions as, "How do people leave this house?" "How do they get on a ship?" "Airplane?" "How is the man getting the heavy barrel onto his truck?"

Now inquire, "What seems to be about the same in all four of these pictures?" Bring out that in each picture there is a slanting way to go up and come down. If no child knows it, the proper inclusive term for three of the four devices is a *ramp* or *inclined plane*. The children may need help to understand that a plane is any flat surface, and that inclined means a slanted or tilted condition.

make inferences

Take a string and stretch it from the upper end of the first inclined plane straight down to the ground.

Now measure with the string the length of the inclined plane. Guide the children to note that the distance is greater. Follow the same procedure in each picture.

Mention that in each picture the people are walking farther than they need to. Why don't they climb straight up a ladder? Wouldn't it be shorter? Someone will probably hypothesize that it is easier to walk or push a load up an inclined plane than to walk or pick something straight up. Ask the pupils how they could find out with the board, box of books, and low table.

suggest hypotheses

select procedures

Help them to reason through the experiment. Two children might first attempt to lift the books onto the table. Then the board can be placed against the table, and the box of books pushed up onto the table. Take care to hold the board so that friction between box and board does not cause the board to slide upward. Bring out from the two participants that it was somewhat easier to use an inclined plane. Encourage others to repeat the experiment to see if they get the same results.

Permit someone to measure with string the distance from table top to floor, and then along the ramp. Develop that while it was easier to use an inclined plane, more distance had to be traveled to get the load onto the table.

make inferences

2. *Materials:* cardboard box of books; 4-foot board; pair of roller skates; low table.

Use this activity to show that friction

Figure 6-2

is reduced if wheels are placed under a pushed box.

Draw out that although the inclined plane was easier to use than lifting the box of books straight up, there was still a large effort needed to push the box onto the table. Bring out that the box and board are rubbing together when the box is pushed. Inform the class that rubbing action is called *friction*—whenever two things rub together there is friction. Inquire as to whether it would be easier to push the box up the ramp if there were less friction. Question how grease, butter, or banana peels could ease the sliding. Since no one wants to make a mess in the classroom, is there another way to reduce friction? If unmentioned, hold up the skates. How could they be used? (Place the skates in tandem under the center of the box.)

develop procedures

Again, guide the children to think through a procedure. First, the box will be pushed up the ramp without wheels, then with wheels. Several children may repeat the experiment to verify accuracy of findings.

Now is a good time to introduce the idea of force within an understandable context. Explain that when we push or pull something we use *force*. A hard push needs a large force behind it. An easy push needs less force. Ask if more or less force was used to push the box when the skates were placed under it. Inquire as to why less force was needed. (There was less friction.)

Bring out that now the children have found two ways to make work easier with a simple machine: take a longer distance to lift something, and lessen friction.

3. *Materials:* roller skates; 4-foot board; a durable rubber band; ruler; paper clip.

This activity brings out that the tilt of the board is related to the force used.

Have everyone recall the ramps shown in the introductory pictures. On the chalkboard, develop that the angles of ramps differ somewhat. Sometimes ramps are slanted like this ⌒. Others are slanted like this ╱ and this ╱. Raise conjecture as to whether the degree of slant is related to the force needed to travel up a ramp. You might say, "If we want to get something like this skate onto our table, does the way the board is slanted make any difference in the force we must use? How many slants should we try?" Perhaps no more than three or four positions should be tried as the differences in force must be large enough to be readily noticeable.

Pupils will probably hypothesize that more force will be required as the slant becomes steeper. Press for why they think this is so. It may be helpful to give them such forced choices as: "Does it take less force to walk up a short, steep hill or a longer, less steep hill?" "Do you go down faster on a steep slide or a longer, less slanty slide, if both are the same height?"

suggest hypothese

Tell the children that since there will be several slants, it may be hard for everyone to see the amount of force required unless they use something to help them. Hold up the rubber band and ask how it can help. Let a child hold the band and stretch it gently, then harder. Ask the class if more or less force is being used the second time. Now, hold a ruler in back of the band and have another pupil read the numeral closest to the end of the band as it is stretched. Bring out that a larger numeral is indicated as the stretch is increased, showing that more force is used.

Attach a rubber band to the skate with a paper clip hook. The skate will be pulled with the rubber band. Encourage class members to plan how they will record the numerals they observe each time the skate is pulled with the ruler held alongside the rubber band. They might begin with either the steepest or the least steep slant, but, of course, should continue in serial progression. Tell them to ignore any part of the board that might project above the table in several positions. A chalk line drawn across the board at table height in each position might help them to understand that they are solely concerned with the portion of the board below the table top. A record on the chalk board might look like this:

Board	Rubber Band
Very slanty	4 inches
Less slanty	3 inches
Least slanty	2 inches

reason quantitatively

Ask the children what the findings seem to mean. Help them conclude that decreasing the slant of an inclined plane reduces the force needed to use it, and that the opposite is also true. Develop that increased distance is the price paid for decreased force. A simple way to summarize this is, "The less the slant the easier it is, but the distance is greater."

4. A variation of this activity is to fasten one end of a rubber band with a nail or tack to the top of the inclined plane. An attached skate will stretch the band to varying lengths depending upon the angle of inclination. Of course, recording the degree of stretch is easier when the band is static than when it is in motion, as in activity 3. Therefore, you may find this variation better suited for less capable children.

make inferences

5. For additional application, draw a hill on the chalkboard with zigzagged lines, as in Figure 6-3.

Inquire if anyone has seen animal trails on steep hillsides that look like the lines in the sketch. Why do animals seem to choose a longer, zigzagged route rather than a shorter, straight-up route? Again

make inferences

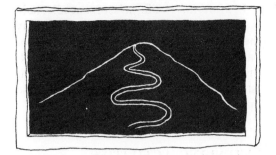

Figure 6-3

bring out the sacrifice of distance to secure decreased effort.

6. *Materials:* projection or sketch of Figure 6-4 A–C; steel wedge and ax (optional).

Help pupils apply their knowledge of inclined planes to wedges.

Show a real wedge or sketch A to the children. What can this object be used for? If no one knows, tell them. Write *wedge* on the chalkboard. Ask them how a wedge is able to split objects apart when struck forcefully.

Show the children a real ax or sketch B. Guide children to note the resemblance between a wedge and an ax. Help them understand that the head of an ax is an example of a wedge. With sketch C, guide them to see that a wedge is like two small inclined planes placed back to back.

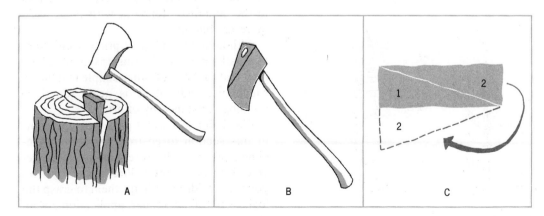

Figure 6-4 A–B–C

309

7. *Materials:* knife; scissors; needle; nail.

Invite different children to describe why these materials can be considered wholly or partly wedges. Have them compare the cutting or puncturing effect of the regular (sharp) and opposite (dull) portions of these materials.

EXTENDING ACTIVITIES

make inferences

1. Set up a bulletin board of pictures that illustrate many "unusual" wedges. Let pupils explain why each is partly a wedge. Some examples are the front of an airplane, the bow of a boat or ship, animal claws (especially digging claws), woodpecker's bill, teeth, plow, head of a rake, spade, carpenter's plane, chisel, can opener, fork, hoe, bulldozer front, trowel, sickle, and saw.

2. Ask your class to find pictures for a scrapbook or bulletin board showing how inclined planes are used in everyday life.

3. Encourage individual children to look for many examples of inclined planes. Each should be ready to tell the class where and how they are used.

Screws. "The screw is just an inclined plane wrapped around a nail." This is what one child said, and it's a fairly accurate description. A common conception of the screw is that of a nail-like object with a spiral thread

which holds together pieces of wood or metal. But other applications of this machine are all around us. There are spiral staircases, roads that wind around a steep hill or mountain, vises for work benches, clamps to hold things together, adjustable piano stools, and the adjustable parts of wrenches, to name just a few. Sometimes its appearance is not readily detectable, as in propellers for ships and airplanes.

When used to lift things, the mechanical advantage afforded by the screw is the greatest of any simple machine. It is relatively easy for a small woman to lift up the front of an automobile with a screwtype jack, and jackscrews employed by housemovers actually lift entire houses off their foundations. As with an inclined plane, however, the price paid for such a gain in force is distance.

Each time a screw is given a complete turn, it advances into a piece of wood or lifts an object only as far as the distance between its threads. This distance is termed *pitch,* and is illustrated in Figure 6-5. The paired drawings show that two screws of similar size, but different pitches, would vary in the number of times turned if screwed into some wood or employed to lift something. We expect a short, steep inclined plane to require more effort than a longer, gradual one when used to ascend to the same height. Likewise, the steeper the pitch of a screw, the more force is needed to make it rotate. However, it advances farther and faster than one with a narrower, more gradual pitch.

Although beyond most primary children, the mathematical relationships involved are identical to those of other simple machines. Mechanical advantage is again found by dividing resistance by effort.

We shall use several paired comparisons in this section to go from the familiar inclined plane to the screw as a related device. Use such a procedure frequently with younger children. It helps them to grasp the logic which links related applications of an idea.

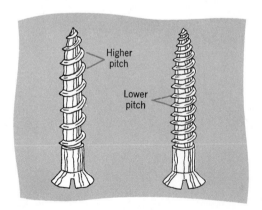

Figure 6-5

Generalization II: Force needed to use a screw changes as its pitch is changed

1. *Materials:* a large sketch for each pair of simple machines shown in Figure 6-6. (Use an opaque projector for easy copying.)

Show sketch A. Which inclined plane needs the least force for a barrel to be pushed to the platform? Establish that though less force is necessary to use the longer inclined plane, the load must be pushed a longer distance.

Show sketch B. How are the two staircases like inclined planes? The class should be able to respond from previous lessons that a staircase is an inclined plane with steps. Which side requires the least force in order to walk to the top? Again establish that additional distance is traveled to gain decreased force.

Exhibit sketch C. Point out that two lighthouses are pictured with inside stairways visible; these, also, are examples of inclined planes. Emphasize that these inclined planes wind around in a *spiral,* and are called spiral staircases. Draw out similar illustrations the children may have seen. Encourage them to indicate the staircase that would require the least force. They should easily recognize that again distance is traded for force.

2. *Materials:* two identical pencils; two tacks; two inclined planes cut from white paper, both 4 inches high, one 6 inches long and the other 9 inches long (Draw a heavy colored line on the outer edge of the long side on each cutout.); for each pair of children, two large wood screws of equal size but different pitches; screwdriver; a small block of soft wood. (Have ready a projection or chalkboard sketch of Figure 6-5.)

Exhibit the screw sketch. Bring out visible differences in *threads* of the screws; one has more spirals or turns. One has a steeper *pitch,* or greater distance between threads. Bring out that the steeper pitch is a steeper "slant." This will help the class to relate the threads to the previous example

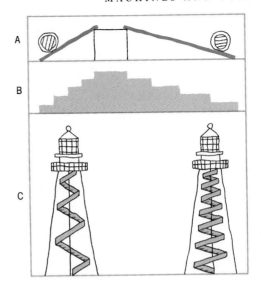

Figure 6-6

of inclined planes. Ask the pupils which previous sketches the spiral threads recall for them. Have someone select the paired lighthouses from among the previous sketches, so that they may be visually compared with the paired screws.

Let children predict as to which screw in the sketch would be easier to screw into a piece of wood, and which would take more turns of a screwdriver. (The screw of lower pitch.) Now distribute the two sets of wood screws and ask that each kind be identified with the sketch example it most resembles. Their prediction can be tested now with the actual wood screws.

Let the children screw the wood screws into the blocks. (It will be helpful to hammer shallow nail holes in the blocks to permit easier starting of the screws.) Have the children count the number of turns made by the screwdriver as the screws go into the wood. Which screw turned most? "Faulty procedure" can result when a child's hands have become tired, one screw is much thicker or longer than the other, screw threads are dull, or when the wood used is of unequal softness.

Why was the screw with more turns of thread easier but longer to turn? Explana-

develop procedures

311

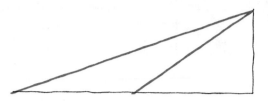

Figure 6-7

tions may be fairly, but probably not wholly, accurate. Use some cut paper inclined planes to insure clear understanding.

Place the smaller inclined plane over the larger, as in Figure 6-7. Review that the longer inclined plane would require less force, but would take longer. Now hold up two pencils. How could two "pretend" screws be made with them and the paper cutouts? Assist two volunteers to roll the paper tightly and evenly around each pencil. Secure paper at the bottom with a small tack or piece of cellophane tape. If both pencils are rolled clockwise, results should look like Figure 6-8. Help the group to summarize: A screw is an inclined plane wound in a spiral. Force required to turn a screw is lessened as pitch is lessened, but the number of turns (distance) is increased.

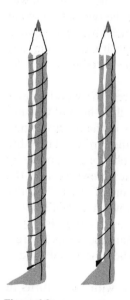

Figure 6-8

3. *Materials:* piano stool or screwtype auto jack; or pictures of these and a house-mover's jackscrew. If available, it would be most interesting for the children to manipulate a piano stool and auto jack (minus the auto!) to observe how screws can be used for lifting heavy objects. Pictures are helpful, also. If possible, locate a picture of a housemover's jackscrew "in action." The class will be impressed with its tremendous mechanical advantage.

EXTENDING ACTIVITY

Let class members locate many actual examples of screws for an exhibit table. Have them tell how each screw is used. Some easy-to-find examples where screws may be wholly or partly employed are the screw-top lid, corkscrew, monkey wrench, C-clamp, nut and bolt, propeller for a toy airplane or boat, desk chair, bit (of a brace and bit), vise, electric fan, and meat grinder. *(make inferences)*

Levers. No one knows who actually first contrived it, but apparently the lever has been known and used for a very long time. The ancient Greek scientist Archimedes is supposed to have said he could move the world, if given an appropriately long lever, fulcrum, and place to stand. It is widely assumed that primitive man also had knowledge of levers, but probably solely in a functional way.

The principles of this simple machine are used in so many ways that a moment's reflection can produce somewhat surprising examples. Thus, the venerable Japanese sport of judo is based on knowledge that the human skeleton is comprised of lever systems. Also, a golfer with long arms is able to develop a speedy club-head movement more easily in his swing than one with shorter arms.

This section includes study of the see-saw, a lever familiar to most children. It has three parts: (1) *fulcrum,* or point on which it pivots; (2) *effort arm,* the part on which the force is exerted; and (3) the *re-sistance* or load arm, that part that bears the load to be raised. When the seesaw is perfectly balanced on the fulcrum, the resistance and effort arms will alternate if two equally heavy riders alternately push against the ground to make the seesaw go up and down.

As with other machines, effort times distance (from the fulcrum) equals resistance times distance (from the fulcrum). This is shown in Figure 6-9. The mechanical advantage in this example is 2. Another way to calculate the mechanical advantage is simply to divide the effort-arm length by the resistance-arm length. Friction is usually so minor in the lever that it does not need to be taken into account.

Primary children can arrive at an intuitive understanding of the foregoing "law of levers" if they are given experience with balancing objects. Of course, the mathematics involved is beyond most primary pupils. In the first activity, we shall provide a gradual introduction to the several ways in which a load may be lifted or balanced with a lever.

Levers are found with parts arranged in three different combinations called *classes*. This is unnecessary to bring out with primary children. But it is helpful for you to know should you wish to teach parts of this unit to older children. Notice the three arrangements in Figure 6-10.

Seesaws, crowbars, and can openers are first-class levers. Two levers of this kind are placed together in such tools as scissors and pliers. By varying the effort-arm length, you change the amount of required force, or gain in speed and distance. This type also changes direction of movement. You exert force in a direction opposite to which the load moves. If both effort and resistance arms are equal, however, a first-class lever can change only the direction of a force. Neither reduced force nor gain in speed and distance takes place.

Second-class levers are illustrated by the wheelbarrow and post-puller. A nutcracker

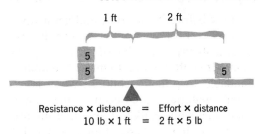

Figure 6-9

illustrates joined, double levers of this type. Speed or distance are not as likely to be considerations when employing a second-class lever as in the previous case.

Should you forget third-class levers, just think of your arm. Your elbow is the fulcrum, your bicep provides the effort at a point just below and opposite the elbow, and your fist represents the load or resistance. Other common applications are found in the broom, baseball bat, fly swatter, and fishing pole, to name just a few. Sugar or ice cube tongs represent double levers of the class. Analysis of this lever reveals that force is sacrificed to provide added speed or distance. With a fishing pole, for example, you want to increase the speed of your hands to hook a nibbling fish

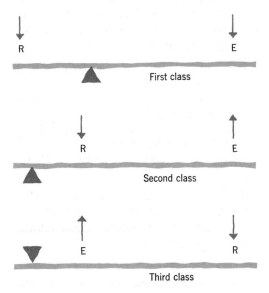

Figure 6-10 Three classes of levers; (R) is resistance, (E) effort.

securely before it can react and get away.

In several following lessons, use, if possible, a sturdy 4-foot board for the experiments. It is often more dramatic and understandable to primary children when large, actual materials are used rather than small, analogous models. For a fulcrum, use a brick or similar-shaped block of wood if children are going to stand on the board. For more delicate balancing, use a large piece of doweling or a round block from a play block set. Two rulers can serve to wedge the fulcrum and keep it from rolling.

Generalization III: Force needed to use a lever changes as length of the force arm is changed; equal lever arms or loads, or combinations, permit objects to balance

1. *Materials:* 4-foot board; round fulcrum and brick fulcrum; five identical books. (On a low table, place the board over a sensitive, rounded fulcrum so that it balances. Put a chalk mark in the center of the board on the edge facing the children, so they can observe that the board is centered on the fulcrum.)

If two identical weights are balanced on a lever with equal arms, the weights will always be the same distance from the fulcrum. Ask questions like the following ones to help pupils discover this fact.

develop procedures

Can you balance the two books? (One on each side of the fulcrum.)
Can you balance the two books on other places on the board?
Can you do the same thing with pairs of books? (One on top of the other.)
How can you balance three separate books? Four? Five?

(In these cases, each book has a counterpart equally distant from the fulcrum.)

Now have them work on the balancing of *unequal* weights with the lever still centered on the fulcrum.

develop procedures

Can you balance one book with two? Two with one?
If you want to balance three books with one

book, where should they go? Four books with one book?

Perhaps the children will have discovered by this time that it is also possible to balance two unequal weights by shifting the board to different positions on the fulcrum. If not, ask if there is another way the unequal weights can be balanced without moving the books from the board ends. Bring up the term *fulcrum* as needed in discussion. Have them try the same combinations as in the last sequence of questions, but now move only the board.

2. See if the children can apply some of their knowledge of the law of levers by using themselves, rather than books, as the weights. For a more stable board, replace the sensitive, round fulcrum with a brick or similar object. As children get on and off the board, have someone stand by at each end to lend support as needed. Instruct participants to get on and off the board in line with the board length, rather than sideways. Otherwise the board may swing around somewhat, and throw the children off balance.

Ask questions like these:

develop procedures

How can you tell who weighs more? (Pick a light girl and a heavy boy.)
Can the board be balanced with only one person on it? (Someone stands astride the fulcrum when the board is centered.)
Can the board be balanced with three people on it? Four? Five?
When the board is centered on the fulcrum, which two people in our class can stand on the ends and be balanced? Which four people?
Will it make any difference if the two persons at one end trade positions? If the two persons at both ends trade at their own end?

(If the paired students on each end differ in weight with each other, balance is impossible if they trade positions at one end only. Remember that balance depends on how the weight is distributed as well as total weight.)

3. *Materials:* chalkboard sketch of Figure 6-11; 4-foot board and fulcrum.

Use a discussion to clarify the idea that force is gained at the expense of distance.

Show the sketch. Explain that "L" means load. With which lever could you lift the *heaviest* load? Have children indicate their choice by holding up one to three fingers. If there is any doubt, try the several positions with a light and heavy pupil. Or, better still, perhaps a small child can lift you.

Bring out that, for the gain in force, the opposite end had to be moved over a greater distance.

4. *Materials:* for each pair of children, lever-type can opener; clean, empty tinned can; two sturdy 12-inch rulers; two 2-foot pieces of heavy twine or masking tape; hammer; several 2-inch nails; a small wood block (into which the nails will be pounded about halfway.)

These activities can give additional meaning to the previous one. By attaching a long handle to a lever-type can opener pupils will find it is easier to puncture the can. In pulling nails out of a board, they will find it is easier when the hammer handle is held near the end rather than toward the head.

Invite the children to puncture a can in two ways. First they should use the can opener alone, then tightly tie the rulers to the opener for a longer handle (Figure 6-12). Also suggest that they experiment with the length of the hammer arm in pulling out nails. (Nails should be pounded about halfway into the wood block.) They can do this by trying different hand positions along the length of the handle, first close to the inverted hammer head, then gradually toward the handle's end.

In a follow-up discussion, bring out again the lessened effort required with the longer handle in each case and the sacrifice in distance at the end of the handle.

5. *Materials:* nutcracker; several small nuts; scissors; tinner's snips (optional but helpful—try asking the custodian); piece of cardboard; chalkboard sketches as in Figure 6-13.

Show the materials as examples of *double levers,* or two levers put together. Permit

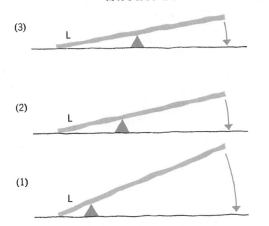

Figure 6-11 Decreasing the effort needed to lift a load requires the effort to be exerted over an increased distance.

pupils to point out the fulcrum, the place where work is done, and effort arms. If they cannot, show them. With the nutcracker, let children predict whether A or B would be the best place to apply force. Make sure they think this through in terms of increasing force-arm length.

If tinner's snips are available besides regular scissors, establish that the greater distance from the fulcrum (i.e., longer force arms) would probably make tin snips more powerful than scissors. Either wire or metal from a can may be used in the comparison.

If scissors alone are available, ask pupils to predict whether it would be easier to cut cardboard at the tips or closer to the fulcrum. Make sure they realize that placing material to be cut close to the fulcrum has the effect of increasing force-arm length.

Figure 6-12

315

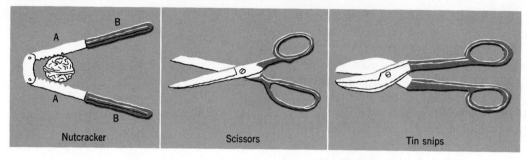

Nutcracker   Scissors   Tin snips

Figure 6-13

(This will be difficult for many primary pupils.) Use thick enough cardboard so the difference in ease of cutting can be readily seen.

EXTENDING ACTIVITIES

1. Invite everyone to gather materials or pictures that are wholly or partly levers.

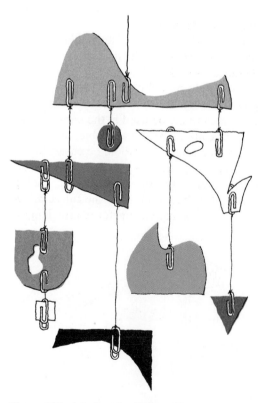

Figure 6-14 A tagboard and paper clip mobile.

Divide the class into groups and assign each several examples. Each group co-operatively locates the fulcrum, effort arm, and where work is done. This information can be reported in turn to the entire class. Examples are the broom, shovel, crowbar, fishing pole, pliers, hedge clippers, ice cube or sugar cube tongs, baseball bat, paper cutter, tennis racket, golf club, hockey stick, bottle cap opener, tweezers, canoe paddle, and boat oars.

make inferences

2. Let everyone make mobiles. This is an interesting way to combine art work with an extension of children's notions of balance. Basic materials needed are a spool of coarse thread; paper clips; scissors; tagboard or a supply of unlined 5- by 8-inch file cards; and art materials to color the figures. Of course, the amount of supplies used will depend on how many figures are used for each mobile. Figure 6-14 shows a seven figure mobile (thirteen paper clips are needed). A simpler mobile might have three pieces (five paper clips), or just one piece (one clip).

To minimize the problem of one suspended figure touching another, use a wider piece of tagboard for the top figure and narrower pieces for the remaining figures, as in the model. Also, each pair of strings can be different in length. Be sure to remind pupils that all strings should be tied to the *narrow* end of each paper clip. To save time, you might want to cut only one 8- by 12-inch piece of tagboard per mobile and to distribute 5- by 8-inch file cards for the figures. Pupils may cut out and then color a group of different-sized birds, whales, fish, airplanes, or abstract figures. It might be best at the beginning to ask that either the top or bottom edge of the suspended card be a straight edge, and be positioned parallel to the floor, as in Figure 6-14. This makes it easy for the child and you to check for proper balance. Later, you might want to skip this restriction.

Children will need adequate working space and a place to suspend the figures while constructing the mobiles. The setup in Figure 6-15 should solve this problem. For a place to store the mobiles when children are not working on them, tightly string some heavy twine across one end of the room. You may need several strings to hold all the mobiles. The strings can also serve as drying "racks" for painted pieces.

To help the children get started, you might have the parts of a disassembled mobile on a table. Ask different individuals to balance various pieces as you hand them over one at a time.

As the children work on their mobiles, they will experience the problems of proper balance, and of figures touching. For solutions, they will need to think about such variables as figure size and shape, string length, best positions for figures, and where to fasten the clips. Use individual and group consultations as needed to assist in finding solutions.

The Wheel and Axle. The windlass or wheel and axle is a commonly misunderstood simple machine. Although similar in appearance to a wagon wheel and axle, a windlass is different. We put wheels on a wagon to reduce friction by lessening the surface area that comes in contact with the road. Its axles are stationary. Greater "leverage" is indeed present in a large wheel, as contrasted with a small wheel. This is why a large wheel can roll over uneven ground more easily than a small wheel. But usually a wagon wheel and axle combination is not regarded as a simple machine.

develop procedures

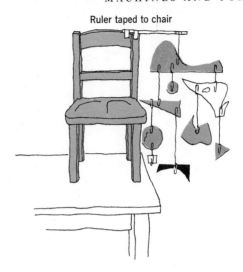

Ruler taped to chair

Figure 6-15 A support for mobile constructions.

In a windlass the axle and wheel are firmly fixed together. Spinning the axle causes the wheel to rotate, and the reverse is also true. By turning the axle, force is sacrificed to gain an advantage in speed and distance on the outside of the wheel. By turning the wheel, an advantage in force is gained, while speed and distance are sacrificed at the axle.

A windlass can be visualized properly as a continuous lever on a continuous fulcrum. Thus, when a handle is placed anywhere on the wheel it becomes the end of the force arm. The axle's radius is the load arm. Figure 6-16 provides an illustration of this idea.

The theoretical mechanical advantage in a windlass is calculated as with a lever. If the effort-arm length is 18 inches, and resistance arm length is 2 inches, mechanical advantage equals 9. Because friction is so great with a windlass, however, actual mechanical advantage is found only through dividing resistance by effort.

Our following lessons develop the same relationship brought out in the lever. Placing the windlass handle ever farther away from the axle decreases needed effort. At the same time, it increases the distance through which the effort is applied.

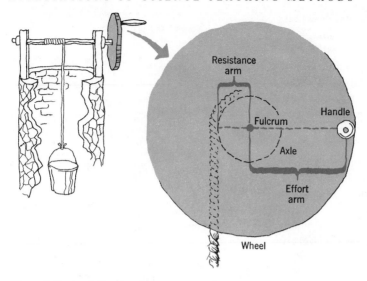

Figure 6-16 A windlass is a lever.

Applications of the relationships involved make it easy for children to understand why a meat grinder needs a longer crank than a pencil sharpener, for example, and why a large steering wheel is easier to turn than a smaller one.

Wheel and axle combinations may be modified to interact with one another by using belts, chains, and toothlike projections on the circumference of the wheel to form gears. The bicycle is a common example of two modified wheels and axles

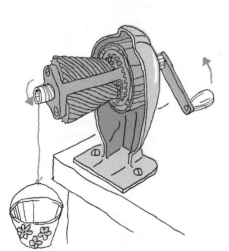

Figure 6-17 A pencil sharpener can be used as a wheel-and-axle.

joined by a chain. Since the front sprocket is larger than the rear sprocket, one turn of the larger sprocket forces several or more turns of the smaller rear one. Older pupils can find the theoretical mechanical advantage of the larger sprocket by counting and comparing the number of teeth on each sprocket. In an upcoming activity with spools and rubber bands, children can discover how the speed and direction of rotation of linked wheels can be changed or predicted.

Generalization IV: Force needed to use a wheel and axle changes with wheel size; the speed and direction of rotation of linked wheels can be changed

1. *Materials:* pencil sharpener (cover removed); sticky tape; 24-inch string attached to a weighted toy bucket. (Set up as in Figure 6-17. Attach string to the end of the sharpener. A tiny piece of sticky tape will prevent it from slipping as the end turns.)

In this activity, the pencil sharpener will be used as a windlass to lift the toy bucket.

Ask someone to turn the pencil sharpener handle and lift the load. Have him do it again with only a forefinger, placed just next to the handle. Suggest that everyone watch his hand movement. Ask him to repeat cranking the handle with his forefinger halfway up the handle, then near where the handle shank is attached to the horizontal shaft.

Let the child describe his increasing difficulty in turning the handle. Point out the decreasing size of the circle his hand appeared to trace as he turned the handle with his finger closer to the horizontal shaft (fulcrum). If no one can identify this part of a sharpener as a *wheel and axle* or *windlass,* inform them. Bring out the relationship to the lever by discussing the effort arm length and varying force needed to turn the crank. Follow through with several other common examples in the next activity.

2. *Materials:* door knob; screwdriver; broom, or any sturdy, polelike object of similar size; masking tape; chalkboard sketch of Figure 6-18. (Mark the center of the broomstick as in Figure 6-18. Place two pieces of tape 6 inches and 18 inches to the right of the center mark, respectively. Do the same left of the center mark.)

Inform the pupils that there are many wheel and axle examples around them. Peer intently at a door knob on the door. Invite them to tell what the example is you are looking at. Unscrew the tiny set screw by the knob and take off the knob. Have someone identify the axle (the part the knob is fastened to) and wheel (the knob itself). Let several pupils try to turn the latch first without, then with, the door knob. Develop the idea of distance and force again.

Hold up a screwdriver. Let a child identify the wheel (handle) and axle (shaft). Request the children to predict as to whose applied force would be more powerful if one child held the shank, another the handle, and each tried to turn the tool in opposite directions. Can they detect that unequal friction of the two surfaces is a lack *develop* of control? Masking tape around both parts *procedures* can help reduce any friction discrepancy. Also note if pupils plan to have the two ex-

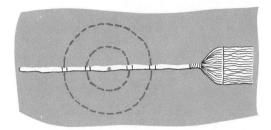

Figure 6-18

perimenters reverse their roles. (Strength is a factor, also.)

Exhibit the broom or pole. Refer to the chalkboard sketch. Explain that this can be considered a spoke of two steering wheels, one large, one small. Question if a larger, rather than smaller, steering wheel makes it easier to turn a car or truck. Entertain predictions. Ask how two children could find out with the broomstick.

Lead them to understand what must be *develop* done. Two children will face each other *procedures* and hold the stick in different places. One child will hold the stick at the inner markings and another at the outer markings. Upon a given signal, each will try turning the broom evenly and steadily in opposite directions. (A few words from you can prevent this experiment from becoming a wrestling match.) Stress that force should be applied smoothly and without excessive strain. Note if reversed roles for the experimenters are planned to control the strength factor. The distance-force relationship should now be quite clear.

3. *Materials:* upturned bicycle.

Use a bicycle to demonstrate how two windlasses can be linked by a chain. Have a child turn the front sprocket of the bicycle. Call attention to the rear sprocket. Why does it turn faster? (It is smaller.) Why is it going in the same direction? (The chain pulls it that way.) Discuss that by linking the two different-sized wheels and axles it is possible to make one go faster.

4. *Materials:* for each small group, a gear board with at least five empty sewing thread spools, four identical and one smaller in size; four small rubber bands. (Set up a

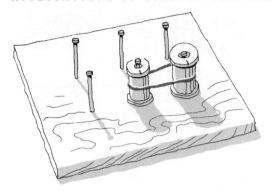

Figure 6-19

model as in Figure 6-19. For the base you will need a half-inch thick board about a foot square. The ends from a discarded vegetable crate are ideal. Pound four to six finishing nails part way into the board, about three inches apart. Make a clear mark on each spool-head rim to make rotations obvious. Rubber bands should fit tightly around the spools.)

Use this activity to let pupils find that both speed and direction of linked wheels can be changed.

Exhibit the model gear board. How are these spools like the bicycle gears? Ask the children to predict the speed (faster or slower) of the smaller spool as the large one is turned.

Can anyone figure out a way to get the small spool to turn *opposite* to the large spool? If no one knows, show how by making one twist in the band. Let the children explore for a while the ways in which they can connect two or more spools.

5. *Materials:* as in activity 4, and a dittoed gear problem worksheet for each child. (See Figure 6-20. Leave off all dotted lines and check marks. Simplify or complicate it according to the ability of your class.)

Follow through activity 4 with a worksheet of problems that need testing. Go over the worksheet directions slowly, to make sure everyone understands the problems. Try to get the children to infer what the problems and procedures are before verifying. Provide these questions and directions:

make
inferences

A. If the left spool is turned, in which

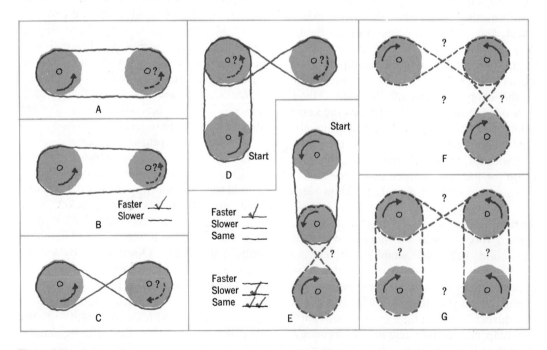

Figure 6-20

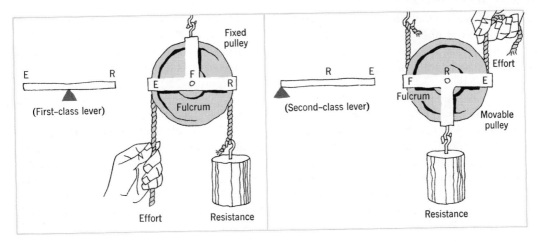

Figure 6-21

direction will the right spool go? They will draw an arrow.

B. In which direction will the right spool go? Will the right spool go faster or slower? They will draw an arrow and make a check.

C. In which direction will the right spool go? Pupils draw an arrow.

D. In which directions will the top spools go? Draw arrows. (Mention that when two rubber bands are to be placed on a single spool one should go around the bottom and one around the top of the spool to avoid binding.)

E. Will the middle spool go faster, slower, or the same? Make a check. How to connect the middle and bottom spools? Draw lines. Will the bottom spool go faster, slower, or at the same speed as the middle spool? Compared with the top spool? Make check marks—two for the last question.

F. How should the spools be connected to make them turn as shown? Draw lines. (Pupils may use three bands when only two are needed. If this happens, see if they can figure out which is the unnecessary band.)

G. How should the spools be connected to make them turn as shown? Draw lines.

6. Encourage the children to invent their own gear worksheet problems and exchange them with classmates. Some may wish to use up to six spools.

EXTENDING ACTIVITY

Invite everyone to find examples of machines that are at least partly the wheel and axle kind, and explain how they work. The children can bring to class names, pictures, or real examples of these machines. Items to look for are a meat grinder, tricycle (front wheel), pepper mill, wall can opener, eggbeater, wrench (in use), skate key (in use), radio and television dials, hand drill, and fishing reel.

make inferences

Pulleys. Elsewhere, it was suggested that miniature models were less usable than larger, real-life materials. Perhaps nowhere is this more so than with pulleys. Tiny pulleys that use thread, currently offered by many scientific supply houses, simply are not practical at the primary level. Often worse are homemade varieties fashioned from wire hangers and thread spools, or similar devices. They are apt to be cumbersome and exhibit much friction. A better solution is to use ordinary clothesline pulleys, or buy at a hardware store two single pulleys of moderate size. Sash cord, or something similar, can serve for rope.

Single pulleys contain but one grooved wheel, or sheave. Some pulleys possess two or more sheaves for combined use with other pulleys in heavy lifting. As its name implies, a *fixed pulley* is securely fastened to some object. A *movable pulley* moves vertically (or laterally as the case may be) with the load.

The pulley's similarity to a lever and windlass is diagramed in Figure 6-21. As with a windlass, the wheel-like arrangement is really a continuous lever. Observe why a fixed pulley can do no more than change the direction of a force. Like a seesaw whose fulcrum is centered, the effort arm and resistance arm are of equal length. There is no useful mechanical advantage. If one foot of rope is pulled downward, the resistance moves upward one foot. This happens, for example, when a flag is raised on a flagpole.

Notice why a movable pulley offers a theoretical mechanical advantage of 2. The resistance arm is only half the effort-arm length. Like a wheelbarrow, this is a variation of a second-class lever. As with other machines, distance is sacrificed for decreased effort. The rope is pulled two feet for each foot the load is lifted.

By placing a fixed and movable pulley in

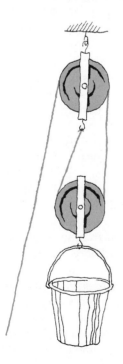

combination, we are able not only to change the direction of a force, but also to decrease the force necessary to lift a load. Such an arrangement is called a *block and tackle*. (See Figure 6-22.) By adding more movable pulleys (or pulleys with two or more sheaves) effort can be reduced even further.

Friction finally limits how far we can go in adding pulleys to reduce effort. It can be partly overcome by greasing or oiling the axle. Let pupils do this in their experiments.

Since each rope in a block-and-tackle setup supports an equal fraction of a load, it is easy to know the theoretical mechanical advantage. Two supporting ropes have a mechanical advantage of 2, three ropes 3, and so on. For practical purposes, however, mechanical advantage must be calculated through dividing resistance by effort.

Use a rubber band (or spring scale) in the following experiments to measure differences in the force needed to lift things as supporting ropes are increased. Because a rubber band otherwise may be inconvenient to attach, fashion a paper-clip hook. Simply pierce the cord at the place where you wish to measure needed force, insert the hook, and attach a rubber band to it. As before, a ruler can measure the amount of stretch.

The following sequence goes from very simple activities to more complex ones. Most primary children should have no trouble understanding the first several activities. The last several activities will be more meaningful to gifted primary pupils or older pupils.

Generalization V: Force needed to use a pulley changes as the number of ropes supporting the load is changed

1. *Materials:* single pulley; heavy twine; heavy rubber band; ruler; toy bucket partly filled with rocks, or substitute; paper clip.

In this investigation, children will compare the force needed to lift a load with and without a single pulley.

Mention that now all but one of the simple machines have been studied. Invite anyone to name or describe the remaining machine. If no one knows, give such clues as: it is used to draw curtains shut; it is used by painters when they paint the outside of a tall building; it is used to raise a sail on a sailboat; it is used to hoist a flag up a flagpole. By the last clue, almost everyone will recognize the machine to be studied. Write *pulley* on the chalkboard and let the class say it aloud. Compare it with a windlass. Now show that a pulley has a movable wheel and stationary axle. Request names of several toys which have the same arrangement: wagons, tricycles (rear wheels), roller skates, and so on.

Point to a hook or nail placed above the chalkboard or other place. Have the class pretend it is alongside the roof of a tall building on which some men are working. Since the men often need materials from workmen below, can the class devise a convenient way in which a pulley and toy bucket can be used to help?

Let the children raise the bucket a few times with a simple pulley. Does it take less force to lift something with a pulley or without one? Guide the class as to what must *develop procedures* be done to find out. For example, ask how a rubber band and ruler might be employed to measure force in using the pulley and then lifting up the same object by hand. In both cases let someone measure any degree of stretch evidenced by the rubber band. When the rubber band is attached to the pulley string, make sure it is pulled smoothly to reduce fluctuations produced by friction and sudden jerks.

make inferences The class will probably be surprised to discover that it requires slightly more force to lift the load with the pulley than by hand. Briefly raise conjecture as to why. If necessary, have the children recall that friction was a retarding force in previous experiments. Bring out how friction might be reduced by greasing or oiling the axle around which the pulley sheave revolves.

Develop that it is more convenient to pull in a downward direction than up because we can use the weight of our bodies to help. Guide pupils to understand that they changed the direction of their applied force. By pulling down, they were able to lift something up. Also, help them to see that there was additional convenience in being able to stay in one spot. For example, discuss the awkwardness of having to climb a flagpole each time a flag is raised or lowered.

Establish that a pulley used in this manner is called a *fixed pulley* — a pulley that stays in one place because it is attached to something. Bring out other common examples of fixed pulleys, such as those used for Venetian blinds, stage curtains, hay hoists, clotheslines, and window weights.

2. *Materials:* two single pulleys; 20 to 40 feet of strong twine; clothespin; handkerchief.

Challenge the children to make a "clothesline" hookup with two pulleys and twine. Who has seen a clothesline with two *develop* fixed pulleys? How can we arrange these *procedures* two pulleys so we can move a load back and forth? Help the class attach the pulleys to two different parts of the room, string the line, and attach the "laundry." Bring out the convenience of remaining stationary while the laundry moves.

3. *Materials:* one single pulley; strong twine; yardstick; toy bucket containing several stones; rubber band; ruler; paperclip hook. (See Figure 6-23 A–B.)

Introduce the idea of a movable pulley with two demonstrations. These will permit the children to compare different data and draw their own conclusions. Tell them they have seen how a fixed pulley works, and found it does not reduce force. Establish that occasionally a single pulley is so arranged that it moves up and down with the load. This is called a *movable pulley.* Inform the children that you are going to do two silent demonstrations. When you are through, they are to tell why a movable pulley might be used to do lifting.

First demonstrate the degree of force needed with a fixed pulley, then with a movable pulley (Figure 6-23 A–B).

There should be little difficulty in deciding that the movable pulley required less force. Now, help the class understand the

323

reason. Request a child to place a yardstick through the bucket handle and lift it. Have him place one end of the yardstick on a desk top and hold the other end horizontally, with bucket centered. Bring out that now he is supporting only half the bucket's weight.

Establish that in a single, fixed pulley the load is supported by a single strand, but that in this movable pulley it is supported by two strands. Therefore, only half the force is required (disregarding friction).

4. *Materials:* one single pulley; yardstick; twine; weighted toy bucket.

Use this activity to show that the lessened effort in using a movable pulley is "paid for" by pulling twice the length of rope needed with a fixed pulley.

Tell the children something is puzzling you. In all their previous experiments they have discovered that whenever force to move a load was made easier, the force was moved over an increased distance. Does the same rule also apply here? How can the yardstick be used to find out? Repeat the demonstrations illustrated in Figure 6-23 A–B, but without rubber bands this time, for greater precision of measurement. Help pupils to measure first the distance the load is raised, then the distance the string is pulled. This should be done with each pulley example. (To avoid confusion, measure each time how far the *hand* holding the string moves. Since a movable pulley moves upward with the load, it is awkward to measure directly how far the string travels.) Deal only with whole numbers unless your group is quite advanced. Record data on the chalkboard:

	Fixed Pulley	Movable Pulley
Distance string pulled	1 foot	2 feet
Distance load raised	1 foot	1 foot

Assist the class to interpret data as needed. Conclude that decreased force was gained at the expense of increased distance. reason quantitative

5. *Materials:* two single pulleys; twine; rubber bands; weighted toy bucket; yardstick.

In this activity, pupils combine two single pulleys to form a block-and-tackle combination.

Let pupils recall that an advantage of the fixed pulley is that a person can pull downward—body weight assists in pulling. Contrast this with upward pulling when the movable pulley was demonstrated. Ask if the class can invent a way in which a fixed pulley and movable pulley together can be

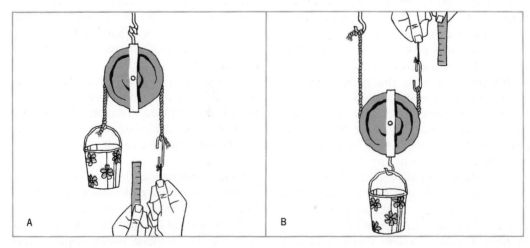

Figure 6-23 A–B

develop
procedures

used. This would give two advantages: less effort and a downward pull.

If difficulty arises, this may be a favorable time for the children to check books, pictures, a film, or filmstrip. Lend assistance if necessary. (See Figure 6-22.) Once the combination pulley is arranged, draw out that any pulling is indeed downward, and the lower pulley is movable. Encourage

reason
quantitatively

measurement of the relative distances between the rise of load and length of rope pulled. Have children compare force required to lift a load with the combination pulley as contrasted with a single fixed pulley.

Ask pupils to note the two supporting ropes (the pull rope is disregarded.) Emphasize that by increasing supporting ropes from one to two, force needed to lift the load is reduced. Bring out, however, that distance of pull is increased at the same time.

6. *Materials:* two sturdy, round sticks from an old broom handle sawed in half; 15-foot clothesline, or other strong rope.

Tell pupils they can see in another way whether adding more ropes to support the load makes it easier to move a load. Tie a rope securely to one broomstick and loop it over the other as in Figure 6-24. Let two boys each hold one broomstick firmly and stand facing each other about 4 feet apart. Instruct a third child to pull on the rope to see if he can force the two boys to come together. They, in turn, are to resist firmly but without excessive strain. (Careful selection of participants in some demonstrations makes the difference between a successful learning experience for all, and unnecessary room control problems.)

It is doubtful whether the boys holding the broomsticks can be pulled together at first. Point out that there is only one supporting rope. Have the class predict what may happen as more loops are made. Let the children experiment with two, three, and four turns of the rope. Each additional loop will, of course, require pulling in a direction opposite to that of the preceding trial. Care should be taken to insure that

Figure 6-24

the ropes do not cross and bind each other.

Elicit from your rope puller and class that additional turns of rope apparently increased his force. You might bring out briefly that the child had to pull on the rope over a longer distance as well.

make
inferences

If a picture of a heavy block-and-tackle rig is available, it would be most interesting for the class to see the four or more ropes used to support the load. They should learn, however, that there does come a time when adding more ropes will not reduce applied force—friction offsets the advantage otherwise gained.

EXTENDING ACTIVITIES

1. Take a study trip to places where pulleys are used. See them in action. Likely locations are construction projects, boatyards, ships or boats, places where painters or roofers are working, auto repair shops, heavy moving projects, and factories.

2. Encourage pupils to collect pictures of pulleys used in different ways.

3. Suspend from some suitable playground apparatus a block-and-tackle rig (Figure 6-22) made up of strong rope and two clothesline pulleys or substitutes. Children will delight in hoisting each other up and down a low, safe height.

Attach a 5-foot rope to the bottom pulley in place of the bucket. Loop and tie the last 18 inches of the rope to form a stirrup. (If you are not sure about the knots, etc., the school custodian might be able to help.)

The Earth's Changing Surface

(Intermediate Emphasis)

UNIT 7

UNIT SEVEN

The Earth's Changing Surface

(Intermediate Emphasis)

SHIFTING SAND DUNES, ERODING HILLSIDES, WEEDS GROWING ON an asphalt playground, muddy water running in gutters—there is evidence all around us that the earth's surface is changing. This unit will help children learn about some of the forces that wear down and build up the earth. In addition, it should increase their understanding and appreciation of soil conservation.

GENERALIZATIONS

I. Weathering and erosion constantly wear down the earth's surface.

II. Topsoil is composed of mineral, vegetable, and animal matter; topsoil conservation benefits everyone.

III. Lava and magma flows, earthquakes, and crustal movements continually build up the earth's surface.

IV. Rocks are formed through the forces that wear down and build up the earth's surface; there are igneous, sedimentary, and metamorphic rocks.

Weathering and Erosion. Perhaps the only permanent feature about the earth's surface is the continuous process of change it reveals. The forces that weather and erode the land are ceaseless and powerful. Strictly speaking, *weathering* refers to the breaking

Credit for chapter opening photograph. **Russ Kinne-Photo Researchers, Inc.**

down of rocks into smaller parts through action of such agents as plants, chemicals, frost, and changes of temperature. *Erosion* is the process of transporting weathered material from one location to another, as in the action of running water, wind, and glaciers. However, the distinction blurs in actual cases, as we shall see.

Plants break down rock in several ways. Growing roots may wedge deeply into a cracked rock and force it apart. As dry plant seeds absorb water, they swell with surprising force, and may perform a similar wedging function. Tiny flat plants called *lichens* grow on bare rock. (Figure 7-1.) Acids released by these plants decompose and soften the rock. Larger plants may then follow in a long succession, each contributing to the rock's destruction.

Oxygen and water in the air combine with rock surfaces to produce "rust." Reddish soils, for example, usually contain oxidized iron compounds.

Falling rain picks up a small amount of carbon dioxide in the air and forms carbonic acid. Although it is well diluted, this substance slowly wears down limestone. Older limestone buildings and statuary have a soft, worn look from the dissolving effect of acidic rainwater. This is especially noticeable in England, where coal burning has been so prevalent. Abnormal quantities of carbon dioxide in the air increase the acidic content of rain and hasten weathering.

Rainwater that percolates into the ground may encounter a limestone formation and dissolve some of it, thus forming a cave. This is how the Carlsbad Caverns of New Mexico, Luray Caverns of Virginia, and Mammoth Caves of Kentucky were formed. Since the surface appearance of a rock is somewhat altered by chemical weathering, we must often chip or break it to note its natural coloration.

Frozen water also contributes to weathering. Many rocks are relatively porous. Water, remember, is one of the few substances that expand in freezing. As ab-

Figure 7-1 Lichens play a part in weathering rock. (John H. Gerard—National Audubon Society.)

sorbed water expands, bits of rock are broken off. In addition, ice may wedge apart cracked rocks.

Stones placed around campfires are sometimes cracked because rocks conduct heat poorly. The difference between a hot surface and cooler interior may produce strains which cause parts to flake off. But some of this *exfoliation,* as it is called, may be from expansion owing to release of pressure. Rocks formed underground are subjected to great pressures. When they finally appear on the surface, because of erosion or other means, there may be a tendency for these rocks to "unsqueeze" slightly, thus starting some cracks.

Moving water is no doubt the most erosive force on earth. Abrasive, water-borne rocks and particles have gradually formed the Grand Canyon over millions of years. Millions of tons of soil daily wash from banks and hills over the world into streams, and are eventually carried into the ocean. Ocean waves unceasingly pound huge cliffs and boulders into sand.

Water running down hills characteristically forms gullies. As the slope angle increases, water moves more swiftly, thus hastening erosion. Rain splashing on near-level fields has a different erosive effect. Broad sheets of soil wash off into lower places without obvious gullying.

Wind erosion became dramatically apparent to millions of Americans in the "Dust Bowl" years of 1934–1935. Prairie lands originally covered by a grassy sod had been broken up for agriculture. A combination of dry weather and marginal farming practices resulted in the most destructive dust storms ever seen in the United States.

Glaciers also contribute to land erosion. Huge snow deposits build up when snowfall exceeds the melting rate. Gradually the snow compacts into ice and flows slowly downhill, in the case of mountain valley glaciers. Continental glaciers are much larger, ranging to thousands of square miles in size. At one time, a large part of North America was buried under snow and ice. Today, much of Greenland and Antarctica are covered by such glaciers. Gravity forces these glaciers to spread out as more and more snow piles on top.

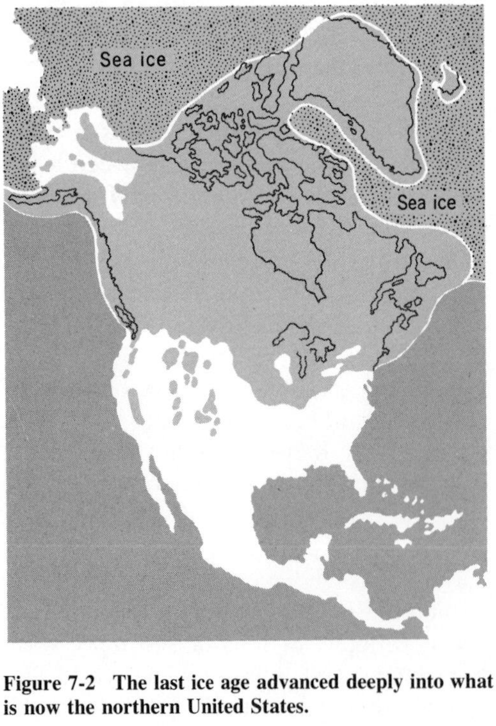

When glaciers move, they scour the land under their tremendous weight, scooping out basins and leveling hills. As they melt, huge deposits of soil and rocks are left at the sides and leading edge. Effects of glaciation may be seen in many parts of our country, particularly in New England and the north central states. (Figure 7-2.)

Although most of the following activities on weathering and erosion can be conducted in the classroom, it will be desirable to use local resources outdoors in teaching them. Signs of weathering and erosion are everywhere. Pupils will be delighted to help look for them.

Generalization I: Weathering and erosion constantly wear down the earth's surface

Contributing Idea A. Plants, chemicals, frost, and temperature changes break down solid rock.

1. *Materials:* small glass jar with screw top; plastic bag; pan; lima beans. (Soak several beans in a glass of water overnight. They will absorb water and swell somewhat. These will be used for comparison with unsoaked beans.)

Inquire about the children's observations of road cuts, deep excavations for building sites, and river banks. Perhaps pictures can be shown. Develop that there is loose soil and rock only a few yards deep. Below that is solid rock. Why isn't it all solid rock? Why is there loose soil and rock on the surface? Encourage conjecture. Bring out that hard rock is probably being broken up in some way. What might do this? Compile a list of possibilities on the chalkboard. Add others, if needed:

suggest hypotheses

Can these things break up rocks?
(1) Plants
(2) Chemicals

Figure 7-2 The last ice age advanced deeply into what is now the northern United States.

(3) Frost

(4) Changes in temperature

If such erosive agents as running water and glaciers are suggested, add them to this list. Or use a separate column and handle them in the B section of this generalization.

How can plants break up the soil? What have they observed? Someone may mention seeing a sidewalk cracked by the growing roots of a tree, or plants growing between rocks. Weeds may be growing in sections of the school's asphalt playground area. If there are examples on or near the school grounds, take the class on a short walking trip.

Mention that sometimes seeds are dropped or blown into a partly cracked rock. Sometimes the crack gets wider and the rock splits even before the seeds grow. How is this possible? Invite discussion. If a clue is needed, display the soaked and dry beans. Is the swelling powerful enough to crack rock?

Point out that it will be easier to make a test of the seeds' swelling power with a glass jar instead of a rock. How shall the *develop* jar and other materials be used? (Fill the jar *procedures* about half-full of water and place inside all the beans it can hold. Screw the cap on tightly and enclose the jar in a plastic bag. Place this material in a pan, to contain water leakage. If a second identical jar is available it can serve as a control. Fill it with seeds also, but omit the water.) Next day, the glass jar with water should be *make* broken. Caution about jumping to conclu- *inferences* sions. This is an analogy. How is it like a real rock? How is it different? Let children read to confirm their inferences.

2. *Materials:* for each group, six bean seeds soaked overnight; two half-pint milk cartons with tops removed (one should be filled with plaster of Paris, the other carton half-filled with garden soil); paper cup of water; small stirring stick; paper towels.

Can seeds push up a man-made rock, such as plaster of Paris? Can they break through solid plaster? To find out, three bean seeds can be buried in one carton containing soil and then covered by an inch or so of plaster. In the second carton, three seeds can be buried in plaster only. The plaster should be mixed with water (added sparingly) to the consistency of thick cream. Bury the seeds before the plaster hardens. Pupils can add a small amount of water to each container the next day only to provide moisture for the seeds. The lifting or splitting actions may take a week or so, if they occur. With living things, there is always the possibility of variation in results.

If there are some lichens on nearby rocks, perhaps someone can bring in a small rock sample. Scrape off some lichens. Have pupils notice that some rock disintegrates at the scraped place. Is it the plant action that crumbles the rock, or is the rock just soft? How can we tell? (Scrape a part that does not have lichens on it.) Inform the pupils that the tiny plants release certain acids which break down the rock. It seems that plants use chemical action, too. Are there other ways chemicals break down rock? They will see another way now.

3. *Materials:* vinegar; small sea shell or piece of limestone; glass container.

Encourage class members who have visited some of the nation's famous limestone caverns to describe these underground wonders. Develop that some of these caves were hollowed out over thousands of years as rainwater soaked deep into the ground. When the water soaked into the soft rock, it slowly dissolved. How can water dissolve this kind of rock? Rainwater has a tiny bit of acid in it.

Demonstrate what happens when vinegar, which is a weak acid, comes into contact with a calcium carbonate. Point out that a sea shell is composed of about the same material as limestone. Pour some vinegar in the glass and immerse the sea shell. Have some pupils listen to the bubbling sounds. Place it on a table for others to examine later.

The next day—or now, if another shell

has been previously soaked for 24 hours — scrape the shell with a knife. It will crumble and break much more easily than a control shell that has not been soaked in vinegar.

4. *Materials:* two small glass jars with screw-top lids; various small rocks (Ask the children to bring these to school.); several containers of water; two heavy paper bags.

How might frost or frozen water break up a rock? Encourage conjecture. Is there anything in the children's experience that might help explain this? Maybe someone has seen frozen milk push out of a milk bottle, or frozen water burst a pipe. It seems as though the water expands. But don't things usually contract, or get smaller, when they get cold?

Perhaps the best thing is to experiment. This can be done at home. How can the glass jar be used? (Fill one with water, and cap tightly. Put it and an empty capped jar — this is a control — in separate paper bags, to contain possible broken glass. Place both in the freezer section of a refrigerator.)

How can the rocks be used? (Answers will vary; provide clues, if needed.) Which rocks are likelier to break, those that soak up much water or a small amount of water? (Much water.) How can we find out which are the most porous, or filled with air? (Place rocks in water and note the bubbles.) Use committees to test and select the most porous and cracked rocks when there are many specimens. Softer rocks will work best. These can be soaked for at least several hours, bagged, and placed in freezer compartments at home.

Similar but unsoaked rocks should be used as controls, to see if the cold alone is responsible for any cracking.

Request reports on results the following day. Probably all the water-filled glass jars used will have burst, and a small percentage of soaked rocks will have cracked and chipped. Uncracked rocks can be lightly tapped with a hammer. They are typically brittle and more easily broken than control rocks. Let the children show

their materials and discuss the results. Emphasize that water is one of the few materials known that expands rather than contracts as it freezes. This expanding action is powerful enough to split rocks, especially over a long time.

5. *Materials:* propane burner; matches; several clear glass marbles; glass of water; pliers. (Clear glass marbles for rocks are suggested for this demonstration because, although rare, it is possible for a rapidly heated rock containing trapped moisture to explode.)

Have someone tell the class a safe way to make a campfire. One technique is to use stones to rim the fire. How about extinguishing the flame? Rangers recommend dousing with water and covering the remains with dirt. Have the children noticed that sometimes stones rimming an extinguished campfire are cracked? Why?

Guide an experiment to test the effects of extreme temperature changes on a simulated rock — a glass marble. How shall it be done? (Hold a marble with pliers in a candle flame for ten seconds or so, then thrust it into water.) Exhibit the results. Many tiny cracks will appear in the marble. Compare this analogy to campfire rocks. How are they alike? Different?

Develop that rock breaks through the continual expansion and contraction caused by extreme differences in temperature. Where are great temperature differences common? (Desert.) Much rock disintegration of this type occurs there. Often gravity assists this action, as when a piece of a rock falls from a high cliff and cracks apart again when it strikes other rocks below.

Emphasize that the actions of plants, chemicals, frost, and temperature changes in breaking down rock are collectively termed *weathering.*

Contributing Idea B. Moving water, wind, and glaciers wear down and move rock.

1. *Materials:* areas on the school grounds and in the adjacent neighborhood which

bear some signs of hillside and sheet erosion.

Have the children recall how places subjected to water runoff look after a heavy rain. Gutters run deep with muddy water. Soil particles and pebbles are strewn in the streets. Where do the soil and rock fragments come from? Encourage discussion. Elicit that the wearing down and shifting of rocks and soil is called *erosion*.

Take the children for a short walk around the school grounds and adjacent land. Have them notice such things as hillside erosion and gullying. Let them see erosion on a steep and a gradual slope with similar or no ground cover. Point out any miniature alluvial fans—fan-shaped depositions of soil and rock at the base of a gully. Have them compare a slope without ground cover to one protected by a profusion of plants or grass. Look for signs of sheet erosion on relatively flat land. Some signs are the partially exposed, upper portions of tree roots, coarser than usual soil, and sparse or no ground cover. Perhaps mud splashes are visible around the bases of some buildings.

If you are unable to leave the classroom, perhaps pictures and slides can be shown. Have pupils recall and discuss their previous observations of these phenomena.

In the following activity, pupils can do their own "hillside" erosion investigations with cafeteria trays containing bare soil and grass-covered soil.

2. *Materials:* glass of water; piece of black construction paper; a weed or similar plant, carefully dug up to preserve soil adhering to the roots; sprinkling can of water; four large cafeteria trays, one containing a sample of soil covered with grass, another containing a sample of similar but loose soil. (Perhaps the school custodian can be coaxed to spade up a square foot or so of grass—enough to fit the dimensions of the tray. Or, at least three weeks before this experiment, plant some rye grass seed in one of the two soil-filled trays. Pupils will enjoy seeing the seeds germinate and watering the soil each day. Leave near a window for

light and warmth during the day. Fill the second tray with soil until it is level with the top.)

Have the class recall some of the possible factors of erosion. Which hillsides had the deepest gullies, those with or without ground cover? (Without.) What effect did greater slope steepness seem to have? (Gullies were deeper.) How can the materials be used first to test for the effect of ground cover? (Prop up or hold both trays at the same angle, with trays below to catch any runoff water. Sprinkle the same volume of water over each. Note any gullies and muddiness of runoff water.) *develop procedures*

How can we set up another experiment to see the effect of slope steepness? (Clean all trays. Put bare soil in two trays. Hold or prop at different angles with trays below as in previous experiment. Pour equal volumes of water over trays containing soil. Note the difference in gullies and runoff water.) If getting additional soil for two trays is inconvenient, simply have the children note the changing speed and more rapid erosive effect of poured water as one tray is held at a low and high angle. *develop procedures*

Invite pupils to explain why a planted hillside erodes less than a bare one. Exhibit the weed roots. Point out the clinging soil. Gingerly soak the roots in a glass of water until the soil washes away. Lay the plant on some black construction paper. The intricate, soil-holding network of delicate roots and root hairs will be visible. A hand lens will help the viewing. Leave these materials on a table for everyone to examine.

The next activity can serve to acquaint pupils with the effects of splash erosion and how it can be reduced or prevented.

3. *Materials:* two clean, flat sticks (tongue depressors are a bit small, but should do); tray of grass sod; tray of soil; several pop bottle caps or coins; sprinkling can of water. (The following activities may be done outdoors at appropriate locations, and with a garden hose.)

Bring up the common observation of mud

splashes around the lower portions of buildings. This reveals the erosive nature of falling water. What can be done to prevent splash erosion? (Plant a thick ground cover to break the impact of the falling raindrops.) How efficient is a grass cover? Invite a test with the trays of grass sod and soil. Have the children do the planning. A stick can be placed upright in each tray sample and equal volumes of water poured from an equal height. Let them note and evaluate the differing degrees of mud splashes on the sticks.

develop procedures

make inferences

Is there much erosion from falling water when the ground is fairly level? Or does the mud just splash? Place several coins or pop bottle caps on the soil tray. What will happen if the water continues to pour onto the soil? Tilt the tray very slightly—virtually no field is absolutely level—and have someone sprinkle several or more cans of water directly over the caps. Remove the caps and have them notice the pedestal effect. This makes it easier to note the *sheet erosion* that has taken place.

4. *Materials:* wall map of the United States; a quart size or larger can with watertight lid (discarded tobacco or paint can); ten to fifteen small, rough rocks (broken pieces of brick are fine); water.

In this investigation children simulate the action of a running stream by shaking containers of rocks and water. They observe the weathering effect of rocks rubbing together.

Invite someone to locate the Mississippi River on the wall map. Bring out that often it is called the "Muddy Mississippi." Where does the mud come from? Develop that this river washes thousands of tons of eroded soil into the Gulf of Mexico. This stream can be considered a gigantic "gully." Let class members identify other significant rivers. Bring out how each river begins as a small stream at an elevated location, gradually increases in size, and ultimately empties into the sea.

Do rivers just carry soil to the sea? Or do they also break down rocks and soil? Hold up some smooth rocks. How did they get that way? Guide the children to reason that, as the rock is pushed along by the river current, it rubs and knocks against other rocks. Also, that a fast current probably breaks down the rock faster than a slower one.

make inferences

Ask the children to think of a way the weathering effect of rocks rubbing in water might be simulated with the available materials. (Put stones in the can. Half fill with water and shake.) They may not realize the necessity of shaking the can many hundreds of times. This can be done by volunteers during the day at recesses.

develop procedures

Request everyone to note how the smaller rock particles gradually increase in number as the rough rocks get smoother. This would be an excellent time to show a picture of the Grand Canyon, if one is available. The class should be impressed by this majestic example of the cutting power of a stream carrying abrasive materials. Be sure to bring out, however, that millions of years were needed.

Why are ocean beaches so sandy? Develop that a similar abrasive effect occurs when waves smash along the shore. Rock particles grind against other particles. Perhaps a picture can be shown in which wave action is undercutting a cliff. Or draw a rough, chalkboard sketch. Pupils will see how continued erosion at the cliff base eventually will cause the jutting, top-heavy portion to collapse into the sea. Here it will be gradually pulverized into sand after many years.

5. *Materials:* sheet of black construction paper; two identical flat stakes about 3 feet long; masking tape or cellophane tape; outdoor lawn and bare soil areas; windy day; desert sand dune picture (optional).

This activity leads into an experiment to see if a grassy ground cover cuts down wind erosion of soil.

Act puzzled. You can see how rivers and ocean waves grind rock into sand, but why are deserts so sandy? Everyone knows that deserts receive very little rain. Show the desert picture, if available. Invite hypotheses. If clues are needed, remind the children that deserts usually have wide temperature ranges. Many children at this point may name expansion-contraction as the main factor. Show them the sand dune picture again or discuss sand dune appearance. Are there any clues which seem to go against this guess? (The sand is distributed into uneven piles, like snowdrifts.) By this time, most pupils will think of wind as a possible factor. Wide temperature ranges create strong winds.

suggest hypotheses

make inferences

Gradually develop that windblown soil or sand is highly abrasive. Some pupils may describe the stinging sensation on their faces when walking into wind whipped dust and sand. Sand blasting crews cleaning building surfaces or removing painted traffic guides from streets may be familiar. Perhaps a child's relative has had a pitted windshield replaced or automobile repainted after a desert or prairie windstorm. Point out that windblown sand can gradually erode away the base of a high cliff. The top-heavy overhang then crashes down and is gradually worn down into sand.

Why isn't wind erosion a major problem where there is more rain? Guide toward the hypothesis that rain permits more vegetation to grow. Perhaps ground cover holds down the soil more than dry, bare terrain or sand. Invite the pupils to design an experiment to test this notion. Indicate the available materials, if needed.

suggest hypotheses

develop procedures

Cellophane or masking tape can be fastened — sticky side out — almost the full length on both stakes. One stake should be placed upright in a dry, bare soil area; the other in a lawn. There are so many possibilities for controls it may be wise to divide the class into small discussion groups to plan this experiment before meeting together to decide on the best plan. Or perhaps several alternate plans can be used.

Help the children if needed. Do the sticky parts on both stakes face the wind? Are both exposure areas about equal in size? Is exposure time the same? Long enough? Are the test areas side by side, or could the wind blow from the bare spot onto the lawn area or the reverse? Are both areas unobstructed? Are the stakes the same height? What do we mean by "height"? An operational definition is needed. Perhaps we should measure from the soil upward in both cases; the grass top may be several inches above the soil. Use as many possibilities for thinking as the class seems able to profit from and enjoy.

state problems

If this experiment is done indoors, use the following materials: an electric fan; cellophane tape; two identical trays (one containing soil, one grass sod); two large cardboard boxes. Fasten tape — sticky side out — on the inside bottom portion of both boxes and tip on the side. Place a tray partly into each box. Turn on the fan before one tray, then before the other tray. Use the same distance, force, and time.

Assist pupils in evaluating their data. Many more particles should appear on the bare soil sample. What conclusions might be drawn about vegetation and wind erosion?

make inferences

This experiment might be extended. Why are the bases of high desert cliffs usually eroded away sooner than the tops? Taller stakes may be needed to note that more and heavier sand particles blow at a lower height than higher up.

develop procedures

Yet another variable might be tried with the tray materials. Does soil *dryness* make a difference? Use a tray of dry soil and one of damp soil, both firmly compacted. Help the class to realize that moisture increases the tendency of soil particles to stick together.

make inferences

Bring out that, in addition to grass lawns and other ground cover, cities and towns have many paved areas and structures which reduce wind erosion. However, even populated areas have many dust particles in the air. Place a piece of black construction paper on a table. Leave exposed to the air a few days. Have pupils observe daily the growing amount of dust that settles on it.

6. *Materials:* wall map of North America.

Trace an imaginary line along the northern United States. Establish that there are huge boulders and rocky soil along this area, especially in the New England States. But these materials are different from the underlying rock. How did the huge boulders get there? Weathering? The boulders are of differing composition. Running water? Is it likely that rivers could move so much rock over so widespread an area?

Develop that *glaciers* were responsible. What are they made of? Where did they come from? Through authority and discussion, bring out some important ideas. Glaciers form when the rate of snowfall exceeds the amount that can melt each year. As more snow piles up, the tremendous pressure turns much underlying snow into ice. The pull of gravity causes the glacier to move. Thousands of years ago, a series of great *continental glaciers* advanced and retreated over much of North America.

Bring out how these huge ice sheets scoured the land, crushing and picking up boulders, rocks, and soil. What are some likely clues of glaciation? Huge deposits of boulders, soil, and rock left along the sides and ends of glaciers as they melted in warm climates; deep, parallel scratches in hard rock layers or boulders; many lakes. Point out the large number of lakes in Minnesota and adjacent states. Develop that there are also smaller, *valley glaciers*. Icebergs are glaciers that reach the coastline, break off, and fall into the sea. Glaciers and icebergs exist today, though not nearly to the extent that they did when the climate was colder.

EXTENDING ACTIVITIES

1. Mention that the materials of which rocks are composed are called *minerals*. Salt is one of many minerals found in rocks. Rains dissolve a tiny amount of salt in the rocks; eventually rivers carry this water to the ocean. But why is the sea so salty when the salt content in river water is so slight? What happens to salty sea water exposed to the air? (It evaporates.) Does salt? Encourage a test. Have someone evaporate a strong solution of salt water. A hot plate will speed this up. Let everyone note the white mineral residue left behind. A taste will confirm it is salt. The seas are gradually getting saltier because most of the salt stays behind as sea water evaporates.

2. Encourage children to bring in old magazine pictures that feature weathering and erosion effects. Help them plan a bulletin board organized around the factors they have studied.

3. Reinforce and extend their study with a film or filmstrip on weathering and erosion.

4. Suggest reading about the great "Dust Bowl" wind erosion disaster of the thirties. What caused it? What measures are being taken today to prevent a recurrence?

5. Man changes the earth's surface, too. What evidence can pupils find of this?

Soil and Its Composition. Weathering and erosion wear underlying rock into small particles. But it is not until decomposed plant and animal matter is added (or manmade chemicals provided) that the soil becomes productive enough to support agriculture. *Humus,* as this organic matter is called, supplies plants with nitrogen, phosphorus, potassium, and other essential elements. The decomposition of organic material is done by soil bacteria. Acids released in decomposition also dissolve other minerals in the soil particles. Humus retains water well, and so keeps soil from drying out rapidly. The darkish color of humus-laden soil absorbs sunlight efficiently, and so it is warmer than light-colored soil. This speeds up plant growth and reduces seed failure.

Earthworms are important to soil for several reasons. They help break up the soil, which permits air, as well as water, to reach the plant roots. Root cells die unless they absorb sufficient oxygen. And, as earthworms eat through soil, they leave castings which contain rich fertilizing ingredients.

The composition of soil is easily studied if we mix some earth in a water-filled jar and allow the jar to stand several hours. Gravity causes the several materials to settle in order. Heavier, coarser particles like pebbles settle first, followed by sand, silt, and clay. Any humus present floats on the water surface.

The best soil for most plants is *loam,* composed of sand (30 to 50 per cent), silt (30 to 50 per cent), clay (up to 20 per cent), and abundant humus. Silt and clay have small particles which retain water well. Having been eroded from rocks rich in minerals, they contain elements plants need for healthy growth. Coarser sand particles make soil porous, thus enabling air and water to reach plant roots. As we shall see in a forthcoming demonstration, a soil composed of sand or clay alone lacks the moderate degree of porosity which seems best for watering plant roots.

Soils differ greatly in their degree of acidity and alkalinity. Strawberry plants thrive in acidic soil. Many grasses grow well in alkaline or basic soils. Clover does best in soil which is neither basic nor acidic, but neutral. In conserving soil minerals and fitting proper crops to the soil, farmers may conduct tests to determine the soil's chemical content. An upcoming activity will demonstrate to pupils how chemically prepared *litmus paper* may be used to determine whether a soil is basic, acidic, or neutral. A strip of blue litmus paper turns to red (or pink) when dipped into an acidic liquid. Red litmus paper turns blue when placed in a basic (alkaline) liquid. You may find that ordinary litmus paper is not sensitive enough to detect the acidity or alkalinity of soil water from your samples. If so, use hydrion paper, available at scientific supply houses.

It may take up to five hundred years for an inch of good topsoil to be produced by natural means. With a rapidly multiplying world population, topsoil conservation is a serious concern. In this sequence, children will be challenged to apply preventive and remedial measures that can be taken in soil conservation. Help them to realize that soil conservation benefits everyone.

Generalization II: Topsoil is composed of mineral, vegetable, and animal matter; topsoil conservation benefits everyone

Contributing Idea A. Topsoil is composed of a thin layer of mineral, animal, and vegetable matter; soil differences result from differences in these materials.

1. *Materials:* hand magnifying lenses; hand trowel; large bucket of rich topsoil; old spoons; newspapers; several tinned cans.

Briefly review weathering and erosion. Then bridge into the present sequence in this manner: "We've seen how rocks are broken down. Is that all soil is, broken and worn down rock? What do you think is in garden soil? Let's examine some and find out."

If there is enough soil and other materials, a useful arrangement is to have a small pile of soil on newspaper for every three or four pupils. Materials can be picked up from wherever they were prepared in the room and carried to working areas. Besides soil, each group should have something with which to pick apart the soil— old spoons or tongue depressors serve well—also, a magnifying lens, and a tinned can in which to put live insects or earthworms. (A moment to set behavior standards before working will usually prevent any excessive reactions to discoveries.)

Bring out the need to organize the materials found. Parts of the newspaper can be used to hold similar things. Circulate around the room as the children work.

After an appropriate interval, list on the chalkboard specific objects found—leaves, twigs, pebbles, small rock particles, sow bugs, and so on. Help the group to organize these into larger categories. Gradually work into the largest categories: mineral, vegetable, animal. Be sure to allow plenty of time. This is an interesting and instructive activity for children.

Mention that the decaying vegetable and animal matter is *humus*. Water soaks into the humus and helps to decay it into very tiny bits, too small to see. In this dissolved form the humus is taken in by the roots. This provides many materials plants need to be strong and healthy.

Have the children do some thinking:

make
inferences a. Are we likely to find much humus in the desert? Why or why not? (With little rain, there are far fewer living things to make humus. Also, since there is little water, what humus there is tends to dry up and blow away.)

Figure 7-3 A soil profile or cross section. Subsoil becomes coarser and contains less humus with depth. (Courtesy USDA Soil Conservation Service.)

b. What, if anything, do earthworms do to the soil? (They burrow into the soil and make holes. This loosens the soil and more air circulates. The humus they eat passes out of their bodies and helps to fertilize the soil. They become part of the humus when they die.)

2. *Materials:* two Mason jars with screw caps, one half-filled with rich topsoil, the other with poor, coarse subsoil; container of water.

Most children have seen roadside cuts and old excavations which expose the subsoil. Perhaps the photograph of Figure 7-3 can be projected. Bring out that one seldom sees wildflowers or weeds growing in the subsoil while there may be a profusion of growing things in the topsoil. Raise conjecture as to why.

Someone may suggest that seeds cannot suggest
hypotheses get lodged as easily on a vertical or tipped surface. This is a reasonable explanation. Are there others? Exhibit the materials. Have the pupils quickly examine the two soils. If the group is large, it is better to put samples in paper cups and pass these around.

Draw out that the subsoil *appears* to lack much humus. How can this be tested? develop
procedure Equal-sized samples are necessary. But how can the humus be separated from the rocky grains of soil? Provide clues, if needed. Is humus likely to be lighter than rock particles? Is humus likely to float? What can be done to find out? (Pour water to within several inches of the top in both jars. Shake jars to separate humus from rock particles. Leave until the material settles. This may take several hours.)

An examination of the results will show much more humus in the topsoil. But why is topsoil likely to contain more humus than subsoil? Bring out the way humus materials develop.

Have pupils describe what else they observe in the two jars. In both cases the soil increases in coarseness toward the jar bottoms. Proceeding from the lower portions of the jars upward, identify the materials:

pebbles, sand, silt, clay, and humus. Have the children notice the different proportions of these materials.

Emphasize that topsoil depth averages but a scant 9 inches in the United States. Initiate a discussion as to its great importance to living things.

(Now would be a good time for groups to begin plant growing experiments with radish seeds in humus-laden topsoil and subsoil. Which is better for plant growth?)

3. *Materials:* labeled, capped jars half-filled with samples of topsoils from various locations: forest floor, beach, garden, and so on; water; microprojector (optional).

Establish that topsoils seem to differ. Some feel loose and crumbly, some closely packed and sticky, and so on. Encourage children to bring in soil samples from many places so that reasons for differences may be examined. Pupils should add water to the samples, shake, and allow the materials to settle overnight, if possible.

At observation time, guide toward an understanding that differences among the samples are mainly the result of differences in the amounts of sand, silt, clay, and humus present. Point out that topsoils often are described as *sandy, silty, clayey,* or *loamy,* depending upon the relative amounts of sand, silt, clay, and humus particles present. *Loam* is topsoil which contains sand, silt, and clay, usually mixed together with much humus.

Emphasize through close observation and discussion the different relative sizes of particles in the sand, silt, and clay. Help the children to understand that the looseness or compactness of a soil depends greatly on the size of its particles. With a microprojector at hand this would be an excellent time to project dried sand, silt, and clay particles onto a screen.

The next activity will show how three soil samples vary in permeability—the degree to which they retain water.

4. *Materials:* three identical, 10-ounce size tinned cans with tops removed; three narrow drinking glasses or glass jars; dry

(margin note: make inferences)

sand, clay, and loam soil; quart of water. (With a small nail and hammer, punch six small holes in the can bottoms. Fill each can two-thirds full of a different soil and place on top of the glasses, as in Figure 7-4.)

Mention to the children that there is another reason why loam is usually considered the best topsoil for growing plants. They may be able to tell what it is by observing closely what happens now. In a moment they will be asked to apply what they see to a problem.

Carefully pour an equal amount of water into each can. Water will run fastest through the sandy soil, then the loam, and slowest in the clay.

Develop a problem for class speculation: A woman puts three healthy, identical plants in three pots, each containing one of the present soil types. She gives each the proper amount of fertilizer, and the same amount of water each day. After a short while, the clay and sand soil plants die. If she digs up and examines the roots of these two plants, how might they look? (It is likely the clay soil plant roots are rotting away. Roots of the sandy soil plant are probably dry and shriveled.)

Bring out that fine clay particles help to hold soil together. But clay alone retains too much moisture. Larger sand particles are good for drainage, but too much drain-

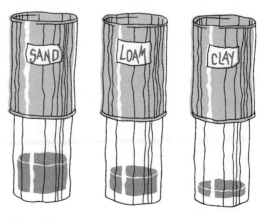

Figure 7-4

age, results in too scant a water supply for most plants. Establish that a mixture of these materials usually works best.

Bring out other applications. Dusty, fine-powdered soil stays muddy for some time after a rainstorm. The surface of a sandy beach may dry in minutes.

If the children can bring their own materials, let them conduct open-ended experiments to see who has the soil samples with the least and most permeability. Pupils will see the need for controls if they are asked to set up "rules" for how the "winning" samples will be determined. (Same volume of soil, water, same time; identical cans and drain holes, procedures; *dry* soil samples.)

develop procedures

Contributing Idea B. Farmers use several methods to conserve and improve topsoil; this benefits everyone.

1. *Materials:* red and blue litmus paper (or hydrion paper); salad oil; baking soda; ammonia; vinegar; six containers of topsoil samples from different locations; pint of distilled water; paper cups.

Through reading or your information, develop that soils also vary according to certain chemicals they contain. Some soils contain *acids*. Acid solutions have a sour taste. Mention citrus products and vinegar as common examples of acids. Acids will turn chemically treated paper called *blue litmus paper* to red. Demonstrate this by partly dipping a strip of blue litmus into some acidic juice.

Explain that some soils contain *bases*. Basic solutions have a bitter taste. Soap, ammonia, and lye are common examples of bases. (Caution children never to taste lye or ammonia.) Bases will turn *red litmus paper* to blue. Demonstrate by dipping a strip into some ammonia.

Point out that soils that are neither basic nor acidic are *neutral*. These do not change the color of either testing paper. Show this by dipping both kinds of litmus paper in some salad oil.

Indicate the six containers of soil. Labels should identify from where they were obtained. Which are acid, basic, or neutral? Let children test with the litmus paper. Since the soil must be wet for litmus paper to work well, what must be done first? When wetting the paper is suggested, see if the children try to do this without first testing the water with litmus paper. If water is added without testing, how will anyone know whether the water or soil affects the litmus paper? Use distilled water, if the local water supply lacks a reasonably neutral condition.

develop procedures

Should enough materials be available, have four or five groups testing portions of all soil samples. Chairmen can record findings. These can be summarized on the chalkboard. Where conflicts occur, let the children follow through on retests.

Point out that some crops grow best in one kind of soil, some in another. For instance, clover grows well in neutral soil, certain grasses in basic soil, strawberries in acidic soil. Farmers add materials to the soil to change its chemical content for different crops. Children in rural areas will be familiar with the widespread practice of distributing powdered lime on fields to reduce soil acidity.

Encourage class members to try to reverse or change the present chemical composition of their samples by adding small amounts of either baking soda dissolved in water (base), or vinegar (acid) to teaspoon-sized samples of identified soils.

2. *Materials:* pictures of contour plowing, strip cropping, terracing, check dams, tall tree windbreaks (all optional, see Figure 7-5).

Mention to pupils they know already many things that erode the land. All concern the farmer; to save topsoil he must be able to apply his knowledge of erosion. Can they do the same? Can they suggest solutions to the following problems?

suggest hypotheses

a. A farm is located on hilly land. Plowing the hill causes gullies to form. Is there a way to plow which will cut down gully formation? (Contour plowing.)

b. A farm is in a windy location. When corn is planted, much of the soil blows away. How can wind erosion be reduced without eliminating corn growing? (By strip cropping. Alternate a strip of a row crop with much exposed bare ground, such as corn, with a ground cover crop, like clover.)

c. There is a small but steep hill on a farm. How can the soil be prevented from sliding down? (By a heavy grass cover, or terracing, if a commercial crop is to be grown.)

d. A gully is increasing in size. Now it is 10 feet across and 5 feet deep. What can be done? (Build check dams of logs and stones. Plant trees and shrubs.)

e. A field is located where a fresh wind blows from about the same direction much of the time. What can be done to protect the field from wind erosion besides using a cover crop? (Plant a row of trees to act as a windbreak.)

Encourage picture research in magazines and books before discussion, if possible. If *develop procedures* there is time, it would be desirable to try out experiments in miniature on the school grounds and in the classroom. For example, the contour plowing problem can be tested with two small mounds of dirt. One hill should have furrows winding around. The other hill's furrows should go straight up and down. An equal amount of water can be poured upon each hill. The other experiments might be performed on a similarly small scale. Stones, twigs, and sticks make excellent check dams across miniature gullies. A row of windbreaking trees can be simulated with popsicle sticks, and so on. By this time, the pupils should have sufficient input to think of some interesting ways to test their notions and make accurate inferences.

3. We have seen some useful ways to save farm soil. But what difference does all this make to people who are not farmers? Why should we care if some farmer's topsoil is washed or blown away? Develop *make inferences* how food prices and the availability of both meat and vegetable products is related to

the abundance of crops. Bring out how various governmental agencies, such as the Soil Conservation Service, have been developed to assist the farmer, and indirectly, everyone else.

EXTENDING ACTIVITIES

1. Have some children study and report on the many different services provided by county, state, and federal agencies for soil conservation. Perhaps they can interview a local agricultural agent.

2. Look into the possibilities of a soil conservation study trip, with a conservation agent in charge. This service is offered to schools in many parts of the country. Or the agent may instead give an illustrated presentation in the classroom.

3. Try this experiment to see how reservoir water sprayed lightly with oil may be conserved through reduced evaporation. Have ready these materials: two clean half-pint milk cartons with tops removed; water; hand atomizer spray containing some light oil.

Point out that many parts of the United States have severe water shortages. Some farms and most cities depend on water reservoirs for much of their water. Sometimes the water surface of a reservoir is sprayed with a very fine, oil-like chemical. *suggest hypotheses* Why? (Maybe this slows down evaporation.) Invite a test with the materials. (Fill *develop procedures* both containers with water. Spray one lightly with the atomizer. Leave both in the same place, check to see which evaporates faster.)

The next day, results should be obviously in favor of the sprayed water. But raise an objection, if no one else does. Doesn't this ruin the water? Who wants to drink water with an oily chemical in it? If thinking bogs down, have the pupils observe the oil carefully. Pour some into a glass. Does oil seem to be everywhere in the water? How could most of the water be removed from the carton without getting

Contour plowing

Terraces

Figure 7-5 Ways of preventing erosion. (Courtesy U.S. Dept. of Agriculture.)

Strip crops

Check dam

Tree windbreak

any oil mixed in it? (From under the surface.)

develop
procedures Have someone with a pencil punch a hole in the oil-sprayed carton near the bottom. Catch some of the escaping water in a clean glass, then replug the hole. Let pupils examine the water. No oil should appear. Bring out that oil is lighter than water, and does not mix. Underwater pipes can remove clean water from a reservoir. Therefore, we are able to get the advantage of a slower evaporation rate without spoiling the water, except for a tiny amount at the surface.

4. Combine an art activity with science by having children draw a large mural of different conservation practices of farmers. Much prior picture "research" will furnish ideas about how to show these practices in pictorial form.

The Building Up of the Land. Careful geological studies show that the powerful forces of weathering and erosion should have long ago worn down the earth's surface to a low-lying plain. Then why are there mountains? Part of the answer is seen in volcanic activity. Fiery molten rock formed deep underground, called *magma,* thrusts up through weak spots and fissures in the earth's crust. When this material reaches the surface it is called *lava.*

Sometimes the accumulation of magma and high-pressure gases is so great the molten rock shoots up to the surface in a spectacular eruption. This can occur under the ocean, as well as land. The Hawaiian Islands are the eroded tops of volcanoes, as are the Azores in the Atlantic Ocean.

Sometimes magma may quietly ooze up through great cracks in the crust and spread out over the ground. Large parts of the Pacific northwest are covered with hardened lava beds to depths of thousands of feet. Similar lava flows have occurred in Iceland.

Several types of magmatic activity are not directly visible until erosion has worn away parts of the crust. Magma may stop flowing and cool before it reaches the surface. Or it may push up part of the crust, thus forming a dome or *laccolith.*

Where does heat energy for volcanoes originate? This remains a matter of speculation. Since the earth possibly was once a mass of fiery molten rock, perhaps it has not yet cooled in certain portions of the rocky mantle. But the popularity of this idea is waning. A more prominent theory is that radioactive rocks are responsible. One radioactive element is uranium, which continually shoots off helium atoms and changes to lead. In the process, a tiny amount of heat energy is generated. If many rocks of this type become concentrated, it is conceivable that they could bring about enough heat energy to melt rocks.

(The known rate of decay of uranium into lead is useful in determining the age of rocks. Since the rate never changes, scientists can determine age by noting the proportion of remaining uranium to lead.)

But magma and lava flows are only partly accountable for the continued mountainous features of the land. Figure 7-6 illustrates another method which may be responsible. As materials erode from a mountain and wash into the sea, the mountain becomes lighter while the sea floor gets heavier from accumulated sediment. The weight forces down the sea floor, which in turn squeezes the underlying plastic rock into an area of less pressure—under the lightened mountain. A new mountain is not produced, but the "floating" equilibrium developed serves to reduce greatly the leveling effect of erosion.

This interesting explanation was included in a broad theory of *isostasy* (i.e., "equal pressure"), first proposed by an American geologist named Clarence Dutton. Although advanced in 1889, it is still widely regarded as an important and useful description of what might have occurred.

Other mountains seem to be made

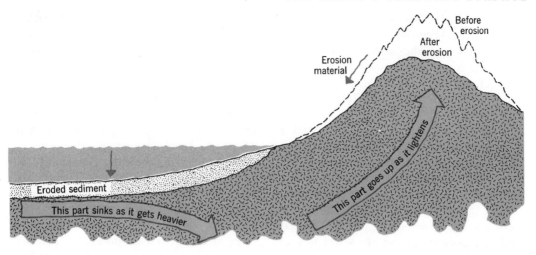

Figure 7-6

through *folding*. The Appalachians are an example. Unknown subterranean forces push parts of the crust into giant wrinkles. Perhaps immense, slow convection currents of plastic mantle materials are responsible. Solid rock behaves oddly under great pressure. If squeezed hard enough, it acquires some of the properties of a near-liquid.

Earthquakes occur when the crust breaks under the strain of its deforming forces. Parts of the crust may move horizontally, diagonally, or vertically along a huge crack or *fault*. Over a long time *block mountains* may develop through tilted or vertical movements along a fault line. This seems to be how the Sierra Nevada range was formed.

Compare Figures 7-8 and 7-12. Note the correlation between regions of volcanic and earthquake activity. For the most part, these are regions of relatively young, high mountains. These are where the greatest strains on the crust are likeliest. Numerous faults and weak spots occur in such regions. Since magma takes the path of least resistance, it is reasonable to expect that volcanic action would often take place here, too.

Generalization III: Lava and magma flows, and crustal movements, continually build up the earth's surface

Contributing Idea A. Lava and magma flows build up the earth's surface.

1. *Materials:* sketch or opaque projection of Figure 7-7; color film or filmstrip or still pictures featuring volcanoes (optional).

Point out that scientists have made careful measurements of how fast weathering

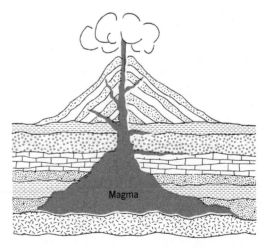

Figure 7-7

and erosion are wearing down the earth's land surface. According to their findings, all the land by now should be worn down to about sea level. Discuss the two implications of this conclusion. Maybe they are wrong. (But this seems unlikely, because there is general agreement among earth science specialists.) Maybe the earth's surface is built up in some way or ways. **suggest hypotheses** Does anyone have some ideas about how this might happen?

Probably someone will mention *volcanoes.* Should others be mentioned list them on the chalkboard, but defer their study temporarily. Valid ideas will fit into the following B sequence. Invalid ideas can be evaluated after study of both A and B sequences.

Draw out what information pupils have about volcanoes. This is an excellent time to exhibit a film or pictures of volcanoes. Show the sketch of Figure 7-7. Explain that some lower parts of the earth's crust become so hot the rock melts even though it is under great pressure. Melted rock is called *magma* when it is below the surface. If there are weak spots or cracks in the crust the magma may suddenly burst through. A volcano is formed. The hot molten rock — now it is called *lava* — and hot gases, cinders, and ashes gradually build up into a mountain. Emphasize that many volcanoes have more gentle eruptions.

Develop that sometimes lava may also come out of long cracks in the earth's surface. Over many years large flat areas or *plains* of solidified lava are built up. Have someone locate on a map the states of Oregon, Washington, and Idaho. Plains of solidified lava up to thousands of feet deep were formed over large portions of these states.

2. *Materials:* opaque projection of Figure 7-8; large map of the world.

Exhibit Figure 7-8. Acquaint pupils with the world's main distributions of volcano-formed land features. Call attention to Hawaii and the Azores as islands of vol-

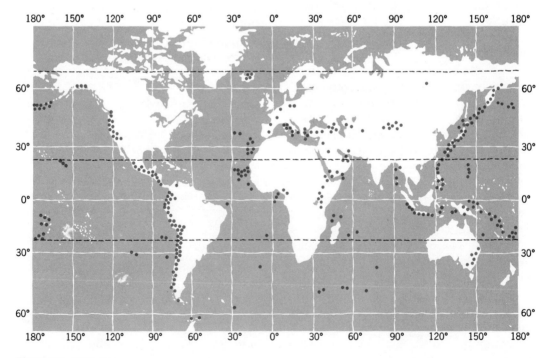

Figure 7-8 Volcanoes.

canic origin. Bring out that several volcanoes remain active in these areas.

Have everyone look at the wall map of the world (it should be the physiographic kind, to bring out land surface features) and the volcano distribution map. Help the children recognize the startling correlation between mountainous areas and volcanoes. See if they jump to conclusions. All mountains may not be made by volcanoes. Shortly, they will find out more about this.

3. *Materials:* unopened soft-drink bottle; hand bottle top opener; suitable outdoor location for a simulated "volcanic eruption."

Discuss the tremendous explosive power of some volcanoes. Develop that powerful gases in the molten rock suddenly expand when released into the air. Under normal conditions the crust's great pressure keeps both gases and rock from expanding.

Bring out the analogy of a soft-drink bottle. It, too, contains a confined gas. When a pop bottle is opened, gas collected at the top escapes with a "pop" when the cap is released. Rising bubbles indicate that more gas is escaping. After the gas escapes, the liquid tastes "flat." The gas, carbon dioxide, is responsible for the tingle.

Continue with the analogy: Let's pretend the liquid is magma. What will happen if we mix all the gas throughout the "magma"? (It may "erupt.") Shake the bottle rapidly several times. Have a child hold it firmly at an angle and pointed away from everyone. An outdoor location is best. Anchor the bottle top opener securely, then quickly flip off the top. An impressive eruption will take place.

make inferences Back in the classroom, draw out likenesses and differences of this analogy.

4. *Materials:* sketch of Figure 7-9; wall map of the United States.

Exhibit Figure 7-9. Point out that a *dome mountain* may be formed when magna develops a "blister" in the crust without breaking through. Emphasize that such a mountain may not look like a dome because of erosion. Have someone locate

on a map the Henry Mountains of Utah, which were formed in this way. Erosion has since worn many parts of these mountains.

Contributing Idea B. Unbalanced forces under the earth's surface cause mountain formation and earthquakes.

1. *Materials:* sketch of Figure 7-6; physiographic world map.

Explain that scientists have found that not all mountains seem to be made from volcanoes. So additional possible explanations, yet unproved, have been made. The class will now have a chance to develop and test an explanation about how some mountains may be formed.

Reveal your sketch of Figure 7-6. Ask the children to study it for a moment. (With a very bright class omit some details.) Invite them to develop an explanation about how a mountain might continue to stand high even though much of it erodes **make inferences** over millions of years. It may be useful to have several discussion groups each form a theory, followed by an evaluative discussion with the entire class.

Guide toward a reasonable approximation of the following ideas. Over many, many years, weathering and erosion cause much of the mountain to wash into the sea. The mountain loses much of its weight. As more and more sediment accumulates, the sea floor sinks under the tremendous

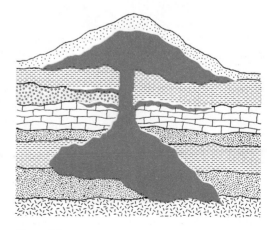

Figure 7-9

weight. The weight forces down underlying, soft, heated rock which then flows to where there is less pressure—under the lightened mountain. This material pushes up the mountain again.

Pull down a wall map of the world's land features. Invite the class to search it carefully for any signs which might give further support to the theory. If clues are needed, remind the pupils that eroded materials were washed in a nearby sea. Be sure to emphasize the mountainous western coastlines of North and South America.

2. *Materials:* opaque projection or sketch of Figure 7-10; 2-inch stack of construction paper of several colors.

Bring out that many mountains are not along coastlines and are not of volcanic origin. How could these mountains have formed? Project Figure 7-10. It is believed this land was once flat. We saw how hot magma could push land up into a dome. But

make inferences

Figure 7-10   An anticline. (Bruce Anderton-Photo Researchers, Inc.)

this seems to have been made in a different way.

Invite the class to speculate how the center portion of the colored construction paper stack might be raised. Let someone push the two ends horizontally toward the center. The center will rise into a miniature, humped anticline. Develop that most of this process begins deep under the crust, where the rocks are heated and more pliable. Many mountains are made through *folding*. But scientists are not sure what forces underground cause this to happen.

3. *Materials:* opaque projection or sketches of Figure 7-11.

Present a projection of Figure 7-11 A–B. Bring out that cracks called *faults* sometimes develop in weakened parts of the crust. When this happens there may be a sideways movement along the *fault line,* as in A. Or sometimes an up or down movement develops along a fault line as in B. If the movement is great enough, mountains may form through *faulting.*

Emphasize that faults usually develop when the earth's surface is squeezed or stretched beyond the breaking point. When this happens the rocks suddenly crack and move in a sideways or up and down direction. Shock waves pass along the earth's surface and through the earth. This is an earthquake. Discuss pupil experiences, if any, with earthquakes.

4. *Materials:* opaque projection of Figure 7-12; physiographic world map.

Project Figure 7-12. Explain that the black areas indicate the world's most intense regions of earthquake activity. Have pupils compare this map with the previous one on volcanic regions. Use the physiographic map to help them see the correlation between these regions and the world's chief mountain formations. Places where volcanoes and earthquakes occur seem to be located mostly where mountain building is taking place.

5. *Materials:* large wall map of North America or world; 16-inch string tied to

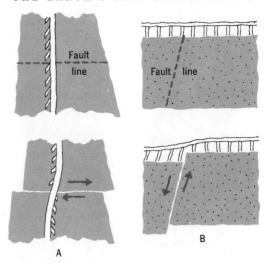

Figure 7-11 Horizontal and vertical faulting.

piece of chalk; opaque projection of Figure 7-13.

Mention that many places where earthquakes begin are unpopulated or under the ocean. How do scientists learn where an earthquake starts? Discuss briefly, then introduce the *seismograph* if no one mentions it. This is a very delicately balanced instrument which continually traces a line on paper or photographic film. Any slight shaking of the earth causes the traced line to become uneven, just as a line drawn by us becomes uneven if someone shakes our desk. Explain that a single earthquake sends out several shock waves, often for thousands of miles on and through the earth, with a time interval between. Since the speed of these shock waves is known, scientists are able to tell how far away the quake is from the seismograph station.

But there is a problem. How can anyone tell where an earthquake is if he knows only the distance but not the direction? Project Figure 7-13. Ask the children to study it and explain the method used.

Bring out that many individual seismograph stations can only detect that a disturbance exists somewhere along a recorded distance. This distance becomes the

make inferences

make inferences

349

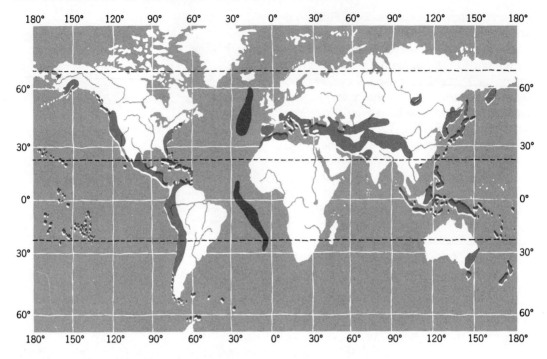

Figure 7-12 Earthquake regions of the world.

radius of a circle. Two stations narrow the location to either of two places that intersect. A third station verifies the exact location. Identify this as the *epicenter*.

Review until the children have these ideas thoroughly in mind. Now invite them to locate an earthquake on their wall map.

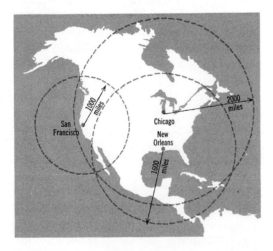

Figure 7-13 Finding the epicenter of an earthquake.

They will need a string to measure distances on the map scale and an attached piece of chalk. Put these data on the chalkboard:

Seismograph Location	Distance Recorded (miles)
New Orleans	1000
Chicago	1300
San Francisco	1050

Have the children discuss how they will locate the epicenter. Help in drawing the circles if the chalk is difficult to see on the map. The three circles should intersect below the Mexican border, near El Paso, Texas. If a perfect intersection does not occur, let the class think of possible faulty procedures. (The string may have stretched a little; perhaps the scale was consulted improperly; the distances may be off slightly.) Develop that scientists also make mistakes. But they make them less often and within a much narrower range of precision.

Before ending this activity, you might mention that in recent years some seismo-

reason
quantitati

select
procedure

350

graph stations have had equipment installed that enable earthquake locations and intensities to be detected independently at each station.

6. *Materials:* wall map of the world.

Invite pupils to solve the following imaginary problem. Tom and Jerry were walking down the street one day. Tom said, "It's so hot and sticky today. It feels like earthquake weather." Jerry said, "That's silly. How can the weather cause an earthquake?" About an hour later an earthquake shook the ground. Who do you think was right, Tom or Jerry? Why? How could we find out whether hot, sticky weather and earthquakes go together? Discuss briefly.

Continue with the story. Jerry thought the weather idea was wrong so he decided to find out more about it. He looked for information and here is what he found (have data ready on the chalkboard but concealed until now by a drawn map):

Place	Earth-quake Year	Temper-ature	Humidity
Coast of Central	1905	warm	high
Ecuador, South	1921	hot	low
America	1940	hot	very high
	1951	hot	low
	1966	warm	medium

Help the children read these data. They may need to know what humidity means, for example. But let pupils draw their own **make inferences** conclusions. Did high humidity go along with earthquakes there? (No.) How about high temperatures? (Yes.) Do earthquakes and hot weather usually go together?

Encourage an evaluative discussion. See if the children detect the flaw in this sample. Lead to an assessment of location. What does a location on the equator usually mean? (Hot weather.) Help them to see the need for further data from other locations not on the equator. Perhaps a temperate zone with all kinds of weather is needed. Where are some temperate zone locations where earthquakes occur? Draw a line below the data and add this information:

Coast of	1910	cool	very low
Central	1921	warm	medium
California,	1943	cold	very low
U.S.A.	1955	hot	very high
	1965	cold	medium

Now, weather and earthquakes seem un- **make inferences** related. Bring out that the examination of many more locations and data would be needed for a more definite conclusion.

If the class is able, bring out through discussion the necessity of determining causation even if a correlation could be found between earthquakes and weather.

(Interestingly, one modern theory suggests that large variations in air pressure on the earth's crust may precipitate some tremors. However, this idea is not generally accepted.)

EXTENDING ACTIVITIES

1. Have a child report on Parícutin, a volcano that developed in a Mexican cornfield in 1943.

2. Encourage children to gather magazine pictures of the great Alaskan earthquake of 1964, and more recent earthquakes.

3. Invite pupils to compile from encyclopedias and trade books a list of large volcanic mountains in the United States. Let them make a large map bulletin board with names of these mountains on the side and strings running from the names to locations.

4. Let some able children make a homemade seismograph. Directions may be found in many children's trade books on earth science.

How Rocks Are Formed. Elementary-school children bring rocks to school by the dozens through the school year. This unit will probably motivate them to bring even more specimens. Of course, the first thing they want to do with their rocks is to identify them. But beyond a few, this is quite difficult. (Figure 7-14.)

351

Figure 7-14 This group is working to identify some rocks brought to class.
(Jane Bergheim—Tom Stack & Associates.)

Rocks are made of *minerals*—natural elements such as copper and carbon, or inorganic compounds such as quartz and mica. The chemical composition of a mineral is much the same anywhere it is found on earth. A pure copper or quartz mineral sample is as recognizable in Asia as in North America.

Geologists have developed many ways of identifying minerals. These means include noting the mineral's color, luster, hardness, cleavage, fracture, specific gravity (its weight compared to an equal volume of water), certain chemical tests, and crystalline structure. (The interesting, pure crystals into which minerals commonly arrange themselves are a direct result of their atomic structure.)

Of the two thousand known minerals, fewer than one hundred make up most of the earth's rocks. But since these can occur in any combination, it takes much study and practice before one can identify any significant number of rocks through their mineral composition.

It is more productive to begin the study of rock identification on an intermediate level with the three basic ways in which they form. *Igneous* rocks are formed from cooled magma and lava; originally, all rocks were igneous. *Sedimentary* rocks are formed largely through depositon of eroded and chemically precipitated materials on the ocean floor. *Metamorphic* rocks are igneous and sedimentary rocks that have been changed through the pressure and heat developed in crustal deformation, such as folding.

In this unit we are concerned with teaching basic ideas. Gradually, as children learn to recognize some rocks through the visible clues related to their origins, they can also learn more sophisticated techniques. For most intermediate pupils, however, these techniques will be more properly taught in later school years.

Although colored pictures of rocks are helpful in teaching, there is no comparable substitute for real specimens. A large number is not needed to acquaint children with the three basic rock types. Try the following dozen. Some, perhaps all, of these rocks may be included in the specimens pupils bring to school. If not, they can be obtained from scientific supply companies, local museums, or rock collectors. If possible, get several examples of each type. This will save time and permit everyone to participate in related activities.

IGNEOUS ROCKS	Description	How Formed
 Pumice	Grayish, fine pores, glassy, frothy, light, floats on water.	From rapid cooling of frothy, surface lava containing gases.
 Volcanic Breccia	Consolidated fragments of volcanic ash, such as glass, pumice, quartz.	From being exploded high into the air from a volcano and settling.
 Obsidian	Black, glassy, no crystals.	From very rapid surface cooling of lava.
 Basalt	Dark, greenish-gray, very small crystals, may have some holes.	From rapid cooling of lava. (See Figure 7-15A.) Escaping gases form holes.

Granite

Coarse crystals, white to gray, sometimes pinkish.

From slow, below surface cooling of molten rock (magma). See Figure 7-15B.

SEDIMENTARY ROCKS	*Description*	*How Formed*

Conglomerate

Rounded pebbles, stones, and sand cemented together.

From loose materials compacted by pressure of overlying sediments and bound by natural cement.

Sandstone

Sand grains clearly visible, gray, yellow, red.

From sand compacted by pressure of sediment, bound by natural cement.

Shale

Soft, smells like clay, fine particles, green, black, yellow, red, gray.

From compacted mud bound by natural cement.

Limestone

Fairly soft, white, gray red, forms carbon dioxide gas bubbles when touched with acids.

From dead organisms that used calcium carbonate in sea water in making body parts; from evaporation of sea water containing calcium carbonate.

METAMORPHIC ROCKS	Description	How Formed
 Marble	Different, mixed colors, may have colored bands, medium to coarse crystals, fizzes if touched with acids.	Formed when pure limestone is subjected to intense heat and pressure.
 Slate	Greenish-gray, black, red, splits in thin layers, harder than shale.	Formed when shale is subjected to intense heat and pressure.
 Quartzite	Very hard, white, gray pink, indistinct grains, somewhat glassy.	Formed when sandstone is subjected to intense heat and pressure.

Generalization IV: Rocks are formed through the forces that wear down and build up the earth's surface; there are igneous, sedimentary, and metamorphic rocks

Review briefly some of the major ideas learned. Emphasize that natural forces are constantly wearing down and building up the earth. These forces also form rocks. How this is done the class will consider more fully now.

Contributing Idea A. Igneous rocks are formed from lava and magma flows.
   1. *Materials:* several specimens each of pumice, volcanic breccia, obsidian, granite, and basalt rock; hand lenses.

Have the children recall how lava and magma flows build up the land. Rocks made in these ways are called *igneous* or fire rocks. Relate to the word "ignite." Show samples of the five types. Indicate all are of igneous origin. But under what conditions were they formed? Allow timé for close observation. Provide two clues. Challenge the class to select two rock types from the five displayed which best seem to match these clues:

   a. Small bits of lava and rock materials were thrown high in the air when a volcano erupted. Which rock may have been formed in this way?

make inferences

355

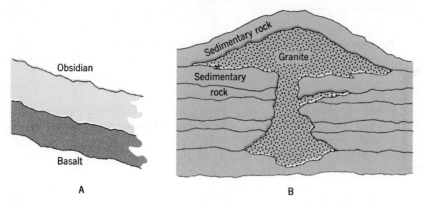

Figure 7-15 A–B

b. Some top parts of a lava flow were whipped into a bubbly foam from gases inside the lava. Which rock may have been formed in this way?

Note their choices. Identify *volcanic breccia* (a) and *pumice* (b). Set aside the samples of these two types.

Identify the *obsidian* specimen as a type of volcanic glass. This forms on and near the top surface of a lava flow. Just below the lava flow surface, *basalt* forms. Hold up this specimen. Now identify a specimen of *granite*. Develop that it cools under the earth's surface, as when a dome mountain is formed. Sketch Figure 7-15 A–B on the chalkboard if clarification is needed.

Pass around hand lenses and samples of these three rocks for close examination. Help the children notice that obsidian has no viewable crystals, basalt has very tiny crystals, and granite large crystals. Raise speculation as to why these conditions obtain. There are some differences in the mineral composition. Could there be other reasons?

Lead the class to consider the ways in which these rocks cooled. Draw out that obsidian should have cooled fastest, then basalt, and granite slowest. Does how fast a rock cools make a difference in crystal size? An experiment can be done to find out.

2. *Materials:* several ounces of alum (sold in drug stores and supermarkets) or table salt; two test tubes; saucepan; news-paper page; two ceramic cups, one containing ice cubes and water.

Boil a cup of water in a saucepan. Add alum and stir until no more will dissolve. Pour the same amount of solution into both tubes. Place one tube in the cup of ice and water. Wrap a newspaper page around the second test tube and place it in the second cup. Leave the materials overnight where they will be undisturbed.

Next day pour off the water and let everyone examine the crystals with hand lenses. Crystals formed in the rapidly cooled test tube should be small and fine; those more slowly cooled should be relatively coarse and large. Which crystals are like basalt? Granite?

The children might want to try this activity at home, if parents agree. They can use salt for crystal formation and the family refrigerator to slow the cooling rate of one solution. Have them bring in and compare their crystals.

Contributing Idea B. Sedimentary rocks are formed through the depositing of sediments which are squeezed and cemented together.

1. *Materials:* conglomerate, sandstone, and shale rock specimens; Mason jar about two-thirds full of equal portions of soil, sand, and pebbles. (Put water in the jar, shake, and allow materials to settle overnight before starting this activity.)

Have the children speculate about what

happens to the tremendous amounts of soil and rock particles which erode and wash from the land into the seas. Develop that the enormous pressure of overlaid materials gradually causes those deeper down to be squeezed together. Chemicals in the water help to cement the particles together.

Exhibit the materials settled in the Mason jar. Draw on the chalkboard a large diagram of the jar and materials. Let children label the levels of mineral content in order, from bottom to top: pebbles (and a little sand), sand, silt, and clay. (Identify the silt and clay as ordinary mud.) Materials like these settle in large bodies of water and are pressed into rocks.

Show the class the conglomerate, sandstone, and shale specimens. Can anyone identify the jar materials which might, under proper conditions, form into these rocks? Before accepting identifications, pass around the rock specimens to enable close observations. Place some water on the shale and have some children smell it. (It smells like mud.) Let someone rub several pieces of sandstone together. Put a piece of black paper underneath to catch the sandy fragments.

make inferences

Let pupils confirm their observations of this analogy through reading. Pebble and sand particles are cemented into *conglomerate* or *puddingstone;* sand becomes pressed and cemented into *sandstone;* mud becomes *shale.* However, layers may not necessarily form in this order—it depends on which materials erode and settle.

Develop that settled particles are called *sediments.* When hardened, they become *sedimentary* rocks.

2. *Materials:* for each group, vinegar; drinking glass; limestone rock.

Have the children learn another major way in which sedimentary rocks are formed. Bring out that in the seas millions of tiny animals take chemicals from the water and make them into shells. When they die these tiny shells settle to the ocean floor and are pressed and cemented into *limestone.* Although limestone does not look like sea shells, we can see how it reacts to the acid test.

Put the limestone in a vinegar solution. Children will notice the bubbles and hear it fizz. (The fizzing action is much more noticeable if small rock fragments are used. Crush with hammer or pliers. Always enclose rocks in a thick cloth or bag before hammering to guard against flying chips.) Recall with them their earlier discussion of limestone caves. Mention that all sedimentary rock materials made from bones and shells of animals give a similar chemical reaction when touched by acid.

Let children read about how wind and glaciers also may form some sedimentary rock deposits.

3. *Materials:* salt; water; sand; pint or quart milk carton.

Demonstrate how to make artificial sandstone. Half fill the carton with sand. Add a few ounces of heavily saturated salt water. (Hot water will permit more salt to dissolve than cold.) Close the top and shake thoroughly. After the sand settles, pour off excess water. Set materials aside. Any remaining moisture will dry within a few days. Remove the dried "sandstone" by slitting open the carton. How is this like real sandstone? Different? Let everyone compare these materials.

Contributing Idea C. Metamorphic rocks are formed when heat and pressure change sedimentary and igneous rocks.

Materials: limestone, shale, sandstone, quartzite, marble, and slate rock specimens; wire clothes hanger; wax crayon; half-full glass of vinegar.

Have your class recall how modeling clay looks after it has been baked in a kiln. If available, show baked and unbaked pieces of clay. Develop that both sedimentary and igneous rocks can be changed into a third kind, called *metamorphic* rock. Resketch Figure 7-15 B on the chalkboard. Point out that hot igneous rock touches surrounding sedimentary rock inside the dome. The adjacent sedimentary rock is baked and changed, almost as if it were in a kiln.

Remind your group of how the earth's surface may be *folded*. The tremendous pressures bend, squeeze, twist, and heat the rock into changed form. Have everyone observe the effect of bending a solid material. Let a child rapidly bend a wire coat hanger back and forth about twenty times. (See Figure 7-16.) Touch some wax at the point indicated. Wax will partly melt on contact with the hot metal. Bring out that the folding of rocks also produces heat, even though it takes place very slowly. The combined heat and pressure changes the rocks into a new and different type.

Pair the sedimentary and metamorphic specimens for comparisons:

a. *Limestone* can change into *marble*. (Will marble fizz like limestone? Have someone check this. Crushed marble fizzes very well. Wrap a piece of marble in some cloth and crush it with a hammer. Immerse the crushed marble in vinegar.)

b. *Shale* can change into *slate*. (Does wet slate also smell like mud? Let someone check this. It does somewhat.)

c. *Sandstone* can change into *quartzite*. (Get children to notice how the distinctness of separate sand grains has diminished through the crushing action of metamorphosis.)

Have pupils rub the paired samples together and also compare their weights if possible. Challenge them to explain why metamorphic rocks seem harder and heavier than the parent rocks. (The heat and pressure have compacted them more; they are denser.) *make inferences*

Have class members summarize the three main ways in which rocks are formed.

EXTENDING ACTIVITIES

1. Let the children identify further examples of the dozen rocks they have studied from miscellaneous specimens brought to class. Get a few trade books to help make other identifications. Some rocks might just be labeled by the location in which they were found. Individual collections may be placed in egg containers, twelve labeled specimens to a carton.

2. An important part of rock identification is accuracy and completeness of description. Here is an activity children will enjoy that will help them to be more precise. Get at least ten large samples of different rocks. Break these into enough smaller rocks so every child has one each of all ten samples. Invite pupils to describe their rocks to partners who will try to pick them out according to these descriptions. Stress that only the rock itself may be described, not its location or order of placement on a table, for example. Also that trial results should not be revealed until all the rocks have been selected. An easy way to communicate descriptions is with charts, such as this one:

Rock	Color	Texture	Scratches	Etc.
A	gray	smooth	no	
B	brown	rough	yes	
C	brown	v. rough	no	
D	black	smooth	yes	
Etc.				

Other descriptive properties children might decide to use are *layers* (yes or no), *crystals* (small, medium, large, none), *holes* (yes or no), *luster* (shiny or dull), and the like. A hand lens and a large nail to

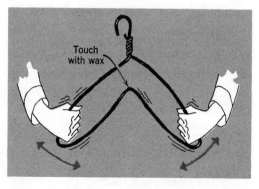

Touch
with wax

Figure 7-16

test hardness (Does it scratch?) will aid pupils to make descriptions. Of course, each child should select which of his rocks should be A, B, and so on, so that only the descriptions can serve to identify the rocks. When or if disagreements come up, pupils will begin to see the need for opera- state
problems tional definitions that relate to the ten specimens. For example, a "very rough" rock might be among the roughest three of the ten samples.

3. Invite a local rock collector to talk about and exhibit his collection. Give him beforehand a list of questions prepared by the children. Perhaps he can advise children how to begin this excellent hobby.

4. Use a study trip as a culminating activity to observe rock examples at a quarry, road cut, or large building excavations. Where possible, have the children apply their observations to major ideas of this unit.

5. Get a comprehensive film on the earth's changing surface. Use it to help reinforce major ideas.

Air and Weather

(Primary Emphasis)

UNIT EIGHT

Air and Weather

(Primary Emphasis)

IN THIS UNIT WE FOCUS ON BASIC ELEMENTS OF WEATHER. CHIL-
dren investigate the interesting properties of air itself, and develop
a heightened awareness of temperature, wind, and the water cycle.
There are many occasions for thought-provoking activities in
weather study. Few other science teaching areas offer more opportunities to take pupils as far as they can go while maintaining
real-life observations.

  Such concepts as heat transfer, heat absorption, evaporation and
condensation, introduced in previous units (Unit 1, page 142 and
Unit 3, page 212), are applicable in the present unit. It may be
useful and interesting to note differences among the several levels
of presentation.

GENERALIZATIONS

  I. Air is real because it moves things and we can feel it; air also
has weight and takes up space.
  II. Air is found almost everywhere around us.
  III. Air presses in all directions around us.
  IV. Wind is moving air; it changes in force and direction.
  V. Temperature is how warm something is; a thermometer read-
ing changes with the temperature.

Credit for chapter opening photograph. **Louis Goldman-Rapho Guillumette**

VI. Water evaporates into the air; evaporation is affected by wind, temperature, and amount of water surface exposed to the air.

VII. Air contains moisture which condenses when it cools; water evaporates and condenses, over and over.

Air and Its Properties. There are so many printed and spoken references to the earth's "ocean of air" it is easy for us to get the impression that pure air is a uniform compound, such as pure water. Actually, the air we breathe is a mixture of several separate and distinct gases, of which the three most important to survival are oxygen, nitrogen, and carbon dioxide.

Oxygen makes up about 21 per cent of the air, and nitrogen 78 per cent. Oxygen is essential to us because it combines readily with sugars in our body cells and releases heat energy. Nitrogen is essential because it is necessary for plant growth. It also dilutes the oxygen we breathe. Continual breathing of pure oxygen speeds up metabolic processes to the point where the body cannot get rid of waste products fast enough to survive. The small amount of carbon dioxide in the air, about $3/100$ of 1 per cent, is needed for photosynthesis to occur in green plants. In addition to these gases, there is less than 1 per cent of such gases as argon, krypton, helium, neon, radon, and xenon. All these atmospheric gases are remarkably well mixed by winds, up to a height of 5 to 10 miles.

But this is not all we breathe. As hay fever sufferers know, there are other substances mixed in the air. Besides the troublesome pollens, there are dust, smoke, and salt particles, water vapor, chemicals, spores, bacteria, and viruses.

Since pure air has no taste, color, or odor, its study at the primary level has an elusive quality not present in many other areas. Therefore, the main intention behind our first sequence of activities is to develop the tangibility of air. Like such other material substances as automobiles, houses, books, and people, air is a real thing. Children can feel it, and see it move things in the form of wind. Air has weight. A blown up balloon shows that air takes up space. Yet no one can see air directly.

The following sequence employs a comparison of air with a real child. It should provide pupils with an understandable, beginning base for further explorations.

An extending activity suggests that the children place in order, according to air capacity, bottles of different sizes and shapes. This will give them many chances to do compensatory thinking. That is, they will have to judge several variables at one time when they make their estimates. A bottle that is tall and narrow may have a smaller capacity than one that is less tall but is very wide. In the second bottle, largeness in one dimension (width) compensates for relative smallness in another (height). You may recall from Chapter 1 that practice in such thinking seems to help children progress to higher stages of mental operations.

Generalization I: Air is real because it moves things and we can feel it; air also has weight and takes up space

Briefly acquaint the children with the nature of the unit. Write the two words "air" and "weather" on the chalkboard if the class can read to some extent; otherwise just state them. Get opinions as to what "weather" means. Ask why the words "air" and "weather" appear together. It may be wise to delay any definitive statements at this time. Simply suggest that, as the unit progresses, the class will understand more and more why the two terms go together.

Try the following bridge to move smoothly into a sequence of activities for the present generalization: "Some children say that it is silly to talk about air because they think there is no such thing as air. They say if air is real, you would be able to see it. Do you think they are right or wrong? Why?"

After a brief discussion, tell the children they may find it helpful in their thinking to decide on what makes something seem real to us. Ask a child to come before the class. Is he real? How do we know? (He can move things; we can touch, see, and hear him.) Have a strong child lift him slightly — he has weight. Draw a circle on the floor with chalk around where the child is standing. Can someone else stand in that exact space while he is in it? Then he also takes up space.

Put some or all of these ideas on the chalkboard:

We know John is real because:
1. We can touch and see him.
2. He can move things.
3. He has weight.
4. He takes up space.

If all the same things are true of air, it, too, would be real. The class can find out now.

1. *Materials:* for each pair of pupils, a leak-proof, clear plastic bag; cardboard fan; some bits of torn paper.

develop procedures

Can we feel air? How can the above materials be used? Children may open plastic bags and then twist the tops closed to prevent air from escaping. They may push against the bag's sides and sit on the bags. They may open the tops slightly and

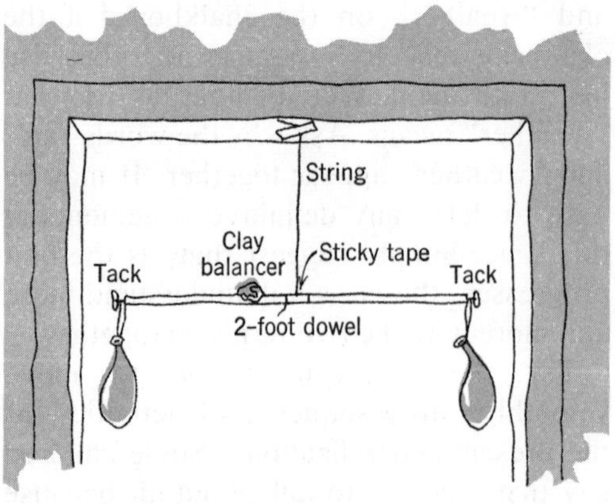

squeeze the bags near other children. Can they feel the escaping air? Other children may decide to swish the cardboard fans through the air. The air currents resulting will be felt by nearby persons.

Can air be seen? Not directly, of course, but as it moves things. Ask for signs that indicate air is moving outdoors. (Leaves moving, flag rippling, smoke drifting.) Pupils can move bits of paper by waving the cardboard close to them. Bring out that air can move things. We can see what air does, although we cannot see air itself.

2. *Materials:* two large balloons; string; 2-foot dowel, about 3/8-inch diameter; two tacks; soft clay pellet; sticky tape. (For the dowel balance needed in this and other activities, see Figure 8-1. If there are enough materials for several groups, their balances may be suspended from rulers taped to chair backs, as on page 317R.)

Summarize the preceding ideas. So far, the things that make a child seem "real" are also true of air. Now the class needs to find out if air has weight. Show the children a suspended balance with two deflated balloons attached by strings. How is it like a seesaw? What would happen if a weight was put on one side? Can anyone think of a way the balance can be used to see if air has weight? (If there are sufficient materials, let each group decide for itself how it wants to proceed. Probably, suggestions will be made to blow up one balloon only and suspend it again. If the balloon is blown up to maximum capacity and attached again, the balance should tip toward the heavy side immediately.)

Help pupils to reason through what happened. Now, can the class think of *two* ways to make the balloons balance again? (Blow up the deflated balloon. Let the air out of the inflated balloon.)

3. *Materials:* half-filled aquarium tank (or large, clear glass bowl); small cork; two identical drinking glasses; sheet of paper.

Have everyone recall that a child takes up space. It is impossible to stand where he stands unless he is pushed out of the way.

Figure 8-1 A wood dowel balance. The clay pellet is used to offset a slight imbalance.

Does air take up space? Everyone will now want to watch the following demonstration carefully.

Hold up an "empty" glass. Bring out that it probably contains air. Turn it upside down. Does it still contain air? Crumple a piece of paper and wedge it far inside the glass.

make inferences

Have a child slowly submerge the inverted glass straight down into the water without tipping it. Encourage the class to predict what will happen to the paper. Let the glass be withdrawn, again without tipping it. Extract the paper. Press for an explanation of why it remained dry. (The air inside the glass took up space, and the water could not enter.)

Point out that it was impossible to tell how far the water rose in the glass because both the water and glass were clear (transparent). Put a cork on top of the water. Invite someone to use it to discover the water level, if any, in the glass. By carefully lowering an inverted glass over the cork, it will be possible to push the cork down to the tank bottom. Establish that air kept the water away.

Remove the floating cork. Push an inverted empty glass straight down into the tank until it is completely submerged. Tip it slightly. Have pupils note the bubbles. Elicit that escaping air causes the bubbles. Ask them to observe what happens inside the glass as more bubbles are released. (More water enters.) Lead them to understand that, as air leaves, additional room within the glass is provided for water to enter.

Hold up both glasses. Caution careful observation of what happens next. Invert one glass and submerge it. Tip it so all the air is replaced by water. Invert the second glass and submerge it without tipping. Place the second glass near and slightly under the mouth of the first one. Now tip and pour the air out of the lower glass into the glass above. (See Figure 8-2.) As one container fills with air, the second fills with water. Reverse the procedure. If no bubbles (air)

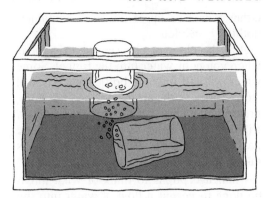

Figure 8-2

are lost, the process may be repeated indefinitely. Give pupils a chance to repeat this demonstration. They will react enthusiastically.

4. *Materials:* small flask (or clear glass baby bottle); small plastic or glass funnel; lump of soft modeling clay. (See Figure 8-3.)

This demonstration will present further evidence that air occupies space. It may be used as a substitute activity for the preceding one. Place the funnel in the flask opening and seal carefully with *dry* clay around the opening's inside edge. There must be no air leakage here. If you find your clay is unsatisfactory, try sealing the connection with Vaseline. When there are no ridges in

Clay

Figure 8-3

365

either funnel or lip of the glass container, nothing is needed.

Ask the class to observe what happens when you pour water into the funnel. Some water will fall into the bottle, but this will stop shortly as the air inside becomes compressed enough to resist any further entry. Fill the funnel. Ask why no water enters the flask. Draw out the probable reason: air is taking up the space inside the bottle.

make inferences

Challenge pupils to think of what might be done to permit a flow of water into the flask. Guide them to reason that a way must be made for air to escape so water can enter. (This can be easily done by tilting the funnel while holding the flask in place.)

develop procedures

Summarize all the preceding activities as they relate to the opening statements about the child. Help the class to conclude that air seems to be real, also.

make inferences

EXTENDING ACTIVITIES

1. Children will be interested in learning how much space air occupies inside their lungs. Encourage them to measure chest expansions with string.

A more engrossing technique is to set up materials as shown in Figure 8-4. You will need a large bowl; 1-gallon bottle; rubber tube; and two small blocks (on which to rest the bottle opening to avoid pinching the tube). Put several inches of water into the large bowl. Fill the bottle with water. Put your hand or a piece of cardboard

Figure 8-4

firmly over the bottle opening. Invert the bottle and lower it into the water. Have someone position the two small wood blocks under the bottle opening as you take away your hand or cardboard. Be sure to have the bottle opening under water at this time.

Let someone blow one long breath into the bottle through the tube. The water displaced represents his lung capacity. Chalk or crayon marks on the bottle will serve to mark the lung capacities of different children. For hygienic reasons, dip the tube end in alcohol and rinse with clean water as additional pupils use the tube.

reason quantitatively

2. From the preceding investigations pupils found that air could replace water and the reverse. In this activity, pupils estimate the relative air capacities of various small bottles of different shapes and composition. They can use the *water* capacities of these bottles to test their estimates. (See Figure 8-5.)

Each group should have at least five small bottles of different shapes but of fairly similar capacity; masking tape; five large identical paper cups; deep bowl of water; paper towels; shoebox (optional).

This investigation works best when the bottle capacity is under five or six fluid ounces—small enough to be quickly filled with water when submerged in a deep bowl. Shoeboxes are handy if groups wish to exchange sets of bottles. The success of this activity depends on how well the bottles are arranged in sets. It is important that the bottles not be conspicuously different in size, but yet be different enough so that a careful estimate of relative capacity is possible.

A good way to develop sets is to ask all the children to bring in miscellaneous, clean small bottles with labels removed. Have several children make sets of five bottles each that seem to be similar in size. You might then make minor adjustments to insure that there are few actual duplicates, openings are large enough to admit water, and so on. Have each group use masking

Figure 8-5 In what order would you place the capacities of these bottles? (Remember that only two dimensions are shown here.)

tape and pencils to label the caps of its five bottles A through E.

To develop the problem, point to an interesting set of bottles and elicit that once they contained a liquid but now they contain air. Which one has the most air in it? The least air? In what order should all five be, going from the least air to the most air? (You can adjust the number of bottles to the ability of your class.) Encourage disagreements. Ask for reasons behind preferences. How can the class find out which *is* the proper order?

develop procedures

After suggestions are made, have the class evaluate them and choose the methods they wish. One workable way to find relative air capacities is to fill each bottle with water by submerging it in a bowl and then to pour the contents into five matched paper cups — one bottle to one cup.

Primary children enjoy this activity most when it is turned into a game. Have each group determine the relative capacities of bottles in its set, make a record, and then exchange with another group. Each group then attempts to place in order, from least to most air capacity, the five bottles in the set. The group should do this first by careful estimation, and then through use of the water test to see if it is correct. Disagreements among groups can be settled by the water test before the entire class, if necessary.

reason quantitatively

The Atmosphere. Space exploration has made us increasingly aware of how dependent we are on our atmospheric environment. Without an air supply, man cannot survive for more than minutes. While we may travel in comfort thousands of miles over the earth's surface, an ascent of only three miles into the sky may require special oxygen apparatus.

How far out does the atmosphere extend? No one knows exactly. But meteorologists have identified four roughly separable layers of differing characteristics, named the *troposphere, stratosphere, ionosphere,* and *exosphere* (Figure 8-6).

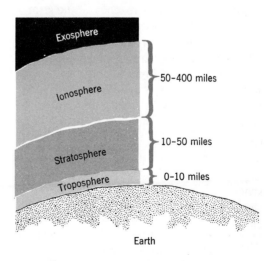

Figure 8-6 The atmosphere has several layers.

367

The troposphere extends to a height ranging from five miles at the poles to about ten miles at the equator. This is the region where practically all weather conditions take place. Why the difference in altitudes? Tropospheric air is coldest at the poles and so weighs more per unit than warmer, equatorial air. Also, the earth spins on its axis. The fastest speed of rotation, about 1000 miles per hour, is at the equator. This offsets the earth's gravitational pull to some extent. The speed of rotation decreases as distance to the poles decreases, just as a person who runs on an inside track can slowly jog along while someone on an outside track must run swiftly just to keep abreast. As the rotational speed slows, gravity has an increasing effect. In the troposphere, stable air temperature decreases about 3.5°F for every thousand feet of altitude.

Immediately above is the stratosphere, which reaches to about 50 miles. This is the layer airlines use for long-range cruising when their advertisements proclaim, "We fly above the weather." The cold, thin air is remarkably smooth and clear, since vertical movements of warmed air, and atmospheric dust particles, are largely confined to the layer below. Air travelers may note some pale clouds of ice crystals, but these are infrequent.

Between the lower reaches of the stratosphere and the troposphere are found winds that vary greatly in force and direction. Most interesting are the so-called *jet streams,* rivers of high velocity air several miles high, and more than a hundred miles wide. They range to thousands of miles in length, and tend to flow from west to east. A pilot can increase the speed of his plane from 100 to 300 miles per hour by locating and staying within a jet stream.

Beyond a height of about 50 miles, the stratosphere gradually blends into the ionosphere. In this region are ions—electrically charged particles formed from collisions of air molecules with high-energy solar and cosmic rays. These harmful rays are largely absorbed at and below this level. Auroras are sometimes visible. Meteors burn to ashes from friction as they strike scattered air molecules.

The ionosphere is an invaluable aid to radio communication on earth. The earth's surface is curved, but radio waves travel in straight lines. One way of overcoming this problem has been to transmit radio waves to the ionosphere, where they are reflected downward to other points on earth. Since solar "storms" frequently disturb the ionosphere and disrupt communication, this has not proved to be a completely satisfactory solution. Radio and television signals reflected from man-made communications satellites are helping to solve this problem.

The exosphere begins at approximately 250 miles and extends to an undetermined distance. A few air molecules have been detected beyond 500 miles, and it is probable that others are scattered thousands of miles beyond. For practical purposes, this region may be considered the beginning of interplanetary space.

While scientists estimate the entire weight of our atmosphere at an enormous five quadrillion tons, over half of all air molecules are concentrated below a height of three and one-half miles. The combination of this enormous pressure and the unimaginably small size of air molecules results in the presence of air in practically everything on or near the earth's surface. Air is found in most soils, water, and even in some rocks. We shall consider the effects of this pressure more fully in the third generalization.

Generalization II: Air is found almost everywhere about us

1. *Materials:* globe; picture of astronaut with helmet, and photographs of the earth's atmosphere taken from a space capsule (*Life* magazine).

Why does a spaceman wear a helmet? Bring out that it is probably used to help the astronaut breathe. If available, exhibit a picture of an air tank strapped to a space-suit. Help the children to realize the significance of a helmet. There probably is not enough air to breathe at some altitude above the earth.

Develop speculation as to how high the air around them extends. Is it as high as the clouds? As high as airplanes fly? Where does it end?

Produce the globe. Help pupils understand it represents the earth they live on, and that the atmosphere envelops the earth. Hold a finger a fraction of an inch above the globe's surface. Inform the children that our atmosphere would go to about that height if the earth were actually as small as the globe. Draw an imaginary circle around the globe to indicate that air envelops all the earth. Exhibit some recent photographs of the atmosphere as taken from space vehicles. Help them understand that there is less and less air as one goes higher.

suggest hypotheses Raise conjecture: Since air is so light and easy to move, why doesn't it all blow away into space? If a hint is needed, ask a child to jump up. Pretend annoyance when he comes down. You asked him only to jump up! Does this give a clue? The child had weight and is attracted to the earth. Children will recall that air has weight, too. If desired, introduce the word *gravity* at this point.

2. *Materials:* for each group, large bowl half-filled with water; pieces of brick, chalk, bread, pumice, sandstone, leather, and several coins.

This activity will permit children to discover that there is air in many objects.

Draw out that since the atmosphere extends all the way around the earth, the children should have no trouble breathing unless they decided to climb the tallest mountains. Air is found everywhere on earth. But how about air *inside* things that are on earth?

Mention that the class has found air in bottles, but how about the other materials on the table? Do they contain tiny spaces that air can get into? Which ones? How can

they find out? If enough materials are available have several committees test these and then compare results. If disagreements occur, materials can be retested.

make inferences Virtually all of the above materials except the coins should release some air bubbles when immersed in water. Guide toward the tentative conclusion that they contain some air.

3. *Materials:* hot plate; flask or small glass bowl (Pyrex); water; fishbowl containing live fish (optional).

Encourage speculation as to whether water contains air. Try to pin down reasons for opinions. Let children carefully observe gill movements of fish, if a fishbowl or aquarium are available. If not, have them recall this phenomenon from past observations. Develop conjecture as to its meaning in the present problem.

make inferences Ask the class to observe the following demonstration for signs of air in water. Place a heat-resistant flask or glass bowl on a hot plate. Within a minute or so, tiny bubbles will appear at the bottom of the bowl, rise to the top, and burst. It seems that water, too, contains air.

Help pupils realize that fish need air. When fish stay continually near or break the water surface, this is a clue that points toward an insufficient amount of air (oxygen) in the water. Emphasize that practically all the air in the water would be driven off by boiling the water for a short time.

The air shortage in boiled water can be indirectly tested with a goldfish (harmlessly). Put it in a jar of boiled water that has been cooled to room temperature. Compare the more rapid gill movements with previous observations. Return the fish to its regular container after several minutes to avoid harming it.

4. *Materials:* glass bowl half-filled with coarse, loosely packed soil; container of water.

make inferences Briefly review the several materials, previously immersed in water, which contained air. How about soil? Are there any signs they can think of which might indicate air

369

spaces? Remind them, if needed, that one sign of air in water was the presence of fishes. Elicit the names of such soil dwellers as insects and earthworms.

Encourage a test for air in soil. Indicate the above materials if thinking bogs down. Have your group note the many bubbles that rise to the surface when water is poured onto the soil.

state problems
But isn't there something wrong? What did the demonstration with water show? (There was air in the water.) How might that get the present experiment mixed up? Bring out that it might be the air in the water, and not the soil, which causes bubbles. If this is so, what must be done to the water first? The input children have received about boiling the water should help them come up with this suggestion. To save time, boil and cool the water in a teakettle during another learning activity. When the water is ready, let the children take several moments out to try their experiment again. Use fresh soil. Bubbles will again appear on the water surface.

develop procedures

EXTENDING ACTIVITY

Help pupils understand that the presence or absence of air in water affects its taste. You will need a clean glass of boiled, cooled water, another glass of water drawn recently from the tap, and a clean Mason jar and lid or substitute. Inform the group that occasionally it is necessary to boil water to destroy harmful germs. Elicit that this practice would also eliminate nearly all the air. Does this make a difference in its taste? Have someone try to distinguish between the tapwater and boiled water. (Several glasses of each will enable more pupils to participate.) The boiled water should taste "flat."

What effect will there be if air is put back into the water? How can this be done? If clues are needed, remind the children of the bubbles that appear when frozen orange juice is shaken in a closed container. After the flat water is thoroughly shaken in a large jar, pour it into a glass.

Will the taster be able to tell which is which? Draw out that he must be unaware of which glass contains the shaken water. Perhaps the class will suggest that he turn his back while the glasses are shuffled. Even if he does detect the shaken water (the use of additional tasters will give more latitude for error) bring out that both glasses of water now taste more nearly alike.

develop procedure

Air Pressure. Since the average weight of air is about 14.7 pounds per square inch at sea level, there may be as many as 20 tons of air pressing against the human body. Why, then, are we not crushed? There are two basic reasons. As with water, air at a given level presses with equal force in all directions. Because there is a counteractive force for every force, the pressure is neutralized. Counteractive pressure also takes place in our bodies. Air molecules are so tiny they dissolve in the blood stream, besides occupying space in our lungs and other body cavities.

Unlike free air, the air in our bodies lags somewhat in building up or reducing counteractive back pressure as atmospheric pressure changes. Have you noticed your ears "pop" while ascending quickly in an elevator of a tall building? This happens because air pressure in the inner ear tends to remain the same while the outside air pressure diminishes with increased altitudes. The result is an uncomfortable outward pushing sensation behind the eardrums. A slow elevator gives more opportunity for inner ear pressure to be adjusted through the Eustachian tube, which connects the inner ear to the nasal passages and mouth.

A similar, but much more dangerous situation is encountered by deep-sea divers. As they descend into the water, air is pumped under increasing pressure into the diving helmet and suit to counteract increasing water pressure. After working for twenty or thirty minutes, the diver's circulatory system contains an abnormal amount of air. If he ascends rapidly to the surface, a region of much lower air pressure, the air in his blood may expand and form bubbles. This causes a very painful and possibly fatal condition known as "the bends."

The lag in adjusting to outside atmospheric pressure may also be an explanation of why some persons complain of aches and pains prior to rainy weather. Outside air pressure usually lessens before a storm. If the body's blood pressure remains the same, the blood will now press outward a little more forcibly than usual against body joints and tissues. It is possible that the slight additional pressure may cause some sensations of discomfort.

At one time, it was thought that atmospheric pressure over any one point was always the same. We now know this is incorrect. Huge masses of air constantly move over the earth, changing the pressure. Cold, dense air piles up in a given area and causes an increase in pressure. In another area, a mass of swirling, warmer air has the opposite effect.

An instrument used for measuring atmospheric pressure is the *barometer*. To understand how it works, let us consider how we drink through a straw. When we draw some air out of a straw, the atmosphere presses down on the liquid's surface and pushes it up into the space formerly occupied by the air.

If you are skeptical, try the following experiments. Place two straws in your mouth, but leave one *outside* the pop bottle or glass. You will find it is now practically impossible to drink the liquid. Why? Air traveling inward through the outside straw restores the pressure in your mouth and drinking straw to normal. For the second experiment, fill a flask with water and seal it tightly with a one-hole stopper containing a glass tube. No matter how hard you sip, no water goes up the tube. There is no air pressing down on the water. With a two-hole stopper, normal drinking is possible. Air pressure is exerted through the second hole. Try these two activities with children, also.

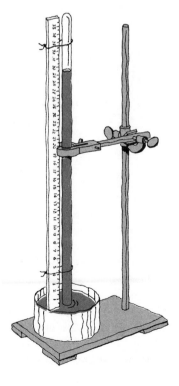

Figure 8-7 Homemade mercury barometer and a manufactured aneroid barometer.

In a *mercurial* barometer, a glass tube closed at one end, about 36 inches long, is filled with mercury and inverted into a dish of mercury. While some of the liquid runs out, a column of about 30 inches remains. This indicates the force of air pressing on the liquid's surface. As air pressure increases, the column will rise higher into the vacuum above. The reverse takes place with reduced pressure.

Since mercurial barometers are easily broken and cumbersome, many weather observers use the *aneroid* barometer (Figure 8-7). This consists of a thin, flexible, metal box from which air has been largely evacuated. As air presses on it with varying degrees of force, the box moves in and out accordingly. A clever linkage and leverage system transfers these movements to a movable indicator on a dial. Since air pressure also changes with altitude, aneroid barometers are used in airplanes to indicate altitude. This is done by merely changing the dial to read in feet rather than inches of mercury. Such a barometer is called an *altimeter*.

As with drinking straws, the phenomena we associate with "suction" are really due to removing or reducing air pressure from one part of a device. Air pressure on all other parts then pushes and performs the work. In vacuum cleaners, for example, the motor whirls a reversed fan which reduces air pressure at the cleaning nozzle. The surrounding air then *pushes* dirt particles into the nozzle. A plumber's force cup or "suction" cup works in a similar way. By pressing down on the pliable rubber cup, most of the air inside is forced out. Air from all other sides pushes against the cup's exterior and holds it fast to whatever surface it has been pressed.

Generalization III: Air presses in all directions around us

Briefly review that air is everywhere around us and has weight. It might be helpful in the discussion to draw a large circle on the chalkboard to represent the earth, and then a larger circle around it to show the earth's atmosphere. Invite pupils to use their knowledge of air to explain the following demonstration.

1. *Materials:* plumber's force cup; a smooth, flat, rigid metal surface (onto which the force cup will be pressed—an upturned dishpan should serve); pencil; toy "suction cup" darts (optional).

Produce the plumber's force cup. Rest it on the upturned dishpan. Draw out that there is air above and inside the cup. What will happen to the air inside when the cup is pushed down? (It will be forced out.) Have someone feel the air as it is squeezed out. Let a child gently try to pull up on the cup. Why is it stuck? Bring out that the air above is pushing down on it.

Invite the children to predict what will happen if some air is allowed to enter between the cup and the metal surface. Let someone take a pencil point and push it gently under the cup. Have pupils identify the subsequent hissing noise as entering air. The cup will be immediately freed. Lead them to reason that the air below pushed up with the same force as the air above pushed down. *[make inferences]*

Attach the force cup with the pan held vertically, and then overhead. Allow someone to introduce air with a pencil in each case. No matter in which position it is held, air pushes in that and the opposite direction. Help the group realize this illustrates that air presses in all directions. If we can remove air pressure on one side of a material, air will press on it from all other sides and hold fast. *[make inferences]*

If a toy "suction cup" dart is available, show it. Or have pupils recall their play with this and similar toys. Bring out that all work on the same principle as the force cup.

2. *Materials:* straw, or glass tube of similar size; glass of water, with food coloring or ink added for easy visibility. (Duplicate materials will permit all pupils to work.)

Announce that the next activity will be

done silently. At its completion, the children are to explain what has happened in terms of air pressure. Dip the straw vertically into the water. Lift it straight out. Whatever water enters the straw immediately flows out. Dip the straw again, but now close a forefinger over the straw's exposed end before lifting it out. Water remains in the straw although it is lifted out of the glass. Remove your finger and the water flows out of the straw. Repeat to insure accurate observation. Why does water remain in the straw? Why does it flow out when the finger is removed?

suggest hypotheses

Develop that air below pushes up the water and helps to keep it from flowing out. However, when air is free to enter the opposite end it pushes down just as forcefully. Since these forces are balanced, the water's weight causes it to flow out.

This is an ideal time to demonstrate how a dip tube is used to remove small food and waste particles from an aquarium. A straw or glass tube may be used. Scatter a few tiny crumbs of bread in a glass of clear water. Shortly, these will settle at the bottom. Place a finger over the tube's open end before dipping the tube into the water. Position the tube over a particle and remove the finger. As the compressed air escapes water will rush into the tube's opposite end and bring the waste material with it. Close the tube's open end again with a finger and remove the tube. Its contents can be released into a nearby container by removing the finger.

EXTENDING ACTIVITIES

1. The following experience will help pupils understand why two holes are often punched into the tops of cans containing liquid. Ask everyone to bring an empty, rinsed-out can which formerly held a liquid. When several cans are assembled, tip them over so pupils may observe the openings made in their tops. Inquire as to what there seems to be in common. (Most have two

make inferences

holes.) Encourage hypotheses to explain. Help the children apply their recently learned ideas to screen hypotheses.

suggest hypotheses

Encourage tests with liquid poured from one and two holes. Invert the cans after filling them with water and stopping up the previous opening with modeling clay. A large nail and hammer can serve to punch holes easily.

Elicit that air pressure prevents or slows down the water from leaving when only one hole is made, just as it did with the dip tube. A second hole permits air to enter the can and neutralize this effect.

What did the class learn? Many children will say, "You have to make two holes for liquid to pour from a can." Help them see the fallacy in this inference by pouring water from a can with only one large opening. Guide toward an amended statement, such as, "There must be enough space for air to enter the can as the liquid is poured."

make inferences

2. Motivate for pictures or names of the many objects around pupils which use air pressure *inside*. Some examples are bicycle, airplane, and auto tires, balloons, air mattresses, auto lifts at service stations, air drills used by construction workers, and air rifles. Suggest a bulletin board be made of pictures brought to school.

Causes of Winds. At early morning off the African coast, hundreds of Arab fishing vessels point out to sea as a fresh land breeze fills their colorful lateen sails. They return in the afternoon with sails taut from a sea breeze blowing in the opposite direction. You have probably experienced a similar shift of winds at the seashore, or by a large lake. How does this happen? (Figure 8-8.)

You remember that warmed air expands and is pushed up by denser, colder air which rushes in and replaces it. All winds are caused by the unequal heating and cooling of the earth's surface. During the day, solar radiation is absorbed by the sea and land. But the land heats up much faster. One reason is that the sun's warmth pene-

Day   Night

Figure 8-8   Winds are caused by unequal heating and cooling of the Earth's surface.

trates only a short distance below the land's surface, while sunlight penetrates more deeply into water. Another is the higher heat capacity of water. After a shor. period of sunlight, air immediately above the earth is heated by conduction and begins expanding. Cooler heavier air from the sea rushes in and pushes the lighter air upward. The reverse occurs at night and until the following morning. During this period, the land cools quickly and stays cool, while the sea remains relatively warmer. As air warmed by contact with the water expands, it is pushed upward by cooler air rushing in from the cooler land.

These air movements are not confined to land and sea settings. The same basic air movements take place between any surfaces that have a temperature difference. As temperature differences increase, the subsequent wind force increases. This is one reason why a large fire is so destructive. It sets up a powerful, localized wind which fans and spreads the flames.

The world's prevailing winds are caused by the same phenomenon on a grand scale. But the earth's rotation adds a complicating factor. If the earth did not rotate, heavy cold air at the poles would flow due south and north in replacing warmed, rising equatorial air. The rotational effect (named the *Coriolis effect*) results in a wind deflection to the right in the northern hemisphere. A deflection to the *left* occurs in the southern hemisphere.

You can see why this happens with a globe and some chalk. Rotate the globe from west to east. While it is moving, draw a line from the North Pole due south toward the equator. Note that the line curves to the right. Draw a line from the South Pole and the curve is reversed.

Detailed understanding of wind patterns requires much more background than can be provided here. For example, we have briefly discussed jet streams. But there are other winds aloft to be studied. It is possible for an airplane pilot to encounter a wind blowing from one direction at 3000 feet and another blowing from another direction several thousand feet higher. You will not want to explore this subject in detail at the primary level. But it will be worthwhile to help pupils learn that wind direction aloft may differ from surface wind direction.

Meteorologists use measuring instruments to observe small, helium-filled pilot balloons as they rise to various altitudes in calculating winds aloft. A cruder method is to observe cloud movements with a *nephoscope,* a circular mirror marked with the points of a compass. Properly aligned, this instrument can indicate the direction of cloud movement as the cloud reflection moves across the mirror. Pupils may employ a makeshift nephoscope in a forthcoming activity.

It will be most worthwhile in the following sequence to explore and emphasize many observational clues as to wind force and direction. With an able group, this should also be an opportune time to introduce the cardinal directions.

Generalization IV: Wind is moving air; it changes in force and direction

1. *Materials:* balloon; cardboard fan; newspaper or large tissue-paper sheet; electric fan; toy pinwheel (optional); ribbon.

Ask class members to recall experiences of riding a bicycle or walking on a windy day. What is wind? Encourage them to define it. Have them recall several activities in which they demonstrated that air could move things. By opening the top of a plastic bag filled with air they could feel the escaping air. By swishing a cardboard through the air they could feel the air on their faces. Now several additional activities will help them to realize more fully that wind is moving air.

Let some air escape from a filled balloon. Direct the air stream against a pinwheel or the hands of several children. Have someone fan a cardboard rapidly, or start an electric fan before the pinwheel or children. Let them feel or see what happens.

Ask a pupil to stand before a moving fan while he holds a single, opened newspaper or tissue-paper sheet against his chest. If the fan is powerful enough, he will be able to release the paper. The wind force will hold it against his body. Let the children compare this with the experience of the wind outdoors blowing against their clothing.

Tie a ribbon or piece of string to a disconnected electric fan. Have everyone notice how it ripples after the fan is turned on.

Invite the children to tell what happened to the air in every case. (It moved.) Were they able to feel the air or did the pinwheel turn when the air was still? (No.) Would the paper have stayed up without air moving against it? (No.) Establish that wind created both in the classroom and outdoors is moving air.

The next two activities are designed to provide some understanding of the causes of winds. After being introduced to an air-current detector (the wind "snake"), pupils will see it applied with miniature winds created by a hot plate and tray of ice cubes.

2. *Materials:* for each child, a large soda straw; wind "snake."

A completed wind snake appears in Figure 8-10. Pupils can make this device turn by blowing through a soda straw. To construct it, trace the cutout pattern in Figure 8-9 on tissue paper, then put the tissue paper pattern on a ditto master. Go over the pattern heavily with a ball-point pen to make legible cutout guidelines. Be sure to draw the arrow as shown. Cut out the pattern from a dittoed sheet of paper. With a pencil, make a small hole at the X. Insert the end of a 2-foot *fine* thread (Figure 8-10). Affix the thread end securely with a tiny piece of sticky tape on the other side of the sheet, opposite the X. When the wind snake is suspended in a current of air moving *upward,* it should turn *clockwise,* or with the arrow. Winds from any other direction will cause it to turn *counterclockwise.* Since this is critical for the success of the activity, you might construct a wind snake yourself to see if it works properly. If it doesn't, simply reverse the side where you inserted the thread; this will take care of it. The setup on page 317R will do for a suspension apparatus. Or pupils can work in pairs, one dangling the wind snake and the other blowing, in turn.

Introduce the wind snake by showing a completed one. What is it? How does it work? Let someone blow steadily through a straw for one long breath at the side of the device. It will turn quickly *against* the arrow's direction. Call this to the pupils'

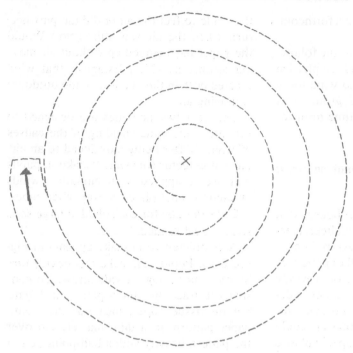

Figure 8-9 **Wind snake cutout pattern. (Actual size.)**

attention. When the child stops blowing, it will reverse directions. Why is it now moving *with* the arrow? (The string is unwinding.)

Have the children cut out and assemble their wind snakes. Pose a problem: Can you get the wind snake to turn *with* the arrow when the air is blowing on it? Pupils will find that this happens when the air current is directed at the bottom of the wind snake. The only other time it occurs (excluding unwinding) is when the suspended device is rapidly moved downward; the relative wind is upward in this case. Let the children discover these things for themselves. Discuss findings after an adequate time period for exploration.

make
inferences

3. *Materials:* hot plate; wind snake; large saucepan and tray of ice cubes.

Suspend a wind snake six inches above an unheated hot plate (Figure 8-9). Ask the children what will happen if the hot plate is turned on. Elicit the direction in which the device may turn. (With the ar-

row, or clockwise.) Turn on the hot plate. Children should reason from their previous knowledge that the air is moving upward. But where is the air coming from to replace the warmed rising air? (From the sides.) How can this be tested? (Hold the wind snake in different locations near the hot plate's sides. The wind snake arrow should move backward.) *Since the horizontal air currents will be weak, only a sensitive wind snake will work.* Therefore, you may wish to skip testing the side locations if you have trouble in trial use.

Show a deep saucepan with a tray of ice cubes inside. (There is no need to remove the cubes from the tray. The object is to cool the air inside the saucepan.) Hold the pan over a suspended wind snake. What will happen when you tilt the pan? See if the children predict a counterclockwise movement of the wind snake as the cold air spills downward from the pan.

make
inferences

But winds are not made by hot plates and ice cubes outdoors. Develop that the sun

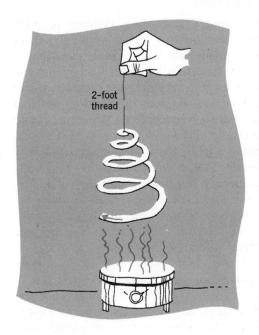

2-foot
thread

Figure 8-10

provides the heat. As it warms the earth some air rises. Other, cooler air rushes in and takes the place of the rising air. To bring out that the ground is heated unevenly, have the children recall their experiences when walking barefoot over grass and sand, or other varied ground surfaces. It may be desirable to place a pie plate of soil and one of water in the sun for ten minutes. Pupils can touch the soil surface and water to learn that soil heats up faster. Since the earth's surface heats and cools unevenly, point out that cooler air usually rushes in and replaces warmer, rising air. This causes local winds.

3. *Materials:* electric fan; wind vane (construct from a chalkboard eraser, pencil, clay pellet, straight pin, bead, straw, and construction paper, as in Figure 8-11); small piece of rope; matches; thin strip of tissue paper or ribbon; small pieces of paper.

Use this activity to acquaint pupils with the many ways to detect wind direction.

Request those who like to fly kites to raise their hands. Point out that when sev-

eral kites are flown at the same time in the same location, all face in the same direction —against the wind. (If a picture is available of several kites flying together, let all pupils notice this for themselves. Better still, should time and space be available, let some of them bring kites to school and discover this.)

Bring out that it is helpful to know in what direction the wind is blowing when flying a kite. It is also helpful for sailboat owners and airplane pilots. Ask for signs which might indicate wind direction. Discuss briefly. Now the class will learn additional things which can indicate wind direction.

Exhibit the above materials. Mention that the electric fan will be the wind source. Invite the children to use as many materials as possible to indicate wind direction. Before any trials, have them first predict what will happen. The wind vane will always point into the wind. (If it does not move freely, wiggle the pin in the hole to reduce friction.) The ribbon or tissue-paper strip will always blow away from the wind, as will smoke from the smoldering rope. Bits of paper will act in the same way when blown.

Guide the children to make a list of ob-

develop procedures

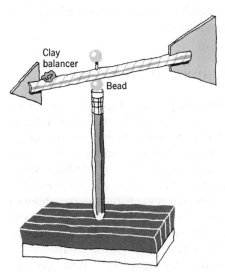

Clay balancer

Bead

Figure 8-11 A straw wind vane.

develop procedures

jects they can observe outdoors which may give them clues about wind direction: flags flying, smoke from chimneys and fires, falling leaves, blown dust or paper, kites flying, clothes on clotheslines, water ripples and waves, wind vanes, and so on. If there is some wind, take them outdoors and let them try to determine its direction. Invite them to give reasons for their inferences, according to the clues just learned.

If your pupils seem able, it will be worthwhile to teach them the four cardinal directions. (Use a technique like that described in Unit 4, page 259.) Develop that a wind is named after the direction from which it comes.

Draw out that wind force is also important when flying a kite. Guide the children to reason about how their wind directional clues would also indicate *no wind,* a *light wind,* a *fresh wind,* and a *strong wind.* If using a daily calendar, extend this information to include the daily weather. It will be more natural and less confusing to pupils to add one item of information at a time as it is studied, rather than to attempt recording everything at once. For example, begin with adding wind force now. Later, include temperature, clouds, and so on. (See page 390 for symbols that can be used for a complete weather chart. If possible, let the children invent some symbols with your guidance.)

EXTENDING ACTIVITIES

1. Encourage class members to collect pictures for a bulletin board which indicate the effects of wind. Some scenes might show storm damage, ocean waves, iceboats and sailboats, windmills, kites, clothes on a line, and so on. After exhibiting all the pictures, encourage the children to classify them in some manner; for example, "pleasant" and "unpleasant" winds, or "light winds" and "strong winds."

2. Raise the question, "Why do airplane pilots usually land their planes into the wind?" Encourage children to bring their inexpensive balsa wood gliders or stick model airplanes. Guide experiments where distances taken for landing into and with the wind are measured through use of a long string. Help the children see that several trials are necessary and that planes must be thrown with the same force at equal heights. Have them observe that both landing speed and distance may be greatly reduced when landing into the wind. This controlled experiment will also provide another opportunity for pupils to estimate wind direction and force for a purpose "that counts" in their view.

reason quantitatively

make inferences

3. Acquaint pupils with a homemade nephoscope. This instrument can be used to detect winds aloft by watching the directions of cloud movements. A mirror (5 × 6″ is a useful size), a pencil, and a small white paper cutout of a "cloud" will be needed. Place the mirror on the floor. Have a child kneel by the mirror and watch the cloud reflection as the cloud is moved overhead in a specific direction by another child. Let the observer point to the direction of movement without lifting his head. The class can check his accuracy by noting how the two directions compare.

After several trials, let children try to track actual cloud movements outdoors. Encourage all pupils to bring mirrors and compare their results of cloud tracking. When results differ, help them to decide how they will improve the accuracy of their observations. One way will be to use some common reference point. If the class seems capable, this may serve as an excellent purpose to teach the cardinal directions.

develop procedures

Air Temperature. In parts of Southern California and Mexico, it is sometimes possible in winter to observe snowy mountain peaks while lying on a warm, sunny beach. Children are curious about conditions like this. ("Aren't the mountain peaks closer to the warm sun?") Most adults know that air temperatures are lower at higher altitudes. But why?

One cause is the varying distance of air molecules from the earth's surface. Air molecules closest to the earth are warmed more easily by conduction and heat waves radiated from the earth's surface than those farther away.

Secondly, as we get closer to sea level, more and more molecules are piled up. This increased weight compresses the air. With reduced space for movement, there is more energy exchange among molecules as they collide. Thus, the heat energy in the denser molecule "population" is concentrated into a relatively low, dense layer.

There is also a third reason. As warmed air rises any great distance it expands and cools as it encounters lower air pressure with the increased altitude. Whatever heat energy is contained in the original air parcel is dissipated throughout an ever larger volume.

The combined effect of these causes results in rising air cooling about five and one-half degrees Fahrenheit with every 1000 feet in altitude. As sinking air is compressed, the opposite happens.

As you saw in Unit 3, the atmosphere is a gigantic greenhouse which retards the loss of heat received from solar radiation. Fortunately, the earth loses and gains about the same amount of heat each day. A narrow temperature range enables life to continue. Since the Industrial Revolution, however, conditions have been developing which may upset this delicate balance.

Up until the 1940's, the lower atmosphere gradually became warmer through increased carbon dioxide from the burning of such fuels as coal and oil. As light waves from the sun warm the earth's surface, heat waves going from the surface into the atmosphere are blocked somewhat by carbon dioxide. Some of the heat energy cannot escape into space. This caused the atmosphere to lose slightly less heat than it gained from solar radiation.

But since the 1940's the trend has been reversed. Now the earth's atmosphere is cooling very gradually. In recent years there has been a large increase in air pollution throughout the world. The greater number of suspended pollutants in the air apparently is causing some sunlight to be reflected away from the earth *before* it reaches the earth's surface. This seems to be overcoming the effect of the increased carbon dioxide.

The total temperature drop amounts to about one-half of a degree Fahrenheit. While this might not seem like much, several scientists think that it is a primary cause of the increased severity of winter storms in parts of the world. Some predict the beginning of another ice age if the worldwide temperature is lowered by only eight degrees.

Thermometers. In the following sequence, pupils can be helped to learn how to measure air temperature with the thermometer. A simple bar graph will show them what happens to air temperature during the day. If desired, measurements can be extended over longer time periods.

Several children may ask why some thermometers have a "silver line" and some a "colored line." Bring out that some contain mercury and others colored alcohol. Whichever is used, be sure that they are placed in the shade, and several or more feet off the ground, when recording air temperatures. When a thermometer is placed in the sun, its glass tube absorbs some heat energy and records a misleading temperature. If too close to the ground, some heat energy coming from the warm ground itself may distort the temperature reading.

Of course, we rely on many indicators other than thermometers to estimate temperatures. Although our skin temperature is a rough but useful indicator, we must rely on other means when observing a distant scene through a telescope or viewing a picture. How people dress, pale slanting sunlight, snowy peaks, denuded trees, the kinds of animal life, and so on, all give temperature clues to the observant person.

Perhaps the most unusual temperature

indicator is the cricket. Being a variable-temperatured ("cold-blooded") animal, its basal metabolism rate is slowed or speeded by comparatively small changes in temperature. Some warm evening, count the number of chirps a cricket makes for exactly 15 seconds. Add 37 to this figure, and then check a reliable Fahrenheit thermometer. Your results should not be off more than several degrees from the thermometer reading.

Generalization V: Temperature is how warm something is; a thermometer reading changes with the temperature

1. *Materials:* two magazine pictures, one showing a child wearing heavy winter clothing, the other light summer clothing; household thermometer; rubber band; glass container of ice cubes and water; candle and matches, or hot plate.

Remind your pupils that they have learned many signs that have helped to indicate the condition of the air. Now they will learn others. Hold up the pictures. What do they probably show about the air? (It may be hot or cold.) Bring out that *temperature* refers to how hot or cold something is.

Exhibit the thermometer. How does this tell about hot and cold? At least some children will recognize its use, but many or most will be in doubt about how it works. Raise conjecture about the colored line. What happens to it when the temperature gets colder? Warmer? Indicate the materials. How can they be used to check what happens?

Before the thermometer is dipped into the ice water, elicit need for a reference point. How will the class tell whether the line goes up or down? A rubber band can mark the former place. The same procedure can be used when this instrument is held over the candle flame or hot plate. (Be sure the thermometer is not held too close, as the liquid may rapidly expand and break the tube.)

If another thermometer is available, have the children duplicate the experiment. Will it work the same way? Guide toward a tentative conclusion about how thermometers indicate the temperature.

2. *Materials:* large cardboard thermometer model. Construct from a piece of chipboard, red and white ribbons, elastic band. Paint numerals black and the bulb red. Probably it will be best to use the Fahrenheit scale, since this is what children are likely to see. (See Figure 8-12.)

Call attention to the model thermometer. Establish that it has numerals similar to those on the real thermometer. Demonstrate how the movable ribbon can simulate a rising and falling liquid column. Have the class practice reading the numerals. Many primary children have no difficulty with multiples of 10. If the class is able, put four equally spaced lines in between the numerals so pupils can make readings in multiples of 2. Multiples of 5 may be more difficult.

Invite someone to look at the real thermometer and adjust the model's ribbon to about the same relative level. A large magnifying glass held over the smaller thermometer will enlarge the numerals for easier viewing by all.

Introduce the term *degrees*. Develop that there are degrees of temperature. Help the

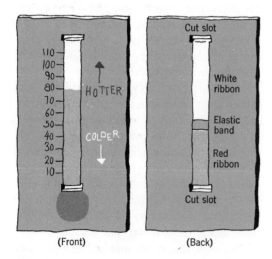

(Front)   (Back)

Figure 8-12

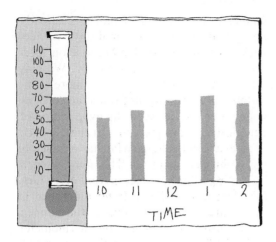

Figure 8-13

children understand that comparisons of temperature in degrees are more useful than the terms "cold" and "hot." Construct questions to get them used to this notion: Is 70° hotter than 80°? Is 40° colder than 50°? What are all the degrees on our model which would be colder than 30°? Warmer than 90°?

reason quantitatively

3. *Materials:* an outside thermometer hung in the shade; scissors; straight pins; cardboard thermometer and tagboard chart. (See Figure 8-13 for completed version.)

The following activity will help show the children that the daily temperature varies, and will provide them a chance to learn how to make and interpret a bar graph.

Initiate a discussion about temperatures during the day. Is the morning cooler than at lunch time? How about dismissal time, etc.? Have children adjust the model thermometer to show the possible temperatures.

Pin the model thermometer to your chart. Draw out how an hourly air temperature record might be kept for this day. How closely will these temperatures agree with those suggested? Two children can check the outside temperature and then adjust the model thermometer ribbon accordingly. Strips of red construction paper can be pinned on the chart each time. For proper lengths, first have each strip placed next to the adjusted model thermometer ribbon

and snipped off at the proper place. Have one red strip ready for each hour the temperature will be taken.

Take a few moments an hour before dismissal time to interpret the resulting graph. At what time was it warmest? Coolest? What were the two hours that showed the greatest change? Least change? Is the three o'clock (dismissal time) temperature likely to be lower or higher than the two o'clock temperature? How can we make sure? (Take a three o'clock reading.)

reason quantitatively

make inferences

If weather records are included with the daily calendar, it may now be useful to add the daily temperature. Or a graph similar to the one in Figure 8-13 may be initiated and kept by the children for a week or longer.

EXTENDING ACTIVITIES

1. Have an exhibition of various thermometers: meat, refrigerator, clinical, candy, aquarium, and household. Encourage pupils to look at oven and automobile thermometers after school. Have them identify the specific purpose of each.

2. Encourage everyone to bring pictures for a bulletin board that show warm and cold places. Bring out some clues in these pictures which might indicate temperatures: vegetation, animal life, snow, slanting sunlight, great heights, and so on. Caution about jumping to conclusions.

make inferences

Evaporation. Many younger children find it hard to believe that a tangible substance, such as water, can disappear into air. Therefore, it is advisable to begin a study of evaporation with examples that are well within the scope of their immediate experiences. The next activity sequence begins with some sketches of an aquarium from which water is disappearing. If an aquarium is handy, it may be desirable to use it for an introductory bridge in place of the suggested sketches.

In Unit 1 (page 152R) you saw that both

heat and atmospheric pressure have an effect on an evaporating liquid. Increased heat energy increases the speed of molecules. Additional speed enables them to overcome the cohesive forces of nearby molecules and greater numbers leave the liquid's surface than before. Any decrease of atmospheric pressure affects evaporation because it tends to "take the lid off." The counterforce of air molecules pressing down on the surface of an evaporating liquid becomes weaker, and more evaporation takes place.

It is easy to see why increasing a liquid's surface area increases the rate of evaporation. There is greater exposure to the air above and a higher probability of more molecules escaping. This is why you have to add water oftener to a rectangular aquarium than to a fish bowl of equal volume. The wind speeds up evaporation, too. When air immediately above the surface of an evaporating fluid becomes quickly saturated, the wind blows it away and replaces it with drier air.

Another factor influencing evaporation is

Figure 8-14 A homemade psychrometer.

humidity, the amount of moisture already present in the air. On humid days we feel sticky and uncomfortable because our perspiration evaporates very slowly. We may turn on an electric fan to feel more comfortable. But moving air from a fan cools us mainly because it speeds up evaporation of perspiration from the skin. In the absence of an evaporating liquid a fan has practically no cooling effect at all. This may be seen by putting a thermometer in front of a whirling electric fan. There is no difference in the before and after readings. But dampen some cotton and stick it to the thermometer bulb. The rapidly evaporating water will now cause a noticeable drop in temperature.

The moisture content of air varies considerably from time to time. The capacity of air to contain moisture is related to its temperature — warm air holds more moisture than cooler air. The amount of moisture present in a given volume of air at a certain temperature, compared to the maximum amount it could hold at that temperature, is called its *relative humidity.* During a period of low relative humidity, our skin moisture evaporates more quickly than it can be effectively replaced. This results in dry, chapped skin.

One reason we have more colds in winter may be directly related to the relative humidity of air in our homes. The cool air of winter holds comparatively little moisture. As it is warmed by heaters, it expands and becomes even drier. Unless the home heating system is equipped to provide additional moisture, the air becomes increasingly dry. The protective mucous film that coats the delicate nasal membrane evaporates, and we may become more susceptible to infections.

Relative humidity is often measured with a wet-and-dry bulb thermometer apparatus called a *psychrometer* (Figure 8-14). Two identical thermometers are placed next to each other. The bulb of one instrument is enclosed in a wet cotton wick which is immersed in water just before use. The wet-bulb thermometer is fanned rapidly until its reading steadies at some lower point. As water evaporates from the wick, it is continually replaced by water traveling upward through the wick by capillary action. Any difference in thermometer readings is translated into the percentage of relative humidity by consulting a reference table.

We close this section with several possibilities for extending pupils' abilities in data gathering and analysis of faulty procedure (controls). It will be worthwhile to get as many suggestions as possible from the children before providing guidance in these experiences.

Generalization VI: Water evaporates into the air; evaporation is affected by wind, temperature, and amount of water surface exposed to the air

1. *Materials:* two identical, wide-mouthed jars with screw caps; water; sketches of Figure 8-15 A–B–C. (Put each sketch on a large, separate card.)

The following bridge may be helpful in getting pupils to identify the problem which leads into the next experiment. We begin with simple evaporation.

"Class, let's say you are in charge of an aquarium for a long time. Here is how it looks." (Show sketch A and have the children briefly identify the two plants and fish. Now put this sketch face down on a table and continue.)

"After a few weeks, here is how the aquarium looks." (Show sketch B but discourage comments. Place this sketch on the table also.)

"After more weeks have passed, here is how it looks. (Show C.) Sometime soon, you are going to have a problem with this aquarium. Does anyone know what it is?" state problems

If no one knows, show the cards again in sequence. If necessary, place them side-by-side for easy comparisons. Some children may immediately say, "The tank is leaking." Help them understand that they could be jumping to a conclusion. Do we *know* the tank is leaking from these pictures? Develop that the only thing these pictures show is that the water level is getting lower. What seems to be the problem? (Why is the water level getting lower?)

Invite possible causes for this condition:

Maybe the tank is leaky. suggest hypotheses
Maybe the tank is "soaking up" the water.
Maybe the fish drank it.
Maybe the water is going into the air.

Help the children screen their hypotheses through discussion and experiments. Guide them toward the last idea: What happens to puddles after a rain? Wet clothes on clotheslines? Encourage a test with the two jars. How can they be used to see if water goes into the air? develop procedures

Both jars can be filled to an identical level, with one capped and the other left exposed to the air. Both should be put in the same place, such as a window sill. The next day there should be a noticeable difference in water levels.

Introduce the term *evaporation.* Let children name many familiar situations in which water may evaporate: wet sidewalks and streets become dry; also wet

A

B

C

Figure 8-15 A–B–C

hands, lawns, rivers, ponds, and so on. Water is going into the air everywhere around them.

2. *Materials:* electric fan, pan of water; two identical handkerchiefs; string; hot plate or sunlight.

To lead into activities showing that evaporation is speeded up by wind and heat, try this bridge. "What are some of the ways in which your mothers dry laundered clothes? When outdoor clotheslines are used, on some days the clothes dry very quickly. At other times, it may take most of the day before they are dry. Why is that?"

suggest hypotheses

Help the children isolate sunny and windy days as possible aids to evaporation. Bring out that sunny days are usually warmer than cloudy days, and that occasionally, wet clothes are hung before heaters. (Develop briefly the possible danger of doing this close to a heater.) Guide toward an experiment with either the hot plate or sun as the source of heat. The two identical handkerchiefs may be soaked in water, and wrung out with equal force. One should be placed on a line stretched over a hot plate or in the sun. The second handkerchief could be placed on the same line but should be away from the hot plate or in the shade. Does the heated handkerchief dry faster?

develop procedures

The same basic procedure will do for testing the effect of wind. Substitute a fan for the hot plate or sun. Guide pupils to do these experiments several times, and to switch handkerchiefs on each subsequent retrial.

To help the group develop beginning notions about the additional effect of humidity on evaporation you might ask: "What are foggy days like? When there is much water in the air will clothes dry as fast as on a sunny, dry day? Whom can we ask to find out? Why would they know? Should we see how many mothers agree?"

make inferences

3. *Materials:* cake or pie tin; two drinking glasses; water.

To introduce the idea of surface area as

it affects evaporation, try the bridge introduced in Chapter 3:

"Does anyone here own a dog? What does it need to have, especially on a hot day? Let me tell you about a girl who found out something very interesting. Each day, she filled her dog's bowl with water. (Draw a cross section of a bowl of small diameter on the chalkboard, with a dotted line to show a near-full water level.) At night, it was usually about half empty. (Draw another dotted line halfway down across the bowl.) One day, though, the bowl got lost and she had to use another one. It held as much water as the old one, but it was shaped in a different way. (Draw a picture of a cake or pie tin now. Or postpone this until later, if you wish to provide fewer clues.) Now each night she noticed that the water in this bowl was almost gone. Why was there always less water left over in this bowl than the other one?"

After such logical guesses as the bowl was cracked, the dog drank more water, and so on, help the children focus on the shape of each bowl. For the experiment, guide them to use a glass for one bowl, and a cake tin for the second. Watch for omission of controls. See if the children can determine a way to pour equal volumes of water into the containers. A bit of tape on the pouring glass can serve to mark any desired water volume.

suggest hypotheses

develop procedures

Have the pupils examine results the next day. Emphasize any disagreement as to which bowl contains the least water. Guide them to see that a precise comparison can be made by carefully pouring the remaining water into two identical glasses. Assist in forming the tentative conclusion that a larger surface area increases evaporation.

make inferences

Guide applications of this idea to pupils' experiences. Why does an opened, spread-out bathing suit dry faster than one that is crumpled into a ball? Why does father sweep out water puddles over a wider area on the driveway? Let them try some applications with actual materials, if possible.

EXTENDING ACTIVITIES

The following experiments will require children to apply much of what they have learned in the preceding activities.

1. Try this procedure to extend pupils' thinking in developing an experiment. Materials needed are a balance made from a dowel, two tacks, string, and sticky tape; also, a paper cup filled with weights (such as small clay pellets and paper clips), a wash cloth, water, and medicine dropper.

Tell the class, "You have found out that water evaporates. If we wet this cloth it will dry. But let's say someone thinks the water just soaks deeply into the cloth, so you can't feel it. How could you show him *develop* that the water has left the cloth and gone into the air?"

develop procedures

Hopefully, the pupils will suggest setting up a balance, as in Figure 8-1, substituting the cup and cloth for the balloons. If clues are needed, have someone feel the weight of the wash cloth before and after immersing it in water. Wring it out to prevent dripping. If necessary, suspend the dowel and ask how it can be used. Pupils' input with previous balance experiments may help them perform a similar experiment now. The wet cloth can be tacked on one end of the yardstick, while the cup containing clay pellets and paper clips is tacked on the other end. Once a perfect balance is achieved—the pellets will help effect small changes in weight—any significant evaporation of water from the cloth should cause a noticeable imbalance *within several minutes*.

Hold up a medicine dropper. How can we tell how much water has evaporated by now? (Add water to the wash cloth with the dropper until it balances again.) Before doing this, you may want to get estimates *reason* from the children about how many water *quantitatively* drops or full droppers of water it will take to achieve a balance.

reason quantitatively

2. Do the activity suggested in Chapter *state* 2, page 31L. This requires pupils to develop *problems* an operational definition for the term "dry"

state problems

before they attempt to dry soaked paper towels in the shortest possible time. Each small group will need a dowel balance with a tack on each end, a bowl of water to submerge towels, and several identical paper towels.

A towel is tacked to each end of the suspended dowel to determine if they balance. Then one towel is removed, soaked in the bowl, and dried as quickly as possible through any acceptable means the group can think of. When the soaked towel appears to be dried, the group tests this by tacking it once again to the dowel. (You may want to remind the children that it is unfair to move the clay pellet balancer after it is initially set.) The first team to achieve a balance wins.

This activity can be done just as well with a towel for each child in the small group and an equal number of unsoaked towels for counterbalancing. Two controls will be especially important. All towels should be equally wet to begin with and everyone should begin at the same time. See if pupils *develop* can design this experiment with the mini- *procedures* mum of help.

develop procedures

This is an exciting activity for children. You may want to develop a few behavior standards before work begins to keep the enthusiasm within reasonable bounds.

3. Gather several shallow containers of widely varying circumferences and fill them with *different* amounts of water. Try to keep the differences in water volume from being obvious. Ask the class to predict the correct order of evaporation from these containers, from most to least, in a day. When unexpected results are obtained, challenge the *suggest* class to detect why. Encourage repeated ex- *hypotheses* periments before conclusions are drawn.

suggest hypotheses

Condensation and the Water Cycle. On many mornings, we see dew drops glistening on lawns, parked automobiles, spider webs, and other surfaces. When the ground cools during the night, its temperature may fall below that of the surrounding air. As the surrounding air loses some heat energy, its molecules slow down. Water vapor molecules in the air slow sufficiently to be attracted to, and condense on, a cool nearby surface. Essentially the same thing happens when water droplets form on a cold pop bottle or cold water pipe.

The relative humidity of air is related to its temperature. Any parcel of air containing some water vapor becomes saturated if cooled enough. The loss of heat energy slows down molecular speed and reduces the range of molecular movement. The attractions of water molecules for one another now draw them together into drops.

The temperature at which condensation takes place is called the *dew point*. In very humid air, as in a steamy shower room, water vapor condenses on walls and mirrors although they may be only several degrees cooler than the air. But comparatively dry desert air may have to be cooled more than 50 degrees before reaching its dew point.

A forthcoming activity calls for observation of dew on the outside of a shiny metal can containing ice cubes and water. If a condition of low humidity exists in the classroom, very little or no moisture may collect on the can unless the can temperature can be reduced. Just add a few spoons of salt to the water. This will cause the ice cubes to melt faster and thus reduce the temperature even more. By substituting dry ice (frozen carbon dioxide), the can temperature will drop below freezing. In this case, condensation will occur in the form of frost. This is what happens to the freezing compartment of a refrigerator; thus, periodic defrosting is needed. Below freezing temperatures also produce frost in place of dew on the ground.

Fog may occur when the surface temperature is low enough to cool air a short distance above the ground to its dew point. In this case, water vapor condenses on tiny specks of airborne dust and remains suspended. Sometimes fog results from the unequal cooling of land and water. Such fog is common over a lake in summer. Cool air from the land flows over warm, moist air rising from the lake. As the warmer air cools to its dew point, condensation occurs and we see fog. Fog can be considered a low cloud.

Clouds at higher altitudes are formed in several ways, but all involve a parcel of air that is cooled to its saturation or dew point. In one method, wind may blow moist air up a mountain slope. As the air rises, it expands because of decreasing air pressure, cools, and condenses on airborne dust particles. If the dew point is below freezing, tiny ice crystals may form. Sometimes air may be pushed aloft when two huge air masses merge. The cooler, heavier air mass will push under the warmer, lighter mass. Again expansion, cooling, and condensation take place. A third method of cloud formation occurs when heat from the ground develops convection currents. The affected air near the ground becomes increasingly unstable, rises rapidly, and cools, and its moisture condenses.

When sufficient moisture is present, the tiny, constantly moving droplets within a cloud collide from time to time and form larger drops. These may fall as rain. In freezing temperatures, ice crystals collect and fall as snow.

Knowledge of the air temperature and its dew point can enable you or upper-grade pupils to roughly calculate cloud heights. Here is how it is done. Suppose the outdoor air temperature is now 88°F. Stir a thermometer around in a metal can of ice water. At the exact instant water droplets occur on the can, read the temperature of the immersed thermometer. This is the dew point. Let us say it reads 66°F, which makes a difference of 22°F between the two figures. Remember that rising air cools at about 5.5°F for each 1000 feet of altitude. Dividing 22 by 5.5 gives a quotient of 4. Multiply this figure by 1000. The bases of nearby clouds should be about 4000 feet high.

Although experts have invented over 200 cloud classifications, even young children can be taught to recognize three basic cloud forms. *Cirrus* clouds are high, wispy formations of ice crystals. *Cumulus* clouds are white, fluffy, and usually associated with clear visibility and fair weather. *Stratus* clouds are lower, darker formations that appear as a dense layer. These clouds may blanket the entire sky and precipitate rain within a short time. (See Figure 8-16.)

If pupils identify clouds, have them use actual clouds and authentic pictures of clouds. Avoid using cotton or hand-drawn cloud models. These seem to develop misconceptions in some children. Should a few able children wish to pursue cloud classification beyond the three basic types, have them consult an encyclopedia for additional illustrations.

The earth's cloud cover provides many clues for weather forecasting. Through use of weather satellites continually orbiting the earth, it is now possible to relay pictures of cloud formations to international data processing centers. As additional information becomes available, increased accuracy of forecasting, particularly long-range forecasting, appears probable.

We shall use several activities in the following sequence to introduce the water-cycle concept. Water evaporates, condenses, and falls without apparent end. The raindrops we see today may have dampened an ancient forest whose remains we now burn as coal. For many pupils, this will be their first conscious encounter with the conservation of matter-energy principle.

It is probable that some children at this level will be unable to understand fully the water cycle or the analogy used to demonstrate how rain occurs. Although it may be too soon to teach for mastery of these ideas, primary pupils should profit from the present exposure.

Generalization VII: Air contains moisture which condenses when it cools; water evaporates and condenses, over and over

1. *Materials:* spoon; sugar; ink; two clean, identical tinned cans; ice cubes; container of water (at about room temperature).

To lead into experiments on condensation, guide children to discuss their experiences with drinking beverages. Have them recall that sometimes the containers holding these liquids feel wet. Draw out that this seems to happen when a container is cool. Does it have to be cool? Invite a test with the provided materials. *develop procedures*

Help them plan. Two cans of water will be used, one with and one without ice cubes. Shortly, a beaded film of water should appear all over the cooler can. It may be wise to postpone much comment until the next phase of this activity is over.

Introduce a related problem: Where does the water come from? Bring out only two places are feasible, from inside or outside the can. Encourage critical thought: If the cooled can is leaking why didn't the other one leak? Perhaps someone will suggest that the contents of the two cans be switched at this point. The same results should occur. *suggest hypotheses*

There are at least four additional ways pupils can test for a "porous" can. Give hints if necessary: *develop procedures*

a. Are there water drops *above* the water level inside the can?

b. How can sugar be used to tell?

c. How can ink be used to tell?

d. How can the water level be used to tell?

Provide needed assistance in if-then thinking. If the can is leaking, then water would probably appear only at or below the water level. If sugar is added to the water inside, and the water outside tastes sugarless, then . . . . If ink is added and the outside water is uncolored, then . . . . Draw out that the water appears to be *make inferences*

Cirrus

Cumulus

Stratus

Figure 8-16 Three basic cloud forms. (Courtesy U.S. Weather Bureau.)

coming from the air surrounding the cooled container.

Identify this event as *condensation*— the opposite of evaporation. Moisture in the air can collect on cooler things. Bring out the children's related experiences with condensation. During a shower or bath, warm moist air *condenses* on the cooler bathroom mirror and walls. Warm, moist air inside a house may condense on the inside of a cooler window. Water in the air condenses on cold water pipes in a basement.

2. *Materials:* sketches of Figure 8-17 A–B–C. (Have all the sketches on one large paper.)

The next several experiences will help pupils connect evaporation and condensation to the water cycle. Exhibit the sketches. Bring out that the warm sun is evaporating water from the ocean in sketch A. Raise a question: With water evaporating from the earth all the time, why doesn't everything dry up? The next two sketches will help the children to think about this. Develop that in B the water vapor has risen far away from the warm earth. As the vapor rises higher it gets colder. The vapor now condenses on tiny bits of dust and clouds are formed. More and more moisture collects and many tiny water drops come together and become larger. In C, the larger drops fall as rain. Point back at A. What happens after the rain? (The clouds disappear and water evaporates into the air again.) Emphasize that this cycle continues without end. The same water is used over and over again.

3. *Materials:* several medicine droppers; several glasses of water; a small piece of waxed paper and a toothpick for each pupil.

Distribute the waxed paper and toothpicks. Have several children use medicine droppers to place four water drops on each piece of waxed paper, an inch or so apart.

Inform everyone that these materials will help them understand how tiny droplets in a cloud become larger and larger before they fall. Let the children push the water drops around the paper. They will discover that when several water drops are close together they suddenly fuse and become a larger drop. Emphasize that in a cloud, the water drops are much smaller. Also, they move around because of air movements in the cloud.

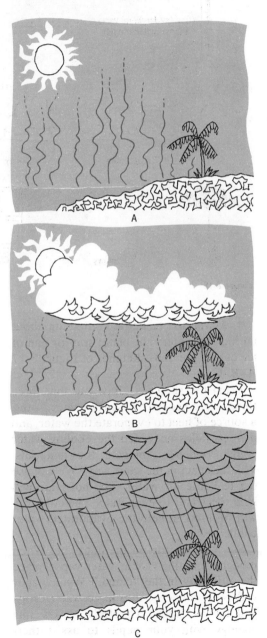

Figure 8-17 A–B–C

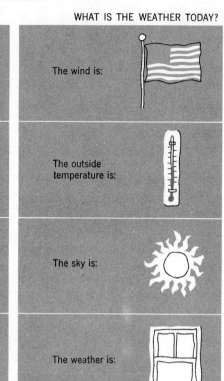

Calm	Breezy	Windy

(Use the large, movable thermometer model)

Sunny	Partly cloudy	Cloudy

Rainy	Snowy	Clear

Figure 8-18

The wind is:

The outside temperature is:

The sky is:

The weather is:

Figure 8-19

4. *Materials:* teakettle containing about an inch of water; hot plate; tray or pan of ice cubes; previous sketches of Figure 8-17 A–B–C.

make inferences From the sketches, draw out that three things were needed for rain to occur: water, a source of heat to evaporate the water, and dust particles on which the cooling water could condense. Indicate the materials. Will these act in the same way? We will use the teakettle for water. The hot plate will help the water to evaporate. The cold tray will be used to help the evaporated water condense.

Set the teakettle on the hot plate. When it begins emitting visible water vapor, place the cold tray in the "cloud." Water vapor will soon condense into large water drops and fall as "rain." Carefully review this analogy with your pupils to assist their understanding.

EXTENDING ACTIVITIES

1. It will be interesting and helpful to continue and extend the daily weather chart to include sky and precipitation reports. Figure 8-18 contains examples of useful symbols. Each morning, have the children decide from their weather observations which symbol is most appropriate among the several categories provided. Figure 8-19 reveals a typical chart for primary children.

2. Discuss how weather affects farmers, sailors, aviators, workers in the building trades, road construction, and transportation. Develop how weather affects everyone. Show a newspaper weather forecast. Bring out how the weather bureau is of service in predicting weather. Leave pupils with the realization that in future grades they will learn more about forecasting and other interesting things about the weather.

The Earth in Space

(Upper Emphasis)

UNIT 9

UNIT NINE

The Earth in Space

(Upper Emphasis)

"THE SKY'S THE LIMIT."
"What goes up must come down."
"Heaven is up above; the other place is down below."

Even tricycle riders today smile at these clichés. Television, space missions, and magazines have given children a beyond-the-earth outlook unknown to previous generations. But few children learn outside of school the basic ideas and physical laws that give meaning to the motions of objects in space. We shall concentrate on several of these in this unit.

Some teachers would ask, *"Can* astronomy units be thoroughly taught at the elementary school level?" Admittedly, there are difficulties. For example, no one can truly comprehend the limitless expanse of space and time represented by the universe. Moreover, tools of instruction are likely to be models and analogies, which demand analytical thinking and reasoned applications—not easy tasks for children.

Yet many teachers do a surprisingly effective job. These persons often use films and filmstrips with their models. They provide for much pupil participation. Their questions are often carefully planned and ordered to help children reason. These practices are especially commended for this unit.

Credit for chapter opening photograph. **NASA**

THE EARTH IN SPACE

GENERALIZATIONS

I. The earth's motions in space cause time and seasonal changes.

II. The relative motions of the sun, earth, and moon bring about moon phases, eclipses, and tides.

III. The solar system contains nine planets which revolve at different distances around the sun; the solar system is only a tiny part of a vast universe.

IV. Gravity and the laws of motion affect the movements of planets, satellites, and rockets.

Time and Seasons. Most upper-grade children know the earth rotates. But few can tell in which direction. Since the rotation apparently causes the sun to rise in a generally eastern direction and set in a generally western direction, at least some good thinkers will figure this out for themselves. Only a west to east rotation produces this effect.

Figure 9-1 shows how a person on the east coast of the United States moves into the sunlight. To him, it looks as though the sun is rising from the horizon, climbing higher as time goes by. Six hours from the time he first observes "sunrise" the sun is closest to being directly overhead. This is noon. Gradually, he continues to rotate counterclockwise. Shadows grow longer. Around 6 P.M. it is almost twilight, and the sun appears to sink into the western horizon. The next 12 hours he spends in darkness, until once again the sun appears to rise. A complete rotation takes 24 hours, or one complete day.

Expect some trouble with the term "day," since it has two meanings—the hours during which it is light, and the time for one complete rotation. Use the terms "complete day" and "daylight" to differentiate between the two; this should eliminate confusion.

Of course, the preceding is an incomplete explanation. We know that summer days are longer than winter days, for ex-

ample. (We shall take up why shortly.) Also, it would be extremely inconvenient to judge time by the sun's apparent passage overhead. Every location more than a few miles away would have a different time as the sun reached its noon position. Though this was not a problem in the days of slow-moving transportation, it became intolerable when railroads were established.

The problem was solved in 1833 by creating four standard time zones in the United States. Figure 9-2 shows those in use today in the continental United States. We set our watches ahead going eastward, and back going westward. The entire globe is now divided into 24 time zones, 15 degrees apart. (This distance was determined by dividing 360°—the earth is a near sphere—by 24 hours.)

Persons in New York on any December 21st experience about 9 hours of daylight and 15 hours of darkness. Six months later the reverse occurs. An even greater difference is found at a higher latitude, such as near Seattle, Washington (50th parallel). To see why, let us first examine Figure 9-3. Notice that the earth's axis is tilted twenty-three and one-half degrees from the plane of the earth's orbit around the sun. As the earth revolves about the sun, its axis continues to point in the same direction—

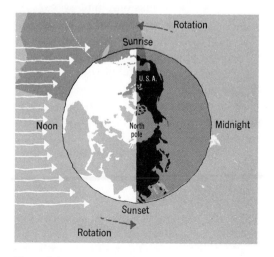

Figure 9-1

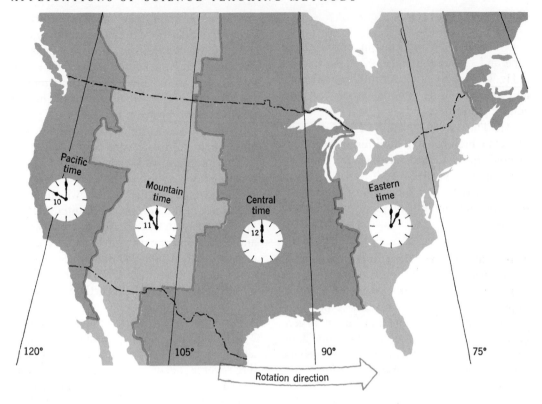

Figure 9-2

toward the north star. Check the winter position. Because of the tilt, the northern hemisphere is in darkness longer than in daylight. One can see this merely by checking the length of the parallels of latitude shown. In the summer position, we see the reverse. Now the same latitude is exposed for a much longer period to sunlight. At the "in between" periods – spring and fall – day and night periods are more nearly equal.

Also observe that the southern hemisphere experiences opposite conditions to those in the northern hemisphere. While New York shivers in December, the beaches in sunny Rio de Janeiro are crowded with swimmers and sun bathers enjoying their summer.

But there is another reason summers are warmer than winters besides increased length of the days. The sun's rays are more

nearly overhead at summer than at other times. Note that we said, "more nearly overhead." Because the earth's axis is tilted, the sun at noon can never be completely vertical (at a 90° angle) north of the Tropic of Cancer or south of the Tropic of Capricorn.

If you ask a pupil to explain why it is warmer in summer than winter, don't be surprised if he replies, "The earth is closer to the sun." This is entirely logical, even though it is wrong. In fact, the opposite is true. The earth's path (orbit) around the sun is a slightly elongated circle, or ellipse, as are virtually all the orbits of celestial bodies. In winter we are 3 million miles closer to the sun than in summer. However, since this distance is relatively small compared to the average distance, about 93 million miles, the effect is generally negligible.

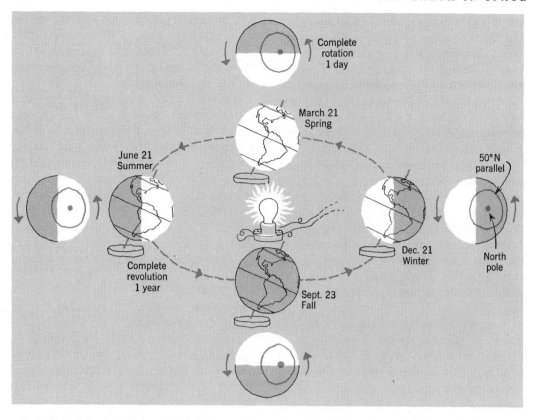

Figure 9-3 Demonstrating the seasons. Outside figures as viewed from above. Note the unequal periods of daylight at the fiftieth parallel except on March 21 (Spring equinox) and September 23 (Fall equinox).

Generalization I: The earth's motions in space cause time and seasonal changes

Contributing Idea A. The earth's rotation in sunlight causes time changes.

Materials: filmstrip projector; darkened room; sketch or opaque projection of Figure 9-2.

Take time to acquaint the children with their new unit and to gain some insight into what they already know. What does "The Earth in Space" mean to them? How does the earth move in space? How does the moon affect the earth? What causes seasonal changes? What are planets and stars? What problems must be overcome to launch a space satellite?

Mention that the pupils already know some of the earth's motions in space. Review how the earth's *rotation* in sunlight causes night and day. This can be demonstrated with a filmstrip projector and globe. But in which direction does the earth rotate? From west to east, or east to west? Review what *north, south, east* and *west* mean if necessary.

Have the class remember that the sun appears to rise in the east and set in the west. Tip the globe toward the class, as in Figure 9-1. Where is the east coast of the United States? West coast? Should the rotation be clockwise or counterclockwise? To find out, we can try it both ways.

Let someone darken the room and turn on the filmstrip projector. Rotate the globe counterclockwise. Establish that the east

make
inferences

coast is experiencing sunrise as it turns into the light. Continue rotating until the west coast disappears into the shadow. This is sunset. Reverse the rotation. The children should see that only a counterclockwise rotation makes the sun seem to rise in the east and set in the west. Establish that one complete rotation takes 24 hours. This is one *complete day*.

Now that we know where sunrise and sunset take place, where is the United States' east coast position at noon? Guide a child to rotate the globe until the east coast is midway between the sunrise and sunset borders. Slowly rotate the globe in the "sun." At each point where the sun is closest to directly overhead it is noon. The midwest has noon next, and the west coast last.

If noon is always where the sun is highest overhead, how can we know what time it is in another nearby city? A town only a hundred miles west of a location where the sun is highest would not have its noontime until several minutes later. What would happen if everyone set his watch at noon only when the sun was highest overhead? (Everyone more than a few miles apart would have different times showing on their watches.) Bring out the ensuing chaos in bus, train, airline, television, and radio schedules.

make
inferences

Exhibit a sketch or opaque projection of Figure 9-2. How is this problem solved? Let the children study the sketch. Draw out that the continental United States is divided into four *standard time zones*. The people living in each zone agree to set their watches and clocks to the same time, whether the sun is directly overhead or not. In this way, a watch needs only to be changed three times as one flies or drives from one coast to another.

Quiz the children to help clinch their understanding: When it is noon in New York what time is it in San Francisco? and so on.

Write *ante meridien* and *post meridien* on the chalkboard. These are Latin words.

The first means before mid-day, the second after mid-day. Can someone guess their abbreviations? Instead of saying or writing "9 in the morning" or "9 in the evening," we use the abbreviations.

Have everyone note that the time zone boundaries are uneven. Help the children notice that otherwise some states and large urban areas would be in two zones, which would be inconvenient. Emphasize that the entire world is divided into 24 time zones of equal size, one for each hour of the complete day.

Contributing Idea B. The earth's tilted axis and revolution about the sun cause seasonal changes.

1. *Materials:* slide projector; 2- by 2-inch piece of wire screen; clay; string; globe; darkened room.

Develop that, in addition to rotating, the earth also *revolves* about the sun. Take the classroom globe and, while rotating it slowly, move around a pupil who acts as the sun. Emphasize that the earth's tilted axis continues to point in one direction—toward the north star—throughout the revolution. The entire revolution takes about 365 days, or one year. That is, the earth rotates 365 times during one revolution.

Pose a problem. On December 21, New York City has about 9 hours of daylight and 15 hours of darkness. On June 21, it has the reverse. Why? Discuss briefly.

Darken the room. Turn on a slide projector or unshaded lamp. (A projector gives a much sharper definition of light and shadow.) Place the globe in the winter position shown in Figure 9-3. Fix a small lump of clay at the position of New York City, so that it may be easily observed. Slowly rotate the globe at a reasonably uniform rate of speed. Is this location longer in darkness or light? Help someone measure with string how much of New York's latitude—the forty-first north parallel—is in darkness and in light. Mark the string with crayon where darkness and light meet. (About $9/24$ is in light, $15/24$ in darkness.) Remove the string. A chalk line can be drawn under the string if it is held taut against the chalkboard.

To estimate the hours spent in daylight and darkness more accurately, divide the chalk line into twenty-four parts. This can be done by the children in four easy steps. Since $3 \times 2 \times 2 \times 2 = 24$, simply divide the line into three segments, then halve each segment three consecutive times.

Now place the globe in the June 21 position. Rotate the globe slowly. The forty-first parallel now seems to be longer in daylight than darkness. Measure again with string. The previous findings should be reversed. Bring out that the unchanging tilt of the earth's axis and opposite orbital positions cause the difference.

make inferences

Let pupils hypothesize about, and then measure, portions of light and darkness at the fall and spring positions. They should be roughly equal in each case. Elicit names of the four seasons as the globe is placed in appropriate positions.

suggest hypotheses

make inferences

2. Is summer warmer only because the days are longer? Winter colder only because days are shorter? What might be another reason? Encourage conjecture based on the children's observations. Hold up a piece of 2- by 2-inch screen material. Place it in the slide projector slot. Shine and focus the projector on the globe positioned in the December location. A sharp grid effect will be seen. Ask what the pupils observe. (The squares become increasingly elongated toward the top and bottom portions of the globe.) Does this give a clue? (The sunlight is more at an angle than at the equator; it is spread out more, and therefore not as intense.)

suggest hypotheses

make inferences

Have someone place paper over the projected rectangle at New York City and trace it with pencil. Will it be the same size at the June position? Place the globe in the June position. The traced rectangle should now be put in the same location and traced again. It will be appreciably less elongated. What does this possibly show about the sun's rays? (In summer, sunlight is more nearly overhead and so is more intense.)

make inferences

If pupils are unaware that vertical sunlight is warmer than slanted sunlight, use extended activity 3 as an experiment at this time.

Let the children notice that a location in the southern hemisphere receives nearly vertical sunlight when New York has slanted sunlight. When the northern hemisphere has winter, it is summer in the southern hemisphere. Conclude by helping them generalize about the causes of seasons. This will be easier if you project Figure 9-3 onto a screen for reference as they talk. But don't press for precision yet. This is a difficult idea for children.

make inferences

EXTENDING ACTIVITIES

1. Show a film on time zones and the seasons. If the film is clear and explicit—as many are—you may want to use it first and the models second. Pupils' relative success with the models will enable you to determine what points need clarification.

2. Invite the pupils to verify the direction of the earth's rotation. You will need a small globe; toothpick and small lump of clay; filmstrip projector. Each pupil team will need a stick about 4-feet long; plumb bob, made from a 4-foot string and weight; pebble marker; hammer; level lawn; one-half hour of afternoon sunshine. The assembly will look like Figure 9-4.

Shine the projector on the globe. Affix a small lump of clay to the globe in the noon position. Push in part of a toothpick so that it is nearly vertical to the surface and casts almost no shadow. Toward which direction will the afternoon shadows go if the earth rotates from west to east? (East.) If the earth rotates from east to west? (West.) Try rotating the globe slowly in each direction. The class will see a clear tendency for the afternoon shadows on the model to go in these respective directions.

Point out the materials. Will a big shadow stick work in the same way with the earth

399

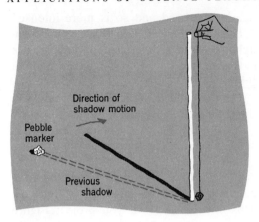

Direction of
shadow motion

Pebble
marker

Previous
shadow

Figure 9-4

itself? Develop conjecture. Help them plan what to do with the materials. A chalkboard sketch will help.

After pounding a stick vertically into the ground, the children should observe where the tip of its shadow falls. A pebble can mark the spot. Allow at least twenty minutes before the second shadow is marked. Since the earth rotates one degree each four minutes, this will permit an angle of five degrees to result going eastward. With a 4-foot stick to cast shadows, the pebble *make* *inferences* and new shadow should be at least several inches apart after this time.

If several teams have used different-sized shadow sticks, see if they can figure out *make* *inferences* why the distance between the recorded shadow tips varies from team to team.

3. Is vertical sunlight warmer than slanted sunlight? Get two identical thermometers and two small pieces of cardboard. Lay one thermometer flat on one cardboard in a sunny place. Next to this, prop up the other cardboard and thermometer against a book so that the sunshine is received *vertically.* (A pencil held at a right angle to the second cardboard surface should cast no shadow.) The cardboard pieces will insure a similar background in both cases. A few minutes in strong sunshine should be enough for a significant difference to appear in thermometer readings.

Moon Phases, Tides, and Eclipses. Why does the moon seem to change its shape? Why does the ocean have tides? What causes eclipses? Children are curious about these things. The next sequence presents opportunities for them to learn how the sun, earth, and moon interact. Let us consider moon phases first.

You are aware that the moon, like our earth, receives and reflects light from the hot, glowing sun. Also, the moon revolves around the earth a little less than once a month. Study Figure 9-5 for a moment. Right drawings show the earth and moon as seen from far out in space. Left drawings of the moon show how it appears as viewed from the earth in each of eight different positions.

Imagine us standing on the earth in the center of this illustration. Gaze at position 1. This is the *new moon* position. The moon's face is now dark to us. But the moon moves on in its orbit. At position 2, we see a *new crescent moon;* at position 3 a *first-quarter moon.* (It is a "first-quarter" moon rather than a "half moon" because we are looking at a sphere, rather than a plane surface. Being a three-dimensional object, its other illuminated one-fourth is "over the hill" and almost wholly out of sight from any relative position on earth.) At position 4 we see a *new gibbous moon;* one side is now almost fully illuminated. At 5 there is a *full* moon. The other positions reverse the sequence of phases—old gibbous, last quarter, old crescent—until once more there is a new moon. As it moves from the new to full positions, more and more of the moon appears to be illuminated; it is said to be *waxing.* But from full to new moon positions, less and less of its illumination is visible from earth, so it is said to be *waning.* Try the moon phase activity on page 405L. Compare the phases you see with those in Figure 9-5.

The interaction of sun, moon, and earth also results in tides. Notice the great difference in water level in the photographs of Figure 9-6. How does this happen? The

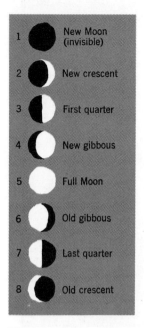
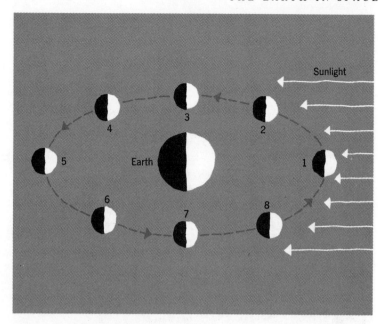

Figure 9-5   Moon phases as seen from the earth (left figures).

law of universal gravitation, first formulated by the great eighteenth-century philosopher and scientist Sir Isaac Newton, provides much of the answer. Briefly stated, *every object in the universe attracts each other; the force of this attraction depends upon the mass of each object and the distance between them.* ("Mass" refers to the amount of matter that makes up the object.)

As shown in Figure 9-7, the mutual attraction between earth and moon causes the ocean to bulge at position 1. This is a *direct high tide.* An *indirect high tide* appears at 3 because it is most distant from the moon, and hence gravitational attraction is weakest here. (We'll add a refinement to this statement shortly.) Also, the land surface is pulled slightly away from this region. Positions 2 and 4 have low tides because these are areas of weak attraction that furnish the extra water making up the high tides.

What causes the tides to rise and fall? Let us put ourselves at position 1. As we rotate on the earth toward 2, the tide will seem to ebb, or fall. We experience a low

tide. Moving from 2 into 3, we gradually come into the bulge. It seems as though the tide is "coming in." We experience a high tide. Rotating onward, we have another low tide before once again arriving at the direct high-tide area. In other words, the oceans tend to bulge continually in the moon's direction, and opposite point as the earth rotates. While the oceans rotate with the land, of course, the effect of the continual bulges creates the illusion that the tides are moving in and out independently.

Since the earth's rotation takes about 24 hours, high tides occur about every 12 hours. (Remember, there is one direct and one indirect high tide simultaneously.) Six hours elapse between low and high tides. Actually, these times are a little longer because the moon itself moves some distance in its orbit while the earth rotates. Because the tidal bulge moves into alignment with the moon as it advances, the earth must rotate an extra 52 minutes each 24 hours before it is again in the direct high-tide zone.

Twice monthly unusually high and low tidal ranges occur. During *spring* tides,

Figure 9-6 High and low tides. (Russ Kinne—Photo Researchers, Inc.)

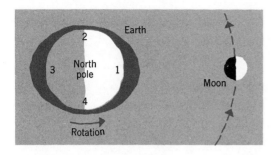

Figure 9-7

high tides are very high, low tides very low. (Incidentally, there is no connection between "spring" and the season. Perhaps the name arose because these tides appear to "spring up" so fast.) A week later, there is much less variation from high to low tides. Tides during this period are called *neap* tides. Figure 9-8 shows how these tides take place. When the sun and moon are aligned (A), the sun's added gravitational attraction causes very high spring tides. This happens when the moon is in either the full or new moon phases. Since the sun is so far away, its tremendous mass contributes only an additional one-third to the force of gravitational attraction. When the sun and moon tend to pull at right angles (B), we have neap tides. This occurs when the moon is in its first- and last-quarter phases.

Interestingly, besides water tides, there are also huge atmospheric tides, and tiny land tides. All occur through the same interaction of sun, moon, and earth. Accurate measurements show that some land portions of the earth rise and fall more than a foot with the tides.

Causes of eclipses are seen in Figure 9-9. Both earth and moon cast conelike shadows. When the moon is in position 1, the tip of its shadow barely reaches the earth. Persons in this small, shadowy area see a *solar eclipse.* A total eclipse is never more than 170 miles across. Sunlight is cut off except for a whitish halo, called the *corona.* The shadow moves quickly over the ground, since both earth and moon are in motion. Sunlight is never blocked for more than 8 minutes.

In position 2, the moon is eclipsed when it revolves into the earth's large shadow. Practically everyone on the earth's dark side can see a *lunar eclipse,* which may last for 2 hours before the moon revolves out of the earth's shadow. There are at least several lunar and solar eclipses each year.

Notice that eclipses can occur in the full and new moon positions. Why, then, don't they occur every few weeks? The reason is that the moon's plane of orbit is tilted about 5° from the earth's orbital plane around the sun. This usually causes the moon to pass above and below the positions required for eclipses.

A 5° tilt would be only a minor deviation from the earth's orbital plane in Figure 9-9, hardly enough to make a difference. But in proper scale, this small deviation is quite significant. With a scale of 1 inch to 1000 miles, the earth's diameter is eight inches,

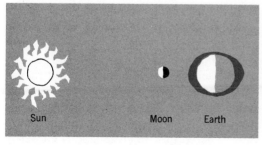

A

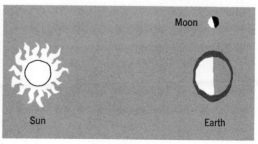

B

Figure 9-8

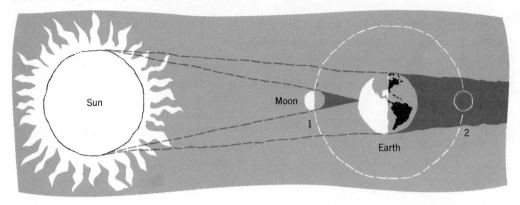

Figure 9-9

the moon's two inches. Their distance apart is 20 feet. This is seldom realized by children. The sun's diameter and distance at this scale are even more surprising. Imagine a sun model 72 feet across, 1½ miles away!

We tend to think of the moon revolving around the earth, but strictly speaking, this is not quite the case. The gravitational attraction of these two objects is such that they are locked together in a revolving system that has a common center of mass (barycenter). To see why this is so, look at Figure 9-10 A–D.

The large ball of clay represents the earth, and the small one is the moon. A paper clip joins the two to simulate their gravitational attraction. If you suspend this system from the middle (A) with a string, the much heavier earth goes down and the moon goes up. The same thing would happen if a heavy adult and a small child got on a seesaw with the fulcrum in the middle. In (B), the balance is improved, but much the same thing happens. In (C), however, a balance is achieved. If you spin the model system with a twisted string, (A) and (B) will wobble and sway unevenly; but (C) revolves uniformly and simulates the motion of the earth-moon system.

Now for the refinement on the cause of indirect tides, promised earlier. In any spinning system such as this, there is a tendency for the two objects to fly apart. The gravitational attraction prevents this from happening. In (D), the side of the earth facing the moon is strongly attracted to the moon. The water moves more easily than the solid earth, so it flows strongly toward the near side and becomes a high tide. The earth's opposite side is attracted less because it is farther away. So the tendency of this far side of the spinning system

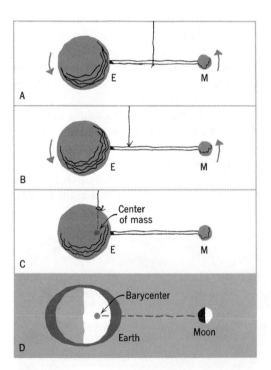

Figure 9-10 A − B − C − D The earth-moon system has a common point of balance or center of mass called the barycenter. (Distance not to scale.)

to fly apart is countered only weakly by the weakened gravitational pull. The result is an indirect high tide.

Our model is imperfect in several ways. The earth's mass is about eighty times greater than the moon's. Also the distance scale is wrong. But if we were to use the proper scale our paper clip connector would need to be at least several feet long. One of the extending activities will allow the children to make a clay earth-moon system, and to discover its common center of mass for themselves.

From an earth reference position it is natural to regard the moon as revolving in a circular path around the earth (or, more accurately, the barycenter). But motion is relative to the observer. If we could see the moon's path from far out in space, it would not look circular. Instead it would weave in an almost S-shaped, undulating motion along the earth's orbit. Since the sun is in motion, a similar pathway is woven by the earth. Is it wrong, then, to say the moon *revolves* around the earth, and the earth around the sun? Not at all. It is just another way of looking at the same set of facts. The closing activity can be used to help pupils learn this idea.

Generalization II: The relative motions of the sun, earth, and moon bring about moon phases, eclipses, and tides

Contributing Idea A. Moon phases appear when the moon revolves around the earth.

1. *Materials:* slide projector or unshaded lamp; darkened room; globe; white volleyball or substitute; toothpicks; several Ping Pong balls or modeling clay; black and white tempera paint; paint brushes; large chalkboard sketch of Figure 9-5. (At present show only empty circles for the eight moon positions. Circles may be drawn conveniently by tracing chalk around the base of a large tinned can. In addition, off to one side draw the eight phases, but scrambled out of sequence. Conceal with a pulldown map until needed.)

What makes the moon shine? Bring out the difference between a body that reflects light and one that generates light, such as the sun.

Does the moon always look the same? Have children draw on the chalkboard some impressions of their observations. If needed to show additional phases, reveal the scrambled drawings made earlier by you. Why does the moon seem to change its appearance? Arouse conjecture.

Reveal a chalkboard sketch of Figure 9-5. Instruct the children to ignore the empty circles for now, and that they will be asked soon to fill in the correct drawings. Bring out that the moon is shown at eight different positions as it revolves around the earth. The entire revolution takes a little less than a month. Encourage discussion and hypotheses about how this revolution might change the sequence of the moon's appearance. You might want to name the phases (but not their order) to aid discussion.

suggest hypotheses

Ask someone to stand in front of the room. He will be an "earthling" looking at the moon as it circles the earth. He will indicate how the moon's shape appears to change.

Darken the room and turn on the slide projector. It should be at the side and pointed toward the child, from at least 10 feet away, to insure a broad field of light. Have him hold a white volleyball "moon" at arm's length and slightly higher than his head. (If the ball is not higher, his head will block off the light as he turns his back to it. Placing the projector at least 5 feet above the floor will also help to prevent light blockage.)

Starting in position 1, let him put the moon through a full revolution as he rotates in place and observes the moon from his position. The other pupils should observe from their seats. Does the moon keep changing shape? The earthling will say "yes." But most of the class should disagree. To them the moon will look much as it does in the sketch. (Turn on the lights for

suggest
hypotheses

discussion.) Why is this so? Draw out that the observers are in different relative positions. Perhaps this is the reason. There is a way that all of us can find out together.

Since only one observer or so at a time can observe the present moon setup, suggest that each person use a painted Ping-Pong ball or clay ball for a moon. A chalkboard sketch of Figure 9-11 will help the children prepare their moon models. If no Ping-Pong balls are available, each child will need some clay to make a ball about an inch in diameter, two toothpicks, a small paint brush, and some black and white tempera paint. Pupils should shape the clay as nearly round as they can, then paint one half of the ball white and the other half black. Guide them to insert toothpicks as shown.

Instruct the children as follows. The white half of the moon model is receiving sunlight. Therefore it must always face toward the sun. Designate one wall as the sun. The top toothpick will remind them to keep the white part facing the proper direction. The bottom toothpick will be used to hold the model.

Have class members stand and view their models at arm's length in position 1. Caution all not to reveal what they see. Have them try all eight positions at least several times. Let each draw his eight observations in sequence on a sheet of paper. Walk around and check these drawings; assist individuals in viewing their models as needed. Encourage pupils to make their own observations and record only what they see.

Ask for a volunteer to now view the projector-volleyball model. Will his observations be the same? At each position, have him stop and draw what he has seen in the empty circle opposite each position number on the chalkboard. The class will enjoy noting agreements and disagreements. Follow through with more experimentation using other pupils.

Acquaint the children with the term *phases of the moon,* if it did not come up before in discussion. The moon's shape appears to go through changes or phases as it is seen in different positions of its orbit around the earth. Bring out repeatedly the name given to each phase. Write these names next to their proper places on the chalkboard sketch: 1. *new moon* 2. *new crescent* 3. *first quarter* 4. *new gibbous* 5. *full moon* 6. *old gibbous* 7. *last quarter* 8. *old crescent.* Compare and emphasize the full and new moon positions. The understanding of these terms will be helpful in the forthcoming activities on tides.

Contributing Idea B. Ocean tides are caused by the gravitational attraction of the earth, moon, and sun.

1. *Materials:* construction-paper model of earth and its tides. (To prepare, see Figure 9-12. Cut out a round piece of tan construction paper about 20 inches in diameter, and a larger blue piece cut into an elliptical form. Number and label as shown. Fasten in the center with a paper fastener. Stick this model to the chalkboard with cellophane tape. Draw on the chalkboard a 5-inch diameter moon about 4 feet away. Leave off for now the arc showing part of the moon's orbit.)

Ask pupils to describe ocean tides. Develop that the ocean recedes for some distance from a beach during low tide. At high tide the water may cover most of a beach. If available, show pictures of high and low tides at the same location. (Perhaps you can project the pictures in Figure 9-6.)

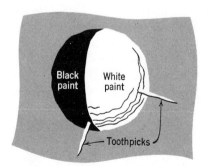

Figure 9-11 A clay model for investigating phases of the moon.

Figure 9-12

Direct attention to the earth-tide model fastened to the chalkboard and its nearby moon. Bring out that the mutual gravitational attraction of earth and moon is chiefly responsible for tides. Each body is like a magnet that attracts. However, gravitational attraction is present with all substances, not just some metals.

Bring out that the earth's oceans are not sturdily in place as is the land. This causes the ocean to bulge out toward the moon. Why is there an opposite bulge? Help the class to understand that this part is farther away and receives less pull. Also, the land itself at the opposite bulge is drawn slightly toward the moon. Rotate the land part of the model. The land rotates but the bulges tend to stay aligned with the moon.

make inferences
Ask questions about the numbered locations. Where is it high tide? (1 and 3; 1 has a direct high tide, 3 an indirect high tide.) Low tide? (2 and 4.) Challenge the children to describe the tides from the X position as it goes through a complete rotation. From 1 to 2, the tide seems to be going out; it becomes low tide. From 2 to 3, the tide appears to be coming in; actually we are moving into the bulge. From 3 to 4, tide going out. From 4 to 1, tide coming in.

reason quantitatively
Ask more questions. How long does it take to rotate completely around from one direct high tide to the next direct high tide? (About 24 hours.) From one high tide to the opposite, indirect high tide? (About 12 hours.) From high tide to low tide? (About 6 hours.)

Now pose a problem. According to our figures, there should be 24 hours between one direct high tide and the next direct high tide. (Rotate location X once to demonstrate.) But records show that the actual period between these two direct high tides is 24 hours and 52 minutes. Why the extra 52 minutes?

suggest hypotheses
Arouse conjecture. Challenge the group to show what might cause this delay. If clues are needed, draw in the arc representing the moon's orbit. Gradually develop that in the 24 hours the earth rotates, the moon moves ahead in its orbit. Draw a dotted-line moon about a foot beyond the present moon figure. Unfasten the cellophane tape and realign the water bulges so they are directly aligned toward the moon's new position. However, take care that land position X still points toward the moon's initial location. Now slowly rotate position X until it is in the exact center of the bulge. Bring out that the moon's orbital movement necessitates 52 additional minutes of earth rotation until position 1 is again in the center of a direct high tide. This would then make 12 hours and 26 minutes between a direct high tide and the indirect high tide, and 6 hours, 13 minutes between high and low tides. Let the children calculate these corrected times if they can.

reason quantitatively

407

Mention that local land conditions may alter these times somewhat. In a seashore community, have someone consult a newspaper for local tide tables. List these data reason on the chalkboard and let the children calculate and contrast actual times of tides with the generalized times developed before. Discuss the importance of ship captains knowing about high and low tides when they enter or leave a seaport. (Sufficient water depth and favorable current.)

reason
quantitatively

2. *Materials:* pencils and paper; chalkboard or chart sketch of Figure 9-8. (Omit the tidal bulges for now.)

Use this activity to teach how spring and neap tides come about.

Introduce drawing A. Bring out that the sun also has gravitational pull. But it is so far away that its pull is much weaker than the moon's, in spite of the sun's far greater size. Emphasize the way that sun, moon, and earth are aligned. Have the children make contrast this alignment with B. In which inferences situation would a high tide be greater? (A.)

make
inferences

Have the class understand that extra high tides would also occur in A if the moon were in an opposite position. Lesser tides would result in B if the moon were opposite its present position. Emphasize that these positions represent the times when tidal ranges are highest and lowest. High tidal variations are *spring tides.* Low tidal variations are *neap tides.*

Invite pupils to draw pictures of what the make moon would look like from the earth during spring tides. A new moon would appear in A; or a full moon in the opposite location. With neap tides, there would be a last-quarter moon in B; or a first-quarter moon in the opposite location. Walk around and note how accurate children's drawings are; review where necessary.

make
inferences

Help them to understand that huge air tides and tiny land tides also occur with water tides.

Contributing Idea C. A lunar eclipse occurs when the earth's shadow falls on the moon;

a solar eclipse occurs when the moon's shadow falls upon the earth.

1. *Materials:* globe; one-foot string attached by tape to a white tennis ball or baseball; slide projector; darkened room; pictures of eclipses (optional); chalkboard sketch of Figure 9-13. (Omit the two moons and numerals for now.)

Ask the children if they have ever seen an *eclipse.* Show pictures, if any. Develop that the term means "to block off light or cast a shadow." A *solar eclipse* happens when sunlight is blocked and cannot reach the earth. A *lunar eclipse* happens when moonlight is blocked.

Refer to the chalkboard sketch. The suggest dotted circle shows the moon's orbit. Seek hypotheses someone to draw the moon's probable position during a solar eclipse, and lunar eclipse. (Have several moons drawn. Make no comment on accuracy. Position 1 will be needed for a solar eclipse, position 2 for a lunar eclipse.)

suggest
hypotheses

Show the materials. How can we test develop with our models to see if these eclipses procedures might occur? (Shine a projector on the globe from 10 feet away. Dangle a ball from a string and move it counterclockwise around the globe.) When the moon is between the globe and projector, it will cast a small shadow on the earth. This is a solar eclipse. When the earth is between the projector and moon, its shadow will obscure the moon. This is a lunar eclipse.

develop
procedures

Why is it that persons living on only a small part of the earth see a solar eclipse? (The moon casts only a small shadow—up to 170 miles wide.) Why is it that people on half the earth at one time can see a lunar eclipse take place? (The earth's large shadow blocks off all the moon. Everyone on the earth's dark or night side can see this happen.) Draw out that the children's make chances of seeing a lunar eclipse are much inferences greater than seeing a solar eclipse. *Emphasize that there are only several solar and lunar eclipses a year.*

make
inferences

2. Referring to the chalkboard diagram,

Figure 9-13

remind the pupils of their preceding work with moon phases. What moon phase occurs in position 1? (New moon.) Position 2? (Full moon.) There is something odd here. What is the problem? (Why isn't there a solar eclipse *each month* at new moon? A lunar eclipse *each month* at full moon?)

Encourage hypotheses. If necessary, have the children recall why the moon-phase demonstrator held the ball slightly higher than his head. Some pupils will immediately suggest a moon orbit above the earth's plane of orbit. Some will have it below the earth's plane of orbit. Let them try these positions with their models. Both suggestions will permit moon phases, but no eclipses are possible. Encourage discussion and experimentation until the children see the likeliest situation. Only a moon orbit which is tilted from the plane of the earth's orbit around the sun will permit monthly moon phases and occasional solar and lunar eclipses.

Caution pupils never to look directly at the sun during a solar eclipse. Even the use of dark glasses or exposed film negatives may not be completely safe. Show them a safe method for indirect viewing. Punch a sharp nail hole in the center of a small piece of cardboard. With back to the sun, focus the sun's rays through the hole onto another cardboard. During a solar eclipse it will be possible to watch the sun's bright disc on the cardboard being obscured by the passing moon.

Contributing Idea D. Relative sizes and distances of the earth, moon, and sun are difficult to draw to the same scale.

1. *Materials:* two small sheets of construction paper, one white and one brown; 20-foot string; yardstick; drawing compass; scissors; paper and pencils for pupils.

Develop that whenever we see drawings of the earth and moon, the moon is usually smaller. Why is this so? (The moon *is* smaller.) Write *8000 miles* on the chalkboard, then *2000 miles*. These are the approximate *diameters* of the earth and moon. Explain this term, if needed. Bring out that, in their eclipse models, the relative sizes of earth and moon are fairly accurate. But how about the distance from earth to moon? How far away is the moon? (About 240,000 miles.) Do the eclipse and moon-phase models give a false picture? (Yes.) Invite children to make an accurately scaled model of the earth and moon, and their distance apart, with the available materials.

Help them choose a scale: 1 inch to 1000 miles is easy to work with. Let them first calculate sizes. The earth will have a diameter of 8 inches and the moon 2 inches. Have a child draw with a compass an 8-inch circle on the brown paper, a 2-inch circle on the white. Cut these out quickly with scissors. Discard the remaining paper.

Now how about the proper distance on this scale? Let the children calculate: 1 inch for 1000 miles. There are 240,000 miles. Dividing 240,000 by 1000 gives 240 inches. How many feet would that be? 240 inches divided by 12 inches = 20 feet. Invite two children to measure off 20 feet of string with a yardstick. Get children to hold the scaled models at opposite ends of the string. Now the earth and moon, and their distance apart, are in proper scale.

It will be instructive to mount the earth and moon models above the chalkboard, 20 feet apart. Have a committee plan and make suitable captions. Labels will be needed for the earth and moon, their

409

diameters, and distance apart. The main caption might read, "A scale model of the earth and moon (1 inch to 1000 miles)."

In the next activity, pupils find that when the sun is added in proper scale to the earth-moon model, considerable space is required.

2. *Materials:* 5-foot string attached to chalk; yardstick; drawing compass (Replace the pencil with a piece of chalk.); a chalkboard at least four and one-half feet high and wide.

Write the sun's diameter (864,000 miles) and average distance away (93,000,000 miles) on the chalkboard. Can the same scale of 1 inch to 1000 miles be used in the *reason* room for the sun? Let the children calculate. *quantitatively* (No. The diameter would be 864 inches, or 72 feet. The distance would be 93,000 inches, almost 1½ miles away.) Give a familiar referent for the diameter, such as the width of a school building. Have someone indicate on a map a location 1½ miles away.

Suggest a scale of 1 inch to 8000 miles. Let the children first calculate the sun, earth, and moon diameters to this scale. *reason* Since the sun is 864,000 miles in diameter, *quantitatively* this will be divided by 8000 miles to yield 108 inches, or *9 feet.* The earth's diameter is 8000 miles. Thus it will be *1 inch* on the scale. At a diameter of 2000 miles, the moon will be only *one-fourth inch* across.

reason Suggest that the children calculate the *quantitatively* distance between sun and earth to scale. 93,000,000 miles divided by 8000 miles = 11,625 inches, or almost 970 feet. The distance between earth and moon is 240,000 divided by 8000, or 30 inches. Since the sun scale is still too large for the room, suggest they make it half as large; that is, have a scale of 1 inch to 16,000 miles.

The above figures are now reduced one-half:

sun: 4½ feet diameter
earth: ½ inch diameter
moon: ⅛ inch diameter
distance from sun to earth: 485 feet
distance from earth to moon: 15 inches

It appears the playground must be used to show distance. First, however, the models will need to be completed. The next activity shows how this may be done efficiently.

3. *Materials:* a string 2 feet 3 inches long tied to a pencil; two 5-foot pieces of butcher paper; cellophane tape; scissors; four bowls of yellow tempera paint; four sponges; white card about 18 inches by 6 inches; 20-foot string; black crayon; yardstick.

A committee can prepare a sun model. Help the members with directions if needed. Connect two 5-foot long pieces of butcher paper with cellophane tape. Draw on this a circle four and one-half feet in diameter with a string connected to a pencil. Cut out the model. Color it with yellow tempera paint. This can be done quickly by applying the paint with sponges. Four children can each take a quarter section, and starting from the center, work out to the edge of the model.

Let someone prepare the earth and moon models. On a white card about 18 inches by 6 inches draw a one-half-inch earth near one end and a one-eighth-inch moon 15 inches away. Label each clearly.

Invite your pupils to show the proper distance between their earth-moon and sun *reason* models on the playground. How many *quantitative* times will a 20-foot string need to be stretched to measure this distance? (Slightly more than 24 times.) If the playground is not long enough, perhaps this can be done on a sidewalk in front of or near the school.

After this activity, let the children mount their models on a bulletin board with appropriate labels and familiar referents. A caption might read, "A scale model of the sun, earth, and moon (1 inch to 16,000 miles). At this scale the earth-moon model and the sun model should be 485 feet apart."

EXTENDING ACTIVITIES

1. Encourage pupils to sketch and label the moon's appearance each night at a

designated time for 30 days. If near a seaport, have them check in newspapers or port records the correlation between a new and full moon, and spring tides. Do the same with a first- and last-quarter moon, and neap tides.

make inferences

2. Write on the chalkboard, "The moon changes its shape as it revolves around the earth." Invite the children to state this sentence more accurately. ("The moon *appears* to change its shape. . . .")

state problems

3. Inform the children that almost one-half of the moon has never been seen from the earth. Yet the moon rotates as it revolves. Why can't all parts be seen? Develop conjecture.

suggest hypotheses

Draw a large circle with string and chalk in front of the classroom. Let someone stand in the center and represent the earth. Have a "moon" child stand on the circle and face him. How can the moon child rotate and revolve in such a way that the earth child never sees the back of his head? (While the moon child revolves he should keep his face toward the earth child.)

develop procedures

But there may be protests. Some may claim the moon child only revolved; he did not rotate. Have the children invent an operational definition for rotate. ("A body faces all directions during a complete turn.") Let the moon child try moving around again. Children will see that he faces all four cardinal directions as he revolves. Therefore, he must also have rotated.

state problems

Have him try revolving around the earth child while facing only *one* direction, such as north. Now the earth child will see all parts of the "moon." Bring out the reason that only about half of the moon's surface is visible from earth: The moon rotates at the same speed it revolves about the earth.

make inferences

Let someone look up in magazines photographs of the moon's opposite face taken through the U.S. lunar exploration program.

4. Invite pupils to make a clay earth-moon model to see how balance affects the way the system spins. Each child will need a handful of clay (enough to make an earth about the size of a Ping-Pong ball and a moon about the size of a small toy marble—relative diameters four to one); straightened-out paper clip; straight pin; ruler; 15-inch string.

After the clay balls are made, the ends of a straightened-out paper clip should be pushed into them; how far in will be determined easily when the model is balanced. Ask pupils to use an edge of their rulers as a fulcrum to find the point of balance between the two clay balls. They will soon discover that the balance point is somewhere inside the larger ball. (Figure 9-10C.) Suggest that the string and straight pin be used to suspend the system. (The pin should always be inserted at a right angle to the suspended string; it will stay in longer.) Have pupils spin and compare the motions of the model system when it is balanced and not balanced. Pins can be placed in various places on the larger ball. Discuss implications for the actual earth-moon system and the ways the model differs from reality.

make inferences

5. This extending activity can help the children to envision the moon's monthly orbit around the earth from an uncommon frame of reference. You will need a chalkboard diagram or opaque projection of Figure 9-14; chalk and chalkboard; ruler; and an earth-moon model cut from construction paper (see Figure 9-15).

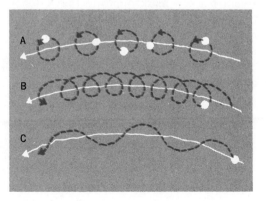

Figure 9-14

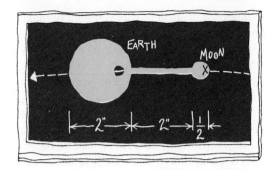

Figure 9-15 Dimensions and alignment of the earth-moon model.

Show Figure 9-14. Remind everyone that the whole earth-moon system is in orbit around the sun while the moon goes around earth each month. The long arc in A, B, and C represents part of the system's orbit. (For our purposes we can consider this to be the earth's path around the sun.) Develop the question. Since the earth is moving, which of these three patterns would most nearly show the moon's path if it could be observed from "above" the sun?

suggest hypotheses

Encourage conjecture and supporting reasons. Suggest that the cutout model can be used to find out. Draw a large arc on the chalkboard, about six feet long. Mark off each foot with ruler and chalk. Align the model on the drawn arc, as far to the right as possible. In what phase is the moon? (First quarter.) Now move the model a foot to the left along the arc and turn the moon counterclockwise to a full moon position. Again place a mark opposite the X location. Move the model another foot, turn the moon to the last quarter position, and again mark opposite the X.

After using the entire length of the arc, and giving the moon a quarter turn for each

foot travelled, have someone draw a line connecting the several marks. A gentle S-shaped curve will appear. Be sure to remind the class that the scale is incorrect and so gives an exaggerated picture, although the principle is correct. Perhaps you can show an opaque projection of Figure 9-16 to help them see a more accurate representation.

The Solar System. The earth is one of nine planets revolving around a medium-sized star, the sun. How did the solar system begin? Scientists are not sure. One prominent theory holds that the sun and planets may have been condensed by gravitation from an enormous swirling cloud of dust and gas.

Mercury is the smallest and closest planet to the sun. It rotates very slowly, only two-thirds around to one complete revolution around the sun. Its small mass results in a surface gravity too weak to retain an atmosphere. As might be expected, Mercury's surface has the largest temperature differences of the planets. (Figure 9-17.)

Venus, next in order from the sun, is enveloped in a dense cloud cover. This reflects sunlight so well that, except for the sun and moon, Venus is the brightest object in the sky. The cloud temperature averages about 130°F, but its surface temperature is believed to be much higher.

Beyond the earth is *Mars*. Its reddish appearance may be the result of "rusted" iron compounds on its surface. Of all the planets, Mars most nearly resembles our earth. However, its thin atmosphere, temperature range, and present lack of oxygen make it an unlikely home for any form of life but the most primitive plants. Two tiny natural

Figure 9-16 The earth and moon orbits drawn to scale.

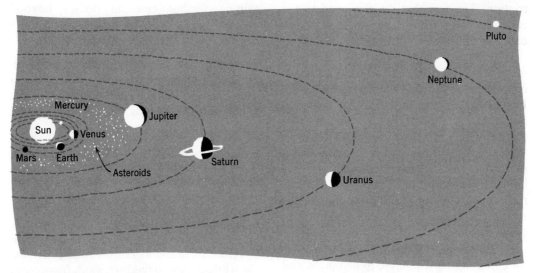

Figure 9-17   The solar system.

satellites (moons) revolve speedily around Mars.

Between Mars and the next planet, *Jupiter,* is an unusually large gap containing several thousand irregularly shaped chunks of stone and metal called *asteroids* (tiny "stars"). Some astronomers think these may be the remnants of a planet which came too close to Jupiter and disintegrated under its powerful gravitational attraction. Ranging from about 1 to 500 miles in size, they are invisible to the unaided eye.

Of the *outer planets,* as the five beyond Mars are called, *Jupiter* and *Saturn* are by far the largest. Saturn is conspicuous because of its rings, believed to be composed of ice particles. *Uranus* and *Neptune* are nearly the same size, about three and one-half times the earth's diameter. *Pluto* is so small and distant it was not discovered until 1930. Its orbital plane is tilted sharply from those of the other planets. All the outer planets but Pluto have natural satellites. All are so distant from the sun, it is probable that at least some of their atmospheric gases are frozen.

Ancient skywatchers were so puzzled by the changing appearance of the planets they named them "wanderers." We realize now that their differences in brightness and position from time to time occur because they revolve at different distances and speeds in their orbits around the sun. But long ago, all such objects were thought to be stars, which ordinarily seem fixed in space. A forthcoming activity will help pupils learn why the movements of planets were misunderstood.

Comets are huge, unstable bodies apparently composed of gases, dust, ice, and small rocks. A few are temporarily visible as they occasionally sweep near the sun and far out again in immense, highly elliptical orbits. They possess so little mass that the pressure of sunlight causes a long streamer or "tail" to flow from the comet head, always in a direction opposite the sun. Like the planets, comets probably originated from the gases and dust of the solar nebula over 4 billion years ago.

Most children have seen "shooting stars." These are fragments of rock and metal, probably from broken-up asteroids and parts of comets, that hurtle through interplanetary space at high speeds. Although most are no larger than a grain of sand, some weigh tons. It is estimated that billions of such *meteors,* as they are termed, daily plunge into the earth's atmosphere and burn into extinction from the heat of air

413

friction. The few that do penetrate to the earth in solid form other than dust are called *meteorites*.

Is there any danger of being struck by a meteorite? Not much. The only recorded instance of anyone ever being injured in the United States was in 1954. An Alabama housewife was grazed by a 10-pound meteorite which crashed through her roof. While records are scanty, it is unlikely that more than one or two additional cases of injury have occurred in recent world history. Since 1900 only two large meteorites and a small one have been witnessed to strike the earth.

By far the most difficult ideas in this unit for children to grasp relate to distances and sizes of objects in space. It will be helpful to their thinking if a large section of the playground can be used in some of the scaled-distance activities that follow. However, even a very large area will be inadequate to demonstrate both distance and size on the same scale. At 1 inch to 8000 miles, for example, Pluto would need to be located about 7 miles away!

Distances are even more astounding as we move beyond the solar system. Now the mile is too tiny a unit of measurement for practical purposes. You will need to acquaint pupils with the *light-year,* defined as the distance a beam of light travels in one year. At 186,000 miles per second, this is almost 6 trillion (6,000,000,000,000) miles.

It has been said that none but the astronomer-philosopher can ever achieve a "sense of the infinite." Yet even a child can begin to grasp some notion of relative perspectives in the universe. Our earth is a huge planet when compared to the limited area we can personally occupy and closely experience. But it is a smallish member of a large solar family. The gigantic source of its energy, the sun, is only one of billions of stars that make up our Milky Way Galaxy. Millions of galaxies are strewn throughout space at incomprehensible distances, con-taining further celestial bodies beyond calculation.

Generalization III: The solar system contains nine planets which revolve at different distances around the sun; the solar system is only a tiny part of a vast universe

Try this introduction:

Some scientists believe that billions of years ago, there was no earth or sun as we know them. Instead, there may have been a huge, slowly rotating cloud of dust and gas in space. Slowly, gravitational attraction caused these materials to come closer together. The speed of rotation increased more and more. As rotating dust and gas particles rubbed together, much friction and heat developed. A large mass in the center became so hot it formed into the sun. Gradually, most of the remaining materials spread out as a result of their spinning and began revolving around the sun. They slowly shrank and cooled into nine separate masses, which became *planets.* Today, we call these planets and the sun the *solar system.*

Discuss briefly with the children how planets differ from stars. Identify the earth as a planet. Show pictures of the planets, if available. Draw a small sun on the chalkboard with nine surrounding orbits at varying distances. Don't be concerned with scale now. Put a small dot on each orbit in a line. Write nearby the planet names in order from the sun: *Mercury, Venus, Earth, Mars, Jupiter, Saturn, Uranus, Neptune,* and *Pluto.*

Contributing Idea A. The planets' different distances from the sun affect their revolution periods and the amounts of solar heat they receive.

Use the first two activities to demonstrate why the planets we see sometimes seem bright and relatively near, while at other times they seem dim and much farther away.

1. *Materials:* 20-foot string tied to chalk; suitable playground location.

Write *planetes* on the chalkboard. Identify it as an ancient Greek word which means "wanderer." From it the term planet was derived. Explain that thousands of years ago, no one knew about planets. People thought all such objects were stars. But these so-called "stars" were a puzzle. They never seemed to stay in place, as did the other stars. Sometimes they would appear dim and far away. At other times they would seem near and bright. In short, these objects seemed to "wander" through the sky.

Call attention to your chalkboard model. Under what conditions would some of these planets look nearer and farther away *suggest* from the earth? Invite speculation. (If the *hypotheses* planets moved at different speeds some might get ahead or fall behind others. If they all moved at the same speed, each inside planet would move ahead of its outside partner.)

Keep erasing and changing positions of various planets in their orbits. Have children come up to the chalkboard and measure with string any changing distances from the earth that result. Suggest a larger demonstration with children taking the roles of planets.

2. Take the class to a suitable location on the playground. It will save time if someone previously has drawn with chalk and 20-foot string nine circles of different sizes to represent planetary orbits. Ignore proper scale for now. Orbits about 1 foot to 2 feet apart should be satisfactory. Let the nine planet-children line up in a row. First test to see what happens to their distance from the planet earth child if they move counterclockwise at different speeds in orbit. After a few seconds, have pupils stop and notice the planets' changing distances from the earth.

Now get them to try moving around in orbit at the same speed. Each outer planet will fall behind its immediate inner planet. Again have pupils stop, notice, and measure the planets' changing distances from the

planet earth. Mention that the three farthest planets are too distant from earth to be visible with the unaided eye; therefore people of ancient times did not see all the planets.

3. *Materials:* lamp with unshielded light bulb; large chalkboard graph grid (See Figure 9-18. Leave off all references and recordings for now.); graph paper for pupils (optional).

In this activity pupils learn that the varying distances of planets from the sun affect planetary temperatures. They also find that temperature data placed on a graph can help them to make some accurate inferences.

Point out that Mercury—the planet closest to the sun in our solar system—may have a temperature of about 770°F. Pluto, the outermost planet, has a temperature estimated at −400°F. Why the difference? Develop discussion. Bring out it is prob-

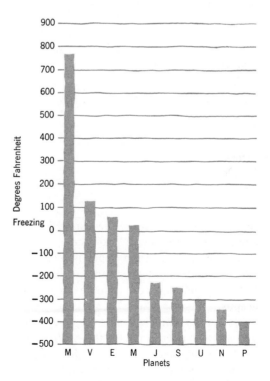

Figure 9-18

415

make inferences

able that planets receive most of their heat energy from the sun. So, it is probable that the farther away from the sun a planet is, the colder it is.

Turn on the lamp. Have several children position their hands at various distances from it. Does it feel warmer when one's hand is close to the lamp? Colder when farther away? So far it seems as though distance would make a difference in the heat received. But this is only a model (analogy). They will need to check further. Ask someone to look up the estimated planet temperatures in an encyclopedia, or reveal them yourself. (See following.)

Write the temperature figures on a long sheet of butcher paper in chart form. Leave enough room for such other future data as distance from the sun, diameter, gravity, speed of revolution, number of satellites, and so on. In this way the pupils will gradually develop an awareness of what our planetary system is like. It will also save the trouble of repeatedly writing planet names.

(Add other columns as needed.)

Planet	Temperature (°F)
Mercury	770
Venus	130
Earth	55
Mars	30
Jupiter	−225
Saturn	−250
Uranus	−300
Neptune	−350
Pluto	−400

reason quantitatively

Suggest that these figures be graphed. How can the chalkboard grid be organized? Help where needed. If graph paper is available, delay a chalkboard recording at this time. First let the children prepare their own graphs. Assist where necessary. After pupils have completed this task, have them prepare a master graph on the chalkboard. They should check their individual graphs for accuracy with the master graph.

Call attention to Mercury's temperature. Are there reasons other than its closeness to the sun that might account for its very high temperature? Have children speculate, then read to find out. Develop that Mercury turns only two-thirds around on its axis during a full orbit around the sun. This means any portion facing the sun gets very hot before it can rotate away from the fierce heat. Reveal that Mercury's dark side may have a temperature lower than −400°F.

Point to the chalkboard graph. All the other figures are average temperatures. Why don't we record an average temperature for Mercury? (It would be misleading.) Cite the case of two persons, one with a million dollars and one with nothing. Wouldn't it be misleading to say that their average wealth is a half-million dollars? Have the children find Mercury's "average" temperature by counting the number of *intervals* on the graph between −400°F and 770°F and dividing by 2. (Averaging negative and positive numbers may be too tricky for most pupils.) Let them estimate the correct figure. (About 185°F.)

reason quantitative

Ask the children if they notice anything else that seems unusual on the graph. Bring out that temperatures of the next three planets are relatively close together. But beginning with Jupiter, there is a radical change. Help them realize that there is probably a huge increase in distance from the sun at this point. Suggest that they find the average planetary distances by reading or otherwise consulting authority. Write their findings on the chart. Starting with Mercury, the distances (in millions of miles) are approximately: 36; 67; 93; 142; 484; 887; 1787; 2792; and 3672.

make inferences

reason quantitative

Guide the class to understand that, at 484 million miles, Jupiter is more than three times as far away from the sun as Mars. Since there is such a great difference in distances at this point, the first four planets are called the "inner planets." Those beyond are the "outer planets."

Contributing Idea B. Relative sizes and distances of the planets are difficult to draw to the same scale.

In the following sequence, pupils first construct a model of the solar system with planet diameters in scale, then planet distances. They find that a model showing both size and distance is impossible for a classroom, because of its huge dimensions. The last activity, done on the playground, enables them to see the largest planet in correct perspective.

1. *Materials:* drawing compass; four and one-half feet of string tied to a pencil; two sheets of butcher paper 5 feet long; cellophane tape; scissors; black crayon; white tagboard sheet; previously begun solar system chart; nine sheets construction paper of assorted colors (Tape these along the chalkboard in a row.); several sponges and yellow tempera paint.

Remind the children how misleading their earlier models of the sun, earth, and moon were in size and distance until they were measured to scale. Have them look on the chart at Mercury's distance from the sun (36 million miles), and Pluto's (3672 million miles). Roughly, how many times *reason* farther away is Pluto than Mercury? (More *antitatively* than 100 times.) Urge them to recall their playground model of planets. They should realize it was grossly out-of-scale. Suggest they make an appropriately scaled model now for a bulletin board.

As before, it will be convenient to start with diameters. Let some pupils look up planet diameters in trade books or other references. Add these to the chart, rounding off figures to the whole number. In miles, they should be as follows: Mercury 3000; Venus 7600; Earth 8000; Mars 4200; Jupiter 87,000; Saturn 72,000; Uranus 32,000; Neptune 27,000; and Pluto 3600 (uncertain). Also have them include the *reason* sun (864,000 miles). Suggest that a scale be *antitatively* selected for diameters alone, appropriate for a bulletin board. 8000 miles to 1 inch should work out well.

Show how to estimate diameter sizes from a scale. Draw a line 11 inches long on the chalkboard and carefully mark off each 1-inch interval. Number each interval on top from 0 to 11. Immediately below each number place the appropriate multiple of eight. (See Figure 9-19.) Place a small mark midway between each interval; these will help in close estimations. Label as shown.

Ask children to estimate the diameter *reason* of Mercury on the scale. It is very tiny; *quantitatively* less than the first half-inch mark on the scale. Take the drawing compass and measure half of this for the radius. Draw the diameter with the compass on the first sheet of construction paper. It is difficult with such a small radius. Continue with the others, each drawn on a separate paper. The largest model will be Jupiter, with a diameter of almost 11 inches, drawn from a radius of nearly five and one-half inches. Distribute scissors and let some pupils cut out these nine models. Someone can cut out a white ring for Saturn. Make sure planet names are labeled on the back to prevent confusion in later handling. (If enough compasses, paper, and scissors can be provided, it would be ideal for each child to make his own models.)

Have a pupil tape the two butcher-paper sheets together. At this scale the sun will be slightly more than 9 feet across. With a four and one-half foot string as the radius, draw a quarter of the sun. Use the upper left-hand corner of the paper as the center of an interrupted circle, as in Figure 9-20. This quarter sun should be cut out and painted with sponges dipped in yellow tempera paint. Other pupils may prepare appropriate labels from white tagboard and printed with black crayon. For the present, leave off any reference to scale in distance, as this will be more understandable after the next activity. Mount materials in bulle

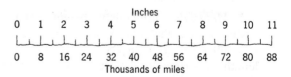

Figure 9-19

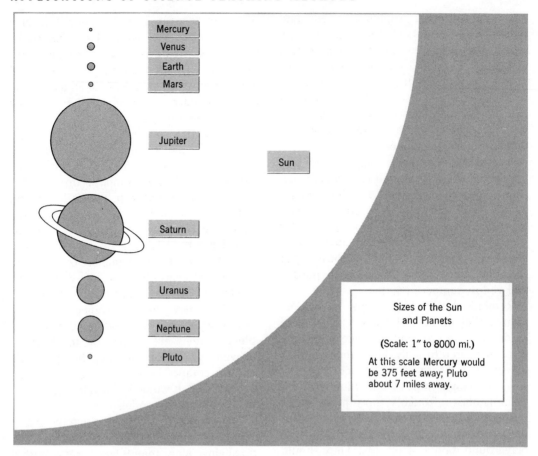

Figure 9-20

tin board form. The completed scaled diameters should be about the same as these:

Sun	9 feet, 3 inches
Mercury	³⁄₈ inch
Venus	1 inch
Earth	1 inch
Mars	½ inch
Jupiter	11 inches
Saturn	9½ inches
Uranus	4 inches
Neptune	4¼ inches
Pluto	½ inch

2. *Materials:* previously begun solar system chart; chalkboard scale of 1 inch to 8000 miles used in activity 1; 50-foot length of string; yardstick; outdoor location at least 50 yards long, preferably 100 yards long (football-field length).

Begin this activity in the classroom: "We didn't have much trouble showing planet diameters on our bulletin board with a scale of 1 inch to 8000 miles. Could we use the same scale to show planet distances from the sun?" (Some should suspect it is impossible.)

Invite discussion. Direct attention to the solar system data chart. How far away from the sun is Mercury? (36 million miles.) How far would that be on the 1 inch to 8000 miles scale? Help the children calculate: 36,000,000 ÷ 8000 = 4500 inches; 4500 inches ÷ 12 inches = 375 feet. Mention that Pluto, at over three and one-half *billion* miles, would be about 7 miles away from the sun with this scale.

Lead toward the adoption of a more

reason quantitativ

usable scale, such as 1 inch to 1 million miles. Children can calculate scale distances by dividing each of the regular distances by 12 inches. Results should be as follows:

Planet	Distances (million miles)	Scale Distances (1 inch to 1 million miles)
Mercury	36	3 ft.
Venus	67	5 ft. 7 in.
Earth	93	7 ft. 9 in.
Mars	142	11 ft. 10 in.
Jupiter	484	40 ft. 4 in.
Saturn	887	73 ft. 11 in.
Uranus	1787	148 ft. 11 in.
Neptune	2792	232 ft. 8 in.
Pluto	3672	306 ft.

Invite a committee to mark off appropriate distances on the playground with chalk or pebbles. A 50-foot string and yardstick will be useful for measuring. This can be done at recess or noon hour, if preferred. If the playground is small, omit several outer planets.

3. *Materials:* rulers for each child; ten small tagboard signs, each bearing the name of a different planet, with one sign for the sun; 25-cent piece; straight pin.

Before going out for a playground demonstration, ask pupils to estimate the sun's diameter on this scale. Let each draw a 1-inch line on paper. This stands for 1 million miles. The sun is 864,000 miles across. How far is that on the line? (About four-fifths.) Hold up the coin quarter. The sun is about this size.

reason quantitatively

How large is Jupiter—the largest planet—on this scale? (Less than one-tenths inch.) Hold up a pin. It is about the size of a pinhead. Help children realize that the small planets would be practically invisible to the unaided eye.

With this perspective established, take the class out to the playground. Place children with signs at the ten appropriate locations. Have the sun child hold up a quarter and the Jupiter child (who is over forty feet away) hold up a pinhead. Many children will never forget this sight. The solar system is tremendously large.

Contributing Idea C. The solar system is a tiny part of a vast universe.

Materials: show, when mentioned below, an opaque projection of Figure 9-21.

Discuss the enormous planetary dis-

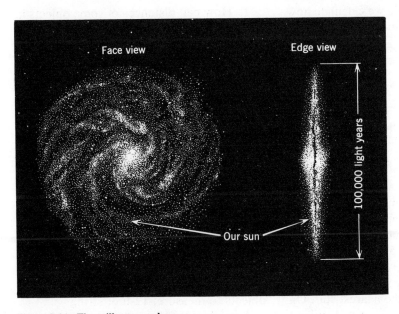

Figure 9-21 The milky way galaxy.

tances represented by the playground scale model. Have the children estimate the amount of time required for a space vehicle traveling at 25,000 miles per hour—that is, 600,000 miles a day—to reach Pluto. (About 17 years.) If they could continue on beyond Pluto, what would they find? (Some children will mention the stars.)

How much longer would it take to reach the nearest star other than the sun? Discuss briefly. Note the variety of specula- *suggest* tion which probably ensues. Some thought- *hypotheses* ful children will want to know how far away the star is before they give a response. Write *Proxima Centauri—four and one-half light-years away* on the chalkboard. Explain that this is the name of the nearest star and its approximate distance from earth.

state Let the class try to define a light-year. *problems* See if the children can reason why the distance is not given in miles. (Distances to the stars are so great, the mile is too small a unit of measurement.) Is it easier to say, "I took a trip of 6,336,000 inches," or, "I went 100 miles"?

Lead to further understanding of what a light-year means. Light travels at about *186,000 miles per second.* Let this sink in for a moment. How could we calculate how far it goes in a year? Guide the children's thinking:

60 seconds = 1 minute
60 minutes = 1 hour
24 hours = 1 day
365 days = 1 year

reason To find out how many miles there are in a *quantitatively* light-year we multiply 186,000 miles × 60 seconds × 60 minutes × 24 hours × 365 days. (This calculation should take about 10 minutes. If there is time, it will be worth it. Many pupils will appreciate more fully the enormity of this measurement unit.) The final product is 5,865,696,000,000 miles per year, or almost *6 trillion miles.*

Help them realize that 27 trillion miles of space separate us from the nearest star. On the playground scale of 1 inch to 1 million miles, *Proxima Centauri* would be over 400 miles away. Have someone locate on a map a landmark at this distance. Traveling at 25,000 miles per hour, it would take about 10,000 years to reach this star. Only much greater velocities would permit man ever to *make* travel to the nearest star. *inferences*

Many pupils will have seen the band of whitish, hazy light in the night sky called the Milky Way. Develop that it is composed of millions of stars in a huge cluster, or *galaxy,* within which the sun and its planets are located.

We can only see part of the Milky Way at any time as we are inside it and the earth is not transparent. Show an opaque projection or sketch of Figure 9-21. Point out that this great galactic cluster is 120,000 light-years long and about 12,000 light-years thick in the center portion. Show the estimated position of the solar system.

Emphasize that there are millions of other galaxies, perhaps more, scattered throughout space. The universe is vast indeed.

EXTENDING ACTIVITIES

1. How can distances of some objects in outer space be measured? Two related extending activities can help your pupils understand that the distances of faraway, inaccessible objects on earth or in space may be measured indirectly by triangulation. The first activity involves a sighting instrument (astrolabe) pupils can use to calculate the heights of buildings and the parallel of latitude of their location. Each pair of children will need a soda straw; 12-inch thread with small weight attached; protractor (an inexpensive cardboard type will do; or use a machine copier to duplicate the protractor in Plate 1a, see following—copies can be glued to thin cardboard and cut out); cellophane tape; graph paper; school flagpole or other tall objects to measure; 12-foot string.

Assemble the instrument as in Figure

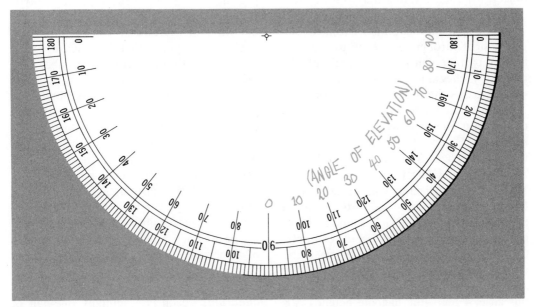

Plate 1a

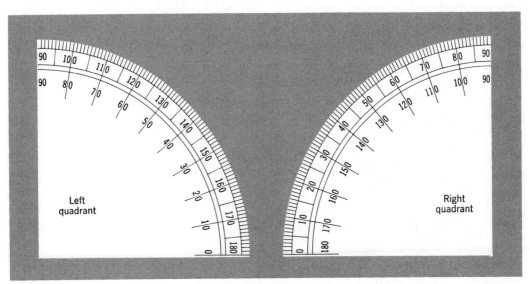

Plate 1b

9-22. Give these directions. (A chalk-board sketch will aid understanding.) To find the height of the flagpole or other tall object, use the 12-foot string to measure a distance of 24 feet from the object's base. This is called the base line. From its end point, sight through the straw to the pole top. A partner can note the angle of elevation by checking where the plumb bob string crosses the protractor markings.

The next step is to make a scale drawing of the base line and angle of elevation, as shown in Figure 9-23. On graph paper, using one space for each foot, mark off a base line of 24 feet from the left margin. Mark off the vertical axis in the same way. Use a protractor (right side up this time) to measure the angle of sight found by looking through the soda straw. In the example, this is 45°. Extend the line until it meets the vertical axis with adjacent numerals. By adding the eye height of the observer—in this case, 4 feet—the flagpole height is 28 feet.

If many sightings are taken of a single object, you might want to take the opportunity to discuss the variations in measurement that are sure to arise. Make a histogram (Figure 9-24) to aid discussion. Analyze it for the range of differences, most probable correct height, and so on. Why is there so much variation? Some will have forgotten to add eye height. Perhaps a very "stretchy" baseline string was used. The protractor may be taped on poorly. Maybe the astrolabe was not held steadily. Bring out ways measurements can be improved.

Suggest to pupils that they measure their parallel of latitude with the astrolabe. This may be done at night by measuring the angle of sight to the north star. Many pupils and parents know how to locate the north star by drawing an imaginary line through the "pointer" stars in the bowl of the Big Dipper. Next day, results can be compared, and then checked by looking at a globe.

2. Inform the class that a similar method of measurement can be used to find the *distances* of inaccessible objects on earth and in space. Each pupil pair will need a piece of chipboard, 28 by 12 inches; four straight pins; ruler; graph paper; two protractors or substitutes. (For substitutes, use the two *quadrants*—each is essentially one-half of a protractor—found in Plate 1b. As before, a machine copier can be used to duplicate this material.)

This distance finder may be assembled as in Figure 9-25.

Place an object on the chalkboard tray in front of the classroom. Have the children use their distance finders from various

suggest hypotheses

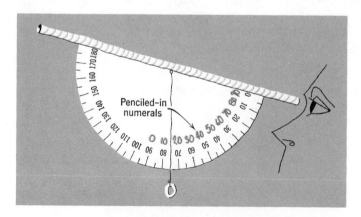

Figure 9-22 A soda straw astrolabe. Notice the penciled-in numerals above the regular markings. Since the protractor is being used upside down, the degree recordings are reversed. The present reading is 14 degrees. (The protractor in Plate 1a includes these extra markings.)

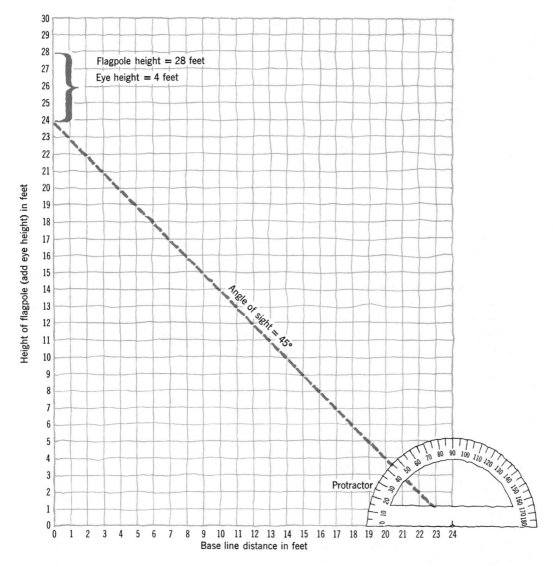

Figure 9-23

places in the room. A sighting is taken from each quadrant by looking over the first (vertex) pinhead to the object and then placing the second pin where it lines up with the object and vertex pin. The second pin should be placed close to the quadrant arc, so the angle of sight may be read accurately. Be sure the distance finder is not moved or jarred until both angles are measured.

After finding the two angles that converge into the object, pupils should make a

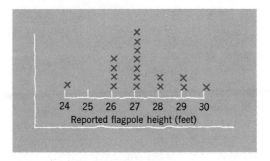

Figure 9-24 A histogram.

423

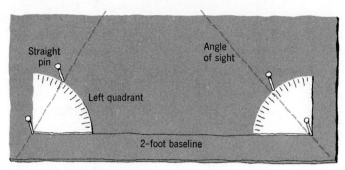

Figure 9-25 Distance finder.

scale drawing to find its distance. As before, a regular protractor is needed to draw the angles. A convenient scale is one inch to two feet. In Figure 9-26, the object was found to be seven and one-half feet away. Have pupils also measure the distance to the object directly, and then compare their measurements.

As the children try to measure objects from farther distances, they will find the measuring device becomes less accurate. A longer base line is needed. For measuring distances to objects outside of class, base lines of ten to fifty feet may be made from strings. Sightings are made as before, but pupils should make sure the chipboard is aligned exactly on the base line at each end before a sighting is made.

make inferences

Explain to the class that, in a similar way, distances to the moon and most planets can be measured fairly accurately. However, the base line used must be huge. For example, when measuring the moon's distance, the diameter of the earth itself may serve, with two astronomers at opposite points on the equator taking a sight at the same time. For planets, an even longer base line may be used, such as the distance from opposite points of the earth's orbit around the sun.

3. Is it possible for other planets in the solar system to support human and plant life without special protection? Develop the general requirements for most living things as we know them — water, air, reasonable temperature range, an environment relatively free of hazards, and so on. Have

small committees investigate individual planets for data. Emphasize that only *data,* not conclusions, are wanted. The class will weigh the evidence as presented in each case, and try to draw reasonable conclusions. After the class has done so, let each committee reveal conclusions, if any, of qualified astronomers.

make inferences

4. Some children will be interested in learning how astronomers are able to detect temperatures of objects in space. One method is to determine the frequency of radio waves received from these bodies. All objects with some heat energy give off radio waves. The frequency of vibrations increases with increased heat.

Another way to find temperatures is by use of a *thermocouple.* Two wires of different metals are twisted to form a junction. The thermocouple is secured to a telescope which focuses the light (and so some heat) from a distant object onto the junction. The heat causes a very weak flow of electricity in the wires, which is recorded by an attached, sensitive galvanometer.

5. Get several children to report on such other objects in the solar system as asteroids, comets, and meteors. If possible, exhibit pictures of meteorites found in museums, and Meteor Crater in Arizona. Perhaps a study trip can be taken to a nearby museum which houses actual specimens of meteorites.

6. Secure several simplified sky charts that contain directions for locating prominent planets at various times of the year.

These are found in many children's trade books, and in such magazines as *Science News* and *Natural History*. (See bibliography.) Point out for pupils approximate locations in the sky and star clues to watch for at a specified time in the evening. Encourage interested, able pupils to learn and report some techniques of "skywatching."

Gravity and the Laws of Motion. It is a good idea when teaching astronomy units to avoid getting involved in the technology of satellites and space vehicles. While this is where the "glamour" is, space technology is intricate and continually changing. It is better for lasting understanding to focus on some principles which undergird technological innovation. The basic scientific laws that govern motions of natural and artificial satellites, planets, and rockets are the same.

This does not mean we should avoid any references to rocket design, propulsion systems, and so on. The motivation and interests of children are broad and should be recognized. And, as suggested in an earlier chapter, the products of technology may furnish a perfect setting through which we can teach principles. It merely suggests where to place the emphasis.

Nobody actually knows what caused the planets to begin moving initially, but the reason they keep moving is readily understandable. There is virtually nothing in space to stop them. But why do they circle the sun? We have already introduced Newton's law of gravitation. Equally important to our understanding is Newton's law of *inertia.* Briefly stated, *any object at rest or in motion remains at rest or continues in motion in a straight line unless acted upon by some outside force.*

Anyone who has ever tried to push a heavy, stalled automobile knows how difficult it is to move a heavy body at rest. It possesses a great deal of inertia. Anyone who has ever tried to stop a heavy, rolling automobile by pushing against it knows how difficult this is. A body in motion possesses the inertia of motion (momentum). The more momentum it possesses, the more difficult it is to stop it.

Figure 9-27 indicates how the laws of gravitation and inertia combine to keep objects in orbit. Although a natural satellite, the moon, is shown in this case, the same factors operate with all bodies that orbit other bodies in space.

If it were unaffected by our earth's powerful gravitational force, the moon would follow a straight path owing to its inertial momentum. Since it is affected, however, the moon follows a path which is a result of each factor countering the other.

A common example of this countering effect occurs when a ball rolls swiftly off a table. Instead of falling straight down, the ball's inertia of momentum keeps it going nearly sideways for an instant until gravity

Object

0   ½   1   1½   2
Baseline (feet)
Scale 1":2'

Figure 9-26

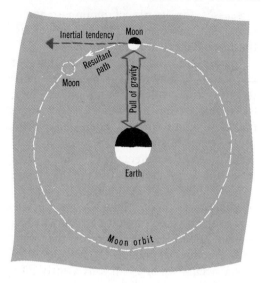

Figure 9-27

satellite, they have no sensation of weight. This is because the pull of gravity is balanced exactly by the counteracting inertia of motion. This *weightless,* or *zero gravity,* condition we sometimes experience on earth for an instant when an elevator starts rapidly downward, or an automobile goes too fast over the crown of a steep hill.

In one science lesson not long ago, a bright child asked his teacher a remarkably astute question: "If we would be weightless in an orbiting satellite, why wouldn't we be weightless on the moon?" The teacher had him reconsider the law of gravitation, especially the part that says ". . . this attraction depends upon the *mass* of each object and the distance between them."

Since the moon has a much smaller mass than the earth its surface gravity is only about one-sixth of the earth's. A 180-pound astronaut weighs a mere 30 pounds. But the moon's mass is almost infinitely greater than that of a space vehicle. The tiny mass comprising a space vehicle has practically no gravity at all.

Since prolonged periods of weightlessness seem unsatisfactory for astronauts, attempts are being made to design space vehicles that create a gravitylike condition. This may be done by rotating the vehicle at a carefully calculated speed. The astronauts' inertia gives them a feeling of gravity as they are slightly pressed against the spaceship's interior. An analogy is the small ball that remains stationary on the rim of a roulette wheel until it stops turning.

Through the ages, men have always yearned to explore what mysteries lie beyond the earth. But until recently, our technology has not been as advanced as our ambitions. Early devices and inventions designed for space travel included such things as hitching a flock of geese to a wicker basket, hand-cranking propellers attached to hot-air balloons, and festooning a box with crude rockets containing gun-

forces it to the floor. The resultant path of its fall is an arc.

In our illustration, both factors are equally powerful. If this were not so, the moon would either be drawn into the earth or pull away from it. This is what happens to an artificial satellite that moves too slow or too fast. Clearly, getting a space satellite into a sustained orbit is tricky. Its velocity and angle of entry into orbit must be calculated closely. Since perfection in these matters is virtually impossible, most orbits are markedly elongated (elliptical).

Because gravity weakens with distance, orbital speeds of one body must be slower as distance from the second body increases in order to maintain balance of the two forces. At 22,300 miles from the earth, for example, the proper orbital speed for a satellite results in one complete orbit each 24 hours. Since this is the period of the earth's rotation, a satellite positioned above the Equator will always stay in the same relative position. With several of these satellites, properly spaced, television and radio signals can be relayed to anyplace on earth.

When astronauts circle the earth in a

powder. Occasionally, such contraptions were personally occupied by their daring inventors, some of whom did depart from this earth, although not in the manner intended.

Because space is a near vacuum, no engine that draws oxygen from the air in burning its fuel can serve in a propulsion system. Instead, rocket engines are used; these carry their own oxygen supply. Rockets work because *for every action there is an equal and opposite reaction*. (Another law of motion by Newton.) When a rocket pushes hot gases out of its combustion chamber (action), the gases push back (reaction) and thrust the rocket ahead. Additional applications are furnished in the activities that follow.

Most rockets today are composed of multiple stages fastened together in a tandem arrangement. The bottom rocket propels all the stages to a point where its fuel is expended, and then drops off. The remaining stages reach ever higher velocities as the process continues, lightening the load each time. The speed of the last stage represents the accumulated sum of speeds attained by each stage. Perhaps future rockets will be efficient enough to reduce or eliminate the necessity for present cumbersome staging techniques.

Although modern rocketry provides the means to reach beyond the earth, travel for the astronaut poses some difficult problems. As the rocket blasts off in a terrifying surge of power, the rapid acceleration pins his body to the seat with crushing force. Once beyond the earth's atmosphere, he needs oxygen and sufficient pressure to keep his body functioning normally. He needs some means of temperature control. Without air conduction of heat energy the side of the spaceship facing the sun grows red hot, the dark side freezing cold. Because of his weightless condition, the astronaut may eat and drink from plastic squeeze bottles. To prevent the space capsule from being burned to a cinder as it enters the atmo-

sphere, he may slow its speed with reversed rocket power and a special parachute. These indicate only some of the problems of space travel.

With so many difficulties, why does man go into space? While his curiosity is one answer, of course, there are many advantages to be gained from continued space efforts. Some additional benefits are improved communications, long-range weather forecasting and possible weather control, astronomers' observation posts beyond the annoying interference of the earth's atmosphere, possible solutions to how the universe was formed, improved mapping and navigation, and more.

Eventually there will be the most important reason of all. It is believed that someday, perhaps two to five billion years from now, the sun's nuclear fuel will be largely depleted. The sun may gradually expand and engulf the planets, or explode in one final cataclysm of fury. Perhaps by then our descendants, whoever they may be, will have found a comfortable haven among the stars.

Generalization IV: Gravity and the laws of motion affect the movements of planets, satellites, and rockets

Contributing Idea A. Gravitational attraction and inertia of motion cause planets and satellites to orbit in space.

1. *Materials:* drinking glass; child's toy marble; piece of rough cloth about a yard long; chalkboard eraser fastened to a 32-inch string, threaded through a spool, and fastened at the opposite end with two additional chalkboard erasers. (We shall call this contrivance the "orbiting eraser model." See Figure 9-28.) For this model to work well, friction between the spool and string must be reduced. Sand smooth the top outside edge of the spool. Use a candle to wax the string, and wax the spool's top outside edge; also around the spool hole.

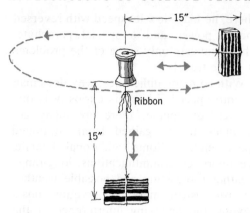

Figure 9-28

suggest
hypotheses
What keeps the nine planets revolving about the sun? Why don't they slow down and stop? Why aren't they pulled into the sun by gravitational attraction? Encourage speculation for several moments.

Mention that the following demonstration may help the class understand why the planets do not slow down and stop. Lay a large piece of roughly woven cloth on the floor. Put a toy marble in a drinking glass. Tilt the glass over and move it quickly in a line toward the cloth. Stop the glass suddenly at the cloth edge. The marble will continue through the glass opening and roll for a short distance on the cloth. Repeat this demonstration without the cloth. The marble will go farther, than gradually stop.

Develop the principle shown: *A moving object tends to keep moving unless it is acted upon by another force.* What finally stopped the marble in each case? (*Friction* from the cloth and floor.) Establish that the tendency of a moving object to keep moving is called the *inertia of motion.* Let pupils recall how they slide forward in an automobile when the brakes are suddenly applied. Help them reason that seat belts are used in automobiles to counter this tendency.

Apply this demonstration to a planet in space. It is moving rapidly. The inertia of motion keeps it going because there is virtually nothing to stop it. Outer space is almost completely empty, and so friction is no problem.

2. But why doesn't the sun's powerful gravity pull the planets into the sun? Why doesn't the earth's powerful gravity pull the moon into the earth? Permit some speculation. Ask pupils to observe a demonstration before they form more specific answers.

Taking the orbiting eraser model in hand, hold the single eraser out at one side about 2 or 3 feet from the spool and parallel to the floor. Hold the string at the spool hole to prevent it from slipping through at this time. Release the single eraser. It will swing down, move briefly to and fro, and stop. What prevents it from staying up when released? (Gravity.) What would happen if the eraser were moving around rapidly—if it had the inertia of motion? (It might stay up.)

Start whirling around the eraser slowly overhead. Gradually increase its orbital speed. Slowly the string length beneath the spool will shorten while the horizontal, orbiting length increases. Slacken speed and the reverse occurs.

Bring out that, at first, gravitational force exceeds the force of inertia. Shortly thereafter, this is reversed. Develop that the planets' speeds are fast enough to keep them from falling into the sun. On the other hand, the sun's gravitational attraction is great enough to keep the planets from leaving its effective field. Since the opposing forces are equally powerful, the planets keep circling the sun. Our moon and artificial satellites circle the earth for the same reason.

Make sure pupils understand that the string simulates the pull of gravity in this demonstration. The children should be familiar enough with magnetism to realize interaction can exist between two objects without a visible connection. But they may need to be reminded.

3. *Materials:* orbiting eraser model (With 6 extra chalkboard erasers. Prepare these for easy attachment to the 2 erasers

already suspended by affixing a rubber band and a paper-clip hook to each. Erasers will be added as needed.); small red ribbon or piece of yarn; watch with a second-hand; previously begun solar system data chart; graph paper (optional).

The following activity will teach pupils that planets close to the sun must travel faster than those farther away. If this did not happen, the tremendous gravitational attraction of the sun would pull inner planets out of orbit and engulf them.

Have someone look up the planets' revolution periods around the sun. Add these data to a new column on the chart: Mercury 88 days, Venus 226 days, Earth 1 year (365 days), Mars 688 days, Jupiter 12 years, Saturn 29 years, Uranus 84 years, Neptune 165 years, Pluto 248 years.

Ask pupils why the revolutionary periods of the planets vary so much. Many children will indicate the increasing sizes of orbits. Guide them to reason that the varying periods could also be caused by different orbital speeds, or both factors. Bring out that gravitational force, like magnetism, decreases with distance. Help the class see the significance of this idea: The sun will *make inferences* pull very strongly on such nearby planets as Mercury and Venus, and more weakly on those farther away.

Can anyone see a problem here? (Why *state problems* aren't the inner planets pulled into the sun?) If a clue is needed to elicit a problem statement ask "What would happen if we placed a steel ball close to a powerful magnet?" Encourage conjecture about the stated *suggest hypotheses* problem. A reasonable hypothesis is that the inner planets' orbital speeds must be greater than those of the outer planets. Suggest that the children put this idea to a test with the orbiting eraser model and extra attachable erasers for weights.

Guide where necessary. Pupils might have 4 different weights to simulate increased gravitational attraction—a 2-, 4-, 6-, and 8-eraser weight. A red ribbon attached to the string about an inch below the spool will remind the model operator to maintain the same orbiting string length in all three trials. Help the children to reason why this control is needed: They already know that decreasing orbit size decreases the revolutionary period. They need to measure the effect of increased gravity on orbital *speeds,* while holding orbital size constant. With the ribbon attached, the orbit radius will be only 15 inches or less. If the model operator keeps his arm stiff he will be able to easily whirl the model in front of him, rather than overhead, which is harder.

We will want to know the number of revolutions per second. How will the speed *reason quantitatively* of revolutions be measured? (Count the number of complete revolutions past a given point for 10 seconds; divide by 10; this will give the number of revolutions per second.) Let the children discover for themselves a useful time period. For example, 1 or 2 seconds will be too short for accuracy. In addition, they might find it useful to average several trials, rather than take only one sample. It will be interesting to have each pupil record his own data, as someone calls out, "Start—stop!" for each agreed time interval. Should discrepancies occur, get the group to determine why.

The children should record their data. For example:

No. of weights	Revolutions in 10 seconds	Revolutions per second	
2	15	1.5	*reason quantitatively*
4	19	1.9	
6	24	2.4	
8	27	2.7	

A graph may be made of the data, as in Figure 9-29. Have the children predict, then test for, revolutions with three, five, and seven erasers.

It seems as though increased gravitational attraction does mean an orbiting body must revolve faster to stay in orbit. *make inferences* But this is only an analogy. Do planets behave the same way? Let someone locate and read the average orbital speeds of the planets. They should be stated in miles per

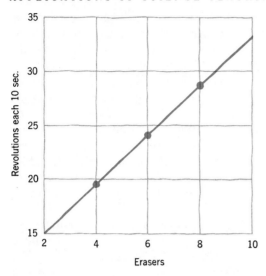

Figure 9-29

second. Record these on the large data chart: Mercury 29.8, Venus 21.8, Earth 18.5, Mars 15.0, Jupiter 8.1, Saturn 6.0, Uranus 4.2, Neptune 3.4, Pluto 2.9. The data appear to agree with our analogy.

make inferences

4. *Materials:* table; rubber ball; picture of an earth satellite (optional); chalkboard sketch of Figure 9-30.

Help pupils understand that the same forces—gravity and inertia—operate on artificial satellites. Roll a ball speedily across a table and let it fall to the floor. Note that it lands a short distance away.

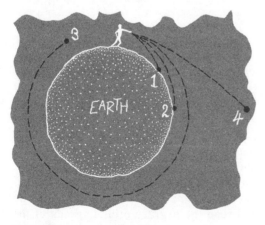

Figure 9-30

Repeat, but now with greater force. The ball will land farther away. Lead children to realize that in each case the ball falls in an arc rather than straight down.

Reveal your sketch of Figure 9-30. Explain that it shows an imaginary child who can throw a ball very, very fast. He throws a ball very swiftly almost parallel to the ground. It travels nearly parallel to the ground briefly through its inertia of motion, but gravity finally pulls it down. He throws a second ball even harder. Its faster speed causes it to remain almost parallel to the ground longer. But gravity forces it down at position 2. The imaginary child now throws a ball at 18,000 miles an hour. It now travels so swiftly that its inertial force is as powerful as the earth's gravitational force. It "falls" continuously in orbit around the earth in a *weightless* condition. Bring out that for this to happen the ball would have to be beyond most of the earth's atmosphere. Otherwise air friction would interfere with its movement.

Have the children recall some of their experiences that simulate briefly a weightless condition. Bring out such common examples as being in an elevator that starts descending a little too quickly, or riding in a car that swiftly rolls over the top of a short, steep hill, and starts downward.

Call attention to position 4 on the chalk sketch. In this case the ball is thrown so swiftly that its inertia of motion is more powerful than the earth's gravitational pull. This permits the ball to escape from orbit. Explain that a space vehicle must travel at least 25,000 miles an hour for this to happen, if it starts from the earth's surface. They should understand from activity 3 that slower escape velocities would be sufficient at increased distances from the earth's surface through lessening gravity.

How are these terrific speeds developed? Draw out that giant rockets are used. How these work they shall consider next.

Contributing Idea B. Rockets operate because for every action, there is an equal and opposite reaction; a rocket's speed may be increased by using stages.

1. *Materials:* roller skates; briefcase containing several books (or several books tied together); 3-foot rope; sausage-shaped balloon; cellophane tape; 20-foot piece of strong thread or smooth string; plastic (to reduce friction) soda straw. (Assemble these last four materials as in Figure 9-31. Thread line through the straw. Secure one end to a high-up wall fixture and tie the other end to a desk leg. The line should be taut and slanted. Blow up the balloon, fold over the end piece, and attach a paper clip to it to prevent air from escaping. Secure the balloon to the straw with several strips of cellophane tape. Leave this apparatus set up and ready for demonstrating how a rocket operates.)

Ask the children how rockets work. After a short discussion, suggest that they observe several demonstrations for additional clarification. Request someone to put on roller skates. Have him stand in front of the classroom with his skates parallel to each other. Give him the loaded briefcase. Direct him to hold it to his chest and throw it to you by pushing both hands forward suddenly and releasing it. (Several children should stand ready to assist him in case he loses balance.) Catch the briefcase, return it, and let him repeat this action. Each time he throws the briefcase forward, he will roll back a few inches on the skates. Draw out what happened. For every *action* (his pushing the briefcase away), there was an opposite *reaction* (his rolling backward). He pushed against the briefcase, and it pushed back at him.

Tie a rope to a chair and have a child sit in it to weigh it down. Let another on skates take hold of the rope and tug it briefly several times. He will move forward each time. Bring out the similarity of this and the preceding demonstration. He pulls backward (action) and moves forward (reaction). He pulls against the rope and the rope pulls back against him.

Draw a chalkboard outline of an inflated

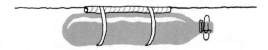

Figure 9-31

balloon with a double-pointed arrow inside along the length. Point to the end through which air will escape. What should happen if the air were suddenly released? The shrinking balloon would push against the escaping air (action), and the escaping air would push back against the balloon interior, making it move (reaction).

Hold the demonstration balloon at the lowest possible point on the line. Remove the paper clip and release the balloon. It should move up the line rapidly, like a miniature rocket. Explain that a rocket works in a similar way. A rocket pushes hot burning gases out of its combustion chamber (action), and the gases push back (reaction), thrusting the rocket ahead.

Let the children read to learn the difference between rocket and jet engines. (Rockets carry their own oxygen supply to support combustion. Jets get their oxygen from the air itself. Since there is no air in space, jets cannot be used for space travel.)

2. *Materials:* playground; piece of chalk; yardstick; 20-foot string; bicycle; rubber ball; chalkboard sketch of Figure 9-32.

Point out on the chalkboard sketch that rockets may be designed to contain three stages. The first and second stages are dropped at certain heights and only the third stage continues in orbit. Or the third stage may release a space vehicle which goes into orbit. Why do scientists bother with three stages? Why not just have one? Arouse speculation. *suggest hypotheses*

Some children should suggest that each preceding stage boosts the speed of the last stage. Does this really happen? Have them think of related, analogous situations in their lives. For example, will a ball thrown from a moving bicycle go faster and farther than a ball thrown from a still position? Invite them to plan a test. (Mark a line on the

Figure 9-32

playground. Have a bike rider pump to a fairly fast speed and coast to the line. As he crosses it, he should throw the ball as hard as he can without losing balance. Measure the distance with a string and yardstick. Have him throw the ball again at the line while sitting on his bike. But this time, the bike is motionless and balanced by a helper. Measure this distance and compare it with the former.)

The additional velocity the thrown ball receives from the bike's momentum should send it far ahead in distance. Help the children understand that such extra distance was due to extra speed. Through a film or follow-up reading and discussion, let them verify their thinking.

Bring out an additional reason why the first two stages of a rocket are discarded. They no longer contain fuel, and so represent dead weight. By discarding these stages the rocket is lighter and thus can go faster. Liken this situation to a runner who must carry someone on his back. He can run faster alone.

EXTENDING ACTIVITIES

1. Present a demonstration of weightlessness. Suspend a book bound with string from a paper clip hooked onto a rubber band. Have a child stand on a chair and hold up this material as high as he can, then let go. Will the rubber band stay stretched as it falls? Have everyone observe closely. (It does not.) Develop that the rubber band-book system was weightless relative to itself as it fell.

2. Explain that a weightless or zero gravity condition may be difficult for astronauts to operate in over long time periods. Can artificial gravity be produced? Ask the children to observe this demonstration and tell how the principle it shows might be used in a space vehicle. Punch a hole in the center of a large cottage-cheese container top. Put this on top of a phonograph turntable and flip on the switch. Place a marble — explain that this is a man — on the rotating container top and move it out to the edge. The slight ridge around the container's edge will prevent the marble from flying off. The marble's inertia will hold it fast against one section of the ridge.

Develop that, in a similar way, a space vehicle may be rotated just fast enough to produce a gravitylike condition.

3. Try this activity to help the children understand how an orbiting satellite must keep a delicate balance between the pull of gravity and its inertial tendency to pull

out of orbit. Have pupils swirl a marble in a smooth bowl. If it is swirled too slowly, it will fall to the bottom. If the marble is swirled too fast, it will fly out of the bowl, into the "outer space" of the classroom.

4. Let the children study some of the conditions and problems which must be overcome for astronauts to survive a trip into space. Include problems of acceleration, air pressure, oxygen supply, temperature, food supply, waste disposal, radiation, and re-entry into the earth's atmosphere.

Seeds and Plants

(Intermediate Emphasis)

UNIT 10

UNIT TEN

Seeds and Plants

(Intermediate Emphasis)

THE OPPORTUNITIES FOR INDIVIDUAL WORK WITH OPEN-ENDED experiments are greater in a unit on plants than in almost any other area of elementary-school science. At the same time, there is more need for planning ahead and keeping track of activities, so that they may be interrelated. Living things take time to grow, and growth rates can seldom be exactly predicted. To take advantage of the numerous things to do in growing plants, both in and out of the schoolroom, this unit should be taught in the spring.

There are many kinds of plants. The simplest forms include bacteria, fungi, and algae. These plants lack roots, stems, and leaves. Mosses have stems and tiny leaflike parts, but are rootless. Ferns and their like resemble the most complex plants, except in reproduction.

Most complex and familiar are those plants that produce seeds, of which there are two basic groups. One group is composed of the *gymnosperms*. These plants are flowerless; they develop seeds which are attached to open scales or cones. Such evergreens as pine, hemlock, spruce, juniper, fir, and redwood are examples. There are about six hundred species. The second and far larger group (about 250,000 species) is composed of the *angiosperms,* or flowering plants. These form their seeds in closed compartments or cases within the flower. In this unit, we shall concentrate on flowering plants.

Credit for chapter opening photograph. **Russ Kinne-Photo Researchers, Inc.**

GENERALIZATIONS

I. Some plants grow from seeds; proper conditions are needed for seed germination.

II. Some plants can be grown from roots, stems, and leaves.

III. To grow well, green plants need water, light, proper temperature, and minerals.

IV. The special ways in which the several parts of a plant work keep the plant alive and growing.

V. Plants respond to gravity, light, water, and touch.

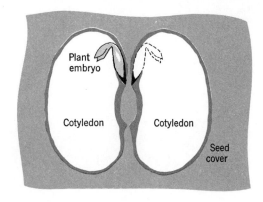

Figure 10-1 Parts of a bean seed.

Seeds and How to Plant Them. Seeds of flowering plants are produced in a central part of the flower called the *ovary*. As the ovary ripens, its seeds become enveloped either by a fruity pulp, a pod, or a shell, depending on the kind of plant. Pears and peaches are fruits whose pulp we eat. Beans, peas, and peanuts are examples of seeds enclosed in pods. When we "shell" string beans, lima beans, peas or peanuts, we are removing these seeds from their pods. Walnuts, pecans, and coconuts have hard outer coverings.

Seeds come in many different shapes, colors, and sizes. But they have three things in common: a protective seed cover, a baby plant (embryo), and a food supply which nourishes the seed as it pushes up through the soil and grows into a young plant. In some plants, such as the bean and sweet pea, the food supply is located in two seed "leaves" or cotyledons (Figure 10-1). In other seeds, such as corn and rice, there is only a single cotyledon.

What happens when a seed grows into a young plant or seedling? For an example, look at Figure 10-2. In A, the seed swells from moisture in the soil. The coat softens and splits. A tiny root and stem start to emerge. In B, the upper part of the stem penetrates the soil surface and lifts the folded cotyledons out of the seed cover. In C, the cotyledons and tiny plant leaves unfold. Roots deepen and spread. In D, roots

become more extensive. The cotyledons are smaller and shriveled. Nearly all the food supply is consumed. The plant begins to make its own food through photosynthesis [1] within its maturing leaves. In a short while, the shriveled cotyledons, then useless, will drop off the growing plant. This growth process, from seed to seedling, is called *germination*. The total time from A to D is about fourteen days in a bean plant.

Many pupils are surprised to find that seeds and recently sprouted seedlings placed in the dark grow as fast or faster for a time than those placed in the light. Light energy seems partly to inhibit rather than stimulate growth in many sprouting seeds until photosynthesis takes place.

Some flowering plants produce thousands of seeds a year. If they all grew into plants, before long there would scarcely be room on earth for anything else. Fortunately, a variety of factors enables only a small percentage of wild seeds to grow. Seeds are destroyed by birds, insects, bacteria, and other organisms. And unless proper conditions of moisture, temperature, and oxygen are present, seeds remain dormant. After several years in a dormant state, all but a few kinds of seeds lose their potential ability to germinate. These few, however, may not lose this ability for hundreds or even thousands of years.

[1] For a review of photosynthesis, see page 451R.

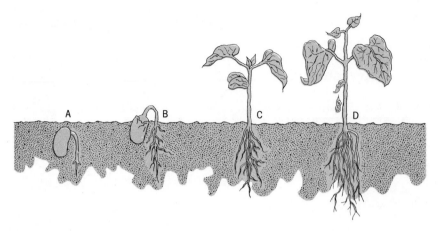

Figure 10-2 From seed to seedling.

Perhaps you have noticed that weeds appear at different times during a growing season. This is because growth conditions of moisture, temperature, and oxygen vary greatly among different kinds of seeds. Of course, this has great survival value. Conditions are never such that all seeds in the soil die at one time.

Two of the most useful seeds for this unit are the lima bean and radish. Always purchase any seeds for growing plants from a nursery or seed store, rather than relying on those purchased for cooking. The latter are less likely to germinate because of certain food processing methods.

Lima beans are excellent to use because they are large, easy to handle, and start germinating within three or four days. One disadvantage is that they are susceptible to fungus growth if overwatered. (Many seeds are sprayed with a fungicide to prevent this. Caution children not to eat seeds intended for planting.) Radish and mustard seeds start sprouting in about two days and grow fast. One minor disadvantage of these seeds is that they are small and therefore a little harder to handle. Germination may be hastened by soaking seeds in water overnight. However, if left in water much longer, some seeds die from lack of oxygen.

Many improvised containers can be used in germinating seeds and growing seedlings

—tinned cans, paper cups, half-pint milk cartons with tops cut off, and cottage cheese cartons. In some experiments water glasses permit better observation. Seeds may be planted next to the glass. If black paper masks the roots from light, they may grow a little faster. (Figure 10-3.)

All containers may be filled with garden soil, sand, sawdust, or vermiculite—an inexpensive insulating material made up of small bits of mica. Only the garden soil will possess minerals needed for healthy growth of plants beyond the seedling stage. For the most part in this unit, however, it will not be necessary to use garden soil as the lessons deal mostly with seedlings. These will still be dependent to a large extent on the plant food within their parent seed. The other foregoing "soil" materials permit more air to circulate around the seed cover and plant roots. They are more porous and hence more difficult to overwater. Plants rooted in these materials may be easily removed, examined, and replanted without serious root damage.

Small holes punched in containers will also aid good drainage. Any water runoff can be caught in a saucer placed below. If holes cannot easily be made, as with a glass jar, be sure to include an inch of gravel in the jar bottom before adding soil. Water only when the soil surface feels slightly dry.

Figure 10-3 Simple, improvised soil containers permit everyone to participate in plant experiments. (Suzanne Szasz.)

Guide pupils to plant radish seeds about one-fourth inch below the soil surface, beans about one-half inch. In all cases, however, follow instructions on the seed package. Since it takes energy to push through the soil, a small seed planted too deeply runs out of food before it reaches the surface. Also, keep the soil loose.

Because there is a lengthy time lag between the beginning and ending of many experiments in this unit, it will be worthwhile to start some seed germination and grow some seedlings well in advance of need. It will also be good practice to make specific recordings as to the purposes of experiments. Once into the unit for a week or so, data should be continually materializing. These are the times when carefully written records can prove useful.

Generalization I: Some plants grow from seeds; proper conditions are needed for seed germination

Contributing Idea A. Seeds need water, air, and the right temperature to sprout.

1. *Materials:* small bag of peanuts; one fresh lima bean pod, if possible; lima beans. (Soak half of the beans overnight to soften the seed coating.)

Use this activity to let the children get acquainted with the parts of some seeds.

Ask the children if they have observed their parents or others start a flower garden or new lawn. Develop that seeds are usually planted in the soil. With proper care for a period of time, the seeds will sprout. What's inside a seed that causes it to grow into a plant? Discuss briefly. Hold up the fresh bean pod. Open it and show the lima beans inside. Explain that some seeds are enclosed in this way.

Distribute one unshelled peanut, and one soaked and one dry lima bean to everyone, if possible. Bring out that the difference in size and softness of the soaked and dry lima beans is because the soaked beans have absorbed much water. Help the children open the soaked beans. A fingernail wedged into the rounded or convex portion will force them open without difficulty. The class will immediately notice the plant embryo. Have children agree on names for the seed's three visible parts, such as, *seed covering, seed halves,* and *baby plant.* Help them reason that the seed coat is protective, and that the baby plant grows into an adult plant. However, withhold verification of the seed halves' function for the present. Let them discover this for themselves.

Does a peanut have the same parts? First, have the children remove the protective pod or "shell." It will be easy to identify the reddish-brown seed cover, the two seed halves, and the baby plant. *make inferences*

2. *Materials:* paper towels; several drinking glasses; half-pint milk cartons with tops removed, containing soil; water, lima beans.

Now lead into a problem. There are many weed seeds in the soil of vacant lots and fields. Yet only during certain times of the year do we see a great many weeds growing in these places. Bring out that perhaps proper conditions for seed growth are found only at certain times of the year.

Paper towels or blotter

Water

Figure 10-4

What conditions are needed for seeds to grow? For one clue, have the children again compare the soaked and unsoaked lima beans. Bring out another clue if needed: What is winter weather like in most parts of the United States? Put the pupils' hypotheses in question form on the chalkboard. Develop discussion about other possibilities they raise that might affect germination. Help the class to plan experiments after all the questions have been raised. Divide the class into small groups to do all the experiments individually and then compare future findings. Some questions and experiments might be:

a. Will seeds sprout when it is cold? (Plant several seeds in each of two cartons of soil. Water each. Place one in a refrigerator at school or home, and the second carton in a relatively warm, dark place.)

Bring out that the second carton must be kept in darkness because the refrigerator interior is dark. Since both seeds are underground, only when plant shoots appear above ground would they be directly affected by light.

b. Will seeds sprout whether or not the seed is "right side up"?

c. Do seeds need soil to sprout? (Questions b and c can be tested at the same time. Line the inside of a water glass with several folded paper towels. Stuff an extra

suggest hypotheses

develop procedures

towel into the center as in Figure 10-4. Wet the paper thoroughly. Leave an inch of water inside the glass. With a pencil push several soaked bean seeds between the glass and towel. Make sure seeds are in various positions, and that all are above water level.)

d. Will seeds sprout in soil that is underwater? (Plant some seeds in a carton of soil. Water often enough to maintain a pool of water on the soil surface.)

e. Will seeds sprout better in light or darkness? (Line the inside of two water glasses with paper towels or cotton. Wet paper and leave about one-fourth of each glass filled with water. Using a pencil, push some soaked seeds between glass and paper. Put one glass in a dark place and another in a light place of equal temperature.)

Since a week or more may be needed for definite findings in these experiments, get pupils to write and attach carefully to their experiments the purpose of each.

Children's findings may lead into some tentative inferences:

a. Only a few bean seeds will sprout when it is cold.

b. Bean seed roots grow down and shoots grow up no matter how the seeds are placed.

c. Bean seeds do not need soil to sprout.

d. Bean seeds will not sprout properly underwater. There may not be enough air.

e. Bean seeds sprout a little faster in the dark than in the light.

If needed, acquaint the class with the term *germinate* (also germinating, germination) to label the concept they have learned while working with the seeds. Invite open-ended experiments with other kinds of germinating seeds under these conditions.

develop procedure

Contributing Idea B. Food material inside a seed provides the energy it needs to germinate.

1. *Materials:* large cardboard carton; six recently sprouted lima-bean seedlings whose seed halves are several inches above

ground, growing in small containers of sand.

Have the class find out now about the function of the bean's cotyledons through a controlled experiment.

Ask pupils to describe a peppy, frisky dog. Explain it has much *energy*—the ability to move around and do things. Where does a dog get its energy? (From the food it eats.) Bring out how humans, too, rely on food for their energy. If animals could not eat, they would gradually use all of their energy supply and die.

How about seeds? Where does a seed get the energy it needs to push up to the surface and grow for the first few weeks or so? Raise conjecture. Develop that we get energy from eating lima bean seeds. Perhaps the same material in the seed that gives us energy also provides energy for the baby plant. Probably some children *suggest hypotheses* will hypothesize that the seed halves contain this food, if there is such. Others may suggest that water is responsible. Some may claim that the soil provides food. If so, have them recall their previous experiments where the seeds grew well for a time without soil.

Have children closely observe seed halves of the six seedlings. Mention that these seed halves seem to be shriveling slowly. What may be causing the seed halves to shrink? (The plant probably is *develop procedures* using the food material.) What could we do to see if the seed halves are providing food material for growth? (Remove some of the seed halves from the plants.)

Removal of a cotyledon can be easily accomplished by bending it back gently and breaking it off. An effective test would be to leave both cotyledons on two plants, remove one from each of two plants, and remove both from the remaining two plants. Figure 10-5 shows three examples.

Place all these seedlings under a large, inverted cardboard carton or in a dark closet. This will prevent photosynthesis. (As an explanation for the time being just say it is a good idea to shield the plants as

Figure 10-5

sunshine might affect the experiment. Let the children find out about photosynthesis in a future activity.) Water all plants as usual.

Within several days, the children will notice that the plants with both cotyledons are healthiest and growing fastest. Those with one cotyledon will be next best. Plants with no cotyledons will be growing the slowest, or not at all.

A line graph (Figure 10-6) may be used to record the comparative growth of each set of three plants. Each line can be colored differently for easy identification. Have the *reason quantitatively* children estimate growth on weekends. Invite them to make predictions about future relative growth. The simpler bar graph may be used if children are not familiar with graphs. Figure 10-7 shows the record of a C seedling. A and B records should be placed next to this one for comparisons. You might have a short discussion each day about the relative growth rates and overall growth.

2. *Materials:* single-edge razor; soaked lima beans and radish seeds; large, tall glass jar (empty peanut-butter jar), three-fourths filled with sand; black construction paper.

It will be worthwhile to run additional experiments at the same time to cross-check results. Show pupils some radish seeds. Emphasize how much smaller they are than lima bean seeds. If a seed contains food material for a growing plant, would there be as much in a radish seed as in a lima bean

441

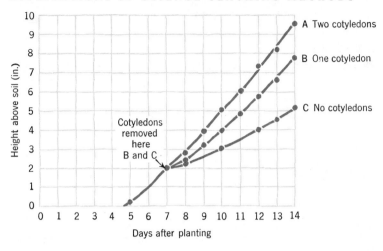

Figure 10-6

seed? (No.) What might happen if we planted both kinds of seeds deep in soil? (The radish plant might not be able to reach the surface.)

Produce a deep glass jar containing sand. Let a pupil push down with a pencil several seeds of each kind to various depths. If seeds are placed next to the glass, it will be possible to observe their growth. Water until the sand is damp, but not saturated. Wrap black paper around the glass to shield the seedling and its roots from the light. Remove paper temporarily as needed for observations. Place on a shelf or table where it will remain undisturbed except for occasional watering.

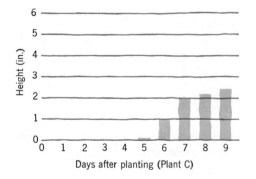

Figure 10-7

Within a week or so, results should be clear. The radish seeds planted deep down will have used their food material before reaching the surface. For some confirmation of results, have children check various seed packages for instructions. They will note that instructions for small seeds usually state shallow plantings. Instructions for larger seeds usually specify deeper plantings. How does this agree with our findings?

3. Yet another verifying experiment can be run simultaneously. Cut off the bottom half of several soaked lima beans. Retain the half containing the plant embryo. By opening one bean, you can learn how to align the other beans to cut off the correct half.

Show these seeds to the class. If seeds really contain food material, will these halves grow as well as whole beans? (Probably not.) The halves can be planted next to whole beans about 2 inches down in sandy, damp soil. They will grow more slowly, and into smaller seedlings. The children might also be interested in seeing if the halves that contain no embryo will grow. (They will not.)

Let pupils experiment further to confirm and broaden their conclusions.

EXTENDING ACTIVITIES

1. Bring up how seeds "travel." We know that people plant seeds in gardens. But people don't plant weeds in fields and vacant lots. Nor do they plant seeds in many other places where plants grow. Where do these seeds come from? Bring out that seeds are produced by plants, but for the time being, dwell on their means of distribution.

Let pupils read or view a film or filmstrip on how seeds travel. Develop that some seeds travel through the actions of animals and people. The sharp hooks or barbs on the cocklebur, wild barley, and beggar tick cling to clothing or animal fur. (Figure 10-8.) Birds eat fleshy fruits but may not digest the hard seeds. The seeds pass out of their bodies some distance away. People throw away fruit pits (which contain seeds), watermelon seeds, and so on. The wind blows many seeds. Some have "parachutes," such as the goldenrod, milkweed, and dandelion. The maple tree seed has "wings." Bring out that water can carry seeds from place to place, since many seeds float. Help pupils understand that seeds travel in many ways.

If possible, have an exhibition of a variety of seeds from green plants. An excellent time to collect many seeds without cost is in the fall. Pupils will be happy to assist.

2. Have an open-ended activity to determine germination times of many different, common seeds: orange, lemon, apple, pumpkin, barley, corn, oats, and so on. Use half-pint milk cartons filled with clean sand. Have children keep track of germination times. Guide them not to jump to the conclusion that a seed is defective because it has not sprouted right away. Some seeds may take several weeks to begin germination.

make inferences

3. Let interested pupils line a shoebox with plastic and fill it with soil from a vacant lot containing many wild plants. Are there seeds in the soil? Pupils can water it for a month or more and find out.

Vegetative Reproduction. It is common to think only of seeds producing new flowering plants. Yet some of the most useful and interesting means of new plant growth occur through the propagation of roots, stems, and even leaves. This is called *vegetative reproduction.*

Consider the orange-colored tap root of the carrot plant—the part we eat. A carrot plant is usually grown from seed in the spring and harvested some months later. If left in the ground, however, all parts above the soil surface die as the weather becomes cold. No growth occurs during this time. As warmer weather approaches tender shoots grow from the tap root and emerge into sunlight. These grow into stems and leaves. Some time thereafter, flowers and

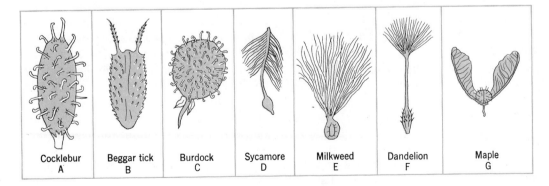

| Cocklebur A | Beggar tick B | Burdock C | Sycamore D | Milkweed E | Dandelion F | Maple G |

Figure 10-8 Seeds.

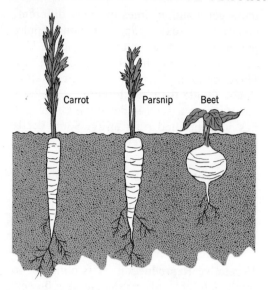

Figure 10-9 Carrots, parsnips, and beets have tap roots.

seeds are produced. Like a seed, a tap root provides the food energy needed for shoots to emerge and grow. Parsnips and beets are other examples of tap roots which grow in this way (Figure 10-9).

New plants may be grown from tap roots in the classroom by imbedding them in moist sand or garden soil. A favorite method of many teachers is to cut off all but the top quarter of a tap root and imbed it in a small bowl containing a layer of pebbles and some water. At least half of the root cutting is above water to assure a sufficient oxygen supply. When sufficient foliage and roots have emerged, cuttings are planted in garden soil for full growth.

A sweet potato is another example of an enlarged root that can propagate a whole new plant. It may be grown in a similar way, described in a forthcoming extending activity.

Most ground cover plants, such as grass, strawberry, and ivy, spread quickly after planting. Each sends out stems or runners which take root, push up shoots, and develop into new plants. These lateral stems may spread above ground, as in the strawberry plant and Bermuda grass, or below

the ground, as in quack grass. The most persistent weed grasses are of the underground-stem variety, as frustrated lawn growers will testify.

New plants may be propagated from stem cuttings of the geranium and begonia. Other common plants whose stems grow independently are the coleus, oleander, philodendron, and English ivy. Dipping the ends of stem cuttings in a commercial hormone preparation may stimulate root growth to occur in half the usual time.

Sometimes upon opening a bag of white potatoes we find some of them beginning to sprout. Usually this happens when the potatoes are left undisturbed for a time in a dark, warm place. White potatoes are swollen parts of underground stems, called *tubers*. The dark spots or "eyes" are buds, from which shoots grow. Farmers today seldom, if ever, use potato seeds in growing crops. Instead, they cut potatoes into several bud-bearing parts and plant these. Each bud grows into a new plant which produces more potatoes.

Occasionally, we see shoots growing from onion bulbs stored in the home pantry. Bulbs, too, are modified stems. All contain thick, fleshy leaves wrapped tightly around a small, immature stem. Tulips and gladioli are typical flowers which may be grown from both bulbs and seeds.

Even leaves may develop into whole plants. If the rex begonia leaf suggested for a forthcoming lesson is unobtainable, a leaf from an African violet, echeveria, or bryophyllum plant may be substituted. Techniques for using these substitutes follow.

Use a fresh African violet leaf with attached petiole (leaf stalk). Put the stalk into an inch of water in a drinking glass. For better support of the leaf, use a card with a hole punched in it placed across the glass rim. Insert the leaf petiole through the hole and into the water.

An echeveria leaf will usually root by merely laying it flat on dry sand. It is a thick leaf which contains much food and water. After it roots, water sparingly. Like most desert plants, this one thrives in semiarid soil.

The bryophyllum leaf is sometimes sold in variety stores under the name "magic leaf." This title is only a slight exaggeration. To propagate, pin it down flat on damp sand with several toothpicks or straight pins. Tiny plants should grow from several of the notches around the leaf rim. A variation of this method is to pin the leaf to a curtain! When some plantlets start growing, cut them out with scissors and plant in damp sand.

Sometimes children ask, "If plants can grow from seeds, why are the other ways used?" There are several reasons. All of these methods result in whole plants in far less time. Also, some things cannot be grown from seed—seedless oranges, for example. In this case branches of seedless oranges are grafted onto an orange tree grown from seed.

But the most important reason is quality control. We can never be sure of the results when we plant seeds of some plants. Vegetative reproduction carries the assurance that the new plant will be very much like the parent plant. If large, healthy potatoes are cut up and planted, for example, we probably can harvest near-identical specimens.

All the foregoing methods of vegetative reproduction are asexual. In other words, reproduction does not require involvement of plant sex organs. Certain lower animal forms also can reproduce themselves asexually. In another exposition, we shall review sexual reproduction in flowering plants; that is, how fertile seeds are produced.

Generalization II: Some plants can grow from roots, stems, and leaves

Contributing Idea A. Root parts from some plants can grow into whole new plants.

1. *Materials:* two fresh carrots with stems and leaves intact; two quart milk cartons with tops removed, containing clean sand; knife; large cardboard carton.

Try a controlled experiment with carrot tap roots.

Hold up a carrot before the class. Elicit that the part we eat is a *tap root,* or main root. Let the children observe the smaller roots, if any, trailing away from the tap root. They will be able to identify the stems and leaves. Bring out that the orange-colored tap root grows just beneath the ground surface. Now develop a problem.

Carrot plants are usually dug up out of the ground when the part we eat is well developed. If a carrot plant is not dug up, all parts of the plant above ground die in winter, when the weather turns cold. In spring, as the weather gets warmer, new stems and leaves grow above the ground. Where does the carrot plant get the energy needed to grow new stems and leaves? Draw out at least three possibilities: *(suggest hypotheses)*

    a. From water in the ground.

    b. From the soil.

    c. From the tap root.

Which of these three seems likeliest? (Tap root. Since seeds store plant food, maybe a tap root works the same way.) Challenge the class to develop an experiment that will test this hypothesis and also tend to rule out the other two at the same time. Give a hint, if needed: We found that a small seed did not have as much energy as a larger seed. Another hint: How large and healthy will the stems and leaves be if only part of the tap root is planted?

Most likely, children will suggest an experiment. (Plant a carrot top and a whole carrot in the same amount of sand. The top of each should be just below the sand surface. Give each carrot the same amount of water.) *(develop procedures)*

Make sure some holes are punched in the cartons for drainage. Cartons should be placed on saucers to catch any excess water. If no one mentions it, suggest that these plantings be covered with a box to prevent sunlight from possibly affecting results.

Within two weeks, results should be obvious. Foliage of the whole carrot will be thicker than that of the carrot top. *(make inferences)*

2. *Materials:* milk cartons of sand; assorted beets, parsnips, turnips; any additional materials from home children may think they need.

develop procedures

Explain that beets, turnips, and parsnips are also tap roots. Encourage a "What will happen if . . ." session. Let the children suggest all the ideas they wish in varying the conditions under which plant stems and leaves might be grown from these roots. Then let them screen and develop tests for their ideas.

Here are some variables one class tried: (1) different kinds of soil; (2) water only, with the tops of these vegetables imbedded in gravel; (3) different solutions in water, such as salt, sugar, and ink; (4) different positions and depths in planting root tops; (5) different temperatures; and (6) different parts of the tap root (top, middle, and bottom).

Contributing Idea B. Stems of some plants can grow into whole plants.

1. *Materials:* nearby outdoor planted area containing grass, strawberry plant, or ivy ground cover.

Begin this activity in class through discussion. Get pupils to recall that a grass lawn is usually planted from seed. Even a few weeks after the seeds have sprouted the grass is sparse. But several months later there is a thick grass cover. How is this possible? A few children may say some kinds of grass "spread." Try to pin down what they mean. If they know what ivy is,

state problems

ask how it also "spreads" from a sparse planting.

Take pupils to a nearby outdoor location. Have them examine closely the underground or above ground grass runners (stems) that gradually branch out and take root. Let them note that ivy and strawberry plants propagate themselves through the extension of stems above ground which take root. When leaves and roots are developed, these new plants also send out stems.

2. *Materials:* cuttings from a geranium, coleus, begonia, or philodendron plant; water-proof containers; water. (Cuttings should be about 4 or 5 inches long. Cut with a sharp knife just below a place where leaves join the stem. This place is called a "node." Remove any leaves from the lower halves of cuttings.)

Ask the children if they have seen their parents plant *cuttings* from a geranium or other plant. It may be necessary to define the term. Explain that, when placed in water or soil, cuttings from some plants may grow roots after a period; under proper conditions these grow into whole plants. Will any of these cuttings grow roots? We shall put them in jars containing several inches of water and find out.

Encourage children to bring in cuttings from other plants to learn if they will grow. Instruct them how to cut below the node. (Children should do this only in the presence of a responsible adult.) Cuttings may need about two weeks in water for good results. They may be planted in rich soil when roots are well developed and cared for in the usual way.

Contributing Idea C. Leaves of some plants can grow into whole plants.

Materials: rex begonia leaf; container of moist sand; sharp knife or single-edged razor; large, wide-mouthed glass jar.

Demonstrate how a leaf may grow new plants. Take a healthy rex begonia leaf and place it underside up. Make one cross cut with the knife across each of the leaf's main veins. Lay the leaf flat, underside down, on moist sand. Press the leaf down gently. If needed, put a few pebbles on top to keep it flat. It will be necessary for the cut parts to be in direct contact with the moist sand. Invert a wide-mouthed glass jar over the leaf to reduce evaporation. Place the container on a window sill or other well-lighted place. In about two weeks, small plants will probably grow at the cross cuts.

EXTENDING ACTIVITIES

1. Leave several healthy white potatoes in a dark place until shoots begin to sprout from the "eyes" or buds. Show them to your pupils. Explain that a white potato is a swollen part of an underground stem of the potato plant. Food for the plant is stored in this stem. Develop that farmers usually do not plant potato seeds to grow new potatoes. Instead, they cut up whole potatoes into several parts and plant them. Which parts are likeliest to grow into potato plants? (The parts with eyes or *buds*.) Does it make any difference how you position the buds? Have pupils plant potato parts that contain buds and some that do not. These should be planted in damp sand just below the surface. After two weeks, have the children dig up these parts and compare them. Growth will have occurred only in the parts with buds and most often when the bud is facing upward.

2. Show the children an onion bulb. Cut it in half, lengthwise. Show the thick leaves and tiny stem. Explain that food in some plants, such as the onion, tulip, and gladiola is stored in a *bulb*. This is a swollen stem-like portion just below the ground surface. Mention that most gardeners prefer to plant a bulb rather than a seed. Can they guess why? (Maybe it will grow faster.)

suggest *potheses*

Let them experiment. Several small onion bulbs may be planted in a container of moist sand and several onion seeds in another. Bulb tops should be just above the soil surface. The bulbs should grow faster and be much more vigorous. Bring out also that a healthy bulb usually produces a healthy plant. When only the seed is inspected, it is more difficult to determine if a plant will be healthy, or even grow.

3. Let some children find out how to grow a sweet potato vine. Place a sweet potato into a jar of water; have the end with no purple buds pointed down. Only about one-third of the potato should be immersed. If the jar rim is too large to support the potato, stick three toothpicks hori-

Figure 10-10

zontally into its sides (Figure 10-10.) Set the jar in a warm, dark location until roots and stems grow (about three weeks). Then place it in sunlight. A large sweet potato may grow for several months in water. At the end of that time, its food supply should be gone. Unless planted in soil or given liquid fertilizer, it will die.

Sometimes sweet potatoes purchased at the grocery store fail to grow because they have been chemically or heat treated before shipping.

Conditions for Plant Growth. The next sequence of activities will help teach that green plants flourish only under proper conditions of water, light, temperature, minerals, and more indirectly, space. As such, these experiences should extend some ideas about growing conditions already developed with seeds.

Children will find that soil-watering requirements for plants are similar to those for germinating seeds. Overwatering causes the plant to die of oxygen deprivation or disease. Underwatering usually results in a droopy, malnourished plant. The absence of vital soil minerals and extremes in temperature also have a weakening, or even fatal, effect on plants.

Crowding of plants is harmful to growth largely because individual plants are de-

447

prived of enough of what they need for good growth through competition. Even the hardiest plants develop to less than normal size under crowded conditions.

Green plants need light energy to manufacture their own food, but not necessarily sunshine. Electric lights may be substituted. Many commercial flower growers take advantage of this fact to regulate the growth rates or blooming times of their flowers to coincide with different holidays. Plants generally grow faster when exposed to light for increased time periods. However, overexposure retards growth and delays normal blooming times.

Light color is also a factor in speed of growth. You remember that white light is composed of several different colors. Each color has a different wavelength. At various stages of growth, from seedling to adult plant, wavelengths of certain colors stimulate more growth than others. But generally of all single colors, red seems to stimulate seedlings to grow most nearly in a normal way. Exposure to white light usually results in the best overall growth patterns.

Strange as it seems, recent experiments show that sound energy may also stimulate plant growth. Sounds of various types are generated near the plant. Some vibration frequencies appear to be more stimulating to growth than others.

Generalization III: To grow well, green plants need water, light, proper temperature, minerals, and space

Contributing Idea A. Green plants need water, light, and the proper temperature to grow.

Review with the children the conditions that were needed for their seeds to germinate. Do plants need the same conditions to grow? Focus on water, light, and temperature at present. This can lead into the next three activities.

1. *Materials:* twelve healthy, young lima bean plants potted in good soil, started three weeks before; five cardboard

shoeboxes; five pieces of cellophane — clear, red, green, blue, and yellow; cellophane tape; large cardboard box.

Most, if not all, children will realize their bean plants need water. But how much? What happens to a plant when it receives only a small amount of water? How do its parts grow, if at all? What does the plant look like? What happens if it is given a very large amount of water? How will this plant compare with a plant watered properly?

Have children plan some experiments to find out the effect of varying a plant's water supply. For example, use three healthy young plants in need of watering. Give one a sparse surface watering once every two days. Give a second plant a "normal" amount of water; that is, water it briefly until no more soaks into the soil. Rewater this plant only when the surface is slightly dry. Saturate the third plant's soil several times a day. Whenever definite results begin to appear (in a week or so) let the children remove the plants from their pots and closely examine roots, stems, and leaves. Both the overwatered and underwatered plants should be yellowish and doing poorly. If not, allow more time. Roots should be somewhat shallow in the underwatered plant. Roots should be unhealthy and in the first stages of decay in the overwatered plant. *develop procedure*

2. Pupils will recall that bean seeds sprouted and grew just as fast or faster for a time in the dark as in sunlight. What about plants that are no longer dependent upon the food in their seeds? Do they need sunlight? Let the class plan a test. One plant can be placed under an inverted cardboard box and a second placed nearby in a well-lighted place. (Or, a small patch of lawn can be covered with black construction paper for several days and then compared with adjacent grass.)

After about three days, results will be obvious. Call attention to the plant's yellowing leaves and droopy appearance. Confirm that a bean plant needs light. But what kind? Is sunlight the only kind of light

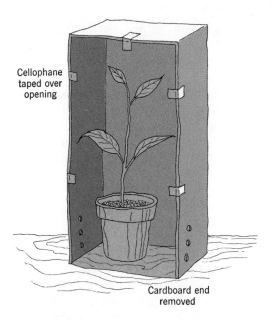

Cellophane
taped over
opening

Cardboard end
removed

Figure 10-11

energy that will work? Will an electric light do? How about colored light? Have the children plan some tests. For experiments to see how filtered light affects the growth of plants, children can use shoeboxes whose openings are covered with clear and different-colored pieces of cellophane. (The clear cellophane is a control.) Unless the plants are large, they will fit nicely in shoeboxes placed on end. Arrange five boxes, each with a different cellophane color, as in Figure 10-11. Punch holes in the sides of each box — near the bottom — for adequate air circulation.

reason ntitatively

Boxes can be slipped off quickly for plant measurements and watering once a day. A graph might be kept of any changes in growth rates. The plant with the red cellophane covering will probably grow most nearly like the one in the clear cellophane box.

Some children might like to try growing plants under artificial light at home. A dark basement will be useful. A gooseneck lamp with 50-watt bulb works well as a light source. This may be placed on books and positioned directly over the plant. There

should be a distance of at least 24 inches between the light and plant to avoid overheating the plant. For safety, stress that a responsible adult must be present when this experiment is set up. If the bulb is left on twenty-four hours a day, children may discover that plant growth slows down.

make inferences

When results are in, develop that once the food material in a seed is gone, a plant is completely dependent upon the food it makes for itself. Through the use of light energy, a plant can manufacture the food it needs from water, materials in the soil, and air. Mention that the class will soon learn more about how this is done.

3. Encourage pupils to think of ways to test the effect of temperature on bean plants. Let everyone carefully evaluate suggestions. For example, placing a plant in the refrigerator is not a valid suggestion unless the light stays on. We want to test temperature alone.

develop procedures

It may be difficult to test the effect of coldness unless the temperature outdoors is sufficiently low during the day. Excessive heat is more easily tested by placing a plant over or near a radiator or hot plate.

Contributing Idea B. Green plants need sufficient minerals and space in which to grow.

1. *Materials:* small bottle of liquid plant fertilizer; six closely matched, young bean plants, a pair potted in rich garden soil, and a pair in each of two separate pots of moist sand.

Exhibit the six plants. Explain that they are entirely dependent upon the food they make for themselves. In which soil will these plants grow best? Garden soil or sand? (Garden soil.) Have children back up their answers by references to what they may have observed or read. Or, if desired, experiment with plants growing in sand and soil.

Bring out that sand generally lacks the decaying vegetable and animal matter called *humus,* found in good garden soil. This material is soaked by rain, partly dissolved, and taken up by plant roots in the water they absorb. Develop that *fertilizers* of various kinds are often put into poor soil to provide the same kinds of minerals naturally furnished by dissolved humus and rock particles. Hold up the bottle of fertilizer. Ask the children to plan a controlled experiment to determine if beans planted in sand with fertilizer added will grow as well as beans planted in rich garden soil.

develop procedures

A satisfactory plan might be as follows. Water each of the three pots the same every day, but add fertilizer to one pot of sand. Follow directions on the bottle label. Leave one pot of sand without fertilizer for comparison of its plants with those in the fertilized sand and garden soil. This is a control.

In about a week, some results should be visible. With proper fertilizing, the treated sand pot plants should compare favorably with those in humus soil. The untreated sand pot plants should be noticeably declining in vigor.

Point out, however, that sandy soil may present a watering problem under normal outdoor conditions. Sand is so porous water may drain too quickly, leaving the roots dry. Humus soil retains moisture to a greater extent. (This would be an excellent time to correlate the material on topsoil found in Unit 7, page 337R.)

2. *Materials:* for each group, about twenty soaked radish seeds; quart milk carton; damp garden soil. (Place the carton down lengthwise, and cut out one of its long sides. Fill the carton with garden soil.)

This activity can help teach that plants need space to grow if they are to develop properly.

Mention that instructions on seed packages usually recommend spacing planted seeds several inches apart, rather than closer together. Why is this done? (They may not grow as well when they are crowded together.) Let the children plan how they will test the effect of crowding on growing plants, using the available materials. (Plant several seeds 1 inch apart in

suggest hypotheses

a straight row at one end of the carton; plant all the rest closely together in a row at the opposite end.)

develop procedur

Within a week the stunting effect of crowding will be apparent. Let some children follow through on this experiment by thinning out some crowded plants in the second week after planting. This should cause the remaining plants at that end of the carton to grow faster.

EXTENDING ACTIVITIES

1. If an outdoor garden plot is available, encourage the children to plan a class garden. They should know enough by now to apply their knowledge and do most of the planning themselves. Quick-growing plants will enable them to take home their harvest in a month or so. Radishes, lettuce, beets, peas, and turnips are all excellent for them to raise.

2. Perhaps a study trip can be taken to a nearby plant nursery or greenhouse. Nursery-men are usually happy to pass on a few tips to eager young gardeners. In addition, there will be opportunities to learn how professionals handle the same problems of lighting, watering, germinating, and so on, that the children themselves have met.

Plant Parts and Their Functions. Children are usually surprised to learn that, besides fruits and vegetables, all the meat they eat has originally been derived from green plants. Flesh-eating animals are dependent upon plant-eating animals. This is true in the ocean as well as on land. Everything alive basically depends upon food synthesized from raw materials in the leaves of green plants. The plant itself is dependent upon the proper functioning of its several parts to produce this food. In this section, we will examine how these parts work. Let's begin with plant roots.

The experience of weeding a garden makes us very conscious of one principal function of roots—they anchor the plant.

Figure 10-12 A seedling has many root hairs. (Courtesy Hugh Spencer.)

the root cap tissue is continually worn off and replaced by new tissue.

Water absorbed by the roots goes into the stems, through which it is transported by narrow tubes to all parts of the plant. Dissolved minerals in the water are deposited within the cells of these parts. When water reaches the leaves, some of it evaporates into the air. Exactly how this continual movement of water occurs in the plant has been a mystery until recent times. Modern molecular theory provides an answer.

As you know, molecules that are alike have an attractive force which binds them together (cohesion). These molecules may also be attracted to unlike molecules (adhesion). The thin tubes that transport water in a plant run from root to stem to leaf. Adhesion of water molecules to the tube walls helps to support the tiny water column. Cohesion causes the water molecules to stick together. As water molecules evaporate into the air, they "tug" slightly at the molecules below because of cohesive attraction. Because of cohesion, all the other molecules rise in a kind of chain reaction.

Should an air bubble get into the tube, the chain reaction is broken. The bubble separates some molecules to a distance beyond their effective cohesive attraction. You will find a way to prevent this from happening in an activity with stems.

A leaf seems thin and simple in structure from the outside. Yet the intricate mechanisms within it, which produce the world's food supply, have never been fully duplicated by man. Inside the leaf cells is a green-pigmented chemical, *chlorophyll.* Chlorophyll enables a leaf to combine carbon dioxide chemically from air and water into a simple sugar. The energy needed to power this chemical synthesis in the leaf comes primarily from sunlight, which is absorbed by the chlorophyll. *Photosynthesis,* as the process is called, literally means "to put together with light."

From the sugar it manufactures, the plant cells make starch, which may be stored in

In addition, we know that food storage in roots enables the plant to survive when food-making cannot occur. Another function of roots is the absorption of soil water.

Plants that are transplanted sometimes grow poorly for a while, or even die. This is usually due to damage done to tiny, very delicate root hairs which grow from the older root tissue. (Figure 10-12.) It is the root hairs which absorb nearly all the water, rather than the older, fibrous material. There may be billions of root hairs on a single plant, enough to stretch hundreds of miles if laid end-to-end. If laid side-by-side, in rows, they would occupy the floor area of an average-size home. Root hairs are so small that they are able to grow in the tiny spaces between soil particles and make direct contact with water and air trapped therein.

Growth takes place very largely at the tip of a root. A tough root cap protects the sensitive growing portion as it pushes through the soil. Since the soil is abrasive,

all parts of the plant. With additional compounds received from the soil and through soil bacteria, plant cells can manufacture proteins and vitamins.

While carbon dioxide is taken up in photosynthesis, oxygen is released as a waste product. However, as a plant consumes the food stored in its cells, it takes up oxygen and gives off carbon dioxide as a waste product, as does man. Fortunately for us, much more oxygen is released to the air through photosynthesis than is used by plants in oxidizing their stored food. In fact, green plants comprise the chief source of the world's present oxygen supply.

How do these gases enter and leave the leaf? Thousands of microscopic openings, called *stomates,* may be found in a green leaf. In land plants these are largely, but not exclusively, located in the leaf's underneath surface. Each *stomate* is surrounded by special cells which regulate the size of

the opening (Figure 10-13). Since water in the leaf evaporates into the air through the stomates, regulation of these openings has great survival value. In dry spells and at night, the stomates stay closed, thereby preventing any appreciable loss of water.

Interestingly, most of the photosynthesis on earth occurs in the ocean, within uncountable numbers of microscopic algae which float on and near the water surface. We have not yet learned to use the tremendous food supply this source potentially affords to a hungry world.

The flower is the reproductive system of a flowering plant. Its two principal organs are the *pistil,* which contain unfertilized egg cells, and *stamens,* which produce dustlike *pollen* cells. (See Figure 10-14.) When a pollen grain lands on the sticky end of a pistil, it begins to grow a tube which "eats" its way down to the pistil base or *ovary.* There it joins onto an egg

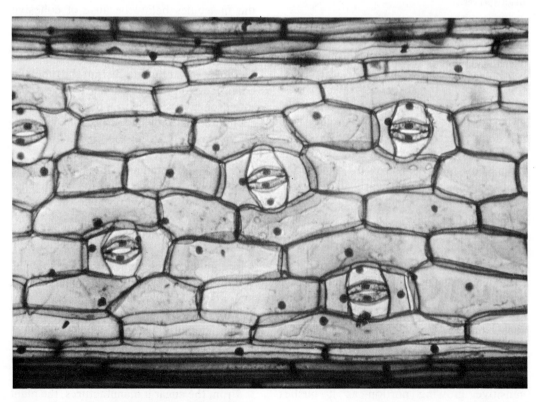

Figure 10-13   (Bruce Roberts — Rapho Guillumette.)

452

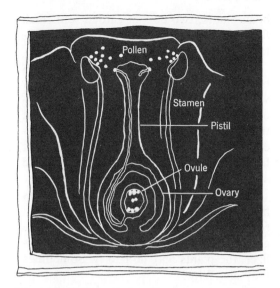

Figure 10-14 Parts of a flower.

cell or *ovule*. A sperm cell released from the pollen grain travels down the tube and unites with the ovule. Other ovules in the ovary may be fertilized by additional pollen in the same way.

The ovules, now fertilized, begin growing into seeds. The entire ovary begins to swell as a fleshy fruit begins to grow around the seeds. As the ovary becomes larger, parts of the flower drop off. Finally, a whole fruit forms. In the apple, the ovary is enveloped by a stem part which swells up around it. When eating an apple, look at the core end opposite the fruit stem. Quite likely tiny, dried-up remains of the pistil and stamens will be visible.

When examining flowers with children in a future activity, use single flowers, such as tulips and sweet peas, rather than composite flowers, such as daisies and sunflowers. The centers of these composite types consist of many tiny flowers, each complete with pistil and stamens. They are too small to be readily observed and may be confusing to the children.

Self-pollination occurs when pollen from a flower's own stamens fertilize the ovules. *Cross-pollination* occurs when pollen from another flower perform this function. How-

ever, pollen must be from the same type of flower for fertilization to take place.

Much pollination is effected through gravity, as when pollen simply fall from tall stamens onto a shorter pistil. Or pollen may fall from a flower high up on a stem to one lower down. Insects are also primary distributors of pollen. As they sip nectar from flowers, pollen grains rub off onto their bodies. In visiting other flowers, these grains may become dislodged. It is interesting to note that bright colored and fragrant flowers are visited by the most insects. Wind is also an important distributor of pollen. In spring, the air contains billions of pollen grains, bringing pollination to plants and hay fever to many people.

Many garden flowers and vegetables grow from seed, then blossom, produce seeds, and die in one growing season. These are known as *annuals*. Examples are petunias, zinnias, beans, and tomatoes. Those that live two seasons are *biennials*. Examples are hollyhocks, forget-me-nots, carrots, and turnips. Plants that live more than two growing seasons are *perennials*. Trees and most shrubs fit into this classification.

Generalization IV: The special ways in which the several parts of a plant work keep the plant alive and growing

Ask the class members to name the several parts of most green plants. (Roots, stems, leaves, and flowers.) Briefly elicit comments about the functions of these parts to learn how much the children already know. Probably it will be best not to comment on their accuracy at this time. However, you might mention that they can do experiments and other activities to find out more about the interesting, special ways in which these parts function.

Contributing Idea A. Roots absorb water, anchor the plant, and store food.

1. *Materials:* three closely matched, vigorous bean seedlings, growing in sep-

arate pots; aluminum kitchen foil; a large tray or pan; hand water sprinkler. (A substitute may be made by punching holes in the bottom of a quart milk carton. If the hinged cap on top is secure, water flow may be stopped by inverting the carton.)

If asked about the functions of roots, almost all intermediate-grade children will mention that roots take up or absorb water. Invite your pupils to cite evidence which might back up this belief. Most will mention that an unwatered house plant dies. But now ask them to think about natural watering—rainfall. Rain falls on the leaves before it soaks the ground. How do we know that the leaves do not take in water? Could it be that leaves also take in water? How could we find out? Challenge the *develop procedures* class to think of an experiment with available materials.

(Use the two closely matched plants. Water the soil of one plant as usual. Keep track of how much water is used. Water only the leaves of the second plant with the same amount of water. To prevent water from dripping onto the soil, waterproof the pot opening. Carefully wrap waterproof foil around the base of the plant and extend it out over the sides of the pot. A tray underneath will contain water runoff.)

Within several days, results should be fairly conclusive. The plant whose leaves only were watered will be drooping. The soil-watered plant should be thriving as usual.

make inferences Evaluate for overgeneralizing from this experiment. Some water absorption might take place in some leaves. In this case water absorption, if any, is not enough to maintain the plant. For further evidence encourage duplicate experiments at home with beans and other plants.

2. *Materials:* a dozen sprouting radish seeds, about three to four days old, with visible root hairs (Prepare by sprinkling the seeds on paper toweling or a sponge placed in a saucer of water. Cover with a moist paper towel.); hand magnifying lenses; two closely matched, potted, healthy bean plants; two pots of garden soil; small flat stick; large, wide-mouthed glass jar containing water.

Exhibit some sprouting radish seeds. A background of black paper will permit easy viewing, as will hand lenses. Have everyone note the root structure. Point out that the tiny root hairs take in water and minerals from the soil. Mention that all the root hairs of a single radish seedling would stretch for miles if placed end to end.

Now develop a problem. Many gardeners have trouble when they dig up plants and replant them somewhere else. Even if the gardeners water carefully and apply ferti- *suggest hypotheses* lizer, the plants may do poorly. Sometimes they die. Why?

When possible root-hair destruction is mentioned, indicate the two bean plants and ask pupils to think of an experiment. Help them to think this through. One plant *develop procedures* might be pulled roughly out of the soil and the other gently lifted out after the soil has been loosened and watered. Roots of both plants can be soaked gently in a container of water to remove any remaining soil. An examination with a hand lens will reveal more root hairs on the gently treated roots. Replant both. The plant with fewer root hairs should not be as vigorous as the other until it grows new root hairs.

Bring out other functions of roots. They store food, children should remember, in the carrot, beet, and sweet potato plant, and in other plants, too. Roots also anchor the plant to the ground. Have children dig up some weeds of various kinds and bring them to school to examine and compare their root systems.

Contributing Idea B. Stems conduct liquids and support leaves.

1. *Materials:* several fresh, firm, celery stalks with many green leaves intact; red and blue food coloring or ink; freshly cut white carnation with at least a 5-inch stem; razor or knife; two glasses containing water.

Mention that we usually water a house plant only at the roots. Yet all parts of the

Figure 10-15

plant seem to contain some water. Why? (The stem carries it from the roots to the plant's other parts.) Show the celery stalk.[2] How could the pupils use it to see how water is transported? (Put it in a glass of water.) But how will they tell if water is moving up the stalk? This is fresh celery. Discuss. Guide toward the use of colored water as an indicator.

Make a new diagonal cut across the stalk base to open any clogged tubes. Immerse *quickly* (to avoid air bubbles) in colored water and place in strong sunlight for several hours. Water should rise in the stalk and enter the leaf veins, leaving a spidery network of colored lines. (Figure 10-15.) Pull apart the stalk and have children examine the individual tubes.

develop procedures Under what conditions will the water rise speed up or slow down? Experiments can be conducted with matched stalks at school or home. Pupils might try stalks with leaves, stalks in darkness and light; also with wind (electric fan) and no wind.

2. Bring out that sometimes florists color their white carnations green for St. Patrick's Day. Can the class guess how this is done?

[2] The celery stalk is a leaf stalk (petiole) which functions like a stem.

(Place a carnation with stem in green-colored water.) How might a florist prepare a carnation with *two* colors? (Maybe the stem can be split in two with each part placed in a glass of different-colored water.) Make a new cut just above the stem base to open any clogged tubes. Now split the stem carefully down the middle. (Figure 10-16.) Place the carnation in sunlight. In several hours, the flower should exhibit both colors.

Occasionally this demonstration does not work because the stem tubes contain air bubbles which block passage of the water. To prevent this, snip off a small piece of the stem end with scissors while it is underwater.

Develop other stem functions. Some stems store plant food, as with asparagus, celery, and white potatoes. Stems also hold up leaves.

Contributing Idea C. Leaves can make plant food; they also store some plant food.

1. *Materials:* hot plate, two tinned cans, one large, one small (to fit inside the larger can); water; alcohol; iodine; drinking glass; tweezers; fresh geranium leaf, or other soft green leaf; a spoonful of sugar and one of powdered starch.

This activity will demonstrate a way to detect starch in a leaf.

Figure 10-16

Get children to recall that a green plant turns yellow when left in the dark. Carefully develop the following ideas:

a. The green material in a plant is *chlorophyll*. It is made by the leaf, but only in the presence of a light. If a plant is placed in darkness it turns yellowish in about three days because the plant's chlorophyll disappears.

b. Chlorophyll is very important. It enables the leaf to make its own food from the air and water that enter the leaf. Sunlight provides the energy for this to happen.

c. The food that is made is stored in different parts of the plant. Some of the stored food is starch. (Show some dried starch. Explain that a potato is mostly starch. When we eat a potato, we use as food what would have been used by the potato plant in its further growth.)

d. Of all living things, only green plants can make their own food. This process is called *photosynthesis*.

Now lead into a demonstration. Mention that leaves also store starch. Hold up the fresh geranium leaf. Will it contain starch? You will demonstrate a way to find out.

First, show that iodine can indicate the presence of starch. Put a drop on some powdered starch. It will turn purple-black. Put a drop on some sugar. The iodine will largely remain its original color. Iodine changes to a purple-black only with starch. Develop that the iodine test can be used to see if a leaf contains starch, but first the green chlorophyll must be removed.

Boil out the green chlorophyll in the leaf with water first, then alcohol. *Since alcohol is flammable, do not boil it directly over a hot plate. Never use an open flame.* A safe method is as follows. Half fill a large can with water, and place on a hot plate. Boil the leaf for about five minutes in the water. Take out the leaf and place it in a small can half-filled with alcohol. Place the smaller can inside the larger one containing hot water. Turn on the hot plate again. The leaf should be almost pale white after about ten minutes in boiling alcohol.

Remove the leaf with tweezers after turning off the hot plate. It will look pale green or near-white. Explain that the boiling alcohol has removed most of the chlorophyll. However, if there was starch in the leaf it should still be there. Put a dozen drops of iodine into a glass of water. If starch is present, the leaf's color will turn purple-black when the leaf is dropped into this solution. Drop in the leaf. It should change to that color.

2. *Materials:* potted geranium plant or one found outside near the classroom; leaf-boiling materials used in preceding activity; glass of diluted iodine; two 2- by 2-inch squares of heavy tagboard or cardboard; paper clip.

Tell pupils that they now have enough knowledge to find out about the importance of chlorophyll for themselves. Any part of a green leaf that does not receive light loses its chlorophyll in about three days. Challenge the class to plan an experiment to answer this question: Will starch be found in a leaf or part of leaf that does not have chlorophyll? If needed, hold up the cardboard squares and paper clip. How could these be used on geranium plant leaves? What experiment can the children design?

(Place the squares on the top and bottom of a growing leaf outdoors. The squares will cover only part of the leaf. In about three days, the covered parts should have little or no chlorophyll. These sections will probably have used all the starch available to them. Test for starch by boiling the leaf in alcohol and then putting it into diluted iodine.)

Children will be pleased to discover that uncovered portions of the leaf will appear blue-black, showing that starch is present. make inferences The previously covered portions will be light brown, indicating no starch is present. It will be interesting to test coleus, silver leaf geranium, and other plant leaves having parts that are not green. These parts generally will not contain starch.

3. *Materials:* microprojector or microscope; razor; fresh lettuce leaf; glass slide

and cover slip; medicine dropper containing water; tweezers.

How does air move into and out of a leaf? The following demonstration will show children the tiny openings in a leaf's underside (stomates). (As an alternative to this demonstration, a drawing can be enlarged by an opaque projector.)

Only a small piece of crisp lettuce leaf is needed for this demonstration, but it must be very thin for light to shine through. Bend the leaf back until it cracks. Pull back this leaf part so that you shear one section over the other. Pull off a small piece from the thin, sheared section. This must be from the leaf's lower surface. With tweezers, place it on the glass slide. Put a drop of water on it and cover with a glass cover slip. Press the slip down slightly to remove air bubbles. With the microprojector, use a low power objective to locate some stomates. Then switch to a higher magnification, if desired.

Point out that these openings permit air to enter and leave the leaf. Each opening is called a *stomate*. Emphasize that the *stomates* are almost entirely on the bottom, not the top surface, of a leaf. Why is this make an advantage? (Dust in the air might settle inferences on the leaf and clog the stomates.) What might happen to a plant if the stomates became clogged? (It might die.)

Continue with questions and ideas. Some plants, like the water lily, have leaves that float on top of water. On which surface of the leaf would stomates probably be found? ⟩ (Top surface because there is more air.)

4. *Materials:* four large, identical water glasses, two containing water; two identical pieces of cardboard, about 5 inches by 5 inches; large, fresh leaf with petiole (leaf stalk) intact; vaseline or soft modeling clay. (Arrange half of these materials as in Figure 10-17. A small hole for the leaf petiole can be punched in the card with a pencil. Be sure to seal around this opening with clay or vaseline.)

Mention that a plant takes in much more water than it can use. What happens to all the extra water when it reaches the leaves? (It may evaporate into the air.) Show the assembled materials. If the leaf gives off moisture what may happen to the inside of the top glass? (Water drops should appear.) Why is the cardboard placed between the two glasses? Why is there vaseline around the opening? (To prevent water evaporation from below reaching the top glass.)

Raise the need for a further control, if no one else does. How shall we know if the water comes from the leaf? It might come from the air. Have pupils recall the many occasions when they have seen condensed water vapor on window panes, bathroom mirrors, and so on. How can the remaining materials help? (Put a cardboard over the second glass of water and an empty inverted glass on top. If water does not appear in this glass, and it does in the glass containing the leaf, we shall know that the leaf has given off moisture.)

After several hours in a well-lighted place water droplets should appear only or largely in the glass enclosing the leaf. Develop that, in addition to taking in and releasing air, water evaporates through a leaf's stomates. Mention that a stomate can open and close. Help children reason when a stomate would shrink in size or close. (Hot weather. This would help to preserve the water supply.)

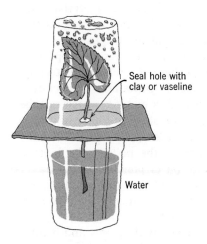

Seal hole with clay or vaseline

Water

Figure 10-17 A transpiration test.

457

This experiment can be done with two leaves, one of which is coated with vaseline to clog the stomates. It can also be done with two plastic bags and plants, as in Figure 10-18.

Contributing Idea D. Flowers make seeds under certain conditions.

1. *Materials:* a class supply of any large single flower, such as a tulip, lily, snapdragon, petunia, or sweet pea; newspapers, if flowers are available for pupils; large chalkboard sketch of Figure 10-14. (Florists are often willing to donate unsellable flowers.)

Raise conjecture as to how seeds are developed. Some children may know seeds are formed in a flower, but press for details. Invite pupils to use the chalkboard sketch as they offer explanations. Mention that it shows the inside parts of a simple flower. If or when it becomes apparent they need more information, let them search for it in in books or other sources and then use the sketch.

Bring out the following ideas slowly and carefully through the drawing and related discussion:

a. A flowering plant usually has two parts —a male and a female part. The female part is called a *pistil*. The male part is the *stamen*. Some flowers have many stamens. The sketch flower has only two.

b. Tiny bits of dustlike material called *pollen* grow on the end of the stamen. These may be shaken off into the air. If a pollen grain lands on the sticky tip of the pistil it stays there. Soon it begins to grow a narrow tube. It grows until it reaches an *ovule*—a tiny bit of material which may become a seed. Ovules are found in a place at the bottom of the pistil called the *ovary*.

c. As soon as the pollen tube joins an ovule, a tiny bit of pollen material travels down the tube. When it touches the ovule, the ovule begins growing. We say that the ovule is *fertilized.*

d. A fertilized ovule grows and forms a seed. Inside the seed is a baby plant.

Figure 10-18

e. When the flower dies and falls to the ground, the seed may grow into another plant, if it has the right conditions of water, heat, and so on.

2. If flowers are available, distribute them now. Have pupils carefully pull away the leaves and identify the several parts. Let them feel the sticky end of the pistil and touch the pollen-bearing part, found at the ends of the stamens. Pupils can split with their fingernails and pull away the pistil wall protecting the ovary. Ovules should be visible.

3. *Materials:* microprojector or microscope; pollen-bearing flowers; glass slides, black construction paper; hand lenses.

Shake off some pollen onto black paper for visibility. Let pupils examine with a hand lens. Use a microprojector to show some pollen grains greatly magnified. An opaque projector may be used, with more limited success, if you shake some pollen onto cellophane tape, sticky side up. Grains will adhere strongly enough not to be blown away.

Summarize children's learnings. Emphasize that they have studied the reproduction method of flowering plants, which includes most trees. However, flowerless plants reproduce in other ways. They will find out more about such plants in future studies.

EXTENDING ACTIVITIES

1. Encourage some children to find out the several ways in which pollen can travel from one flower to another: wind, insects, water, and gravity.

make
inferences Have children carefully observe the kinds of flowers visited by insects. These will be mostly fragrant flowers with bright colors.

2. Develop a bulletin board on the parts of plants we eat, from pictures brought in by the children. Let them work out a classification scheme, such as:

Seeds — oats, barley, beans, etc.
Fruits — peach, pear, apple, etc.
Leaves — lettuce, cabbage, spinach, etc.
Stems — asparagus, celery, white potato, etc.
Roots — sweet potato, carrot, radish, etc.

3. Initiate a discussion about what the earth would be like without green plants. Focus on food. What difference would it make to a meat eater who doesn't like vegetables, anyhow? Bring out food chains.

Plant Responses. If you were asked to invent a plant, what adaptive characteristics would you want it to have for survival value? Whatever your design, it would be wise to have your plant regulate itself to some extent according to its needs. Assume it has the same needs as other plants. Since it requires water, and water soaks down into the soil, you would want the plant roots to grow downward. But what if there were no water below the roots? You would want roots that could overcome the pull of gravity and grow toward a water source, even if the source were to one side or above the roots.

Since the plant needs light, you would want the stem to be able to grow toward a light source if light became blocked or dimmed. At the same time it would be desirable to design the leaf stalk to give maximum exposure of the leaf to sunlight. An efficient stalk should be able to grow longer if another leaf blocks its light. It might also

turn the leaf perpendicular to the sun's rays as the sun appears at different positions in the sky.

You would also want to consider the obstructions which the plant might encounter in its growth both above and below the ground. It would be helpful for survival if the plant roots and stem could grow around these obstacles to some extent when they touch them.

Of course, there is no need to invent plants like this, as they exist now everywhere around us. Most green plants are responsive to gravity, water, light, and touch. These responses are called plant *tropisms*. Let us see why tropisms occur.

Figure 10-19 shows a radish seedling growing on wet blotting paper inside a water glass. The glass has been placed on its side for twenty-four hours. Notice that the seedling shoot or stem is beginning to curve upward, while the root is starting to grow downward. *Both* reactions are responses to gravity.

Why the opposite directions? Check the magnified sections of the seedling. Gravity causes a concentration of plant hormones (*auxins*) all along the bottom cells from the beginning of the stem to the root tip. The cells along the bottom of the stem are stimulated by the hormones to grow faster than cells above. Growth of these cells is fastest by the stem tip (left inset). As these bottom cells become elongated, the stem

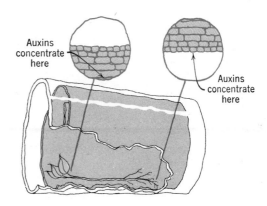

Auxins concentrate here

Auxins concentrate here

Figure 10-19

begins to curve upward. Root cells, however, are much more sensitive than stem cells. Therefore, the concentration of hormones along the bottom root cells has the opposite effect; it inhibits cell growth. Top cells are least affected and elongate faster, so that the root tip begins to curve downward. Cell growth is fastest by the tip (right inset).

Tropistic responses seem to be the result of plant hormones that concentrate in various parts of the plant. As we have seen, this causes some cells to grow faster than others. Such responses can occur only in growing tissue.

It is always easy and tempting to think of plants and animals as responding to stimuli the way man does. (Remember the discussion of anthropomorphism in Chapter 2.) When we are thirsty, we consciously seek water. Does the plant? The literature on living things contains thousands of references to plant and animal behavior that suggest anthropomorphism. Although most of the time no harm is done, anthropomorphism does encourage loose thinking. Perhaps the best reason we should be aware of anthropomorphic statements is because they are unwarranted inferences from a set of facts. It seems sensible to discourage faulty inferences wherever or whenever they occur.

Generalization V: Plants respond to gravity, light, water, and touch

Contributing Idea A. Gravity influences plant roots to grow down and stems up.

Materials: small, potted geranium or bean plant; six-day-old radish seedling growing between a moist paper towel and side of a drinking glass.

Show the children a chalkboard sketch of Figure 10-20. Can they solve this problem? A man wants to plant some trees and shrubs on a steep, bare hill to hold the soil in place and prevent landslides. He has planted one young tree in A. Before he can plant any more, it rains hard and the loose earth on the hill shifts downward. The tree and roots now look like sketch B. If there are no further landslides, will this tree and its roots continue to grow in a slanty way? Raise conjecture.

Some children may recall that bean seedling roots grow down and the shoots grow up no matter how the seed is positioned. Will growing plants do the same? Hold up the growing radish seedling. How could it be used to find out what might happen to the farmer's slanted tree? (Put the glass on its side. The stem will change direction and grow up; roots will change direction and grow down.) The paper towel should be moistened several times a day. Let a fast-dripping faucet drip onto the inside surface of the toweling. When it is moist, quickly put the glass on its side again.

How could the potted geranium be used in a substitute experiment? (Place it on one side, except for watering once a day. Notice the new direction the stem takes. Take the plant out of the pot to examine its roots.) Good results should be visible in both experiments within four or five days.

Develop that gravity influences plant roots to grow down. Stems are influenced in the opposite way. Encouraging pupils to apply their findings in observing foliage on hills and bluffs around the neighborhood. Generally, roots grow down and standing stems grow vertically, relative to the earth's horizontal surface.

make inference

Figure 10-20

Contributing Idea B. Plant stems above ground grow toward light.

Materials: quart milk carton; garden soil; six radish seeds; large shoebox; razor. (Slice the milk carton in half lengthwise. Discard one-half unless you wish to have two experiments going at one time. Place the remaining half down flat and fill with garden soil. Plant six seeds in a straight row, about an inch apart. In about five days, they will be sufficiently grown for this experiment. Take the large bottom section of the shoebox and invert it. With a razor, cut a narrow slot one-fourth inch wide running the length of the box. The slot should be about one inch from the top of the box. Except for the slot cutting, let children prepare these materials, preferably well in advance of need. See Figure 10-21.)

You might begin with this bridge: "When we buy a house plant to put on a window ledge, sometimes we are told to turn the plant halfway around every two or three days. Why is this advice given?"

Guide the discussion as needed. Let the class investigate classroom plants and note how the leaves and flowers are oriented. Help the children to focus on the light factor. If a plant grows toward the light, its stem will become curved rather than straight. How could the materials be used to find out if plants grow toward the light? develop ocedures (Place the seedlings on a table in a well-lighted location. Put the inverted shoebox over the seedlings with the slotted side opposite the window. Seedlings should bend and grow toward the slot.)

A definite bending toward the light source will be noticeable within a day or two. Let make nferences children evaluate their data. What makes it seem likely that the light was responsible? (All six seedlings are bent the same way.) What could we do to make sure? (Reverse the box. See if the plants start growing the develop rocedures opposite way.) To be as evident, the reversal may take somewhat longer than the initial experiment.

Let all the children try their own light experiment, if possible. This can be done with a radish seed planted in soil contained in a small paper cup. Cover with a larger, inverted paper cup that has a small hole punched in the side with a pencil. Should there be inconsistencies in results, get suggest hypotheses pupils to analyze why. If other seeds are used, conclusions can be broadened. Otherwise, have everyone read for further confirmation.

Contributing Idea C. Plant roots grow toward their source of water.

Materials: aquarium tank or substitute containing soil; three soaked lima beans.

Tell the pupils they will find it interesting to learn more about how roots grow. Invite them to consider a problem that happens occasionally with underground pipes. Develop briefly how some large underground pipes near the children's homes are used to transport water and sewage. Some of these pipes are made of clay and some of iron. Occasionally, the clay pipes get clogged or broken from tree roots growing in and around them. This may happen even if the pipe is 30 or 40 feet away to one side of the tree. Yet almost never does this happen to iron pipes, even if they are closer. What causes the roots to grow in and around the clay pipes?

Hint about the porosity of clay, if needed. When water is mentioned as the

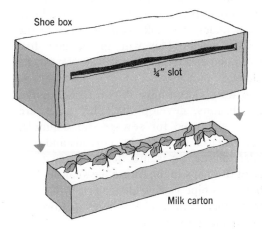

Shoe box

¼" slot

Milk carton

Figure 10-21

attraction, ask the children about gravity. Doesn't gravity cause plant roots to grow down? If water does "attract" roots, it would have to pull against gravity to some extent in this case. Can it do this? Develop a discussion.

develop procedures Divide the class into six "task forces." Ask the groups to design an experiment with available materials to see if water will cause plant roots to grow sideways. If necessary, mention that the glass tank could be used to make root growth visible. But give as few hints as are necessary to keep the children thinking. Let the chairmen present their groups' strategies. The whole class can screen these ideas and choose the one that seems best. Focus on the logic of all "arguments" for one or another strategy. Now is the time when "if-then" thinking can flourish with guidance.

An experimental setup like the following should work well. Plant three soaked lima beans close to one end of the tank. They should be planted 1 inch apart, and against the glass, about 2 inches below the soil surface. Water directly over the seeds until they sprout and are growing well. From then on water only slightly and in the far opposite corner. In about a week, there should be a noticeable change in root direction, particularly with the roots nearest to the water.

To hasten this experiment, have the seedlings already growing. Also, to make the roots visible at all times, put one book each under the tank corners opposite the planted seeds. This will tip the tank forward and cause the roots to stay next to the glass.

After children have drawn some limited conclusions, develop that clay pipes are often still used for sewage, for example, because iron pipes tend to corrode and rust. Also plastic pipes are being increasingly used. Perhaps in the future we shall seldom hear of a pipe getting clogged or broken by tree roots. (For a related investigation, see extending activity 5.)

Contributing Idea D. Plants respond to touch.

1. *Materials:* large glass jar of soil in which a bean seedling is growing (The seed should have been planted next to the glass, so that the roots are currently visible.); several stones or sticks.

Mention that there is another problem with roots which the children can think about. What does the ground look like below the first few inches of topsoil? (It becomes rockier.) What happens to a root when a rock or something else gets in its way? (It may go around the rock.) Will roots move around something that gets in their way? Invite a test. (Put some rocks or sticks under the root tip. We shall see whether the root moves around or through these things.)

Unless many obstructions are used, the root should go around or through them and continue to grow. Bring out that the root seems to be sensitive to touch.

Since this is another potential open-ended experiment, encourage children to try individual tests, varying seedlings and obstructions. Tall glass jars or paper cups might be used. If paper cups are used, have children examine roots by cutting the cups in two and gently picking at the soil with pencils. develop procedure

2. *Materials:* vigorous, potted bean seedling; two rulers; a dozen or so books.

What would happen if there were something in the way of a growing plant *above* ground? Say a plant is growing directly under a railing. What would happen when it touches the railing? (It might go around.) Let the children suggest experiments to find out. Perhaps one will look like Figure 10-22. (Put the seedling between two stacks of books. Lay two rulers close together across the stacks. The seedling tip should almost touch the rulers' undersides. Adjust stack heights as needed.)

The seedling should grow around the obstacle. However, it might push the rulers aside unless they are weighted down. What

develop
procedures
if four rulers are used? What if different obstacles are used? Different plants? There are many possibilities for open-ended, individual experiments and subsequent reports.

Summarize by discussing the survival value of all four tropisms studied.

EXTENDING ACTIVITIES

1. For a dramatic example of a plant's sensitivity to touch, borrow a mimosa plant from a nurseryman. Touch the narrow leaves with a pencil. They will suddenly contract or fold together. This will not harm the plant, although it may take several hours for the leaves to return to their former position.

2. Have pupils grow a climbing plant, such as a sweet pea or morning glory. The narrow tendrils of these plants will curl around a stick or string and "lead" the rest of the plant. If a tendril's sensitive underside is stroked, it will curl within minutes.

3. Take the class on a study trip around the school or neighborhood to observe leaf arrangements of trees and bushes. Have the children notice how branches and even leaf petioles vary in length. This permits almost every leaf to have direct exposure to sunlight. Discuss how useful this is for survival.

4. Show a film which features time-lapse photography of plant tropisms and other plant movements.

5. For another investigation in which the stimulus of water seems to be greater than gravity to plant roots, see Figure 10-23. Get a plastic berry basket with a mesh type construction. Plant inside four soaked bean seeds in about an inch of either peat moss or vermiculite. Suspend this from strings and water normally. After the roots grow through the basket bottom, they will begin to turn upward toward the moist peat moss. How can we be fairly sure that it is the water that is causing the roots to curl

develop
procedures

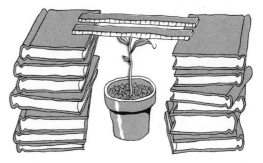

Figure 10-22

upward? (A plastic or paper cup containing water might be affixed just under the basket. The plant roots should touch the water surface. If so, roots will grow downward.)

6. Help children become sensitive to anthropomorphic statements. Is it accurate to say that plant roots are "searching" for water? Why or why not? They should realize that a conscious purpose is probably not involved. Have them compose a more desirable statement. Let them search for such expressions in trade books, make reports on their findings, and discuss how these expressions could be rewritten. Sharp thinkers will particularly enjoy and profit from this activity.

make
inferences

Figure 10-23

Animal Groups

(Primary Emphasis)

UNIT ELEVEN

Animal Groups

(Primary Emphasis)

THIS UNIT CAN HELP CHILDREN LEARN HOW TO OBSERVE AND classify animals. But our intention goes beyond this. Children should discover that despite their tremendous diversity, animals share certain characteristics and needs. Careful observation of how animals are built enables us to place them into common groups. These groupings permit us to learn many of the interesting adaptations and ways of animals without the need to study every individual group member.

The unit will particularly interest and teach children if several live animals are kept in the classroom. We shall provide a variety of suggestions for doing so in the pages which follow. To take full advantage of the teaching possibilities, begin this unit in the spring.

GENERALIZATIONS

I. There are many kinds of animals; they may be grouped in different ways.

II. Mammals are warm blooded, have some fur or hair, and milk glands.

III. Birds are warm blooded, have feathers, and two wings.

IV. Reptiles are cold blooded, and have a dry, scaly skin; some have a shell.

V. Amphibians are cold blooded, and have either a smooth or

Credit for chapter opening photograph. **Marc and Evelyn Bernheim-Rapho Guillumette** bumpy skin; most hatch from jellylike eggs laid in water.

VI. Fishes are cold blooded, live and breathe in water, and are usually covered with scales.

VII. There are many animals without backbones; insects make up the largest group.

Classifying Animals. Of some 1 million 250 thousand different forms of living things, animals make up almost 1 million. They run, walk, crawl, fly, slither, and swim. They range in size from a microscopic protozoan to the blue whale, 100 feet long. Their colors embrace all shades of the spectrum. In almost any way one can imagine, the diversity of animals is truly amazing. How do scientists keep track of them? A system developed by the great Swedish naturalist, *Carolus Linnaeus* (1707–1778), provided the base for modern classification. Fundamentally, it takes into account the physical structure of the living thing. Six main categories are used, which range from the general to the particular description of group characteristics. For example, let us classify a dog. Parenthetical remarks refer to the general meaning of each category.

Kingdom — Animalia (The subject belongs to the animal, not the plant kingdom.)
Phylum — Chordata (It has a backbone or a notochord.)
Class — Mammalia (It is a mammal.)
Order — Carnivora (It eats meat.)
Family — Canidae (It belongs to a group with doglike characteristics.)
Genus — Canis (It is a coyote, wolf, or dog.)
Species — Canis familiaris (It is a common dog.)

Such a system has important advantages to biologists. It is possible to pinpoint most living things and to note relationships which otherwise might be easy to miss. Since the system is accepted by scientists the world over, accuracy of communication is realized.

For elementary-school science, however, you will want to work with a more simplified classification scheme. The following one should be useful, and will fit nicely into any more formal structure the child may develop later in high school and college. Although in this unit children will not study all the groups described, seeing the overall classification scheme should be helpful to you.

We can divide the entire animal kingdom into two huge groups, each with a manageably small number of subgroups:

Animals with Backbones (Vertebrates)
Mammals (man, dog, horse, etc.)
Birds (sparrow, penguin, eagle, etc.)
Reptiles (turtle, lizard, snake, etc.)
Amphibians (frog, toad, salamander, etc.)
Fishes (carp, bass, minnow, etc.)

Animals without Backbones (Invertebrates)
Echinoderms — animals with spiny skins (sand dollar, starfish, sea urchin, etc.)
Arthropods — animals with jointed legs
   insects (fly, moth, grasshopper, etc.)
   arachnids (spider, scorpion, tick, etc.)
   crustaceans (crab, lobster, crayfish, etc.)
   myriapods (millipede and centipede)
Mollusks — animals with soft bodies (clam, snail, octopus, etc.)
Worms (flatworm, roundworm, segmented worm, etc.)
Sponges and Jellyfish (sponge, jellyfish, sea anemone, coral, etc.)
Protozoa — one-celled animals (paramecium, ameba, foraminifera, etc.)

When primary children use the term "animal," they are inclined to mean mammal, or at best, another animal with a backbone. Yet the five main vertebrates make up a scant 5 per cent of the animals in existence. Insects, which make up 70 per cent of all animals, represent by far the largest class of invertebrates. There are more than 700,000 species. (A species is a group whose members can generally reproduce only among themselves.)

In daily contact and interest, the vertebrates and insects compose most of the animal world for primary children. Therefore, we shall concentrate in this unit on making children more aware of these particular animal groups and their fascinating adaptations.

Some of the forthcoming activities will require about twenty colored pictures of animals. Most, if not all, can be gathered by the children. One primary teacher who worked with this unit reported that over two hundred pictures had been brought in by the class! Children's trade books represent an additional source. Moreover, any children's encyclopedia is sure to have many animal pictures, located in one convenient section. These can be exhibited with an opaque projector.

The *Golden Nature Guides* (see page 96L), contain excellent pictures of animals in color. In addition, helpful descriptions and other data accompany each picture. These, too, can be used with an opaque projector. Both readers and non-readers can thumb through these guides and classify specimens.

All of the animals mentioned in this unit's activities can be furnished through the children, pet shops, or biological supply houses. The unit contains many suggestions for maintaining these animals in the classroom. But you may wish to have even more detailed and comprehensive directions than can be provided in this book. One biological supply house offers free-of-charge to teachers an excellent set of leaflets [1] on

---

[1] Turtox Service Leaflets: No. 5, *Starting & Maintaining a Fresh-Water Aquarium;* No. 11, *Plants for the Fresh-Water Aquarium;* No. 23, *Feeding Aquarium & Terrarium Animals;* No. 48, *Aquarium Troubles: Their Prevention & Cure;* No. 10, *The School Terrarium;* No. 40, *The Care of Rats, Mice, Hamsters & Guinea Pigs;* No. 28, *Reptiles in the School Laboratory;* No. 7, *The Care of Frogs & Other Amphibians;* No. 34, *The Care of Living Insects in the School Laboratory;* No. 35, *Studying Ants in Observation Nests;* No. 13, *Rearing the Silkworm Moth.* Employed teachers can obtain all these and several more leaflets free-of-charge. On school stationery simply request the *Turtox Elementary School Leaflet Set* from the General Biological Supply House, 8200 South Hoyne Ave., Chicago, Illinois 60620.

the care of living things in the classroom.

If there is a natural history museum nearby, don't overlook the possibility of borrowing preserved animal specimens. In addition, some museums arrange free guided tours and consultant services for individual classes.

The intent of the first sequence is to make pupils more aware that there is much diversity among animals, and that animals may be classified in many ways. We shall provide opportunity for children to invent their own classifications—pets, farm animals, and the like. Children enjoy and learn from chances to classify objects based on their own criteria and value systems. From these they can move gradually into a more involved scheme of classification by body structure, with its consequent relationships to adaptation and life needs. Help pupils realize that we classify things according to our purposes. Different purposes may demand different classification schemes.

Generalization I: There are many kinds of animals; they may be grouped in different ways

1. *Materials:* 18 to 24 cut-out, colored magazine pictures, including several from each of these groups—mammals, birds, reptiles, amphibians, fishes, insects. (Place all pictures on a large bulletin board. Arrange in even rows and columns, but not in definite groups at this time. Put a different numeral on a small white card under each picture, for quick reference. Have this question mounted at the top of the board: *Which animals make good pets?*)

Mention that the children are going to find out many interesting things about animals during this unit. There will be many chances to work with different animals in the classroom. But first, they will want to find out the kinds of animals that are easy to work with and fun to observe.

Ask for the hands of those who have animal pets at home. Invite these pupils to name and describe their animals, and how they take care of them. Try to have a variety of pet animals described. Bring out some reasons why these animals make good pets: tameness, size, interesting habits, and so on.

After some discussion, direct attention to the bulletin board and caption. Are there any animals pictured here which make good pets? Ask pupils to use the picture numerals for handy reference, and the animal's name, if known. Get the class to screen each suggestion according to the pet criteria just established. Develop that some animals are too wild, large, difficult to feed, or have other characteristics which make them undesirable as pets.

make inferences

To summarize, write "Good for pets" and "Not good for pets" on the chalkboard. Draw out appropriate numerals of the animal pictures for each heading and list them in columns. Include animal names, if known.

2. Develop that the class has divided the bulletin board animals into . two large *groups,* according to their usefulness as pets. A group is a collection of things. Animals in the pet group belong together because they are alike in some ways. Elicit that there are many other ways the children can group animals. One other way is by size. Invite them to group the animals on the bulletin board according to size: *small, middle-size,* and *large.*

state problems

Be alert for chances to establish operational definitions. What is a "small" animal? A bear is small compared to an elephant. A bear is large compared to a mouse. Guide toward the use of three representative animals on the bulletin board to establish a workable definition for each of the three sizes.

make inferences

Encourage suggestions for other classifications of animals; for example, how they move. Some fly, swim, walk, or run.

3. *Materials:* pictures of two different birds, and two different fishes.

Now lay the groundwork for further study. Hold up a picture of a small fish and another of a bird. Tell the class about a boy who owned these animals. Establish that he probably kept the fish in a fish tank and the bird in a cage. One day the boy thought these animals must be tired of living in the same old places, so he decided to change things around. He thought he would put his bird in the fish tank and his fish in the cage. Is this a good idea? What would happen?

The boy found out from a friend that the bird would drown and the fish would die, so he did not switch them. But he had two other pets. (Show the second pair of pictures.) Could he switch *these* two around— bird in the tank and fish in the cage? (No!)

Develop that although the boy's two fishes are somewhat different in appearance, they are built in much the same way and have many of the same life requirements. This is also true of his birds. Point out that there are many different kinds of animals; more kinds of animals than there are children in the school, or in the whole neighborhood, or for many miles around. We will never be able to study each and every animal alive. There are too many. But we can study groups of animals. Although animals may look different at first, their bodies are often much the same. Animals with similar bodies often act and live in similar ways.

EXTENDING ACTIVITIES

1. Through use of many picture books of animals, have children look up and determine common names for any animals not identified on the bulletin board: panther, alligator, salamander, and so on.

2. Encourage pupils to invent additional ways to group the bulletin board pictures. Some classifications commonly used by primary pupils are farm animals, skin covering, number of feet, and kind of food eaten—animal or plant.

develop procedures

You might want to take this opportunity to develop a simple coordinate system so pictures can be quickly located on the bulletin board. For example, pupils may put their pictures in rows labelled with numerals and columns headed by capital letters. Pictures can then be identified as B4 (second column, fourth row down), A2 (first column, second row down), and so on. With a little help, pupils may develop a system like this themselves.

Mammals. Look around long enough, and you will find animals everywhere: below the ground (mole, gopher, woodchuck); on the ground (man, giraffe, elephant); in trees above the ground (monkey, sloth, tree squirrel); in the air (bat); and in the water (whale, seal, dolphin). What can such a diverse collection of creatures have in common? All of these are *mammals*. That is, all have some fur or hair; all have milk glands. To be sure, you will not find much hair on a whale—only a few bristles on the snout. And sometimes fur or hair is greatly modified, as with the porcupine's quills. But look closely enough, and, if it is a mammal, it has hair.

Both male and female mammals have mammary, or milk glands. (You can see how the term "mammals" originated.) Ordinarily, of course, only the female produces the milk used in suckling the young.

Another distinction of mammals is their intelligence, the highest of all animal groups. But other unique characteristics are few and subtle.

Mammals are usually born alive. The embryo develops within the mother from a tiny egg fertilized by a sperm cell from a male of the same species. During its development the embryo is attached to the female by a placenta, or membranous tissue. Water, oxygen, and food pass from female to embryo through this tissue. In turn, liquefied waste materials flow the other way. These are absorbed into the female's blood stream, sent to the kidneys, and eliminated. The navel pit in the abdomen of humans is a reminder of this early stage of our development.

The two known exceptions to this reproductive pattern are the spiny anteater and duck-billed platypus, both of Australia.

Each lays eggs. The hatched young, however, are cared for and suckled by the female much in the manner of other mammals.

Mammals are warm blooded and have efficient hearts with four definite chambers. These characteristics are shared by only one other group, the birds. Their blood temperatures stay at relatively the same level, whether the air warms or cools. Animals of lesser complexity are cold blooded. That is, their blood temperature changes as their environmental temperature changes.

It is both an advantage and disadvantage to be warm blooded. Vigorous activity is possible within most air temperature ranges. But the body heat of mammals must be conserved, else death occurs. In cold climates, thick blubber or fur performs this function, as does hibernation, and, in some cases, migration. In warm climates, humans perspire. Some animals estivate. That is, they become relatively inactive for a period in whatever suitably cool refuge can be found.

Some cold-blooded animals can withstand great cold or heat, but most are dependent on a narrow temperature range for normal activity or survival. We shall go into more detail later with several specific animals.

Although the terms are still relative, it is more accurate to say "constant temperatured" and "variable temperatured," rather than "warm blooded" and "cold blooded," when we refer to animals. In hot weather, for example, a "cold-blooded" animal might have a higher body temperature than a "warm-blooded" one.

The teeth of mammals are particularly interesting to observe, since they are apparently adapted to specific functions. We can see the four main kinds of teeth by examining our own in a mirror. In front are the chisel-like incisors. On both sides of these teeth are the conelike canines. Farther back are the front molars, and last, the back molars. Now let us note how these teeth are used by several kinds of mammals.

Prominent, sharp incisors are characteristic of gnawing mammals—rats, mice, gerbils, guinea pigs, hamsters, muskrats, beavers, and rabbits. The incisors of these rodents grow continuously at the root, and are worn down at the opposite end by gnawing. When prevented from gnawing, incisors may grow so long the animal cannot close its mouth, and so starves to death.

The flesh eaters (carnivores), such as cats, dogs, and seals, have small incisors and prominent canines, sometimes called "fangs." Their molars have curved, sharp edges. The canines are useful for tearing meat. The molars are suited for chopping it into parts small enough to swallow.

Plant eaters (herbivores), such as the horse, goat, and sheep, have wide, closely spaced incisors, and large, flat-surfaced molars. Canines do not appear. The incisors work well in clipping off grasses and plant stems. The molars grind this material before swallowing.

Man is an omnivore, in other words capable of eating both plant and animal matter. Human teeth include all four types.

A forthcoming activity suggests that children examine a dog's teeth. Besides this, they might look at trade books that show pictures of teeth of other animals.

An extending activity suggests the breeding of white rats or mice in the classroom. You can also breed gerbils (jur-bils), an increasingly popular pet, in the same way. This is an interesting experience for youngsters, and furnishes the basis for a wholesome and intelligent attitude toward reproduction in all animals, including man. We recommend use of white rats, mice, or gerbils over such common classroom animals as hamsters and guinea pigs. Mating is more uncertain to come about with captive hamsters. They seem a little more inclined to bite, although this is not so with young, well-handled hamsters. Guinea pigs are a bit large for small classroom cages, and their comparatively long gestation period (63 days after mating) is inconvenient.

Although simple cages for rodents can be homemade from strong screening ma-terial, a commercial cage is usually more secure and better suited to the animals' needs. Rodents are typically quite active and may deteriorate in health unless an exercise wheel is provided. A small, inverted water bottle with tube, affixed to the cage, will present a clean, long lasting water supply. A commercial cage, like that in Figure 11-2, should serve well and last indefinitely. It may be purchased at most pet stores and scientific supply houses, as can white rats, mice, and gerbils. (In some states, gerbils may be banned to prevent a wild pest population from developing.)

One last point. Never house a rodent in a wood or cardboard container. Remember those incisors!

Figure 11-1 Gerbil. (Gordon Smith-National Audubon Society.)

Figure 11-2

Generalization II: Mammals are warm blooded, have some fur or hair, and milk glands

1. *Materials:* several pictures of mammals, such as a seal, dog, rat, and horse; pictures of a cow with full udder of milk, and any animal suckling its young; several pictures of different birds, with one showing a parent bird feeding its young, if possible. (Affix these illustrations in no apparent order on a flannel or bulletin board.)

Use this activity to identify some properties of mammals.

Call attention to the pictures. Mention that all the animals shown may be divided into two large groups. Challenge the children to note likenesses and differences. Let them separate the pictures. Discuss reasons for their choices. Bring out that one group has feathers and is made up of *birds*. Have pupils note carefully that the remaining animals all possess some fur or hair. If a picture of a cow is available, draw out that the udder is a milk gland used by the cow to nurse its young. This is also where the milk we drink comes from, before it is put into cartons or bottles.

Develop that all the animals on the bulletin board which are not birds are called *mammals*. All have some fur or hair. Mother mammals have live babies and feed

make inferences

their babies milk from their milk glands.

2. *Materials:* gentle female dog, preferably one that has had puppies; dog owner.

Have the owner lift his dog's front feet up from behind so the class can see the dog's milk glands. Let him describe how his dog feeds its puppies, how often, and how long. Perhaps he can tell some other ways in which the dog takes care of its young. Encourage other children to describe pups or kittens born to their pets—number in the litter, how the newborn animals looked, when they were able to walk around, and so on.

Have several children feel the dog's skin and note its warmth. Establish that mammals have warm blood in their bodies. Whether the air gets hot or cold, the blood of mammals stays at about the same warm temperature. Mention that this is true of only one other group of animals, which they will study shortly. In all other animal groups, we find cold-blooded animals. That is, the temperature of their blood is usually about the same as the air temperature around them. As the air gets warmer, their blood gets warmer. As the air gets colder, their blood gets colder.

Elicit that the dog needs air, food, and water. Then let its owner open the dog's mouth. Discuss how the teeth are well suited for chewing meat. Bring out how the fur coat keeps the dog warm.

Summarize on a chart how to identify a mammal: warm blooded, fur or hair, and milk glands. Have pupils use these criteria to test if man is a mammal.

make inferences

EXTENDING ACTIVITIES

1. Inform pupils that they can raise mammals in class. Tell them two white rats (or mice) are available; a *male* ("He will become the father"), and a *female* ("She will become the mother"). Demonstrate how to prepare the cage and care for the animals. If some children have raised

472

small mammals, let them contribute suggestions. Be sure pupils understand the reason for each action taken whenever possible.

Cage—Use a commercially produced cage with exercise wheel and inverted water bottle as recommended in the exposition. Cover the floor with a four-page thickness of newspaper. Distribute a generous covering of sawdust, wood shavings, peat moss, or shredded newspaper over the paper. Remove the floor covering and replace with fresh materials twice a week, or oftener if a pronounced odor develops. The cage should be in a draft-free location, as rodents are quite susceptible to colds. Ideally, the temperature should not fall below 60°F. However, a deep floor covering usually provides some insulation against the loss of heat energy since the animals will burrow into it.

Food—Dry pellets for small laboratory animals, including rats, are obtainable at most pet and feed stores. In addition, feed bits of carrots, lettuce, and bread. Avoid feeding rats raw meat as sometimes this makes them vicious. A constant supply of pellets and other nonperishable food may be left in a small, flat container in the cage. However, remove any perishable food within an hour after offered. A fresh bottle of water and tray of pellets should last over weekends, but provisions for feeding will need to be taken for longer periods.

Handling—White rats and mice are typically very gentle, likable creatures. They should be handled daily for a short period. This tames them and accustoms them to being around children. If a tiny bit of peanut butter or carrot is offered on the tip of a toothpick, they can be enticed into the children's hands. Although there is virtually no chance of the animals biting if treated gently, caution children to wear gloves when handling them. (Notify the school nurse immediately if *any* classroom animal should bite a child. Although the bite itself is usually very minor, germs the animal may harbor in its mouth may cause infection unless the wound is promptly treated.)

Breeding—Rats and mice usually breed within a few days. Provide some loose cotton or shredded newspaper which the female can use in preparing a nest. Remove the male rat from the cage after it appears obvious that the female is pregnant. It may eat the young or agitate the female to do the same. Return the male to the pet store, or give it to the Humane Society, or confine it to a separate cage until the young are a month old. About three weeks after mating, the female will give birth to six or more young in the nest. Do not disturb the female for several days after this event.

The newborn young will be blind and hairless. They may be weaned gradually to a regular diet after they are about three weeks old. Feed them milk which contains soft bread crumbs for a week, and adult food thereafter.

All rats should be given to a responsible source for disposal after completion of this activity. Abandoned rodents become wild and add prolifically to the local pest population within a short time.

During the seven or eight weeks of working with this activity, be sure to provide opportunity for frequent, short, class discussions about the behavior and habits of the caged rats. Particular emphasis should be placed on the birth, appearance, care, feeding, and physical development of the young. You may note rapid day-to-day improvement in children's oral reporting skills as they tell the latest news about their rats.

Use a chart with rotating names for assigning such tasks as replacement of water, paper, and food. Most primary children are delighted to serve. This may be an excellent opportunity to motivate a problem child or help him achieve a greater sense of responsibility.

2. Encourage the class to bring in pictures of as many different kinds of mammals as it can. Pictures should be screened by class members for accuracy of classifica-

tion. If disputes arise about whether an animal is a mammal, have them use picture books and illustrated identification books for verification. Let an able class committee plan a bulletin board featuring unusual mammals and where they come from.

Birds. "A bird is an animal with feathers." This is a primary child's definition, but really cannot be much improved. Almost all other characteristics we see in birds may be found here and there among other animal groups, though not in the same combinations. The coloring and construction of their feathers vary tremendously, from the luxuriant plumage of a peacock to the scruffy covering of a New Zealand kiwi.

Although we ordinarily think of birds as fliers, chickens and road runners seldom fly, and some birds—the ostrich, penguin, and kiwi, for example—cannot fly at all.

"He eats like a bird." How often we have heard a person who eats sparingly described this way. It is hardly fitting. Few other animals possess such voracious appetites for their size. Many birds must eat their weight in food each day just to stay alive.

To see why this is so, examine a small, flying bird closely. Notice that its body volume is relatively small when compared to the large surface area of its skin. As body volume decreases in size, the relative size of skin surface increases. If this seems unclear, inspect a pint and quart milk carton. The small carton holds only half as much, but clearly has more than one-half the surface area of the larger carton. A large skin surface area causes heat energy to radiate rapidly away from the body. This is bad when the body volume is small because the heat generating capacity is also small. To generate enough heat energy for normal functioning when heat energy is quickly being radiated away, a high metabolic rate (the rate at which food is oxidized and assimilated) must be maintained. The rapid burning of fuel causes body temperatures in birds of 102° to 110°F, highest of any animal group.

Mammals are also affected in this way. Smaller mammals usually eat more for their size than larger ones. As we travel toward the earth's polar regions, we can observe a general increase in mammals' body size. As body volume increases, the relative size of skin surface decreases. Comparatively less heat energy is radiated away.

The bodies of most birds are well suited for flight. Inside are several air sacs connected to the lungs. Many bones are hollow, or nearly so, and further reduce body weight. Even a chicken has relatively little marrow in its longer bones. It is said that the great evolutionist Charles Darwin had a pipe stem made from a wing bone of an albatross.

The body of a bird is streamlined and closely fitted with three kinds of feathers. Next to the skin are fluffy, soft, down feathers. These contain numerous "dead-air" pockets which help conserve body heat. Contour feathers hug the body closely, and large flight feathers help to propel and steer the bird as it flies.

Most birds continually preen their feathers. This is done by using the bill to press a drop of oil from a gland located just above the tail, and then spreading it over the feathers. A shiny, waterproof coating results. It is so effective that a duck can float for many hours without becoming waterlogged. If the oil were removed, a swimming duck would disappear into the water like a slowly submerging submarine. If you can locate a large, recently molted feather, dip it in water before and after washing in soap or detergent. Let the children notice how water soaks in after the washing. (You can use the dowel balance on page 364L to measure the weight change.)

The thick white meat or breast section on poultry is partly the result of selective breeding by man. But virtually all birds have their largest and strongest muscles in this section, since they control the major wing movements. We shall provide an activity to help children realize how important these muscles are for this function.

The remarkably keen eyesight of birds has been well advertised. Less known is that they have three eyelids. Two shut the eye, and the third—a transparent membrane—sweeps back and forth, cleaning away dust or other foreign matter without need for blinking. Eyes of most birds are located on the sides of the head. Thus, they must continually cock the head to one side to see directly forward. Their hearing is also acute despite the lack of outer ears. But birds do not appear to discriminate well among various odors or tastes.

Most birds have horny beaks, whose various shapes show great diversity of function. Although all known modern birds are toothless, fossil records indicate that a variety of toothed birds lived in ancient times. The feet of birds are equally diverse in form. On the legs we find scales, which indicate their evolutionary connection to the reptiles.

As in mammals, sexual reproduction begins with an egg cell fertilized within the female by a sperm cell. However, fertilization is not necessary for an egg to be laid. Many chickens lay an egg every day. We eat these unfertilized eggs.

An egg acquires its hard shell in the lower part of the hen's oviduct, or egg-conducting tube. Glands produce a limy secretion which gradually hardens over a period of hours before the egg is laid. The shell is porous and permits both oxygen to enter and carbon dioxide to leave. In a fertilized egg, this is essential for life in the developing chick embryo.

Your pupils will thoroughly enjoy a chick-hatching activity, described later in some detail. You will need fertilized eggs and an incubator. Get the eggs from a hatchery or farmer. Buy a small incubator, usually priced at several dollars and up, from a pet shop or scientific supply house. Although it is possible to make an incubator with a glowing light bulb and insulated cardboard container, few seem to work

Figure 11-3 Children enjoy the chick-hatching activity. (Courtesy La Mesa-Spring Valley School District.)

satisfactorily. It is essential to success that a near-constant temperature of 101–103°F be maintained for the 21-day incubation period. Homemade incubators typically fluctuate in temperature well beyond permissible limits.

Generalization III: Birds are warm blooded, have feathers, and two wings

1. *Materials:* five or six pictures of birds. (Place on flannel or bulletin board.)

Ask the children to note several ways in which the pictured birds differ in coloring, marking, size, shape, and so on. Now ask them to note at least three ways in which they are the same. Develop that all have feathers, two wings, two legs and feet. Children may also observe that all have *bills*.

make inferences

Probably some class members have handled chicks, parakeets, or ducks. Draw out that these animals feel warm to the touch. What might this tell us about their blood? (They are warm blooded, like mammals.) Draw out that their feathers can also keep them warm in cold weather. Perhaps some child has a blanket at home filled with downy feathers. Let him describe how warm it is.

475

Many children will be aware that young are hatched from eggs, laid by the mother bird in some kind of nest. If they become curious and interested about this at the present time, you may want to start immediately on a chick hatching activity (extending activity 1).

2. *Materials:* large stuffed bird specimen (or a large picture of a bird); several clean, dry, long bones from a chicken.

Ask for the hands of pupils who like to eat chicken. Who likes the dark meat? Light meat? Point to the bird specimen or picture. Where would most of the light meat be found on this bird? (Breast.) Let someone indicate this area.

Bring out that the light meat section on a bird is the thickest part of its body, and is made up of chest muscles. But why are the muscles so thick and large here? Encourage speculation briefly. Ask the children to stand and hold their arms out to the side,

parallel to the floor. Arms should be straightened and elbows locked. Have all rapidly move their arms forward and back, no more than a foot or so. In less than half a minute pupils will feel a tightening and slightly strained effect on their upper chest muscles (pectorals) and shoulders. Draw out that the bird's wings are moved mainly by the chest muscles. The exercise of pushing against the air develops strong, large chest muscles.

Break open a few long bones from a chicken. Let the children closely examine them. Develop that the bones are relatively hollow, in contrast with mammal bones, which are thicker and filled with a heavy marrow. Mention that a few kinds of birds have some bones which are completely hollow. Help pupils reason that the lightness of hollow bones is an advantage in flying. Mention that many flying birds have several air pockets inside their bodies, which also help to make birds light for their size.

Ask the children to speculate why a bird cocks its head to one side as it looks at something directly ahead. Why doesn't it stare straight ahead? Have children examine the specimen and available pictures. Develop that most birds' eyes are located on the sides of their heads. This makes it difficult or impossible to see something directly in front. Let the class discover through pictures that owls are the commonest exception.

suggest hypotheses

make inferences

Point out the eyelids on the stuffed specimen. There is an upper and lower lid, like on humans. Explain that, in addition there is a third eyelid which is clear (transparent). It sweeps from the back to the front of the eye, and wipes away dust.

Does a bird have ears? Ask a child to take a pencil and probe gently around the stuffed specimen's head. He should find an opening on each side of the skull. Explain that a bird does not have outside (external) ears, but does have hearing organs inside that work very well. The outside holes help to let in sounds.

Figure 11-4 (A) Duck, (B) woodpecker, (C) sparrow, (D) hawk.

3. *Materials:* opaque projector; Figure 11-4.

This is an appropriate time to develop adaptations of bills and feet of birds. Project Figure 11-4 onto a screen. Have the third column masked with some black paper at present. It can be revealed later to verify pupil hypotheses. Ask the children to study the first and second columns,

suggest hypotheses and then to guess the kind of food each bird eats. To make this easier, you might slowly say, "One of these birds cracks open seeds; another eats small mammals; another scoops up plants and tiny fish from water; another punches holes in the bark of trees and digs out insects."

make inferences Bring out the following ideas:

a. The bill of bird A is useful in scooping up plants and small fish in water, because it is like a little shovel. The scooped-up water spills out through the uneven sides of the bill, but the food remains inside.

b. The bill of bird B is like a large, pointed nail. It can dig into tough tree bark and catch insects. (Point out that the bills of most other insect eaters are slenderer.)

c. The bill of bird C is small but strong. It can crack open seeds and some nuts. (A child may have a pet canary whose seed-cracking ways might be described.)

d. The bill of bird D is like a sharp hook. It can tear the meat from bones of small mammals.

suggest hypotheses Let children speculate how specialized feet help the birds. After some discussion, reveal the third column of Figure 11-4. Identify the birds: duck (A), woodpecker (B), sparrow (C), and hawk (D). Develop these ideas: Webbed feet of the duck are useful for paddling in water. The woodpecker's feet can dig securely into a vertical tree trunk. The sparrow's feet are useful for perching. They automatically close around a tree limb or similar perch. It requires no effort and the bird may sleep in this position without danger of falling. The hawk's feet are useful for grasping an animal and holding it securely.

EXTENDING ACTIVITIES

1. Have a chick-hatching activity. Get several fertilized eggs from a hatchery or farmer, and an egg incubator. Discuss the fact that birds hatch from eggs. Describe the behavior of a hen after it lays one or more eggs. The hen settles over the egg and keeps it warm. Several times a day it turns the egg. This keeps the growing chick from sticking to the shell. After twenty-one days, the chick breaks open the shell and comes out.

Show the incubator. It can keep the eggs warm, too. We can turn the eggs twice a day—once in the morning, and once at dismissal time. Will chicks hatch? We shall see. Help the children to realize that a mark placed on the egg will assist in keeping track of egg positions.

In twenty-one days, or sooner if the eggs have not been freshly laid, the hatching will take place. This process may take from a few hours to perhaps ten or more. Since some hatching may occur at night, it is good to have several eggs. This will increase the chance that a few chicks will hatch during school hours.

Let the children observe how a chick breaks out of its shell by using a tiny "egg tooth" on top of its beak. This drops off shortly after the chick emerges. The chick will look wet and scraggly until its downy feathers dry. (Figure 11-5.) No food is necessary for at least twenty-four hours as it will have digested the egg yolk and some egg white before breaking out of the shell. (Many children have the misconception that an egg yolk *is* the undeveloped embryo, rather than its principal food.)

Chicks need constant warmth. This is furnished by a brooder, or warm box. An incubator can be used temporarily if the lid is raised, but may be too confining after a few days. If the chicks are to be kept for more than several days, use a cardboard box with a shielded, goose-neck lamp shining into it. Chick feed may be pur-

Figure 11-5 (Lynwood M. Chace — National Audubon Society.)

chased at a pet store. Leave some feed and clean water in dishes within the brooder at all times. A fresh newspaper floor cover each day will keep the brooder clean. Give the chicks to a farmer or hatchery after a week or two. Proper conditions become increasingly difficult to provide in a classroom as chicks become older.

2. Invite pupils to bring in pictures of various birds. On the basis of the bills, let the children tentatively divide the birds into such categories as "seed eaters," "insect eaters," and "meat eaters." Picture book research will confirm how accurate they are. Let the class discover that some birds cannot be classified in just one category.

make inferences

Reptiles. Many children know that snakes are reptiles, but are unaware that the term also includes turtles, lizards, alligators, and crocodiles. What do these animals have in common? Typically they have dry, scaly skin. Those with feet have five toes, which

bear claws. All are lung breathers, which means that even an aquatic turtle will drown if placed underwater for an extended time period.

Reptiles have well developed hearts with three chambers (some have almost four). Unlike mammals and birds, reptiles are cold blooded. In winter, reptiles in relatively cold climates hibernate below ground; they become unable to move when the temperature drops very low. It is no accident that reptiles are rare in regions beyond the temperate zones, and grow prolifically in the tropics.

Reproduction in reptiles begins with internal fertilization of an egg, similarly to mammals and birds. But the process thereafter is different enough to warrant our attention. All of the turtles and most of the lizards and snakes lay eggs in secluded areas on land. The eggs have tough, leathery covers, and for the most part are dependent upon the sun's warmth for ef-

478

fective incubation. Some snakes and lizards retain the egg internally until the incubation period is complete. The young are then born alive. However, the process should not be equated with the development of mammalian young. In mammals, as we noted, the embryo is attached to the female and nourished directly through a placental membrane. In the case of reptiles, there is no internal attachment. The egg incubates until the growing embryo inside is sufficiently developed to hatch and so leave the female.

Turtles and most lizards have three eyelids, as do birds. Snakes have no eyelids. A transparent, horny cover over the eye protects it from injury as the animal moves among sticks and vegetation. Just before a snake sheds it skin—up to several times a year—the transparent eye cover becomes milky in color. Interestingly, the only easy way to tell the difference between the several species of legless lizards and snakes is to note if the eyes blink.

Children may bring lizards to class, often "swifts." (See Figure 11-6.) In the southwestern United States, it is common for them to bring the gentle and easily tamed horned "toads." (Horned lizards.) Nearly all lizards may be housed satisfactorily in a terrarium containing some sand, placed where it is sunny. (*Caution: leave the top open to avoid excessive building of heat.*) The anole, or American chameleon—the kind often bought at fairs and pet shops—is more suited to a woodland terrarium, described on page 115R.

Chameleons are fun for children to ob-

Figure 11-6   A typical small lizard: Eastern Fence Swift. (Howard Earl Uible-Photo Researchers, Inc.)

serve. Like many lizards, they change body color under different conditions of light, temperature, and excitation. However, the color change is greater in chameleons than in most other lizards. It is brought about by dilation and contraction of blood vessels in the skin. To distinguish the male, look for a loose fold of skin at its throat. (Figure 11-7.)

Many lizards have fragile tails which break off easily when seized. In some species, the broken-off tail part wriggles about animatedly, thereby often distracting the attention of a would-be captor until the lizard escapes. Lizards can grow back (regenerate) new tails.

If possible, try to obtain a small, tame snake for at least a short period during this unit. Let the children touch it and learn that it has a dry, cool skin, rather than a slimy coating. Children should be taught that nearly all snakes in this country are highly beneficial to man, that snakes consume many thousands of destructive rodent and insect pests each year. At the same time pupils should learn an intelligent respect for snakes. If poisonous snakes appear locally, show pictures of what they are like. Caution the class never to hunt for snakes unless accompanied by a responsible and informed older person. In the continental United States only the rattlesnake, copperhead, water moccasin, and coral snake are dangerous to man.

Generalization IV: Reptiles are cold blooded, and have a dry, scaly skin; some have a shell

Figure 11-7 American chameleon. (William M. Stephens—Photo Researchers, Inc.)

1. *Materials:* two small aquatic turtles; deep, glass baking dish or dishpan; gravel. (To make a suitable home for the turtles, put some gravel in the container. Pile it gradually at one end to form a slope. Pour in several inches of water. The turtles will now have a pond for swimming and a land surface to crawl onto for resting.)

Show the children the turtles. Write *turtle* on the chalkboard when children mention the word. Place the turtles on a low table top and have everyone observe the way they walk. Touch their heads gently with a pencil. Draw out that withdrawal of the head and legs into a shell is a form of protection. Pass the turtles around for close examination. If each is first placed in a small dish, it will aid observation. (It is a good policy to have children wash their hands afterward if they handle animals without gloves.) Have pupils describe what they see. Bring out these features: four webbed feet, bearing tiny claws; hard shell, no teeth, eyelids, and scaly dry skin. Emphasize the scaly skin appearance. Turn over the turtles. Have everyone observe how they achieve a right side up position. Ask why turtles feel cool to the touch. (They are cold blooded.) Their blood is as warm or cold as the air around them.

If some pupils have had turtle pets, invite them to tell how these may be cared for. Establish the following procedures:

develop procedures

Feeding—Once a day; commercial turtle food, bits of raw meat and lettuce, dropped into the water. Aquatic turtles feed under water. Remove all uneaten food from the tank after 15 minutes to keep the water clean. (Or, present this as a problem: How can we keep the water clean? The best solution is to remove the turtles from the tank and put them into a deep glass dish of water. After 15 minutes for feeding, return them to the tank.)

Care of tank—Change the water twice a week. Wash off the gravel each time.

Sunshine—Most turtles are healthiest where they can get several hours of sunshine each day. But if they become too warm, they may die. Part of the container should be in the shade.

Ask the children why the gravel is slanted in the container. Develop that turtles are air breathers, like humans. They must be able to crawl out of the water to rest.

2. *Materials:* American chameleon; hand magnifying lens; woodland terrarium. (The one described on page 115R is ideal for this lizard.)

Introduce this animal as a "mystery guest." It is an animal, but we will need to find out more about it before we can say for sure what it is. If a child calls it a lizard, ask him how he knows. Suggest personal observations if authority alone is cited. Let the children observe that its skin is dry and consists of tiny scales. The feet bear tiny claws on five toes. Draw out that the small holes on the head are ear openings. A hand lens will aid observations.

Put the animal into the terrarium. Ask pupils to observe its behavior during their individual free-time periods and occasionally during the day. Feed it some live insects or a mealworm daily. After several days, ask pupils what they have found out. (The animal changes color sometimes. It can climb on a branch very well with its padded feet. It laps water drops from the plants. We can see it breathing. It has a flap under the throat which swells up sometimes. And so on.) Encourage use of picture books to find its identity. Guide children to compare critically the data they have gathered through observation with data accompanying the picture. Let them locate pictures of other *lizards*.

make inferences

3. *Materials:* various pictures of turtles, lizards, and snakes.

Invite the children to name these animals. Explain that all belong to the same group, called *reptiles*. There are many different kinds of turtles, snakes, and lizards. All reptiles have a dry, scaly skin. All are cold blooded and breathe air. Nearly all hatch from eggs which are laid on land by the female (mother) reptiles.

Figure 11-8 Toad (left) and frog. Notice the external ear drum, just behind and below the eye.

(Verna R. Johnson-Photo Researchers, Inc. Ron Winch-Photo Researchers, Inc.)

If a film is available which goes into the characteristics of reptiles, it may assist in developing some ideas. But pose a few thought-provoking questions before showing it. For example, what happens to these cold-blooded animals when the weather gets freezing cold? What happens when the weather gets too warm?

EXTENDING ACTIVITIES

1. Use a glass tank to house a small, tame snake for a week. It will not be necessary to feed it. Put sand and a low pan of water on the tank floor. Arrange inside several rocks of various sizes and shapes and a strong, branched stick. The snake should be able to retreat under or between the rocks. The branch can be used in climbing. Put a fine-meshed screen over the tank top. Weigh it down at the four corners with bricks or heavy books.

Help the children to understand that nearly all snakes are beneficial to man because they eat mostly insect and rodent pests. In our country only four kinds are dangerous. Let them observe that the snake's skin is scaly, dry, and cool, like that of the other reptiles they handled. Permit them to handle or touch the snake gently, but only if they want to. The important

thing at this level is to circumvent, or at least diminish, unreasoning fears about these reptiles.

2. Provide a variety of picture books on lizards, snakes, and turtles. Divide class members into three groups. Help each child to find an interesting picture and fact about one type of reptile. Let him show the picture and report the fact to the entire class.

Amphibians. These are animals that typically spend part of their lives in water and part on land. The principal kinds are frogs, toads, and salamanders. Amphibians represent an interesting evolutionary link between fish and reptiles, and indeed have many characteristics of both groups. If animal life originally began and evolved in the sea, as is generally supposed, it is probable that early amphibians were the first vertebrates to emerge from the water and live successfully on land.

Amphibians are cold blooded, and have hearts with three chambers. Like other cold-blooded animals, they hibernate in cold weather, usually by burrowing in the ground or mud. The adults breathe through lungs, but are also able to absorb some oxygen through the skin. The latter method of breathing is especially useful in hibernation. But skin breathing is inadequate for sustained activity, and even a frog will drown eventually if forced to remain underwater.

Frogs and salamanders usually have moist, smooth skins which must remain moist if they are to survive. For this reason a bowl of water is needed in a terrarium that houses these creatures.

One day a child may show you a small amphibian and ask, "Is this a toad or a frog?" Although it is hard to distinguish between them all the time, a toad usually has dry, rough skin. Its body is broad and fat, and the eyelids more prominent than those of frogs. Another indicator is the location where it was caught. Frogs are likelier to live by water, whereas toads are mostly land dwellers. (Figure 11-8.)

Can toads cause warts? Many children think they can. The toad's warty-looking tubercules are glands which secrete a fluid that can sicken attacking animals. But the substance cannot cause warts. It may, however, irritate a child's eyes if he should rub them after handling a toad. Advise pupils to wash their hands after playing with a toad.

Salamanders are less common than frogs and toads; chances are that few pupils will have these as pets. Most have four legs of the same size, and long, tubular bodies with tails. Superficially, they resemble lizards and are often mistaken for them. They differ from lizards in several ways: the forelegs of salamanders have four toes instead of five; they have no claws; and typically the skin is smooth, rather than rough.

Perhaps the most striking difference of amphibians from the other groups we have examined is in their means of reproduction. Female amphibians lay their eggs in water, or in very moist places on land. The males fertilize the eggs immediately after they are laid by shedding sperm over them. Thus, fertilization is external, unlike that in higher animals.

A single female frog or toad may lay several thousand eggs at one time. The eggs are coated with a thick, jellylike substance which quickly absorbs water and swells in size. This substance protects the developing embryo and serves as an initial source of food.

The embryo hatches after one to two weeks as a tadpole or "polliwog" which looks completely unlike the adult. It is only after several months to several years, depending on the species, that tadpoles acquire the adult form. (See Figure 11-9.) This process of changing forms, called metamorphosis, is another distinct departure from the growth and development pattern of higher animals.

In their initial growth stages, tadpoles breathe like fishes — they obtain oxygen from water through tiny gills. Therefore, be sure to "age" tap water for at least twenty-four hours to rid it of chlorine before adding it to the container in which they are kept. But use tap water only if pond water is not available.

Generalization V: Amphibians are cold blooded, and have either a smooth or bumpy skin; most hatch from jellylike eggs laid in water

Figure 11-9 Metamorphosis of the frog.

1. *Materials:* small, live adult frog in a small glass jar; large glass jar half-filled with aged water; terrarium (described on page 115R): dead insect: thread: live insect.

Let pupils identify their new visitor as a *frog*. Mention that there are many interesting things they can notice about a frog's body if they observe carefully. Have several children touch its skin. Let them describe it. How might a smooth, slippery skin help a frog get away from an enemy? (It is hard to hold onto.) Is the frog probably warm blooded or cold blooded? (The skin is cool; it is probably cold blooded.)

<small>make inferences</small>

Direct attention to the frog's eyes. A thin, transparent membrane will periodically come up from the lower eyelid, sweep the eye, and go down again. Slowly draw the eraser end of a pencil near one eye. An upper and lower lid will close the eye, and the frog may retract the eyeball somewhat into its head. Let children describe these behaviors.

Explain that a frog can hear sounds, but it does not have ears like ours. Can anyone find the places which serve as outside ears for the frog? (The round-shaped piece of skin below and back of each eye.)

Let everyone examine the frog's legs. The forelegs are small and have four tiny toes, but no claws. The hind legs are larger and longer, with five webbed toes. Some pupils will remember that several birds have webbed feet. Draw out that the hind legs may be used more in swimming than the forelegs. They can see if this is so, shortly.

<small>make inferences</small>

Does the frog breathe air? Challenge the children to find any indications of air breathing. (Tiny nostril vents near its snout, and throat movements.) Will it breathe underwater? Hold the frog securely by its hind legs and submerge it completely for a few seconds in a large jar of water. (The nose holes close, and throat movements stop.) Develop that while the frog cannot breathe air directly, some air in the water goes through its skin. However, it cannot keep alive for long on this tiny amount of air except during special times.

Release the frog. Wait briefly until it floats quietly. Children will observe that its nose vents are open and above water and the frog is again visibly breathing. They may also notice that the frog's eyes are above water as it floats. Help them reason that in this way it can see better what is going on above the water surface. Compare to the eyes of a floating hippopotamus and alligator if pictures are available.

Rap the jar sharply with a pencil. The frog probably will begin swimming. Have everyone observe how the powerful hind legs propel it along.

Take the amphibian out of the water and place it in a smaller jar. Drop in a live ant, mealworm, or other nonflying insect. Children will be astonished at how quickly the frog's tongue lashes out, catches the insect, and withdraws into its mouth. Several trials may be needed before everyone observes this action. Develop that the tongue is attached to the *front* of the lower mouth, unlike the tongues of other animals.

Put a dead insect inside the jar. Why doesn't the frog eat it? Raise conjecture. Tie a piece of thread loosely around a leg of the dead insect. Swing it slowly in front of the frog. It may eat the insect. Bring out that frogs usually do not eat something unless it moves.

<small>suggest hypotheses</small>

Place the frog in the woodland terrarium. Be sure there is a bowl of water inside. Explain that a frog's skin must be moist if it is to survive. Schedule volunteers to supply it with several live earthworms and insects each day.

2. *Materials:* pictures of a frog, toad, salamander, and lizard (or live animals, if possible).

Ask the children to compare a frog with a *toad*. How is the toad different? (Toad's skin is bumpy. Its legs are shorter. The body is wider.) How is it alike? (Same general appearance, same number of toes, no claws.) Mention here that both animals

<small>make inferences</small>

hatch from jellylike eggs laid in water. Stress that each is an *amphibian*—an animal that usually spends part of its life in water and part on land.

Show the salamander and lizard, but do not identify them at present. Mention that one is an amphibian—a member of the same group as the frog and toad. Another is a reptile. Which is which, and why? Children should determine that the salamander is more closely related to the frog and toad because it has the same number of toes, no claws, and a smooth skin. Identify the *salamander*. Explain that the salamander often hatches from jellylike eggs laid in ponds, or in moist places on land.

make nferences

EXTENDING ACTIVITIES

1. Encourage a few pupils who have their parents' approval to gather some eggs of frogs or toads. These can be found in spring and summer among the weeds in ponds and marshy places close to shore. Frogs' eggs will be in jumbled clumps, often floating on or near the water surface. Toads' eggs will be laid in strings, often wrapped around some water plants.

Wide-mouth jars can be used to scoop up and contain the eggs. Stress that only several eggs should be taken—for two reasons. Many frogs and toads should grow from the remaining eggs and destroy insect pests. Also, a crowded container may prevent some eggs from hatching or cause some tadpoles to die. A few small water plants and some pond water should be taken at the same time. Microscopic, waterborne matter will serve as the tadpoles' food supply until they are developed enough to eat tiny bits of lettuce and fish food. The plants will furnish a place for the newly hatched tadpoles to cling to until they become strong enough to swim freely.

Tadpoles can be kept in large, open glass jars or in a fishless aquarium tank. It may be necessary to change most of the water

every several weeks and clean out the container. If so, replace with more pond water or as a last resort, aged, chlorine-free water.

Encourage the children to observe and discuss tadpole development as it proceeds. You might record for them the unfolding sequence of events as they describe them: tadpoles with tiny gills emerging from the eggs; clinging to the plants; body and tail increasing in length; hind legs appearing; gills disappearing; front legs developing; tails shrinking; and so on. When the front legs appear, place the tadpoles in a semi-aquatic environment, like that recommended for the aquatic turtle. As its gills disappear, the tadpole develops lungs. Rest periods out of the water become increasingly necessary or the tadpoles may drown.

Since the time period for complete metamorphosis varies with each species, the tadpoles may not have grown into adult form when the school term ends. If so, let some responsible children take the tadpoles home, or release them where the eggs originally were found.

2. If the preceding activity cannot be done, show a film on the metamorphosis of amphibians. Develop some speculation first, before running the film, about the possible physical development of a frog or toad from egg to adult.

Fishes. Next to mammals, fishes are the vertebrates that present the greatest diversity in appearance, adaptations, and habits. Certainly fishes are most numerous, both as individuals and in numbers of species. (When only one species is referred to, "fish" is both singular and plural. "Fishes" means those of several species.) Fossil records indicate that these creatures were the first animals with true backbones.

Fishes are cold blooded and have hearts of only two chambers. Only they among the adult vertebrates breathe through gills, instead of lungs. Gills are composed of thousands of blood vessels contained in hairlike filaments, located in back of the head on both sides. We cannot easily see these filaments on a live fish, as gill covers conceal them.

A fish breathes by opening and closing its mouth. In the process, water is taken in then forced out of the gill openings. As water passes over the gills, oxygen dissolved in the water filters into the filaments and blood vessels, then circulates throughout the body. At the same time, carbon dioxide passes out of the filaments and is swept away.

One of the advantages in carefully classifying living things by structure is that it enables us to see relationships we might otherwise miss. In fishes, for example, an organ called the "air bladder" appears to be a forerunner of the lung. The bladder is an air-filled sac usually located in the middle of a fish, between its kidney and stomach. By compressing and expanding its air bladder, a fish can rise and descend in the water.

In the odd lungfish, this organ has been modified into a crude lung, enabling it to breathe air directly, in addition to gill breathing. A lungfish typically lives in a muddy pond or marsh, which may dry up in summer. It survives by burrowing into the mud and breathing air supplied through a hole in the mud cover. When its pond fills again with seasonal rainfall, the lungfish resumes the behavior we are accustomed to expect of fish.

The lungfish is found in Africa, South America, and Australia, and is of no commercial importance. But to a student of evolution, it is a most interesting animal. The lungfish appears to be a clear link between fishes and amphibians in the long evolutionary march of vertebrates from the sea.

The body of a fish is well suited for its environment. Its streamlined contours offer a minimum of resistance to the water. A slimy, mucuslike secretion that exudes between the overlapping body scales further reduces friction and insulates the skin from attack by microorganisms. A

large tail fin, wagged from side to side, propels it through the water. Vertical fins on top and bottom keep the fish on an even keel while it is moving. Two pairs of side fins, one pair near the gills (pectoral fins), and the other pair farther back (pelvic fins), balance the fish when it is stationary. These fins are also used to assist turning, in the manner of oars, and for swimming backward. When held out laterally, they brake the swimming fish to a stop. Pectoral fins correspond to forelegs, and pelvic fins to hind legs, in other animals.

The eyes of a fish are always open since it has no eyelids. Focusing is accomplished by shifting the pupil forward and back, rather than changing the lens shape, as in humans. Although there are no external ears, fish hear with auditory capsules deep within the head. In many fishes, a lateral line of sensory scales extends along both sides of the body from head to tail. These scales are particularly sensitive to sounds of low pitch. Some expert fishermen claim that a fish can hear heavy footsteps (Always of other, inexpert fishermen, of course!) on a nearby bank. The taste sense appears to be mostly lacking, but a fish is sensitive to smells. Nostril pits on the snout lead to organs of smell just below. The whole body seems to be sensitive to touch, especially the lips. In species like the catfish, extra touch organs are found in the form of "whiskers."

Reproduction of fishes is accomplished by either external or internal fertilization of the egg, depending on the species. The female goldfish, for example, lays eggs on aquatic plants. The male fertilizes the eggs by shedding sperm cells over them. Goldfish usually reproduce only in large tanks or ponds.

Guppies and many other tropical varieties use internal fertilization. The male has a modified anal fin which carries sperm. The fin is inserted into a small opening below the female's abdomen and sperm cells released. Fertilized eggs remain in the female's body until the embryos hatch and are "born." Many of the young guppies are eaten by the adult fish, unless sufficient plant growth makes it difficult to detect them.

To raise as many guppies as possible, place the pregnant female and some plants in a separate container. After the young are born, remove the mother. The young may join the adult guppies safely in about one month. Try not to be too efficient at breeding guppies, however. Someone good at arithmetic has calculated that a single pair will become three million guppies in a year, assuming all generations and offspring stay alive. A female guppy may produce several dozen young every four to six weeks at a water temperature of 70° to 80°F.

Male guppies are readily distinguishable from the females in several ways. They are about half the size (exclusive of the tails), much narrower in body, and more brilliant in color. (Figure 11-10.)

Generalization VI: Fishes are cold blooded, live and breathe in water, and are usually covered with scales

1. *Materials:* three quart jars of aged water, each containing a live goldfish; three ice cubes.

Assist pupils to observe various physical properties of a goldfish.

Cluster one-third of the class around each jar, so each child can closely observe a fish. Ask some questions to determine pupil knowledge and to guide observations. What are these animals? How do we know? Seize any opportunity to improve reasoning. For example, someone may mention that these animals swim in water. Don't some of the other animals we studied? How do fish differ?

Have the children observe the overlapping body scales. Bring out that fish scales differ from reptile scales in that they overlap like house roof shingles; reptile scales do not overlap in this way.

Continue with other observations. How does a fish get its air? Draw attention to the

related movements of the mouth and *gills.* Develop that a fish takes in water through its mouth. The water goes out through gill openings on each side of the head. Gills remove air from the water and also expel used air the fish exhales. Emphasize that, of all full-grown animals, only fish can breathe in this way.

Have groups compare the rate of gill movements before and after an ice cube is dropped into each jar. Can they infer how temperature variation affects the fishes' breathing rate? (Use two ice cubes on a warm day, but do not severely chill the water as this may be harmful to the fish.)

make inferences

Some children may observe two tiny nostrils in the snout. Raise conjecture about their use. Children might find out through a film shown later that these openings are used in smelling rather than breathing. Let them search in vain for external ears. Perhaps the same film may reveal that fish do

Figure 11-10 Male (right) and female guppy. (Courtesy of the American Museum of Natural History.)

not have ears as such, but that they can sense some sounds.

Pupils will observe that the fish do not close their eyes. Draw out that there are no visible eyelids. Challenge them to determine how they might discover whether a fish sleeps. After some discussion, tell them that there is no perfect way to know at this time. Scientists are still working on the problem.

Raise questions about how the fish propel themselves in the water; also, how they turn and stop. Sharp-eyed observers may notice that they move quickly forward only when the tail is lashed from side to side. Why doesn't a fish turn partly over on one side when it stops swimming? For a clue have a child stand balanced on one foot. Bring out how he uses his arms laterally to stabilize himself. What does a fish use? Develop that the side fins are employed in somewhat the same way, but that they push against the water.

Perhaps some children have handled live fish. Let them recall how cool and slippery the skin feels. Develop that fish, too, are cold-blooded animals. Caution everyone not to handle a live fish with dry hands, since this rubs off the scales' protective, slippery coating.

2. *Materials:* pictures of a variety of fishes; simple film which shows some fish adaptations.

Exhibit many pictures of fishes in identification books or trade books. Let children discuss the many ways in which these fishes are different and alike—in coloring, marking, probable size, shape, and so on.

Use a film to confirm earlier observations and to furnish information for unanswered questions. Emphasize that fishes are usually covered with scales, breathe and live in water, and are cold-blooded animals.

EXTENDING ACTIVITIES

Help children set up several small aquaria for observation at school or home. For each aquarium they will need a wide-mouth glass jar of at least one-quart capacity, two guppies (a male and female), an aquatic snail, a small water plant, and a large-size soda straw. If a child or another teacher has a large guppy aquarium, chances are they will gladly give up a dozen or more guppies to reduce the rapidly increasing population, and some plants to thin out the thickening aquarium foliage. Use a small dip net or glass to scoop out the guppies. Transfer them to a jar containing water taken from their present home.

Show pupils what to use for their aquaria. Develop why these materials are used, when possible:

a. A wide-mouth glass jar, of at least one-quart capacity. A wide-mouth jar will let more air into the jar than a narrower one.

b. Water that is "aged" (left standing for one or two days). This warms the water to room temperature. Cold water may kill the fish. Also, this lets out chemicals that are put into the water to kill germs. Sometimes these chemicals kill fish.

c. Two guppies (a male and a female, identify by size and coloring). They may have young and we can see how baby guppies are born.

d. A small, rootless water plant. When baby guppies stay among the plant leaves, the big fish cannot see them and eat them. (Also, the plant helps to provide extra air; this will be meaningless, however, at the primary level.)

e. A water snail. It will help to keep the jar clean. (Establish that the fish should be given only a tiny pinch of fish food, three or four times a week. Explain that uneaten food spoils the water after a while.)

f. A straw dip tube. Show how it is used to remove debris from an aquarium. Drop a small crumb into a glass of water; it should sink quickly. Take a straw and close the top open end with a forefinger. Place the bottom opening of the straw over the crumb. Open briefly and then close again the top end with your forefinger. Withdraw the straw and captured crumb. Re-

Figure 11-11 There is nothing like telling a friend about events happening in one's own, personal aquarium. (Courtesy San Diego City Schools.)

lease your finger; the crumb and water will rush out of the straw.

Encourage the children to observe their guppies and snails carefully, and to report any interesting changes, including birth, growth, death, and decay. When some baby guppies appear, develop that some fishes are born alive while others hatch from eggs laid in the water. Guide pupils to transfer some guppies when an overcrowded condition appears. Occasionally observe pupils' fish jars to help them figure out how to prevent or reverse unwanted changes. (See page 114R.)

Insects and Life Cycles.

Insects

They eat our carpets and munch our clothes,
Spread disease and damage our homes,
Spoil our picnics and wreck our fun,
I'd like to get rid of every single one!

(Sandra, age 11)

This brief verse sums up the opinion of many persons about insects. But it is only one side of the story. "Get rid of" all insects and some very undesirable consequences take place. Here are only a few: Probably half of all the flowering plants on earth would disappear—bees, flies, moths, and butterflies help to pollinate them. Most of the land birds would vanish—their principal source of food is insects. Biological research would be hampered—the short life cycles of insects are ideal for quick results in medical and hereditary studies.

As mentioned, insects make up an astounding 70 per cent of all animal species. Hundreds of new species are discovered each year. They are found virtually everywhere on earth. What makes them so successful? How do we tell a "real" insect from a pseudo insect?

The first thing we might note about insects is that they have jointed legs. Instead of an internal skeleton, such as we find in vertebrates, they have an external skeleton, made of a crusty substance called chitin. Muscles and other body parts are attached inside to this semirigid exterior. To continue growing, an immature insect must molt or shed its outside covering from time to time. We can see that the need for molting greatly limits insect size. A heavy body would collapse before the soft, new covering hardened. These two characteristics — jointed legs and external skeleton — are also typical of the several other classes which make up the arthropods. (See page 467R.)

The easiest way to distinguish an adult insect is to look for six legs and three body parts: head, thorax, and abdomen. (Figure 11-12.) Notice that this leaves out spiders, which have eight legs, and many other arthropods — sow bugs, centipedes, scorpions, and so on. The head contains a primitive "brain," and mouth parts which vary considerably among insect orders. Most insects have two compound eyes, which are aggregates of many lenses, and several simple eyes as well, each of which has only one lens. The eyes are always open, since there are no eyelids. Two hairlike antennae, sensitive to touch and sometimes smell, are

also found on most insect heads. The middle section or thorax is where the six legs and wings are attached. Some insects have two wings, others four; a few have none. The abdomen contains the organs of digestion, excretion, and reproduction. Tiny holes (spiracles) in the thorax and abdomen furnish air for breathing. The air is piped into the internal organs by a network of connected tubes.

There are several reasons why insects have survived so successfully. Most are capable of flight. This provides a great range for potential food. Insects typically have very sensitive nervous systems; they are particularly sensitive to odors related to their food. The thorax of an insect may be packed with striated muscles — the kind that contract immediately upon signal. This makes many insects difficult to catch. The compound eyes add to this difficulty because they cover a wide-angle view. Although insects are cold blooded, as are all known invertebrates, their small size often permits them to secure adequate shelter when the weather becomes cold. Many pass through the winter months in a resting or inactive stage. Perhaps most important for their survival as a group is the rapidity with which they produce new generations.

The life cycles of insects are most interesting. Eggs are fertilized internally and hatched externally. In most species the insect goes through a complete metamorphosis of four stages as it matures: egg, larva, pupa, and adult. The hatched larva (caterpillar) eats almost continually, and sheds its skin several times as it grows. Then it either spins a cocoon (moth larva, for example) or encases itself in a chrysalis (a butterfly larva, for example) and enters the pupa stage. The body tissues change during this "resting" period. Sometime later — it varies with the species — an adult insect emerges.

Some insects, such as the grasshopper, cricket, termite, and aphid, go through an incomplete metamorphosis of three stages:

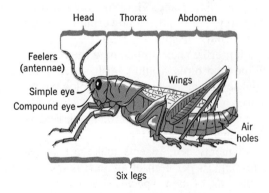

Head   Thorax   Abdomen

Feelers (antennae)

Wings

Simple eye

Compound eye

Air holes

Six legs

Figure 11-12

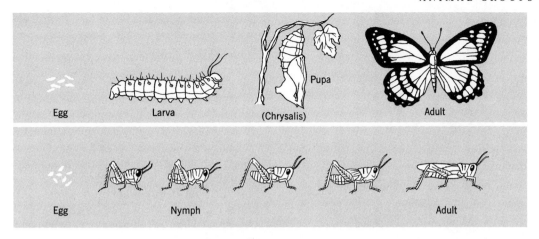

Figure 11-13 Grasshopper and butterfly metamorphoses.

egg, nymph, and adult. The hatched young, or nymphs, resemble the adult except that they appear out of proportion and lack wings. As they grow, molting takes place at least several times. There is no pupa stage. (See Figure 11-13.)

Pupils will relish observing some insects go through several stages of their life cycles and will learn from this procedure. They will not be able to locate eggs, as these are usually too small to see, but they should be able to find and bring in caterpillars, cocoons, and chrysalises. Remind them to take several leaves from the plant on which the caterpillar was feeding when captured. A fresh supply may be needed every few days. Use a glass jar or similar container to house each of these specimens. (Figure 11-14.) Place some soil inside, and an upright twig from which the larva might suspend its chrysalis. Either a cheesecloth lid secured with an elastic band, or a perforated jar top, should provide enough air. Moisten the soil occasionally for cocoons and chrysalises, as they may dry up without sufficient humidity.

For a larger, more elaborate insect terrarium, see Figure 11-15. You will need two cake pans, a section of wire screen, paper fasteners, an upturned jar lid (for water), several twigs and leaves, and some

soil. Roll the screen into a cylinder to fit inside the cake pans. Secure the screen seam with several paper fasteners. Put soil in the base. To make the base heavier and to firmly implant a small branch, you may want to pour some mixed plaster of Paris into the bottom cake pan before adding the soil.

To show the entire life cycle of an insect from egg to egg, raise some silkworm moths

Figure 11-14

491

Cake pan

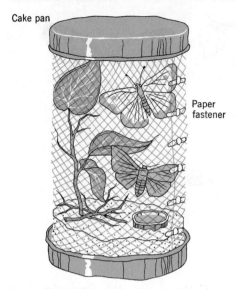

Paper fastener

Figure 11-15

in class. Within about eight weeks, children will see larvae hatch from the eggs, feed busily for a time, spin cocoons and pupate, emerge from the cocoons as adult moths, mate, lay eggs, and die. Eggs and specific instructions can be purchased inexpensively from a biological supply house. (See page 91R.) The mulberry leaves on which the larvae feed are found in most parts of the continental United States. Another insect with a short (six to eight weeks) life cycle is the greater wax moth. It may be purchased from several supply companies, including the Macalester Scientific Corporation, 60 Arsenal Street, Boston, Massachusetts 02172.

The grain beetle (Tenebrio molitor) also undergoes a complete four-stage metamorphosis. This insect has a particularly interesting larval stage, during which time it is called a mealworm. Mealworms shed their skin from ten to twenty times during the four or five months they remain in the larval stage. The entire metamorphosis takes about six months, which may be too long for some classroom situations. Cultures of this insect can also be secured from biological supply houses.

Generalization VII: There are many animals without backbones; insects make up the largest group

1. *Materials:* 18 to 24 colored, magazine illustrations, featuring members of the five animal groups with backbones, and several insects. (Use the same pictures suggested for activity 1 of the first generalization if others are unattainable. Scatter pictures in no apparent order on the right half of a large bulletin board. Put numbered white cards under each, so they may be quickly located. On the left side of the bulletin board space, place five cards in a column, bearing the titles *Mammals, Birds, Reptiles, Amphibians, Fishes.*)

Challenge pupils to classify the animal pictures according to the five listed groups. Each child can do this individually by writing the numerals on a piece of paper. Walk around and note how successful they are. After an appropriate time interval, initiate a discussion. Encourage class members to evaluate their choices with reasons. Place pictures in rows next to their corresponding headings. *(make inferences)*

Mention that there seems to be disagreement and hesitation about several pictures (indicate the insects). In which group do these animals belong? Raise conjecture. *(suggest hypotheses)* Many children will know that these are insects or "bugs," but will be unaware that they belong in a group as yet unstudied. Develop that these animals—*insects*—do not seem to fit into any of the five classifications. Does anyone know why? Give some hints: There is something inside children's bodies which all the animals studied have, but not insects. After we eat chicken, what is left on the plate? Continue with meals of lamb chops, rabbits, and fish. Do reptiles and amphibians have bones, too? (Yes.) How about ants and flies? (No.)

Develop that the five groups of animals they have studied all have bones inside their bodies. Many bones of each animal are joined to a *backbone,* which runs along the animal's back. Let each child feel his own backbone. Let some children recall feeling a pet's backbone.

Emphasize that all animals may be divided into two very large groups, those with and without backbones. They have studied the five kinds of animals with backbones. Now the class will find out about some animals which do not have backbones. Mention that study will begin with insects, which make up the largest group of animals without backbones. Later, the class will find out about some others.

Encourage children to bring to school the next day any dead animals in good condition which they think are insects. Suggest use of tin cans or paper sacks for containers, rather than breakable glass jars. Advise everyone to scoop up the insects with a small card or stiff piece of paper, rather than handle them with their fingers.

2. *Materials:* large sketch of Figure 11-12 (Keep concealed until needed for use.); a quantity of different dead insects and pseudo insects; toothpicks; white paper; three- by five-inch cards; hand magnifying lenses. (Distribute equal quantities of materials among several or more groups, so each child can actively participate. Insects should be on white paper for easy observation, with a hand magnifying lens alongside. Several toothpicks and small cards will permit insect handling without direct contact.)

state problems

Mention that of the many different animals on the white papers *most* are insects. What is an insect? (Answers will probably vary considerably.) Capitalize on disagreements to arouse need for an operational definition. Develop that, although there are many kinds of insects, they mostly have the same body parts. Can the class find out what these parts are? Give hints, if needed. Let pupils carefully study their specimens for a time to note common characteristics.

Guide discussion about their findings. Note how close they are to an accurate description of insects as a group. Try to guide further observations as needed, without directly telling the children what to look for. Summarize their findings on a chart or chalkboard:

We think an insect has:
6 legs;
3 body parts;
2 feelers;
(add others as given)

make inferences

How close did we come to finding out how scientists describe an insect? Exhibit the sketch of Figure 11-12. Let the class evaluate agreements and disagreements. Emphasize that grownup (mature) insects have three body parts, six legs, and usually, two feelers. The feelers are sometimes used for smelling as well as touching. Many insects have two kinds of eyes—point out the simple eye and compound eye. Many, but not all, have wings. Point to the spiracles in the sketch. Mention that these are air holes, through which an insect breathes. State that the sketch shows a simplified grasshopper.

Which animals are left that do *not* fit our description of insects? Most likely children will have included in their original collections such organisms as spiders, millipedes, centipedes, small worms, pill bugs or sow bugs, and perhaps ticks. It is not important to name these creatures. Children should simply realize that these do not fit the criteria they have developed for defining an insect.

If a microprojector is available, show some enlarged insect parts—wings, antennae, and so on. If a dead bee is in the collection, children will find it interesting to examine the stinger. This can be removed by pushing down on the abdomen with a pencil eraser and pulling lightly on the stinger with tweezers.

Perhaps a child can bring in a live grasshopper. Let him hold it steadily in front of a filmstrip projector shining on a screen. Have children observe closely the abdomen's greatly enlarged silhouette. It will expand and contract visibly as the insect breathes.

3. *Materials:* two pint-size, identical,

loosely capped jars; four recently captured, live flies (two enclosed in each jar); deep pan containing ice water and ice cubes.

Bring out that we see very few, if any, flies in the winter. But there are many flies around in spring and summer. Arouse con- *suggest hypotheses* jecture as to why. Bring out that the weather is usually colder in the winter and that this may affect flies. How does cold- *develop procedures* ness affect a fly? Point to the materials. How can we find out? (Put one jar in the ice water for a while. Leave the other jar alone for the same time. Then take off the caps and see how the flies in both jars act.)

Use a book to weigh down the immersed jar. If the jar is left in ice water for about ten minutes, the flies inside should become noticeably sluggish and unable to escape. Flies in the warm jar should escape im- mediately. Will the cold flies be able to fly away if they get warm again? Remove the jar from the pan. Within a short time, they will probably fly away.

Develop that flies are cold-blooded ani- mals, as are all animals without backbones. When they get cold, flies move more slowly or not at all. Many cold-blooded animals die when the weather get very cold.

EXTENDING ACTIVITIES

1. Let pupils observe the life cycle of the silkworm moth, or stages in the life cycles of other insects. See the preceding exposition for details.

2. Try the protective coloration experi- ment on insects found on p. 52R. You can easily adapt it to a primary class if fewer variables are considered.

3. Encourage pupils to locate pictures of some common invertebrates other than in- sects. It may be desirable to check out from the school or district library some picture books containing illustrations of snails, earthworms, spiders, crabs, starfish, clams, jellyfish, and so on. Let small committees of pupils do the initial locating and screening of what they think are animals without

backbones. Then have the entire class evaluate their selections.

4. During the entire unit, pupils will be learning many descriptive properties of the animals they observe and work with. Set up a game in which class members individually describe an animal from among many bulle- tin board pictures and the rest of the class attempts to identify it. To prepare them for the game, and to give much practice in both describing and identifying, you might have pupils first work in pairs for a while.

For a second approach, you might have children try to identify an animal you are thinking of by asking you questions that are mostly answerable by yes or no. Be sure to have the children search for *physi- cal properties,* rather than related func- tions. Notice the difference:

Does it fly?
I can't tell you.
Does it have feathers?
Yes.
Does it eat insects?
I can't tell you.
Does it have a long, thin, pointy beak?
No.
Does it have a short, curved beak like a hook?
Yes.
Is it C-5 (on the bulletin board coordi- *make inferences* nate system)?
Yes. (The child has indicated a hawk.)

For more practice, pupils can also play this game in pairs. You might want to assist them with descriptive words as needed. This can be an absorbing and challenging game for children of all ages by varying the number of picture specimens and the sub- tlety of differences in physical properties.

5. Plan a trip to a local zoo or natural history museum as a culminating activity for this unit. Through consultation with a zoo official, concentrate class attention on only several of the most diverse animals within each of the five vertebrate groups. This will be more effective than trying to observe everything.

Human Growth and Nutrition

(Upper Emphasis)

UNIT 12

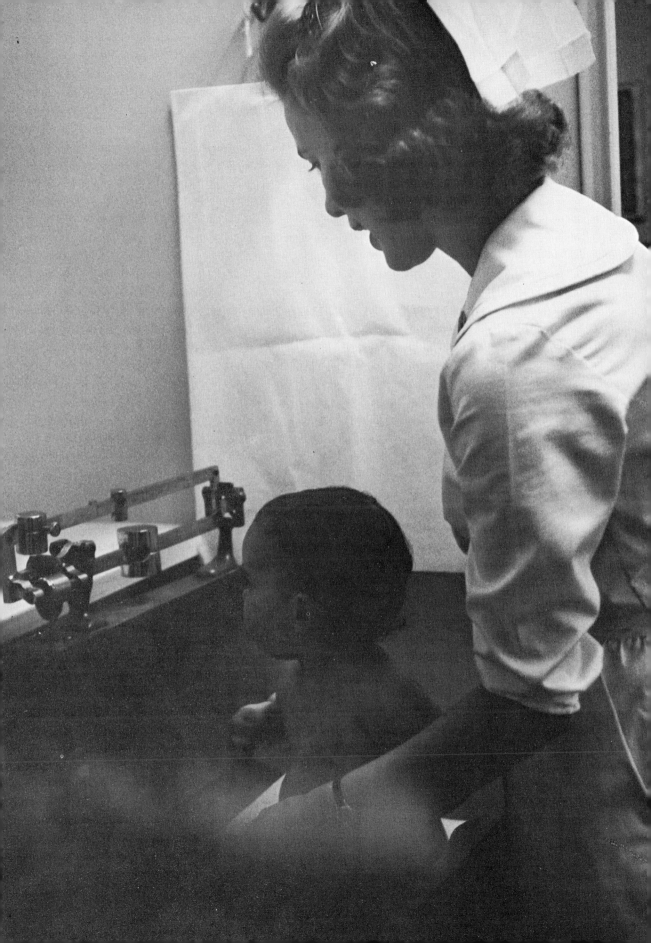

UNIT TWELVE

Human Growth and Nutrition

(Upper Emphasis)

MANY NUTRITION SPECIALISTS CLAIM THAT BETWEEN THE AGES
of 12 and 20 young Americans have the poorest diets of their lives.
Significantly, this is the time of increasing personal independence
and freedom of choice. How do we educate children to make
intelligent decisions about their health? One way is to begin teaching good health habits early, when receptivity is high and "sophistication" low. Health and nutrition lessons are often begun in the
primary grades. Another way to reach children is to develop
scientific reasons for actions — reasons that can be discovered and
demonstrated in ways that make sense to young minds.

GENERALIZATIONS

  I. Growth takes place as living cells divide or enlarge; the
amount of growth children have depends upon several things.
  II. Several food nutrients are needed for health and growth of
body cells; tests can be used to identify them.
  III. Food is digested in the alimentary canal and then transported
to cells, where it is oxidized, changed into body materials, or stored.
  IV. For a healthful diet, one should choose wisely from a variety
of foods.

Credit for chapter opening photograph. **Eve Arnold-Magnum.**

Growth and Cells. One day in 1665 an English botanist named *Robert Hooke* examined a very thin section of cork under his crude microscope. To his surprise he saw what appeared to be tiny, empty compartments with thick walls. Since they resembled cells, this is what he named them. He learned through subsequent investigations of many other materials that living things are composed of cells. He soon realized that, unlike dried cork, these cells are filled with a fluidlike substance. We know today that this substance is the cell's living material, protoplasm.

Most children are unaware that their bodies and most other living matter are composed of cells, and that growth itself is a result of cell division and enlargement. It will be instructive for them to examine cells with a microprojector or microscope.

For examination of plant cells, the inside skin of an onion will do nicely. Slice an onion ring, and peel off a bit of thin skin from one of the inside layers. Put a water drop on a slide and lay a piece of skin section in it. To make cell details clear, stain the specimen by putting a drop of diluted iodine on it with a medicine dropper. Cover with a cover slip. Leaves of elodea, a very common aquarium plant, are also thin enough for cell study. No stain is necessary.

Human skin cells — *epithelial* cells — are interesting to show for contrast. These may be gotten by gently scraping the inside of a cheek with a blunt toothpick. Spread the whitish material on a slide and put a drop of diluted iodine on it. Cover with a glass cover slip.

Pupils will find that the most obvious difference between animal and plant cells is in how they are enclosed. Plant cells are surrounded by a wall composed chiefly of cellulose. This is tough, fibrous, nonliving substance indigestible to man. A thin membrane within the wall is almost invisible. Animal cells are enclosed by only a thin, living membrane, permeable to some fluids and gases. Both animal and plant cells contain a dense spot called the *nucleus,* which controls the cell's vital activities. (Figure 12-1.)

Children are usually very interested in examining single-celled animals, or protozoa. These tiny creatures carry on all the vital activities of living things: food taking, digestion, oxidation, excretion, responses to stimuli, growth and reproduction. The *paramecium,* one of the larger, easily observed protozoa, is especially interesting to watch. Children may note how hairlike cilia propel it through the water. (Ciliated cells within the human respiratory system sweep up irritants to where they can be coughed out.) The class may see an occasional paramecium divide, and become two paramecia. Growth by cell division is also characteristic of human cells. However, some human cells, such as those that compose nerve and muscle tissue, may merely enlarge somewhat or grow longer.

A culture of protozoa may be developed by making a *hay infusion.* Drop a handful of dry grass, hay, or leaves into a quart glass jar of pond water. If no pond water is available, use aged water or boiled, cooled water. Leave the jar lid loose for air. Place the jar in a well-lit place but out of direct sunlight. Within a week or two several varieties of protozoa should appear. Drop a few grains of rice or a pinch of Pream (powdered cream substitute) into the jar. This will stimulate a bacterial population on which the protozoa can feed.

For viewing protozoa, use a well slide — one with a shallow depression in the center. The depression prevents the tiny organisms from being crushed when a cover slip is added. If only standard slides are available, you can paint a small ring with nail polish on a slide and put the cover slip over that. Or you may omit a cover slip if you don't mind the fast evaporation rate of slide liquids when a microprojector is used. It is handy to transfer protozoa from culture jar to slide with a medicine dropper. One drop should do if you have a rich culture. Most

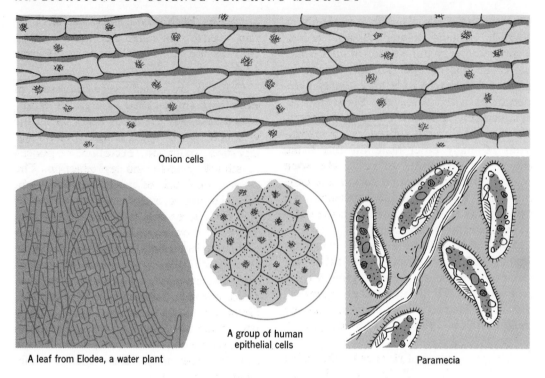

Onion cells

A leaf from Elodea, a water plant

A group of human epithelial cells

Paramecia

Figure 12-1   Cells.

protozoa will be concentrated near the jar bottom.

Where do protozoa come from? They are found almost everywhere there is moisture. When dry conditions occur, these animals lose much water. The cell membrane dries into a hard, cystlike cover. The animals may survive this dormant condition

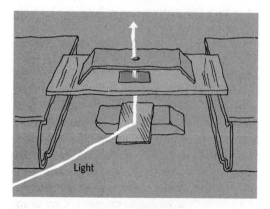

Light

Figure 12-2   A waterdrop microscope.

for years until at last there is sufficient water to soften the cell cover and resume usual functions.

If microscopes are not available, let each pupil make his own water-drop microscope, as in Figure 12-2. Basic materials needed are a glass slide, strip cut from a tinned can, and a small mirror. For the lens, use a nail to punch a small hole in the strip. A drilled hole is superior, but not essential. Put a water drop in the hole with a medicine dropper. If the hole is perfectly round, the water-drop lens may magnify up to 100 times. This is sufficient for viewing gross features of the cells previously described. Focusing is accomplished by slightly bending the strip up or down. For best viewing, the eye must be very close to the lens. For the best light conditions, adjust the mirror so light reflects upward through the lens. Then lean the mirror at the proper angle against an eraser or other small object.

Boys	43.9	46.1	48.2	50.4	52.4	54.3	56.2	58.2	60.5	63.0	65.6	67.3	68.2
Girls	43.6	45.8	47.9	50.0	52.0	54.2	56.5	59.0	60.6	62.3	63.2	63.5	63.6
Age:	5	6	7	8	9	10	11	12	13	14	15	16	17

Figure 12-3 Average height in inches of students in seventeen states.

Although children's cells are growing continually, they should realize that rates of growth—really, the speeds at which different cells divide—vary greatly at various periods of childhood. It is natural for upper-grade children to be concerned about their heights. From about age 10, this is a period when girls begin to grow faster than boys. Several years later the boys start to catch up, and by age 14, usually exceed the girls in height.

Pupils will be interested in a table of average heights, from age 5 to 17, presented in a forthcoming activity. (See Figure 12-3.) The table is based on data released in 1953 by the United States Office of Education. Figures are averages of almost 300,000 students then living in 17 states and the District of Columbia. Future activities will suggest that the class use its own average heights and other data to make present comparisons with the children of almost a generation ago. Be sure to bring out that these figures are averages. Individual pupils may be taller or shorter. Get the children to understand that they inherit many characteristics of their parents, including height tendencies.

The graph on page 505 (Figure 12-6) is an estimate of the increasing heights of young adults in succeeding generations. It is based on a composite of several studies, old and new. Children seem to be growing taller than their parents, almost 1 inch taller every 25 years. Unsurprisingly, growth of feet and hips appears to be keeping pace with overall gains in height. Besides medical evidence, shoe manufacturers report increased sales of extra-large shoes. Theater owners now must install seats which are several inches wider than those designed twenty or so years ago.

What are the reasons for increased stature and size? It is difficult to know exactly although some general factors seem clear. We know that better living conditions and reduced illness help children to attain better growth. Some persons claim that increased size is an evolutionary tendency. Certainly, a main factor is improved nutrition. Studies in England and France before, during, and after the Second World War clearly show that improved nutrition results in increased growth. There are many other researches which reveal the same evidence.

Generalization I: Growth takes place as living cells divide or enlarge; children's growth depends upon several things

Contributing Idea A. Living things are composed of cells; growth takes place as cells divide or enlarge.

Materials: baby picture of a class member; microprojector or several microscopes; prepared slides of onion skin, elodea, epithelial cells, and protozoa. (See preceding exposition for details. If microscopes are available, children will enjoy and gain from preparing their own slides.)

Use this activity for careful observation of several kinds of cells.

Ask for the hands of children who have at some time cut or scraped their skin. Discuss the varying lengths of time these wounds required to heal.

Show the baby picture. Ask the child whose picture it is to stand. Look at the difference!

Emphasize the wondrous quality of these

events. What causes wounds to heal? What makes a baby increase in size? Arouse conjecture. After some discussion, mention that observation of some microprojector slides will be useful in finding out.

Exhibit a stained onion skin slide. Children will immediately notice the cell-like structure. Explain that they are looking at a very small and thin section taken from a living thing. The small compartments are called *cells*. Point out the *cell wall* and *nucleus*. Have the children try to guess for a moment the living thing from which the slide specimen was taken. Now let them see how the slide was prepared. Show an unstained onion skin slide briefly for contrast, and then replace it with the stained slide. reason quantitatively Lay a single human hair across the specimen so pupils can estimate cell size.

Follow with a projection of elodea leaf cells. Children will immediately note the contrast in size and color of the cells.

Do animals also have cells? Show slides of epithelial cells, stained and unstained. Have pupils try to guess their origin. Develop that these cells are like plant cells except that in place of a thick cell wall there is a thin, *cell membrane*. This is true of most animal cells, although they have many different shapes and sizes. Demonstrate how to prepare these slides.

Now project a slide of living *protozoa*. Mention that they are looking at some of the world's smallest animals. Each is made up of only one cell. Try to isolate a *paramecium*. Children may be able to detect how it uses its hairlike *cilia* for locomotion. Develop that there are many cells with cilia in our lung passages. The cilia brush irritating particles into the throat where they can be coughed out. (However, stress that ciliated cells in the respiratory tract are not protozoa.)

If there are many paramecia, some may divide as the children are observing. State that most growth in animals and plants takes place when cells divide. Food material dissolved in water enters through the thin cell membrane. Some of the food material is changed into part of the cell itself. The cell grows a little larger, then divides into two cells. Each new cell looks like the old cell but is a little smaller for a while. Some cells do not divide in this way, but just grow larger or longer. Mention that new cells continually replace old, injured, and worn-out cells.

If pupils have microscopes, let them prepare and view many slides to discover what they can about cells.

Contributing Idea B. Growth varies with age, sex, heredity, and nutrition.

1. *Materials:* opaque projection or chart of Figure 12-3; graph paper; chart paper; yardstick. (Reveal when appropriate.)

Help children realize the significance of cell division: wounds heal; worn cells are replaced; physical growth results. Now ask them to think carefully. Do body cells always grow at the same rate when we are children, or do they slow down and speed up at times? What evidence can they point to which might help answer this question? Bring out that their shoes and clothing sizes often change radically in a short time period, after a long period of no change. Some children may observe that lately several boys and girls are growing taller than their classmates. Mention that it is a usual thing for growth to speed up and slow down. By looking at a chart the class will be able to find out more about the time periods when this happens to most children.

Reveal the projection or chart of Figure 12-3. Mention that these were found to be the average heights of thousands of children of 17 states in our country. Invite the children to study the chart carefully for five minutes. What can they observe about amounts of growth and growth rates? Ask reason quantitatively them to write down all the important things they think the data reveal. Suggest that they make graphs from these data to aid interpretations. (See Figure 12-4 for an example. Have each child save his graph as it will be needed later.)

In the discussion, bring out three of the

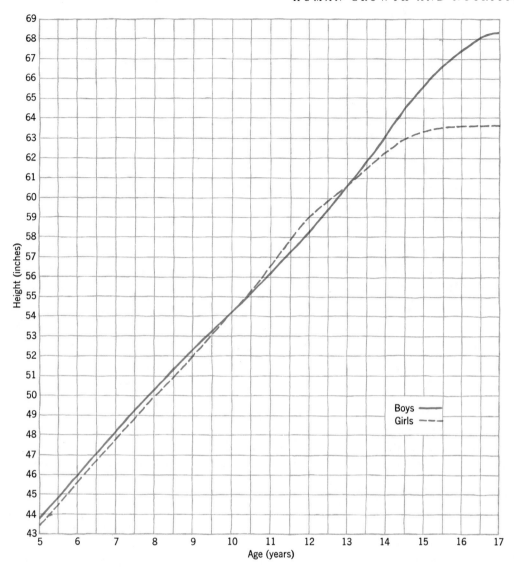

Figure 12-4

more important generalizations: (1) Until the age of 10, boys and girls grow at about the same rate. (2) After age 10 until age 13, most girls grow faster than boys. (3) From 13 on most boys grow faster than girls.

Stress the average nature of these figures. Does this mean *all* girls are taller than *all* boys at age 12? Develop further the idea of deviations. Children of tall parents will tend to be taller than average. Children of short parents will tend to be shorter. These tend-

encies run in families; that is, we *inherit* the qualities of tallness and shortness, just as we inherit dark eyes or hair color. These tendencies are determined mostly by *heredity*. Clarify this term as needed.

2. Now bring up a surprise. These data are about twenty years old. Were the heights of children at that time the same as today's children of the same age? Are there any ways to find out? (For the time being you might concentrate on the age group of

Figure 12-5

your class.) One suggestion may be to find the average heights of both boys and girls in the class.

What procedures can be used? One large, paper height chart (Figure 12-5) can be prepared for the boys and one for the girls to speed up measurements. Anticipate a few problems:

"How will we measure tenths of an inch?"

"What about people with lots of hair?"

"Should you wear shoes?"

"How do you find the average height?"

"I'm *almost* twelve. What group am I in?" and so on.

develop procedures See if the pupils can think through procedures without help. An operational definition of "years old" (age) will be *state problems* needed. Time to nearest birthday probably will be best. For example, if it is less than six months for an eleven-year-old, the child is considered to be twelve. Tenths will be hard to estimate, although half-inch marks on the measuring charts will help. A book can be placed on top of the head of the child being measured to press down his hair. A second child can hold it level to help some-

one make a careful reading of the height chart.

Probably there will be some variation in the data your pupils collect and data on the Figure 12-3 chart that correspond with your pupils' age levels. How do they account for these differences? Encourage *suggest hypotheses* conjecture. Try to bring out, among other ideas, that this class may not be entirely representative of boys and girls of their ages. How could a more exact (representative) sample be taken? (Probably only a short discussion will be profitable, as statistical sampling procedures are beyond most children.)

Ask the children to look again at the individual graphs they made of data in Figure 12-3. What would the growth curves look like for present-day American children, ages five through seventeen? Where can we get newer data to graph? Which *develop procedures* authorities should have new data? Why would these persons know? (Perhaps cited will be a public health officer, school nurse, or school district physician. If any of these persons will provide official *data*, rather than a completed report, the class will be most impressed.)

If new data are available, suggest that everyone make new graphs and compare these with their previous graphs. Encourage pupils to note similarities and dif- *reason quantitative* ferences. Individual interpretations can be discussed in small groups and then with the entire class. Are the rates of growth about the same now as then? (Probably yes.)

3. *Materials:* opaque projection or chart of Figure 12-6.

Ask the children to look at Figure 12-6. There is something odd here. These are the average heights of young adults. What *state problems* seems to be happening with each new group as the years go on? (The average 21-year-old is becoming taller; about 1 inch every 25 years.) Arouse conjecture as to why. Some of the same hypotheses may be advanced as in the preceding activity. Gradually draw out the concept of better, more

504

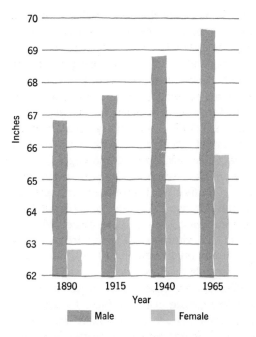

Figure 12-6 **Estimated average heights of 21-year-olds in the United States.**

healthful living conditions. Contrast the great variety of modern, nutritious foods with the limited, less nutritious foods of years past. Emphasize that healthful foods can help bring out the most that is passed on to each person through heredity. In this unit class members will find out a great deal about foods which will be useful for their growth and health throughout their lives.

EXTENDING ACTIVITIES

1. Invite pupils to look in trade books and encyclopedias for pictures of cells of different human tissues. If microscopes are available, let them bring in plant and animal cell materials to examine.

2. Some children may want to set up and maintain their own protozoa cultures. *develop procedures* Under what conditions does the population increase or decrease? Light, temperature, population size, and type of food are a few factors that pupils should be able to con-

sider. Encourage reports on this interesting open-ended activity.

3. Exhibit a motion picture film on the topic of cells and cell growth.

4. Encourage each child to bring in several pictures of himself taken at various ages. The set of pictures for each person might be arranged in a row, from younger to older, in a pocket chart. For an interesting "Guess Who?" arrangement, *make inferences* turn over all pictures in each set but the first. The object is to discover the child's identity while turning over again the fewest successive pictures.

Foods and Nutrition. We may eat hundreds of foods, combined in thousands of ways. But nutritionally speaking, there are four kinds: sugars, starches, fats, and proteins. Some persons would add three more: vitamins, minerals, and water. These seven nutrients may be combined into three groups:

(1) Foods for energy—sugars, starches, and fats.
(2) Foods for growth and repair of cells—proteins.
(3) Foods for regulation of body processes—vitamins, minerals, and water.

If we heat table sugar in a test tube, the sugar gradually turns black and water vapor is driven off. The black material is carbon. The water is formed as hydrogen and oxygen atoms given off by individual sugar molecules combine. Heat some starch, and again carbon and water appear. Both sugar and starch are *carbohydrates,* a name that means "carbon and water."

Although sugar and starches are composed of the same elements, these elements may appear in various combinations, and form relatively small to large molecules. "Simple" sugar molecules, for example, are the smallest carbohydrate molecules. They may be found in grapes and many other fruits. When two simple sugar molecules become attached, a complex sugar is formed, such as table sugar. A starch mole-

505

cule is nothing more than a long chain of sugar molecules tightly attached to one another.

In digestion carbohydrates are broken down into simple sugars. Only in this form are these molecules small enough to pass through cell membranes into the cells, where they "burn" and release energy. The "burning" is a result of *oxidation,* a process where oxygen chemically combines with fuel—in this case sugar—and releases heat energy. (Rusting is a form of slow oxidation; fire is very rapid oxidation.) The oxygen comes from the air we breathe.

Fats are also composed of carbon, hydrogen, and oxygen. But fat molecules have relatively fewer oxygen atoms than carbohydrates. Since they are oxygen "poor," fat molecules can combine with more oxygen atoms and yield about twice as much energy as carbohydrates.

Foods rich in carbohydrates and fats provide our principal source of energy. But when we eat more than we need of these materials the cells store any excess in the form of fat. Fat storage does not occur uniformly throughout all body cells, as every figure-conscious person knows. In another exposition, we shall discuss the different energy needs of persons.

Proteins are extremely complex, large molecules. A single molecule may contain thousands of atoms. Like the preceding nutrients, proteins are composed of carbon, hydrogen, and oxygen. But in addition, proteins contain nitrogen, and typically, sulphur. Proteins are the main source of materials (amino acids) needed for growth and repair of body cells. Excess proteins can be oxidized in cells and so provide energy.

Unfortunately, there does not appear to be a truly effective and reliable test for protein that children can do independently. Perhaps the easiest test is to burn tiny food samples, such as meats. If the odor is like that of burning feathers, protein is indicated in the burned sample. If you and your chil-

dren do not mind the odor, perhaps you can add this test to the several that will be suggested shortly for other nutrients.

Though all animal and some plant foods (mainly beans, peas, nuts) contain proteins, few plant proteins contain sufficient amino acids for complete growth and repair of body cells. This causes many vegetarians to supplement their diets with such animal products as milk, cheese, and eggs.

Vitamins are essential because they regulate cell activities. These chemicals are not digested or used directly, but permit biochemical processes to take place. We can get all the vitamins we need from a balanced diet (see page 518L) without extra vitamin pills or capsules.

Minerals are essential because they also help to regulate cell activities. In addition, some minerals are incorporated into body tissue. Calcium and phosphorus form the hard portions of our bones and teeth. Milk is especially rich in these two minerals. Iron and copper help form red blood cells. A proper amount of iodine is needed in the thyroid gland for normal oxidation to take place in cells. Salt is often iodized to prevent goiter, an iodine deficiency. Some minerals cannot be used by cells unless specific vitamins are present. Most fruits and vegetables are rich in vitamins and minerals.

There are many reasons why water is essential to life and good nutrition. It changes chemically to form part of protoplasm. Water is the chief component of blood. It cools the body and carries away accumulated poisons. It is important to digestion and excretion. About two-thirds of the body itself is composed of water.

Besides drinking water directly, we take in much water in the food we eat. For example, celery is about 95 per cent water, fresh bread about 35 per cent water. Pupils can learn how to determine the proportion of water present in a food. To do this properly, they will need a sensitive balance.

A sensitive, handmade balance is shown in Figure 12-7. Materials needed for its construction are a plastic soda straw,

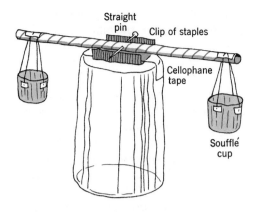

Figure 12-7 A soda straw balance.

straight pin, small clip of staples, drinking glass, cellophane tape, thread, two small paper cups, and a small piece of modeling clay. First, affix with cellophane tape a small clip of stuck-together staples to the bottom of an upturned drinking glass. (Or fold and affix a stiff piece of cardboard with similar dimensions.) Then push a straight pin through the center of a straw and place it on the clip as shown. The straw should almost balance if it is well-centered. Next, suspend two paper cups from the straw ends with thread. Use cellophane tape to secure the thread on both cups and straw ends. To correct any slight imbalance, place a tiny bit of modeling clay at some point near the pivot.

To find the fraction of water in food, put into one paper cup ten light, identical objects. Pins work well, but washers, brads, B-B's, etc. may be used instead. Put into the other cup several small, thin slices of food. Remove bits of food until there is a perfect balance. The food should now be taken off and dried. Also remove the pins (or substitute objects) from the second cup. When completely dry, place the food back into a cup. Carefully, drop one pin at a time into the opposite cup until there is a balance. If three pins balance the food, for example, you will know that seven-tenths (70 per cent) of the food originally was water.

If more precision is desired, children can use more pin units to balance larger quantities of food. Very small samples tend to give unreliable data, as children may discover. If your class understands percentages, use 100 pin units. However, the counting of many small units takes time. One way to speed this up is to fasten a tiny bit of cellophane tape around each group of ten pins, brads, or other weight unit used. The tape's extra weight should be negligible.

In forthcoming activities we shall present other ways in which pupils may test foods. Encourage everyone to bring materials from home. This will permit all to participate.

Generalization II: Several food nutrients are needed for health and growth of body cells; tests can be used to identify them

Contributing Idea A. Starches, sugars, and fats are needed for energy.

The following investigation is divided into two parts. First, pupils learn how to detect the presence of starch, sugar, and fat in foods. With this input, they then engage in an open-ended activity to discover which of a variety of foods contain these three nutrients.

Materials: for each group, Benedict's solution (order through drug stores); iodine; spoons; brown wrapping paper; medicine droppers; alcohol burner; test tubes; small drinking glasses and paper cups; variety of foods brought in by the children—starches, sugars, fats.

Write on the chalkboard the words, "You are what you eat." Ask for interpretations of this idea. Develop that the body cells convert food into more living cells, and energy. How well body cells are constructed depends upon the materials that go into them. Persons who lack pep often do not eat the right foods.

What specific foods give us most of our energy? Start a discussion but withhold verification of children's guesses at this time. Develop that foods rich in *starches, sugars,* and *fats* are needed for energy. The children can discover for themselves which specific foods are rich in these substances by several simple tests. Demonstrate these now.

Starch Test. Put a few drops of iodine on some dry cornstarch and on a sugar cube. Which contains starch? Bring out that iodine changes into a blue-black color when much starch is present.

Show how to test liquids for starch content. Mix some starch in a little water; dissolve some sugar in another glass containing water. Place a few drops of iodine in each glass. Which contains the starch? (The liquid that turns blue-black.)

Sugar Test. Dissolve some brown sugar in a test tube one-third filled with water. Add a half-inch of Benedict's solution. Heat over an alcohol burner until the solution boils. (Demonstrate the proper method of holding a test tube over a flame. Grip the tube with tongs or pliers and point the open end away from you and the children.) The solution will gradually turn a yellow or orange color. Let the children describe this color. It indicates the presence of a simple sugar.

This test does not work with complex sugars. Point out to the children that some sugar molecules are arranged in such a way that this test does not affect them. Table sugar and the sugar in pineapples are examples of foods which do not react to this test. (Prolonged, intense heating may partly break down these sugars.) Demonstrate with table sugar. If someone suggests tasting substances to detect sugar, bring out that some poisons look perfectly harmless.

Fat Test. Rub a bit of margarine and a small piece of carrot on brown paper. Explain that the shiny, translucent spot made by the margarine came from oil, or melted fat. The wet spot made by the carrot will quickly dry and look largely as it did before the test.

In a second test crush a peanut into a fine powder, and pour this into a glass containing some water. Have children notice the oil film on the water surface.

Set up an open-ended activity. Which foods contain starches, sugars, and fats? Either of two ways may be used to organize the class for finding out. For example, have the entire class test only for starches, then sugars, then fats. Or let them test for all three at one time. This is more complex to administer, but more fun for the children. In either case, divide the class into several groups. Let each group chairman carefully record data on the chalkboard. When results are in, have children evaluate results by cross-checking all data. When there are disagreements among groups ("Does bread really have starch in it?") let the groups run retests.

Pupils might summarize their findings in three columns on a large butcher-paper chart. Of course, their notations may differ from the following according to the foods they bring and test:

make inference

Has Starch	*Has Sugar*	*Has Fat*
potato	prune	bacon
white bread	raisin	peanut
spaghetti	grape	lard
corn	corn syrup	salt pork
soda cracker	fresh orange	olive
oatmeal	juice	mayonnaise
rice	honey	milk
	onion	

Or, the class might organize data by having each group record its identifying numeral next to the samples it tested. In this way conflicts can be spotted immediately:

Food	*Starch*	*Sugar*	*Fat*
potato	1, 3, 4, 5, 6	2	—
corn syrup	1, 3	2, 4, 5, 6	—
salt pork	—	5	1, 2, 3, 4, 6
corn	1, 2, 3, 4, 5, 6	—	—
etc.			

Be sure everyone understands that a fatty food can also contain some sugar, and so on. Few foods will be wholly composed of one substance.

Have some children consult encyclopedias and trade books to check their food classifications. Encourage them to add to the chart names of other foods rich in starch, sugar, or fat as they are found.

Contributing Idea B. Proteins are needed for growth and repair of body cells.

Materials: various trade books and other reading materials on nutrition.

Point out that athletes eat foods containing sugar and starch for energy, but that they are especially likely to eat many foods that are rich in *proteins*. Develop that proteins are food materials which enable the body to build new cells and replace worn-out cells. This is particularly important for athletes because they need to build strong muscles. Help pupils to reason why it is important for them to eat proteins. A growing child needs this food material to build tissue. Explain that surplus proteins may also be stored in the body in another form and later converted into energy.

Let children speculate as to which foods are rich in proteins. Discourage blind guessing. To aid their thinking encourage wise use of clues they already know. Which foods are athletes likeliest to eat? Which foods are often recommended for children? Which foods tend to be alike? If one kind of food is rich in proteins, perhaps similar ones also are.

suggest hypotheses

Ask everyone to check written references. Encourage them to make a chart of findings on which they might agree. Other high-protein foods may be added to the list as learned.

Contributing Idea C. Minerals and vitamins regulate body processes; some minerals are used in growth and repair of cells.

1. *Materials:* a clean, chicken leg bone; capped fruit or peanut-butter jar containing fresh vinegar. (Prepare materials in advance of this lesson. Place the chicken bone in the jar and cap tightly. In about a week,

acetic acid in the vinegar will dissolve most of the hard mineral structure of the bone.

Write on the chalkboard: *Energy foods, Proteins, Minerals.* Review briefly why energy foods and proteins are essential to health. Point out that minerals in the diet are also essential to good health. Discuss with the class what minerals are—the materials of which rocks and soil are made. But we don't eat rocks. How could minerals get into our bodies? Develop that some minerals dissolve in rainwater and are taken into plants as they soak up the water. We eat plants and some animals which feed on plants.

Ask, "Can anyone think of one reason why our bodies need these materials?" For a clue remind the class that rocks are hard. When bones are mentioned, produce the vinegar jar and bone. Rinse the bone in water and dry it. Explain that the bone has been placed in a mild acid for a week. Acid dissolves much of the mineral matter in a bone. Can the children guess what has happened to the bone? Show them how flexible it is now. Bend it, or tie it in a knot!

suggest hypotheses

Explain that, in addition to helping build bones and teeth, tiny amounts of minerals aid in the formation of blood and many other substances in the body. Some minerals are needed for body cells to work properly.

Point out that *calcium* is one of the most important minerals for building bones. Ask the class to locate in books names of foods rich in calcium. In addition, mention that salt is often iodized—that is, the mineral element iodine is added. Invite several volunteers to find out why.

2. *Materials:* cornstarch; saucepan; hot plate; tincture of iodine; cup of water; small glass jars or glasses (such as baby food jars); medicine droppers; several assorted liquids containing vitamin C, such as orange, lime, lemon, grape, potato, tomato, carrot, and cabbage juice.

To test liquids for vitamin C, prepare a test indicator as follows. Add to a cup of boiling water about one teaspoon of cornstarch. Boil for several minutes. Pour off the clear starchy liquid into a jar. This will be used. Put fifteen drops of the starchy liquid into half a *glass* of water. (Do not use paper cups as the paper becomes stained and masks any color change.) Add one drop of iodine. The mixture will turn blue in a spectacular way! To test for vitamin C, drop into the mixture some fresh fruit juice, one drop at a time. Gradually, the blue color will disappear.

It will be helpful to stir the mixture a bit and pause briefly after every five or six drops to assess the chemical reaction. When a liquid without vitamin C is tested, the test mixture color remains unchanged, or takes on the color of the added liquid if enough is used.

You might begin by adding the word *vitamins* to the several nutrients already listed on the chalkboard. Develop that, like minerals, these chemical substances also help to promote health and growth of body cells. Mention that one of the most important of these substances is vitamin C. During the lengthy voyages of slow sailing ships long ago, many sailors suffered badly from a disease called scurvy. Their body joints would swell painfully, gums bleed, and teeth fall out. Yet once again on land, the sailors usually recovered quickly.

Which foods were probably missing on these ships? Invite hypotheses. Probably fresh fruits or vegetables will be suggested. Use a sample liquid, such as lemon or orange juice to demonstrate the vitamin C test. Mention that British naval doctors discovered 200 years ago that a daily ration of juice from limes or lemons would prevent scurvy.

Show the class any assorted fruit and vegetable juices you may have. Do all contain vitamin C? If so, is the vitamin present in equal amounts? Have groups test these liquids. Perhaps not all will show a positive reaction. Suggest that the groups place in order, from least to most vitamin C content, the several liquids that reacted positively to the test. This can be done in a crude way

by counting the number of drops it takes for the blue color to disappear. Encourage critical appraisal and cross-checking of group work. An easy way to do this is to list on the chalkboard all the liquids tested in one column. Have each group leader write the rank order given by his group in another single column, one appropriate numeral adjacent to each liquid.

Invite some open-ended experiments. *suggest hypotheses* Why did some liquids not indicate vitamin C? Why were some weak? Does a food lose its vitamin C content? What conditions might bring this about? Pupils may suggest cooking, leaving a container uncovered, deterioration from age, freezing (freshly made frozen juice appears to have the same *develop procedure* vitamin C content as fresh juice), and other conditions. These can be tested if variables are thoughtfully controlled.

Contributing Idea D. About two-thirds of the human body is composed of water; most foods we eat contain water.

In this investigation pupils use soda-straw balances to find out the percentages of water in some common foods.

Materials: soda-straw balances (see preceding exposition); a variety of fresh, thinly sliced foods—apple, orange, tomato, potato, bread, bologna, etc.; goose-neck lamp; metal kitchen foil.

Ask pupils to imagine themselves on a small desert island. There will be no rescue for three weeks. They can have either 1 pint of water each day, or a slice of bread each day; nothing else. Which would they choose, and why?

During discussion, establish that water is the wiser choice. The body can draw upon stored fat for energy, and even use up muscle or organ tissue if necessary. The average person might survive for three or four weeks without food. But water is needed within several days.

Stress reasons why water is so important. It makes up most of our blood. It cools the body, most noticeably as we perspire. Water permits the body to get rid of poisons that accumulate. It is essential for cells to function properly. There are other important reasons they will find in later study.

Back to the desert island. What if the children had a choice of three fresh apples a day or a daily pint of water? Establish that apples are a better choice because they contain sugar, minerals, vitamins—and water, too. How much water? Encourage children to express their guesses in either percentages or tenths, depending upon their knowledge of arithmetic. Hold up some of the other food samples. List the foods and estimated percentages of water on the chalkboard. Ask how they think the water content can be found. Draw out that the foods can be weighed, then dried, and weighed again.

reason quantitatively

Demonstrate how to use the soda-straw balances. Divide children into as many groups as there are balances. This will allow much pupil participation, and permit later cross-checking of results. Group chairmen should carefully record weights of various food slices.

Thin slices of many foods may be dried satisfactorily overnight with a goose-neck lamp. Put the slices on some kitchen foil and position the lamp shade about 18 inches away. If no lamp is available, oven-dry the slices or leave them exposed to air and sunshine for three or four days. Lastly, thin food slices can be dried within ten minutes if enough alcohol burners are available and the children are permitted to use them. Slices can be placed on small trays made from metal foil. Pupils can hold the trays with clipped-on clothespins. Care should be taken to hold the tray far enough away from the flame to dry the food rather than burn it. Since there will be slight variations in procedures, results may not be as uniform as with the other drying methods suggested.

After the materials are dry they should be weighed again. The difference between before-and-after-drying weights will represent water loss.

reason quantitatively

Have children cross-check their results. Then let them compare their results with findings for the same foods recorded in nutrition books or trade books. Encourage them to analyze why differences appear. Guide them to treat their theories as hypotheses which can be tested.

suggest hypotheses

EXTENDING ACTIVITIES

1. Ask able pupils to look up the major diseases that result from vitamin deficiencies and how these diseases are prevented.

2. Encourage at-home testing of additional foods for starch or other nutritive materials. Have children make reports on their findings.

Digesting and Using Food Nutrients. We can eat food, but when is it within the body? The answer to this seemingly simple question depends upon whose point of view we take. Most of us would say that food is inside the body once it is swallowed. To biochemists, however, any food still within the 30-foot digestive tube they call the *alimentary canal* is considered outside the body. This underlines the uselessness of foods we eat until they are digested—that is, chemically broken down and dissolved into a form that can be used in the cells. The digestive system is marvelously suited to this function. Let us examine how it works. (See Figure 12-8.)

The digestive process begins when we start chewing food. Our front teeth (incisors and canines) cut and tear the food. Back teeth (molars) crush it into small particles. At the same time, saliva pours into the food from six salivary glands in and near the mouth. Saliva softens the food and begins the chemical breakdown of starches. A gradual, sweetening flavor is experienced when we chew starchy foods, such as cooked potato, soda cracker, or bread. The saliva contains an enzyme called ptyalin, which reduces large starch molecules into simple sugar molecules. (An enzyme is a chemical that brings about or speeds up chemical reactions without being changed itself.) In addition to ptyalin, several other enzymes in the body's digestive system play important roles in the reduction of food to usable form.

Swallowed food passes into the esophagus, or food tube. It is squeezed down into the stomach by regular, wavelike contractions of smooth muscles which surround the esophagus. Similar muscles are located all along the alimentary canal. Since it is muscle action (peristalsis), not gravity, which moves the food inside the canal, it is possible to eat and swallow while standing on our heads.

Peristaltic motions continue in the stomach. The food is churned slowly in gastric juices secreted from the stomach lining. Several enzymes and diluted hydrochloric acid break down most of the proteins. Digestion of starch stops, because acid prevents ptyalin from working. Some fats are broken down, but for the most part fats go through the stomach undigested.

The stomach's hydrochloric acid is powerful indeed. (Almost every television viewer has seen at least one drug advertisement in which hydrochloric acid burns holes in a handkerchief!) Why doesn't this corrosive liquid digest the stomach itself? Only in recent years have researchers pinpointed the reason. A small amount of ammonia—this is an alkali or base—is secreted in the lining of the stomach. It effectively neutralizes acid next to the lining without interfering with the acid's digestive action elsewhere in the stomach. We use the same principle of neutralizing an acid when we drink seltzer or soda water to settle a "sour" stomach.

After about two to six hours in the stomach, depending upon what and how much has been eaten, the partially digested food materials are pushed into the small intestine. Here, glands within intestinal walls produce digestive juices with enzymes which begin working on the food. Additional digestive juices are secreted into the intestine from small tubes connected to the liver and pancreas.

Throughout the small intestine, peristaltic motion continues as digestive juices complete the breakdown of carbohydrates into simple sugars, proteins into amino acids, and fats into fatty acids and glycerine. At various portions of the small intestine the sugars and amino acids are absorbed into blood vessels within its lining. Digested fats are first absorbed into the lymph system and then later transported into the blood stream.

Nondigestible material or waste, composed chiefly of cellulose, passes into the large intestine. Much of the water contained in waste material is absorbed into

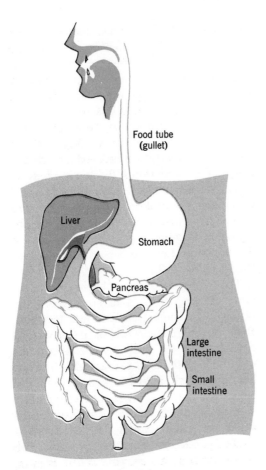

Figure 12-8 The digestive system.

the intestinal walls. The remaining substance is eliminated from the body.

Food products dissolved in the blood are distributed to cells after they are processed by the liver. In the cells these products are oxidized, changed into protoplasm, or stored as fat. Many children find it difficult to believe that oxidation ("burning") takes place in cells. We shall provide several activities to aid their understanding.

Generalization III: Food is digested in the alimentary canal and then transported to the cells, where it is oxidized, changed into body materials, or stored

Contributing Idea A. Digestion begins in the mouth, continues in the stomach, and is completed in the intestine.

1. *Materials:* model of human torso, or chart of human digestive system, or opaque projection of Figure 12-8.

Begin with a quick summary of digestion to help pupils grasp the big picture. Point out that although we can enjoy eating a delicious hamburger or peanut-butter sandwich, these foods cannot reach our body cells and give us energy until they are changed in form. Before food can be used, it must be in a *dissolved* form that can pass through the cell membranes. (Dissolve some salt in a glass of water if pupils are unacquainted with the term.) Indicate the chart or substitute material. Who can describe what happens when food is broken down or *digested* in the body?

Briefly develop the course of food in the alimentary canal: Digestion begins in the mouth. Chewing breaks food into small particles. Saliva from the mouth is added to the food and it is swallowed. The swallowed food passes through the *gullet* into the stomach. From there it goes to the *small intestine* where digestion is completed. Some water and solid wastes go into the *large intestine.* Much of the water is absorbed into the body. The remaining waste matter is passed from the body.

Mention that, in the next several activities, the children will look more closely at what happens during digestion.

2. *Materials:* sugarless soda crackers or small slices of potato; iodine; several test tubes; test tube holder; Benedict's solution; alcohol burner and matches.

This activity should help pupils learn that saliva changes starch into sugar. They should be already aware that soda crackers contain starch. If this has not been discovered in preceding activities, test some crackers for starch before starting the following lesson.

Ask several children to chew some soda crackers or small potato slices, but not to swallow them for at least one minute. Do they notice any change in taste as they chew? Draw out that the taste gradually becomes sweeter. Is there sugar in a chewed cracker or do they just imagine that it is sweet? How can it be tested for sugar? (Put part of a chewed cracker in a test tube and add saliva. Pour inside an inch of Benedict's solution and heat over an alcohol burner. If the mixture turns yellow-orange it contains sugar.) See Figure 12-9.

develop procedures

After sugar is identified, continue. Have pupils recall that at first there was no sugar taste. Where did the sugar come from?

Figure 12-9

Some pupils will say from saliva, others, from the cracker itself. How can we find out if saliva contains sugar? (Put some by itself in a test tube and test for sugar.) How can a cracker be tested for sugar? (Crush part of a cracker, put it into a test tube, add some water and once again heat with Benedict's solution.) Raise an objection, if no one else does: How will we know if the *water* is sugar-free? (Water can first be tested by itself.)

develop procedures

Children will be puzzled by negative results of all three tests. Where does the sugar come from? Have them speculate. Some children may reason that there is something in saliva that changes the starch to sugar. Develop this idea. There is a chemical in saliva which changes large starch molecules into smaller, simple sugar molecules. As they have found out, the chemical itself does not contain sugar.

suggest hypotheses

3. *Materials:* two glasses; water; dry cornstarch; sugar; spoon.

Remind pupils that before food can be used by body cells, it must be in a dissolved form. Does changing a *starch* into a *sugar* help the dissolving process? Which of the two dissolves more completely in water? Indicate the materials. How can they be used to find out? (Put one spoonful each of sugar and starch in separate glasses. Add the same amount of water to each glass and stir the same number of times.)

Pupils will find that no matter how long the starch is stirred it will not dissolve. Help them to understand that starch must be broken down into a soluble form before it is usable. This is accomplished when it is changed to sugar.

4. *Materials:* two balloons; water; four small cubes of sugar; two empty glasses.

Have the class recall that swallowed food goes down the gullet or food tube to the stomach. There, further digestive juices, including a strong acid, break down proteins that may be in the chewed food. Also muscles in the stomach cause it to churn the food inside. How does the churning motion help to break down food?

Point to the materials. We will pretend the balloons are stomachs. We can use water for digestive juice. Sugar cubes can be the food to be digested. Can anyone think of a controlled experiment to see if churning helps to break down food? (Put two sugar cubes in each balloon with equal amounts of water. Squeeze and unsqueeze one balloon continually to imitate churning action. Leave the second balloon alone. After a few minutes, pour the contents of each balloon into separate glasses and check which sugar cubes have dissolved the most.)

develop procedure

Children will learn that the churning action results in faster dissolving. But this is an analogy. Let them read before conclusions are drawn. Bring out, too, that thorough chewing of food in the first place would speed up digestive action in the stomach.

The next investigation has two parts, a and b. In a, pupils learn how to use red and blue litmus paper to identify bases and acids. Also they learn how to neutralize these substances. In activity b, they put their knowledge to work.

5a. *Materials:* red and blue litmus paper (sold in drug stores); ammonia; vinegar; medicine dropper; salt water solution in a glass; two empty glasses.

Explain that digestive acid released from the lining of the stomach is so powerful that it may break down meat into a semiliquid form within an hour or two after eating. Let pupils recall how even a weak acid in vinegar dissolved bone minerals in an early experiment. Why isn't the stomach itself digested by this powerful acid? Allow some speculation, then give further information for the children's thinking. Scientists have discovered that, besides the acid, a tiny amount of ammonia is released all along the stomach lining. Point out that ammonia is one of a group of chemicals called *bases*. Mention that a strong *basic* chemical is corrosive. Children may recall that their mothers use ammonia for dissolving thick grease spots.

Show children how to identify an acid. Dip blue litmus paper into the acid. It will turn red. Try it with red paper and it remains unchanged. Now demonstrate how to identify a base. Dip red litmus paper in some ammonia and it will turn blue. Try blue paper; it will remain blue. Hold up and identify the salt water. Is it an acid or a base? Dip in both red and blue litmus paper. Both will remain unchanged. Explain that salt water is one of many *neutral* materials. It is neither an acid nor a base, but a substance "between" these two.

Refer to the original question. Does anyone now have an idea why the stomach is not digested by its own acid? (Maybe the ammonia neutralizes the acid.) How can we test this? (Add ammonia drops to some vinegar a little at a time. Keep testing with both red and blue litmus paper. Neither should change color when or if the mixture becomes neutral.)

Follow through by pointing out that the neutralizing effect takes place chiefly at the stomach lining. It does not materially weaken the acid's digestive action on the food itself.

The next activity is related to this one. You can develop a two-part problem: Which of six "mystery" liquids are acidic or basic? Can the children determine the relative strengths of these liquids and place them in rank order?

5b. *Materials:* for each group, medicine dropper; a popsicle stick (or substitute); red and blue litmus paper; tablespoon of baking soda in a plastic cup; small amount of vinegar in a plastic cup; six plastic cups, three containing acidic and three basic mixtures.

You might have several children help you prepare the mixtures. First, half-fill all the empty cups with water. In each of three cups put vinegar—five, ten, and fifteen drops, respectively. Label these cups A, C, and E. In each of the three remaining cups put ammonia—five, ten, and fifteen drops, respectively. (Probably only you should handle the ammonia bottle.) Label these cups B, D, and F.

Each group can test the contents of its six cups by using different-colored litmus

paper as in activity 5a. After pupils identify the three basic and three acidic mixtures, they can try to determine their relative strengths. The acids can be gradually neutralized with *tiny* amounts of baking soda picked up with the popsicle stick. If pupils have sensitive soda straw balances, these will measure the relative amounts used. If not, pupils may simply count the number of "stickfuls" they need to neutralize each acidic mixture. The basic mixtures may be neutralized by adding varying numbers of vinegar drops with a medicine dropper. Continual testing is required to determine when each mixture becomes neutralized. If the litmus paper strips are torn in half, the supply will go farther.

Have groups compare their results. If there are different findings, what may be responsible? How can these ideas be tested? *suggest hypotheses*

6. *Materials:* yardstick.

Explain that digestion is completed in the small intestine by additional digestive juices released there. Remind children that the small intestine is coiled. Invite speculation as to its length in an adult. Reveal that it is about 22 feet long while the large intestine is about 5 feet in length. Have several children measure off these lengths to provide accurate, visible referents.

Contributing Idea B. Digested food is transported by the blood to the cells, where it is oxidized, changed into body materials, or stored.

In the next activity children use limewater to test for carbon dioxide in their breath. This helps to indicate that digested food may be oxidized in the body. It also leads into a problem which they identify and attempt to solve.

1. *Materials:* several straws; pocket mirror; limewater (sold in drug stores); two jars with caps; two small candles and matches. (Prepare materials beforehand. Drip some melted wax from a burning candle onto the inside base of two uncapped jars. Blow out the candle and attach it upright to the inside base of one jar

before the wax hardens. Attach a second candle similarly inside the other jar. Pour about an inch of limewater into each jar and cap securely as in Figure 12-10.)

Through pupil reading or your exposition, reveal that dissolved, digested food molecules seep through the walls of the small intestine and enter the blood stream. There the food, and oxygen picked up from the lungs, are transported to body cells. Inside the cells, the oxygen combines with the food molecules and releases heat energy. This process is called *oxidation;* it is a very slow kind of burning. A waste product, *carbon dioxide* gas, is given off by the cells and absorbed by the blood. The blood circulates back to the lungs and releases it. We then breathe out the carbon dioxide. You may have to go over the steps in this process several times before it seems reasonably clear.

Mention that many children find it hard to believe oxidation takes place in their bodies. Several demonstrations may help to convince them.

Hold up the two capped jars containing candles. Remind pupils that a burning object releases carbon dioxide. Explain that there is a special kind of liquid called *limewater* inside the jars. When carbon dioxide dissolves in limewater, something happens. Ask the children to look carefully at the limewater—and also the jar—to see if any changes take place when one candle

is lighted. Draw out why only one candle should be lit. (The second setup will serve as a control.) *develop procedures*

Uncap one jar, light the candle (you might use a burning soda straw if the jar is narrow and deep), and quickly recap the jar. Shortly the flame will die. Children may notice that the limewater becomes whitish in appearance. Sharp observers may see a few water droplets condense inside on the glass. The control jar will remain unchanged. If the limewater reaction is slow, shake both jars gently for a few seconds. Establish that limewater turns milky white when carbon dioxide is dissolved in it.

Say, "If oxidation is taking place in our bodies, we should be breathing out some carbon dioxide. How can we find out?" (Blow through a straw into clear limewater; see if it turns white.) Results will be positive and obvious within a minute.

Now lead into a problem. If we are breathing carbon dioxide into the air, the air should contain carbon dioxide. Hold up the clear limewater. There is something *state* strange here. What is the problem? (Why *problems* doesn't the limewater turn white *without* blowing into it?) Encourage a reasonable hypothesis. (Maybe there is only a tiny amount.) Let the class develop a long-range *suggest* test, such as leaving some limewater in a *hypotheses* wide-mouthed open container for a week. It *develop* should change appearance within this time. *procedures* A second tightly capped jar of limewater can serve as a control.

Bring out that some water droplets condensed in the jar after the candle went out. *make* Where did these come from? You may need *inferences* to explain that another product of burning is *water vapor*—that is, water in gaseous form that condenses into liquid water again when it strikes a cool object. Do we give off water vapor, too? What available material could we use to find out? (Blow warm breath against a mirror surface.) Have the class recall how water vapor in the breath condenses in air on cold days.

2. *Materials:* clinical thermometer; alcohol; water; cotton.

Figure 12-10

The following activity can be used to demonstrate that exercise increases body temperature.

Press for additonal evidence that slow burning may be going on in our bodies. Draw out that a warm body temperature is a strong indication. Develop that when we blow air on a fire, the increased oxygen makes the fire burn hotter and fuel is consumed faster. Explain that when we exercise we breathe harder and take in more oxygen than usual. Hard exercise uses up energy fast. Oxidation of food in cells should therefore take place faster than usual. Can the children think of any evidence that this happens when they engage in hard exercise? For example, how do they feel after running hard? (Hot and sweaty.)

develop procedures Hold up the thermometer. How can we find out if exercise does increase body temperature? (Measure temperatures of someone before and after a few minutes of hard exercise.) Guide pupils to see the *reason quantitatively* wisdom of taking temperatures of several persons and averaging them. (The thermometer can be cleaned with alcohol-soaked cotton and rinsed in water each time.)

Help the class understand that increased activity requires increased food consumption. Explain, however, that eating more food than is required results in fat storage in the cells. How the children can select the right foods, in proper amounts, they shall consider shortly.

EXTENDING ACTIVITIES

1. Children will enjoy discovering for themselves places on their tongues which give the four chief sensations of taste: sweet, sour, salt, and bitter. Each child will need a paper towel; paper cup of water; a pocket mirror (unless he works with a partner); about six cotton swabs; and four accessible containers of solutions to be tasted. There should be one container

each of salt water, sugar water, diluted vinegar, and a bitter solution prepared by dissolving half of an aspirin tablet in a half-glass of water. Each group of four containers can be shared by several or more children, *provided they do not reuse a swab that has been placed in the mouth.*

To simplify charting of taste spots on the tongue, you might put a sketch of Figure 12-11 on the chalkboard. Or, provide a dittoed tongue map for each child. However, do not write in letter labels until children have revealed their results. Direct pupils to use only a tiny bit of solution on the swab, and to touch lightly various parts of the tongue. To promote accuracy of taste, pupils might sip water and blot their tongues with a paper towel before each time a different solution is tried.

How can differences in our findings be explained—and tested? Be sure children *suggest hypotheses* realize that people's taste sensors may differ. Agreement with your tongue map is not required.

2. Pupils will recall how tasteless foods seem when they have colds. Develop a controlled experiment with them to determine how well they can detect the names of foods without use of their noses. Use tiny cubes of apple, carrot, potato, onion, and other common foods of about the same consistency. Pupils should try first to identify *develop procedures* the foods by taste with noses pinched, and

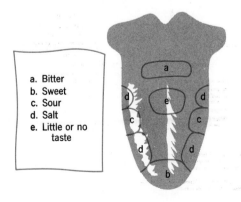

a. Bitter
b. Sweet
c. Sour
d. Salt
e. Little or no taste

Figure 12-11

then with noses free. Eyes should be closed during both series of trials.

A variation of this test is interesting and reveals how much we rely on odors to "taste" things. With eyes shut, have a pupil chew a tiny cube of one kind of food (apple) while a large piece of another food (pear) is held close to his nose. Most pupils will be misled about what they are tasting. See if someone insists that chewers should also try to identify food cubes when food is *not* held by the nose. ("How else can we compare?")

develop
procedures

3. Show a film on the digestive process in humans to help summarize and extend the preceding ideas.

Choosing a Healthful Diet. Does an apple a day keep the doctor away? It helps—but

it had better be included in a balanced diet. No single food contains all the essential nutrients for good health. A balanced diet consists of carbohydrates, fats, proteins, vitamins, minerals, and water, in proper amounts. Even milk falls a bit short in several of these essentials.

It is desirable for persons to know that balanced nutrients are needed. But how is this knowledge transferred into action? For instance, can we rely on taste alone to be the guide? Try asking your class what they would prefer eating for a steady diet. As you might suspect, a list of their preferences usually resembles a chronicle of gastronomical horrors.

Even adults who want to may have some difficulty in selecting balanced foods. For this reason, the federal government years ago asked nutrition specialists to prepare a simple Daily Food Guide. The guide originally contained seven basic food groups. Recently, these have been consolidated to form the "Basic 4," consisting of a meat group, vegetable-fruit group, bread-cereal group, and milk group. (Figure 12-12.) When eaten in suggested quantities and with sufficient water, these foods constitute a healthful diet for normal persons.

By "healthful diet for normal persons" we mean nothing else is needed for optimum health—no yogurt, vinegar and honey, organically grown vegetables, vitamin pills, brewer's yeast, or the other nutrients advertised as special health foods.

Will knowledge of the "Basic 4" really improve children's diets? Sometimes the objection is raised that there is not much value in teaching nutrition to children. After all, what they eat is controlled by their parents. How valid is this reasoning? Admittedly, the home does exercise control to a great degree. But no one can completely control a normal child—in food habits, or anything else—as many parents will ruefully testify. Even in homes where good diets are found, securing children's cooperation through understanding is usually more effective than the admonitory,

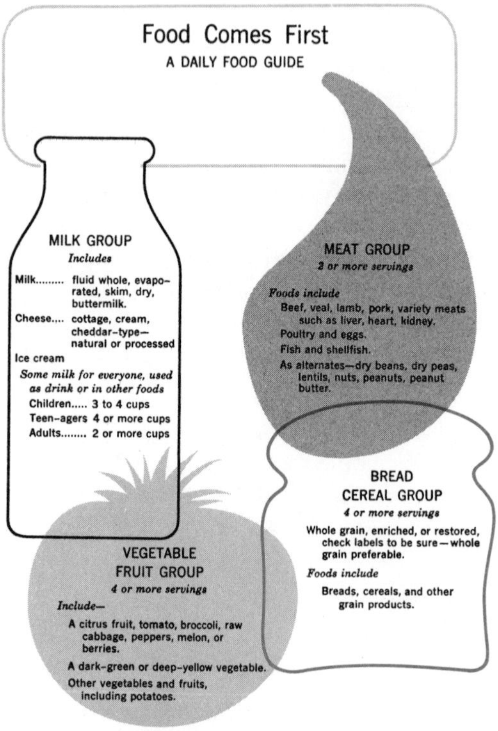

Food Comes First
A DAILY FOOD GUIDE

MILK GROUP
Includes

Milk......... fluid whole, evaporated, skim, dry, buttermilk.
Cheese.... cottage, cream, cheddar-type—natural or processed
Ice cream
Some milk for everyone, used as drink or in other foods
Children..... 3 to 4 cups
Teen–agers 4 or more cups
Adults........ 2 or more cups

MEAT GROUP
2 or more servings

Foods include
Beef, veal, lamb, pork, variety meats such as liver, heart, kidney.
Poultry and eggs.
Fish and shellfish.
As alternates—dry beans, dry peas, lentils, nuts, peanuts, peanut butter.

BREAD CEREAL GROUP
4 or more servings

Whole grain, enriched, or restored, check labels to be sure—whole grain preferable.
Foods include
Breads, cereals, and other grain products.

VEGETABLE FRUIT GROUP
4 or more servings

Include—
A citrus fruit, tomato, broccoli, raw cabbage, peppers, melon, or berries.
A dark–green or deep–yellow vegetable.
Other vegetables and fruits, including potatoes.

Plus other foods as needed to complete meals and to provide additional food energy and other food values.

Adapted from Food for Fitness, Leaflet No. 424, U. S. Department of Agriculture

Figure 12-12 The daily food guide.

eat-it-because-it-is-good-for-you approach. And most children do have some influence on food purchases, even in households with low budgets. Balanced meals can be prepared inexpensively. Finally, as children grow, they have more opportunity to exert their increasing independence in food selection. How wisely this is done is influenced by their knowledge, attitudes, and previous habits.

Although a balanced diet is essential to good health, care should be taken to eat only the amount of food that maintains proper bodyweight. People feel better and seem to live longer when their bodyweights are reasonably close to those recommended in height-weight tables.

How fat or thin we are largely depends on the amounts of carbohydrates, fats, and proteins we eat. These are the only nutrients that "burn" in our cells and provide energy. When we take in more of these materials than the body can burn most of the excess is stored as fat in various cells.

The amount of heat energy that any food can produce is measured in *calories*. You may remember from another unit (page 158L) that a food calorie is the amount of heat required to raise the temperature of 1000 grams of water 1 degree centigrade. In more familiar terms, 1 calorie will raise the temperature of a quart of water almost 2 degrees Fahrenheit.

The caloric value of a food is determined by burning it in an enclosed, insulated container called a *calorimeter* (Figure 12-13). A small, known weight of food is placed inside an oxygen-filled chamber surrounded by water. An electrically heated wire ignites the food and it burns completely. The heat given off raises the water temperature. A mechanical stirrer keeps the water temperature uniform throughout the container. The degree of temperature rise indicates how many calories are in the burned food.

How many calories should people have daily? The proper number of calories for each of us is a highly individual matter,

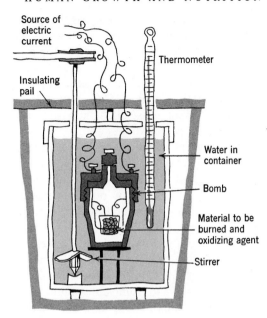

Figure 12-13   A calorimeter.

since it depends on several varying factors: age, size, physical activity, and environmental temperature. Temperature is included because we lose more body heat as the weather becomes colder. Recent evidence indicates that heavy work performed in hot temperatures also requires many additional calories. Apparently, the body works so hard at keeping cool a vast expenditure of energy occurs.

The last sequence closes with an activity to help pupils reason how the several factors combine to determine the amount of food one should eat.

Generalization IV: For a healthful diet, one should choose wisely from a variety of foods

Contributing Idea A. Nutrients from the four basic food groups can provide a balanced diet.

1. Use the following activity to make pupils aware that food preferences alone are likely to be an unsatisfactory guide for healthful nutrition.

You might say, "Boys and girls, suppose you had the chance to select all the kinds of food you wanted to eat, each day for the next five years. What would you choose?" Rapidly write on the chalkboard food preferences as they are given. One or two class secretaries might assist in chalkboard writing to speed up recordings.

After several moments, have the pupils assess their choices. These foods would taste very good. But how good would they be for their health? Draw out the several nutrients needed for sound health: carbohydrates, fats, proteins, vitamins, and minerals. Do the foods selected have all the required nutrients? (Probably not.) Develop that a *balanced diet* includes all these nutrients and sufficient water.

Invite the children to plan three meals —breakfast, lunch, and dinner—which together might contain all the essential nutrients. Provide a few minutes for them to think about this task. Most children will realize the assignment is too difficult without reference to a guide of some kind. Bring out this need during discussion. Mention that many adults also are often uncertain about how to plan meals or select proper

foods in the absence of a nutrition guide.

2. *Materials:* large chart of basic foods as in Figure 12-12. (Or project this Figure.)

Exhibit the chart. Explain that it is based on recommendations of nutrition experts to help people select a balanced diet more easily. Let pupils analyze briefly the main nutrients of each group. The meat group is mostly rich in proteins. The vegetable-fruit group is richest in vitamins and minerals. Bring out that starches predominate in the bread-cereal group. Develop that milk is probably the most complete of these foods. It is rich in fat, has some protein, sugar, and several important minerals.

Remind pupils that the guide was developed to make food selection easier. Will it help them plan a nutritious breakfast, lunch, and dinner? Invite them to write down a balanced menu for one day. Walk around and help individual students. Suggest to the faster workers that they plan for several days, with as great a variety of foods as possible.

For variation, challenge both boys and girls to plan diets according to different-sized budgets. What is the lowest budget they can operate with without having monotonous meals? (After this experience many pupils appreciate more the skills needed to shop wisely.)

When appropriate, organize the class into small groups to make possible specific evaluations of each pupil's plans. However, provide sufficient time for pupils to evaluate their own plans before further appraisal. *(make inferences)*

3. Ask children to collect and bring in colored, cutout, magazine pictures of foods belonging to the four basic groups. Have them sift through and classify the pictures according to basic groups. This can be done first within small committees, and then with the entire class for a final check. Let pupils plan a bulletin board to show the variety of foods within each broad category. *(make inferences)*

Contributing Idea B. People need different amounts of food, depending on age, body size, physical activity, and temperature.

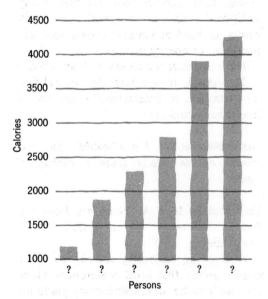

Figure 12-14

1. *Materials:* opaque projection of the calorimeter in Figure 12-13.

Have pupils recall that the basic food guide recommends a certain number of food portions, as well as food types, for daily meals. Raise the question: If a person has a balanced diet, what difference does it make if he eats a great deal, or very little? Bring out that overweight or underweight may result.

Mention that many persons, especially those placed on strict diets by their doctors, watch carefully the number of *calories* in foods they eat. Define a food calorie in familiar terms: One food calorie will provide enough heat energy to raise the temperature of a quart of water almost 2 degrees Fahrenheit.

How is the food burned? Project the calorimeter picture in Figure 12-13. See if pupils can figure out how it works before your explanation.

make inferences

2. *Materials:* large copy of the graph in Figure 12-14.

Use this activity to bring out several factors which determine how many calories different persons need. Write the following data on the chalkboard before beginning this lesson:

Person	Age (yrs.)	Weight (lbs.)	Where Lives
(1) Boy or girl	2	27	Iowa
(2) Male lumberjack	40	175	Alaska
(3) High-school boy	16	150	New York
(4) Boy or girl	11	72	Texas
(5) Female office worker	25	110	Wisconsin
(6) Male office worker	26	175	California

Pin up the graph next to the preceding data. Inform children that the graph shows the number of calories needed by the six persons described. But there is a problem here. Before the graph can be used, something will need to be done. (To which

state problems

column in the graph does each of the six belong?) How can this be determined?

Have pupils speculate about the relative importance of the several factors described. Would a heavy, older man need more energy than a child? And so on. After some small group discussion, challenge pupils to write the numerals of persons in the order in which they should probably appear on the graph. When this assignment is completed, have the children compare their choices. Notice the explanations they give. Then reveal the most probable order: (1), (5), (4), (6), (3), (2).

make inferences

Help pupils to reason through the factors involved. Age, body size, amount of physical activity, and environmental temperature all would have some bearing on total calories needed. Stress that for most healthy children, their own appetite is an excellent guide as to how many calories must be consumed. Calorie watching is mostly for persons who are trying to gain or lose weight according to doctors' instructions.

EXTENDING ACTIVITIES

1. Introduce the idea that many persons believe certain foods increase their intelligence. Challenge pupils to criticize and set up an imaginary experiment to test this statement: "Fish food will make you smarter." Draw out that an operational definition is needed for "smarter." Also elicit that smarter implies a comparison— but to whom? to what? After these ideas have been explored, let the children design an imaginary, controlled experiment. This activity can stimulate deep thought if given a chance.

state problems

develop procedures

2. Invite the school nurse to discuss with the class how proper nutrition, exercise, and rest are the foundations upon which growing bodies depend for maximum growth and health.

3. Encourage class artists to design a freehanging art mobile in which the four basic food groups form a "balanced" diet.

SOME EXPERIMENTALLY DEVELOPED PROGRAMS

Part III

SOME
EXPERIMENTALLY
DEVELOPED
PROGRAMS

The Science Curriculum Improvement Study

CHAPTER SEVEN

The Science Curriculum Improvement Study

SINCE THE EARLY 1960'S, GOVERNMENT AND PRIVATE FOUNDA-tions have invested millions of dollars in elementary science curriculum projects. The general goal of all is the same: to make science education more relevant to the modern world. The work of three of these groups is nearing the final stages. Sooner or later, you and your colleagues will want to make some decisions about tryout teaching, evaluating, and choosing among the projects' programs. What are their objectives? Which program is best? How will they affect what you do in the classroom? Where does your present knowledge fit in? In this chapter we shall examine the *Science Curriculum Improvement Study* (SCIS). The next two chapters feature two other programs of national importance. The final chapter considers the merits of these programs and some possible choices you face in teaching science.

A child does more than merely observe the physical world about him. He continually builds concepts to make sense out of what he experiences. But most of his concepts are based on common sense. Some are valid, some are not. The school science curriculum must contend with these naturally developing (and often invalid) ideas. But since the curriculum typically consists of reading or direction and information from others, it competes only feebly. The hazy abstractions resulting from such a program are seldom applied out of school and soon fade away. What a child needs, then, is first-

Credit for chapter opening photograph. **Courtesy Science Curriculum Improvement Study**

hand experience within an unfolding structure of powerful concepts—ideas that will allow him to get much more mileage out of what he observes than would happen naturally. By gradually building a broad conceptual structure and vocabulary, the child understands and assimilates his later experiences more adequately, whether through direct observation or secondhand sources, such as books or television. This conceptual knowledge has been called "scientific literacy." It is both the goal and the rationale of the *Science Curriculum Improvement Study.*[1]

SCIS was begun in 1962, under the leadership of Robert Karplus, a theoretical physicist at the University of California. Since then, several hundred scientists, teachers, consultants, and other persons have contributed to the project. The curriculum development plan is to develop ungraded, sequential programs in both physical and life science for children of ages five through twelve. The activities used typically begin with suggestions from scientists that involve important science concepts. These are adapted to the elementary level and tried in classrooms. After several carefully evaluated trials and revisions, the units are published.

The conceptual framework of SCIS is shown in Table 1. Concepts within the units unfold in a sequential way. That is, ideas introduced in early units are refined and extended in later ones within both the physical and life science programs. However, the sequence reflects more than just a straightforward, logical pattern. The mental abilities of children are also taken into account. SCIS has been strongly influenced by the work of Jean Piaget and by the several American psychologists who have extended and applied his theories to the classroom. Above all, the activities are designed to be interesting enough to do for

[1] Robert Karplus, *Theoretical Background of the Science Curriculum Improvement Study,* Berkeley: Science Curriculum Improvement Study, University of California, 1965, page 8.

Table 1 Units of the SCIS Program

Unit Level	Physical Science	Life Science
K–3[a]	Material Objects	Organisms
2–4	Interaction	Life cycles
3–6	Relativity	Populations
	Systems and subsystems	
4	Position and motion	Environments
	Approaches to equilibrium	
5	Energy	Food (energy)
	Phases of matter	transfer
6	Periodic motion	Natural selection
	Models for electric and	Ecosystem
	magnetic interaction	

[a] The unit levels listed are roughly equivalent to grade levels. Unit relationships are adapted from the *SCIS Unit Chart,* Copyright 1968 by the Regents of the University of California; and *Organisms* Teacher's Guide, Preliminary Edition (SCIS) Boston: D. C. Heath, 1968, page 3. (Unit titles may change.)

their own sake. Let's examine now the physical science units, then those in life science.

PHYSICAL SCIENCE UNITS

Material Objects (K–3). This first unit introduces the primary child to concepts that pervade all the other units: *object, property,* and *material.* Objects are tangible substances made up of matter, such as water, steel, fish, air, toys. They differ from emotions (joy, fear) and actions (walking, looking). Objects contain properties that can be used to describe and classify them, such as weight, size, color, texture, and shape. (See Figure 25.)

After learning these concepts through many observations, the children find that different objects may be composed of different materials. While these objects may share some properties, such as shape and size, they may differ in others—weight and texture, for instance. Comparisons are then made of one property at a time, such as texture. The children sort the objects and arrange them in various serial orders.

527

**Figure 25   Classifying objects by size and shape. (From *Material Objects*. Courtesy
Science Curriculum Improvement Study and The D. C. Heath Co.)**

Later in the unit, pupils work with rock candy, sugar, and ice. They find that, even though the objects may be changed in form, their material identity remains unchanged. Rock candy tastes as good in one form as in another!

Interaction (2–4). Consider the idea of change for a moment. How does it happen? SCIS attempts to teach changed conditions as evidence of *interaction* between two or more identifiable objects. Take this page, for instance. If you turn it too fast, it may tear. The main objects interacting are your hand and the page. The torn page is evidence of the interaction.

During a variety of activities, pupils create many changes through chemical interactions (such as dissolving crystals), and electrical interactions (by starting and stopping toy motors). Also introduced is *interaction-at-a-distance,* the concept that direct contact need not be made for changes to occur. Activities with magnets and static electricity provide several examples. (Figure 26.)

An important part of the unit teaches the concept of *system*. When a change occurs, it's confusing and inefficient to consider the entire environment. A better way is to isolate the objects that seem to be most closely involved in the change. These objects may then be viewed as a system with interacting parts one can experiment with and observe. A system also may consist of objects one can combine into some pattern—a flight of birds, for example.

The use of systems appears to help children focus their attention and organize their perceptions. The same advantage is realized by adults who use the approach. If you take your car to a garage for engine work,

528

notice how the mechanic diagnoses the trouble. After observing the engine, he isolates a system—fuel, electrical, or cooling system, for instance—and then gets down to details.

Relativity (3–6). A person who says the sun "rises" may think of the earth as a stationary *frame of reference*. But if he could stand on the sun, that is, have a sun-fixed reference frame, the sun would appear to stand still. As you sit inside a railroad car and peer out the window, suddenly the station may seem to move backward. This is because you use the car window as a fixed frame of reference. Once the train accelerates and you feel it moving, however, the perception of motion is transferred back to the train.

It is hard for us to see position and motion from other than our customary reference systems. It goes against common sense, and the tendency to see things from our own personal frame of reference. This is especially so with young children. To help them work with problems of position and motion, an artificial observer called "Mr. O" is used. (See page 543.) This card-

board observer is very self-centered. He always describes the locations of objects relative to himself. By trying to see things from Mr. O's reference frame, the children gradually improve in their capacity to consider other points of view. A treasure hunt with Mr. O giving directions provides a powerful need to learn his reference system.

Systems and Subsystems (3–6). Here, the systems concept is extended to include *subsystems*. A bicycle can be thought of as a single system that includes steering, propulsion, braking, and main-frame subsystems. Each of these, in turn, may be composed of *sub*-subsystems. The process can go on with even smaller subsystems, until one gets to the subatomic level.

The strategy in this unit is to teach a variety of grouping patterns, and how to keep these in proper perspective. The child combines these experiences with his previous ones involving causation and conservation of matter. This helps him to make the transition from intuitive thinking to the next mental stage.

Figure 26 Interaction of two magnets mounted on roller skates. (From *Interaction*. Courtesy Science Curriculum Improvement Study and The D. C. Heath Co.)

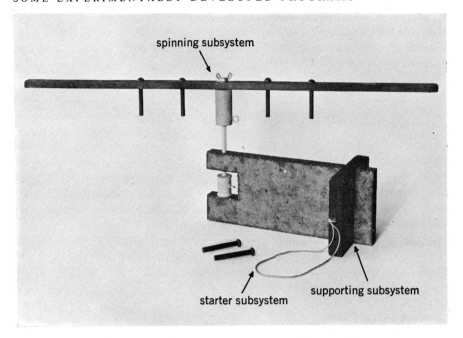

Figure 27 The whirly bird. (Courtesy Science Curriculum Improvement Study.)

As part of the strategy, the identification and control of variables, and how to reproduce data, are introduced through a simple device called the "Whirly Bird." (See Figure 27.) Notice how the parts can be separated into subsystems: base, spinner, starter. This makes it easy to identify the variables affecting the system: the number of turns the starter is wound, the number of rivets attached to the spinner subsystem, and their location on the spinner. The need comes up to identify and control these variables when pupils get different results as they manipulate their Whirly Birds. They use histograms to record and compare their data.

Position and Motion (4). How will J. P., an average American boy, and Homer, an average American dog, find their way around Yellowstone Park? They discover that they need *reference systems*. Work begun in the relativity unit is extended here. J. P. (and the class) learn that, to describe a position, a starting point and a reference direction are needed. When *polar coordi-*

nates are used, one measures the degree of angle from the reference point and the distance. When *rectangular coordinates* are used (as with road maps) two distances are measured to locate an object, one each along a horizontal and vertical axis.

Children are also introduced to *reference landmarks,* those objects used to describe the position of other objects. These become familiar as pupils:

Swim to the Island;
Guide the Camels to the Oasis;
Lead the Archaeologists to the Lost City; and
Search for the Lair of the Dragon.

After these educational games, a map is made of equipment locations on the school playground, and further practice is given with coordinates.

The final activities consist of plotting the paths of rolling steel spheres. A sheet of white paper is placed under a sheet of carbon paper to give a permanent track of the spheres' motions. The children apply their knowledge of reference systems to

530

reproduce the motions on flip-books. They learn to make inferences about the sizes and weights of the spheres, their collisions, and resultant paths of travel.

Approaches to Equilibrium (4). This is the second of two physical science units taught in the fourth year. In it children investigate several phenomena approaching *equilibrium* (a state of balance, either static or dynamic). Several activities include working with pendulums, and making graph records of heated objects as they approach thermal equilibrium with adjacent materials or the surrounding environment. (Figure 28.)

The SCIS way of combining interest with scientific value in learning materials is reflected in the "stopper popper." This is a toy popgun given to each of several class teams for the purpose of continuing the study of variables begun in previous units.

Of course, the *children's* purpose is to see how far they can shoot the stopper. In competing with their rivals, everyone becomes concerned with the variables: How high should we aim the popgun? How far in should we push the stopper? How far in should the plunger go? These ideas about equilibrium and variables are considered again in later units.

Energy (5). The children learn how energy is transferred as they experiment with combustion, ice melting, and the heat conduction properties of different materials. An ice *calorimeter* is used to measure the amount of heat energy absorbed by ice from a burning candle and nut. This useful device is made up of a container to hold the ice, and a chimney to confine the heat given off by the flame. It also provides a crude and indirect measure of the total

Figure 28 Observing a change toward thermal equilibrium. (Courtesy Science Curriculum Improvement Study.)

Figure 29 (Courtesy Science Curriculum Improvement Study.)

amount of energy given off by the burning material.

Variations in data show up when the children make a histogram of the final weights of nuts they have burned. They realize the need to control the weight variable if they are to learn how much energy a burning nut contains. The solution? They make measurements in units of energy per gram rather than per nut. (Figure 29 shows a sensitive spring balance children use to learn about the weight variable.)

Phases of Matter (5). This is a beginning chemistry unit in which the concept of *phase* emerges from the activities. It is *not* equivalent to the states of matter: solid, liquid, gas. A phase is a particular kind of material, different from other materials, even though it may share the same state. For example, corn syrup and water are both liquids but, when in a common container,

each may have a distinct identity (phase), as you saw in the light energy unit. The children experiment with different phases of matter within one state and among all three states. They discover that some interactions produce a uniform, clear mixture (a solution); sometimes there is an intermingling of a solid phase and a liquid phase and each is identifiable (a suspension); and sometimes two phases react to form a third phase (a precipitate). They also produce solutions with greater and lesser concentrations of matter and learn how to detect the differences.

Some of the experiments require work with *closed systems,* that is, those to which nothing is added or taken away. When the children make a solution from a liquid and solid, for instance, the total weight is the same before and after the operation. In this way the children learn more about the conservation of matter concept.

The unit ends with a number of exciting investigations into the nature of gases. Fizzing, bubbling, and color-changing liquids provide evidence of their interactions with gases. Here, as with the other experiments, pupils use their own observations to make inferences.

Periodic Motion (6). This is one of the final units of the physical science program, and is in the exploratory stage at the time of this writing. Some activities include investigating the motions of falling objects through the air and down inclined planes. The results of these experiments lead to the invention of *gravitational field* as an explanatory concept.

Their growing understanding of this concept and supporting information help the children to analyze the periodic motion of two systems: a pendulum, and a solid sphere which rolls on an upright, U-shaped track. Each moves back and forth (oscillates) in a measurable way. How to study the timing of the sphere's motions? A carbon track of its movement helps the analysis. How to vary the timing of the pen-

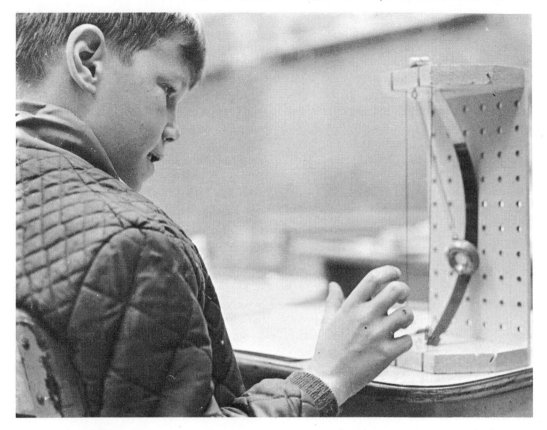

Figure 30 Controlling the motion of a pendulum. (Courtesy Science Curriculum Improvement Study.)

dulum? Pupils quickly realize the need to identify and control the several variables affecting its motion. (Figure 30.)

Models for Electric and Magnetic Interaction (6). As you saw in Chapter 1, by age eleven many children are ready to work with the formal operations of logic. The work of Piaget and others has confirmed this many times. This unit takes advantage of the readiness of sixth-level boys and girls by providing them with chances to create mental models.

The chief devices used are electric circuit puzzle boxes. Children have to develop theories about possible interactions inside the boxes as they test exposed terminals with a battery-bulb-wire apparatus. The concept of *model system* is introduced by

the teacher to fix attention on the thinking process they are using in the puzzle box activities. As they finally compare their model systems with the actual systems in the puzzle, pupils begin to realize that several different model systems may explain, predict, and control a phenomenon equally well. For the same reason, they realize that successful models may not need to duplicate the actual system being investigated.

LIFE SCIENCE UNITS

The SCIS life science program is based wholly on concepts developed from the children's own observations and experiments with living things. Its unifying idea is the *ecosystem:* interactions of plant and animal life with each other and the surrounding environment. The main strategy of the entire unit sequence is to begin with a study of whole but miniature ecosystems (aquaria and terraria), to separate the whole into parts where individual organisms and groups can be studied in some detail, and then to end with applications to the larger ecosystem outside the classroom.

Organisms (K–3). Most of the time in the first unit is devoted to observing different aquaria. Pupils see animals "born," grow, and die. They see feeding, digesting, and excreting in tiny fresh water animals. They learn how waste material enriches the soil by planting seeds and watching their growth in a controlled experiment.

Study of a simple *food chain* (guppies, water fleas, algae) leads to the introduction of *food web,* with its broader applications. The concept of *habitat* is revealed as the place in an ecosystem where an organism lives. *Diversity of organisms* is brought out as various organisms within the miniature ecosystem are compared for likenesses and differences. The children use magnifiers and observe film loops of several animals to note their parts and movements in greater detail.

The first life science unit is truly introductory. Nearly all of the ideas met are continued and enlarged in later units.

Life Cycles (2–4). How do you tell if an object is alive? This question is not as simple as it appears. Growth? Crystals grow in a saturated solution. Reproduction? A fire can reproduce itself. Motion? Clouds move. In this unit the approach is first to help pupils learn the similarities and differences of plants and animals. The similarities are then used to differentiate between living and nonliving things.

The beginning lessons focus on a large picture of a farm pond. Pupils are asked to identify the many objects in the picture as living or nonliving. As disagreements and related discussions occur, the broad problem is raised about the properties of living things.

Most of the activities deal with the life cycles of both plants and animals. Seven kinds of plants are grown from seed. Vegetative reproduction is examined with the planting of bulbs (onions, tulips, and daffodils), corms (crocus, gladiolus), and tubers (white potatoes). In addition, the life cycles of several interesting animals are observed: fruit fly, cricket, and grain beetle. (The short life cycles of insects are ideal.) Other organisms are suggested for supplementary work. Some of the main concepts that emerge from these observations are *metamorphosis, life cycle,* and *generation.*

One of the most valuable concepts is wisely left unlabeled at this stage: *biotic potential*—the capacity of a species to produce young. Since frogs lay so many eggs why isn't the world soon covered with them? The children begin to see that over the long run, other organisms and the environment may keep the biotic potential in check. (Perhaps even in man, one might add.)

Populations (3–6). While the previous unit emphasized the individual organism, this one is about *populations.* A population is the number of organisms of the same kind that live in an area. In nature, usually several populations occupy the same area. The term *community* is used to include several or more interactive populations. A key factor in the interactions is food— what eats what? Such concepts as food chain and food web, begun in the first unit, are taken up now in more detail. Green plants are revealed as the primary food producers.

As they observe such animals as chameleons and crickets, dragonfly nymphs and water fleas, pupils see that one population may consist of *predators,* another the *prey.* They see how each of the several animal and plant populations making up the community may control the sizes of

Figure 31 Setting up a habitat. (Courtesy Science Curriculum Improvement Study.)

other populations. Although the miniature ecosystems they observe cannot expose the whole picture, children begin to realize that the sizes of community populations stabilize only when births and deaths are equal. In addition, pupils are introduced to a subtler idea, considered again in later units: it is the nonliving, environmental elements — air, sunlight, temperature, moisture and nutrients — that ultimately control the community's populations.

Environments (4). Conditions are seldom the same in an environment. Short- or long-range variations in moisture, light, temperature, and other conditions influence the organisms within the affected habitats. Some organisms respond within the habitat:

trees lose their leaves; animals shed or grow more hair and feathers, estivate, hibernate. Some respond by migrating to a more favorable environment.

This unit is about adaptations children can observe for themselves. One activity they do throughout the study is to keep track of rainfall and temperature changes, and to relate observations at home or outside the school to their collected data. An especially engaging activity to the pupils is working with isopods. (An isopod is a tiny, insect-like crustacean.) After gathering much data about the sensitivity of isopods to temperature, soil surface, light, and moisture, the children are invited to set up habitats that will favorably support their isopods. (Figure 31.) This calls for them to thoughtfully interpret and apply their own data.

Food (Energy) Transfer (5), **Evolution** (6) **and Ecosystem** (6). The last three life science units are incomplete at the time of this writing. Tentative plans for the fifth level unit are to stress the two ends of the food chain: plants as primary producers at one end; at the other, such organisms as bacteria and fungi which decompose dead plants and animals. This will expose the cyclical nature of materials transferred within an ecosystem.

A unit is tentatively planned at the sixth level to present the process of natural selection—the evolutionary changes that lead to the adaptations of individual organisms. Activities will include experiments to illustrate how variations in individuals may increase their chances of survival in the ecosystem.

Plans for perhaps the last unit are to relate the contents of earlier units to the larger, natural ecosystem of the children. Some of the relations studied may be the effects of local weather and climate, the kinds of living things and their habitats, and man-made influences on the ecosystem.

SAMPLE LESSONS

Each of the concepts in the SCIS program is taught through lessons organized in three parts: *exploration, invention,* and *discovery*. In the exploratory part, children are given objects to observe or manipulate. At times these observations are guided by the teacher; otherwise the children observe and manipulate the objects as they wish. You may recognize this procedure as being similar to the "arranged environment" idea, introduced in an earlier chapter.

Explorations allow firsthand contact with the phenomena under study, and provide a basis for the children to use language. At the same time, the need arises for an explanation to make sense out of what has

been observed. This is taken up in the second part of the lesson sequence. If the children are not able to give an accurate description or explanation of their observations, the teacher "invents" (introduces) a concept for them that does.

Following the invention, the children are given a variety of further experiences within which they discover many applications of the concept. These extend and reinforce their knowledge. (The discovery part is like many of the extending activity sections of Part II in this text.) Here is an example of the three procedures drawn from a biology lesson with six-year-olds:

The biology lesson was started by bringing six aquaria into the classroom. The aquaria were half-gallon jars containing water with about one-half inch of white sand on the bottom, a few guppies, snails, and water plants. They were scattered about the room so that each child could get close enough to observe what was inside.

The teacher directed the children's attention to the water in the aquarium by asking, "What can you tell me about the water in this jar?" From the discussion that followed, it was apparent that at least some of the children knew the difference between fresh water and salt water and that the ocean contained salt water.

The next day the teacher set up a new aquarium with seawater and marine organisms including crabs, starfish, fish, and clams. By means of the "taste test," the children identified the seawater as salt water and differentiated it from the fresh water in the other aquaria. They also recognized that the animals in the marine aquarium were different from those in the fresh water. At this point, the teacher introduced a new word "habitat," telling the children that a habitat was where organisms lived, and that fresh water was a habitat for certain organisms while seawater was a habitat for other organisms. This was an invention—the introduction of a new concept on the basis of what the children had observed.

Discovery follows invention. Could the children apply the new concept to different situations? To achieve this, the teacher normally brings other examples into the classroom; but this time she tried a different approach. She

1 Observation of Aquaria

Objectives
To identify parts of an aquarium.
To describe contents and events in an aquarium.
To discuss observations of an aquarium.
To ask questions that can be answered by experimenting with parts of an aquarium.
To use the term "organism" to refer to a plant or animal.

Preparation
Order the organisms 3 weeks in advance (postcard A).
Age the tap water for 24–48 hours.
Allow 1 hour for preparing the six aquaria.
Use a scissors to shorten the tip of the baster by one inch.

Prepare the aquaria as described on pages 93–94. Label the aquaria and place them in different parts of the classroom so that there is room for groups of children to gather around them. Be sure that three of the aquaria are placed near the windows or a foot away from artificial lights, while the other three are placed in a darker part of the room (see page 95). The reason for this is that the water in those near the window will eventually become green (due to proliferation of algae) while the water in the others will not. This difference becomes a problem which the children will investigate later in the unit. Take care of the aquaria as described on page 95.

Materials
6 one-gallon containers, each with:
    2 cups rinsed white sand
    aged tap water
    2 sprigs of waterweed (page 118)
    2 sprigs of eelgrass (page 118)
    duckweed (page 118)
    3 small pond snails (page 115)
    1 live-bearing snail (page 115)
    2 male and 2 female guppies (page 114)
    6 drops of Chlamydomonas (page 119)
    10 drops liquid plant food
pH test kit
medicine dropper
dip net
6 labels
magnifier for each child (see page 96)
fish food
baster (with one inch of tip cut off)

Teaching Suggestions
Divide the children into six groups so that each child can closely observe an aquarium. While the children are observing the aquaria, move from group to group and listen to their comments and questions. You can use these to plan the discussion that follows. Rather than answering the questions directly, encourage the children to observe and to talk to each other freely about what they see. The vocabulary developed by the children who have worked with the *Material Objects* unit will be employed as they describe contents and events in aquaria.

PART ONE / NATURAL EVENTS IN AQUARIA

asked the children if they could think of other habitats.

The immediate response was disappointing, but the next day the children were literally bursting with habitats. The teacher suggested that they take their crayons and draw habitats. The various drawings included the sea, a stream, the air with birds, a barn with a rabbit, the Steinhart Aquarium, a forest with "Christmas trees and a tiger," "grass with a snake, caterpillars, and a long worm."

Later, the children decided they wanted to paint a mural which would illustrate different habitats with animals and plants in them. The result was a painting three feet wide and nine feet long, containing habitats from the mountains to the ocean.[2]

Various learning materials are used for the exploration and discovery phases: real objects, pictures, film loops, models, and the like. Soft-cover workbooks are provided for the pupils, but these contain no descriptive information. Instead, they contain suggestive questions to assist observations, to make recordings, or to clinch learnings connected with previous observations. Lesson descriptions for the teacher are provided in a soft-cover guide. In some lessons, related pupil workbook pages are reproduced in the teacher guide for handy reference. On page 537, then 539–542, is an example of an exploration lesson found in the *Organisms* Teacher's Guide.[3] Notice the flexible organization of this introductory lesson. Follow-up lessons depend on the children's responses.

The next sample is an invention lesson taken from the *Relativity* Teacher's Guide.[4]

[2] Chester A. Lawson, *So Little Done—So Much to Do,* Berkeley: Science Curriculum Improvement Study, University of California, 1966, pp. 7, 11. By permission.

[3] Science Curriculum Improvement Study, *Organisms,* Teacher's Guide, Preliminary Edition, Boston: D. C. Heath and Company, 1968, pp. 20–23. By permission.

[4] Science Curriculum Improvement Study, *Relativity,* Teacher's Guide, Preliminary Edition, Boston: D. C. Heath and Company, 1968, pp. 42–45. By permission.

(See pages 543–546.) Observe how work in the student manual is tied to the lesson.

PROCESS SKILLS

Perhaps you became aware when you examined both sample lessons that there were no process skill statements. Their omission is intentional. SCIS views process learning as the natural, inseparable by-product of concept learning.[5] As the unit concepts increase in sophistication, so does the thinking used to learn them. The project staff feels that any separation of the two creates an artificial division that is incompatible with concept development. (Remember that the SCIS program is based on continual experiments, discussions, and analyses by the children. The claim may not be supportable for other programs unless similar activities exist.)

A process list is not furnished by SCIS and does not seem to be needed. Even so, it may be worthwhile to identify several skills used in the lessons with what you have learned before in this book. If you can examine some SCIS units with these in mind, it can speed up your understanding of the program. At all levels, look for these process opportunities in the lessons:

- Observing and classifying
- Suggesting and appraising hypotheses
- Recording data
- Interpreting data and making inferences
- Making operational definitions
- Reasoning quantitatively
- Controlling variables

Notice in particular how the processes are geared to the children's developmental levels. Younger children deal with a more restricted scope; their choices within a process are relatively more limited; they are more likely to apply the processes than to "invent" them. While the teacher may

[5] Robert Karplus and Herbert D. Thier, *A New Look at Elementary School Science,* Science Curriculum Improvement Study, Chicago: Rand McNally & Company, 1967, page 72.

- Discussion. After about ten minutes, gather the children together and ask them to describe what they observed in the aquaria. Encourage and accept all responses. If children disagree about something, do not try to resolve the difference but let them argue. You may also ask them to tell what they might do to find the answer. The point of the reporting and discussion is to create an atmosphere in which children feel free to talk, discuss, and argue about what they observe and what they think about their observations.

  Questions such as, "What did you observe? Did anyone observe something else? What makes you think such-and-such? How could we find out? Does anyone have any questions to ask Howard about his report?" help to promote discussion.

  Encourage the children to use the term "organism" to refer to a plant or animal whose name they do not know.

- "What is on the bottom of the aquarium?" Do not tell children that it is sand, but be alert to any disagreements the children may have about the identity of this material. This question should be followed immediately by Part Four (page 45), for it introduces one of the basic concepts of the life science program: habitat.

  The following activities can be carried out informally by small groups of children or the entire class when there is opportunity to observe the aquaria.

- Magnifier. Give each child a magnifier so that he can more closely examine the contents of the aquaria. Show the children how to increase the magnification by holding two or more magnifiers together. (See page 96.)

PART ONE / NATURAL EVENTS IN AQUARIA

- Unanswered questions. When the children raise questions which they want to investigate, it is helpful to record these questions in a place where children can frequently refer to them throughout the unit.

  Occasionally ask the children if they have any questions about what they have observed. "What do you wonder about?" may elicit a great array of questions from them. Throughout this guide you will find suggestions for helping children answer some of their questions. They probably will raise other questions which are not covered by this guide. Try to set up experiments to answer these as well. (See page 92.)

- Feeding the fish. The food relationships among organisms will be the subject of Part Seven, Food Web. The children can carry out introductory work here by feeding the guppies and watching them eat. No more than the smallest pinch of food (about 1/32 teaspoon) should be put in each aquarium each day. The children can do the feeding, but you should supervise them to see that they don't overfeed the fish. (See page 95.)

- Snail eggs. Transparent clumps of tiny spheres will appear on the plant leaves and on the sides of the aquarium. The children will have many ideas about what these may be, and Chapter 2 (page 24) makes some suggestions about how to proceed.

- Baby guppies. Eventually at least one of the aquaria will contain baby guppies. If your guppies give birth to young, the children may note, with much excitement, that the young are eaten by the adults. Plants often serve as places of escape for young fish. To prevent all the young from being eaten, you can put the adult guppies into another aquarium. (See page 24.)

- Tadpoles or guppies? Some children may think the guppies, particularly the young ones, are tadpoles. Ask them how they might find out, and follow up their suggestions. You might also transfer a few young guppies to another container where they can be observed more carefully. (See page 24.)

- Male and female. The birth of young guppies is likely to raise the question, "Which are the mothers and which are the fathers?" Chapter 3 (page 25) contains an experiment designed to help answer this question.

- Death of a fish. Some fish will die, and this may happen very soon after you set up the aquaria. If so, leave the dead fish in at least one aquarium so that the children can see what happens. If there are dead fish in several aquaria, remove them from all but one. (See page 27.)

- "What is the black stuff?" Some children may almost immediately notice dark material (detritus) on the sand. Use the baster to collect some of this material, and put it in the depression of an inverted tumbler where it can be observed more easily by the children. Let the children speculate about the identity of this material, but do not pursue this question at this time. It is the subject of Part Eight. (See page 87.)

- Record of the aquaria. The children may find it helpful to make a record of the aquaria, to which they can refer later when some change has taken place. This record can be a list of the aquarium contents, drawings, Polaroid photographs, or whatever the children suggest. Many teachers have found that children enjoy making these records *if* it is optional.

- Water level. Because the aquaria are not covered and thus are exposed to the air, water will evaporate and the water level will gradually go down. When the children notice the change in water level, you might ask them what happened to the water. The topic of evaporation will come up again in Chapter 10 and in later units of this program. Do not change the water. Simply add enough aged tap water to replace that which has evaporated. You will find it convenient to have one or two gallons of aged tap water on hand at all times.

  If children want to prepare aquaria of their own at home, tell them that it is best to let the water "age" in an open container for a day or two. This way, the chlorine (which is put into drinking water to kill small organisms that might be harmful to humans) will have time to escape and will not harm the fish.

- Names of organisms. When children have distinguished the different kinds of organisms in an aquarium, they often will ask for names of particular ones. By all means, tell them these names. (See pages 113–120.)

- Word chart. Children will be introduced to new words as they pursue the activities in this unit. Because children sometimes confuse terms as they talk about their observations, your class might construct an appropriate word chart with pictures to help them as they are introduced to the new vocabulary. The Glossary (pages 134–136) distinguishes these terms.

- "How do fish breathe?" This question is frequently raised, but we decided not to pursue it in this unit. The explanation involves many complex ideas about gases dissolved in water which we have found children unable to deal with at this age.

- Next activity. The foldout chart (back cover) is your guide to the order in which the various parts of the unit may be taken up. Depending on the children's response to what happens in the aquaria, you will proceed next to:
  Part Four, Habitat ("What is on the bottom of the aquarium?") page 45;
  Chapter 2, Birth and Growth of Guppies and Snails, page 24;
  Chapter 4, Death in an Aquarium, page 27; or
  Part Five, Algae ("What makes the water green?") page 59.
  Two groups of activities which are independent of events in the aquaria can be introduced at any time. They are:
  Part Two, Seeds and Plants (page 29) and
  Part Three, Diversity of Organisms (page 35).

PART ONE / NATURAL EVENTS IN AQUARIA

2 Birth and Growth of Guppies and Snails

Objectives   To observe and discuss the appearance of young guppies and snail eggs.
To observe that the young grow and in turn become adults that look like the other adults in the aquarium.

Materials   aquaria prepared in Chapter 1
fish food
dip net
crayon (provided by teacher)
magnifier for each child

Teaching Suggestions   Guppies in your classroom aquaria will undoubtedly give birth to young, and snails are also likely to reproduce. The observations which the children make in this chapter will provide a basis for the study of life cycles in the second-year life science unit.

• Guppies.   In at least one of the aquaria, guppies (see page 114) should give birth to young. There is no way of predicting exactly when this might occur; but if you see a female with a bulging belly, you can expect young guppies soon. The children probably will not see the birth process. More likely they will notice very small guppies in an aquarium where there had been none the day before.

If young guppies are born, it may be necessary to transfer the adults to another aquarium because the adults frequently eat the young.

If the young guppies survive and are fed daily the tiniest pinch of food, they should grow. If the children do not notice this, ask them to look for a change in size. Measurement of fish is very difficult and need not be attempted. Be satisfied if children notice and report that young guppies do increase in size.

When young fish appear, some children may think that these might be tadpoles. Ask the children to suggest ways of finding out, and follow up their ideas. Comparing these organisms with pictures of guppies and tadpoles, and waiting many weeks to see what happens, may help the children decide. More careful observation can be encouraged if these organisms are transferred to a separate container.

If the birth of young gives rise to the question, "Which are the mothers? Which are the fathers?" turn to Chapter 3.

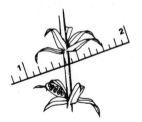

• Snail eggs.   Clusters of yellowish, transparent spheres, each one the size of a pinhead, may appear on the sides of the aquaria and on the leaves of the plants. (See page 115.) These are eggs laid by the snails, but the children will probably not know where they came from. Let them speculate. To focus their attention on eggs which have been laid against the aquarium wall, encircle the eggs with a crayon mark on the outside of the aquarium. A leaf on which eggs have been laid can be moved to a separate container for observation.

If eggs appear, have the children watch them through a magnifier. Eventually a small, brown, opaque spot will appear in each sphere and become larger day by day. After a week or two, a very small snail will hatch out of the transparent sphere.

PART ONE / NATURAL EVENTS IN AQUARIA

CHAPTER 3   Invention of Mr.O

Synopsis

In this chapter you introduce the Mr.O figure for describing relative position. Because the tasks are somewhat abstract and there are limited opportunities for the children to participate actively, you should plan to use several short sessions for this chapter. The introduction of Mr.O might be done in one session, the review chart and page 10 may be enough for the second session, and page 11 along with an Optional Activity might occupy the third session.

Teaching Materials

For each child:
    Student Manual pages 10–12
For demonstration purposes:
    3 Mr.O figures
    wood block
    ball
    book*
    box (to conceal Mr.O)
For the class:
    Mr.O chart
*(provided by teacher)

Teaching Suggestions

Advance Preparation. Make a word list on the chalkboard to assist children in spelling their answers in the student manual. You may base the list on the phrases the children used in Part One, or on the flash cards that will be used in Chapter 4. Fold the box to be used for concealing Mr.O.

Meet Mr.O. Gather the children near the demonstration table and show them a Mr.O figure. Identify Mr.O's front (with buttons), back, right arm (painted), and left arm. Explain to the children that they will pretend Mr.O is an observer who reports the position of objects relative to himself. Mr.O describes the position of an object by using words that tell the direction from him toward the object and the distance from him to the object. Mr.O never uses reference objects other than his own figure. In this way Mr.O is much like the child who played the role of Blindman in Chapter 1.

To illustrate, choose an object such as a block, a book, or a small box, and tell how Mr.O reports the position of that object relative to himself. The rules that Mr.O uses for giving a direction and a distance to describe the position of an object are explained in the Background Information on page 41 of this guide.

To involve the children in the activity, choose an object, place a Mr.O near it, and ask a child to tell how Mr.O would report the position of the object. Do this several times with Mr.O in various orientations relative to the class. Be sure to arrange his placement, however, so that the object is in a major direction from Mr.O. For example, Mr.O might report, *The box is to my right and very close.* or *The lamp is under me and far away.* Not acceptable under Mr. O's rules are descriptions such as *The lamp is near the ceiling.* or *The fire station is near the church.* Both of these descriptions make use of reference objects (the ceiling, the church) other than the figure of Mr.O.

Review chart about Mr.O. After you display the chart entitled "Meet Mr.O," demonstrate a cardboard Mr.O, and compare it with the description of Mr.O on the chart. Then have several children set up the displays pictured at the bottom of the chart, and ask them to describe what Mr.O would report about the positions of the objects. Let the children compare their reports with those printed on the chart. The third picture introduces a situation which combines two major directions. This will be more difficult for some children than the use of only one major direction. The chart also introduces the problems on pages 10 and 11. Display the chart for the remainder of the unit so that the children may read it, and refresh their memories about Mr.O at unscheduled times and during later science sessions.

The block is to my right and very close.

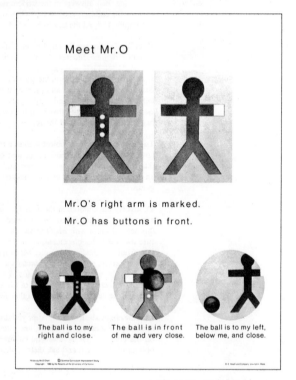

Meet Mr.O

Mr.O's right arm is marked.

Mr.O has buttons in front.

The ball is to my right and close.

The ball is in front of me and very close.

The ball is to my left, below me, and close.

CHAPTER 3 / INVENTION OF MR.O

544

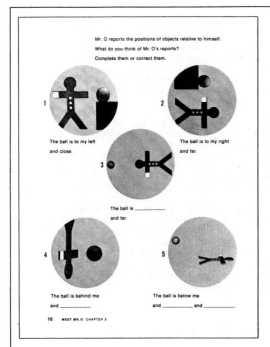

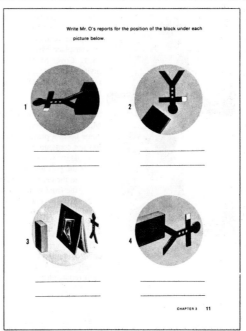

Student manual page 10. The illustrations on page 10 are similar to those at the bottom of the chart. Read this page with the class, and let children compare reports that they would make with those that are printed in the book. You may help to resolve disagreements by having the children use Mr.O figures to duplicate the situations in the pictures.

Some children will discover that they can get a better view of an illustration if they rotate the manual. This is an excellent discovery. The pictures are circular to make it easier to view them from all sides, and to keep the corners of the picture from serving as reference objects.

Student manual page 11. The children are to describe the position of the small cardboard block relative to Mr.O. You may wish to use the photographs for discussion; you may wish to have children write Mr.O's reports on the lines under the pictures; or, you may wish to use both of these activities.

In picture C a visual barrier is placed between Mr.O and the block. Children may wonder how Mr.O can report the position of the block if he cannot "see" the block. Explain to the children that Mr.O is not a real person, and that you pretend he knows the relative position of objects whether or not he can "see" them.

Mr.O in the box. To help convey the idea that Mr.O need not "see" objects in order to describe their positions, and to challenge the children with a new kind of problem, ask questions about the position of an object relative to Mr.O

PART TWO / MEET MR.O

while Mr.O is covered by a box and the object is outside the box. The children will have to remember the orientation of Mr.O, and they will have to imagine the spatial relation of the object to Mr.O. Be sure all the children are watching as you place Mr.O in some orientation on your table (upright, lying down, etc.). Cover Mr.O with the box, select an object (book, flag, globe), and invite a child to report the position of the object relative to Mr.O. The children must observe Mr.O's orientation before he is covered; otherwise, they will be unable to make the reports for Mr.O.

Student manual page 12. Page 12 deals with the idea that two or more Mr.O's may observe the same object and give different reports. If this idea has come up in a previous discussion, you may proceed directly to page 12. If it has not come up, you may like to use one of the following activities first.

1. Have several children who are sitting far apart in the classroom report the position of the same object (such as a flower pot placed on a desk in the center of the room), pretending that each child is a Mr.O facing the front of the room.
2. Place several Mr.O figures near an object, and ask the children to tell how each Mr.O describes the position of the object.
3. Place one Mr.O near an object, and challenge the children to place other Mr.O's so they make similar or very different reports.

After this introduction, the children open their manuals to page 12. Let the children discuss the reports made by each of the Mr.O's. The children are to supply the parts of the reports that have been omitted. The letter ahead of each report identifies the Mr.O making that report.

also present process methods for older pupils, they have greater opportunities in their lessons to create mental models or otherwise do more abstract thinking. Piaget's ideas, of course, are influential in an overall sense. But the workable details found in every lesson clearly bear the mark of feedback from rigorous classroom testing.

LEARNING MORE ABOUT SCIS

With many units now completed, the project is giving increased attention to classroom evaluation techniques, and teacher education in the SCIS approach. Four trial centers have been set up to demonstrate and further evaluate the SCIS program, and to develop new methods for in-service and preservice teacher education. These are located at the University of Hawaii, University of Oklahoma, Teachers College of Columbia University, and Michigan State University. Numerous elementary schools in the trial center areas are using and evaluating project materials in collaboration with the centers.

A substantial part of the SCIS materials is available in commercial form. Kits containing preliminary editions of printed materials and needed laboratory equipment have been prepared and are distributed by the Raytheon Education Company, 285 Columbus Avenue, Boston, Massachusetts 02116. (Figure 32.)

Figure 32 (From *Systems and Subsystems.* Science Curriculum Improvement Study and D. C. Heath and Company.)

The publisher and distributor of SCIS units in the final edition is Rand McNally and Company, P.O. Box 7600, Chicago, Illinois 60680.

Two paperback books are indispensable for a deeper understanding of the SCIS program. You will find it worthwhile to read:

A New Look at Elementary Science, by Robert Karplus and Herbert D. Thier (Chicago: Rand McNally, 1967); and

SCIS Elementary Science Sourcebook, by Willard Jacobson and Allan Kondo (Berkeley, California: Science Curriculum Improvement Study, University of California, 1968.)

Science—A Process Approach

CHAPTER EIGHT

Science — A Process Approach

THIS K–6 PROJECT WAS BEGUN IN 1962 BY THE COMMISSION ON Science Education of the American Association for the Advancement of Science. The association is the largest society for the scientific professions in the United States. From its beginning the AAAS program, *Science — A Process Approach,* has attracted much attention because of its unique structure.

Usual practice in developing the scope and sequence of a science curriculum is to use subject matter (product) as the base. Process skills are then introduced as needed within the various subject matter contexts. This program reverses the procedure: it uses process skills as the base for scope and sequence, and selects subject matter mainly to aid in developing these skills.

Why a process approach? Robert Gagné, a learning psychologist and one of the principal architects of this design, has claimed there are several advantages.[1]

First, children learn to cope better with reading and arithmetic when they are systematically taught skills in these subjects than they do when instruction is less organized. Why not also study science skills in an organized way to achieve improved results? To deal adequately with the objects and events of the natural enviornment, the child must be able to measure, predict, describe, and use other intellectual skills. These are basic ways of dealing with the natural world. When such processes are taught in an organized program

Credit for chapter opening photograph. **Bob S. Smith-Rapho Guillumette**

[1] This section is based on a speech given by Robert M. Gagné, "Process in Science for the Elementary Grades," at the 1968 convention, National Science Teachers Association, Washington, D.C.

they gradually become generalized intellectual strategies. As such, they should be useful throughout a child's entire life and within many content fields, provided sufficient content is learned in these fields.

Also, intellectual processes can be built up gradually, from simple to complex procedures. The result is that these do not have to be unlearned at other levels because, at all stages, what the child does is what the scientist does. In other words, a scientific skill such as observing may be conducted at simple to complex levels, depending upon a scientist's purpose. The simpler observations of the child can be basically the same as the scientist's, if the school program teaches the skills. On the other hand, when a principle or concept is learned by a child, it is more likely that aspects will need to be unlearned when, in later grades, they are found to be erroneous or oversimplified.

Finally, the selection of a content curriculum for children is difficult; there is so much subject matter, and one does not know what the child will need to learn in later years. By emphasizing processes general to all the sciences, the child learns what will be helpful in any content field he encounters later. Formal study of subject matter content might well begin in junior high school.

THE PROCESSES

In kindergarten through grade three, the following processes are taught:

1. Observing.
2. Using space/time relationships.
3. Using numbers.
4. Measuring.
5. Classifying.
6. Communicating.
7. Predicting.
8. Inferring.

In grades four through six, subtler skills are introduced which build upon and extend the abilities developed in the lower grades. These "integrated processes" are:

1. Formulating hypotheses.
2. Controlling variables.
3. Interpreting data.
4. Defining operationally.
5. Experimenting.

Subskills for each of the processes have been identified in the form of pupil behaviors and arranged in carefully tested sequences. The method used to develop the skills was to identify the process behaviors of scientists and then to logically break down the behaviors into orders in which they might be learned best. For example, before a child can describe an object he observes in terms of color and two-dimensional shape, he probably must (1) be able to identify the primary and secondary colors, and (2) be able to identify common two-dimensional shapes. Figure 33 shows part of the subskill hierarchy for the process of observing. The planned progression of this hierarchy is such that mastery of the later subskills depends upon mastery of the previous subskills. The combined hierarchies of process behaviors are the framework of *Science — A Process Approach*, and govern the selection and ordering of lessons in the entire program. Let us now examine the general features and sequences of all the processes.[2]

Observing. The child begins by identifying objects and their properties. By the first grade he is able to identify a cone, cube, cylinder, oval, rectangle and other shapes. (Figure 34.) He goes on to describe changes occurring in physical systems, such as solids changing to liquids. He orders a series of observations taking place over a given time period. One of the final exer-

[2]As based on AAAS Commission on Science Education, *Science — A Process Approach*, Parts A–C, 1967, Parts D and E, 1968, New York: Xerox Education Division; and Parts 6 and 7, Fourth Experimental Edition, 1967, Washington, D.C.: American Association for the Advancement of Science.

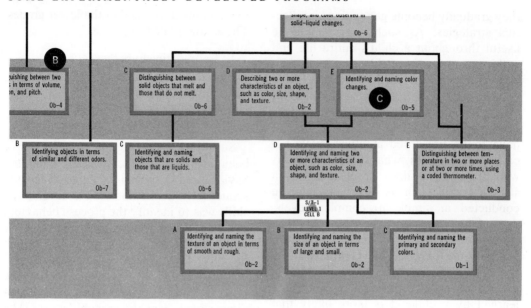

Figure 33 (Courtesy *Science—A Process Approach,* AAAS Commission on Science Education and Xerox Corp.)

cises requires him to make controlled observations, as he manipulates the shapes of several materials and studies the time they take to fall to the floor. During the sequence, he learns to use all his senses when observing, to separate observations from inferences, to use measurement for more exact descriptions, and to notice changes that occur when two or more objects interact.

Using Space/Time Relationships. How do we know that a far planet is not mostly two-dimensional, such as a cutout piece of cardboard? Or a closed cylinder with one end pointed toward the earth? In this sequence, pupils study how to draw three-dimensional objects and to detect such objects from projections of their shadows. They learn to recognize symmetry in the shapes of animals. They find out how to measure angles and time intervals. Later, the children learn to identify changes in the position of objects relative to the position of another observer. (Recall "Mr. O" in the SCIS unit on *Relativity.* The learning objective here is similar.)

Using Numbers. By now, nearly everyone recognizes the close relationship between modern science and mathematics. But why not teach the needed quantitative skills separately and apply them, rather than teach them within the science program?

Figure 34 (Courtesy Howard Jones.)

Figure 35   (Courtesy Howard Jones.)

Apparently, there are several reasons. For one thing, this insures that the children will have the needed number of skills for the related science exercises. It is more likely that the close relationship between the two subjects will be appreciated. Also, there is some evidence that pupils learn better how to use their numerical skills in science if science-related mathematics is taught in sequences especially designed for the purpose.[3]

The mathematics emphasis of this project is strong; up to a third of the lessons, depending on how one views them. However, the mathematics taught in *Science — A Process Approach* is designed to supplement or complement the regular mathematics program, not to replace it. Ap-

parently, teachers find that the science exercises provide excellent opportunities for children to apply what they learn in the regular program.

As early as kindergarten, sets and their members are introduced, along with cardinal and ordinal numbers. This is followed by use of the number line, consisting of positive and negative integers. (Figure 35.) Ideas learned here are applied to reading temperature scales, for example. Subsequent work includes finding averages, using decimals, and expressing large numbers as powers of ten. Later, the concept of probability is introduced in simple concepts dealing with heredity. For instance: What is the probability that a person is a taster or nontaster (of a selected chemical)?

Measuring. We have used standard measurements for so long that it is easy to forget the often arbitrary manner in which they were invented. Some of the present English

[3] See John R. Kolb, "Effects of Relating Mathematics to Science Instruction on the Acquisition of Quantitative Science Behaviors," *Journal of Research in Science Teaching,* Vol. 5, No. 2, 1967–1968, pp. 174–182.

units of length—inch, foot, yard, rod—can be traced back thousands of years to the *cubit*. This was the length of a man's forearm, from elbow to middle fingertip.

The measuring sequence of *Science—A Process Approach* begins with the arbitrary nature of measurements and brings out the need for standard units. The metric system is introduced early and used exclusively in the program. Besides learning how to measure length, mass, and time, the children discover how all other measurements may be derived from these basic units. For example, speed is derived from distance traveled within a specified time period. Other measurements are made to determine area, volume, temperature, and force. In addition, the children make estimates of basic and derived measures. They learn more about measuring angles, and apply their knowledge to light reflections. One of the final techniques learned is how to measure the sizes of microscopic objects.

Classifying. The child begins this sequence with the invitation to sort simple objects such as leaves, shells, and blocks into groups according to their similarities and differences. He learns to divide a set of objects into two or more subsets on the basis of one property. He finds that each of these subsets can be further subdivided on the same basis. (The child in Figure 36 is classifying all the objects making up the room aquarium.)

Gradually, the child realizes that all classifications are arbitrary, and that they may be based on either the properties of objects or their uses. He progresses to where he can use multistage classifications and code them on punch cards for rapid tabulation. This is a skill that would appear to have broad uses.

Communicating. The process of communicating is perhaps the most comprehensive of all; it involves descriptions that require knowledge of the other processes. *Replication* is at the root of communication in science: Can one investigator tell another what he did so exactly that the second person can perform the operation and get the same results?

Pupils begin to sharpen their communication skills with exercises in description. By carefully describing several properties of an object, they find that another person can identify it without being told what the object is. They learn to describe and order according to time intervals the changes observed in a plant. Graphs are found to be convenient ways to efficiently communicate much information. (Figure 37.) But in the process, pupils learn that certain conventions must be followed when constructing graphs if their data are to be communicable. The children discover that tables and charts are also efficient ways to display data. Maps and other coordinate systems are found to be ideal for precisely reporting locations. One of the final exercises in the sequence teaches how to describe in writing an entire investigation: purpose, method, materials, procedure, and results.

Predicting. Many adults and children think of the terms "predict" and "guess" as

Figure 36 (Courtesy Howard Jones.)

554

being the same. There is a significant difference, as used in *Science—A Process Approach*. Predictions are the expectations one has that an event will occur (or has occurred) based on previous observations. A guess is a shot in the dark; it is made when there is little or no evidence to draw upon. The formal sequence of this process is short—fewer than a half dozen exercises. However, predicting is found in combination with many other lessons throughout the entire program.

The children begin the sequence with a survey of the animal preferences of their class. The data are put on a bar graph and compared with the preferences of another class. From this information, pupils predict what a poll of a different grade will reveal. In another exercise, the children try to describe the motion of a bouncing ball. They construct a graph which helps them to realize that a ball's bounce is directly related to its drop height. From this they predict the bounce heights of a ball dropped from several untried heights. In "The Suffocating Candle" exercise which follows, pupils measure how long a candle will burn under different-sized jars. Using graphed data again, the children predict when the candle will go out with other, untried jars. They follow through by testing their predictions and revising them as new evidence is gathered.

Final lessons in the sequence call for predicting the motions of swinging pendulums; predicting the number of objects needed to balance an equal-arm balance; and studying the frequency of vibrations of a suspended spring as different weights are attached.

Inferring. One reason the adage, "Seeing is believing," can mislead us at times is that it omits the accompanying interpretation process. The chief intent of this sequence is to teach the difference between observations and the inferences drawn from them. In an initial lesson, pupils try to infer the identity of objects concealed in packages.

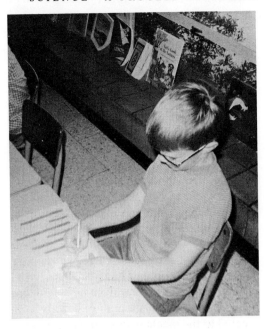

Figure 37 (Courtesy Howard Jones.)

By using several senses to make observations, they begin to discover enough properties of the objects to make intelligent inferences about what they are. A following exercise introduces the class to Andrew and Mike, two boys shown in a series of cartoons. Both boys mix their statements of observations with inferences. The job of the class is to properly classify these statements, and to note the kinds of observations upon which they are based.

Another exercise shows how inferences are used in animal biology. The children inspect a colored slide projection of a woodland scene in which varying animal tracks and traces are shown. They select from a group of suggested animals those that might have caused these observed clues. Other activities include observing water drops collecting on the outside of a cold glass and inferring their origin; designing ways to test inferences about water loss in plants; and inferring electric circuit patterns from indirect evidence gathered through testing hidden circuits.

Formulating Hypotheses. The first of the integrated processes extends children's previous work with inferences. They learn that generalized hypotheses may yield more information than specific ones. For example, the limited hypothesis, "A geranium plant needs light energy to grow" will yield a limited inference. A broader hypothesis, "Green plants need light energy to grow" permits a broader inference, assuming the proper tests take place.

In some activities, pupils gain experience in developing and modifying hypotheses from indirect observations. For instance, they hypothesize about the hidden contents of push-rod boxes (containers with simple mechanisms inside). They see the need to change their hypotheses from new evidence gained as they push and pull rods connected to the mechanisms, shake and otherwise examine what may be inside. Pupils are encouraged to describe in words, pictures, or actual constructions their hypotheses (mental models) of the hidden mechanisms.

In sixth-grade activities, hypothesizing takes place in combination with all the other integrated processes as the children engage in complete experiments.

Figure 38 (Courtesy Howard Jones.)

Controlling Variables. Many of the primary level activities on observation and measurement include some attempt to control variables. The difference now is mainly one of precision. A beginning exercise requires the careful observation of liquid movement in different materials: blotters, fabrics, and sand. What properties in these materials will change the rates of movement? How will we know? The possible variables must be identified and controlled. Each is manipulated and the responding event observed.

Some other investigations requiring the testing and control of variables are these: finding out how practice affects the memorization of words; learning some factors that influence chemical reactions; discovering the conditions that affect a rolling cylinder (Figure 38); and observing the changes brought about in living things by environmental variables.

Interpreting Data. Again the basic processes play a large role. Especially important is the ability to separate inferences from observations. All the preceding exercises involving reasoning from data equip the child for further data interpretation at the upper grade levels. The integrated exercises require reasoning with predictions, hypotheses, and inferences. Several lessons include the interpretation of simple statistics and probability.

A description of one exercise may illustrate the typical use of this process. The child begins by interpreting a graph on which he has recorded the various time records of guinea pigs in running a maze. He analyzes the data relative to the number of trials and makes predictions about further trials results. In so doing, he must relate the data to these hypotheses. After testing his hypotheses, he then carefully draws conclusions from his findings. If challenged to explain his conclusions, he interprets his data in a logical way that supports his conclusions.

Defining Operationally. The children begin by distinguishing between operational and nonoperational definitions. Later in the sequence they detect the need for, and then construct, such definitions.

The exercises dealing with this process develop two criteria for judging or constructing an operational definition: (1) it must include what one *does,* and (2) what one *observes.* In one typical example, the children are to decide if various metal rods are "good" conductors of heat. To meet the two criteria for operational definitions, they (1) describe how they will attach a marble to each rod with wax and hold each rod end in a flame, and (2) observe if each marble falls off in three minutes or less.

Experimenting. This process is actually a combination of all the basic and integrated processes and is met in "pure" form only in the sixth grade exercises. Of course, the children by this time have conducted many investigations and experiments. But seldom before this level are they asked to do whole experiments that require them to use all the processes in combination. In nearly every exercise, the children:

1. observe;
2. construct questions to be investigated;
3. construct hypotheses;
4. identify the variables;
5. construct operational definitions;
6. construct and test hypotheses;
7. collect and display data;
8. interpret data;
9. modify hypotheses as needed; and
10. repeat part or all of the cycle as needed.

LESSON STRUCTURE

The entire program is divided into seven parts, A through G, adaptable for either graded or nongraded schools. Part A might be used in kindergarten, Part B in first grade, and so on. Each part has a teacher's guide. This is a box of twenty to twenty-five lesson booklets, called exercises. (Figure 39.)

The exercises follow this format:

Title of the exercise

Objectives — the behaviors a child should exhibit by the end of the exercise.

Sequence — how the exercise fits into the sequence, what led to the present one, and what comes next.

Rationale — a description of the exercise and its relationship to others; also extra subject-matter information as required.

Vocabulary — a list of the words children will learn.

Materials — the instructional equipment and supplies needed for the exercise.

Instructional Procedure — suggests how to introduce the exercise through questions or problems and lists the activities.

Generalizing Experience — an activity that contains different subject matter but which requires an application of the same process skill; this helps to insure process transfer to new situations.

Appraisal — suggests tasks for the children so the teacher can see how well they have achieved the exercise objectives.

Competency Measure — an oral or written test for individuals or a class.

See pages 560–571 for a sample exercise from Part D.[4]

Lesson Topics. In most programs organized on a subject-matter basis, a unit topic or theme reflects the continuity of subject matter within the lessons. An electricity unit may present several different ideas, but all of the lessons are about electricity. As mentioned earlier in the chapter, *Science — A Process Approach* selects subject matter mainly to aid in developing process skills. This results in exercises (lessons) that may

[4] *Science — A Process Approach,* Part D, New York: Xerox Education Division, 1968. By permission.

Figure 39 (Courtesy *Science — A Process Approach*, **AAAS Commission on Science Education and Xerox Corp.**)

have little or no *subject-matter* continuity. For example, note the twenty-two consecutive topics of the exercises in Part D [5] (the numeral after each process indicates the order of the exercise in each process sequence):

a. Inferring 3 "Observations and Inferences"

b. Inferring 4 "Tracks and Traces"

c. Predicting 3 "Describing the Motion of a Bouncing Ball"

d. Using Numbers 10 "Dividing to Find Rates & Means"

e. Inferring 5 "The Displacement of Water by Air"

f. Measuring 13 "Describing the Motion of a Revolving Phonograph Record"

g. Measuring 14 "Measuring Drop by Drop"

h. Using Numbers 11 "Metersticks, Money, and Decimals"

j. Communicating 11 "Describing Location"

[5] Ibid.

k. Measuring 15 "Measuring Evaporation of Water"

l. Inferring 6 "Loss of Water from Plants"

m. Predicting 4 "The Suffocating Candle"

n. Observing 16 "Magnetic Poles"

o. Using Space/Time Relationships 14 "Rate of Change of Position"

p. Measuring 16 "Describing and Representing Forces"

q. Observing 17 "Observing Growth from Seeds"

r. Communicating 12 "Reporting an Investigation in Writing"

s. Using Space/Time Relationships 15 "Two-Dimensional Representation of Spatial Figures"

t. Classifying 10 "Using Punch Cards to Record a Classification"

u. Using Space/Time Relationships 16 "Relative Position and Motion"

v. Observing 18 "Observing Falling Objects"

Notice however, that there is some continuity of *process* in this sample list. And remember that continuity of process is carefully built into the entire program through the elaborate process hierarchies. Is the comparative lack of subject-matter continuity a handicap? We shall examine this and other issues in the final chapter.

SUBJECT MATTER CONTENT

Although continuity of subject matter is not stressed in this program, children are exposed to a considerable amount of subject-matter content. Exactly how much is learned of concepts and principles is hard to say. There are no formal procedures to assess these learnings like those for the processes. Nevertheless, the exercises contain a broad array of important content ideas.

Physical Sciences. The early grades feature simple activities selected from elementary physics, with some chemistry and earth science activities making up the rest. This emphasis is reversed in the upper grades. Many of the primary-level exercises contain investigations of material objects. In some ways these lessons are similar to those of SCIS. Pupils observe the properties of solids, liquids, and gases. They extend their growing knowledge of properties to include density, viscosity, and compressibility. They learn to describe changing properties through observing chemical reactions and changes of state taking place.

Also investigated are the effects of temperature and wind on evaporation rate. Some activities involve work with the concepts of temperature and heat. The calorie is learned as a basic heat unit and applied in related measuring exercises. Other investigations include the concepts of force, motion, inertia, acceleration, and energy. Further concepts are met in exercises involving magnetism and electricity, levers, light energy, and lenses.

Biological Sciences. Interaction of living things and their environment is a theme that apparently influences many exercises of biological content. Early work with various organisms leads to the properties and functions that distinguish living from nonliving objects. Pupils also learn how structure is related to function in animals and plants. Life cycles are introduced by grade two and brought up again several grades later.

The concept of biotic potential is met with the rapid reproduction of imaginary animals called "glurks." Effects of environmental changes on a population come up as the children experiment with hatching and growing brine shrimp. Other environmental influences are discovered that change the growth of green plants, molds, and yeasts. Study is also made of hereditary transfer of dominant and recessive traits in several generations of fruit flies.

Several topics and concepts included in the exercises are related to psychology and

SCIENCE—A PROCESS APPROACH / PART D

INFERRING 6

LOSS OF WATER FROM PLANTS

OBJECTIVES

At the end of this exercise the child should be able to

1. *CONSTRUCT* appropriate inferences about water loss from plants based on observations of investigations demonstrating water uptake and loss.

2. *CONSTRUCT* situations to test such inferences.

3. *CONSTRUCT* predictions from a graph about water loss from plants over a given period of time.

SEQUENCE

```
┌─────────────────────┐        ┌─────────────────────┐
│ Constructing inferences │     │   Describing the    │
│ concerning the shape │        │  expected outcome of │
│   of an object on the │       │ future observations  │
│ basis of observations │       │  based on inferences │
│ of transverse, slant, │       │ formulated and tested│
│   and longitudinal    │       │    by the child.     │
│ sections of the object.│      │                      │
│                       │        │     Inferring 7      │
│      Inferring 8      │        │                      │
└─────────────────────┘        └─────────────────────┘
              ▲                            ▲
              └──────────────┬─────────────┘
                   ┌─────────────────────┐
                   │    Constructing     │
                   │  situations to test │
                   │  inferences made    │
                   │    by the child.    │
                   │                     │
                   │    THIS EXERCISE    │
                   │                     │
                   │     Inferring 6     │
                   └─────────────────────┘
                            ▲
                   ┌─────────────────────┐
                   │ Demonstrating that  │
                   │ inferences may need │
                   │  to be altered on the│
                   │  basis of additional │
                   │    observations.    │
                   │                     │
                   │     Inferring 4     │
                   └─────────────────────┘
```

RATIONALE

Children already know that plants need to be watered. However, they may not know where the water goes after the plant is watered and they probably do not know how much water a plant uses. The study of transpiration in plants (a process in which moisture is given off through the porous surfaces of leaves and other parts) will give them an excellent opportunity to make careful observations, to make inferences, and to design situations in which they can test their inferences.

The activities here will also give them important background about the general phenomenon of water loss, which will arise frequently in the child's study of living systems, physical environments, and ecological relationships.

(**Note:** Two weeks before you expect to start *Activity 1*, plant a number of wax bean seeds—or have the children plant them—in two pots containing potting soil or vermiculite. Put the pots in a well-lighted area that is free from drafts, and water them daily. In two weeks the plants should be growing well.)

VOCABULARY

transpire
transpiration

stomate (STOW-mate)

RELATED MATERIALS

Listed below are the materials required to conduct this exercise.

Some items cannot be supplied at all or are not supplied by Xerox in the Standard Kit. These are designated as *NS*. Note, however, that many items so designated are supplied in the Comprehensive Kit. A separate list of these items is included with the comprehensive materials.

It should be noted that some supplied items are expended in the course of this exercise. These expendable items are designated as *EXP.*

Items too large for the Exercise Drawer will be found in the Teacher Drawer and are designated as *TD.*

Bean seeds, 100 (EXP)
Flowerpots, 2 (EXP)
Vermiculite, 1 package (TD, EXP)
Geranium plant, 1 (NS)
Celery stalks, 30 (NS)
Dishpan, 1 (NS)
Single-edge razor blade, 1 (NS)
Red food coloring, 1 bottle (EXP)
Plastic cups, 30 (EXP)
Large pail, 1 (NS)

Leafy shoots of willow, pine, privet, sycamore, cottonwood, tomato, or geranium, 10, approximately 35 cm long (NS)
Flexible plastic tubing, 8 pieces
Masking tape, 1 roll (NS)
Cardboard, 10 pieces, 25 × 50 cm or larger (NS)
Modeling or florist clay (NS)
3-decimeter metric rules, 10 (found in Exercise "i" drawer)
Graph paper, 2-mm squares printed in green ink, 100 sheets (TD, EXP)
Plastic bags, 8 (EXP)
White petroleum jelly, 1 tube (NS)
100× microscope or a microprojector, 1 (NS)
Microscope slides, 6 (NS)
Cover slips for slides, 6 (NS)
Potted plants, 2, 15 to 20 cm high (NS)
Illustrations (as in Figure 4), 1 copy
Graph (as in Figure 5), 1 copy

INSTRUCTIONAL PROCEDURE

Introduction

Show the class a healthy geranium plant and ask, **What are some of the things a plant needs to live and grow?** From their previous experience, the children will probably say that a plant must have air, proper temperature, soil, sunlight, and water. Ask if they have any idea what happens to the water when a plant is watered. **Where does it go? Does all the water stay in the soil, or does it go into the plant? Will a plant live very long without getting more water? How long?**

Activity 1

Set the two pots of growing bean plants on a table in front of the class. Ask, **How could we use these plants to discover whether plants require water?** (Give water to one pot of plants but not to the other.) Tell the children to mark one pot "To be watered" and the other "Not to be watered," to put both plants in a well-lighted place, to schedule the daily watering of one pot, and to keep a simple record for a week or so, as in the following example:

Date	Time	Watered Plants	Unwatered Plants
Monday, 3/4	9:00 AM	Appear healthy	Appear healthy
Tueday, 3/5	9:00 AM	Appear healthy	Appear healthy
Wednesday, 3/6	9:00 AM	Appear healthy	Becoming limp
Thursday, 3/7	9:00 AM	Appear healthy	Droopy leaves; losing color
Friday, 3/8	9:00 AM	Appear healthy	Bent over
Monday, 3/11	9:00 AM	Appear healthy	Leaves are dry

Discuss these observations with the children. **Do your observations give you any information about where the water went?** (No, they indicate only that plants will not live very long without water.)

Activity 2

Remind the children of the potted plants they observed in *Activity 1.* Ask, **Where did the water go that we gave the plants that remained healthy?** (Into the plant, or it evaporated.) **Are these observations or inferences?** (Inferences.) **Can we test these inferences?** Discuss any ideas the children have. Then say you know one way they might like to try.

Put a number of celery stalks with leaves and a large dishpan of water on a table at the front of the room. Tell the children they are going to see what happens when you put a cut celery stalk in colored water and let it stand for a while. Say, **You should observe everything that happens and write your observations down on a piece of paper.**

Divide the class into groups of four children. Then give each group (or each child, if you have enough celery) a plastic cup about half full of water colored with red food coloring. Have each group or child, in turn, bring a cup (or cups) of red-colored water to your supply of celery stalks and water. As the group watches, submerge the lower part of a stalk in the pan of water; then, with a razor blade or a sharp knife, make a slant cut completely through the stalk about 2.5 centimeters from the bottom.

Discard the small piece you have cut off. (You must make the cut under water to prevent air from getting into the conducting tubes in the stem. Also, the blade must be sharp enough to make a clean cut and to prevent the tubes from being crushed or pushed together and thereby closed.)

Ask a group representative (or each child) to quickly transfer the cut stalk with the leaves from the pan to his cup of colored water. Tell him to label his cup, put it in a brightly lighted place in the room, and leave it there for several hours.

As soon as they notice a change in the color of the leaves, have the children retrieve their cups. Tell them to remove the stalk from the water and observe the color in the stem and in the leaves. If they hold the leaves up to the light, they will be able to observe the color pattern more closely. Then cut across the stems in several places for the children and ask them to find the tubes in the stem that carry the water to the leaves. Also, tell them to break a piece lengthwise and to try pulling out the dyed strings (conducting tubes).

Ask the children to review their list of observations. **Do your observations support and verify the inference that the water moves into the celery plant?**

Activity 3

Before the class begins, cut one leafy shoot of a plant for each group of children. It should be about 6 millimeters in diameter and 35 to 40 centimeters long, and it should have several leaves. Branches of willow, pine, privet, sycamore, cottonwood, or tomato are all suitable, although branches with a woody, sturdy stem are better. A local greenhouse could supply them if you conduct the investigation in the winter and cannot find branches with leaves attached. Geranium plants also work well.

When the branches are cut from the plant, submerge the cut end immediately in a large pail of water. Then immediately make a second diagonal cut under water, 2.5 to 5 centimeters from the cut end. The purpose of this second cut is to remove any air bubbles that may be left in the water-conducting tubes of the plant after the first cut. Discard the small pieces of stem. Keep the cut end of each branch under water.

(Start this activity early in the day.)

Ask the children whether a plant draws up into its leaves and stem all the water that is put on the soil. From their previous experiences with evaporation and water vapor, some may suggest that some of the water evaporates from the soil. If so, tell them that this is true. Then ask, **Does some water move into the plant itself?** (Yes.) **Does some water evaporate from the plant after moving into it? How much water does a plant take up?**

Divide the class into groups of four children and give each group a piece of clear, flexible plastic tubing, 50 centimeters long. Have a child from each group, in turn, fill the plastic tube with water from a sink or a large, shallow pan. The child can put one end of the tube in the water and suck on the other end, or he can lower one end of the tube vertically and hold it under the water while the rest of the tube is gradually submerged, making sure no kinks or bends develop to prevent the water from filling the tube. After the tube is completely full, tell the child to put a finger over each end so that the water does not drain out and to submerge the entire length. If there are any large bubbles, the procedure has to be repeated more carefully. However, tiny pinhead-size bubbles that cling to the inner surface of the tube will not influence the experiment and can be ignored, and small bubbles can be pinched toward the end of the tube.

Now have all the children watch the next procedure. Quickly transfer one of the branches to the container of water. While the stem and tubing are still under water, fit the end of the branch into one end of the plastic tube. Again check to see that the tube is full of water and has no air bubbles. Carefully remove the branch and the attached tube from the water, and fasten each with cellophane tape or masking tape in a U-shaped position to a piece of cardboard already on the bulletin board. (See Figure 1.) To prevent loss of water at the connection between the tube and the branch, mold a little bit of modeling or florist's clay around the end of the tube. Then attach a ruler to the cardboard beside the plastic tube so that its zero end is in line with the water level in the tube. (You could also use a strip of lined paper or graph paper, with the divisions numbered.) Adding a drop of food coloring to the water will make it easier to read the water level.

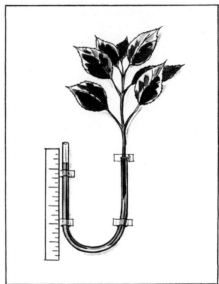

FIGURE 1

Have the children keep an hourly record of the water level throughout the day. The record might look something like this:

Time	Total distance (in cm) the water dropped in tube	Distance (in cm) the water level dropped from the previous level
9:30 AM (Start)	0.0	0.0
10:30 AM	1.0	1.0
11:30 AM	2.6	1.6
12:30 PM	4.6	2.0
1:30 PM	6.0	1.4
2:30 PM	7.7	1.7
3:30 PM	8.2	0.5

After the observations are completed (in five or six readings), discuss the data with the children. **What total amount did the water level drop during the day? How much did it drop each hour?** (Different amounts, probably.) If the data show it, point out that the amount of water the plant used each hour changed at different times during the day. (This may not be apparent, though, if the classroom temperature and lighting are relatively constant.) Now ask the children to graph their results. Discuss with them what they should plot on the horizontal and vertical axes. Then make sure that they label the axes appropriately, indicating the units of measurement (hours, centimeters). Afterward, you might reproduce some representative graphs on the chalkboard.

The graphs in Figure 2 show two ways to graph the data. The first one illustrates the *total amount* of water used as time passes. The second shows how the plant's rate of water uptake varied during each hour of the day. Although both graphs are based on the same data, they emphasize different aspects, and the children may have some difficulty seeing the relationship between them. If so, point out that the second graph shows the distance (vertical) between two successive points on the first graph.

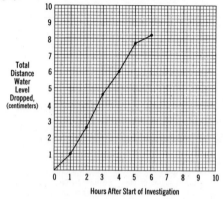

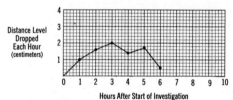

FIGURE 2

Ask different groups to compare their results. They should conclude that although their actual measurements varied, the trends are similar: Large plants used more water than small plants, and all plants used more water during the warm, bright part of the day. Ask the children whether their conclusions are inferences or direct observations. You might point out that their measurements do not show the volume of water the plant uses. To find this, they could fill different lengths of tubing with water and then pour the water into a graduated cylinder and measure the volume.

Ask volunteers to use their graphs to predict where the water level will be at 9:30 AM tomorrow morning. If they predict that it will be below the bottom of the scale, suggest that before they leave the setup for the day, they may add water to the tube so the level is up to the top of the scale. They can measure the water level at 9:30 the next morning. Their measurement probably will not agree with the predicted value, since the plant does not transpire as much water at night as it does during the day. The failure of the prediction should stimulate both discussion and disagreement. This is good, provided the discussion remains logical and is not random guessing. Persistent questioning of a child who has an explanation should reveal, however, whether his idea is based on thought or guesswork.

Save the experimental setups so you can use them again in *Activity 4*.

Activity 4

After *Activity 3*, various related questions may arise. The children should realize that they still do not know what happens to the water the plant takes up or why the plant continues to need water. They may ask if some of the water gets out of the leaves and stems somehow. They may want to know which loses more water, the leaves or the stems. Or they may ask if both sides of the leaves lose water. Try to elicit these or related questions if the children do not ask them first. Also, let them explore any ideas they have about finding answers to their questions.

Wherever possible, the children should use the equipment from *Activity 3* and the same technique to carry out further investigations. You will need to cut more branches as you did in *Activity 3*. If the children do not make any suggestions for tests, briefly propose the following procedures, but try to get them to work out the details themselves.

Where does the water from the plastic tube go? Tell them to add food coloring to the water in the tube. They should observe the change in the coloring of the plant parts and infer that the water went into these. Point out the similarity of this investigation to the one in *Activity 2*.

Does water get out of the leaves and stems? Tell them to wrap a polyethylene bag tightly around the plant and to examine this bag after a few hours. (They should see droplets of water condensing on the inner surface of the bag.) **Where did this water come from?** Have them draw inferences from their observations.

Which loses more water, the leaves or the stems? Have the children cover the leaves with a waterproof layer of vaseline to prevent evaporation. Then tell them to compare the amount of water the plant used before and after the leaves were covered. **What inferences can you make from these comparisons?**

Do both sides of the leaves lose water? Two groups should cooperate on this test, each preparing similar setups with twigs of about the same size and having the same number of leaves. One group should cover the upper surfaces of all the leaves with a thin film of vaseline; the other group should cover the lower surfaces of the leaves. Tell the two groups to collect their data and to compare the amount of water used in the two setups. **What inferences can you make from these investigations?**

Encourage the children to keep whatever records they feel will help them later in communicating their procedures and results to the rest of the class. Have them use graphs wherever possible.

Tell group representatives or individuals to describe their tests, results, and conclusions to the rest of the class. Point out any instances of missing information or information that was not recorded. Then discuss with them whether the conclusions are observations or inferences. At the end of the discussion, identify the process by which plants give off moisture as *transpiration*. In summary, ask, **What parts of the plants you have observed transpire the most?** (The underside of the leaves.)

Activity 5 (Optional)

(You should include this demonstration if you have a microscope or a microprojector.)

Remind the children that they have inferred from their observations of *Activity 4* that water has left the stem and the leaves of the plant in a process called transpiration. Ask, **How do you suppose this happens?** Give each child a leaf. (Geranium leaves or crisp lettuce are excellent.) Say to the child, **Examine the surface of your leaf. Do you see any holes?** (No.) **Suppose we look more closely, as we can do with a microscope.**

Prepare a microscope slide as follows, describing what you are doing as the class watches: Carefully peel off first the upper surface and then the lower surface of a leaf. You can do this by bending the leaf until it cracks and then shearing one section over the other. The thin, transparent surface should separate from the rest of the leaf. Mount each of the peeled surfaces in a drop of water on a microscope slide, cover the specimens with cover slips, and identify the slides with appropriate markings.

Now put one of the slides in the microscope or micro-projector and examine the surface of the leaf. Try to find the small openings (the stomates). (See Figure 3.) Let the children come, in turn, to look through the microscope, or project the image for the whole class to see. Be sure each child identifies the stomates. Show them both the top and the bottom surface of the leaf.

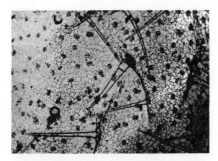

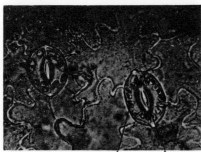

FIGURE 3   Guard Cells   Stomate

Then ask, **What inferences can you make from these observations? What inferences that you made in Activity 4 are strengthened by your observations?** If necessary, ask, **For example, what inference can you make about the difference in the number of stomates on the two sides of a leaf?**

GENERALIZING EXPERIENCE

Have the children use the setup in *Activity 3* to test such questions as these:

Would another kind of plant use water as this one did?

Would the water in the tube drop faster or more slowly if the plant were in the dark?

Would the plant use water faster if a breeze from a fan were blown over the leaves?

Would the water level in the tube continue to drop if all the leaves were stripped from the plant?

Do flowers use water?

After each test, conclude by asking the children, **What inferences can be made from an investigation such as this?**

See Back Cover for
APPRAISAL and
COMPETENCY MEASURE

NOTES

APPRAISAL

Tell the children that you saw six carnations in a vase at the florist's shop and that three of the blooms were white and three were green. The florist told you that when he cut these carnations, all six were white. Ask the children to infer how the florist might have changed the color of the flowers.

Show the children a properly labeled graph, similar to one of those in *Activity 3,* that indicates the rate of water uptake during each hour, and the base line of which shows the hours when readings were taken. Say, **Suppose one half of the plant's leaves had been removed before the study was begun. Predict what the water level would have been at each of the designated hours, and mark points on the graph to represent your predictions. What observations did you use to make them? What inferences are these predictions based on?**

FIGURE 4

COMPETENCY MEASURE

(Individual score sheets for each pupil are in the Teacher Drawer.)

Show the child the following drawing (see Figure 4) and say, **This drawing shows two potted plants, labeled $\underline{A}$ and $\underline{B}$, that are the same size. Plant $\underline{B}$ was completely enclosed in a large, airtight plastic bag. At 1:00 PM, the two plants were placed one at each end of an equal-arm balance, which was then level. (Plant $\underline{A}$ balanced Plant $\underline{B}$.) But by 3:00 PM, the balance was no longer level.**

TASKS 1, 2 (OBJECTIVES 1, 2): Ask, **What inference can you make to explain why the plant that was not in the plastic bag, Plant $\underline{A}$, weighed less than the plant inside the plastic bag, Plant $\underline{B}$, after two hours?** Put one check in the acceptable column for Task 1 if the child says that water was lost from some part of Plant *A* (the soil, the leaves, or the stem), but that the plastic bag prevented loss of the water that evaporated from Plant *B*. Then say, **Tell me a way to test your inference.** Put one check in the acceptable column for Task 2 if he suggests an appropriate test.

Show the child a copy of Figure 5, which shows data from an investigation like the one described in *Activity 3.* TASKS 3, 4 (OBJECTIVE 3): Say, **Predict how far the water level measured in this investigation will have dropped after six hours.** Put one check in the acceptable column for Task 3 if the child says "Six centimeters," or "About six centimeters." Then say, **Predict how far the water level will have dropped after eight hours.** Put one check in the acceptable column for Task 4 if he says "Eight centimeters," or "About eight centimeters."

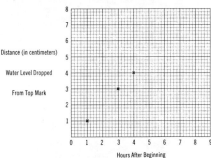

FIGURE 5

the social sciences. For example, pupils study changes in learning times of guinea pigs placed in a maze and, later, how interference affects human learning. They see how perceptual judgment is affected by optical illusions, and how conflict lengthens the time in which one can make a decision.

Of course, mathematical concepts also make up an important part of *Science—A Process Approach.* We have already seen in the process descriptions such topics as geometry (space/time relationships), graphing, numbers and number notation, measurement, and probability.

LEARNING MORE ABOUT SCIENCE—A PROCESS APPROACH

With all the basic parts of the program completed, the AAAS Commission on Science Education is refining and testing an in-service education program. Attention is also being given to further work in evaluation. The field testing has been very extensive and encouraging.

Science—A Process Approach is available in commercial form from the Xerox Education Division, Dept. SB, 600 Madison Ave., New York, New York, 10022.

Figure 40 (Courtesy *Science—A Process Approach,* **AAAS Commission on Science Education and Xerox Corp.)**

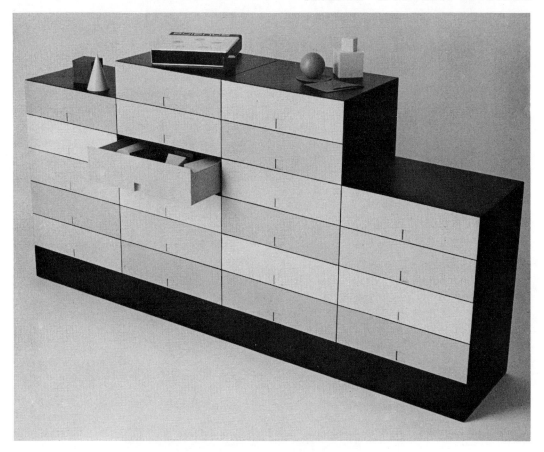

Figure 41 (Courtesy *Science — A Process Approach,* AAAS Commission on Science
Education and Xerox Corp.)

Besides the teaching guides and hierarchy charts, there is a classroom laboratory kit for each of the seven parts. (Figure 40 shows the materials in Part A. Figure 41 shows how materials are stored in a kit.) The laboratory kit comes in two versions. A standard kit contains all the basic experimental materials needed for a class of thirty pupils except for some locally-obtainable materials. An expanded version includes everything but perishable items. As in the SCIS program, no written ma-

terials are provided for children except for data worksheets.

Two paperback publications will help you to learn much more about this uniquely constructed and important program:

The Psychological Bases of Science — A Process Approach, Second Edition, 1967; and

Commentary for Teachers, Third Experimental Edition, 1968. Available from AAAS Commission on Science Education, 1515 Massachusetts Ave. N.W., Washington, D.C. 20005.

The Elementary Science Study

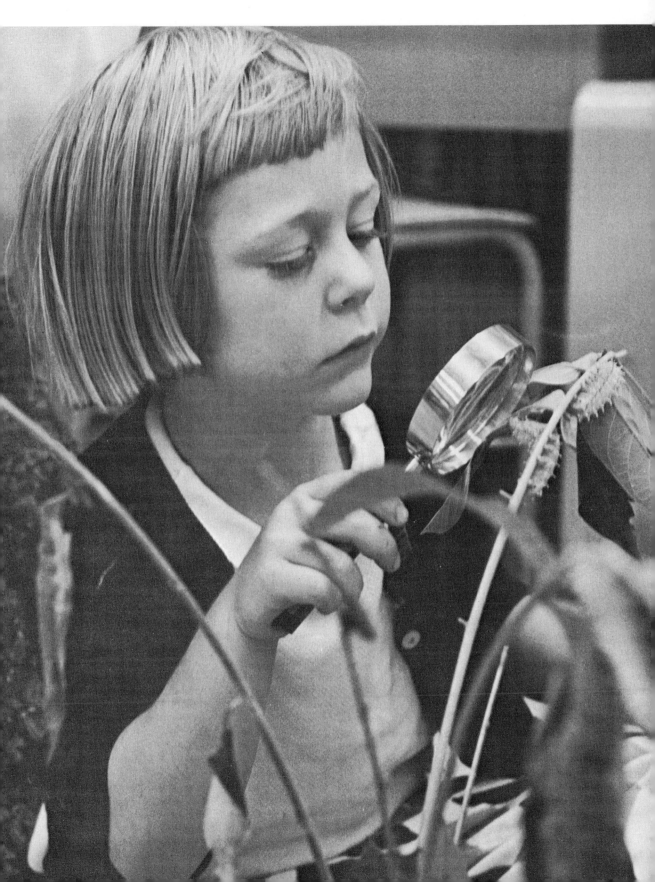

CHAPTER NINE

The Elementary Science Study

THE ELEMENTARY SCIENCE STUDY (ESS) IS ONE OF MANY CURRICU-
lum improvement projects of the Education Development Center
(formerly Educational Services, Inc.), a nonprofit organization
devoted to generating new ideas for education. The aim of ESS is
to develop a variety of thoroughly tested units that personnel in local
school districts can choose from. It has no curricular master plan for
scope and sequence. Instead, units stand independently for the most
part. Why this approach? As ESS explains:[1]

The enormous variety of schools and school systems in this country
suggests that no group—ESS or any other—can design a single curriculum that will satisfy all conditions. Planning a curriculum involves decisions which can be made only with specific knowledge about the teachers,
principals, students, parents, and finances in each case. We feel that the
healthiest situation is one in which each school system decides what it
wants to teach at every level and what it expects of students; into such a
framework it can then fit those units that are most appropriate to the
situation.

Many ESS units are based on a specific event or object that can
be exploited to arouse children's curiosity and also teach useful
skills or basic concepts. In other words, the unit developers are just
as likely to conceive a unit from *objects* children can observe or play
with as they are from subject matter ideas. ESS has found (as many

Credit for chapter opening photograph. **Courtesy Educational Development Center,
Newton, Mass.**

[1] Elementary Science Study, *Introduction to the Elementary Science Study,*
Watertown, Mass.: Educational Services, Inc., 1966, n.p. By permission.

teachers have found) that meaningful activities often are hard to invent for children when one begins with a logical framework of subject-matter principles. Not surprisingly, several unit titles seem to reveal the manner in which they were conceived: "Kitchen Physics," "Balloons," "Ice Cubes," and "Mystery Powders," among others.

The ESS approach is frankly child-centered. It appears to have captured well the essence of wonder, curiosity, and natural play that is so characteristic of childhood. While the teacher guide for each unit suggests an overall structure, the pupils determine largely in which directions the activities go and how much time is spent on individual activities. Therefore, most classroom procedures are open-ended and exploratory. These features permit the units to be used by pupils who vary greatly in age, intelligence, and background.

Most of the activities require the children to use reasoning processes after beginning explorations have taken place. But there is little problem solving for the specific purpose of clinching subject-matter principles. Instead, more attention is given to finding out ways to test questions that arise as materials are manipulated: Where should the stick be placed to be balanced? Will the mealworm be able to find where we hid its food? What will happen if we add moisture to this mold? An intuitive, "messing about" spirit characterizes many of the activities, especially in the early stages of a unit. ESS believes that learning occurs best when children are free to use their own unique styles without overstructuring and premature closure from adults; that there are many paths to success. The rationale is interesting: [2]

Learning theorists are quick to remind us that they do not yet fully understand which approach, which experiences, in which sequences produce the situation that makes an individual

[2] Elementary Science Study, *Introduction to the Elementary Science Study,* Boston: Houghton Mifflin Company, 1965, p. 7. By permission.

child or group of children respond. Jerome S. Bruner, Professor of Psychology at Harvard, emphasizes two ways of learning, knowing, and acting, which he calls the "right-handed" and "left-handed." The right-handed is rational, deductive, purposeful, straightforward; the left-handed is intuitive, hypothetical, playful, witty, imaginative, and sometimes simply wrong. Both ways are useful.

Confronted by such variables and unknowns, we feel that our approach should follow a mixed strategy—one that does not even pretend to be perfectly planned and leaves occasional decisions to chance and to the opportunities of the moment for a particular child, teacher, and classroom. Our materials therefore provide situations for traditional, rational, "right-handed" learning and situations suited more to the intuitive, playful, "left-handed" approach. They are designed to appeal to all the senses, to the imagination and artistic instincts, and through the wordless experimental equipment as much as through the printed or spoken word.

UNIT COMPOSITION

About fifty units are completed or in trial version form at the time of this writing. About four or five more are contemplated. The units exhibit much variety. Many require little equipment except that usually found around the home or school. A few are best taught with materials designed especially for the unit. Some might take fifty or more hours to complete, others a fifth of that time. Some involve mostly the learning of process skills, others are weighted toward concept learning. Other variations exist in structure and format. Several units cannot even be included under the heading of "science," but are more suited for topics like "logic," or "general education."

A "typical" unit (an arguable term, such is the variety) consists of an instructional package of related materials—a teacher's guide, a kit of supplies and equipment, data sheets for the children, film loops and, in a few units, one or two information booklets. The teacher guides are likely to provide suggestions for flexible management of the class, and some subject-matter background. Objectives seldom appear in specific form. Instead, notes to the teacher give possible problems to pursue and activities that have proven to be worthwhile in classroom trials. Look now at descriptions and excerpts from two of the guides, *Colored Solutions* and *Microgardening*. Notice in particular the easygoing instructional style.

Colored Solutions (Grades 3–6). This unit introduces the children to the concept of density and the phenomenon of "layering." When two liquids of different densities are put into a container without any mixing taking place, a distinct boundary is revealed between the liquids. The children dissolve salt in water and find they are able to float a food-coloring solution on top of the salt water. The salt water is denser and so supports the food coloring. By working with four colored solutions of different densities, pupils find that they can make a four-layer liquid "sandwich." Naturally, each layer above must be less dense than the layer below. If a mistake is made and this order is violated, a mixture occurs and the layering effect is spoiled.

Early "messing about" with colored solutions in this unit provides pupils with enough experience for them to make some predictions about the layering behavior of the solutions. By Part IV, they are ready to experiment with ordering liquids in a soda straw so that layering occurs. Examine pages 579–583 to see how the needed activities are discussed in the teacher's guide.[3]

Microgardening (Grades 4–7). In contrast with the preceding unit, *Microgardening* is an extensive investigation into five related problems concerning the growth of molds. The total teaching time needed

---

[3] Elementary Science Study, *Colored Solutions Teacher's Guide.* Copyright 1968 by Education Development Center, Inc. Published by Webster Division, McGraw-Hill Book Company, pp. 26–30. Reprinted by permission.

might range from fourteen to nineteen weeks, assuming a one-hour lesson three days a week. The five problems for investigation, and related activities, are described on pages 584–585.[4]

The first part of the sequence (see pages 586–589) suggests ways to introduce pupils to molds. This arouses questions from them and plans to find out some possible answers. Observe the natural ways in which the control of variables comes up.[5]

Subject-matter scope of the many ESS units is extensive. This is necessary if school districts are to have sufficient freedom to develop the programs that seem best suited to local requirements. Examine now descriptions[6] of the units. These will be divided into three groups — physical science, life science, and general education (logic, science-related mathematics, esthetics, and other areas).

PHYSICAL SCIENCE UNITS

Spinning Tables (Trial Edition, Grades K–3). This unit introduces children to circular motion. Small groups work with hand-driven turntables on which they can draw or spin marbles, blocks, and containers of liquids and powders. A maximum of eight children can work with the equipment at any one time. No set length of time is required for the unit.

Light and Shadows (Grades K–3). A beginning unit on spatial relationships — technically, "geometric optics." Children use objects of many shapes and their own movements to examine shadows and light

---

[4] Elementary Science Study, *Microgardening Teacher's Guide.* Copyright 1968 by Education Development Center, Inc. Published by Webster Division, McGraw-Hill Company, pp. 4–5. Reprinted by permission.

[5] *Ibid.,* pp. 12–15. By permission.

[6] Descriptions are adapted from a 1968 ESS report to the International Clearinghouse on Science and Mathematics Curricular Developments, College Park, Md.; and information supplied by ESS to the author.

IV. Liquid Layers in Soda Straws

SUMMARY OF THE ACTIVITIES

By placing a transparent soda straw into the four different colored liquids in a certain order, children can make "sandwiches" of two, three, or four layers of liquids that will not mix readily. Utilizing the results of the experiments in Section III, children can predict which liquids can and cannot be layered in a soda straw. They can also arrange these liquids into an upness-downness scale.

MATERIALS

In addition to materials in the *6-Student Kit* and the four liquids used in Section III, the children will need:

transparent soda straws

CLASS ACTIVITIES

Liquid Layers (1-3 class periods) If children in your class have noticed that they were sometimes able to get colored layers in their eyedroppers, their observation can be used as a lead into this activity.

If no one has noticed the layering of liquids, you can introduce it by making a two-layered sandwich in a soda straw and asking the children how many different kinds of two-layered sandwiches they can make. Holding a piece of white paper behind your straw will enable the class to see the layers a little more clearly.

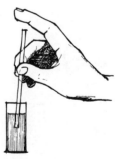

Dip the straw about a half inch into the blue liquid. The top of the straw is open.

Don't expect the children to answer your question immediately. They will need some time to learn how to manipulate the straws, as shown below.

Can you make a red on blue sandwich? How many two-layered sandwiches can you make? How many two-liquid combinations will *not* form layers?

Even if you perform the demonstration very slowly, some children will find it difficult to manipulate the straw in the manner needed to make liquid layers. Some of them will enjoy finding out how to use the straws for themselves. Some may try sucking the liquids into the straws, which is unadvisable. Some may try to put liquids into the straws with eyedroppers. This is a very time-consuming process which usually results in layers of the *blue-air-red* or *red-air-blue* type. Such air layers are interesting, but the pressure effects involved are difficult for children to understand.

A child's problem in obtaining layers of liquids in a straw can usually be traced to one or more of the following:

(1) failure to put his finger or thumb firmly over the opening at the top of the straw

(2) failure to release his finger or thumb when the straw is in the liquid

(3) lowering the straw all the way to the bottom of the first liquid, so that there is no room for the second liquid

(4) failure to lower the straw more deeply in the second liquid than in the first

(5) failure to lower the straw into the lighter liquid first (For example, he may put the straw into the red and *then* into the clear or into the green and then into the red, etc.)

(6) tendency to hold the straw horizontally rather than vertically

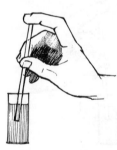  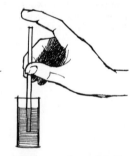 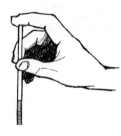

Place your finger firmly over the top of the straw, and remove the straw from the liquid. A half-inch layer of blue liquid will remain in the straw.

Keeping your finger on top, lower the straw about one inch into the red solution.

Release your finger. A half-inch layer of red solution will move into the straw, pushing the blue layer up to the level of the solution in the tube.

Again, put your finger over the top of the straw, and remove the straw from the red solution. You will have a blue on red sandwich.

Just as there are a number of problems in making liquid layers, there are ways of coping with the problems.

(1) You may ask the children who have mastered the technique to help those who haven't.

(2) You can work individually with the children who are experiencing difficulty, asking them questions such as these:

Will the liquid go up the straw if you keep your finger over the top of the straw?

How can you make the liquid stay in the straw when you take the straw out of the container?

How high does the liquid rise in the straw?

If you lower the straw all the way to the bottom of the first liquid, will there be any room for the second liquid?

(3) If there is widespread difficulty, you might direct leading questions to the whole class.

As the children learn to manipulate the straws and begin to get liquid layers, you may hear such comments as these:

You can make blue on green layers, but if you put green in first, it all mixes.

That's pretty!

You can't get green on top.

You can't get blue on the bottom.

Blue stays on red, but red goes down in blue, so that one won't work.

The last comment is very significant. The student was relating what he had learned in earlier experiments to his work with layers. He realized that because drops of red liquid go down in the blue solution, it would be impossible to layer red above blue in the straw.

In one trial class, a boy found that when he put a straw with the green solution into the clear solution, the green ran out before he even lifted his finger from the straw. He said, "The food coloring falls out of the green liquid when you put it in the clear liquid."

"How do you know it isn't the green falling down and the clear going up?" the teacher asked.

After some thought, the boy tried putting the straw containing green liquid into the red solution. The green again fell out, but this time he could see the red solution going up the straw to replace the green. He then asked if he could color the clear liquid. The teacher gave him some yellow food coloring. When he put a straw containing the green liquid into the yellow liquid (formerly clear), he saw the yellow liquid rise as the green fell out. He decided that the green *liquid*, not just the food coloring, fell out. He then realized that green drops go down in the clear solution and that he could expect the green liquid in a straw to behave in the same way. By encouraging this sort of inquiry as it arises, you will help the children to have richer, more rewarding, experiences.

As your students progress in making liquid layers, you might encourage them to record in their notebooks, on paper, or on the chalkboard, the kinds of two-layered sandwiches that they can and cannot make. It is important, of course, that children have time to become adept at making sandwiches that persist (those in which the layers don't mix), before they begin recording data.

Encourage the children to use the information they obtained in Section III to predict and explain why some sandwiches can be made and others can't.

Be sure they record the sandwiches they actually made, not just what they did. Some students will tend to record "green on blue," meaning that they put the straw in the green solution and then in the blue, but not that they actually made a green on blue sandwich.

You might like to prepare a Prediction Sheet similar to the one shown below. Such a sheet is not essential, but it may provide some direction for children who have not been able to organize the results of their experiments. If your children have had difficulty with such symbolism as $B \uparrow G$, $G \downarrow B$, or $\dfrac{B}{G}$, $\dfrac{C}{R}$, etc., you can use less abstract symbols, such as pictures of liquid layers in straws.

PREDICTION SHEET

Name_____

Which of the two-layered liquids below can be made so that the layers stay and do not mix? Make your predictions by drawing a *circle* around those you think can be made. Draw an X across those you think cannot be made.

$$\frac{B}{G} \quad \frac{B}{R} \quad \frac{B}{C} \quad \frac{C}{B} \quad \frac{C}{R} \quad \frac{C}{G} \quad \frac{R}{B} \quad \frac{R}{C} \quad \frac{G}{G} \quad \frac{G}{B} \quad \frac{G}{R}$$

After the children have had time to prepare their liquid layers and, if you use the Prediction Sheet above, to check their predictions, a class discussion of their results will probably reveal that they have successfully made the following two-layered sandwiches:

$$\frac{B}{G} \quad \frac{B}{C} \quad \frac{B}{R} \quad \frac{C}{G} \quad \frac{C}{R} \quad \frac{R}{G}$$

Colored chalk or crayons will enable the children to draw colored pictures of their results that may be more meaningful to some than the letters B, C, R, and G.

Some students may suggest such layerings as:

$$\frac{C}{B} \quad \frac{R}{B} \quad \frac{G}{B} \quad \frac{G}{C} \quad \frac{R}{C} \quad \frac{G}{R}$$

If other students disagree, ask the class to try to make those sandwiches.

Three- and Four-layered Sandwiches (1-2 class periods) By this time, some students will probably have discovered that they can make three-layered sandwiches, and you might use their results as a lead into this activity.

Some students will be able to *predict* which three-layered sandwiches are possible. You might encourage all the children to list or draw pictures of the three- and four-layered sandwiches that they think they can make. Colored pencils or crayons may be helpful. As you move about the room looking at their predictions, encourage those students who are having difficulty to apply what they have learned in previous experiments to this situation. What do they think would happen if they placed drops of the green solution on top of the blue solution, or drops of the red solution on the clear solution, etc.

Those children who grasp the problem quickly will want to get started checking their predictions. You might let them begin, or you might encourage them to talk with others who are having difficulty making predictions. Probably, a few will correctly predict all four possible three-layer sandwiches and the one four-layered sandwich. Others will predict only a few of those possible, while still others may predict some layers of liquids that they will find are impossible to make.

After the children have had time to check their predictions, you can have them draw their sandwiches on the chalkboard.

Questions such as, "Which is the most 'up' liquid? What's the most 'down' stuff? Which is a more 'up' liquid, clear or red?" may help children to see that they can establish an upness-downness order, such as the one shown below:

UP

Blue	B
Clear	C
Red	R
Green	G

DOWN

The idea of an upness-downness order may be too abstract for some youngsters to verbalize, but colored chalk will help. The four-layered sandwich is a good illustration of such an order.

If some children want to keep their liquid layers, they can do so by gently forcing one end of a straw into a soft clay base. How long will the layers remain distinct?

MICROGARDENING IN THE CLASSROOM

THE FIVE AREAS OF INVESTIGATION

I What Are Molds Like?
(Four activities, about 1–2 weeks)
With hand lenses, the children observe mold growing on bread and discuss what they see. The class starts a mold garden to determine what things will mold. Challenged to grow mold on a piece of bread and given the freedom to try whatever they think will work, children immediately become involved with basic questions. As their bread begins to mold, they try to sort out the reasons for this development. If microscopes are available, the students can examine the details of mold structure and make comparisons among different kinds of molds.

II What Influences the Growth of Molds?
(Four activities, about 4–5 weeks)
The children are encouraged to set up experiments to show the factors that influence the growth of molds. At first their experiments may be indeterminate and confusing, but through mistakes and successes they encounter the need to sort out and test variables, such as water, light, and temperature, one at a time. The children are given a chance to apply the knowledge thus gained by investigating how to prevent mold from growing on bread.

III Where Do Molds Come From?
(Five activities, about 4–5 weeks)
The children are introduced to a fundamental technique—sterile procedures. The children expose containers of sterile media to the air and discover a flourishing growth of mold a few days later. They then try to grow just one kind of mold by placing spores on sterile media. Further experiments confirm the fact that spores, although invisible, are nearly everywhere; but they are not to be found in healthy living tissue. These experiences help the children to grasp the significance of historic events, such as Pasteur's experiments on the presence of spores in the air, and to understand some of the principles of aseptic surgery and the germ theory of disease.

IV What Influences the Rate of Mold Growth?

(*Three activities, about 2–3 weeks*)

This area offers an opportunity for experimentation with more precision. Using growth tubes containing sterile potato agar inoculated with pure cultures of molds, the children compare rates of growth of various molds. They also investigate the effect of alternating daylight and darkness on the rate of spore production of certain molds. With the growth tube as a tool, children with special interest and motivation can go on unendingly devising experiments, as time and equipment allow.

Looking further into what molds can do, the children refer again to the mold garden and discuss the role of molds in breaking down materials.

V What Can Molds Do?

(*Three activities, about 3–4 weeks*)

The children grow pure cultures of a species of *Penicillium* which produces penicillin and then seed the cultures with harmless bacteria. The results of this experiment lead to a discussion of antibiotics in general and of Fleming's discovery of penicillin.

After observing some seedlings that have begun to mold, the children develop the idea of isolating the mold, growing it, and then inoculating healthy seedlings. Having thus followed the historic steps of establishing that a microorganism such as a mold can be the cause of disease, they discuss the story of Robert Koch, who first worked out this procedure.

I

GETTING ACQUAINTED WITH MOLDS

1

Note: The length of time required for this bread to mold will indicate, somewhat, how mold reacts in your location.

Propionated bread has also worked successfully for classes unable to find unpropionated bread.

1 GETTING ACQUAINTED WITH MOLDS

The children discuss what they know about molds.

They look at moldy bread, then put it out of sight, and describe how the mold looked.

The children look at the mold more closely with a hand lens.

Each child is challenged to grow mold on a piece of bread.

About one week later, the children discuss their attempts to get mold to grow.

They plan experiments to find out what influences the growth of molds.

Their plans lead directly into the activities of Area II.

MATERIALS

For each child

hand lens

moldy piece of bread in plastic box

folder or loose-leaf notebook

piece of unmolded bread in plastic box

Advance preparations needed
7–10 days before starting this activity

To grow mold on bread, you will need white bread that does not contain sodium propionate (PROH-pee-on-ayt) or calcium propionate to retard spoilage. If either of these chemicals has been added to commercial bread, it will be mentioned on the label. Small bakeries usually do not use these chemicals and therefore are a good source of bread for the purposes of this unit.

Place a piece of bread in a plastic box for each child. Add water until the bread is moist but not soggy. Keep the boxes closed at room temperature. Mold should appear in 7–10 days.

I

GETTING ACQUAINTED WITH MOLDS

1

TYPICAL CLASS DISCUSSIONS

At the start of the first activity in our trial classes, the children were asked where they had seen molds before.

On oranges.

On hot dog rolls.

At the beach last summer.

The teacher then passed out the plastic boxes, each containing a piece of bread with a vigorous growth of mold. He suggested that the children look closely and carefully.

He also reminded them to keep the lids on the boxes so that mold dust would not be scattered in the air.

After the children had examined the moldy bread and made a few comments, the teacher told them to put the boxes out of sight. Then he asked:

What did the moldy bread look like? What did you see?

I saw something that was black with kind of yellow spots.

Mine has two shades of green.

I think what I saw was dusty.

Mine smelled.

There were drops of water on the inside of the box.

There are little black spots.

The teacher let the various observations of the children emerge, and then asked a child whether he thought the black spots were part of the bread or part of the mold. A discussion developed as the children disagreed among themselves.

The teacher suggested that they take a second look at the moldy bread.

Does anyone see something he didn't notice before?

Many more children began to respond. Some commented on the black dots, or the color, or some of the things others had already reported.

Meanwhile, the teacher was putting hand lenses on the desks. As the children eagerly began

to use them, he moved about the room talking with the students individually, encouraging them to make sketches of what they saw.

After about ten minutes, the teacher showed the class a loaf of fresh bread and some plastic boxes.

Here's a challenge for you, he said. *There is no mold on the bread now, and there is enough bread for each of you to have a piece. Which of you will be able to get the bread to mold?*

There were many questions and comments.

But I don't know how.

Can we do anything we want to?

Do anything you want to, the teacher said. *Start your bread molding today, tonight. Let's see who gets the most mold.*

About a week later, the results of the experiment were discussed.

How many have mold on their piece of bread? the teacher asked.

I

GETTING ACQUAINTED WITH MOLDS

1

Many hands were waved enthusiastically.

I put mine in a dark and wet place, and then put it under the radiator.

I put mine in the closet where it did not mold.

The teacher made two columns on the board, and labelled one "Moldy," and the other "Not Moldy." In these columns he listed the children's descriptions of conditions under which the bread either had or had not molded.

Of course, there were no clear and obvious patterns that could be drawn. "Wet" and "dark" appeared in both columns. The teacher did not attempt to force any conclusions, but began to capitalize on the uncertainties, dissatisfactions, and questions that the children raised.

One boy had looked molds up in the encyclopedia and read that molds need air. Someone disagreed.

No, that is not right. I looked it up in the encyclopedia and it said "no air."

At this point, three or four other students entered the discussion on whether air is necessary or not.

Someone else said that he grew mold without water. The children then became involved in an animated debate on whether they thought molds need water or not.

You need water or the bread gets stale and hard. There's moisture in the air. If it has no air, it has to have water.

The teacher listened patiently. The class disagreed, soon became repetitious, and was getting nowhere. The teacher then helped to focus on a question:

What can we do to find out if molds actually do need water?

The children began suggesting some things they might do.

I would take a stale piece of bread, put it in air with a few drops of water, and keep it in a dark, warm place.

That sounds like a good idea, responded the teacher, *but if we try this and mold grows, what will we have found out?*

We will have found out that mold needs water.

There was discussion and disagreement. One child then suggested, *We could put one piece of bread with water on it in one box and another piece of bread without water on it in another box.*

The teacher nodded encouragingly, but not many children seemed to grasp the significance of the "control" included in this last suggestion.

Then the teacher suggested that each child write in his notebook a plan for finding out if molds do need water.

If someone likes his plan so well he wants to start right away at home, he can, the teacher added, *but make some plans and write them down.*

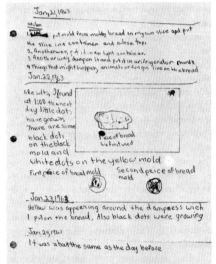

Behold the Mold

She forgot it in the bread box

And the bread grew old

It was dark in the bread box

And not to cold

It stayed for days in the bread box

As I was told

And when I opened the bread box

"Behold the Mold"

Grade 5 and 6
Talmadge School

COMMENT ON THE CLASS DISCUSSION

Some teachers reading about this class or teaching this activity for the first time have felt that the class was confusing, that the children never did get a clear-cut answer from the teacher on any point or get a directive as to what they should do or find out.

Other teachers have stated that their students brought up other factors that might affect mold growth, and they were unable to lead the class to focus on whether molds need water. The children wanted to investigate air, light, the food, as well as water. These teachers did not know whether to let them do this all at once or to direct them toward looking first at one factor.

Such probing queries bear thinking about. To what extent can a teacher let the children seek on their own, make mistakes, and gradually come to a refinement of technique?

The teacher in the reported class was trying to let the children think for themselves and to start their own lines of inquiry. There are many ways to do this. His way was to lead them to work as a class on a single factor. Another teacher might have been equally effective by dividing the class into groups and letting each group work on a different question.

But whatever method you choose, the value to the child will be greater if he is led to see that he can learn some verifiable truths through his own senses and activities.

If the students, like those in the reported class, have never had an opportunity to try to answer their own questions by experiment, of course there will be some confusion when they realize that the expected direction may not be forthcoming, that what is done is up to them. Once launched on this course, however, their enthusiasm and ideas are unlimited. Remember, as you teach, it took man most of the time he has been on earth to develop experimental approaches. It is only fair to allow the children a bit of time to work these out for themselves.

sources on the playground and in the classroom. Printed matter: teacher's guide.

Mirror Cards (Grades 1–7). This unit could extend the work begun in *Light and Shadows,* if desired. It uses mirrors and cards with carefully designed patterns on them to help children learn something about the geometry of image reflections and concepts of symmetry. (Figure 42.) Equipment: cards, mirrors. Printed matter: teacher's guide.

Drops, Streams and Containers (Trial Edition, Grades K–4). A guide to play and investigation with liquids. Children examine flow, drop formation, and other properties of water, soapy water, oil, and other available liquids, using a variety of containers, surfaces, drops, and tubes. Equipment: plastic bottles with holes, caps with holes, eye droppers, medicine caps, tubing, paper towels and wax paper. Printed matter: teacher's guide.

Balance Book (Including Mobiles) (Grades 1–3). This unit provides some special equipment with which the child can investigate balance and weight explicitly. By working with an assortment of balances— seesaws, pan balances, equal-arm and un-equal-arm balances—the child can develop increasingly sophisticated notions of balance and weight. Equipment: walk-on boards, 4-foot boards, pan balances, things to weigh. Printed matter: teacher's guide (The Balance Book), booklet (Mobiles).

Where Is the Moon? (Grades 2–6). An introduction to observational astronomy. During a period of three months the children are given approximately forty notes called "Reminders." Each note describes an event that the children can see in the sky. The children's observations of the moon, sun, a bright planet, and a few easy-to-find stars are the basis of the study. Printed matter: teacher's guide, booklet (Moon Book), reminders.

Mystery Powders (Grades 3–4). This unit deals with the properties of various substances and the use of indicators in detecting their presence. Students try to identify some unknown white powders by tasting, smelling, feeling, and comparing them with known substances. Additional investigations with heat, iodine, and vinegar identify specific reactions with several of the powders. To conclude, the children attempt to determine the presence of individual powders when two or more are mixed together. Equipment: sugar, salt, baking soda, starch, plaster of Paris, vinegar, iodine, heat source, containers. Printed matter: teacher's guide.

Clay Boats (Trial Edition, Grades 3–5). An attempt is made to acquaint children with some of the problems associated with buoyancy, density, and volume displacement in liquid. Children are given lumps of clay and asked to see if they can make them sink or float. Eventually children form the clay into boat-like shapes, load them, sometimes sink them, and discover some properties associated with various shapes, sizes, thicknesses and weights. Equipment: clay, containers, loading materials. Printed matter: teacher's guide.

Figure 42 Reproducing a two-figure pattern with a mirror and one figure. (Courtesy Education Development Center, Newton, Mass.)

Rocks and Charts (Grades 3–5). Each pair of children receives a set of twenty-one rocks. The children establish ways of comparing these rocks and set their own standards to define certain properties such as hard and soft, and heavy and light. They make charts telling the rocks' characteristics, and then exchange charts to see if they can understand each other's. Equipment: rocks, balances, streak plates, hand lenses and others. Printed matter: teacher's guide.

Whistles and Strings (Trial Edition, Grades 3–6). Children explore basic musical sounds. Starting with pieces of plastic tubes, children investigate different ways of making sounds from a column of air, and go on to produce complicated musical instruments and devices of their own design. With strings, fishline, and pieces of wood, children work out their own stringed instruments, and investigate the ways in which sounds made by strings can be altered in pitch, or made more resonant.

Sink and Float (Trial Edition, Grades 4–6). The materials in this introduction to density of solids and liquids consist of things that sink and things that float in tap water and salt water. Among the things that sink in tap water are some that float in salt water. By working with materials and liquids of different densities and by varying densities, e.g., by adding Plasticine to a solid object or salt to water, it becomes apparent that whether or not an object will or will not float depends jointly upon its density and the density of the liquid into which it has been placed. Construction and use of hydrometers is one possible extension. Equipment: containers, Plasticine, materials of different densities, salt. Printed matter: teacher's guide.

Pendulums (Trial Edition, Grades 4–6). This unit uses a frame that supports two pendulums. Working in pairs, children compare the effects of length of string, weight of bob, and amplitude. They find out how long to make the strings in order to double, triple, or quadruple the pendulum's period. They study factors that make pendulums die down faster and they also add couplings between the two strings. Equipment: frame, string, bobs. Printed matter: teacher's guide. Film: five 8 mm loops, color: *Sand Pendulum I: Drawing Circles, Lines and Ellipses; Sand Pendulum II: Drawing on a Turntable; Sand Pendulum III: Drawing Lines on a Traveling Table; Sand Pendulum IV: Slowing Down; Sand Pendulum V: Pouring Sand into Soda Straws.*

Ice Cubes (Grades 4–6). This unit deals with variations of the general question, "What makes an ice cube melt faster or slower?" Children determine how long it takes an ice cube to melt in the air and in different amounts of water. They see who can keep an ice cube the longest; they explore the melting rates of "funny-shaped" ice cubes and begin to develop intuitive ideas about surface-volume relations. They collect data and learn a good deal about plotting tables and graphs. Equipment: thermometers, ice, containers. Printed matter: teacher's guide.

Colored Solutions (Grades 4–6). By using various concentrations of salt solutions identified by color, this unit attempts to introduce children to some phenomena which will lead them to perform experiments associated with the ideas of density and the layering of liquids. The results of their experiments form a foundation of facts from which they may make predictions and draw conclusions as they tackle new activities. Equipment: plastic trays and cylinders, salt solutions, eye droppers, and food coloring. Printed matter: teacher's guide.

Balancing (Senior) (Trial Edition, Grades 4–7). Children hang washers on strips of pegboard suspended from a nail. They learn how to identify problems involving balance and to make use of various strategies to solve the problems. An intuitive understanding of the principles of balance and center of mass underlie the study. Equipment: pegboard, nails, washers, and others. Printed matter: teacher's guide, cards.

Balloons (Trial Edition, Grades 4–7). Children prepare gases which are captured in plastic bags, balloons, and weather balloons. The gases are weighed and tested by various chemical means so that children become aware of the relative densities and methods of identifying the gases. By weighing air, "lung" air, carbon dioxide, and hydrogen in different atmospheres, the buoyant effect comes into play. By weighing balloons filled with different liquids in "atmospheres" of various liquids, children become capable of predicting the relative densities of the liquids. They then test their predictions. Equipment: balances, balloons, plastic bags and containers, flasks, and various chemicals. Printed matter: teacher's guide, worksheets, experiment sheets.

Batteries and Bulbs (Grades 4–8). This provides an introduction to the study of electricity and magnetism. The children investigate such things as ways to light several bulbs with one battery, what happens when more than one battery is used, whether varying lengths and types of wire influence the brightness of bulbs, and the effects different patterns of wires, bulbs, and batteries have on the brightness of bulbs. Equipment: flashlight batteries, small bulbs, various kinds of wire, compasses, magnets. Printed matter: teacher's guide.

Slips and Slides (Trial Edition, Grades 5–6). Children establish "slipperiness" orders by determining the force needed to move blocks with different surfaces along several types of horizontal planes. Additional problems include the effects of weight and surface area on frictional forces; the effect of an inclined plane on the forces

needed to move bodies; the use of wheels in reducing friction, and the need for experimental controls. Children are asked to predict on the basis of the test data they have acquired. Reading involving some classical experiments in friction, as well as some theories of friction, are provided along with experiments which can be performed at home.

Kitchen Physics (Grades 5–7). This is a first course in science drawn from the child's environment. The student investigates the properties of common liquids—typically water, soapy water, oil, alcohol, and syrup. He considers a number of questions about the behavior of these liquids which directs his attention to such attributes as the way they are absorbed, evaporate, drop, stream, and interact with various surfaces. (Figure 43.) Equipment: drip tubes of varying diameters, liquids, balances, droppers, container. Printed matter: teacher's guide, worksheets. Film: three 8 mm film loops, color: *Beading of a Water Column, Water Rise in Blotter Strips of Graded Width, Water Rise in Blotter Strips Exposed and Enclosed.*

Gases and "Airs" (Grades 5–8). This is an introductory unit examining some properties of gases in a series of closely linked laboratory experiments in which children analyze the interaction of air with "things" in the environment. Equipment: tubes, candles, steel wool, seeds. Printed matter: teacher's guide, worksheets. Film: one 16 mm, black and white, sound: *Gases and "Airs" in the Classroom* (for teachers), four 8 mm loops, color: *Candle Burning Techniques, Candle Burning I, Candle Burning II, The Mouse and the Candle.*

Optics (Trial Edition, Grades 5–8). This is aimed at acquainting children with the ideas of reflection, refraction, color, and variations of optical path using many different materials. Experiments with narrow and broad light beams, multiple reflections,

**Figure 43 Observing the beading distance of a water column. (Courtesy Education
Development Center, Newton, Mass.)**

colored shadows, and refraction through
water lenses are devised and examined.
Equipment: light source, mirrors, containers. color filters. Printed matter:
teacher's guide.

LIFE SCIENCE UNITS

Growing Seeds (Grades K–3). In this unit
children plant a collection of seeds and
nonseeds to see which ones grow. They
dig up some of the seeds to find out what
happens underground. Then each student
plants a new corn seed and cuts a strip of
paper daily showing the height of his plant.
(Figure 44.) Children find that the collection of strips can tell much about the way

their plants grew. Equipment: seeds, soil,
containers. Printed matter: teacher's guide.
Film: two 8 mm loops, color: *Bean Sprouts,
Plant Growth-Graphing*.

Beans and Peas (Trial Edition, Grades
K–4). This is a booklet to enable teachers
to grow beans and peas in their classrooms.
Bean seeds of many different varieties obtained from the local grocer's shelf will
grow into adult plants in about six weeks.
Any classroom in practically any weather
can boast of flowering bean plants which
bear pods with seeds. The booklet is primarily designed to insure the class a supply
of healthy plants. It also contains teaching
suggestions for children's observations and
individual projects. Photographs of the

Figure 44 (Courtesy Education Development Center, Newton, Mass.)

plant at various stages of its development and accounts of the laboratory experience give the teacher an idea of what to expect and when.

Starting from Seeds (Trial Edition, Grades 1–7). This unit deals with the responses of oat seedlings to light and gravity. Children do experiments to establish changes in direction of growth of stem and roots and the rate at which they occur under controlled conditions. Equipment: oat seedlings, containers, vermiculite, slides, cellophane tape. Printed matter: teacher's guide.

Eggs and Tadpoles (Grades K–8). The natural development from fertilized egg to adult frog is examined under classroom conditions. The care and fostering of the animals and the total development of the frog require only a few minutes observation and handling each day, plus an occasional period for discussion and summary. Equipment: fertilized frog eggs, aquaria, pond water. Printed matter: teacher's guide. Film: two 16 mm, color, silent: *Frog Development: Fertilization to Hatching; Frog Development: Hatching through Metamorphosis;* 8 mm loops, color: *Frog Egg I: First Cell Division to Early Neural Fold; Frog Egg II: Development of the Body Regions; Frog Egg III: Continued Development to Hatching; Frogs: Pairing and Egg Laying; Artificial Fertilization of Frog Eggs; Frogs: Pituitary Preparation; Tadpoles I: Tadpoles II.*

Changes (Grades 1–4). Children predict what things will change when left by themselves. They make up lists of things that they think will or will not change and then proceed to bring these into class to verify their predictions. During the course of several weeks food becomes garbage, wet metals rust, liquids become cloudy, maggots may appear, and rocks remain rocks. From the nature and timing of these processes the children develop their own sense of biological and physical changes. Equipment: plastic boxes, baby food jars, foods, liquids, metals, crystals, powders, seeds, and other materials. Printed matter: teacher's guide.

Brine Shrimp (Trial Edition, Grades 1–7). Brine shrimp are tiny, salt lake arthropods, whose eggs remain viable when dried. Younger children observe the eggs and the minute larvae when they hatch, then watch them grow into adults. Older children can, in addition, explore a number of questions: Do brine shrimp eggs hatch faster in salt water than in fresh? How do the reactions of brine shrimp toward light change as they grow older? What is their rate of swimming? Because it is so easy to raise hundreds of these animals, statistical answers to many behavioral questions can be found. Equipment: brine shrimp eggs, salt water, containers. Printed matter: teacher's guide. Film: one 16 mm, color, silent: *Brine Shrimp;* two 8 mm loops, color: *Brine Shrimp I, Brine Shrimp II.*

Activity Wheels (Grades 2–5). These are exercise wheels for small animals, to which are attached counters to measure the number of turns the wheel makes. Using an activity wheel, it is possible to gather data on the activity of animals under varying conditions. Some of the factors that can be tested are the effect on activity of: hunger, age, size of cage, noise, night and day, number of animals, and type of animal. Equipment: activity wheel with counter, cage, animals. Printed matter: teacher's guide.

Crayfish (Trial Edition, Grades 3–6). This unit uses the common, readily available crayfish as a typical representative of the fresh water environment. It yields to the students an understanding of the feeding habits, reactions, and relations to the environment of these animals. They are readily managed, maintained, and observed in the classroom. Equipment: crayfish, containers. Printed matter: teacher's guide.

Pond Water (Trial Edition, Grades 3–8). This unit uses as basic material the teeming plant and animal life of fresh water ponds. It gets the students to participate in following the development of representative plants and animals. It brings out the interdependence of organisms concerned and familiarizes the children with representative forms, from microscopic plants and animals to the more familiar larger forms. Equipment: pond water, containers, microscopes. Printed matter: teacher's guide, study cards.

Budding Twigs (Trial Edition, Grades 4–6). In this unit, children observe the first budding of a large collection of twigs. Water supply, light, temperature, length of twig, position of bud, and other such possible growth factors are considered. Equipment: twigs, containers. Printed matter: teacher's guide, children's book (*Buds and Twigs*),

Behavior of Mealworms (Grades 4–6). This unit stimulates children to ask questions about the observable behavior of an unfamiliar animal and then directs them to ways of finding answers for themselves. Equipment: mealworms, food, containers. Printed matter: teacher's guide, two student booklets (*How Barn Owls Hunt* and *How A Moth Escapes from its Cocoon*), set of pictures. Film: one 16 mm, black and white, sound: *How to Make a Mealworm Back Up* (for teachers).

Bones (Grades 4–6). The students become familiar with a variety of bones, notice similarities and differences, and assemble skeletons. Equipment: unassembled skeletons, assorted bones. Printed matter: teacher's guide, two student booklets (*Bones Picture Book, How to Make a Chicken Skeleton*). Film: five 8 mm loops, black and white: *X-ray Motion Pictures Head and Neck, X-ray Motion Pictures Shoulder, X-ray Motion Pictures Knee and Elbow, X-ray Motion Pictures Hand, X-ray Motion Pictures Foot.*

Microgardening (Grades 4–7). Children gain familiarity with the rapid growth and the remarkable diversity of molds. They become familiar with and readily develop pure culture procedures adequate for carrying out experiments that lead to understanding the reasoning of the great pioneers in medicine, agriculture, microbiology, and food technology. They gain appreciation of the importance of molds and other microorganisms in the great cycles of growth and decay. Equipment: containers, nutrient media. Printed matter: teacher's guide, booklet (*Illustrated Handbook of Some Common Molds*).

Earthworms (Trial Edition, Grades 4–7). This is one of a group of activities which offer children the opportunity to uncover various relationships between an organism and the environment. They perform experiments which evaluate the organism's response to a choice of environmental factors. In this unit children learn something of the behavior and biology of earthworms on a statistical basis by placing them in inexpensive plastic "choice" tubes. Various living conditions are established at either end of the tubes, e.g., dry sand versus damp humus, light versus dark. The children insert earthworms into the tubes at midpoint and note preferences when the worms are given choices of conditions.

Small Things (Grades 5–7). This unit introduces the child to the microscopic world, the instruments needed to make it accessible, and the differences in appearance and structure of nonliving and living things. Equipment: microscopes (Figure 45), slides, stains, plants, crystals, pond cultures. Printed matter: teacher's guide, student booklet (*The Faithful Eye of Robert Hooke*), worksheets, set of pictures. Film: one 16 mm, color, sound: *Paramecium, Euglena,* and *Amoeba* (for children); one 16 mm, black and white, sound: *A Small Things Classroom* (for teachers); eleven 8 mm loops, color: *Paramecium, Euglena, Amoeba, Budding of Yeast Cells, Blepharisma, Stentor, Rotifer, Vorticella, Volvox, Stylonychia, Comparative Sizes of Microscopic Animals.*

Euglena (Grades 6–8). Children are challenged to grow the micro-organism euglena, eventually by themselves, in sterile culture. It is an extension of *Small Things* for project-oriented students. The activities are organized around such questions as: How do they reproduce? How fast do they grow? Are they plants or animals? Do cultures always die out? Why? Equipment: small bottles, flasks, transfer loops, cotton, microscope slides, pipettes, euglena broth powder. Printed matter: teacher's guide. Film: one 8 mm loop, color: *Euglena Dividing.*

GENERAL EDUCATION UNITS

Playframes (Grades K–2). These are pieces of equipment which provide opportunities for both mechanical and dramatic play within the classroom. Equipment: playframes and accessories. Printed matter: teacher's guide.

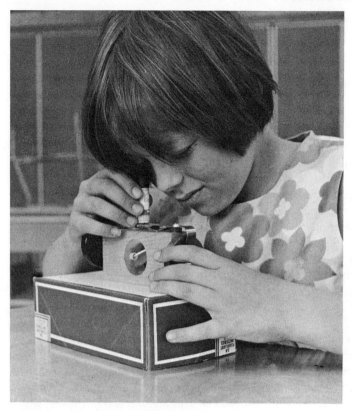

Figure 45 A specially designed, inexpensive microscope is available to every child in this unit. (Courtesy Education Development Center, Newton, Mass.)

Printing Press (Grades K–2). This is a movable-type press on which children compose, select, type, and print their work. The press can support work in all subject matter areas in addition to science. Lower grade children, particularly, are stimulated to learn to read and write and observe. Equipment: press, type, printing ink, type rack, ink rollers, and accessories. Printed matter: teacher's guide.

Pattern Blocks (Grades K–5). This unit consists of a set of blocks of wood in the shapes of regular polygons: triangles, squares, trapezoids, diamonds, hexagons, with each shape painted its own color. There are many patterns and designs which can be made with these blocks, and this gives great scope for children to build large triangles or diamonds or trapezoids out of the blocks. Arithmetical questions arise, such as the relation of the length of the side of the figure to the number of blocks needed. A group of elegant geometrical questions can be posed about repeating patterns and symmetries. Equipment: blocks. Printed matter: teacher's guide.

Geo Blocks (Trial Edition, Grades K–5). These blocks were designed to provide children with manipulative materials and experience related to such subjects as: geometric relations; classification; linear, area, volume measurement and equivalents; and others. A wide variety of shapes and sizes is provided to stimulate expressive building and imaginative visual-

597

ization of more detailed problems. Equipment: blocks. Printed matter: teacher's guide.

Attribute Games and Problems (Grades K–8). The subject matter of this unit is logic, but the emphasis is on developing problem-solving skills and attitudes. Children explore problems of classification and become skillful in dealing with the relationships between classes. These materials are designed for use from kindergarten through junior high school by small groups of children. Older children may work independently; the teacher introduces the games and problems to younger children. (Figure 46.) Equipment: three kinds of blocks, loops. Printed matter: teacher's guide, problem cards.

Tangrams (Grades K–8). This is an ancient Chinese geometrical puzzle. Seven pieces are formed from the dissection of a square: two small triangles, a medium triangle, two large triangles, a square and a rhomboid. A great many geometrical arrangements can be made from these seven pieces.

This unit is an adaptation which starts with various subsets of the full seven piece set and supplies "analysis" cards which will help children become familiar with certain basic combinations. There is a wide range of difficulty in the hundred or so cards which are provided along with the geometrical shapes. Equipment: tangram pieces. Printed matter: teacher's guide, card sets.

Sand (Trial Edition, Grades 2–5). This unit uses graded, colored sand which, appealing aesthetically, invites a wide variety of explorations of a scientific nature. Sand can be thought of as analogous to water, and poured, measured, and dripped. Sand can also be sorted, piled, looked at through a hand lens, rolled down various surfaces, strained, crushed, and weighed. Children make sand clocks, sandpaper, sand sculpture, and sand pendulums. Sand is seen as an inviting material for primary classrooms. Children can explore it, write about it, use it as an art medium, and in various ways interrelate it to many aspects of their school day.

Figure 46 A problem in classification: In which loop should a certain block go? (Courtesy Education Development Center, Newton, Mass.)

Structures (Trial Edition, Grades 3–7). In this unit children are allowed to work leisurely with materials. As the children build with materials (newspaper, clay, sticks, Scotch tape, and others) they begin to see the relationship between material, function, and form. By slowly working with a set of various materials, a wide range of experience is provided. Equipment: clay, straws, string, Plasticine, paper, tape, and other. Printed matter: teacher's guide.

Peas and Particles (Grades 4–6). This consists of a series of classroom activities in counting and estimating. Starting with low numbers and progressing towards "millions and billions," the children estimate beans on a paper, rice grains in jars, and more. They develop and criticize their own indirect counting methods. Equipment: rice, beans, balls, containers. Printed matter: teacher's guide, charts, set of pictures.

Outdoor Mapping (Trial Edition, Grades 5–6). Children examine ways to change and transmit various types of information (particularly two-dimensional representations of three-dimensional objects). Useful mapping concepts emerge: pattern recognition, scaling, congruence, ordering, discreteness, similarity, barriers, boundary conditions, and distortions. Vehicles for learning include: student-gathered information about their "world," maps, air photos, stereoscopic still pictures, sand-stream tables, and numerous other tools.

PROCESS SKILLS

The preceding descriptions reveal a wide array of process learnings as well as concepts, without the dominance of any single subject matter field. ESS believes that a broad sampling of science experiences should come before the study of any specific science discipline. So it mixes its subject matter and stresses the "common denominators" (processes) of science: inquiry, evidence, instrumentation, measurement, classification, and deduction. Since the units develop around topics in which the common processes of science stand out, the choice of subject matter is relatively unimportant. ESS feels that any subject is acceptable for a unit, if some important processes and concepts can be brought out, and if it can be related to a child's environment.[7]

The ESS position on process is like that of SCIS—skills and concept learning go together. Processes are not separately identified with units, nor are they stated as objectives for individual lessons. About the closest ESS comes to stating process objectives for lessons is in the summary descriptions of activities, found in several units. For example, see this statement about work with the surface tension of liquids in *Kitchen Physics:*[8]

The children perform several experiments involving absorption and evaporation of different liquids in different materials to reveal still another aspect of *grabbiness*—cohesive and adhesive forces at work. In the process, they become aware of the need to design experiments with only one variable. . . .

Of course, descriptions of lesson activities rather than detailed objectives are entirely consistent with the ESS approach. How can one state specific objectives when lessons are designed to encourage open-ended and divergent thinking in children of different ages?

It is easy to identify and select units on the basis of process as well as product learnings. For beginning graphing, there is *Growing Seeds*. Classification at all levels is found in *Attribute Games and Problems*. *Behavior of Mealworms* stresses observation and controlling variables. Predic-

[7] Elementary Science Study, *Introduction to the Elementary Science Study,* Boston: Houghton Mifflin Company, 1965, page 11.

[8] Elementary Science Study, *Teacher's Guide for Kitchen Physics,* Experimental Edition, Boston: Houghton Mifflin Company, 1965, page 49.

tions based on previous data are made in *Changes,* and so on. Either the skills listed in this book or some of those in the two other projects described can be taught with these units. The unique feature of ESS is the way processes are handled. There is a definite attempt in most lessons to prompt the imaginative, creative, "left-handed" way.

LEARNING MORE ABOUT ESS

Like the two preceding projects, ESS is paying increasing attention to problems of teacher education, both pre- and in-service. Also, more work is being done on evaluation. Understandably, ESS has found present evaluation measures fall short in measuring some of the creative learnings in children that it values; especially the long-range effects. However, the units as such have had extensive field trials, and have been revised from feedback gathered in a variety of schools—urban, suburban, and rural. A large supply of these units is now available.

The commercial developer and distributor of ESS units is the Webster Division, McGraw-Hill Book Company, Manchester Road, Manchester, Missouri 63011. A list of current materials purchasable may be requested at that address. Materials for most of the available units appear in kit form; some units require only locally obtainable items and no kits are manufactured. Kits appear in two sizes: the classroom size contains supplies and equipment

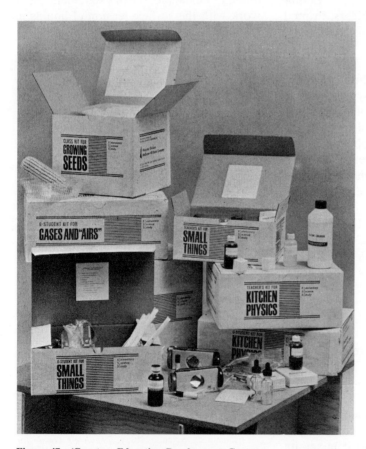

Figure 47 **(Courtesy Education Development Center, Newton, Mass.)**

for thirty children; a smaller kit provides materials for six children. A few units have a teacher kit for dispensing additional supplies. (Figure 47.) As mentioned, each unit includes a teacher guide and, when appropriate, pupils worksheets, booklets, and film loops or films.

ESS has a book with further details of the program: *A Working Guide to the Elementary Science Study.* It is available from ESS, 55 Chapel Street, Newton, Massachusetts 02160. The book contains an introduction to the project and descriptions of all the units, booklets, films, and filmstrips which ESS has produced. There is also a chart of the units by subject matter, another by grade level, and a chart of the units dealing with materials and cost. The book includes descriptions of the ways ESS has been implemented in various school districts throughout the country.

If you can, also read an essay written by a former director of ESS. He has managed to describe the elusive spirit that touches all ESS activities; a quality that must be understood before one can appreciate what this project has tried to do. Read: "Messing About in Science," by David Hawkins, in *Science and Children,* Volume 2, Number 5, February 1965.

Science in Elementary Education: Analysis and Summary

CHAPTER TEN

Science in Elementary Education: Analysis and Summary

MORE AND MORE, TEACHERS ARE ASKING FOR AND RECEIVING A greater share of decision-making responsibility in matters that affect their teaching. But with the responsibility comes the need to be informed, as well as to understand the issues and the possible consequences of decisions made. Because of this, we shall take up some factors to consider when looking over the merits of different curricula. First, we shall analyze ways to evaluate the three project programs, then inspect a growing trend in the teaching of science, and finish with a discussion about your role in the curriculum selection and teaching process.

WHICH PROGRAM IS BEST?

The simple question, "Which program is best?", becomes more complicated upon examination. Since each is organized on a different basis, no direct comparison is possible. Is a process-based program better than a concept-based one? Is "messing around" with phenomena likely to be better than either? This begs the question, better for what? A sounder way to valid appraisal is to

Credit for chapter opening photograph. **Rebecca Snyder-Monkmeyer**

604

ask two related, but different, questions: How well have the projects accomplished their immediate objectives? and, How well do they meet the criteria of individual school districts?

Answering the first question is easy. Judging from reports of trial schools, and examining the curriculum materials, the projects have accomplished their objectives very well. No doubt some of the enthusiasm and appeal of the programs comes from the fact that it is more fun for children to manipulate objects than it is to decode abstract symbols in books. But the massive effort to produce interesting, teachable, and learnable lessons has clearly been successful in each case; relatively far more so than teachers have come to expect from efforts with textbook programs. While no other project's field testing compares with the enormous evaluative efforts of the AAAS program,[1] all have tested their materials in a variety of schools and places. It is safe to say that no previous science curricula have undergone such rigorous classroom trials.

What is less known are the considerations that should be weighed before school districts attempt to fit these programs into their specific situations. *Here, critical comparisons are possible* and should be made. When there is a good match between a program and a district's needs or capacities, things should go well. Some of the questions that local people need answers to are these:

Which program is most compatible with district objectives?

Which can be most smoothly installed? How long will it take?

Which requires the most in-service education?

How will pupil and teacher turnover affect performance?

What about cost? Time needed? Effects on the rest of the school program?

[1] See AAAS Commission on Science Education, *An Evaluation Model & Its Application*, Second Report, Washington, D.C.: The Association, 1968.

Which program best fits individual differences of learners and teachers?

How well do graduates of the program perform in junior and senior high school?

Local trials can answer most of these questions. In time, results can be shared among similar districts. So far, there is little reliable evidence because the programs are still too new.

Since the three programs reflect different points of view about how to teach elementary science, perhaps it is inevitable that some confusion and controversy would develop over the ways in which they have been organized. Take the idea of behavioral objectives, for instance. When stated very specifically, they permit you to observe the effects of instruction or diagnose the "readiness" of a child or class for a lesson. This takes much of the guesswork out of teaching. But for specific behavioral objectives to be reliably attainable, they must be tied to a tightly controlled lesson structure. If you adopt one, you must adopt the other, including a detailed sequence of activities.

Occasionally, someone talks or writes about "improving" a flexibly structured program (ESS, for example) by developing behavioral objectives for it. This misses the point. A loosely knit, open-ended unit cannot validly have behavioral objectives because there is no way to be reasonably sure in advance what will be specifically accomplished by each child. Its very reason for being may be to promote the divergent talents of individuals. (There may be a valid compromise position, however: the "pervasive" kind of behavioral objectives suggested in Chapter 4.)

Here is a related issue: Is a tightly organized structure better than a loosely organized one? Almost everyone is automatically for flexibility, in the way that everyone is for health, happiness, and Friday afternoons. Not well understood is that, as curriculum structure is made increasingly flexible and "creative," a corresponding demand is made upon the resources, security, and imagination of the teacher. While this is fine for those who can handle it, disappointing variations in teaching performance may happen with others.

Another issue is the place of content in a process program, specifically in *Science — A Process Approach*. As you saw in the content analysis of this program, a considerable number of important concepts is taken up. But the subject-matter content may vary from day to day as the exercises change; there is little follow-through on the content learning that may take place. Critics say that content and process should be developed together, or else either is learned unrealistically and imperfectly. The project position, you may recall, seems to be that formal study of subject-matter structure might well begin at the junior high school level; then, equipped with a broad array of process abilities, the child should master content swiftly and with genuine understanding.

Fortunately, the issue is at least partly answerable by research. Before long, it will be possible to observe in students who have gone on to junior high school and beyond the merits of arguments on both sides. In the meantime, going from one subject to another as the exercises change does not seem to bother the children, although it does appear to annoy a few teachers.

Other Experimentally-developed Programs. The fact is plain that science specialists agree on the need for intellectual activity and the exploration of basic ideas with real materials; but they disagree on how to organize curricula. This reveals that some differences do exist in specific objectives, and that there is still much unknown about how best to instruct children. Additional projects are under way that use other criteria than those of the three projects described. Their programs have not been detailed because they are not as far along as those we have examined.

The Minnesota Mathematics and Science Teaching project (MINNEMAST) is designing a completely coordinated science and mathematics curriculum for grades K–6. The Conceptually Oriented Program in Elementary Science (COPES), another K–6 project, is centered on the major conceptual schemes of science: conservation of matter-energy, gene theory of heredity, and so on. An interesting K–12 design for science is being produced by the Educational Research Council of America. This is a nonprofit research organization, supported by grants and affiliated school districts, whose headquarters are in Cleveland, Ohio. A list of these and other programs, including addresses, may be found on page 610R.

THE RISE OF SYSTEMS APPROACHES

The government-supported projects represent a great step forward in science curriculum construction. They are providing solid evidence of what children can do and a variety of fresh approaches to instruction. Perhaps their biggest contribution has been to greatly accelerate the changing role of the learner — from a passive receiver of information to an active investigator who can generate and reason-through his own data.

This trend is forcing changes in the materials provided the learner. Direct experiences require more manipulative materials and fewer printed materials, especially in the lower grades. As part of the trend we are seeing a shift toward integrated instructional systems using multimedia rather than texts alone. Also, firsthand work with inquiry methods requires more expertise than most elementary-school teachers have needed with older science curricula. Thus, much ingenuity is going into ways of making each system easy to work with and ways to give in-service, or even preservice, education related to the system.

Many elementary-science textbook series now feature a broad group of integrated materials: kits of equipment and supplies, tests, pupil workbooks, and audio-visual aids. Does the traditional text approach in elementary science have a declining function? It appears so, especially at the primary level. Future efforts to improve science instruction probably will continue to stress firsthand experiences and intellectual activity. But many educators are convincingly skeptical that firsthand investigations alone will give the children all they need to learn in the short time available for science.

A main reason anyone fails to acquire usable skills or generalizations is simply insufficient practice. Traditional texts were inadequate to provide such practice because they were not geared to firsthand experiences, and because they contained the polished, orderly conclusions of the authors' thinking.

Instead of this, the newer written materials are serving to reinforce and extend concepts through many applications; and to reinforce skills by letting children reason with *data* (written, numerical, pictorial, symbolic). The data require the same thinking children use when manipulating things firsthand. In other words, the newer written materials are providing such practice as extensions of activities that occur first with laboratory and real-life materials.

Why doesn't every school district adopt a multimedia system? Probably cost is the main reason. Commercial versions of the project programs we examined earlier are estimated to cost at least three times as much to install as a text series, and perhaps five or six times as much to maintain each year.[2] A systems package may be beyond the reach of many districts for some time, even with financial help from state and federal sources.

The awkward part about a systems cur-

riculum is that you must adopt all of it for best results. This is why it is the policy of some science projects not to permit their curricula to be adopted piecemeal by school districts. Some programs (ESS, for instance) do allow for smaller bite sizes. In effect, the local district has the option of selecting and organizing individual unit "subsystems" into an overall system. But the system's overall effectiveness will vary with the number of units selected and the ways in which they have been interrelated.

With a text-series package a district can also adopt a less-than-complete program—the basic textbooks, and then as many complementary materials as the budget allows. Here again, we cannot expect best results unless the entire package is adopted.

Teachers with only a text-series for a curriculum are not necessarily doomed to mediocre teaching. With proper methods, good results may be obtained with a soundly-organized series. More on this shortly.

YOUR ROLE— NOW AND THE FUTURE

In the past, most elementary teachers have either used a textbook or a local curriculum guide for teaching science. The text alone has been inadequate for the main reason that no single teaching tool can do the whole job. Most locally-developed curricula have been ineffective, also. With some heroic exceptions, these have been put together with "scissors-and-paste" procedures by science committees of tired teachers meeting a few afternoons a week after school. Everyone worked on the basis of intuition—if something seemed like a good idea, it was put in. In some cases, feedback and revisions occurred, but usually the follow-up was sketchy. Many districts have never had a science guide of any substance.

Even today it is common in districts for someone to ask a student teacher to make

[2] Commission on Science Education, *News Letter,* Washington, D.C.: American Association for the Advancement of Science, Vol. 4, No. 2, March 1968.

an original unit from A to Z, such as a "tidepool unit," or the like. Several frustrating weeks later, the student teacher has aimlessly gathered several pictures and filmstrips, an illustrated book on marine life, and a promise from several children that they will bring in their seashell collections. The "unit" begins.

Yet there has always been good teaching of science by some teachers. Their methods involve knowing how to make the best of all the components available to them — how to integrate these into their personal teaching systems. You can do the same thing. In a curricular jet age, there is no need to reinvent the wheel. When the curriculum is inadequate, use a GAB-BAG approach (Chapter 6). You will recall that it is a simplified way to change a text approach into an inductive teaching system.

Upon close examination, most schools have a number of teaching resources — films, filmstrips, trade books, people, study-trip sites, miscellaneous supplies, and so on. What is needed is to smoothly fit these resources into a system. This is not hard to do *if you can start with a well organized base,* which a modern textbook and its accompanying teacher's manual may provide. With the GAB-BAG system, in- stead of *creating* activities and an organization, which is difficult, you *gather* activities or resources and relate them to an already organized structure. The teaching then goes on as it would in any other system. You can use the textbook as one helpful resource from time to time, or not at all, as you judge.

Even a GAB-BAG approach is not going to consistently produce the same results you would get from a tested multimillion dollar system, developed after years of hard work by hundreds of outstanding professionals. Eventually, perhaps you can help your school district try out some of the newer programs, whether derived from government-supported projects, groups of leading school districts, or commercial sources.

The chances are becoming fewer of your serving on a district or school science committee to *construct* a curriculum. However, there is and will be a continuing need for capable teachers to select, try out, evaluate, modify, and integrate local resources into the new science programs. This role informed teachers should do very well. The overall result should be excellent for everyone.

Bibliography

PROFESSIONAL BOOKS

Blough, Glenn O., and Julius Schwartz, *Elementary School Science and How to Teach It,* fourth edition, New York: Holt, Rinehart and Winston, 1969. Includes subject matter and methods. The subject matter is exceptionally well written and extensive in scope.

Carin, Arthur, and Robert B. Sund, *Teaching Science Through Discovery,* Columbus, Ohio: Charles E. Merrill, 1964. Describes methods and materials for elementary science. Includes lesson plans grouped by basic science areas.

Craig, Gerald S., *Science for the Elementary-School Teacher,* fifth edition, Waltham, Mass.: Blaisdell Publishing Company, 1966. A comprehensive book, especially in subject matter content. Good reference volume.

Hone, Elizabeth B., Alexander Joseph, and Edward Victor, *A Sourcebook for Elementary Science,* New York: Harcourt, Brace and World, 1962. Very extensive collection of classroom activities, with specific accompanying instructions.

Hurd, Paul DeHart, and James Joseph Gallagher, *New Directions in Elementary Science Teaching,* Belmont, California: Wadsworth Publishing Company, 1968. A well-written report of new programs in elementary science and their theoretical foundations.

Kuslan, Louis I., and A. Harris Stone, *Teaching Children Science: An Inquiry Approach,* Belmont, California: Wadsworth Publishing Company, Inc., 1968. Particularly strong in the analysis and synthesis of research that supports modern teaching.

Piltz, Albert, and Robert Sund, *Creative Teaching of Science in the Elementary School,* Boston, Mass.: Allyn and Bacon, Inc., 1968. This book is one of a series, on several elementary subjects, designed to foster open-ended and creative activities for pupils.

Renner, John W., and William B. Ragan, *Teaching Science in the Elementary School,* New York: Harper and Row, 1968. Among other things, considers science instruction in the elementary school's total setting.

Schmidt, Victor, and Verne N. Rockcastle, *Teaching Science with Everyday Things,* New York: Mc-Graw-Hill, 1968. A delightfully conceived and illustrated book on how to teach science with common objects.

Sund, Robert B., Leslie W. Trowbridge, Bill W. Tillery, and Kenneth V. Olson, *Elementary Science Teaching Activities,* Columbus, Ohio: Charles E. Merrill, 1967. Suggested laboratory experiences in elementary school science for college and in-service courses.

Tannenbaum, Harold E., Nathan Stillman, Albert Piltz, *Science Education for Elementary School Teachers,* second edition, Boston: Allyn and Bacon, 1965. Focuses mainly on methods of science teaching. Contains excellent material on how child development relates to science instruction.

Victor, Edward, *Science for the Elementary School,* second edition, New York: Macmillan, 1970. Methods and activities. Features an extensive presentation of subject matter in outline form.

PAMPHLETS

Blackwood, Paul E., *Science Teaching in the Elementary Schools, A Survey of Practices,* U.S. Office of Education Publication 29059, Washington, D.C.:

Government Printing Office, 1965. A thorough report of science teaching in elementary schools of the United States.

Dunfee, Maxine, *Elementary-School Science: A Guide to Current Research*, Washington, D.C.: Association for Supervision and Curriculum Development, National Education Association, 1967. Sets forth research findings and recommended practices in elementary science.

National Science Teachers Association, *How To Do It Series*. Several titles, designed to give practical help toward the improvement of elementary and secondary science instruction:

"How to Utilize the Services of a Science Consultant," by Kenneth D. George (No. 471-14286);

"How to Care for Living Things in the Classroom," by Grace K. Pratt (No. 471-14288);

"How to Teach Science Through Field Studies," by Paul DeHart Hurd (No. 471-14290);

"How to Record and Use Data in Elementary Science Instruction," by Mary Clare Petty (No. 471-14292);

"How to Individualize Instruction in the Elementary School," by Theodore W. Munch (No. 471-14294);

"How to Teach Measurements in Elementary School Science," by Neal J. Holmes and Joseph J. Snowble (No. 471-14580).

Each copy 35¢, three copies for $1. Order from: National Science Teachers Association, 1201 Sixteenth Street N.W., Washington, D.C. 20036. (Payment must accompany orders of $2 or less.)

PERIODICALS

Cornell Science Leaflet, Cornell University, Research Park, Building 7, Ithaca, N.Y. (3 issues a year for $1). A 32-page booklet for teachers of grades 4–7. Practical, classroom-tested activities and background information on a variety of science topics.

Journal of Research in Science Teaching (Journal of the National Association for Research in Science Teaching), John Wiley and Sons, Inc., 605 Third Ave., New York, N.Y. (Quarterly). Scholarly articles on research and practice at all levels of science education.

Natural History, The American Museum of Natural History, Central Park West at 79th St., New York, N.Y. (Monthly, October through May; bimonthly June to September). Interesting articles on a variety of nature subjects, including conservation.

School Science and Mathematics, Central Association of Science and Mathematics Teachers, P.O. Box 246, Bloomington, Indiana (9 issues a year). Frequently contains articles on elementary science.

Science and Children, National Science Teachers Association, 1201 Sixteenth St. N.W., Washington, D.C. (8 issues a year for $4). Journal articles of interest and value to elementary-school teachers. A $5 subscription includes elementary membership in NSTA with voting privileges and periodic receipt of materials packets.

Science News, Science Service, 1719 N Street N.W., Washington, D.C. (Weekly). Brief reports on current findings of scientific research. Articles are short and fairly easy to read.

Scientific American, Scientific American Company, 415 Madison Ave., New York, N.Y. (Monthly). Interesting, thorough reports on recent scientific developments. Requires some science background of the reader.

CURRICULUM IMPROVEMENT PROJECTS

American Association for the Advancement of Science: Science—A Process Approach, Commission on Science Education, 1515 Massachusetts Ave. N.W., Washington, D.C. 20005.

Arlington County Schools: K–12 Curriculum Project, Associate Superintendent for Instruction, 4751 N. 25th St., Arlington, Virginia 22207.

Education Development Center: Elementary Science Study, 55 Chapel St., Newton, Massachusetts 02160

Educational Research Council of America: ERC K–12 Science Program, Rockefeller Building, 614 Superior N.W., Cleveland, Ohio 44113.

Florida State University: Child-Structured Learning in Science, Department of Science Education, Tallahassee, Florida 32306.

New York University: Conceptually Oriented Program for Elementary Science (COPES), 4 Washington Place, Room 502, New York, N.Y. 10003.

University of California (Berkeley): Science Curriculum Improvement Study, Lawrence Hall of Science, Berkeley, California 94720.

University of Minnesota: Mathematics and Science Teaching Project (MINNEMAST), 720 Washington Ave. S.E., Minneapolis, Minnesota 55414.

Index

cal advantage, 306; pitch, 311, defined, 310, (*ill. Fig. 6-5*), 310; pulleys, 321-322, number of ropes relationship, 322-325, extending activities, 325; ramp, 307, *see also* Inclined planes; rotation, changing, 318; screws, 310, pitch relationship, 311-312, extending activity, 312, spiral, 311; "streamlining," 306; trading distance for force, 305; two types, 304; uses, 305; wedges, 306; wheel and axle, 317-318, wheel size relationship, 318-319, extending activity, 321; windlass, *see* Windlass; "work," 304-305

Magazines, 96, 98, 113, 128, 394

Magic, 36

Magma, defined, 346

Magma flows, 328, 344, 345

Magnetic poles, 258-262

Magnetic theory, 262

Magnetic transparency, 252-254

Magnetism, 14, 182, 592; cause, 262; electricity, 289, *see also* Electromagnets; residual, 290

Magnetite, 247

Magnets and their properties, 244-264, 528; *alnico*, 247; arranged-environment, study, 28-29; artificial, 247; bar, 247, 248 (*Fig. 4-1*); brass, 249; care of, 262-264, extending activities, 264; cause, 262; compass, 247, 258-262; cylindrical, 247, 248 (*Fig. 4-1*); domains, 262; electro, 247, 256-257; field of force, 250-251, extending activity, 251-252; generalizations, 69, 246-247; horseshoe, 247, 248 (*Fig. 4-1*); iron and steel magnetism, 254-255, extending activities, 255-256; magnetic poles, 258-261, extending activities, 261-262; magnetic theory, 262, making, 254; natural, *see* Lodestones; objects attracted to, 247-249, extending activities, 249-250; poles, 250, properties, 246; theory, 262; "tin" cans, 247; transparency, 252-253, extending activities, 253-254; *U*, 247, 248 (*Fig. 4-1*); *V*, 247, 248 (*Fig. 4-1*); *see also* Magnetism

Magnifier, purchase guide, 92

Magnifying glass, 212, 224, 239-240; refraction, 227

Mammals, 470-474; characteristics, 466, 470-472; examples, 467; reproduction, 470

Mammoth Caves (Kentucky), 329

Maps, 427, 554; outdoor mapping (ESS), 599; physiographic, 347, 349; road, 530; study, 63-64

Marble, 355, 358

Marconi, Guglielmo, 294

Marine geology, 119

Mars (planet), 412-413; diameter, 417; orbital speed, 430; revolution period around sun, 429; temperature, 416

Mass, 10; earth-moon center (barycenter), 404

Material (concept), 527-528; changes in, 606-607; material-function-form relationship, 599

Materials, providing and using, 88-119; aquarium, 114-115, *see also* Aquarium; assumptions about, 48; audio-visual aids, 97-107; bulletin boards, 110-114; classroom facilities, 107-116; constructions, 106-107; demonstrations, 51; equipment and supplies, 90-93; free and inexpensive, 107; microscopes and microprojectors, 102-105, suppliers, 105; nonreading, 97-107, *see also* Audio-visual aids; opaque projector, 98; pictorial, 97-102, 110; pupil participation, 90-91; *Purchase Guide*, 91-92; Pyrex, 145; quantity, 92; reading, 93-97; recordings, 105-106; resource groups, 118-119; school and community resources, 116-119; science kits, 92-93; science-supply room, 93; slides, 104; sources, 90-91; substitutions, 46-47; television, 105; terrarium, 115-116, *see also* Terrarium; use of easy-to-get objects, 110

Mathematics, 60, 119; concepts (process approach), 572; programs, 61, 91; science, 553-554; symmetry, 214; *see also* Arithmetic

Matter, 14; changing states of, 152-154; composition, 143; conservation of (concept), 532; energy conservation, 606; molecular theory, 143, 295; phases, 532; states, 532

Matter and Energy (publication), 128

Mealworms, 595; experiment, 86-87

Measurement, 60-61, 599; estimation, 60-64; instruments, 62-63; light-year, 414; variations in, 63

Measuring (process), 553-554

Mechanical energy, 14, 166, 167-168

Medicine, 596; folk, 36

Megalopolis City, 17

Mental Measurement Yearbooks, The, 81

Mental models, 45-46, 533

Mental operations, categories, 71

Mercurial barometer, 372

Mercury (planet), 412, 414; diameter, 417; distance from sun, 417, 418; orbital speed, 430; revolution period around sun, 429; temperature, 415, 416

"Messing About in Science," 601

Metals, conductors of electricity, 280; magnets, relationship, 247-249

Metamorphic rocks, 328, 352, 355, 357-358

Metamorphosis (concept), 534

Meteor Crater (Arizona), 424

Meteorites, 414, 424

Meteorologists, 367, 374

Meteors, 368, 413-414

Meter, 61

Methodology, 56

Metric system, 61-62

Metropolitan Achievement Tests, 81

Mexico, 351, 378

Michigan State University, 547

Microbiology, 596

Microgardening, 596; mold, sample lesson, 584-589